AMERICAN FOREIGN RELATIONS
1975
A DOCUMENTARY RECORD

COUNCIL ON FOREIGN RELATIONS BOOKS

The Council on Foreign Relations, Inc., is a non-profit and non-partisan organization devoted to promoting improved understanding of international affairs through the free exchange of ideas. Its membership of about 1,700 persons throughout the United States is made up of individuals with special interest and experience in international affairs. The Council has no affiliation with, and receives no funding from, the United States government. The Council does not take any position on questions of foreign policy.

The Council publishes the quarterly journal, *Foreign Affairs*. In addition, from time to time, books and monographs written by members of the Council's research staff or visiting fellows, or commissioned by the Council, or written by independent authors with critical review contributed by a Council study group, are published with the designation "Council on Foreign Relations Book" or "Council Paper on International Affairs." Any book or monograph bearing that designation is, in the judgment of the Committee on Studies of the Council's board of directors, a responsible treatment of a significant international topic worthy of presentation to the public. All statements of fact and expressions of opinion contained in Council books, monographs, and *Foreign Affairs* articles are, however, the sole responsibility of their authors.

AMERICAN FOREIGN RELATIONS 1975

A DOCUMENTARY RECORD

Continuing the Series
DOCUMENTS ON AMERICAN FOREIGN RELATIONS
THE UNITED STATES IN WORLD AFFAIRS

Edited by RICHARD P. STEBBINS and ELAINE P. ADAM

A Council on Foreign Relations Book

Published by

New York University Press • New York • 1977

PREFACE

This volume offers a condensed historical narrative together with a selection of documents reflecting salient aspects of the foreign relations of the United States in 1975. Continuing the series of foreign policy surveys initiated by the Council on Foreign Relations in 1931 under the title *The United States in World Affairs,* the volume also maintains the service provided annually for more than three decades by the separate *Documents on American Foreign Relations* series, inaugurated by the World Peace Foundation in 1939 and taken over by the Council on Foreign Relations in 1952. The fusion of narrative and documentation, commenced on a trial basis with the inception of the present series in 1971, is designed to provide a single, comprehensive, and nonpartisan record of American foreign policy as it develops during the bicentennial decade and beyond.

The interests of orderly presentation have appeared to be best served by the combination of an introductory essay with a series of brief chronological chapters, each focused on one or two outstanding developments in a single area of foreign policy concern. Within the chapters, the story is told in part by the editors (whose contributions are enclosed within square brackets) and in somewhat greater detail by the documents themselves, which are presented in authoritative texts and accompanied by whatever editorial apparatus seems necessary for independent reference use. Footnote citations are presented in condensed form, and publications referred to by abbreviated titles are fully identified in the Appendix, which lists the principal sources used in preparing the volume. All dates refer to the year 1975 unless a different year is specifically indicated.

The editorial procedure described above admittedly involves the exercise of a substantial measure of individual judgment, and demands all possible objectivity in the handling of controversial events and data. While hopeful that the volume will not be found wanting in this regard, the editors wish to emphasize that the editorial viewpoint is of necessity a personal one and in no way seeks to reflect the outlook of the Council on Foreign Relations or any of its officers and directors, members, or staff.

Among their immediate associates, the editors would note their special indebtedness to John Temple Swing, Vice-President and Secretary; Grace Darling Griffin, Publications Manager; and Janet Rigney, Librarian, of the Council on Foreign Relations; and to Despina Papazoglou, Associate Managing Editor, and other friends at NYU Press. They are also indebted to various official agencies which have provided documentary material; to Howard

PREFACE

Sperber, who designed and executed the map to illustrate the Sinai disengagement agreement; and to *The New York Times* for permission to reprint texts or excerpts of documents appearing in its pages. As always, the editors themselves are responsible for the choice and presentation of the documents as well as the form and content of the editorial matter.

R.P.S.
E.P.A.

June 15, 1977

CONTENTS

INTRODUCING 1975

NINETEEN SEVENTY-FIVE will be remembered as the year when the "North-South" relationship between industrialized and developing countries drew even with the "East-West" rivalry of Communist and democratic states as a preeminent concern of American foreign policy. A period of dawning recovery from the world's most serious postwar economic recession, 1975 was none the less a year of bitter frustration at the difficulties of organized existence on a shrinking planet whose ability to go on supporting existing life patterns had become increasingly problematical.

Not many years earlier, it had been the fashion in more prosperous countries to bemoan the evils of excessive abundance that were becoming evident with the advent and consolidation of the "affluent society." But such concerns seemed oddly irrelevant to the new conditions that had been inaugurated by the fourfold increase in the price of crude petroleum imposed in 1973 by members of the thirteen-nation Organization of Petroleum Exporting Countries (OPEC). This action, in conjunction with a months-long embargo on oil shipments from Arab countries to the United States and certain other consumer nations, had suggested a lively possibility that humanity had been deluding itself in gearing its expectations to an age of ever-increasing ease and abundance. Scarcity, rather than excess, once more began to be perceived as the most likely determinant of the human future. Inflation, unemployment, declining living standards, a deteriorating "quality of life" began to seem the inescapable lot of most of the earth's 4,000,000,000 inhabitants, not necessarily excluding the 213,000,000 people of the United States.

Americans had been doomed by recent experience to find special difficulty in adjusting to a world in which their country had invested so many hopes and had, of late, sustained such bitter disappointments. Less than two years had elapsed since the signature in Paris, on January 27, 1973, of the Vietnam peace agreement that had sealed the nation's withdrawal ("with honor," as its leaders

1

had insisted) from its longest, most divisive, and least successful foreign war. Less than one year had gone by since the President who had framed this withdrawal—and who, for reasons mainly unrelated to foreign policy, had subsequently been faced with almost certain impeachment and conviction under the "high crimes and misdemeanors" provision of the Constitution—had resigned his office in order, as he said, to spare the nation further travail "in a period when our entire focus should be on the great issues of peace abroad and prosperity without inflation at home."[1]

Still mired in the psychic wreckage of Vietnam and Watergate, Americans would face new trials in what was to be the first full year of President Gerald R. Ford's administration—a year in which American foreign policy once again would bear the personal imprint of Dr. Henry A. Kissinger, the Secretary of State and, until November, Assistant to the President for National Security Affairs. Notable among the year's events would be the final overthrow of U.S.-supported governments in South Vietnam, Cambodia, and Laos and the establishment of Communist-dominated regimes in all three of those countries in what would represent the first important territorial enlargement of the Communist domain since the accession of Fidel Castro's Cuba to the Communist camp at the beginning of the 1960s.

Yet it would be idle to pretend that Americans as a people were reduced to despair by this final defeat of a cause for which so many of them had fought and over 46,000 had given their lives. For most Americans, the war had ended years earlier with the withdrawal of American forces under President Nixon's "Vietnamization" policy. Although the events of 1975 would write a tragic finish to this important chapter of American history, such new developments as the European summit conference in Helsinki and the opening of the "North-South" dialogue in Paris would signal a departure for novel destinations whose character was only dimly forseeable.

A World of Violence

Some unattractive characteristics of the emerging post-Vietnam era could nevertheless be glimpsed amid the smoke and fire of daily events. Violence, both rhetorical and physical, quite obviously still remained a favorite recourse of nations as of individuals, unchecked in most instances by religious creeds or secular traditions. To the civil conflict that had raged since 1969 between the Catholics and Protestants of Northern Ireland was added, in 1975, the commencement of an even more murderous internal war in Lebanon, a

[1]Nixon resignation speech, Aug. 8, 1974, in *AFR, 1974*: 280.

Middle East republic hitherto renowned as an island of forbearance in an otherwise violence-prone region. Two other internecine struggles in Asian countries were concluded in 1975, at the cost of untold suffering for members of the Kurdish minority in Iraq and of an almost biblical form of deportation and enslavement for those Cambodians who had failed to support the victorious, Communist-led "Khmer Rouge" insurgency. Black Africans, in large if indeterminate numbers, succumbed to tribal and religious persecution—notably, it was alleged, in the Uganda of President Idi Amin Dada, the self-made chief of state whose characterization as a "racist murderer" by the *New York Times* of October 3, 1975 could be publicly endorsed by an incumbent U.S. Representative to the United Nations.[2]

Arbitrary arrest and torture of political prisoners continued to be frequently reported from numerous countries in Latin America and elsewhere. Murder itself, moreover, was no respecter of rank or station in the world of 1975. Political leaders in four of the world's 150-odd nations met violent death in 1975, either as victims of internal power struggles or for obscure personal causes: King Faisal of Saudi Arabia, Sheikh Mujibur Rahman of Bangladesh, President François Tombalbaye of Chad, and Major General Gabriel Ramanantsoa of the Malagasy Republic. A fifth national leader, General Yakubu Gowon of Nigeria, was ousted in a bloodless coup. Those chiefs and ex-chiefs of state who died naturally during the year—like President Chiang Kai-shek of the Republic of China, General Francisco Franco of Spain, and former Emperor Haile Selassie of Ethiopia—belonged to a select minority already more celebrated as historical figures than as contemporary statesmen. Of comparable note was former President Eamon de Valéra, a leader of Ireland's fight for independence earlier in the century.

American Contributions

Even the new President of the United States, a man not given to arousing personal antagonisms, became the object of two successive assassination attempts in the single month of September 1975. That the world's leading democratic nation was not immune to a sinister involvement with violence and fanaticism was, of course, well known to all who remembered the assassination of President John F. Kennedy, the murders of Senator Robert F. Kennedy and the Reverend Martin Luther King, Jr., and the bombings, kidnappings, and other violent manifestations of the late 1960s and early 1970s. Some critics of American society had gone so far as to portray the whole Vietnam engagement as a manifestation of some

[2]*New York Times* editorial, Oct. 3, 1975; San Francisco address by Ambassador Daniel P. Moynihan, Oct. 3, quoted in same, Oct. 4, 1975.

obscure criminal trait within the body politic. Even those who still insisted on their country's inherent moral superiority could not, by 1975, ignore the mounting evidence that while some Americans had striven with might and main to advance the rule of law in world affairs, other important organs of American society and government had themselves contributed to the worldwide growth of lawlessness and violence.

This phenomenon, as gradually brought to light through the mid-1970s, was broader in scope and implications than the Watergate scandals that had already caused such disillusionment. The improprieties and illegalities ascribed to President Nixon and his circle could still be viewed as an historical aberration, a collective surrender to the temptations of office on the part of individuals whose lust for power had stifled any ethical standards they might originally have possessed. What 1975 would reveal beyond the possibility of doubt was that conventional ethical standards had in any case been far less widely honored than had been popularly supposed—that Watergate and its attendant evils were part of a much broader pattern that antedated the Nixon administration, involved both public and private agencies, acknowledged few if any legal or moral constraints, and exerted a "global reach" extending far beyond America's borders.

Abundant indications of the questionable political role of some large U.S.-based corporations had been developed over the past year or two by the U.S. Senate Subcommittee on Multinational Corporations, a unit of the Foreign Relations Committee chaired by Democratic Senator Frank Church of Idaho. The Church committee's most sensational disclosures to date had been concerned with the protracted campaign conducted by officers of the International Telephone and Telegraph Corporation (ITT), abetted to an undetermined extent by U.S. Government agencies, against the left-wing political movement led by the late President Salvador Allende of Chile.[3] By 1975, the focus of the Church committee, and of related investigations by such bodies as the Securities and Exchange Commission, had shifted to the bribes and similar questionable payments doled out by U.S. corporations as an aid to business at home and particularly abroad. Among the year's developments in this area were an admission by the United Brands (formerly United Fruit) Company that it had paid $1,250,000 to a "high Honduran official"—assertedly President Oswaldo López Arellano, who was removed soon afterward by a military coup—to obtain a reduction in the banana export tax; acknowledgment by the Gulf Oil Corporation of similar payments totaling $5,000,000 in Bolivia, South Korea, Italy, and Lebanon (and $5,300,000 in the

[3]Cf. AFR, 1971: 481; same, 1973: 119 and 409-10.

United States) over the past ten years; and an admission by the government-supported Lockheed Aircraft Corporation that it had disbursed no less than $22,000,000 in payments to foreign officials and political organizations since 1970.[4]

Assassination Plots

Though these disclosures would exert explosive and long-lasting political effects in some of the countries named, for most Americans they paled before the concurrent revelations of illegal and improper activities by the Central Intelligence Agency (CIA) and other components of the U.S. "intelligence community." None but the most naïve, of course, had been unaware that the CIA had on occasion engaged in clandestine political warfare against forces hostile to the United States in such "third world" countries as Iran or Guatemala; and it was already widely recognized that the CIA and other American official agencies, as well as private interests, had been deeply involved in the anti-Allende campaign in Chile. What had not been previously known was the fact that the CIA, in addition to engaging in large-scale espionage and harassment directed aginst American citizens, had actually joined in planning the assassination of various foreign leaders whose elimination had been thought potentially advantageous to the United States.

Evidence of such activities gave rise to more than one inquiry by specially constituted panels. A Commission on CIA Activities Within the United States, chaired by Vice-President Nelson A. Rockefeller, conceded in June that while "the great majority of the CIA's domestic activities comply with its statutory authority," the agency nevertheless had "engaged in some activities that should be criticized and not permitted to happen again—both in light of the limits imposed on the Agency by law and as a matter of public policy." Some of these activities, the commission noted, had been "initiated or ordered by Presidents, either directly or indirectly"; some of them fell within a doubtful area between mandated and prohibited activities; others, however, "were plainly unlawful and constituted improper invasions upon the rights of Americans." Many of these activities, the commission added, had been terminated on the agency's own initiative within the past couple of years.[5]

Rather more serious was the indictment brought by the Senate's Select Committee to Study Governmental Operations with Respect

---

[4]Details in *Keesing's*: 27377 (1975) and 27840 (1976).
[5]*Report to the President by the Commission on CIA Activities within the United States, June 1975* (Washington: GPO, 1975): 10.

to Intelligence Activities, set up in January 1975 and once again chaired by Senator Church. In a heavily documented preliminary report made public on November 20, this group disclosed that the CIA had been directly involved during the early 1960s in plots to assassinate Prime Minister Fidel Castro of Cuba and the late Prime Minister Patrice Lumumba of the Congo (Zaïre); had engaged in covert activity against two other assassination victims of the period, former President Rafael L. Trujillo of the Dominican Republic and President Ngo Dinh Diem of the Republic of Vietnam; and was at least tenuously linked to other assassination plots against the late President Sukarno of Indonesia and the late President François Duvalier of Haiti. Although it also described in some detail an unsuccessful attempt to bring about a coup against President-elect Allende in 1970, the committee reported that it found no evidence of direct U.S. complicity in the events that actually culminated in Allende's deposition and death in September 1973.[6]

President Ford was quick to note that his administration did not condone assassination attempts and would "not participate under any circumstances in activities of that sort."[7] This resolution did not, however, appear to mitigate the President's fear that overzealous investigation by outsiders might impair the effectiveness of the intelligence services in carrying out their legitimate functions. "Under no circumstances," Mr. Ford later insisted, ". . . will I permit the dismantling or the destruction of an intelligence agency or community because that does involve our national security."[8]

Animated by this determination, the Ford administration showed little enthusiasm for the ongoing disclosures of official wrongdoing. Though it avoided major friction with the Church committee, it later became seriously embroiled with the separate House Select Committee on Intelligence chaired by Democratic Representative Otis Pike of New York. That body, frustrated in its demands for information withheld by Secretary Kissinger on policy grounds, attempted to cite the latter for contempt and ultimately completed a report so broadly critical of the intelligence agencies, and of Dr. Kissinger personally, that its publication was formally banned by the House. The contents, however, quickly became available in

---

[6]U.S. Senate, 94th Cong., 1st sess., Select Committee to Study Governmental Operations with Respect to Intelligence Activities, *Alleged Assassination Plots Involving Foreign Leaders: An Interim Report* (S. Rept. 94-465, Nov. 20, 1975; Washington: GPO, 1975).
[7]News conference, South Bend, Mar. 17, in *Presidential Documents*, 11: 275.
[8]News conference, Oct. 1, in same, 11: 1092.

unauthorized versions leaked to the *New York Times* and the *Village Voice.*[9]

International Terrorism

If the recent record of American foreign policy did not lack overtones of violence and illegality, a series of international conventions concluded as the result of American initiative bore witness to the fact that the central thrust of American action had none the less been unequivocally directed toward restraining violence, not encouraging it. Intensified as a response to the terrorist outrages of the early 1970s, such efforts nevertheless seemed not to have inhibited significantly those groups that looked on terror as a legitimate weapon against whatever displeased them in the existing social and political order.

Testimony to the undiminished vitality of the international terrorist movement were such sensational incidents of 1975 as the January bombing of Fraunces Tavern in New York by the Puerto Rican "National Liberation Armed Forces" (FALN); the February 27 kidnapping of Peter Lorenz, Christian Democratic candidate for the post of Governing Mayor of West Berlin, presumably by remnants of the so-called Baader-Meinhof gang; the evasion of arrest by the notorious "Carlos" (a pseudonym for the Venezuelan Ilich Ramírez Sánchez) in a Paris shootout on June 21; the action of two South Moluccan groups in the Netherlands at the beginning of December in hijacking a train and seizing the Indonesian Consulate General in Amsterdam; and the kidnapping on December 21, apparently by "Carlos" associates acting as the "Arm of the Arab Revolution," of eleven Arab and South American oil ministers attending an OPEC meeting in Vienna. Comparable in impact, if not in inspiration, were the terrorist killings of U.S. Consular Agent John Patrick Egan in Cordoba, Argentina, on February 28; of two U.S. Air Force colonels in Tehran on May 21; and of Richard S. Welch, a high official of the U.S. Embassy who had been publicly identified as a CIA representative, in Athens on December 23.

The Battle of "Zionism"

A remarkable feature of the terrorist records of 1975 is the fact that most of the year's spectacular incidents seemed only tenuously connected, if at all, with the Palestinian campaign against the state of Israel, the inspiration of innumerable hijackings, bombings, and killings in the earlier 1970s. But the hatreds and enmities associated

[9]*New York Times*, Jan. 26, 1976; *Village Voice* (New York), Feb. 16 and 23, 1976. The position of Secretary Kissinger and the Department of State with reference to the committee's demands is set forth in *Bulletin*, 73: 599-601, 645-8, and 748-50.

with the Arab-Israeli struggle continued to fester none the less virulently as progress toward a "just and lasting peace" in the Middle East showed signs of slowing to a halt with Israel still in possession of most of the territories occupied in the war of 1973. In a final *tour de force* of his personal "shuttle diplomacy," Secretary of State Kissinger succeeded late in the summer in organizing an elaborate, second-stage military disengagement between Egyptian and Israeli military forces in the Sinai Peninsula. But nothing further seemed likely to be accomplished by the Kissinger "step-by-step" route, and major obstacles still blocked the way to a comprehensive peace settlement such as might theoretically be sought at a reconvened session of the Geneva peace conference that had met briefly in December 1973.

With Israel still refusing any return to the 1967 cease-fire lines, the worldwide, Arab-organized political, economic, and rhetorical campaign against the Jewish state not only attained new peaks of intensity but gained a number of new recruits among "third world" countries, particularly African nations that were feeling the pinch of higher oil prices and, in addition, desired Arab backing for their own campaigns against colonialism and racial discrimination in Southern Africa. The United Nations, racked in 1974 by vehement controversies about the status and rights of the Palestine Liberation Organization (PLO), resounded during 1975 with rhetorical assaults on "Zionism," a movement widely extolled in earlier years but now for the first time bracketed by many countries, non-Arab as well as Arab, with such familiar bugbears as imperialism, colonialism, neocolonialism, racism, and apartheid.

Surfacing during the spring at the Conference of the International Women's Year in Mexico City, the anti-Zionist campaign attained its apogee with the adoption by the General Assembly on November 10 of what purported to be a formal determination "that zionism [with a small Z] is a form of racism and racial discrimination."[10] Decried by one American delegate in such terms as "obscene act," "supreme act of deceit," and "one of the most grievous errors in the 30-year life of this organization,"[11] the resolution was denounced with almost equal vigor by President Ford and by both houses of Congress. It marked what may well have been an all-time low in the relationship between the United States and over 100 U.N. member countries, mainly from the "third world" and Communist groups, that either voted for its adoption or failed to oppose it.

[10]General Assembly Resolution 3379 (XXX), Nov. 10, adopted by a vote of 72-35 (U.S.)-32; text in Chapter 37, Document 56.
[11]Statement by U.S. Representative Leonard Garment to the Third (Social, Humanitarian and Cultural) Committee, Oct. 17, in *Bulletin*, 73: 789.

More "Third World" Frictions

That the United States of the 1970s was seldom in harmony with the outlook of the "third world" nations was no secret to anyone who had observed the recent course of world affairs, particularly since the Arab oil embargo of 1973 and the commencement of U.S. efforts to counter the tactics of OPEC, the oil exporters' association, by welding together a powerful bloc of industrialized, oil-consuming countries. Such activities, it was widely asserted, could only be inspired by a sinister determination to deprive "third world" countries of their legitimate rights. Secretary Kissinger, in a much-quoted interview with *Business Week* at the beginning of the year, had caused a sensation in the "third world" and elsewhere by leaving open a possibility that the United States might even resort to military action should there be "some actual strangulation of the industrialized world" through interruption of the flow of Mideast oil.[12] A sense of hostile confrontation was seldom absent from U.S.-"third world" relations in 1975, a year when the latter group's already numerous ranks were swelled by the accession to independence of no fewer than seven new countries—the former Portuguese territories of Mozambique, Cape Verde, Sao Tomé and Principe, and Angola; Australian-administered Papua New Guinea; Dutch Surinam; and the French Comoro Islands. (Among other dependent or semidependent territories that underwent a change of status in 1975, Sikkim was absorbed by India, Portuguese East Timor was occupied by Indonesia, and the Spanish or Western Sahara was partitioned between Morocco and Mauritania.)

Matching the hostile criticism of many aspects of American policy was a growing readiness on the part of the United States to "talk back" to its critics and even, on occasion, to counterattack by citing such "third world" shortcomings as the widespread disregard for human rights and political freedoms, exemplified in 1975 by the establishment of one-party states in Bangladesh and Iran and, even more notoriously, the introduction of harsh emergency rule by the government of Mrs. Indira Gandhi in India. This new American combativeness found a conspicuous exemplar in the person of Ambassador Daniel Patrick Moynihan, a former envoy to India and experienced critic of "third world" attitudes who succeeded John Scali in June 1975 as U.S. Representative to the United Nations. Much of his activity at the United Nations, Ambassador Moynihan later asserted, had been successfully directed toward what he described as "a basic foreign policy goal . . . of breaking up the massive blocs of nations, mostly new nations, which for so

---

[12]*Business Week,* Jan. 13, 1975; text in *Bulletin,* 72: 101.

long have been arrayed against us in international forums and in diplomatic encounters generally." Any lack of complete success in this regard, in Mr. Moynihan's judgment, was to be ascribed not to any deficiency of zeal on his part but rather to a lack of support for his endeavors from within the Department of State.[13]

Economic Discussions

But though the political relationship between the United States and many of its "third world" friends continued to deteriorate in an alarming fashion, there were at least some indications of improving relations in the area of economic policy, dominated as it was by the demands of the developing countries for more favorable treatment at the hands of the wealthy industrialized nations. Although the United States did not disguise its dislike for such ideological statements as the Declaration on the Establishment of a New International Economic Order and the Charter of Economic Rights and Duties of States, both adopted by the United Nations on "third world" initiative in 1974,[14] to many observers it seemed that Washington nevertheless was growing somewhat more amenable to seeking accommodation on the practical plane.

Moving with a caution attributed by some to the conservative influence of Secretary of the Treasury William E. Simon, the American Government and Secretary of State Kissinger began in the course of 1975 to display what seemed a growing sympathy for developing country views on such crucial issues as development financing, the developing countries' debt burden, and the relative prices of raw materials and manufactured goods. A wide variety of constructive suggestions was laid before the U.N. General Assembly at a special session on development problems in September, and a sympathetic approach to issues of particular interest to developing nations continued to characterize the American position at the December opening of the Paris Conference on International Economic Cooperation (CIEC). Notable in the American approach was a recognition of the particularly difficult plight of those developing countries, sometimes referred to as "most seriously affected" (MSA) or "fourth world" countries, that were compelled to import the bulk of their petroleum requirements and to pay the same exorbitant prices as the developed nations.

Within the industrialized world itself, recession-year economic strains did not prevent a measure of recovery from the frictions of the past two or three years. Passage of the long-pending U.S. Trade Act of 1974[15] cleared the way for formal commencement of the

---

[13]Cablegram, Jan. 23, 1976, in *New York Times*, Jan. 28, 1976.
[14]Cf. Chapter 7 at notes 1 and 2.
[15]Public Law 93-618, Jan. 3, 1975; cf. Chapter 1 below.

long-contemplated "Tokyo Round" of multilateral trade negotiations, now pointed toward belated completion by the end of 1977. Cooperation in energy matters was being strengthened within the framework of a new International Energy Agency (IEA). In May, the major industrialized countries participating in the Organization for Economic Cooperation and Development (OECD) renewed their pledge to refrain from unilateral trade restrictions and artificial trade stimulation; and fears that the Labour government headed by Harold Wilson might take Great Britain out of the European Economic Community (EEC) were laid to rest soon afterward by a 2 to 1 majority of British voters in a national referendum. Key decisions relating to the projected comprehensive reform of the international monetary system preceded the holding at Rambouillet, France, on November 15-17 of an "economic summit" of leading industrial countries that marked a new stage in the closer coordination of their economic and financial policies. If some American authorities continued to express anxiety about the overall trend of Western affairs, their apprehensions now centered less on economic matters *per se* than on the growing strength of the Communist parties and movements in Western Europe and the possibility that Communists might soon be claiming a government role in such countries as Portugal or Italy.

The Proliferation Issue

One special anxiety that had begun to affect American relations with both industrialized and developing countries was the reviving threat of nuclear proliferation that had accompanied the increasing worldwide reliance on nuclear power and the development of techniques for converting spent nuclear fuel into weapons-grade plutonium. India's recent acquisition of a nuclear capability as an outgrowth of its nuclear power program had set an example which might, despite the restraints imposed by the Nuclear Nonproliferation Treaty of 1968,[16] be followed by at least a dozen other countries unless they could be persuaded that their economic and security needs would be met by other means.

Intertwined with the security issue were the commercial interests and ambitions of the United States, West Germany, France, and other countries in a position to export nuclear equipment, technology, and fuel. Discussed in general terms at an international conference convened in May to review the 1968 Nonproliferation Treaty, these issues were later taken up in greater detail by the members of the so-called "Nuclear Suppliers' Conference," an informal grouping of the major nuclear nations that had been

[16]Cf. Chapter 13 at note 1.

organized on the initiative of the United States. Indicative of the acuteness and complexity of the issues, which were destined to cause severe headaches for Washington policy-makers over the next few years, was the conclusion during 1975 of a large-scale nuclear cooperation agreement between the Federal Republic of Germany and Brazil, followed soon afterward by a more modestly scaled agreement between France and Pakistan.

Relations with the Communist World

Participation by the Soviet Union in the Nuclear Suppliers' Conference bore witness to the Soviet leaders' recognition, in common with the leaders of the principal Western governments, that certain interests in the contemporary world were shared by governments and peoples in both the Communist and Western camps. Not in several years, however, had the extent of these common perceptions appeared so difficult to gauge as in 1975, a year of high theatrics but little substantive improvement in the overall relations between East and West.

Two events of the summer of 1975 combined to set a crown upon the external processes of détente as they had developed since the beginning of the decade. A climax to more than three years' preparation was the successful linkup on July 17 of the American *Apollo* and the Soviet *Soyuz* spacecraft, followed by exchanges of visits by crew members over the next two days. To Leonid I. Brezhnev, the General Secretary of the Soviet Communist Party and Moscow's most unchallengeable authority, this long-planned event was fraught with "historic significance as a symbol of the easing of international tension and the improvement of Soviet-U.S. relations on the basis of the principles of peaceful coexistence."[17] American comment was less effusive.

Two weeks later occurred the concluding sessions, "at the summit," of the Conference on Security and Cooperation in Europe (CSCE), an event whose background encompassed a full generation of postwar history. Meeting in Helsinki, Finland, on July 30-August 1, the leaders of 35 nations in Europe and North America signified their acquiescence in the existing European political and territorial setup and endorsed, with varying degrees of conviction, a broad assortment of principles and procedures aimed generally at reducing tension and promoting freer intercourse among Europe's peoples.[18]

What robbed the Helsinki summit of its hoped-for impact was the realization that the Soviet Union and its Communist allies in

[17] *Keesing's*: 27315.
[18] Text in Chapter 25, Document 42.

reality were still acting on radically different principles—and, quite possibly, pursuing radically different aims—to those that actuated the democratic nations of the West. Moscow's denial to its own citizens of various human rights and freedoms that were professedly held sacred in the West had become increasingly notorious at the very time the Helsinki declaration was under negotiation. Aleksandr I. Solzhenitsyn, perhaps the most eminent among contemporary Russian critics of the Soviet system, had already been forced into exile, and was warning all who would listen about the dangers of Soviet-style "peaceful coexistence." A second outstanding dissident, the physicist Andrei D. Sakharov, still continued his agitation for human rights within the Soviet Union, defying a formidable campaign of intimidation and harassment that would, among other things, prevent his going to Norway to accept the Nobel Peace Prize awarded him late in 1975.

Moscow's treatment of its own citizens had already exerted a chilling effect upon the progress of U.S.-Soviet détente. American unwillingness to countenance restrictions on Jewish emigration from the Soviet Union had found expression in specific legislative actions which would severely limit the expansion of economic relations between the two powers. Increasingly, the whole philosophy of détente was being called in question in the United States by people who had from the first been skeptical of Soviet intentions and, in some instances, appeared particularly incensed by President Ford's refusal, supposedly on the advice of Secretary Kissinger, to receive Solzhenitsyn at the White House shortly before the President's departure for Helsinki.

Potentially of more lasting significance was a growing doubt about the genuineness of Moscow's commitment to peaceful relations with the West, a commitment theoretically symbolized by the bilateral Strategic Arms Limitation Talks (SALT) initiated early in the Nixon administration. Building upon the so-called SALT I agreements concluded at the time of President Nixon's visit to the U.S.S.R. in May 1972,[19] President Ford and General Secretary Brezhnev had agreed at Vladivostok in November 1974 upon the outlines of a ten-year "SALT II" agreement that would limit the numbers and types of strategic offensive delivery vehicles available to the two sides through the end of 1985.[20] But far from reducing the agreement to final form, as both leaders had professed to hope, the negotiations carried on through 1975 served only to reveal the existence of fundamental differences regarding the applicability of the Vladivostok ceilings to such novel weapons as the American cruise missile and the Soviet "Backfire" bomber.

[19]Cf. notes 11 and 12 to Chapter 13.
[20]Cf. Chapter 13 at note 14.

Both sides, meanwhile, continued to press forward with the development of still more sophisticated and deadly weapons; and to Americans, at least, it seemed that the strategic balance was increasingly tending to shift in favor of the Soviet Union, with its heavy missiles now being equipped with multiple independently targetable reentry vehicles (MIRVs). With growing frequency, American officials and legislators cited a possibility that Moscow, no longer satisfied with a "rough equivalence" of strategic nuclear power, might actually be aiming at a position of outright superiority that would enable it to launch a devastating "first strike" against the United States and still hope to survive the inevitable American retaliation.

An equal measure of uncertainty surrounded the intentions of the Soviet Union and its Warsaw Pact allies with regard to the European military balance under discussion at the Vienna conference on Mutual and Balanced Force Reduction (MBFR)—officially, the Conference on Mutual Reduction of Forces and Armaments and Associated Measures in Central Europe. Formally opened in October 1973 after years of preliminary maneuvering, the Vienna talks had not yet moved beyond the initial positions outlined by the NATO and Warsaw Pact participants. While each side pressed a formula that called for reductions principally by the other party, the U.S.S.R. and its allies had continued to augment their forces in Europe in a manner that was causing growing anxiety in NATO military quarters. The military superiority that was by now conceded to the Warsaw Pact on the continent of Europe, moreover, was obviously part of a wider build-up of Soviet military and naval strength in the Mediterranean and Middle East, the Indian Ocean, and the Pacific that testified to Moscow's resolve to become a world power in the fullest sense of the term.

Developments in East Asia

Contrasting with the indeterminate state of relations with the Soviet bloc were the sharply altered political patterns in Asia and the Western Pacific that resulted from the Communist victories in Indochina. Neither Peking nor Moscow could be held directly responsible for the overthrow of the U.S.-supported regimes in South Vietnam, Cambodia, and Laos and their replacement by frankly Communist or Communist-dominated governments. The conquest (or, in Communist terms, the "liberation") of all Indochina was essentially the achievement of the Communist-ruled Democratic Republic of Vietnam, the Hanoi-based government which—aided, to be sure, by local forces, and with ample material support from both China and the U.S.S.R.—had successfully withstood the military might of the United States until the victorious completion of its decades-long campaign to extirpate "imperialism" and its "puppets" from the Indochina region.

Commensurate with the magnitude of the Communist victory in Indochina was the depth of the humiliation inflicted upon the United States, whose earlier withdrawal from active participation in the war had been predicated upon the ability of the local governments to hold their own with such material assistance as might be provided by the American Congress. The subsequent failure of the Congress to vouchsafe the funds requested by Presidents Nixon and Ford would leave it an open question whether the Saigon and Phnom Penh governments could have maintained themselves even if American funding had been more lavish. Once South Vietnam and Cambodia had succumbed to the Communist military onslaught, as happened with startling suddenness in April 1975, it could be only a matter of time before Laos, too, would be subjected to Communist rule through an internal takeover by local Communist forces, completed in the course of the autumn.

Developments in Indochina, in turn, inevitably focused attention on the possibility of further Communist advances as predicted by the so-called "domino theory." A fear lest waning confidence in the United States contribute to such developments undoubtedly helped to inspire the vigorous American reaction, not many days after the fall of Saigon, to the seizure and temporary detention of the U.S. containership *Mayagüez* by the new Cambodian authorities. But even this exhibition of American decisiveness did not entirely reassure those Southeast Asian countries that had previously chosen to link their destinies with that of the United States. Thailand, formerly counted as one of the stanchest of U.S. allies, had been especially upset by developments in Cambodia, and not only insisted on an accelerated withdrawal of U.S. military forces from its own territory but joined the Philippines in promoting a "phasing out" of the South-East Asia Treaty Organization (SEATO), established in the 1950s as the principal safeguard of collective security in the region.

The unsettling effect of developments in Indochina extended even to the Korean peninsula, where the U.S.-supported Republic of Korea under President Park Chung Hee appeared to have good reason to fear the growing militancy of the northern Communist government headed by President Kim Il Sung. In spite of some distaste for President Park's authoritarian methods of rule, the United States continued to maintain a substantial military presence in South Korea as well as furnishing its government with material and diplomatic support. Protection of the *status quo* in South Korea was also an important element in the United States' relations with Japan, which had been severely shaken in the early 1970s but had by now regained sufficient stability to permit a long-planned

visit to the United States by Emperor Hirohito and Empress Nagako that took place in the autumn of 1975.

With U.S.-Soviet relations a prey to increased uncertainty, the
United States' *rapprochement* with the People's Republic of China
also failed to advance significantly beyond the generalities of the
so-called Shanghai communiqué, composed on the occasion of
President Nixon's visit in February 1972.[21] Still generally responsive to the moderate, pragmatic administrative style of the ailing
Premier Chou En-lai and his right-hand man, Deputy Premier
Teng Hsiao-ping, China already was affected by the subterranean
tensions that were to burst into the open with the deaths of Chou
En-lai and Chairman Mao Tse-tung in the following year. Although a visit to the People's Republic was among the highlights of
President Ford's Pacific trip in November 1975, no major movement in Sino-U.S. relations could be expected at a time when
Chinese attention was focused on the coming succession struggle
and, more important, the United States was unwilling to diminish
its remaining ties with the rival Chinese Nationalist government on
Taiwan.

Other Regional Issues

As has already been suggested, the United States experienced
some further erosion of its political standing in other areas of the
world where its activity was perceived as less than 100 percent supportive of popular aspirations. The Latin American countries, by
and large, remained profoundly dissatisfied with the attitude of
their northern partner, notwithstanding Washington's endeavors to
pay heed to their economic concerns, to expedite agreement on a
new Panama Canal treaty, and to accommodate the widespread desire for a normalization of relations with Castro's Cuba. In Africa,
American policies were harshly criticized not only by such eccen-
trics as President Idi Amin[22] but also—albeit more in sorrow than
in anger—by moderate black leaders like Zambia's President Ken-
neth Kaunda, who took the opportunity of an official visit to the
United States to complain of what he saw as American lukewarm-
ness toward the African liberation movement.

"What gives Zambia and Africa great cause for concern," the
Zambian chief declared at a White House dinner in April, "is, Mr.
President, America's policy towards Africa—or is it the lack of it,
which, of course, can mean the same thing . . . . You will forgive
us, Mr. President, for our candor if we reaffirmed on this occasion
our dismay at the fact that America has not fulfilled our expectations . . . . To achieve our aim, we need America's total commit-

[21]*AFR, 1972*: 307-11.
[22]Quoted in *UN Monthly Chronicle*, Nov. 1975: 93-4.

ment, total commitment to action consistent with that aim. So far, American policy, let alone action, has been low-keyed. This has given psychological comfort to the forces of evil . . . . America, once an apostle in decolonization, must not be a mere disciple of those which promise but never perform and thus give strength to evils of colonialism and apartheid."[23]

Americans were themselves divided about the justification for such criticisms. Still more divisive, nationally and internationally, was the potentially explosive situation that developed during the latter part of 1975 as the result of the breakup of Portugal's former African empire and the emergence in its various component territories of radical nationalist regimes which, in some instances, showed definite Marxist traits and strong susceptibility to Soviet-type influences. In Angola, a struggle among three rival nationalist groups precipitated a major crisis late in the year in which the leftist Popular Movement for the Liberation of Angola (MPLA), led by Agostinho Neto and actively supported by the Soviet Union and Cuba, was able to establish its preeminence over rival groups supported in varying degrees by Zambia, Zaïre, China, South Africa, and the United States. This threatened intrusion of "cold war" rivalries into Africa, in which Cuba apparently acted as a Soviet cat's-paw in sending at least 6,000 troops to aid the MPLA, not only cut short an incipient improvement in U.S.-Cuban relations but posed a new and clearly serious threat to détente between the United States and the U.S.S.R.

Problems with the Congress

A deeper American involvement in the Angola problem was prevented mainly by the negative attitude prevailing in the American Congress, many of whose members had become distrustful of administration policies in the international field and professed to fear the emergence of a "new Vietnam" in the heart of Africa unless the interventionist proclivities ascribed to Secretary Kissinger and President Ford were drastically curbed. Capitol Hill had not forgotten the record of the 93rd Congress, in 1973-74, in halting the Vietnam involvement and enacting the celebrated War Powers Resolution limiting the President's authority to order the armed forces into combat.[24] The new 94th Congress, younger in membership and even more heavily dominated by the Democratic Party, had not failed to display its independence in ways that emphasized its role as an essential but sometimes mercurial partner in the conduct of foreign policy.

For weeks in the spring of 1975, while the American-supported

---

[23]*Presidential Documents*, 11: 411-12.
[24]Public Law 93-148, Nov. 7, 1973, in *AFR, 1973*: 485-90.

regimes in South Vietnam and Cambodia were fighting their final battle for survival, the Congress had delayed to act upon the administration's pleas for emergency assistance to help save the two endangered governments. In the end, the problem had been solved not by congressional action but by a Communist conquest that made the question of further American aid irrelevant from any but a humanitarian standpoint.

Almost as dramatic had been the prolonged executive-legislative struggle over military aid to Turkey, an old-established NATO ally whose military intervention in Cyprus, aided by weapons acquired under the American military assistance program, had shocked America and the world in the summer of 1974. Continued Turkish occupation of some 40 percent of the island republic had not only alienated Greece from the United States and NATO but had caused extremely adverse reactions in the Congress, which had eventually insisted upon a suspension of military aid to Turkey despite administration warnings that such action could only make matters worse. A crisis was reached in the summer of 1975 when Turkey, infuriated by the failure of Congress to restore the arms flow, assumed direct control of the important U.S. military installations on its territory and in effect deprived the United States of facilities urgently needed for the monitoring of Soviet military activity. Although the situation was eventually alleviated to some extent by the passage of compromise legislation, the issue of principle remained unresolved; nor was any remedy found for the weakening of NATO's eastern flank that resulted from the continuing Greek-Turkish confrontation over Cyprus and other regional questions.

Other problems in executive-congressional relations reflected a similar difficulty in reconciling the demands of military security with the traditional American concern for human rights, fundamental freedoms and the rule of law. Divergences between a security-minded, "pragmatic" executive and a Congress that sometimes inclined to doctrinaire positions repeatedly cropped up in virtually every area of foreign affairs. A classic example had been the congressional refusal, embodied in the Trade Act of 1974, to authorize most-favored-nation commercial treatment or credits for the U.S.S.R. while the latter maintained its restrictions on Jewish emigration. Equally distasteful to many members of Congress was the furnishing of military aid to repressive foreign regimes like those currently in power in Chile, South Korea, the Philippines, and (as some felt) Iran. The revulsion against what was interpreted in some quarters as a deliberate support of foreign dictatorships had inspired a growing number of legislative restrictions on both grants and sales of military equipment, which had expanded greatly in recent years and were widely thought to exacerbate the danger of military conflict.

The Energy Nettle

A specially difficult area of legislative-executive relations had been opened up by recent experience in the field of energy and the realization that the shortages that had occurred at the time of the Arab oil embargo of 1973-74 were only the beginning of a global supply-demand crisis of indefinite duration. Since then, a vigorous, American-inspired effort to organize the principal energy-consuming nations for common action had met with considerable success, and an eighteen-nation International Energy Agency (IEA) was already functioning in Paris under the auspices of the Organization for Economic Cooperation and Development (OECD). Among its early achievements was the approval of plans for emergency oil sharing and for the establishment of a special $25 billion financial support fund to help cope with balance-of-payments problems related to the global price increases of recent years.

Much less successful, to date, had been the administration's quest for support of its endeavors to reduce the United States' dependence on foreign energy supplies. President Nixon, in November 1973, had called for the development "by the end of this decade" of "the potential to meet our own energy needs without depending on any foreign energy sources."[25] President Ford, in an updated program submitted to Congress in January 1975, proposed the somewhat more modest goal of making the nation "invulnerable to cutoffs of foreign oil" by 1985.[26] Designed to bring about a steep reduction in daily oil imports over the next two years, his program called among other things for a system of increased license fees for imported petroleum as well as the abrogation of price controls on domestically produced oil.

Enactment of the program as submitted was blocked, however, by strong congressional objections to a plan that would admittedly increase the cost of oil and gasoline and thus exert additional upward pressure on consumer prices. While Congress and the President proceeded from one confrontation to another, petroleum imports regained their pre-recession volume and the OPEC countries, meeting in Vienna in September, decreed another 10 percent price increase for the nine-month period beginning October 1. [27]

---

[25]*AFR, 1973*: 527.

[26]State of the Union address, Jan. 15, in Chapter 2, Document 4.

[27]A 10 percent increase in the price of "marker" (Arabian light) crude oil for the period Oct. 1, 1975-June 30, 1976 was announced Sept. 27, 1975 at the conclusion of an OPEC ministerial meeting in Vienna. Expressed in terms of an increase from $10.46 to $11.51 per barrel in the price of "buyback" or "participation" oil—i.e., oil sold directly by governments under participation agreements—the change was equivalent to an increase from $11.251 to $12.376 in the "posted price" used in calculating taxes and royalties.

Not until December 22 was the President able to sign a compromise Energy Policy and Conservation Act[28] that would permit rescission of the import fee and decontrol of domestic crude oil over a 40-month period. "For nearly a year," Mr. Ford complained, "the American people and many of our friends abroad have been waiting to see whether the executive and legislative branches of our Government could reach agreement on the basic framework of a national energy policy. It has long been apparent that further delays and indecision would only prolong our Nation's vulnerability to foreign energy producers. Since the oil embargo of 1973, we have in fact become more dependent upon foreign oil, and our total payments to foreign producers have continued to increase at an intolerable rate." Although "by no means perfect," Mr. Ford stated, the new legislation would make it possible "to set up a strategic oil storage system, convert more utility and industrial plants to coal, and take other steps to increase production and promote energy conservation." In this way, he said, it provided "a foundation upon which we can build together toward our goal of energy independence."[29]

The American Outlook

Reluctance to grasp the energy nettle was presumably one more manifestation of the state of mind which, despite official exhortations, had so limited the national response to developments in Indochina and, later, Angola. Undoubtedly the nation as a whole still suffered from a degree of psychic exhaustion after the tumultuous experiences of the past decade. Imperfectly recovered from the Vietnam trauma and preoccupied as seldom before with the immediate realities of crime, inflation, and unemployment, the average American was in no mood to go afield in search of additional problems that originated in unfamiliar parts of the world, had little visible bearing on daily existence, and might conceivably entrap a whole new generation in much the same way that Vietnam had entrapped the generation that was now beginning to step into the leadership.

This feeling of aloofness was tempered, in some measure, by what amounted to a continuation of the familiar "hawk-dove" division of Vietnam days. A substantial body of Americans continued to exhibit not only a wide-ranging interest in international affairs but a settled preference for cooperative action and the maintenance of conciliatory postures toward both friends and adversaries. At the same time, there was evidence of a contrary trend that

---

[28]Public Law 94-163, Dec. 22, 1975.
[29]*Presidential Documents*, 11: 1392.

featured a somewhat undifferentiated type of patriotism and leaned toward vigorously unilateral affirmation of American interests. A kind of nationalistic backlash, undoubtedly fed by the reverses in Indochina and the disillusionments of détente, created special hazards for an administration that was glad to welcome patriotic support in the *Mayagüez* affair or the defense of the intelligence agencies, but was visibly embarrassed when the same elements denounced an intended "giveaway" of U.S. interests in the Panama Canal or a "sellout" of Eastern Europe under the Helsinki declaration. Although this type of criticism did not appear to reflect majority sentiment, it would continue to exert a recognizable influence on the American scene in coming months as the nation prepared to celebrate its bicentennial year and to choose its leaders for the remainder of the decade.

In most respects, the year 1976 was to see a continuation of the healing process that was fast obliterating the scars of Vietnam and Watergate and had already reduced the recent energy emergency to a barely remembered nightmare. Emerging more or less unscathed from the travail of the mid-decade, the nation could look forward to a further easement of at least some of the strains that had weighed upon its recent foreign relationships. Despite the stresses of an election year, the somewhat more equable temper prevailing through most of 1976 would afford a favoring environment for the progress of such American initiatives as those associated with the Sinai disengagement agreement and the new departures in economic development policy announced at the special General Assembly session. It would, in addition, provide the opportunity for some overdue adjustments of America's international stance, particularly in relation to the increasingly insistent problems of Southern Africa. Essential background on these and other foreign policy developments of the mid-1970s will be found in the chapters that follow.

1. THE TRADE ACT OF 1974

(January 3, 1975)

[Five months after President Nixon's resignation and President Ford's assumption of office as the nation's 38th chief executive, the condition of the United States quite obviously left much to be desired from both a domestic and an international viewpoint. As President Ford would shortly point out in his annual address to Congress,[1] the State of the Union was definitely "not good" at this period when the outlook for all of the industrialized democracies was clouded by a formidable array of economic, political, and military problems. One symptom of the nervousness pervading the international front was the worldwide furor touched off by Secretary Kissinger's intimation in *Business Week* that the United States did not exclude the possibility of using military force to ensure the continued flow of Mideast oil in the unlikely event of an attempted "strangulation" of the industrialized world.[2] Another of the ambiguous manifestations that obscured the American foreign policy horizon during these weeks was the peculiar content of the Trade Act of 1974,[3] the last significant piece of legislation to have been bequeathed the nation and the world by the expiring 93rd Congress before its adjournment in December.

Not only the oil-producing countries but also the Soviet Union had reason to be dissatisfied with some of the provisions of the new Trade Act, the legislation originally requested by President Nixon in April 1973 as the basis for American participation in the new round of multilateral trade negotiations to be undertaken under the auspices of the General Agreement on Tariffs and Trade (GATT). Despite repeated warnings by Secretary Kissinger and others, the

---

[1] Chapter 2, Document 4.
[2] Cf. Introduction at note 12.
[3] Public Law 93-618, Jan. 3, 1975.

legislation as finally passed by Congress in the closing days of 1974 included a number of unsolicited provisions which, while obviously important to their congressional sponsors, were seriously troubling to the administration and were deprecated once again by President Ford as he reluctantly signed the measure on January 3, 1975 **(Document 1)**.

One of these legislative additions, optimistically captioned "Freedom of Emigration in East-West Trade," incorporated the gist of the celebrated Jackson-Vanik amendment barring most-favored-nation (MFN) tariff treatment and government credits to Communist countries that restricted freedom of emigration—a practice notoriously characteristic of the Soviet Union, particularly with regard to its citizens of Jewish faith. Another provision of the Trade Act limited to $300 million the amount of routine trade credits that could be made available to the U.S.S.R. without prior congressional approval.[4] The Soviet Union's unexpectedly vehement response to these restrictions, revealed by Secretary Kissinger on January 14 **(Document 2)**, was an indignant repudiation of the bilateral trade agreement (and, by implication, the lend-lease settlement) negotiated by the two countries in 1972 as a central element in President Nixon's détente policy.

The governments of some of the Latin American countries, meanwhile, had taken equally passionate exception to another provision of the Trade Act[5] that offered a partial fulfillment of President Nixon's 1969 promise to institute a system of generalized trade preferences for developing countries. In enacting this provision, Congress had deliberately excluded from its benefits all members of the Organization of Petroleum Exporting Countries (OPEC), the "oil cartel" whose recent price manipulations were held responsible for many of the economic problems now besetting both industrialized and developing countries. In a remarkable display of solidarity with Ecuador and Venezuela, OPEC's two Latin American members, the Latin American countries as a group denounced this action in a special resolution of the Council of the Organization of American States (OAS).[6] Other manifestations of Latin American anger, which would simmer for months to come, included the indefinite postponement of a meeting of American Foreign Ministers that was to have been convened in Buenos Aires in March to pursue the inter-American "dialogue" initiated at Secretary Kissinger's suggestion in 1973 **(Document 3)**.]

[4]Secs. 402 and 613, Public Law 93-618; for background see *AFR, 1974*: 374-89 and 562-77.
[5]Sec. 502, Public Law 93-618; cf. *AFR, 1974*: 570-71.
[6]Resolution CP/RES. 131 (150/75), Jan. 23, in OAS Document OEA/Ser. G, CP/SA.CP/RES, vol. 28 (English): 4-7.

*(1)   Statement by President Ford on Signing the Trade Act,
        January 3, 1975.*[7]

The Trade Act of 1974, which I am signing into law today, will determine for many, many years American trade relations with the rest of the world. This is the most significant trade legislation passed by the Congress since the beginning of trade agreement programs some four decades ago.

It demonstrates our deep commitment to an open world economic order and interdependence as essential conditions of mutual economic health. The act will enable Americans to work with others to achieve expansion of the international flow of goods and services, thereby increasing economic well-being throughout the world.

It will thus help reduce international tensions caused by trade disputes. It will mean more and better jobs for American workers, with additional purchasing power for the American consumer.

There are four very basic elements to this Trade Act: authority to negotiate further reductions and elimination of trade barriers; a mandate to work with other nations to improve the world trading system and thereby avoid impediments to vital services as well as markets; reform of U.S. laws involving injurious and unfair competition; and, improvement of our economic relations with nonmarket economies and developing countries.

Our broad negotiating objectives under this act are to obtain more open and equitable market access for traded goods and services, to assure fair access to essential supplies at reasonable prices, to provide our citizens with an increased opportunity to purchase goods produced abroad, and to seek modernization of the international trading system.

Under the act, the Administration will provide greater relief for American industry suffering from increased imports and more effective adjustment assistance for workers, firms, and communities.

The legislation allows us to act quickly and to effectively counter foreign import actions which unfairly place American labor and industry at a disadvantage in the world market. It authorizes the Administration, under certain conditions, to extend nondiscriminatory tariff treatment to countries whose imports do not currently receive such treatment in the United States

This is an important part of our commercial and overall relations with Communist countries. Many of the act's provisions in this area are very complex and may well prove difficult to implement. I will, of course, abide by the terms of the act, but I must express my reservations about the wisdom of legislative language that can only

[7]Text from *Presidential Documents*, 11: 10-11.

be seen as objectionable and discriminatory by other sovereign nations.

The United States now joins all other major industrial countries, through this legislation, in a system of tariff preferences for imports from developing countries.

Although I regret the rigidity and the unfairness in these provisions, especially with respect to certain oil-producing countries, I am now undertaking the first steps to implement this preference system. By this summer, most developing countries are clearly eligible, and I hope that still broader participation can be possible by that time.

As I have indicated, this act contains certain provisions to which we have some objection and others which vary somewhat from the language we might have preferred. In the spirit of cooperation, spirit of cooperation with the Congress, I will do my best to work out any necessary accommodations.

The world economy will continue under severe strain in the months ahead. This act enables the United States to constructively and to positively meet challenges in international trade. It affords us a basis for cooperation with all trading nations. Alone, the problems of each can only multiply; together, no difficulties are insurmountable.

We must succeed! I believe we will.

This is one of the most important measures to come out of the 93d Congress. I wish to thank very, very generously and from the bottom of my heart the Members of Congress and members of this Administration—as well as the public—who contributed so much to this legislation's enactment.

At this point I will sign the bill.

(2)   Shelving of the U.S.-Soviet Trade Agreement: News conference statement by Secretary of State Kissinger, January 14, 1975.[8]

Secretary Kissinger: Ladies and gentlemen, I am sorry to get you all together at this hour. We had originally agreed with the Soviet Government to make a statement, which I am about to read, on Thursday [January 16]. But there have been a number of inquiries this afternoon which led us to believe that there might be stories that were based on inadequate information and perhaps based on misunderstandings. And in order to avoid exacerbating the situation, and in an already rather delicate moment, we asked the Soviet Embassy whether we might release the statement this evening.

[8]Department of State Press Release 13, Jan. 14; text from *Bulletin*, 72: 139-40. (Questions and answers appear in same: 140-43.)

So I will now read a statement, of which the Soviet Government is aware, and we will have copies for you when you leave. Now, the text of the statement is as follows:

Since the President signed the Trade Act on January 3, we have been in touch with the Soviet Government concerning the steps necessary to bring the 1972 U.S.-Soviet Trade Agreement[9] into force.

Article 9 of that agreement provides for an exchange of written notices of acceptance, following which the agreement, including reciprocal extension of nondiscriminatory tariff treatment (MFN) would enter into force. In accordance with the recently enacted Trade Act, prior to this exchange of written notices, the President would transmit to the Congress a number of documents, including the 1972 agreement, the proposed written notices, a formal proclamation extending MFN to the U.S.S.R., and a statement of reasons for the 1972 agreement. Either House of Congress would then have had 90 legislative days to veto the agreement.

In addition to these procedures, the President would also take certain steps, pursuant to the Trade Act,[10] to waive the applicability of the Jackson-Vanik amendment. These steps would include a report to the Congress stating that the waiver will substantially promote the objectives of the amendment and that the President has received assurances that the emigration practices of the U.S.S.R. will henceforth lead substantially to the achievement of the objectives of the amendment.

It was our intention to include in the required exchange of written notices with the Soviet Government language, required by the provisions of the Trade Act, that would have made clear that the duration of three years referred to in the 1972 Trade Agreement with the U.S.S.R. was subject to continued legal authority to carry out our obligations. This caveat was necessitated by the fact that the waiver of the Jackson-Vanik amendment would be applicable only for an initial period of 18 months, with provision for renewal thereafter.

The Soviet Government has now informed us that it cannot accept a trading relationship based on the legislation recently enacted in this country. It considers this legislation as contravening both the 1972 Trade Agreement, which had called for an unconditional elimination of discriminatory trade restrictions, and the principle of noninterference in domestic affairs. The Soviet Government states that it does not intend to accept a trade status

[9]Text in *Bulletin*, 67: 595-603; summary in *AFR, 1972*: 122-5.
[10]Cf. *AFR, 1974*: 563.

that is discriminatory and subject to political conditions and, accordingly, that it will not put into force the 1972 Trade Agreement. Finally, the Soviet Government informed us that if statements were made by the United States, in the terms required by the Trade Act, concerning assurances by the Soviet Government regarding matters it considers within its domestic jurisdiction, such statements would be repudiated by the Soviet Government.

In view of these developments, we have concluded that the 1972 Trade Agreement cannot be brought into force at this time and that the President will therefore not take the steps required for this purpose by the Trade Act. The President does not plan at this time to exercise the waiver authority.

The administration regrets this turn of events. It has regarded and continues to regard an orderly and mutually beneficial trade relationship with the Soviet Union as an important element in the overall improvement of relations. It will, of course, continue to pursue all available avenues for such an improvement, including efforts to obtain legislation that will permit normal trading relationships.

Now, since undoubtedly a number of you will raise questions and some of you have already raised questions about the implications of this for our political relationships with the Soviet Union, let me make a few observations:

The problem of peace in the nuclear age must be of paramount concern for both nuclear powers. The question of bringing about a more stable international environment depends importantly on improved relations between the United States and the Soviet Union. This essentially bipartisan effort will be continued by this administration.

We have no reason to believe that the rejection of the provisions of the trade bill has implications beyond those that have been communicated to us. It goes without saying that, should it herald a period of intensified pressure, the United States would resist with great determination and as a united people. We do not expect that to happen, however, and as far as the United States is concerned, we will continue to pursue the policy of relaxation of tensions and of improving or seeking to improve relationships leading toward a stable peace.

As far as our domestic debate is concerned, we see no point in reviewing the debate of recent months. We want to make clear that there was no disagreement as to objectives. We differed with some of the Members of Congress about the methods to achieve these objectives—these disagreements are now part of a legislative history.

As far as the administration is concerned, it will pursue the objectives that I have outlined in a spirit of cooperation with the Congress.

And when I have testified before the Senate Foreign Relations Committee on Friday, I will seek their advice as to the steps that in their judgment might be desirable in promoting the cause and the purposes which we all share.

And now I will be glad to answer your questions.

* * *

(3) Postponement of the Meeting of American Foreign Ministers: Department of State statement, January 27, 1975.[11]

The United States regrets that the Government of Argentina, in consultation with the other countries of the hemisphere, has postponed the Buenos Aires meeting of Foreign Ministers scheduled for late March.

The proximate cause of the postponement is the apparent exclusion of all OPEC countries, including Ecuador and Venezuela, from the new tariff preference system. As is well known, the administration opposed this and other restrictions contained in the trade bill and has pledged to work with the Congress to correct them. The President and Secretary of State Kissinger so stated publicly, as did our Representative to the Permanent Council of the Organization of American States last week.

Given these statements regarding our views and intentions, we cannot but consider it inappropriate that some Latin American countries have insisted on conditions for the Buenos Aires meeting which they know to be incompatible with our constitutional processes, as well as substantively unjust.

There is no question—and we have emphasized this to our Latin American friends—that, despite certain deficiencies in the Trade Act, there are many benefits. For example, under our proposed system of tariff preferences, we estimate that more than 30 percent by value of dutiable Latin American exports to the United States will be granted tariff-free treatment. In absolute amounts, tariffs will be eliminated on over $750 million worth of Latin American exports to the United States. It should also be noted that Latin American exports to the United States have more than doubled in value since 1972.

The Trade Act also authorizes us to begin the multilateral trade negotiations in Geneva.[12] These negotiations will lead to reduction

---

[11]Text from *Bulletin*, 72: 214-15; for background cf. *AFR, 1973*: 407-17 and *1974*: 117.
[12]For background cf. same, *1974*: 144.

of tariff and nontariff barriers to trade of great importance to all the developing countries, including Latin America. Moreover, they will benefit Latin America and, indeed, the entire world trading community by providing a deterrent to protectionism around the world—a matter of vital import given today's economic climate.

The United States, in the fall of 1973, began a new dialogue with Latin America to improve relations with our traditional friends in the Western Hemisphere. We hoped that both sides would develop a closer understanding of each other's problems. Over the past year we have jointly made significant progress toward this objective. In this process the United States has renounced any method of pressure as obsolete and inappropriate to the new relationship we seek. We believe this is a reciprocal obligation. Pressure from the south is as inappropriate as pressure from the north.

We will continue to work with our Latin American friends on the problems which have arisen in connection with the Trade Act in a spirit of friendship. We will address cooperatively the many issues which comprise the agenda of the new dialogue in the same spirit of conciliation and friendship.

2. THE STATE OF THE UNION

(January 15, 1975)

[Economic issues were understandably awarded first place in President Ford's address on the State of the Union, delivered on January 15 before a Joint Session of the new 94th Congress elected the preceding November. In voicing his widely quoted opinion that the State of the Union was "not good" in this sixth month of his tenure as chief executive, President Nixon's successor seemed not to be referring to the psychic aftermath of the Vietnam years, the Watergate agony, or the ongoing disclosures of questionable conduct by American intelligence agencies and business firms. Matter more than sufficient for one address could be found in the still deepening recessionary trends which had already halted the normal growth of the nation's real gross product, denied employment to over 5 million Americans, yet failed to spare American households a year of double-digit inflation that had brought a 12.2 percent increase in the consumer price index.

Announcing his intention to recommend a one-time, $16 billion tax reduction, including a $12 billion cash rebate to individuals, the President also outlined a new national energy program designed to supersede President Nixon's "Project Independence"[1] and substitute for the Nixon goal of energy self-sufficiency by the end of the 1970s the more modest but possibly more realistic objective of ending "vulnerability to economic disruption by foreign suppliers" by 1985. The details of the new energy strategy, subsequently spelled out by Secretary Kissinger in an address to the National Press Club,[2] would reverberate throughout the year as one of the central concerns of national and international affairs.

Other significant elements in the administration's current thinking were also left to be elaborated in subsequent messages. One that was of fundamental importance was the President's conviction that

[1]Cf. Introduction at note 25.
[2]Chapter 5, Document 8.

31

notwithstanding the encouragement derived from his recent meeting with General Secretary Brezhnev in Vladivostok, the nation could no longer maintain an arbitrary ceiling on its defense expenditures but must substantially increase its national defense outlays in order to maintain preparedness and manpower levels in the face of rising costs. This point would be explained at some length in the annual budget submitted at the beginning of February.[3] Likewise reserved for a subsequent message[4] was the administration's rising concern over the military situation in South Vietnam and Cambodia, two states whose preservation within the "free world" had hitherto been numbered among the more noteworthy achievements of the incumbent Republican administration.]

(4) . *The State of the Union: Address by President Ford before a Joint Session of the Congress, January 15, 1975.* [5]

(*Excerpts*)

Mr. Speaker, Mr. Vice President, Members of the 94th Congress, and distinguished guests:

Twenty-six years ago, a freshman Congressman, a young fellow with lots of idealism, who was out to change the world, stood before Sam Rayburn in the well of the House and solemnly swore to the same oath that all of you took yesterday, an unforgettable experience, and I congratulate you all.

Two days later, that same freshman stood at the back of this great Chamber, over there someplace, as President Truman, all charged up by his single-handed election victory, reported as the Constitution requires on the state of the Union.

When the bipartisan applause stopped, President Truman said, "I am happy to report to this 81st Congress that the state of the Union is good. Our Nation is better able than ever before to meet the needs of the American people, and to give them their fair chance in the pursuit of happiness. [It] is foremost among the nations of the world in the search for peace."[6]

Today, that freshman Member from Michigan stands where Mr. Truman stood, and I must say to you that the state of the Union is not good.

Millions of Americans are out of work. Recession and inflation

[3]Chapter 4, Documents 6 and 7.
[4]Chapter 3, Document 5.
[5]Text from *Presidential Documents*, 11: 45-53.
[6]*Documents, 1949*: 1.

are eroding the money of millions more. Prices are too high, and sales are too slow.

This year's Federal deficit will be about $30 billion; next year's probably $45 billion. The national debt will rise to over $500 billion.

Our plant capacity and productivity are not increasing fast enough. We depend on others for essential energy.

Some people question their Government's ability to make hard decisions and stick with them. They expect Washington politics as usual.

Yet, what President Truman said on January 5, 1949, is even more true in 1975. We are better able to meet our peoples' needs. All Americans do have a fairer chance to pursue happiness. Not only are we still the foremost nation in the pursuit of peace but today's prospects of attaining it are infinitely brighter.

There were 59 million Americans employed at the start of 1949. Now there are more than 85 million Americans who have jobs. In comparable dollars, the average income of the American family has doubled during the past 26 years.

Now, I want to speak very bluntly. I've got bad news, and I don't expect much, if any, applause. The American people want action, and it will take both the Congress and the President to give them what they want. Progress and solutions can be achieved, and they will be achieved.

*   *   *

To bolster business and industry and to create new jobs, I propose a one-year tax reduction of $16 billion. Three-quarters would go to individuals and one-quarter to promote business investment.

*   *   *

Cutting taxes now is essential if we are to turn the economy around. A tax cut offers the best hope of creating more jobs. Unfortunately, it will increase the size of the budget deficit. Therefore, it is more important than ever that we take steps to control the growth of Federal expenditures.

Part of our trouble is that we have been self-indulgent. For decades, we have been voting ever-increasing levels of Government benefits, and now the bill has come due. We have been adding so many new programs that the size and the growth of the Federal budget has taken on a life of its own.

*   *   *

I have just concluded the process of preparing the budget submissions for fiscal year 1976.[7] In that budget, I will propose legislation to restrain the growth of a number of existing programs. I have also concluded that no new spending programs can be initiated this year, except for energy. Further, I will not hesitate to veto any new spending programs adopted by the Congress.

As an additional step toward putting the Federal Government's house in order, I recommend a 5 percent limit on Federal pay increases in 1975. In all Government programs tied to the consumer price index—including social security, civil service and military retirement pay, and food stamps—I also propose a one-year maximum increase of 5 percent.

* * *

Economic disruptions we and others are experiencing stem in part from the fact that the world price of petroleum has quadrupled in the last year. But, in all honesty, we cannot put all of the blame on the oil-exporting nations. We, the United States, are not blameless. Our growing dependence upon foreign sources has been adding to our vulnerability for years and years, and we did nothing to prepare ourselves for such an event as the embargo of 1973.

During the 1960's, this country had a surplus capacity of crude oil which we were able to make available to our trading partners whenever there was a disruption of supply. This surplus capacity enabled us to influence both supplies and prices of crude oil throughout the world. Our excess capacity neutralized any effort at establishing an effective cartel, and thus the rest of the world was assured of adequate supplies of oil at reasonable prices.

By 1970, our surplus capacity had vanished, and, as a consequence, the latent power of the oil cartel could emerge in full force. Europe and Japan, both heavily dependent on imported oil, now struggle to keep their economies in balance. Even the United States, our country, which is far more self-sufficient than most other industrial countries, has been put under serious pressure.

I am proposing a program which will begin to restore our country's surplus capacity in total energy. In this way, we will be able to assure ourselves reliable and adequate energy and help foster a new world energy stability for other major consuming nations.

But this Nation and, in fact, the world must face the prospect of energy difficulties between now and 1985. This program will impose burdens on all of us with the aim of reducing our consumption of energy and increasing our production. Great attention has been paid to the considerations of fairness, and I can assure you that the burden will not fall more harshly on those less able to bear them.

[7]Chapter 4, Document 6.

I am recommending a plan to make us invulnerable to cutoffs of foreign oil. It will require sacrifices, but it—and this is most important—it will work.

I have set the following national energy goals to assure that our future is as secure and as productive as our past:

— First, we must reduce oil imports by 1 million barrels per day by the end of this year and 2 million barrels per day by the end of 1977.
— Second, we must end vulnerability to economic disruption by foreign suppliers by 1985.
— Third, we must develop our energy technology and resources so that the United States has the ability to supply a significant share of the energy needs of the free world by the end of this century.

* * *

Now let me turn, if I might, to the international dimension of the present crisis. At no time in our peacetime history has the state of the Nation depended more heavily on the state of the world. And seldom, if ever, has the state of the world depended more heavily on the state of our Nation.

The economic distress is global. We will not solve it at home unless we help to remedy the profound economic dislocation abroad. World trade and monetary structure provides markets, energy, food, and vital raw materials—for all nations. This international system is now in jeopardy.

This Nation can be proud of significant achievements in recent years in solving problems and crises. The Berlin agreement, the SALT agreements, our new relationship with China, the unprecedented efforts in the Middle East are immensely encouraging. But the world is not free from crisis. In a world of 150 nations, where nuclear technology is proliferating and regional conflicts continue, international security cannot be taken for granted.

So, let there be no mistake about it. International cooperation is a vital factor of our lives today. This is not a moment for the American people to turn inward. More than ever before, our own well-being depends on America's determination and America's leadership in the whole wide world.

We are a great Nation—spiritually, politically, militarily, diplomatically, and economically. America's commitment to international security has sustained the safety of allies and friends in many areas—in the Middle East, in Europe, and in Asia. Our turning away would unleash new instabilities, new dangers around the globe, which, in turn, would threaten our own security.

At the end of World War II, we turned a similar challenge into an historic opportunity and, I might add, an historic achievement. An old order was in disarray; political and economic institutions were shattered. In that period, this Nation and its partners built new institutions, new mechanisms of mutual support and coopera- tion. Today, as then, we face an historic opportunity. If we act, imaginatively and boldly, as we acted then, this period will in retro- spect be seen as one of the great creative moments of our Nation's history.

The whole world is watching to see how we respond.

A resurgent American economy would do more to restore the confidence of the world in its own future than anything else we can do. The program that this Congress passes can demonstrate to the world that we have started to put our own house in order. If we can show that this Nation is able and willing to help other nations meet the common challenge, it can demonstrate that the United States will fulfill its responsibilities as a leader among nations.

Quite frankly, at stake is the future of industrialized democ- racies, which have perceived their destiny in common and sustained it in common for 30 years.

The developing nations are also at a turning point. The poorest nations see their hopes of feeding their hungry and developing their societies shattered by the economic crisis. The long-term economic future for the producers of raw materials also depends on coopera- tive solutions.

Our relations with the Communist countries are a basic factor of the world environment. We must seek to build a long-term basis for coexistence. We will stand by our principles. We will stand by our interests.We will act firmly when challenged. The kind of a world we want depends on a broad policy of creating mutual incentives for restraint and for cooperation.

As we move forward to meet our global challenges and opportu- nities, we must have the tools to do the job.

Our military forces are strong and ready. This military strength deters aggression against our allies, stabilizes our relations with former adversaries, and protects our homeland. Fully adequate conventional and strategic forces cost many, many billions, but these dollars are sound insurance for our safety and for a more peaceful world.

Military strength alone is not sufficient. Effective diplomacy is also essential in preventing conflict, in building world understand- ing. The Vladivostok negotiations with the Soviet Union[8] represent a major step in moderating strategic arms competition. My recent

[8] *AFR, 1974:* 501-17.

discussions with the leaders of the Atlantic community, Japan, and South Korea[9] have contributed to meeting the common challenge.

But we have serious problems before us that require cooperation between the President and the Congress. By the Constitution and tradition, the execution of foreign policy is the responsibility of the President.

In recent years, under the stress of the Vietnam war, legislative restrictions on the President's ability to execute foreign policy and military decisions have proliferated. As a Member of the Congress, I opposed some and I approved others. As President, I welcome the advice and cooperation of the House and the Senate.

But if our foreign policy is to be successful, we cannot rigidly restrict in legislation the ability of the President to act. The conduct of negotiations is ill-suited to such limitations. Legislative restrictions, intended for the best motives and purposes, can have the opposite result, as we have seen most recently in our trade relations with the Soviet Union.

For my part, I pledge this Administration will act in the closest consultation with the Congress as we face delicate situations and troubled times throughout the globe.

When I became President only 5 months ago, I promised the last Congress a policy of communication, conciliation, compromise, and cooperation. I renew that pledge to the new Members of this Congress.

Let me sum it up. America needs a new direction, which I have sought to chart here today—a change of course which will:

— put the unemployed back to work;
— increase real income and production;
— restrain the growth of Federal Government spending;
— achieve energy independence; and
— advance the cause of world understanding.

We have the ability. We have the know-how. In partnership with the American people, we will achieve these objectives.

As our 200th anniversary approaches, we owe it to ourselves, and to posterity, to rebuild our political and economic strength. Let us make America once again and for centuries more to come what it has so long been—a stronghold and a beacon-light of liberty for the whole world.

Thank you.

3. AID FOR SOUTH VIETNAM AND CAMBODIA

(January 28, 1975)

[Undoubtedly the greatest foreign policy disappointment of the mid-1970s had been the failure of the United States' protracted efforts, military and diplomatic, to restore the peace and ensure the permanent independence of the Republic of Vietnam and the neighboring Indochinese states of Cambodia and Laos. Contrary to the hopes that had been widely expressed at the time, the signature on January 27, 1973 of the Paris Agreement on Ending the War and Restoring Peace in Vietnam,[1] buttressed as it had been with guarantees of the "fundamental national rights" of Cambodia and Laos, had failed to moderate the oft-proclaimed determination of Communist-ruled North Vietnam to establish its ascendancy throughout Vietnam and Indochina. Nor had it lessened the determination of the anti-Communist South Vietnamese government of President Nguyen Van Thieu (and the equally anti-Communist Cambodian regime of President Lon Nol) to defeat the internal insurrectionary elements that had been endeavoring, with liberal North Vietnamese support, to do away with the existing political and social order. Only in Laos had there been achieved at least a temporary modus vivendi, in the form of a coalition government headed by the veteran Prince Souvanna Phouma and encompassing all of the country's significant political elements.

Having painfully extricated itself from active military involvement in Indochina during President Nixon's first administration, the United States had watched with growing dismay the rapid disintegration of the "peace with honor" it had initially been disposed to glorify as one of the outstanding achievements of American diplomacy. Not only had North Vietnamese and Vietcong military units outraged the American Government by their continuing disregard of the "standstill" obligations imposed by the military ceasefire. Even the status of more than 2,400 Americans listed as missing

[1] *AFR, 1973*: 39-52.

in action in Southeast Asia had remained unclarified as North Vietnam withheld its promised cooperation in determining their fate—yet insisted at the same time on scrupulous fulfillment of an alleged American commitment to contribute $3.25 billion in aid of its postwar reconstruction.[2]

Though precluded by Act of Congress from recommitting American military forces to combat in Indochina,[3] the U.S. administration had hoped it might still assist in maintaining a modicum of stability in the area through generous allotments of military and economic aid to the threatened South Vietnamese and Cambodian governments. But even this intention had been frustrated by the contrary attitude of the Congress, which had shown no taste for continuing the U.S. involvement, had sharply reduced both military and economic assistance to South Vietnam, and had restricted aid to the beleaguered Lon Nol government with even greater severity. For the ongoing fiscal year ending June 30, 1975, Congress had authorized $1 billion in military aid to the Republic of Vietnam but had appropriated only $700 million.[4] For Cambodia, it had authorized a total of $377 million for both economic and military assistance, but had limited assistance in the latter category to a maximum of $200 million.[5]

Though Washington may not have been aware that the North Vietnamese were currently preparing what was to their final military offensive against the rival southern regime,[6] American authorities could have few illusions about Saigon's staying power in the absence of continuing infusions of U.S. aid. Even less could they doubt that Cambodia's anti-Communist government, already cut off from most of the country by the encircling "Khmer Rouge" forces, was doomed to early extinction unless its minimum needs could be supplied on an urgent basis. The need for prompt congressional action to avert impending catastrophe was the theme of the special message addressed to Congress by President Ford on January 28, the first in a series of escalating appeals that were to end

[2]Cf. *AFR, 1973*: 14-15. The document on which this claim was based—a letter of Feb. 1, 1973 from President Nixon to North Vietnamese Premier Pham Van Dong—was subsequently published in the *New York Times* of May 20, 1977 and in *Bulletin, 76*: 674-5 (1977).

[3]*AFR, 1973*: 342-3.

[4]Department of Defense Appropriation Authorization Act, 1975 (Public Law 93-365, Aug. 5, 1974); Department of Defense Appropriation Act, 1975 (Public Law 93-437, Oct. 8, 1974).

[5]Foreign Assistance Act of 1974 (Public Law 93-559, Dec. 30, 1974).

[6]Van Tien Dung, "Great Spring Victory: A Summation of Senior General Van Tien Dung of the Combat Situation in the Spring of 1975," excerpted in *New York Times*, Apr. 26, 1976.

only with the complete debacle of the anti-Communist cause in the two countries a quarter of a year later.]

(5)   Supplemental Aid for South Vietnam and Cambodia: Message from President Ford to the Congress, January 28, 1975.[7]

To the Congress of the United States:

Two years ago the Paris Agreement was signed, and several weeks later was endorsed by major nations including the Soviet Union, the United Kingdom, France and the People's Republic of China.[8] We had succeeded in negotiating an Agreement that provided the framework for lasting peace in Southeast Asia. This Agreement would have worked had Hanoi matched our side's efforts to implement it. Unfortunately, the other side has chosen to violate most of the major provisions of this Accord.

The South Vietnamese and Cambodians are fighting hard in their own defense, as recent casualty figures clearly demonstrate. With adequate U.S. material assistance, they can hold their own. We cannot turn our backs on these embattled countries. U.S. unwillingness to provide adequate assistance to allies fighting for their lives would seriously affect our credibility throughout the world as an ally. And this credibility is essential to our national security.

VIETNAM

When the Paris Agreement was signed, all Americans hoped that it would provide a framework under which the Vietnamese people could make their own political choices and resolve their own problems in an atmosphere of peace.

In compliance with that Agreement, the United States withdrew its forces and its military advisors from Vietnam. In further compliance with the Agreement, the Republic of Vietnam offered a comprehensive political program designed to reconcile the differences between the South Vietnamese parties and to lead to free and supervised elections throughout all of South Vietnam. The Republic of Vietnam has repeatedly reiterated this offer and has several times proposed a specific date for a free election open to all South Vietnamese political groups.

Unfortunately, our hopes for peace and for reconciliation have been frustrated by the persistent refusal of the other side to abide by even the most fundamental provisions of the Agreement. North Vietnam has sent its forces into the South in such large numbers

[7]Text from *Presidential Documents*, 11: 109-11.
[8]*AFR, 1973*: 58-63.

that its army in South Vietnam is now greater than ever, close to 289,000 troops. Hanoi has sent tanks, heavy artillery, and anti-aircraft weapons to South Vietnam by the hundreds. These troops and equipment are in South Vietnam for only one reason—to forceably impose the will of Hanoi on the South Vietnamese people. Moreover, Hanoi has refused to give a full accounting for our men missing in action in Vietnam.

The Communists have also violated the political provisions of the Paris Agreement. They have refused all South Vietnamese offers to set a specific date for free elections, and have now broken off negotiations with the Government of the Republic of Vietnam. In fact, they say that they will not negotiate with that Government as it is presently constituted, although they had committed themselves to do so.

Recent events have made it clear that North Vietnam is again trying to impose a solution by force. Earlier this month, North Vietnamese forces captured an entire province [Phuoc Long], the population centers of which were clearly under the control of the South Vietnamese Government when the Paris Agreement was signed. Our intelligence indicates, moreover, that their campaign will intensify further in coming months.

At a time when the North Vietnamese have been building up their forces and pressing their attacks, U.S. military aid to the South Vietnamese Government has not been sufficient to permit one-to-one replacement of equipment and supplies used up or destroyed, as permitted by the Paris Agreement. In fact, with the $700 million appropriation available in the current fiscal year, we have been able to provide no new tanks, airplanes, trucks, artillery pieces, or other major equipment, but only essential consumable items such as ammunition, gasoline, spare parts, and medical supplies. And in the face of the increased North Vietnamese pressure of recent months, these supplies have not kept pace with minimally essential expenditure. Stockpiles have been drawn down and will soon reach dangerously low levels.

Last year, some believed that cutting back our military assistance to the South Vietnamese Government would induce negotiations for a political settlement. Instead, the opposite has happened. North Vietnam is refusing negotiations and is increasing its military pressure.

I am gravely concerned about this situation. I am concerned because it poses a serious threat to the chances for political stability in Southeast Asia and to the progress that has been made in removing Vietnam as a major issue of contention between the great powers.

I am also concerned because what happens in Vietnam can affect the rest of the world. It cannot be in the interests of the United

States to let other nations believe that we are prepared to look the other way when agreements that have been painstakingly negotiated are contemptuously violated. It cannot be in our interest to cause our friends all over the world to wonder whether we will support them if they comply with agreements that others violate.

When the United States signed the Paris Agreement, as when we pursued the policy of Vietnamization, we told the South Vietnamese, in effect, that we would not defend them with our military forces, but that we would provide them the means to defend themselves, as permitted by the Agreement. The South Vietnamese have performed effectively in accepting this challenge. They have demonstrated their determination and ability to defend themselves if they are provided the necessary military materiel with which to do so. We, however, may be judged remiss in keeping our end of the bargain.

We—the Executive and Legislative Branches together—must meet our responsibilities. As I have said earlier,[9] the amount of assistance appropriated by the previous Congress is inadequate to the requirements of the situation.

I am, therefore, proposing:

— A supplemental appropriation of $300 million for military assistance to South Vietnam.

The $300 million in supplemental military assistance that I am requesting for South Vietnam represents the difference between the $1 billion which was authorized to be appropriated for fiscal year 1975 and the $700 million which has been appropriated. This amount does not meet all the needs of the South Vietnamese army in its defense against North Vietnam. It does not, for example, allow for replacement of equipment lost in combat. It is the minimum needed to prevent serious reversals by providing the South Vietnamese with the urgent supplies required for their self-defense against the current level of North Vietnamese attacks.

I believe that this additional aid will help to deter the North Vietnamese from further escalating their military pressure and provide them additional incentive to resume the political discussions envisaged under the Paris Agreement.

All Americans want to end the U.S. role in Vietnam. So do I. I believe, however, that we must end it in a way that will enhance the chances of world peace and sustain the purposes for which we have sacrificed so much.

[9] *AFR, 1974*: 576.

CAMBODIA

Our objective in Cambodia is to restore peace and to allow the Khmer people an opportunity to decide freely who will govern them. To this end, our immediate goal in Cambodia is to facilitate an early negotiated settlement. The Cambodian Government has repeatedly called for talks without preconditions with the other Khmer parties. We have fully supported these proposals as well as the resolution passed by the United Nations General Assembly calling for early negotiations among Khmer parties.[10]

Regrettably, there has been no progress. In fact, the Communists have intensified hostilities by attacking on the outskirts of Phnom Penh and attempting to cut the land and water routes to the capital. We must continue to aid the Cambodian Government in the face of externally supported military attacks. To refuse to provide the assistance needed would threaten the survival of the Khmer Republic and undermine the chances for peace and stability in the area.

The Cambodian Government forces, given adequate assistance, can hold their own. Once the insurgents realize that they cannot win by force of arms, I believe they will look to negotiations rather than war.

I am, therefore, proposing:

— Legislation to eliminate the current ceilings on military and economic assistance to Cambodia, and to authorize the appropriation of an additional $222 million for military aid for Cambodia, and
— An amendment to the fiscal year 1975 budget for the additional $222 million.

To provide the assistance necessary, the present restrictions on our military and economic aid to Cambodia must be removed and additional money provided. The $200 million in military assistance currently authorized was largely expended during the past six months in response to the significantly intensified enemy offensive action. In addition, I have utilized the $75 million drawdown of Department of Defense stocks authorized by Congress for this emergency situation. Since the beginning of the Communist offensive on January 1, ammunition expenditures have risen and will exhaust all available funds well before the end of this fiscal year. To meet minimum requirements for the survival of the Khmer Republic, I am requesting an additional $222 million in military assistance and the elimination of the present $200 million ceiling on military

[10]General Assembly Resolution 3238 (XXIX), Nov. 29, 1974.

assistance to Cambodia. I am also requesting elimination of the $377 million ceiling on overall assistance to Cambodia. This is necessary to enable us to provide vital commodities, mostly food, under the Food for Peace program, to assure adequate food for the victims of war and to prevent the economic collapse of the country.

I know we all seek the same goals for Cambodia—a situation wherein the suffering and destruction has stopped and the Khmer people have the necessary security to rebuild their society and their country. These goals are attainable. With the minimal resources and flexibility I am requesting from you, the Congress, we can help the people of Cambodia to have a choice in determining their future. The consequences of refusing them this assistance will reach far beyond Cambodia's borders and impact severely on prospects for peace and stability in that region and the world. There is no question but that this assistance would serve the interests of the United States.

GERALD R. FORD

The White House,
    January 28, 1975.

4. THE BUDGET FOR FISCAL YEAR 1976

(February 3, 1975)

[President Ford's request for extra funding for South Vietnam and Cambodia was directed to immediate requirements that would, if Congress acted, involve a modification of the Federal Budget for the ongoing fiscal year ending June 30, 1975. The President's longer-range expectations with respect to Federal revenues and expenditures were set forth in the Budget for Fiscal Year 1976, presented to Congress on February 3, 1975 and covering the twelve-month period from July 1, 1975 to June 30, 1976. In conformity with arrangements adopted the previous year, the Fiscal Year 1976 Budget also contained a projection of expenditures for a further three-month period extending from July through September of 1976, the so-called Transition Quarter that would precede the opening of the succeeding fiscal year on October 1, 1976.

As the President had intimated in his State of the Union address,[1] the salient feature of his budget for the Fiscal Year 1976 was the $16 billion tax cut that was thought necessary to spur a revival of economic activity—even though it was also expected to increase the Government's deficit for the twelve-month period to a record peacetime figure of $51.9 billion. A second outstanding feature of the 1976 budget, not emphasized in the State of the Union address but explained at some length in the February 3 Budget Message **(Document 6)**, was a modification of the recent trend which had seen defense expenditure consuming a decreasing share of the gross national product, while nondefense spending, particularly in the form of benefits to individuals and grants to state and local governments, had been increasing in terms of constant as well as current dolllars. To maintain a "military balance . . . essential to our national security and to the maintenance of peace," the President now revealed, the Department of Defense was planning to increase its outlays for military functions and foreign military assistance from $84.8 billion in the current fiscal year to $92.8 billion in fiscal 1976. New obligational (spending) authority for the latter year, the President further urged, should be provided in the unprecedented amount of $104.7 billion.

A part of the rationale for this increase was set forth in the detailed analysis that accompanied the President's message (**Document 7**). Even more illuminating, however, were the views of Secretary of Defense James R. Schlesinger as presented some days later in his annual "Military Posture Statement" to the relevant committees of the Congress. A continuing build-up of Soviet armed power, Secretary Schlesinger made clear, had been the crucial influence on American military calculations. "Despite detente and its opportunities," Dr. Schlesinger asserted, the U.S.S.R. was outspending the United States "in most of the significant categories of defense"; was currently engaged upon "the largest initial deployment of improved strategic capabilities in the history of the nuclear competition"; and had in addition continued to strengthen its general purpose forces and to provide large amounts of military assistance to other states.[2] American perceptions of this mounting Soviet capability, with the resultant uncertainties about Moscow's ultimate intentions, would continue to influence not only the form and scale of the American defense program but also the course of the bilateral U.S.-Soviet negotiations aimed at a new Strategic Arms Limitation (SALT) agreement to implement the understandings reached at Vladivostok in November 1974.]

(6)   Budget Message of the President to the Congress, February 3, 1975.[3]

(*Excerpts*)

To the Congress of the United States:

The year 1976 will mark the bicentennial of this country. With this budget we shall begin our third century as a Nation.

In our first two centuries we have developed from 13 struggling colonies to a powerful leader among nations. Our population has increased from three million to more than 213 million. From a sim-

[2]U.S. Department of Defense, *Report of Secretary of Defense James R. Schlesinger to the Congress on the FY 1976 and Transition Budgets, FY 1977 Authorization Request and FY 1976-1980 Defense Program, February 5, 1975* (Washington: GPO, 1975): I—4-5.

[3]Text from Executive Office of the President, Office of Management and Budget, *The Budget of the United States Government, Fiscal Year 1976* (Washington: GPO, 1975): 3-14.

ple agricultural society we have grown into a complex industrialized one.

Our Government—and its budget—have grown with the Nation, as the increasing complexity of modern society has placed greater responsibilities upon it. Yet our society has remained free and democratic, true to the principles of our Founding Fathers.

As we approach our third century as a Nation, we face serious economic difficulties of recession and inflation. I have a deep faith, however, in the fundamental strength of our Nation, our people, our economy, and our institutions of government. I am confident that we can overcome today's challenges as we have overcome others in the past—and go on to greater achievements.

My budget recommendations are designed to meet longer-term national needs as well as immediate, short-run objectives. It is vital that they do so. Because of the size and momentum of the budget, today's decisions will have far-reaching and long-lasting effects.

The recommendations set forth in this budget are an integral part of the broader series of proposals outlined in my State of the Union address.[4] These proposals provide for:

— fiscal policy actions to increase purchasing power and stimulate economic revival, including tax reductions and greatly increased aid to the unemployed;
— a major new energy program that will hold down energy use, accelerate development of domestic energy resources, and promote energy research and development;
— an increase in outlays for defense in order to maintain preparedness and preserve force levels in the face of rising costs;
— a one-year moratorium on new Federal spending programs other than energy programs; and
— a temporary 5% ceiling on increases in pay for Federal employees, and on those benefit payments to individuals that are tied to changes in consumer prices.

These policies call for decisive action to restore economic growth and energy self-reliance. My proposals include a one-time $16 billion tax cut—$12 billion for individual taxpayers and $4 billion for businesses—to stimulate economic recovery.

Total Federal outlays are estimated to increase 11% between 1975 and 1976. It is essential that we keep a tight rein on spending, to prevent it from rising still further and making tax reduction imprudent. I believe that tax relief, not more Government spending, is the key to turning the economy around to renewed growth.

[4]Chapter 2, Document 4.

I regret that my budget and tax proposals will mean bigger deficits temporarily, for I have always opposed deficits. We must recognize, however, that if economic recovery does not begin soon, the Treasury will lose anticipated receipts and incur even larger deficits in the future.

My energy program calls for an increased fee on imported oil, and an excise tax on domestically produced petroleum and natural gas. The proposals also call for decontrol of oil prices—coupled with a windfall profits tax—and deregulation of prices on new natural gas. These measures will discourage excessive energy use and reduce our dependence on imported oil. The $30 billion in receipts these measures will produce will be refunded to the American people—refunded in a way that helps correct the distortions in our tax system created by inflation. Special provisions will ensure that low-income Americans and State and local governments are compensated equitably. All of these compensatory measures will be in addition to the $16 billion in tax relief I have proposed.

My budget recommendations provide for total outlays of $349.4 billion in 1976, an increase of $35.9 billion over 1975, and anticipate receipts of $297.5 billion, an increase of $18.8 billion over 1975.

The Congressional Budget and Impoundment Control Act of 1974[5] provides for major reforms in the budget process. As part of these reforms, it changes the fiscal year for the Federal budget from the present July-through-June basis to an October-through-September basis, beginning with the 1977 fiscal year. This requires that there be a separate transition quarter, extending from July through September of 1976, after fiscal year 1976 ends and before fiscal year 1977 begins. Estimates for the transition quarter are included in this budget. In general, they anticipate continuing the 1976 program levels unchanged for the additional three months. Because outlays and receipts vary seasonally—that is, they do not occur at uniform rates during the year—the estimates for this quarter (and particularly the deficit) are not representative of a full year's experience.

* * *

BUDGET TRENDS AND PRIORITIES

The Federal budget both reflects our national priorities and helps to move the Nation toward their realization. Recent years have seen a significant shift in the composition of the Federal budget. The proportion of the budget devoted to defense has declined substan-

[5]Public Law 93-344, July 12, 1974; cf. *AFR, 1974*: 375.

tially since 1964, with a corresponding increase in the nondefense proportion of the budget. This shift has been particularly rapid since 1969, due in part to the end of American combat involvement in Vietnam.

Defense outlays remained virtually level in current dollar terms from 1969 to 1974, absorbing substantial cost increases—including the pay raises necessary to establish equitable wage levels for our servicemen and women and to make possible the transition to an all-volunteer armed force. Defense programs have undergone large reductions in real terms—reductions of about 40% since 1969 in manpower and material. In consequence, defense outlays have been a decreasing share of our gross national product, falling from 8.9% in 1969 to 5.9% in 1976.

At the same time, Federal nondefense spending has increased substantially in both current and constant dollar terms, growing from 11.6% of the gross national product in 1969 to an estimated 16.0% in this budget. In the process, the form that Federal spending takes has shifted dramatically away from support for direct Federal operations and toward direct benefits to individuals and grants to State and local governments. About a third of the latter also help to finance payments to individuals. Both legislated increases and built-in program growth have contributed to the doubling of outlays for domestic assistance in the past five years. The sharp drop in defense manpower and procurement has helped make this possible without tax increases or larger deficits.

It is no longer realistically possible to offset increasing costs of defense programs by further reducing military programs and strength. Therefore, this budget proposes an increase in defense outlays in current dollars that will maintain defense preparedness and preserve manpower levels in the face of rising costs. These proposals are the minimum prudent levels of defense spending consistent with providing armed forces which, in conjunction with those of our allies, will be adequate to maintain the military balance. Keeping that balance is essential to our national security and to the maintenance of peace.

In 1969, defense outlays were nearly one-fifth more than combined outlays for aid to individuals under human resource programs and for aid to State and local governments. Despite the increase in current-dollar defense outlays, this budget—only seven years later—proposes spending twice as much money for aid to individuals and State and local governments as for defense.

* * *

NATIONAL SECURITY AND FOREIGN RELATIONS

The ultimate goal of American foreign policy is to ensure the freedom, security, and well-being of the United States as part of a peaceful and prosperous international community. Our diplomacy, backed by a strong national defense, strives to strengthen this international community through the peaceful resolution of international disputes, through arms control, and by fostering cooperation and mutual restraint. We seek a healthy world economy through expanded trade, cooperative solutions to energy problems, and increased world agricultural production to meet mankind's need for food. In today's interdependent world, each of these objectives serves our own national interest even as it helps others.

National security.—The Vladivostok understanding, which I reached with General Secretary Brezhnev of the Soviet Union,[6] represents a major step on the long and arduous road to the control and eventual reduction of nuclear arms. For the first time, we have reached an understanding on specific and equal limitations on strategic nuclear weapons. Once we have concluded an agreement based on these understandings, we will be prepared to take the next step—to seek further reductions, as we have already done in the case of antiballistic missile launchers.

The progress we have already made along the road to eventual strategic arms reductions has been possible only because we have remained strong. If we are to make further progress, we must act to preserve our strategic strength. My defense proposals provide for necessary force improvements, and for the development of strategic alternatives necessary to maintain, within the limits of the Vladivostok agreement, a credible strategic deterrent.

More attention must now be given to maintaining an adequate balance in general purpose forces. In this area we share the burden of defense with our allies. The United States has entered into negotiations between members of NATO and of the Warsaw Pact on mutual and balanced force reductions. If those negotiations are successful, some U.S. forces stationed in Europe could safely be withdrawn. For the time being, however, the United States and its allies must maintain present manpower levels and continue to strengthen conventional combat capabilities.

In an effort to increase efficiency and achieve greater combat capability with existing manpower levels, the Army has undertaken to provide 16 active combat divisions by June of 1976 with approximately the same total number of Army personnel [785,000] as was authorized for 13 divisions in June of 1974. This 16-division combat force will require additional equipment, which is provided for in my budget recommendations.

Because the welfare and survival of the United States and its

6Cf. Chapter 13 at note 14.

allies depend upon the flow of ocean-going trade and supplies, strong naval forces are required. In recent years, the number of Navy ships has decreased, primarily as a result of the retirement of many aging ships built during World War II. The savings from this action have been used to strengthen the combat capabilities of the remaining force. This budget provides for a vigorous program of new ship construction and modernization necessary to maintain the naval balance in the future.

Foreign relations.—In addition to maintaining a strong defense capability, the United States strives, through its diplomacy, to develop and maintain peaceful relationships among nations. Foreign assistance is both an expression of our humanitarian concern and a flexible instrument of diplomacy. Our assistance in Indochina is making an essential contribution to the security and reconstruction of the countries in that region. Additional military assistance is now necessary to enable the South Vietnamese and Cambodian Governments to defend themselves against increasing military pressure.[7] Our assistance in the Middle East is an integral part of our diplomatic effort to continue progress toward a peaceful solution to the area's problems. An increasing portion of our economic aid program is devoted to helping developing countries improve their agricultural productivity.

Higher oil prices, widespread food shortages, inflation, and spreading recession have severely strained the fabric of international cooperation. The United States has undertaken several major diplomatic initiatives designed to help restore international economic stability. Our diplomatic efforts were instrumental in the establishment of the International Energy Agency and its program, which provides for emergency oil sharing, conservation efforts, and development of alternative energy sources.[8] More recently, the United States proposed a $25 billion special financing facility to assist industrialized countries in dealing with balance of payments difficulties.[9] This new facility will supplement expanded operations of the International Monetary Fund. At the World Food Conference, in Rome,[10] the United States proposed a number of measures to deal with the world food problem, including creation of an international system of grain reserves.

In addition, the Trade Act passed by the Congress last December[11] will make possible a strengthening of international trade rela-

[7]Cf. Chapter 3.
[8]*AFR, 1974*: 466-90.
[9]Same: 453-65; cf. Chapter 5 below.
[10]*AFR, 1974*: 427-42.
[11]Cf. note 3 to Chapter 1.

tions by enabling the United States to work with other nations toward reducing tariff and nontariff barriers to trade and improving access to supplies.

The strengthening of international trade and financial cooperation is essential if we and other nations are to cope successfully with current economic stresses. It is a prerequisite for renewed economic progress at home and abroad.

* * *

(7)   The Federal Program by Function: National Defense.[12]

(Excerpt)

Peace and international stability are major United States objectives. National security programs contribute to these goals by helping to maintain the worldwide military equilibrium that is essential to peace. This equilibrium requires a balance in strategic forces between the United States and the Soviet Union, a balance in conventional forces in Central Europe between the NATO and Warsaw Pact nations and a balance in naval strength between the United States and the Soviet Union. A presence in Northeast Asia will also be required, as will an ability to provide weapons and munitions rapidly to allies and friends. Total outlays for national defense[13] will increase from $85.3 billion in 1975 to $94.0 billion in 1976 to maintain defense preparedness and preserve personnel levels in the face of rising costs.

To achieve and maintain a military balance, United States forces must be strengthened. Improved strategic nuclear forces and the development of possible strategic systems for future deployment are planned in order to maintain clear strategic deterrents against the spectrum of potential threats. The fighting power of the general purpose forces will also be strengthened, but with little or no increase in present personnel ceilings. This will be accomplished by shifting personnel from support activities to combat functions and by modernizing weapon systems and equipment. The major change planned is an increase in the number of active Army divisions from 13 in June 1974 to 16 by September 1976. The reserve and guard forces, which augment the active forces, will receive better training, improved equipment and an increased share of combat responsibilities. The tactical air forces will be modernized by the replacement

[12]Text from The Budget of the United States Government, Fiscal Year 1976: 70-76.
[13]Including atomic energy defense activities and other items outside the military budget of the Department of Defense.

of older aircraft with newer and more capable aircraft. A vigorous shipbuilding program is planned to improve and expand the fleet.

Department of Defense. Outlays for Department of Defense military functions and military assistance will increase $8 billion in 1976. This increase is necessary to cover pay and price increases and to maintain defense preparedness.

Under existing law, civilian and military pay raises and military retirement annuity increases would amount to $3.0 billion in 1976. Legislation is proposed to limit these increases to 5% through June 30 of next year. This policy will save $1.8 billion in defense outlays in 1976. This proposal recognizes that Federal employees enjoy greater job security than the average worker under current economic conditions and that increases in recent years in retirement annuities have been well in excess of the rate of inflation.

To aid in planning national security needs, military forces are grouped, regardless of service, according to the major missions to be accomplished. The following table[14] summarizes the defense program on the basis of these major missions in terms of total obligational authority (TOA). Total obligational authority includes budget authority enacted each year by the Congress, plus the authority granted in earlier years that is transferred to subsequent years.

Strategic forces.—The primary objective of the strategic forces is deterrence. In order to constitute credible deterrents across the spectrum of potential threats, these forces must be:

- able to absorb a first strike and respond with devastating effectiveness against any aggressor;
- prepared to execute a range of appropriate attacks, including attacks limited in terms of targets and numbers of weapons;
- perceived as equal in overall capability to the forces of any opponent or combination of opponents so that no one could hope to use a nuclear threat to gain diplomatic or military advantage over the United States and its allies; and
- equivalent to the forces and programs of any other nations in payload, accuracy and reliability.

The Vladivostok negotiations with the Soviet Union are a significant achievement. For the first time in our negotiations with the Soviet Union we have reached an understanding on specific and equal limitations on the total number of strategic delivery vehicles

[14]Omitted; see source document, p. 73.

and missiles with multiple independently targetable warheads (MIRVs). By establishing overall quantitative limits, a substantial expansion of strategic forces can be avoided. Within the limits of the agreement, the United States will continue to deploy an effective combination of strategic bombers, land-based missiles and submarine-launched missiles, and will develop options for the deployment of improved systems in the future. The 1976 strategic program, including systems funded in the research and development program, will permit us to:

- continue engineering development of the B-1 strategic bomber and begin full scale production in 1977 if performance goals in relation to costs are achieved;
- proceed with the Trident submarine system to be deployed in 1979 and design a lower cost alternative to the Trident;
- develop options for future deployment of improved intercontinental ballistic missiles that could be launched from fixed silos or mobile launchers;
- continue development of ballistic missile warhead accuracy improvements and long range cruise missiles;
- maintain technology for ballistic missile defense systems and improve the capability for surveillance and early warning of nuclear attack;
- improve the command, control and communications of the strategic forces.

General purpose forces.—Most land, air and naval forces are designed to perform the general purpose mission of deterring or repelling attacks not deterred by the threat of strategic nuclear retaliation. These threats range from isolated incidents to major assaults by a combination of opponents.

Between 1968 and 1975, the general purpose forces were sharply reduced following the United States disengagement from the conflict in Vietnam. As shown in the summary of active military personnel and forces,[15] military personnel was reduced by 1.4 million, from 3.5 million in 1968 to 2.1 million in 1975. This is the lowest level since before the Korean war and 556,000 less than in 1964 prior to the Vietnam conflict. The number of active divisions, tactical air wings and warships has also been reduced below pre-Vietnam war levels.

The United States has initiated negotiations between the NATO Alliance and the Warsaw Pact on mutual and balanced force reduc-

---

[15]Source document, p. 79. Estimated strengths as of June 30, 1976 were given as: Army, 785,000; Navy, 529,000; Marine Corps, 196,000; Air Force, 590,000; total, 2,100,000.

tions.[16] If these negotiations are successful, some U.S. forces stationed in Europe could be withdrawn. For the time being, however, the United States and its allies must maintain present manpower levels and strengthen conventional combat capabilities. This will be accomplished by shifting manpower from support activities to combat functions, and by modernizing weapon systems and equipment. Increased standardization of weapons will also be emphasized.

With little or no increase in present manpower ceilings, combat capabilities will be strengthened by an increase in the number of active combat elements and an offsetting reduction of headquarters and general support activities. More extensive use of reserve combat components will further augment the active forces. This will result in greater combat power in the early days of a conflict. The major change planned is an increase in the number of active Army divisions from 13 in June 1974, to 16 by September 1976.

Production of modern equipment for the *land forces* will increase in 1976 with emphasis on tanks and antitank weapons. Other procurement priorities include armed helicopters, armored personnel carriers, and air defense weapons. These production increases are necessary, in part, to replace equipment and weapons that were delivered to Middle East nations to rebuild their forces following the Yom Kippur War; in particular the supply of tanks, armored personnel carriers, self-propelled artillery and antitank weapons. At the same time, the Middle East War demonstrated that previously planned inventory levels were too low to sustain United States forces in a conflict that might be fought in the European area. Therefore, production rates will be increased in 1976 to replace the equipment, munitions and spare parts shipped to the Middle East and to build up to the new inventory objectives.

The retirement of many aging ships built during World War II, together with the rapid growth in the Soviet Navy, requires that the United States maintain a vigorous program of new ship construction and modernization for the *naval forces*. Procurement of 10 guided missile frigates will help maintain an appropriate naval balance. The ship construction program for 1976 also includes two more nuclear attack submarines, a DLGN class nuclear-powered guided missile cruiser and two patrol hydrofoil missile ships. A number of destroyer tenders, tankers, and ocean tugs will also be acquired to provide for the adequate maintenance and supply of the fleet.

The *tactical air forces* support the land and naval forces by protecting them from air attack, providing close air support and preventing enemy resupply and reinforcement. Maintaining the superi-

[16]*AFR, 1973*: 552-3 and 557-63.

ority of the tactical air forces is essential to offset the numerical advantages that the Warsaw Pact nations have in land forces and ship-to-ship cruise missiles.

Continued procurement of aircraft is planned in 1976 to replace older systems. Additional production of Air Force F-15 fighters is planned to maintain air superiority. Development of the F-16 air combat fighter will continue. Full scale production of the new A-10 is proposed for close air support of ground forces. Carrier-based F-14s equipped with the Phoenix missile, A-7 and A-6 attack aircraft, EA-6B electronic warfare aircraft and E-2C early warning and surveillance aircraft will be purchased to strengthen Navy and Marine Corps air capabilities. Purchase of S-3A and P-3C aircraft is planned for antisubmarine search and destroy missions. Increased purchases of air-to-air and air-to-ground missiles are also proposed for all tactical air forces.

Increased use of flight simulators for air crew training continues as a high priority. These simulators duplicate the actual flight environment and train pilots in bombing, air combat maneuvering, and emergencies without using aviation fuels or risking men and aircraft.

Airlift and sealift forces.—The transfer of a large amount of supplies on short notice during the October 1973 Middle East War demonstrated the effectiveness of airlift for strategic purposes. Recent improvements in midair refueling have increased the load that can be airlifted over great distances without landing. Several efforts initiated in 1974 to improve the strategic airlift capability will be pursued in 1976.

Guard and Reserve.—The National Guard and Reserves are the initial and primary sources of manpower to augment the active forces during an emergency. Army Guard and Reserve units designated to augment the active divisions will be maintained in the Selected Reserve at a high level of readiness and will train with the active units to which they are affiliated. Air Force Guard and Reserve units will participate for the first time in the strategic mission of refueling. Tankers are transferred from the active forces to the Air Guard and Reserve.

Guard and Reserve recruiting is more successful than anticipated and a large number of individuals with prior service have joined the Selected Reserve. However, an intensified recruiting campaign may be needed to offset the significant number of reservists expected to leave the service during 1975 and 1976 as the last of the draft-inspired enlistees are discharged.

Research and development.—An increase in total obligational authority is necessary to continue the research and development programs that keep U.S. forces modern and maintain technological superiority.

In addition to the strategic development programs discussed earlier, major increases are planned for tactical programs. These include development of an advanced air combat fighter for the Navy and Air Force. This system should be available for procurement in 1978 as a low cost fighter to complement the highly sophisticated F-14 and F-15 aircraft now being deployed by the Navy and Air Force. Work will continue on the development of a new battle tank, armored infantry combat vehicle and attack helicopter system to overcome the Warsaw Pact advantage in armored strength. Naval development programs will emphasize antisubmarine warfare and fleet air defense systems. The Air Force will increase efforts to improve its capability to penetrate and suppress enemy air defenses, and to attack enemy ground forces beyond the reach of friendly ground forces.

There will also be increased emphasis on exploratory research and technology to identify new concepts and to maintain technological superiority.

*   *   *

5. ANATOMY OF THE ENERGY CRISIS

(February 3, 1975)

[It was only recently that energy had come to be generally recognized as the key to continued prosperity, and even long-term survival, for the United States and its partners of the industrial world. The widening gap between prospective energy supplies and the constantly increasing demands of the economically advanced nations had been an object of intense concern to governments since the beginning of the decade. In 1973, it had been brought to the attention of a wider public as member governments of the Organization of Petroleum Exporting Countries (OPEC) imposed a fourfold increase in the export price of crude petroleum and Arab oil-exporting countries declared an outright embargo on crude oil shipments to the United States, the Netherlands, and certain white-ruled African countries.[1]

Although the embargo against the United States and the Netherlands had been lifted in the course of 1974, the possibility of its reimposition at some future date had been difficult to ignore, and there had been much discussion in the United States and elsewhere about the possible reactions of the American Government were this to happen. Secretary of State Kissinger, as already noted, had deprecated—yet not entirely excluded—the idea of U.S. military intervention in the Middle East in such an eventuality.[2] Authoritative Arab spokesmen had commented that any such attempt would be countered by deliberate destruction of the oil installations.

Even without a new embargo, the drastic price increases imposed in 1973—and maintained, with some further upward adjustment, in 1974—had caused immense dislocation throughout the world economy, thus bringing home to all the

[1]*AFR, 1973*: 498-501.
[2]Cf. Introduction at note 12.

industrial nations the need to develop new approaches to the whole problem of energy supplies and use. President Ford, as previously noted, had given high priority to this effort in his January 15 address on the State of the Union.[3] It fell to Secretary of State Kissinger, in an address to Washington's National Press Club on February 3, to trace the international ramifications of the energy problem, describe the steps already taken in conjunction with allied and friendly nations, and outline certain additional measures now contemplated by the U.S. Administration—among them a highly controversial plan to encourage new investment by keeping oil prices high.]

(8)   "Energy—The Necessity of Decision": Address by Secretary of State Kissinger before the National Press Club, Washington, February 3, 1975.[4]

I appreciate this opportunity to speak to you on the question of energy.

The subject is timely, for this week marks an important moment in both our national and international response to the energy crisis.

On Wednesday [February 5], the Governing Board of the International Energy Agency (IEA) convenes in Paris for its monthly meeting. This organization, which grew out of the Washington Energy Conference,[5] represents one of the major success stories of cooperation among the industrialized democracies in the past decade. In recent months it has begun to mobilize and coordinate the efforts of the industrial democracies in energy conservation, research, and development of new energy sources. The IEA already has put in place many of the building blocks of a coordinated energy policy. At the forthcoming meeting, the United States will advance comprehensive proposals for collective action, with special emphasis on the development of new energy sources and the preparation of a consumer position for the forthcoming dialogue with the producers.

Equally important, we are now engaged in a vital national debate on the purposes and requirements of our national energy program. Critical decisions will soon be made by the Congress, decisions that will vitally affect other nations as well as ourselves.

The international and national dimensions of the energy crisis are crucially linked. What happens with respect to international energy policy will have a fundamental effect on the economic

---

[3]Chapter 2, Document 4.

[4]Department of State Press Release 42, Feb. 3; prepared text and titles from *Bulletin*, 72: 237-45.

[5]*AFR, 1974*: 33-48. For the formation of the IEA cf. same: 451-90.

health of this nation. And the international economic and energy crisis cannot be solved without purposeful action and leadership by the United States. Domestic and international programs are inextricably linked.

The energy crisis burst upon our consciousness because of sudden, unsuspected events. But its elements have been developing gradually for the better part of two decades.

In 1950, the United States was virtually self-sufficient in oil. In 1960, our reliance on foreign oil had grown to 16 percent of our requirements. In 1973, it had reached 35 percent. If this trend is allowed to continue, the 1980's will see us dependent on imported oil for fully half of our needs. The impact on our lives will be revolutionary.

This slow but inexorable march toward dependency was suddenly intensified in 1973 by an oil embargo and price increases of 400 percent in less than a single year. These actions—largely the result of political decisions—created an immediate economic crisis, both in this country and around the world. A reduction of only 10 percent of the imported oil, and lasting less than half a year, cost Americans half a million jobs and over 1 percent of national output; it added at least 5 percentage points to the price index, contributing to our worst inflation since World War II; it set the stage for a serious recession; and it expanded the oil income of the OPEC nations from $23 billion in 1973 to a current annual rate of $110 billion, thereby effecting one of the greatest and most sudden transfers of wealth in history.

The impact on other countries much more dependent on oil imports has been correspondingly greater. In all industrial countries, economic and political difficulties that had already reached the margin of the ability of governments to manage have threatened to get out of control.

Have we learned nothing from the past year? If we permit our oil consumption to grow without restraint, the vulnerability of our economy to external disruptions will be grossly magnified. And this vulnerability will increase with every passing year. Unless strong corrective steps are taken, a future embargo would have a devastating impact on American jobs and production. More than 10 percent of national employment and output, as well as a central element of the price structure of the American economy, would be subject to external decisions over which our national policy can have little influence.

As we learned grimly in the 1920's and 1930's, profound political consequences inevitably flow from massive economic dislocations. Economic distress fuels social and political turmoil; it erodes the confidence of the people in democratic government and the confidence of nations in international harmony. It is fertile ground for conflict, both domestic and international.

The situation is not yet so grave. But it threatens to become so. The entire industrialized world faces at the same time a major crisis of the economy, of the body politic, and of the moral fiber. We and our partners are being tested—not only to show our technical mastery of the problems of energy but, even more important, to show if we can act with foresight to regain control of our future.

For underlying all difficulties, and compounding them, is a crisis of the spirit—the despair of men and nations that they have lost control over their destiny. Forces seem loose beyond the power of government and society to manage.

In a sense we in America are fortunate that political decisions brought the energy problem to a head before economic trends had made our vulnerability irreversible. Had we continued to drift, we would eventually have found ourselves swept up by forces much more awesome than those we face today.

As it is, the energy crisis is still soluble. Of all nations, the United States is most affected by the sudden shift from near self-sufficiency to severe dependence on imported energy. But it is also in the best position to meet the challenge. A major effort now—of conservation, of technological innovation, of international collaboration—can shape a different future for us and for the other countries of the world. A demonstration of American resolve now will have a decisive effect in leading other industrial nations to work together to reverse present trends toward dependency. Today's apparently pervasive crisis can in retrospect prove to have been the beginning of a new period of creativity and cooperation.

One of our highest national priorities must be to reduce our vulnerability to supply interruption and price manipulation. But no one country can solve the problem alone. Unless we pool our risks and fortify the international financial system, balance-of-payments crises will leave all economies exposed to financial disruption. Unless all consuming nations act in parallel to reduce energy consumption through conservation and to develop new sources of supply, the efforts of any one nation will prove futile, the price structure of oil will not be reformed, and the collective economic burden will grow. And unless consumers concert their views, the dialogue with the producers will not prove fruitful.

The actions which the United States takes now are central to any hope for a global solution. The volume of our consumption, and its potential growth, are so great that a determined national conservation program is essential. Without the application of American technology and American enterprise, the rapid development of significant new supplies and alternative sources of energy will be impossible.

There is no escape. The producers may find it in their interest to ease temporarily our burdens. But the price will be greater dependence and greater agony a few years from now. Either we tackle our challenge immediately, or we will confront it again and again in increasingly unfavorable circumstances in the years to come. If it is not dealt with by this Administration, an even worse crisis will be faced by the next—and with even more anguishing choices.

History has given us a great opportunity disguised as a crisis. A determined energy policy will not only ease immediate difficulties, it will help restore the international economy, the vitality of all the major industrial democracies, and the hopes of mankind for a just and prosperous world.

The Strategy of Energy Cooperation

We and our partners in the International Energy Agency have been, for a year, pursuing strategy in three phases:

—The first phase is to protect against emergencies. We must be prepared to deter the use of oil or petrodollars as political weapons, and if that fails, we must have put ourselves in the best possible defensive position. To do this, we have established emergency sharing programs to cope with new embargoes and created new mechanisms to protect our financial institutions against disruption. This stage of our common strategy is well on the way to accomplishment.

—The second phase is to transform the market conditions for OPEC oil. If we act decisively to reduce our consumption of imported oil and develop alternative sources, pressure on prices will increase. Measures to achieve this objective are now before the International Energy Agency or national parliaments; we expect to reach important agreements on them before the end of March.

—Once the consumer nations have taken these essential steps to reduce their vulnerability, we will move to the third stage of our strategy: to meet with the producers to discuss an equitable price, market structure, and long-term economic relationship. Assuming the building blocks of consumer solidarity are in place, we look toward a preparatory meeting for a producer-consumer conference before the end of March.[6]

Our actions in all these areas are interrelated. It is not possible to pick and choose; since they are mutually reinforcing, they are essential to each other. No emergency program can avail if each

[6]Cf. Chapter 7.

year the collective dependence on OPEC oil increases. New sources of energy, however vast the investment program, will be ineffective unless strict measures are taken to halt the runaway, wasteful growth in consumption. Unless the industrial nations demonstrate the political will to act effectively in *all* areas, the producers will be further tempted to take advantage of our vulnerability.

In recent months we and our partners have taken important steps to implement our overall strategy. Two safety nets against emergencies have been put in place. In November, the IEA established an unprecedented plan for mutual assistance in the event of a new embargo.[7] Each participating nation is committed to build an emergency stock of oil. In case of embargo, each nation will cut its consumption by the same percentage, and available oil will be shared. An embargo against one will become an embargo against all.

And in January, the major industrial nations decided to create a $25 billion solidarity fund for mutual support in financial crises— less than two months after it was first proposed by the United States.[8] This mutual insurance fund will furnish loans and guarantees to those hardest hit by payments deficits, thus safeguarding the international economy against shifts, withdrawals, or cutoffs of funds by the producers.

The next steps should be to accelerate our efforts in the conservation and development of new energy sources. Action in these areas, taken collectively, will exert powerful pressures on the inflated price. No cartel is so insulated from economic conditions that its price structure is invulnerable to a transformation of the market. Because of the reduced consumption in the past year, OPEC has already shut down a fourth of its capacity, equaling 9 million barrels a day, in order to keep the price constant. New oil exploration, accelerated by the fivefold-higher price, is constantly discovering vast new reserves outside of OPEC. The $10 billion in new energy research in the United States—on the scale of the Manhattan project and the moon-landing program—is certain to produce new breakthroughs sooner or later.

As the industrialized nations reduce consumption and increase their supply, it will become increasingly difficult for OPEC to allocate the further production cuts that will be required among its members. Even now, some OPEC members are shaving prices to keep up their revenue and their share of the market. Indeed, it is not too soon in this decade of energy shortages to plan for the possibility of energy surpluses in the 1980's.

The strategy we have been pursuing with our partners since the

[7] *AFR, 1974*: 465.
[8] Group of Ten communiqué, Washington, Jan. 16, in *Bulletin*, 72: 193-4. For background cf. *AFR, 1974*: 460-61.

Washington Energy Conference has linked our domestic and international energy policies into a coherent whole. We have made remarkable progress, but much remains to be done. The question now is whether the industrialized countries have the will to sustain and reinforce these promising initiatives. Conservation and the development of new sources of energy are the next priorities on our common agenda.

Conservation

Unconstrained consumption of cheap oil is the principal cause of the present vulnerability of the industrial countries. Neither the United States nor other consumers can possibly reduce their dependence on imports until they reverse the normal—which is to say wasteful—growth of consumption.

There is simply no substitute for conservation. Alternative energy supplies will not be available for five or ten years. In the next few years conservation, and only conservation, will enable us both to absorb the present burden of high energy costs and to begin to restore the balance of consumer-producer relations.

Only a determined program of conservation can demonstrate that we and our partners have the will to resist pressures. If the industrialized nations are unwilling to make the relatively minor sacrifices involved in conservation, then the credibility of all our other efforts and defensive measures is called into question.

Some say we face a choice between conservation and restoring economic growth. The contrary is true. Only by overcoming exorbitant international energy costs can we achieve reliable long-term growth. If we doom ourselves to 50 percent dependence on imported energy, with the supply and price of a central element of our economy subject to external manipulation, there is no way we can be sure of restoring and sustaining our jobs and growth. These decisions will depend on foreign countries for whom our prosperity is not necessarily a compelling objective.

To be sure, conservation—by any method—will have an economic cost. The restructuring away from production and consumption of energy-intensive goods which it entails incurs shortrun dislocations. At a time of recession, this must concern us. Yet these costs are small compared to what will be exacted from us if we do not act. Without conservation, we will perpetuate the vulnerability of our economy and our national policy. And we will perpetuate as well the excessive international energy prices which are at the heart of the problem.

At present, the United States—in the midst of recession—is importing 6.7 million barrels of oil a day. When our economy returns to full capacity that figure will rise; by 1977, it will be 8 or 9 million barrels a day in the absence of conservation. Imports will continue to grow thereafter. Even with new production in Alaska and the outer continental shelf, this import gap will remain if we do not reduce consumption significantly and rapidly.

With these prospects in mind, President Ford has set the goal of saving a million barrels a day of imports by the end of this year and 2 million by 1977.[9] That amounts to the increase in dependence that would occur as the economy expands again, in the absence of a conservation program.

Our conservation efforts will be powerfully reinforced by the actions of our IEA partners and of other interested countries such as France. Their collective oil consumption equals ours, and they are prepared to join with us in a concerted program of conservation; indeed, some of them have already instituted their own conservation measures. But any one country's efforts will be nullified unless they are complemented by other consumers. This is why the United States has proposed to its IEA partners that they match our respective conservation targets. Together we can save 2 million barrels a day this year and at least 4 million barrels in 1977.

If these goals are reached, under current economic conditions OPEC will have to reduce its production further; even when full employment returns, OPEC will have surplus capacity. More reductions will be hard to distribute on top of the existing cutbacks of 9 million barrels a day. As a result, pressures to increase production or to lower prices will build up as ambitious defense and development programs get underway. By 1977, some oil producers will have a payments deficit; competition between them for the available market will intensify. The cartel's power to impose an embargo and to use price as a weapon will be greatly diminished.

But if America—the least vulnerable and most profligate consumer—will not act, neither will anyone else. Just as our action will have a multiplier effect, so will our inaction stifle the efforts of others. Instead of reducing our collective imports, we will have increased them by 2-4 million barrels a day. OPEC's ability to raise prices, which is now in question, will be restored. In exchange for a brief respite of a year or two, we will have increased the industrialized world's vulnerability to a new and crippling blow from the producers. And when that vulnerability is exposed to public view through a new embargo or further price rises, the American people will be entitled to ask why their leaders failed to take the measures they could have when they should have.

One embargo—and one economic crisis—should be enough to underline the implications of dependency.

[9]Chapter 2, Document 4.

The Importance of New Supplies

Conservation measures alone, crucial as they are, cannot permanently reduce our dependence on imported oil. To eliminate dependence over the long term, we must accelerate the development of alternative sources of energy. This will involve a massive and complex task. But for the country which broke the secret of fission in five years and landed men on the moon in eight years, the challenge should be exciting. The Administration is prepared to invest in this enterprise on a scale commensurate with those previous pioneering efforts; we are ready as well to share the results with our IEA partners on an equitable basis.

Many of the industrialized countries are blessed with major energy reserves which have not yet been developed—North Sea oil, German coal, coal and oil deposits in the United States, and nuclear power in all countries. We have the technical skill and resources to create synthetic fuels from shale oil, tar sands, and coal gasification and liquefaction. And much work has already been done on such advanced energy sources as breeder reactors, fusion, and solar power.

The cumulative effort will of necessity be gigantic. The United States alone shall seek to generate capital investments in energy of $500 billion over the next 10 years. The Federal Government will by itself invest $10 billion in research into alternative energy sources over the next five years, a figure likely to be doubled when private investment in research is included.

But if this effort is to succeed, we must act now to deal with two major problems—the expense of new energy sources and the varying capacities of the industrialized countries.

New energy sources will cost considerably more than we paid for energy in 1973 and can never compete with the production costs of Middle Eastern oil.

This disparity in cost poses a dilemma. If the industrial countries succeed in developing alternative sources on a large scale, the demand for OPEC oil will fall, and international prices may be sharply reduced. Inexpensive imported oil could then jeopardize the investment made in the alternative sources; the lower oil prices would also restimulate demand, starting again the cycle of rising imports, increased dependence, and vulnerability.

Thus, paradoxically, in order to protect the major investments in the industrialized countries that are needed to bring the international oil prices down, we must insure that the price for oil on the domestic market does not fall below a certain level.

The United States will therefore make the following proposal to the International Energy Agency this Wednesday:

In order to bring about adequate investment in the development of conventional nuclear and fossil energy sources, the major oil-importing nations should agree that they will not allow imported oil to be sold domestically at prices which would make those new sources noncompetitive.

This objective could be achieved in either of two ways. The consumer nations could agree to establish a common floor price for imports, to be implemented by each country through methods of its own choosing such as import tariffs, variable levies, or quotas. Each country would thus be free to obtain balance-of-payments and tax benefits without restimulating consumption, if the international price falls below agreed levels. Alternatively, IEA nations could establish a common IEA tariff on oil imports. Such a tariff could be set at moderate levels and phased in gradually as the need arises.

President Ford is seeking legislation requiring the executive branch to use a floor price or other appropriate measures to achieve price levels necessary for our national self-sufficiency goals.

Intensive technical study would be needed to determine the appropriate level at which prices should be protected. We expect that they will be considerably below the current world oil prices. They must, however, be high enough to encourage the long-range development of alternative energy sources.

These protected prices would in turn be a point of reference for an eventual consumer-producer agreement. To the extent that OPEC's current high prices are caused by fear of precipitate later declines, the consuming countries, in return for an assured supply, should be prepared to offer producers an assured price for some definite period so long as this price is substantially lower than the current price.

In short, the massive development of alternative sources by the industrial countries will confront OPEC with a choice; they can accept a significant price reduction now in return for stability over a longer period, or they can run the risk of a dramatic break in prices when the program of alternative sources begins to pay off: The longer OPEC waits, the stronger our bargaining position becomes.

The second problem is that the capacities of the industrialized countries to develop new energy sources vary widely. Some have rich untapped deposits of fossil fuels. Some have industrial skills and advanced technology. Some have capital. Few have all three.

Each of these elements will be in great demand, and ways must be found to pool them effectively. The consumers therefore have an interest in participating in each other's energy development programs.

Therefore the United States will propose to the IEA this Wednesday the creation of a synthetic fuel consortium within IEA. Such a body would enable countries willing to provide technology and capital to participate in each other's synthetic energy projects. The United States is committed to develop a national synthetic fuel capacity of 1 million barrels a day by 1985; other countries will establish their own programs. These programs should be coordinated and IEA members should have an opportunity to share in the results by participating in the investment. Qualifying participants would have access to the production of the synthetics program in proportion to their investment.

In addition, the United States will propose the creation of an energy research and development consortium within IEA. Its primary task will be to encourage, coordinate, and pool large-scale national research efforts in fields—like fusion and solar power—where the costs in capital equipment and skilled manpower are very great, the lead times very long, but the ultimate payoff in low-cost energy potentially enormous.

The consortium also would intensify the comprehensive program of information exchange which—with respect to coal, nuclear technology, solar energy, and fusion—has already begun within the IEA. We are prepared to earmark a substantial proportion of our own research and development resources for cooperative efforts with other IEA countries which are willing to contribute. Pooling the intellectual effort of the great industrial democracies is bound to produce dramatic results.

When all these measures are implemented, what started as crisis will have been transformed into opportunity; the near-panic of a year ago will have been transformed into hope; vulnerability will have been transformed into strength.

Mutual Interests of Consumers and Producers

Consumer solidarity is not an end in itself. In an interdependent world, our hopes for prosperity and stability rest ultimately on a cooperative long-term relationship between consumers and producers.

This has always been our objective. It is precisely because we wish that dialogue to be substantive and constructive that we have insisted that consumers first put their own house in order. Collective actions to restore balance to the international economic structure, and the development in advance of common consumer views on the agenda, will contribute enormously to the likelihood of the success of the projected consumer-producer dialogue. Without these measures, discussions will only find us restating our divisions and tempt some to seek unilateral advantages at the expense of their partners. The result will be confusion, demoralization, and inequity, rather than a just reconciliation between the two sides.

A conciliatory solution with the producers is imperative for there is no rational alternative. The destinies of all countries are linked to the health of the world economy. The producers seek a better life for their peoples and a future free from dependence on a single depleting resource; the industrialized nations seek to preserve the hard-earned economic and social progress of centuries; the poorer nations seek desperately to resume their advance toward a more hopeful existence. The legitimate claims of producers and consumers, developed and developing countries, can and must be reconciled in a new equilibrium of interest and mutual benefit.

We must begin from the premise that we can neither return to past conditions nor tolerate present ones indefinitely. Before 1973, market conditions were often unfair to the producers. Today, they are unbearable for the consumers; they threaten the very fabric of the international economic system, on which, in the last analysis, the producers are as dependent for well-being as the consumers.

As the consumers approach their preparatory meeting with the producers, what are the basic principles that should guide them?

The United States will propose the following approach to its partners in the IEA:

First, we should explore cooperative consumer-producer action to recycle the huge financial surpluses now accumulating. The oil producers understand that these new assets—which are far greater than they can absorb—may require new management mechanisms. At the same time, the industrial nations know that the stability of the global economic structure requires the constructive participation of the producers.

Second, and closely related to this, is the need to examine our internal investment policies. The oil producers need productive outlets for their revenues; the industrial democracies, while they should welcome new investment, will want to retain control of essential sectors of their economies. These needs can be reconciled through discussion and agreement between consumers and producers.

Third, we must help the producer nations find productive use for their wealth in their own development and in reducing their dependence on a depleting resource. New industries can be established, combining the technology of the industrialized world with the energy and capital of the producers for their own benefit and that of the poorer nations. The creation of fertilizer and petrochemical plants is among the more promising possibilities.

Fourth, the oil-producing countries and the industrial consuming countries share a responsibility to ease the plight of the poorest nations, whose economies have been devastated by

OPEC's price increases. Technology and capital must be combined in an international effort to assist those most seriously affected by the current economic crisis.

Fifth is the need to provide consumers with a secure source of supply. Another attempt to use oil as a weapon would gravely threaten the economies of the industrial nations and destroy the possibilities of consumer-producer cooperation. Oil-sharing arrangements by the consumers would blunt its impact at first, but over time an atmosphere of confrontation would be inevitable. Thus, if the producer-consumer dialogue is to be meaningful, understandings on long-term supplies are essential.

A central issue, of course, will be price. It is vital to agree on prices for the long run which will satisfy the needs of consumers and producers alike. The balance-of-payments crisis of the consumers must be eased; at the same time, the producers are entitled to know that they can count on a reasonable level of income over a period of time.

The United States is ready to begin consultations with the other major consuming nations on this agenda. We will be prepared to expand on these proposals and will welcome the suggestions of our friends so that we can fashion together a common and positive program.

In sum, consumers and producers are at a crossroads. We have the opportunity to forge new political and institutional relationships, or we can go our separate ways, each paying the price for our inability to take the long view. Mutual interest should bring us closer together; only selfishness can keep us apart. The American approach will be conciliatory.

The implications for the structure of world politics are profound. If we act with statesmanship we can shape a new relationship between consumer and producer, between developed and developing nations, that will mark the last quarter of the 20th century as the beginning of the first truly global, truly cooperative international community.

The Need for United Action

The United States will soon celebrate the 200th anniversary of its independence. In those 200 years Americans have gloried in freedom, used the blessings of nature productively, and jealously guarded our right to determine our fate. In so doing, we have become the most powerful nation on earth and a symbol of hope to those who yearn for progress and value justice. Yet now we sometimes seem uncertain of our future, disturbed by our recent past, and confused as to our purpose. But we must persevere, for we have no other choice. Either we lead, or no one leads; either we succeed, or the world will pay for our failure.

The energy challenge is international; it can only be met by the cooperative actions of all the industrial democracies. We are far advanced with our partners toward turning a major challenge into bold creation and determined response.

But our hopes for the future rest heavily on the decisions we take on our own domestic energy program in the days and weeks ahead. Our example—for good or ill—will chart the course for more than ourselves alone. If we hesitate or delay, so will our partners. Undoing measures already instituted, without putting an alternative program in their place, will have implications far transcending the immediate debate.

The United States bears world responsibility not simply from a sense of altruism or abstract devotion to the common good, although those are attributes hardly deserving of apology. We bear it, as well, because we recognize that America's jobs and prosperity—and our hopes for a better future—decisively depend upon a national effort to fashion a unified effort with our partners abroad. Together we can retain control over our affairs and build a new international structure with the producers. Apart we are hostages to fate.

A domestic program that will protect our independence, a cooperative program with other consumers, and accommodation with producers—these are the indispensable and inseparable steps toward a new equilibrium of interest and justice. No one step can succeed in the absence of the other two.

It is the glory of our nation that when challenged, we have always stepped forward with spirit and a will to dare great things. It is now time to do so again and in so doing to reaffirm to ourselves and to the world that this generation of Americans has the integrity of character to carry on the noble experiment that began two centuries ago.[10]

---

[10]For further developments see Chapter 17.

6. SETBACK IN THE MIDDLE EAST

(March 6-23, 1975)

[One way to lessen the danger of another Arab oil embargo was to promote an acceptable peace settlement in the Middle East, a goal to which the United States had in any case been dedicated since the very beginning of the Arab-Israeli conflict in the late 1940s. After each of the major military clashes between Israel and its Arab neighbors—in 1948-49, in 1956, in 1967, and in 1973—American diplomacy had resumed the painstaking endeavor, sometimes alone and sometimes in concert with others, to get the parties to agree on a set of basic conditions under which they could coexist in peace and friendship for the foreseeable future.

In the latest phase of this effort, developed during and since the so-called Yom Kippur War of October 1973, the United States had joined with the Soviet Union in sponsoring a formal peace conference, the Geneva Conference on the Middle East, which had met for two days in December 1973 and had then adjourned to enable Secretary of State Kissinger to pursue his ongoing effort to bring about a disengagement of the Egyptian and Israeli military forces in the Suez Canal-Sinai Peninsula area.[1] In a virtuoso performance that had been everywhere classed among the diplomatic marvels of the decade, the American Secretary of State had succeeded in persuading the Israelis and Egyptians—and, later, the Israelis and Syrians, whose armies confronted one another in the Golan Heights region—to separate their respective military forces and permit the stationing of multinational contingents under United Nations command in the intervening demilitarized zones.[2]

These successful exercises in "step-by-step" diplomacy had not, however, resolved the basic issues that had thus far separated Israel from its Arab neighbors—among them, the question whether Israel should or should not be required to withdraw from every part of

[1] *AFR, 1973*: 603-13.
[2] *AFR, 1974*: 13-20 and 153-64.

the extensive territories it had occupied in the June War of 1967. Nor had the step-by-step method proved well suited to the special conditions prevailing in the Israeli-Jordanian sector, where the situation was complicated by intensely emotional issues concerning the city of Jerusalem, by the volatile temper of the Arab-populated, Israeli-administered West Bank territories, and by the increasing international acceptance—contrary to the wishes of both Israel and Jordan—of the so-called Palestine Liberation Organization (PLO), headed by Yasir Arafat, as the accredited spokesman of the Palestinian Arab people.[3]

Faced with these difficulties on other fronts, the United States had been engaged since late 1974 in trying to promote a second-step Egyptian-Israeli agreement that would involve some further eastward withdrawal of the Israeli forces in the Sinai desert and would permit the Egyptians to recover a further slice of Israeli-occupied territory east of the Suez Canal. Despite strong indications that the desiderata put forward by the two sides would be extremely difficult to reconcile, Secretary Kissinger devoted the better part of sixteen days, from March 6 to March 23, 1975, to still another "shuttle" mission involving repeated conferences with the Israeli Cabinet, headed by Prime Minister Yitzhak Rabin, in Jerusalem, with Egyptian President Anwar al-Sadat and his advisers in Aswan, and with other Middle Eastern leaders in Damascus, Amman, and Riyadh.[4]

In contrast to his earlier successes, Dr. Kissinger in this instance was unable to bridge the distance between the opposing parties. The Egyptians, it soon appeared, were especially insistent that Israel withdraw from the strategic Gidi and Mitla passes and permit free access to the oil fields in and around Abu Rudeis on the Gulf of Suez. The Israelis, however, not only were most reluctant to evacuate the passes, where they had installed an elaborate network of electronic early-warning equipment, but intimated that if the Egyptians were unwilling to conclude a formal peace agreement, they must at least issue a formal declaration of nonbelligerency or "nonuse of force." This, however, was a demand to which the Egyptians felt unable to agree, if only because of the critical attitude of other Arab countries.

In spite of strong American pressure to exhibit greater "flexibility"—including, it is said, an urgent telegram from President Ford suggesting that the United States might otherwise be compelled to reassess its whole policy in the area—the Israelis still stood firm on their demands as Secretary Kissinger made ready to return to the United States on Sunday morning, March 23. In an

[3]Same: 414-23.
[4]Details in *Bulletin*, 72: 471-90; Sheehan, *The Arabs, Israelis, and Kissinger*: 154-63; Golan, *The Secret Conversations of Henry Kissinger*: 227-40.

exchange of airport courtesies with Prime Minister Rabin (**Document 9**), the Secretary of State did not conceal his feeling that it was "a sad day for America" as well as for Israel, and that "different methods and new forums" would now be needed in the continuing search for a just and lasting peace.

The "reassessment" theme came through more strongly as President Ford and Secretary Kissinger met next day, March 24, with the bipartisan leadership of Congress (**Document 10**). By Wednesday, March 26, when Dr. Kissinger held one of his regular news conferences at the State Department, it had come to be widely inferred that "reassessment" meant punishment of Israel, and that the punishment would take the form primarily of reduced American aid to that country. Both in his prepared remarks and in his answers to questions (**Document 11**), the Secretary of State was at pains to combat this impression, which had, apparently, been encouraged in some measure by his own off-the-record comments. In insisting that the United States was not a country that abandoned its friends, Dr. Kissinger made clear his concern not only for Israel but also for the Republic of Vietnam, whose situation had become acutely endangered as the result of new developments that had occurred while he himself was occupied in the Middle East.[5]]

(9) Suspension of Negotiations for an Interim Agreement Between Egypt and Israel: Remarks by Israeli Prime Minister Yitzhak Rabin and Secretary of State Kissinger, Jerusalem, March 23, 1975.[6]

Prime Minister Rabin

Mr. Secretary, I have come to see you off on your way back to Washington as an expression on behalf of the Government of Israel and the people of Israel for the special, unique relations that have existed and will continue to exist between our two countries. I believe that the relations between your country and our country have been based on many common concepts and interests, and I am sure that what has been done in 26 years will continue to be developed.

I have come here, Mr. Secretary, to express our deep appreciation to you. I know you, for many years, from my term as Ambassador of Israel to the United States. I know you as Secretary of State and especially in the last efforts to move this area from war toward peace. I know that you have done more than a human being can do in the efforts to move from war toward peace. I am sorry

[5]For Vietnam developments see Chapter 8; for further Mideast developments see Chapter 29.
[6]Department of State Press Release 166, Mar. 23; text from *Bulletin*, 72: 489-90.

that the present efforts to bring about an interim agreement between Egypt and Israel have been suspended. I am sure that the United States and you will continue to find every possible option, every avenue, to move, or to help the parties to move, from war to peace.

Please accept our great respect, appreciation, and admiration for what you have done.

Secretary Kissinger

Thank you. Mr. Prime Minister, on behalf of my colleagues, let me express our appreciation for your consideration in coming to the airport to see us off. We have worked together for two weeks in the traditional spirit of friendship to move this area toward a peace that no people needs more than the people of Israel, gathered here after 2,000 years of dispersion and a generation of struggle. This is a sad day for America, which has invested much hope and faith, and we know it is a sad day also for Israel, which needs and wants peace so badly.

But the necessities that brought about this effort continue and the need to move toward peace cannot be abandoned. We will now have to look for different methods and new forums, but in any event the United States will do its utmost to contribute to a just and lasting peace in this area. We have had no other goal except to enable the young people in this area to grow up without the fear of war. And, as we leave, we wish the people of Israel all the best. And I want to thank, particularly, my old friend the Prime Minister for the wisdom with which he has conducted himself, for the friendship he has shown to us, and for the dedication that has animated all his action.

(10) Briefing of Bipartisan Congressional Leadership: Remarks by Ron Nessen, Press Secretary to the President, March 24, 1975. [7]

MR. NESSEN. The President began the meeting by saying he did not intend to assign blame for the suspension of the Middle East peace talks. The President gave a short history of efforts to help Israel and Egypt to take another step toward peace. The President said he was greatly disappointed that the talks had been suspended without agreement.

The President said that the parties involved now will assess how to proceed toward peace. The President praised Dr. Kissinger for his "skill and patience"—using his words—and said that everyone was grateful for his efforts.

Dr. Kissinger reviewed in some detail the course of the negotiations. He concluded that the United States will now consider how to further the cause of peace, including the possibility of negotiations at Geneva. . . .

At that point, the President announced that the United States will reexamine the Middle East situation and will keep Congress fully informed on the results of that examination.

REPORTER. Did he use the word "reassess" at that point?

MR. NESSEN. I think both words were used.

The President said that this reexamination or reassessment was being undertaken as a result of the situation which has developed in the last few days, that the reexamination will look into all aspects and all countries in the Middle East.

(11) *Reassessment of Policy in the Middle East: News conference statements by Secretary of State Kissinger, March 26, 1975.* [*]

(*Excerpts*)

I would like to begin with a brief statement concerning the suspension of the Middle East peace talks.

The step-by-step approach pursued by the United States attempted to separate the Middle East problem into individual and therefore manageable segments. Now that approach has suffered a setback, and the Middle East issues have to be dealt with comprehensively, under more difficult circumstances.

A moment of potentially great danger is not the time to assess blame between the parties or to indulge in recrimination. We need a calm appraisal of the situation and the U.S. policy best suited to the new conditions. Let me sum up the U.S. position:

— With the end of the step-by-step approach, the United States faces a period of more complicated international diplomacy. Consequently, a reassessment of policy is essential. This reassessment has been ordered by the President.

— The dangers which produced the need for progress toward peace are still with us. The United States therefore is determined to continue the search for peace in the Middle East. It is prepared to go to Geneva and will be in touch with the cochairman of the conference, the U.S.S.R., in the near future.

[*]Department of State Press Release 172, Mar. 26; text from *Bulletin*, 72: 461-4.

— The United States is prepared to consider any other approach acceptable to the parties.
— The United States remains fully committed to the survival of Israel.
— The search for peace can be nurtured only in an atmosphere of calm. The parties involved in the Middle East conflict thus have a responsibility to moderate words and deeds and to refrain from threatening acts.
— All outside powers have a responsibility to exercise restraint and to follow a course of moderation.

We face a difficult situation in the Middle East and throughout the world. The times demand a renewed sense of national purpose.

We must understand that peace is indivisible. The United States cannot pursue a policy of selective reliability. We cannot abandon friends in one part of the world without jeopardizing the security of friends everywhere.

We cannot master our future except as a united people. Our energies should be directed, not at recriminations about the past, but toward a vigorous and constructive search for a lasting peace. And to this, the Administration is dedicated.

Now I'll take questions.

*   *   *

Reassessment of Middle East Policy

Q. Mr. Secretary, is the reassessment of U.S. policy toward the whole Middle East primarily aimed at prompting Israel to adopt a more relaxed or less intransigent negotiating posture?

Secretary Kissinger: At this moment, there are no negotiations going on, and therefore we would have no concrete proposals to make to Israel, even if Israel asked us what negotiating posture it should adopt.

The assessment of our policy that is now going on is made necessary by the new circumstances. Our policy had been designed, as I pointed out in this statement, to segment the issues into individual elements, to negotiate each element separately, and therefore to permit each party to adjust itself domestically and internationally to a process of gradual approach toward peace.

Now that this approach has to be abandoned, we face an entirely new situation in which, in all probability, all problems will have to be negotiated simultaneously, and in which, instead of a forum in which Israel deals with one Arab country through the mediation of the United States, the strong probability is that Israel will have to deal with all Arab countries in a multilateral forum.

The assessment of our policy is not directed against Israel. It is not designed to induce Israel to alter any particular policy. It is designed to develop a position that the United States can take in order to prevent an increasing radicalization in the area and an increasing tension and, above all, in order to avoid a war in which inevitably the United States would be involved at least indirectly, given the international circumstances.

Q. A very quick followup. You and your spokesmen have denied that this reassessment contemplates a cutoff, but I don't think anybody has denied that it might contemplate a reduction. Can you respond to that?

Secretary Kissinger: There is no level of aid right now that has been set for next year's—for the next year. And therefore the question of a reduction is an entirely academic one.

We have before us an Israeli request of rather large size which at this moment is being staffed on the entirely technical level and has been staffed on the entirely technical level for weeks. It has not yet reached either my desk or the President's desk.

We will make our decisions on aid to Israel on the basis of our national objectives and on the basis of the statement that I made here, that we remain committed to the survival of Israel.

Of course whatever conclusions we come to will be submitted to the Congress, and the Congress can make its independent judgment.

We are not approaching the reassessment with an attitude of cutting aid. And we are approaching it with the attitude of looking at the overall situation in the Middle East to determine what the best course might be.

Q. Mr. Secretary, now that you have written an obituary on step-by-step negotiating, does that mean that you are writing off the possibility of unilateral American action in the Middle East? Are you now going to be walking step-by-step with the Soviet Union? What will be your approach?

Secretary Kissinger: Our approach will be whatever is most likely to lessen the dangers of war and to produce steps toward peace.

As I pointed out in our statement, the United States is prepared to go to Geneva. The United States is prepared also to go along with any other approach that the parties may request of it. So, we are not insistent on any particular approach. We will follow whatever approach is most likely to be effective and is requested by the parties. The obvious forum that is now open is Geneva, but we are prepared to look at other approaches.

* * *

7. A NORTH-SOUTH CONFRONTATION
(Paris, April 7-15, 1975)

[The negative outcome of Secretary Kissinger's Mideast shuttle mission was not the only diplomatic failure of these early months of 1975. A much more ambitious undertaking, encompassing nothing less than the whole complex "North-South" relationship between the world's industrialized and developing countries, also came to grief during these early spring weeks while world attention focused with increasing anxiety on the victorious advance of the North Vietnamese Communists and their local allies in South Vietnam.

The existence of serious disagreements between the advanced industrial countries, including the United States, and the hundred or more developing countries included in the U.N. "Group of 77" had been evident ever since the mid-1960s, and had moved to center stage with the onset of the world oil crisis in late 1973. Within the developing world itself, moreover, the fourfold price increase decreed by the Organization of Petroleum Exporting Countries (OPEC) had opened a fissure between exporting and importing nations, placing the latter at a radical disadvantage reflected in a collective designation as "most seriously affected" (MSA) or "fourth world" countries.

These same events had further exacerbated the differences between the developing countries as a group and the developed, industrialized countries, among which the United States as usual occupied the most conspicuous position. By 1974, it had begun to appear that the developing "North-South" relationship would be governed by a spirit of outright confrontation contrasting markedly with the more equable temper of contemporary East-West relations. Sharp ideological clashes had occurred at the United Nations during that year in connection with such successful developing country initiatives as the Declaration on the Establishment of a New International Economic Order[1] and the Charter of Economic

[1] *AFR, 1974*: 103-7.

Rights and Duties of States,[2] both of which had been adopted by substantial majorities even though unacceptable to the United States and some other industrialized countries.

Although it was widely agreed that the two groups must eventually sit down together and try to reconcile their differences, the United States had consistently taken the position that a meeting between oil importing and exporting countries—or between developed and developing nations generally—should be deferred until such time as the former group had organized its own affairs on the basis of a comprehensive, long-term energy policy. France, on the other hand, had urged with equal persistence that the two groups should get together at the earliest opportunity and attempt to resolve their disagreements in a spirit not of "confrontation" and "domination," but of "concertation" and "negotiation." At a press conference on October 24, 1974, President Valéry Giscard d'Estaing had suggested specifically that a conference of ten or twelve countries, including exporting, industrialized, and developing nations, be convened in 1975 to examine both the central problem of petroleum pricing and the readjustments that would be needed in the world economy as a whole. Meeting the French President in Martinique in mid-December, President Ford had agreed that provided certain basic conditions were met, a preparatory meeting between producers and consumers could be held as early as March 1975 in order to develop an agenda and procedures for a later consumer-producer conference.[3]

Such was the origin of the "Preparatory Meeting for the International Conference Proposed by the President of France," more familiarly known as "Prepcon" or "Prepcon I," which took place in Paris on April 7-15 with a slate of ten participants representing three separate groups: producing countries, industrialized consumer countries, and developing consumer countries. Charles W. Robinson, U.S. Under Secretary of State for Economic Affairs, headed the American delegation, which also included Thomas O. Enders, the Assistant Secretary of State for Economic Affairs and one of the architects of the new International Energy Agency.

Disappointingly for both observers and participants, nine days of "intense and grueling negotiations" in this restricted group proved insufficient even to accomplish the primary task of preparing an agenda for a later full-scale conference. As Assistant Secretary Enders noted after the delegates had separated, there had been "a basic difference of view" between those who, like the United States, envisaged a conference that would be sharply focused on "energy and energy-related issues," and those who con-

[2]Same: 528-41.
[3]Same: 559-60.

tinued to insist on "a much broader conference, extending to all aspects of the relationship between the industrialized countries and the developing world."[4]

The nature of this basic difference, the thinking behind the U.S. position, and the outlook for the coming months were more fully elaborated by Under Secretary Robinson in a subsequent appearance before the Subcommittee on International Resources, Food, and Energy of the House Committee on International Relations (**Document 12**).]

(12) *Preparatory Meeting for the International Conference Proposed by the President of France (Prepcon I), Paris, April 7-15, 1975: Statement by Charles W. Robinson, Under Secretary of State for Economic Affairs, before a congressional subcommittee, May 1, 1975.*[5]

I am pleased to have this opportunity to appear before your subcommittee to provide testimony on the recently concluded preparatory meeting between oil producing and consuming nations and to discuss in broad terms the relationship of this meeting with our overall energy policy.

At the Washington Energy Conference in February 1974, the United States and 12 other industrialized nations agreed that, at the appropriate time, they should meet with developing consumer states and producing countries to explore possibilities for mutually acceptable solutions to the energy problem. The International Energy Agency (IEA), created nine months later, has as one of its goals the institution of contacts and dialogue with the producing nations.[6]

We realized, however, that meaningful discussions could take place only after consuming nations had proved that they would not remain helpless over time to the arbitrary manipulation of the world oil market by the OPEC states. Before we could negotiate effectively, or even gain the necessary respect for serious discussions, we had to undertake unified actions in the energy field that would demonstrate strength and consistency of purpose.

Consequently, our international energy efforts since the Washington Energy Conference have concentrated on the creation of a framework of close consumer-country cooperation. Through this effort, we seek to reduce, and eventually eliminate, our vulnerability to manipulation of our oil supply and oil prices.

Substantial progress has been made in building consumer solidarity over the past 14 months. In the IEA, we have agreed on

[4]*Bulletin*, 72: 621.
[5]Text and subtitles from *Bulletin*, 72: 688-91.
[6]For background cf. note 5 to Chapter 5.

emergency provisions that will enable a unified and coordinated response to any future embargo. Along with other OECD countries, we have agreed to create within the OECD a $25 billion support fund to act as a lender of last resort to industrialized countries suffering severe balance-of-payments costs because of high oil prices.

These efforts, basically short-term insurance policies, are complemented by essential longer term programs to reduce IEA members' collective dependence on imported oil. We have established as a conservation target the reduction of IEA oil imports by 2 million barrels a day by the end of 1975, and similar objectives will be established for later years. We have agreement in principle on a series of interrelated measures to accelerate the development of indigenous energy supplies; it is anticipated that implementation programs will be developed and approved by July 1.

The Paris preparatory meeting of April 7-15, or "Prepcon," took place as a result of a French initiative. Last fall the French President proposed a meeting of a small number of industrialized, developing, and producing countries in Paris to plan a multilateral conference on energy; invitations to such a meeting were issued in March. The French proposal was similar to one made earlier by Saudi Arabian Petroleum Minister [Ahmad Zaki] Yamani, and the French invited the same countries to the Prepcon that Minister Yamani had originally proposed. The Shah of Iran had also shown interest in a producer-consumer conference.

In December at Martinique, President Ford conditioned the participation of the United States in a producer-consumer conference on a sequential four-stage approach, which the IEA subsequently endorsed. In the first stage, consumer cooperation would be strengthened in the areas of finance, conservation, and accelerated development of energy; as I mentioned earlier, concrete programs in these areas have been agreed to. The second stage was to be the Prepcon. Stage 3 would involve intensified consumer cooperation and the development of common consumer positions. Stage 4 would be the holding of the conference. In the light of progress made toward consumer solidarity, we agreed in late March to proceed with the preparatory meeting.

Issues Discussed at Preparatory Meeting

The task of the Prepcon was to agree on the procedures and participants for the energy conference to be held later this year. The 10 participants included representatives from the industrialized countries (the United States, Japan, and the nine members of the European Community represented through a single spokesman), the developing consumer countries (Brazil, India, and Zaïre), and the OPEC nations (Saudi Arabia, Iran, Venezuela, and Algeria). As host, France, which has declined to join the IEA, provided the "technical chairman"; the French were also represented in the European Community delegation.

We went to Paris determined to be cooperative and constructive. We believed that the conference should be one in which rhetoric was minimized and real work toward concrete solutions was maximized. Therefore it was essential, in our view, to have an agenda for the conference that was manageable in size and which offered the promise of real progress.

Despite nine days of intense and grueling negotiations, the 10 delegations at the Prepcon could not reach agreement on the procedural issues for the conference. The talks failed to resolve the fundamental question of what type of conference it would be. The United States, the European Community, and Japan, unanimously supported by other members of the IEA, maintained that the conference should focus on energy and energy-related matters as proposed in the French invitation. The OPEC and LDC [less developed countries] representatives were willing for the conference to discuss energy but only if equal status were given to a wide range of problems relating to the economic relations between developing countries and the rest of the world. Specifically, they insisted that the conference treat raw materials, monetary reform, and assistance to most seriously affected countries on the same basis as energy.

The industrialized countries demonstrated considerable flexibility in the negotiations, offering to interpret quite broadly the topics that could be considered under the general energy rubric. We offered in addition to treat all non-energy-related subjects in other appropriate fora where work on them was already underway. We were not willing, however, to agree, as the OPEC and LDC representatives seemed to want, to create another unproductive forum to discuss the "new international economic order."

Even though the talks adjourned because of disagreement over this basic issue, several other issues were left undecided. The OPEC and LDC representatives sought specific agenda references to maintaining the purchasing power of export earnings and the real value of investments; i.e., indexation of prices and investments. We argued that we could not accept such references since they prejudged the outcome of the conference. We said, however, that we were prepared for them to raise these subjects for discussion at the conference under an agenda formulation that was neutrally cast. Since the Prepcon's mandate was only procedural, we did not attempt to engage in substantive debate over indexation.

Spearheaded by Algeria, the OPEC and LDC states also opposed IEA attendance as an observer at the full conference. They maintained that IEA is a confrontational organization whose existence is not recognized by the OPEC nations. They argued that the presence of the IEA would give the conference too much of an energy orientation and that OECD presence at the conference should suffice for IEA representation. With unanimous support from other IEA members, the United States, the European Community, and Japan were prepared to condition their attendance at the conference, and acceptance of any agreed agenda, on IEA presence as an observer with the right to speak. We believed that to agree on IEA exclusion would be to accept implicitly the confrontational charge. Furthermore, IEA exclusion would prevent representation at the conference (via IEA) of many important consuming countries. This issue was not settled before the conference adjourned.

Let me note parenthetically that it was clear early in the first week that compromise on these fundamental differences was unlikely. Nevertheless the participants continued their negotiations for several extra days and nights in order to explore all possibilities for accommodation. The adjournment of the Prepcon was not accompanied by recrimination among the participants.

Major Conclusions Drawn From Meeting

Mr. Chairman, it is not correct, I think, simply to characterize the Prepcon as a failure. It is true that the main purpose of the meeting was not achieved. On the other hand, all participants gained a much greater appreciation of the others' views which may have a salutary effect on future bilateral and multilateral relations.

What are the major conclusions we have drawn from the Prepcon?

First, the OPEC states have succeeded in linking their interests with those of the LDC's even though high oil prices are seriously damaging the economies of many developing nations. Some LDC nations unfortunately find attractive the idea that they can help solve their economic problems by following the OPEC example; i.e., cartelizing and demanding higher prices for all raw materials. We expect the OPEC-LDC bloc under OPEC leadership to be a strong and vocal force in future international fora, at least until developing countries come to recognize that widespread cartelization will be neither practical nor productive.

Second, the industrialized nations demonstrated strong consumer solidarity, proving the tremendous progress that has been made in the IEA over the past 14 months. During the Prepcon, we coordinated our positions closely with other IEA members. The decision to hold firm in insisting on an energy conference and on IEA participation received unanimous endorsement from the IEA Governing Board, which is composed of representatives from the 18 member countries.

Finally, it appears that the timing is not yet right for a multilateral dialogue on key energy issues. The producers at the Prepcon showed little willingness to engage in serious discussion on energy unless the industrialized nations would consider at the same time the broader issues of LDC relations.

Effect of Meeting on U.S. Energy Policy

We regret that the Prepcon did not succeed. We remain willing to participate in a multilateral conference if one can be arranged that concentrates on energy. But we do not expect our own energy policies to be affected in a major way by the suspension of the Prepcon talks.

Our overall energy policy, pursued both in the United States and in coordination with other IEA countries, will continue to be to bring about a basic shift in the supply-demand balance in the world oil market. This will reduce our vulnerability to foreign supply disruptions, reduce the ability of a small group of countries to manipulate world oil prices arbitrarily, and enable prices to approach their long-term equilibrium level.

The focus of our international efforts will remain in the IEA. We intend to insure that momentum is maintained as we press ahead to implement the conservation and accelerated-development programs.

The Prepcon proved that other IEA members share our belief in the necessity of consumer solidarity. They, too, believe the IEA has a key role to play in dealing with the energy problem. They will, we think, work with us to insure that the IEA's importance and influence will increase in the future.

Given the leading role which the United States has played in the development of the International Energy Agency, it is most important that the United States accede to the Agreement on the International Energy Program[7] without reservation. The United States is now applying the agreement provisionally pending adoption of the requisite implementing legislation by Congress. Unfortunately, the legislation currently under consideration in the House of Representatives would not permit us to adhere to the International Energy Program without reservation. Specifically, this legislation does not fully meet vital IEA requirements relating to demand restraint; that is, conservation, the allocation of petroleum in case of another embargo, and the establishment of a petroleum reserve.

[7]Done at Paris, Nov. 18, 1974 (TIAS 8278); text in *AFR, 1974*: 466-90. The U.S. notification of consent to be bound by the agreement was communicated Jan. 9, 1976, and the agreement entered into force definitively Jan. 19, 1976. For further energy policy developments see Chapter 17.

The antitrust provisions of the legislation under consideration are also deficient. While this subcommittee is not immediately concerned with this legislation, may I take this opportunity to urge you and your colleagues in the House to make every effort to promptly approve legislation which will permit the United States to accede to the Agreement on the International Energy Program.

In the months ahead, we will also seek to intensify our cooperative bilateral relations with producing governments. We have many common interests which provide important opportunities to work together. For instance, our joint commissions with Saudi Arabia and Iran are making significant progress in identifying key areas for cooperation. As we build on and broaden the scope of our activities with these two producers and with other OPEC states, we will create in time a set of economic and political relationships that should enable us to help them achieve important national goals and to appreciate more fully their responsibility for pursuing oil policies that lend stability to the international economy.

We are convinced, Mr. Chairman, that the oil crisis will not simply go away. Our policies are designed to meet the challenge of that crisis. They will, if properly and vigorously pursued, permit us to achieve our two fundamental objectives: an international price of oil set by free market forces and substantial U.S. self-sufficiency in energy.

8. THE STATE OF THE WORLD

(April 10, 1975)

[A feature of the conduct of foreign policy by the Nixon administration had been the issuance each spring of a comprehensive, book-length report on the "State of the World," prepared in the President's name for the purpose of informing Congress and the public about the entire range of the nation's global activities and commitments. Suspended in the turbulent Watergate spring of 1974, this practice was revived in modified form by President Ford when he went before a joint session of the Congress on April 10, 1975, to deliver a foreign policy address of comparable length and scope to the State of the Union address he had delivered under similar auspices on January 15.

But any notion of presenting to the Congress a detached and balanced account of the progress of world affairs had been decisively outmoded by the "vast human tragedy" which, in Mr. Ford's words, had "befallen our friends in Vietnam and Cambodia" in the ten weeks and two days that had elapsed since his January 28 appeal for supplemental military aid amounting to $300 million for the Republic of Vietnam and $222 million for the Khmer Republic.[1] The North Vietnamese offensive which President Ford had apprehended in January had in fact materialized in early March with a series of sharp attacks in the Central Highlands that had led directly to the capture of Ban Me Thuot on March 11 and, later in that same week, to the abrupt decision of South Vietnamese President Thieu to order the evacuation of Kontum, Pleiku, and the entire Central Highlands region.

This unexpected move had been followed over the next fortnight by the virtual cessation of South Vietnamese resistance in the northern provinces. By late March, Quang Tri, Hue, Da Nang, and Quang Ngai were being evacuated, in most cases without a fight, as countless thousands of refugees took to the roads and the Com-

---

[1] Chapter 3, Document 5.

munists, their control of the interior already assured, pushed southward through Qui Nonh and Nha Trang to the very outskirts of the
Saigon area. While President Thieu denounced the United States
for its alleged passivity and failure to live up to its pledges— an apparent reference to the secret assurances conveyed to him by President Nixon on a personal basis before the signature of the Paris
peace agreements[2]—the U.S. Air Force initiated a controversial
evacuation of Vietnamese war orphans that is now remembered
chiefly because of the crash on April 4 of a giant C-5A transport
that caused the death of 143 children and 63 adults.

In Cambodia, meanwhile, intensified insurgent attacks on
Phnom Penh had created a near-desperate situation in which most
of the foreign embassies were already washing their hands of the
Khmer Republic and preparing to come to terms with the insurgent
National United Front, still nominally headed by the exiled Prince
Norodom Sihanouk. Under pressure from leading figures in his
own government, President Lon Nol had departed the country on
April 1, leaving Major General Saukham Khoy, the President of
the Senate, to assume the reins of government and mingle vain appeals to the enemy with equally futile pleas to the United States to
provide the "vital resources" Cambodia so desperately needed. By
the time President Ford was ready to address the Congress on the
evening of April 10 (**Document 13**), the situation in Phnom Penh
was already building toward a final denouement that would see the
emergency evacuation of most U.S. personnel on April 12 and the
fall of the capital to the "Khmer Rouge" insurgents a scant five
days later.

In addition to a passionate plea for emergency aid to South Vietnam and Cambodia, President Ford laid heavy emphasis in his
April 10 address on the need to correct the unsatisfactory relationship between the United States and Turkey that had developed in
the wake of that country's military intervention in Cyprus in the
summer of 1974. A congressionally mandated cutoff of U.S.
military aid to Turkey had taken effect, after several false starts, on
February 5, 1975, but, as Secretary Kissinger and others had
predicted, had heightened rather than softened the intransigence of
the Turkish Government as well as the leaders of the Turkish
Cypriot community, who had soon afterward established what
amounted to a separate Turkish Cypriot state in Turkish-occupied
northern Cyprus.

With Turkey threatening a shutdown of U.S. military installations or even a withdrawal from NATO, the Senate Foreign Relations Committee had approved a bill that would permit the President to lift the suspension of military aid and would also require

[2]Cf. *AFR, 1973*: 14 and 19-20.

him to report to Congress at 30-day intervals on progress toward a Cyprus peace settlement. Sponsored, among others, by Democratic Majority Leader Mike Mansfield of Montana and Republican Minority Leader Hugh Scott of Pennsylvania, the bill (S. 846) was reported to the Senate on the very day of the President's address, although the situation was subsequently to go from bad to worse and several more months were to elapse before even a preliminary adjustment could be reached.]

(13) United States Foreign Policy: Address by President Ford before a Joint Session of the Congress, April 10, 1975.[3]

Mr. Speaker, Mr. President,[4] distinguished guests, my very good friends in the Congress, and fellow Americans:

I stand before you tonight after many agonizing hours in very solemn prayers for guidance by the Almighty. In my report on the State of the Union in January,[5] I concentrated on two subjects which were uppermost in the minds of the American people—urgent actions for the recovery of our economy and a comprehensive program to make the United States independent of foreign sources of energy.

I thank the Congress for the action that it has taken thus far in my response for economic recommendations. I look forward to early approval of a national energy program to meet our country's long-range and emergency needs in the field of energy.

Tonight it is my purpose to review our relations with the rest of the world in the spirit of candor and consultation which I have sought to maintain with my former colleagues and with our countrymen from the time that I took office. It is the first priority of my Presidency to sustain and strengthen the mutual trust and respect which must exist among Americans and their Government if we are to deal successfully with the challenges confronting us both at home and abroad.

The leadership of the United States of America since the end of World War II has sustained and advanced the security, well-being, and freedom of millions of human beings besides ourselves. Despite some setbacks, despite some mistakes, the United States has made peace a real prospect for us and for all nations. I know firsthand that the Congress has been a partner in the development and in the support of American foreign policy, which five

---

[3]Text from *Presidential Documents*, 11: 359-70.
[4]Speaker of the House Carl Albert and President of the Senate Nelson A. Rockefeller.
[5]Chapter 2, Document 4.

Presidents before me have carried forward with changes of course but not of destination.

The course which our country chooses in the world today has never been of greater significance for ourselves as a nation and for all mankind. We build from a solid foundation.

Our alliances with great industrial democracies in Europe, North America, and Japan remain strong with a greater degree of consultation and equity than ever before.

With the Soviet Union we have moved across a broad front toward a more stable, if still competitive, relationship. We have begun to control the spiral of strategic nuclear armaments.

After two decades of mutual estrangement, we have achieved an historic opening with the People's Republic of China.

In the best American tradition, we have committed, often with striking success, our influence and good offices to help contain conflicts and settle disputes in many, many regions of the world. We have, for example, helped the parties of the Middle East take the first steps toward living with one another in peace.

We have opened a new dialog with Latin America, looking toward a healthier hemispheric partnership. We are developing closer relations with the nations of Africa. We have exercised international leadership on the great new issues of our interdependent world, such as energy, food, environment, and the law of the sea.

The American people can be proud of what their Nation has achieved and helped others to accomplish, but we have from time to time suffered setbacks and disappointments in foreign policy. Some were events over which we had no control; some were difficulties we imposed upon ourselves.

We live in a time of testing and of a time of change. Our world— a world of economic uncertainty, political unrest, and threats to the peace—does not allow us the luxury of abdication or domestic discord.

I recall quite vividly the words of President Truman to the Congress when the United States faced a far greater challenge at the end of the Second World War. If I might quote: "If we falter in our leadership, we may endanger the peace of the world, and we shall surely endanger the welfare of this Nation."[6]

President Truman's resolution must guide us today. Our purpose is not to point the finger of blame, but to build upon our many successes, to repair damage where we find it, to recover our balance, to move ahead as a united people. Tonight is a time for straight talk among friends, about where we stand and where we are going.

A vast human tragedy has befallen our friends in Vietnam and Cambodia. Tonight I shall not talk only of obligations arising from

[6]Address of Mar. 12, 1947, in *Documents, 1947*: 7.

legal documents. Who can forget the enormous sacrifices of blood, dedication, and treasure that we made in Vietnam?

Under five Presidents and 12 Congresses, the United States was engaged in Indochina. Millions of Americans served, thousands died, and many more were wounded, imprisoned, or lost. Over $150 billion have been appropriated for that war by the Congress of the United States. And after years of effort, we negotiated, under the most difficult circumstances, a settlement which made it possible for us to remove our military forces and bring home with pride our American prisoners. This settlement, if its terms had been adhered to, would have permitted our South Vietnamese ally, with our material and moral support, to maintain its security and rebuild after two decades of war.

The chances for an enduring peace after the last American fighting man left Vietnam in 1973, rested on two publicly stated premises: first, that if necessary, the United States would help sustain the terms of the Paris accords it signed 2 years ago,[7] and second, that the United States would provide adequate economic and military assistance to South Vietnam.

Let us refresh our memories for just a moment. The universal consensus in the United States at that time, late 1972, was that if we could end our own involvement and obtain the release of our prisoners, we would provide adequate material support to South Vietnam. The North Vietnamese, from the moment they signed the Paris accords, systematically violated the cease-fire and other provisions of that agreement. Flagrantly disregarding the ban on the infiltration of troops, the North Vietnamese illegally introduced over 350,000 men into the South. In direct violation of the agreement, they sent in the most modern equipment in massive amounts. Meanwhile, they continued to receive large quantities of supplies and arms from their friends.

In the face of this situation, the United States—torn as it was by the emotions of a decade of war—was unable to respond. We deprived ourselves by law of the ability to enforce the agreement, thus giving North Vietnam assurance that it could violate that agreement with impunity. Next, we reduced our economic and arms aid to South Vietnam. Finally, we signaled our increasing reluctance to give any support to that nation struggling for its survival.

Encouraged by these developments, the North Vietnamese, in recent months, began sending even their reserve divisions into South Vietnam. Some 20 divisions, virtually their entire army, are now in South Vietnam.

The Government of South Vietnam, uncertain of further American assistance, hastily ordered a strategic withdrawal to more defensible positions. This extremely difficult maneuver, decided upon without consultations, was poorly executed, hampered by floods of refugees, and thus led to panic. The results are painfully obvious and profoundly moving.

In my first public comment on this tragic development,[8] I called for a new sense of national unity and purpose. I said I would not engage in recriminations or attempts to assess the blame. I reiterate that tonight.

In the same spirit, I welcome the statement of the distinguished majority leader of the United States Senate [Mike Mansfield] earlier this week, and I quote: "It is time for the Congress and the President to work together in the area of foreign as well as domestic policy."

So, let us start afresh.

I am here to work with the Congress. In the conduct of foreign affairs, Presidential initiative and ability to act swiftly in emergencies are essential to our national interest.

With respect to North Vietnam, I call upon Hanoi—and ask the Congress to join with me in this call—to cease military operations immediately and to honor the terms of the Paris agreement.

The United States is urgently requesting the signatories of the Paris conference to meet their obligations to use their influence to halt the fighting and to enforce the 1973 accords. Diplomatic notes to this effect[9] have been sent to all members of the Paris conference, including the Soviet Union and the People's Republic of China.

The situation in South Vietnam and Cambodia has reached a critical phase requiring immediate and positive decisions by this Government.

The options before us are few and the time is very short.

— On the one hand, the United States could do nothing more; let the Government of South Vietnam save itself and what is left of its territory, if it can; let those South Vietnamese civilians who have worked with us for a decade or more save their lives and their families, if they can; in short, shut our eyes and wash our hands of the whole affair—if we can.
— Or, on the other hand, I could ask the Congress for authority to enforce the Paris accords with our troops and our tanks and our aircraft and our artillery and carry the war to the enemy.

[8]San Francisco address, Apr. 4, in *Presidential Documents*, 11: 343.
[9]*Bulletin*, 72: 539-40.

There are two narrower options:

— First, stick with my January request that Congress appropriate $300 million for military assistance for South Vietnam and seek additional funds for economic and humanitarian purposes;
— Or increase my requests for both emergency military and humanitarian assistance to levels which, by best estimates, might enable the South Vietnamese to stem the onrushing aggression, to stabilize the military situation, permit the chance of a negotiated political settlement between the North and South Vietnamese, and, if the very worst were to happen, at least allow the orderly evacuation of Americans and endangered South Vietnamese to places of safety.

Let me now state my considerations and my conclusions.

I have received a full report from General [Frederick C.] Weyand [Chief of Staff of the Army], whom I sent to Vietnam to assess the situation. He advises that the current military situation is very critical, but that South Vietnam is continuing to defend itself with the resources available. However, he feels that if there is to be any chance of success for their defense plan, South Vietnam needs urgently an additional $722 million in very specific military supplies from the United States. In my judgment, a stabilization of the military situation offers the best opportunity for a political solution.

I must, of course, as I think each of you would, consider the safety of nearly 6,000 Americans who remain in South Vietnam and tens of thousands of South Vietnamese employees of the United States Government, of news agencies, of contractors and businesses for many years whose lives, with their dependents, are in very grave peril. There are tens of thousands of other South Vietnamese intellectuals, professors, teachers, editors and opinion leaders, who have supported the South Vietnamese cause and the alliance with the United States to whom we have a profound moral obligation.

I am also mindful of our posture toward the rest of the world, and particularly of our future relations with the free nations of Asia. These nations must not think for a minute that the United States is pulling out on them or intends to abandon them to aggression.

I have, therefore, concluded that the national interests of the United States and the cause of world stability require that we continue to give both military and humanitarian assistance to the South Vietnamese.

Assistance to South Vietnam at this stage must be swift and adequate. Drift and indecision invite far deeper disaster. The sums I had requested before the major North Vietnamese offensive and the sudden South Vietnamese retreat are obviously inadequate. Half-hearted action would be worse than none. We must act together and act decisively.

I am, therefore, asking the Congress to appropriate without delay $722 million for emergency military assistance and an initial sum of $250 million for economic and humanitarian aid for South Vietnam.

The situation in South Vietnam is changing very rapidly, and the need for emergency food, medicine, and refugee relief is growing by the hour. I will work with the Congress in the days ahead to develop humanitarian assistance to meet these very pressing needs.

Fundamental decency requires that we do everything in our power to ease the misery and the pain of the monumental human crisis which has befallen the people of Vietnam. Millions have fled in the face of the Communist onslaught and are now homeless and are now destitute. I hereby pledge in the name of the American people that the United States will make a maximum humanitarian effort to help care for and feed these hopeless victims.

And now I ask the Congress to clarify immediately its restrictions on the use of U.S. military forces in Southeast Asia for the limited purposes of protecting American lives by ensuring their evacuation, if this should be necessary. And I also ask prompt revision of the law to cover those Vietnamese to whom we have a very special obligation and whose lives may be endangered should the worst come to pass.

I hope that this authority will never have to be used, but if it is needed, there will be no time for Congressional debate. Because of the gravity of the situation, I ask the Congress to complete action on all of these measures not later than April 19.

In Cambodia, the situation is tragic. The United States and the Cambodian Government have each made major efforts, over a long period and through many channels, to end that conflict. But because of their military successes, steady external support, and their awareness of American legal restrictions, the Communist side has shown no interest in negotiation, compromise, or a political solution. And yet, for the past 3 months, the beleaguered people of Phnom Penh have fought on, hoping against hope that the United States would not desert them, but instead provide the arms and ammunition so badly needed.

I have received a moving letter from the new acting President of Cambodia, Saukham Khoy, and let me quote it for you:

Dear Mr. President, he wrote, As the American Congress reconvenes to reconsider your urgent request for supplemental assistance for the Khmer Republic, I appeal to you to convey to the American legislators our plea not to deny these vital resources to us, if a nonmilitary solution is to emerge from this tragic 5-year-old conflict.

To find a peaceful end to the conflict we need time. I do not know how much time, but we all fully realize that the agony of the Khmer people cannot and must not go on much longer. However, for the immediate future, we need the rice to feed the hungry and the ammunition and the weapons to defend ourselves against those who want to impose their will by force [of arms]. A denial by the American people of the means for us to carry on will leave us no alternative but inevitably abandoning our search for a solution which will give our citizens some freedom of choice as to their future. For a number of years now the Cambodian people have placed their trust in America. I cannot believe that this confidence was misplaced and that suddenly America will deny us the means which might give us a chance to find an acceptable solution to our conflict.

This letter speaks for itself. In January, I requested food and ammunition for the brave Cambodians, and I regret to say that as of this evening, it may be soon too late.

Members of the Congress, my fellow Americans, this moment of tragedy for Indochina is a time of trial for us. It is a time for national resolve.

It has been said that the United States is over-extended, that we have too many commitments too far from home, that we must re-examine what our truly vital interests are and shape our strategy to conform to them. I find no fault with this as a theory, but in the real world such a course must be pursued carefully and in close co-ordination with solid progress toward overall reduction in world-wide tensions.

We cannot, in the meantime, abandon our friends while our adversaries support and encourage theirs. We cannot dismantle our defenses, our diplomacy, or our intelligence capability while others increase and strengthen theirs.

Let us put an end to self-inflicted wounds. Let us remember that our national unity is a most priceless asset. Let us deny our adversaries the satisfaction of using Vietnam to pit Americans against Americans. At this moment, the United States must present to the world a united front.

Above all, let's keep events in Southeast Asia in their proper perspective. The security and the progress of hundreds of millions of people everywhere depend importantly on us.

Let no potential adversary believe that our difficulties or our debates mean a slackening of our national will. We will stand by our friends, we will honor our commitments, and we will uphold our country's principles.

The American people know that our strength, our authority, and our leadership have helped prevent a third world war for more than a generation. We will not shrink from this duty in the decades ahead.

Let me now review with you the basic elements of our foreign policy, speaking candidly about our strengths and some of our difficulties.

We must, first of all, face the fact that what has happened in Indochina has disquieted many of our friends, especially in Asia. We must deal with this situation promptly and firmly. To this end, I have already scheduled meetings with the leaders of Australia, New Zealand, Singapore, and Indonesia, and I expect to meet with the leaders of other Asian countries as well.

A key country in this respect is Japan. The warm welcome I received in Japan last November[10] vividly symbolized for both our peoples the friendship and the solidarity of this extraordinary partnership. I look forward, as I am sure all of you do, with very special pleasure to welcoming the Emperor when he visits the United States later this year.

We consider our security treaty with Japan the cornerstone of stability in the vast reaches of Asia and the Pacific. Our relations are crucial to our mutual well-being. Together, we are working energetically on the international multilateral agenda—in trade, energy, and food. We will continue the process of strengthening our friendship, mutual security, and prosperity.

Also, of course, of fundamental importance is our mutual security relationship with the Republic of Korea, which I reaffirmed on my recent visit.[11]

Our relations with Europe have never been stronger. There are no peoples with whom America's destiny has been more closely linked. There are no peoples whose friendship and cooperation are more needed for the future. For none of the members of the Atlantic community can be secure, none can prosper, none can advance unless we all do so together. More than ever, these times demand our close collaboration in order:

— to maintain the secure anchor of our common security in this time of international riptides;
— to work together on the promising negotiations with our potential adversaries;
— to pool our energies on the great new economic challenge that faces us.

[10]*AFR, 1974*: 491-6.
[11]Same: 496-500.

In addition to this traditional agenda, there are new problems involving energy, raw materials, and the environment. The Atlantic nations face many and complex negotiations and decisions. It is time to take stock, to consult on our future, to affirm once again our cohesion and our common destiny. I therefore expect to join with the other leaders of the Atlantic Alliance at a Western summit in the very near future.[12]

Before this NATO meeting, I earnestly ask the Congress to weigh the broader considerations and consequences of its past actions on the complex Greek-Turkish dispute over Cyprus.[13] Our foreign policy cannot be simply a collection of special economic or ethnic or ideological interests. There must be a deep concern for the overall design of our international actions. To achieve this design for peace and to assure that our individual acts have some coherence, the Executive must have some flexibility in the conduct of foreign policy.

United States military assistance to an old and faithful ally, Turkey, has been cut off by action of the Congress. This has imposed an embargo on military purchases by Turkey, extending even to items already paid for—an unprecedented act against a friend.

These moves, I know, were sincerely intended to influence Turkey in the Cyprus negotiations. I deeply share the concern of many citizens for the immense human suffering on Cyprus. I sympathize with the new democratic government in Greece. We are continuing our earnest efforts to find equitable solutions to the problems which exist between Greece and Turkey. But the result of the Congressional action has been:

— to block progress towards reconciliation, thereby prolonging the suffering on Cyprus;
— to complicate our ability to promote successful negotiations;
— to increase the danger of a broader conflict.

Our longstanding relationship with Turkey is not simply a favor to Turkey; it is a clear and essential mutual interest. Turkey lies on the rim of the Soviet Union and at the gates of the Middle East. It is vital to the security of the eastern Mediterranean, the southern flank of Western Europe, and the collective security of the Western Alliance. Our U.S. military bases in Turkey are as critical to our own security as they are to the defense of NATO.

I therefore call upon the Congress to lift the American arms embargo against our Turkish ally by passing the bipartisan Mansfield-Scott bill now before the Senate. Only this will enable us to work with Greece and Turkey to resolve the differences between our allies. I accept and indeed welcome the bill's requirement for month-

[12]See Chapter 19.
[13]Background in *AFR, 1974*: 377-8 and 571-7.

ly reports to the Congress on progress toward a Cyprus settlement, but unless this is done with dispatch, forces may be set in motion within and between the two nations which could not be reversed.

At the same time, in order to strengthen the democratic government of Greece and to reaffirm our traditional ties with the people of Greece, we are actively discussing a program of economic and military assistance with them. We will shortly be submitting specific requests to the Congress in this regard.

A vital element of our foreign policy is our relationship with the developing countries in Africa, Asia, and Latin America. These countries must know that America is a true, that America is a concerned friend, reliable both in word and deed.

As evidence of this friendship, I urge the Congress to reconsider one provision of the 1974 Trade Act which has had an unfortunate and unintended impact on our relations with Latin America where we have such a long tie of friendship and cooperation. Under this legislation, all members of OPEC were excluded from our generalized system of trade preferences.[14] This, unfortunately, punished two South American friends, Ecuador and Venezuela, as well as other OPEC nations, such as Nigeria and Indonesia, none of which participated in last year's oil embargo. This exclusion has seriously complicated our new dialog with our friends in this hemisphere. I therefore endorse the amendments which have been introduced in the Congress to provide Executive authority to waive those restrictions on [in] the Trade Act that are incompatible with our national interest.

The interests of America as well as our allies are vitally affected by what happens in the Middle East. So long as the state of tension continues, it threatens military crisis, the weakening of our alliances, the stability of the world economy, and confrontation with the nuclear super powers. These are intolerable risks.

Because we are in the unique position of being able to deal with all the parties, we have, at their request, been engaged for the past year and a half in the [sic] peacemaking effort unparalleled in the history of the region. Our policy has brought remarkable successes on the road to peace. Last year, two major disengagement agreements were negotiated and implemented with our help. For the first time in 30 years, a process of negotiation on the basic political issues was begun and is continuing.

Unfortunately, the latest efforts to reach a further interim agreement between Israel and Egypt have been suspended.[15] The issues dividing the parties are vital to them and not amenable to easy and to quick solutions. However, the United States will not be discouraged.

[14]Cf. Chapter 1 at note 5.
[15]Cf. Chapter 6.

The momentum toward peace that has been achieved over the last 18 months must, and will, be maintained. The active role of the United States must, and will, be continued. The drift toward war must, and will, be prevented.

I pledge the United States to a major effort for peace in the Middle East, an effort which I know has the solid support of the American people and their Congress. We are now examining how best to proceed. We have agreed in principle to reconvene the Geneva Conference. We are prepared as well to explore other forums. The United States will move ahead on whatever course looks most promising, either towards an overall settlement or interim agreements should the parties themselves desire them. We will not accept stagnation or stalemate with all its attendant risks to peace and prosperity and to our relations in and outside of the region.

The national interest and national security require as well that we reduce the dangers of war. We shall strive to do so by continuing to improve our relations with potential adversaries.

The United States and the Soviet Union share an interest in lessening tensions and building a more stable relationship. During this process, we have never had any illusions. We know that we are dealing with a nation that reflects different principles and is our competitor in many parts of the globe. Through a combination of firmness and flexibility, the United States, in recent years, laid the basis of a more reliable relationship, founded on mutual interest and mutual restraint. But we cannot expect the Soviet Union to show restraint in the face of the United States' weakness or irresolution.

As long as I am President, America will maintain its strength, its alliances, and its principles as a prerequisite to a more peaceful planet. As long as I am President, we will not permit détente to become a license to fish in troubled waters. Détente must be—and I trust will be—a two-way relationship.

Central to U.S.-Soviet relations today is the critical negotiation to control strategic nuclear weapons. We hope to turn the Vladivostok agreements[16] into a final agreement this year at the time of General Secretary Brezhnev's visit to the United States. Such an agreement would, for the first time, put a ceiling on the strategic arms race. It would mark a turning point in postwar history and would be a crucial step in lifting from mankind the threat of nuclear war.

Our use of trade and economic sanctions as weapons to alter the internal conduct of other nations must also be seriously reexamined. However well-intentioned the goals, the fact is that some of our recent actions in the economic field have been self-defeating, they are not achieving the objectives intended by the Congress, and they have damaged our foreign policy.

[16]Cf. Chapter 13 at note 14.

The Trade Act of 1974 prohibits most-favored-nation treatment, credit and investment guarantees and commercial agreements with the Soviet Union, so long as their emigration policies fail to meet our criteria. The Soviet Union has, therefore, refused to put into effect the important 1972 trade agreement between our two countries.[17]

As a result, Western Europe and Japan have stepped into the breach. Those countries have extended credits to the Soviet Union exceeding $8 billion in the last 6 months. These are economic opportunities, jobs, and business which could have gone to Americans.

There should be no illusions about the nature of the Soviet system, but there should be no illusions about how to deal with it. Our belief in the right of peoples of the world freely to emigrate has been well demonstrated. This legislation, however, not only harmed our relations with the Soviet Union but seriously complicated the prospects of those seeking to emigrate. The favorable trend, aided by quiet diplomacy, by which emigration increased from 400 in 1968 to over 33,000 in 1973 has been seriously set back. Remedial legislation is urgently needed in our national interest.

With the People's Republic of China, we are firmly fixed on the course set forth in the Shanghai communique.[18] Stability in Asia and the world require our constructive relations with one-fourth of the human race. After two decades of mutual isolation and hostility, we have, in recent years, built a promising foundation. Deep differences in our philosophy and social systems will endure, but so should our mutual long-term interests and the goals to which our countries have jointly subscribed in Shanghai. I will visit China later this year[19] to reaffirm these interests and to accelerate the improvement in our relations, and I was glad to welcome the distinguished Speaker and the distinguished minority leader of the House[20] back today from their constructive visit to the People's Republic of China.

Let me talk about new challenges. The issues I have discussed are the most pressing of the traditional agenda on foreign policy, but ahead of us also is a vast new agenda in an interdependent world. The United States, with its economic power, its technology, its zest for new horizons, is the acknowledged world leader in dealing with many of these challenges.

If this is a moment of uncertainty in the world, it is even more a moment of rare opportunity:

[17]Cf. Chapter 1, Document 2.
[18]*AFR, 1972*: 307-11.
[19]Cf. Chapter 40.
[20]Speaker Carl Albert and Minority Leader John Rhodes.

—We are summoned to meet one of man's most basic challenges—hunger. At the World Food Conference last November in Rome, the United States outlined a comprehensive program to close the ominous gap between population growth and food production over the long term.[21] Our technological skill and our enormous productive capacity are crucial to accomplishing this task.

—The old order—in trade, finance, and raw materials—is changing and American leadership is needed in the creation of new institutions and practices for worldwide prosperity and progress.

—The world's oceans, with their immense resources and strategic importance, must become areas of cooperation rather than conflict. American policy is directed to that end.

—Technology must be harnessed to the service of mankind while protecting the environment. This, too, is an arena for American leadership.

—The interests and the aspirations of the developed and developing nations must be reconciled in a manner that is both realistic and humane. This is our goal in this new era.

One of the finest success stories in our foreign policy is our cooperative effort with other major energy consuming nations.[22] In little more than a year, together with our partners,

—we have created the International Energy Agency;

—we have negotiated an emergency sharing arrangement which helps to reduce the dangers of an embargo;

—we have launched major international conservation efforts;

—we have developed a massive program for the development of alternative sources of energy.

But the fate of all of these programs depends crucially on what we do at home. Every month that passes brings us closer to the day when we will be dependent on imported energy for 50 percent of our requirements. A new embargo under these conditions could have a devastating impact on jobs, industrial expansion, and inflation at home. Our economy cannot be left to the mercy of decisions over which we have no control. And I call upon the Congress to act affirmatively.

In a world where information is power, a vital element of our national security lies in our intelligence services. They are essential to our Nation's security in peace as in war. Americans can be grateful

[21]Cf. Chapter 4 at note 10.
[22]Cf. Chapter 5.

for the important, but largely unsung, contributions and achievements of the intelligence services of this Nation.

It is entirely proper that this system be subject to Congressional review. But a sensationalized debate over legitimate intelligence activities is a disservice to this Nation and a threat to our intelligence system. It ties our hands while our potential enemies operate with secrecy, with skill, and with vast resources. Any investigation must be conducted with maximum discretion and dispatch to avoid crippling a vital national institution.

Let me speak quite frankly to some in this Chamber and perhaps to some not in this Chamber. The Central Intelligence Agency has been of maximum importance to Presidents before me. The Central Intelligence Agency has been of maximum importance to me. The Central Intelligence Agency and its associated intelligence organizations could be of maximum importance to some of you in this audience who might be President at some later date. I think it would be catastrophic for the Congress or anyone else to destroy the usefulness by dismantling, in effect, our intelligence systems upon which we rest so heavily.

Now, as Congress oversees intelligence activities, it must, of course, organize itself to do so in a responsible way. It has been traditional for the Executive to consult with the Congress through specially protected procedures that safeguard essential secrets. But recently, some of those procedures have been altered in a way that makes the protection of vital information very, very difficult. I will say to the leaders of the Congress, the House and the Senate, that I will work with them to devise procedures which will meet the needs of the Congress for review of intelligence agency activities and the needs of the Nation for an effective intelligence service.

Underlying any successful foreign policy is the strength and the credibility of our defense posture. We are strong and we are ready and we intend to remain so. Improvement of relations with adversaries does not mean any relaxation of our national vigilance. On the contrary, it is the firm maintenance of both strength and vigilance that makes possible steady progress toward a safer and a more peaceful world.

The national security budget that I have submitted[23] is the minimum the United States needs in this critical hour. The Congress should review it carefully, and I know it will. But it is my considered judgment that any significant reduction, revision would endanger our national security and thus jeopardize the peace.

Let no ally doubt our determination to maintain a defense second to none, and let no adversary be tempted to test our readiness or our resolve.

[23]Chapter 4, Document 7.

History is testing us today. We cannot afford indecision, disunity, or disarray in the conduct of our foreign affairs. You and I can resolve here and now that this Nation shall move ahead with wisdom, with assurance, and with national unity.

The world looks to us for the vigor and for the vision that we have demonstrated so often in the past in great moments of our national history. And as I look down the road,

—I see a confident America, secure in its strengths, secure in its values—and determined to maintain both.

—I see a conciliatory America, extending its hand to allies and adversaries alike, forming bonds of cooperation to deal with the vast problems facing us all.

—I see a compassionate America, its heart reaching out to orphans, to refugees, and to our fellow human beings afflicted by war, by tyranny, and by hunger.

As President, entrusted by the Constitution with primary responsibility for the conduct of our foreign affairs, I renew the pledge I made last August:[24] to work cooperatively with the Congress. I ask that the Congress help to keep America's word good throughout the world. We are one Nation, one government, and we must have one foreign policy.

In an hour far darker than this, Abraham Lincoln told his fellow citizens, and I quote: "we cannot escape history. We of this Congress and this Administration will be remembered in spite of ourselves. No personal significance or insignificance can spare one or another of us."

We who are entrusted by the people with the great decisions that fashion their future can escape neither responsibilities nor our consciences. By what we do now, the world will know our courage, our constancy, and our compassion.

The spirit of America is good and the heart of America is strong. Let us be proud of what we have done and confident of what we can do.

And may God ever guide us to do what is right.

Thank you.

[24]Cf. *AFR, 1974*: 283-6.

9. "FINDING STRENGTH THROUGH ADVERSITY"
(April 17, 1975)

[The collapse of American policy in Indochina during this month of April 1975 proved almost as sharp a blow to national self-complacency as the domestic scandals of the previous year. The ill success of other diplomatic endeavors—the failure of Secretary Kissinger's Mideast mission, the stalemate in "Prepcon I," and the deteriorating relationship with Greece and Turkey[1]—contribued their share to a spreading disillusionment in which past assumptions regarding policies and individuals seemed increasingly open to question. Even Dr. Kissinger, the nation's foremost foreign policy symbol and the architect of the Paris peace agreement, was beginning to lose his "Superman" image and to exhibit some of the limitations that had characterized other Secretaries of State.

In another vital foreign policy area, the path of East-West détente was becoming increasingly obscured by difficulties relating to the negotiations on mutual and balanced force reduction (MBFR) in Europe and the ongoing Strategic Arms Limitation Talks (SALT) between the United States and the U.S.S.R., now focused on the elaboration of a long-term limitation of strategic offensive arms along the lines agreed upon at Vladivostok in November 1974.[2] While Washington and Moscow had both agreed in principle at Vladivostok on an upper limit of 2,400 strategic delivery vehicles, 1,320 of which could be "MIRVed" or equipped with multiple independently targetable reentry vehicles, a complex and potentially time-consuming question had now arisen with respect to the inclusion (or noninclusion) under these ceilings of such novel weapons as the United States' cruise missile and the Soviet "Backfire" bomber.

These and other weighty foreign policy matters—not least, the outcome of the current military operations around Saigon—re-

[1]Cf. respectively Chapters 6, 7, and 8.

109

mained in a state of anxious uncertainty as Secretary Kissinger, in one of the major foreign policy statements it was his habit to deliver at approximately three-week intervals, appeared before the American Society of Newspaper Editors in Washington on April 17 to read an address devoted to the timely theme of "Finding Strength Through Adversity." With the President's emergency aid requests still pending before the Congress, the Secretary of State passed lightly over the issues of the moment in order to concentrate on a psychological assessment of America's recent experiences and their relationship to the continuing obligations of the post-Vietnam era.]

(14) "U.S. Foreign Policy: Finding Strength Through Adversity": Address by Secretary of State Kissinger before the American Society of Newspaper Editors, Washington, April 17, 1975.[3]

I am here to sound a note of hope about the future of our foreign policy despite the fact that we are now going through a period of adversity.

A nation facing setbacks can submerge itself in acrimony, looking for scapegoats rather than lessons. It can ignore or gloss over its difficulties and fatuously proceed as if nothing serious had happened.

Or it can examine its situation dispassionately, draw appropriate conclusions, and chart its future with realism and hope.

President Ford has chosen this latter course.[4] A week ago he called upon Congress and the American people to turn this time of difficulty into a demonstration of spirit—to prove once again our devotion and our courage and to put these into the service of building a better world.

For the entire postwar period our strength and our leadership have been essential in preserving peace and promoting progress. If either falters, major shifts in political alignments will occur all around the world. The result will be new dangers for America's security and economic well-being. The Middle East war and oil embargo of 1973 demonstrated how distant events can threaten world peace and global prosperity simultaneously. A reduction of American influence in key areas can have disastrous consequences.

How other nations perceive us is thus a matter of major consequence. Every day I see reports from our embassies relaying anguished questions raised by our friends. What do events in Indochina, the southern flank of NATO, and the Middle East signify

[3]Department of State Press Release 204, Apr. 17; prepared text and titles from *Bulletin*, 72: 557-63.
[4]Chapter 8, Document 13.

for America's competence—constancy—credibility—coherence? How will Americans react? What are the implications for future American policy? We can be certain that potential adversaries are asking themselves the same questions—not with sympathy, but to estimate their opportunities.

It is fashionable to maintain that pointing to dangers produces a self-fulfilling prophecy, that the prediction of consequences brings them about. Unfortunately, life is not that simple. We cannot achieve credibility by rhetoric; we cannot manufacture coherence by proclamation; and we cannot change facts by not talking about them.

We can do little about the world's judgment of our past actions. But we have it within our power to take charge of our future: if the United States responds to adversity with dignity, if we make clear to the world that we continue to hold a coherent perception of a constructive international role and mean to implement it, we can usher in a new era of creativity and accomplishment. We intend to do just that.

I know that it is not easy for a people that faces major domestic difficulties to gear itself up for new international efforts. But our economic future is bound up with the rest of the world—and with international developments in energy, trade, and economic policy. Our economic health depends on the preservation of American leadership abroad.

This country has no choice. We must, for our own sake, play a major role in world affairs. We have strong assets: a sound foreign policy design, major international achievements in recent years, and the enormous capacities of an industrious and gifted people. We have the resources, and the will, to turn adversity into opportunity.

Indochina

Let me start with our most tragic and immediate problem.

I can add nothing to the President's request for military and humanitarian assistance for the anguished people of South Viet-Nam. I support this appeal and have testified at length to that effect before congressional committees over the past several days.

The time will come when it will be clear that no President could do less than to ask aid for those whom we encouraged to defend their independence and at whose side we fought for over a decade. Then Americans will be glad that they had a President who refused to abandon those who desperately sought help in an hour of travail.

In Indochina our nation undertook a major enterprise for almost 15 years. We invested enormous prestige; tens of thousands died, and many more were wounded, imprisoned, and lost; we spent over

$150 billion; and our domestic fabric was severely strained. Whether or not this enterprise was well conceived does not now change the nature of our problem. When such an effort founders, it is an event of profound significance—for ourselves and for others.

I, for one, do not believe that it was ignoble to have sought to preserve the independence of a small and brave people. Only a very idealistic nation could have persevered in the face of so much discouragement.

But where so many think that the war was a dreadful mistake, where thousands grieve for those they loved and others sorrow over their country's setback, there has been sufficient heartache for all to share.

The Viet-Nam debate has now run its course. The time has come for restraint and compassion. The Administration has made its case. Let all now abide by the verdict of the Congress—without recrimination or vindictiveness.

The Design

Let us therefore look to the future. We start with a sound foreign policy structure.

We are convinced that a continuing strong American role is indispensable to global stability and progress. Therefore the central thrust of our foreign policy has been to adjust our role in the world and the conceptions, methods, and commitments which define it to the conditions of a new era—including an America fatigued by Indochina.

The postwar order of international relations ended with the last decade. No sudden upheaval marked the passage of that era, but the cumulative change by the end of the 1960's was profound. Gone was the rigid bipolar confrontation of the cold war. In its place was a more fluid and complex world—with many centers of power, more subtle dangers, and new hopeful opportunities. Western Europe and Japan were stronger and more self-confident; our alliances needed to be adjusted toward a more equal partnership. The Communist world had fragmented over doctrine and national interests; there were promising prospects for more stable relations based on restraint and negotiation. And many of our friends in other parts of the globe were now better prepared to shoulder responsibility for their security and well-being, but they needed our assistance during the period of transition.

At home, the American people and Congress were weary from two decades of global exertion and years of domestic turmoil. They were not prepared for confrontation unless all avenues toward peace had been explored.

The challenge for our foreign policy has been to define an effective but more balanced U.S. role in the world, reducing excessive commitments without swinging toward precipitate and dangerous withdrawal.

We have come a long way.

Our major allies in the Atlantic world and Japan have grown in strength politically and economically; our alliances are firm anchors of world security and prosperity. They are the basis for close cooperation on a range of unprecedented new problems, from détente to energy.

We have launched a hopeful new dialogue with Latin America.

We are looking to a new era of relations with Africa.

We have taken historic steps to stabilize and improve our relations with our major adversaries. We have reduced tensions, deepened dialogue, and reached a number of major agreements.

We have begun the process of controlling the rival strategic arms programs which, unconstrained, threaten global security. When the Vladivostok agreement is completed, a ceiling will have been placed for the first time on the level of strategic arsenals of the superpowers.

We have helped to ease longstanding political conflicts in such sensitive areas as Berlin and the Middle East.

And we have taken the major initiatives to mobilize the international response to new global challenges such as energy, food, the environment, and the law of the sea.

In all these areas the American role has frequently been decisive. The design still stands; our responsibilities remain. There is every prospect for major progress. There is every reason for confidence.

The Domestic Dimension

If this be true, what then is the cause of our problem? Why the setbacks? Why the signs of impasse between the executive and the Congress? What must we do to pull ourselves together?

Setbacks are bound to occur in a world which no nation alone can dominate or control. The peculiar aspect of many of our problems is that they are of our own making. Domestic division has either compounded or caused difficulties from the southern flank of NATO to the Pacific, from the eastern Mediterranean to relations between the superpowers.

Paradoxically, herein resides a cause for optimism. For to the extent that the causes of our difficulties are within ourselves, so are the remedies.

The American people expect an effective foreign policy which preserves the peace and furthers our national interests. They want their leaders to shape the future, not just manage the present. This requires boldness, direction, nuance, and—above all—confidence between the public and the government and between the executive and the legislative branches of the government. But precisely this mutual confidence has been eroding over the past decade.

There are many causes for this state of affairs. Some afflict democracies everywhere; some are unique to America's tradition and recent history. Modern democracies are besieged by social, economic, and political challenges that cut across national boundaries and lie at the margin of governments' ability to control. The energies of leaders are too often consumed by the management of bureaucracy, which turns questions of public purpose into issues for institutional bargaining. Instant communications force the pace of events and of expectations. Persuasion, the essential method of democracy, becomes extraordinarily difficult in an era where issues are complex and outcomes uncertain. A premium is placed on simplification—an invitation to demagogues. Too often, the result is a disaffection that simultaneously debunks government and drains it of the very confidence that a democracy needs to act with conviction.

All of this has compounded the complex problem of executive-legislative relations. In every country, the authority of the modern state seems frustratingly impersonal or remote from those whose lives it increasingly affects; in nearly every democracy, executive authority is challenged by legislators who themselves find it difficult to affect policy except piecemeal or negatively. Issues become so technical that legislative oversight becomes increasingly difficult just as the issues become increasingly vital. The very essence of problem-solving on domestic issues—accommodation of special interests—robs foreign policy of consistency and focus when applied to our dealings with other nations.

Statesmen must act, even when premises cannot be proved; they must decide, even when intangibles will determine the outcome. Yet predictions are impossible to prove; consequences avoided are never evident. Skepticism and suspicion thus become a way of life and infect the atmosphere of executive-legislative debate; reasoned arguments are overwhelmed by a series of confrontations on peripheral issues.

America faces as well the problem of its new generation. The gulf between their historical experience and ours is enormous. They have been traumatized by Viet-Nam as we were by Munich. Their nightmare is foreign commitment as ours was abdication from international responsibility. It is possible that both generations learned their lessons too well. The young take for granted the great postwar achievements in restoring Europe, building peacetime alliances, and maintaining global prosperity. An impersonal, technological, bureaucratized world provides them too few incentives for dedication and idealism.

Let us remember that America's commitment to international involvement has always been ambivalent—even while our doubts were being temporarily submerged by the exertions of World War II and the postwar era. The roots of isolationism, nourished by geography and history, go deep in the American tradition. The reluctance to be involved in foreign conflicts, the belief that we somehow defile ourselves if we engage in "power politics" and balances of power, the sense that foreign policy is a form of Old World imperialism, the notion that weapons are the causes of conflict, the belief that humanitarian assistance and participation in the economic order are an adequate substitute for political engagement— all these were familiar characteristics of the American isolationism of the twenties and thirties. We took our power for granted, attributed our successes to virtue, and blamed our failures on the evil of others. We disparaged means. In our foreign involvement we have oscillated between exuberance and exhaustion, between crusading and retreats into self-doubt.

Following the Second World War a broad spectrum of civic leaders, professional groups, educators, businessmen, clergy, the media, congressional and national leaders of both parties led American public opinion to a new internationalist consensus. Taught by them and experience of the war, the nation understood that we best secured our domestic tranquillity and prosperity by enlightened participation and leadership in world affairs. Assistance to friends and allies was not a price to be paid, but a service to be rendered to international stability and therefore to our self-interest.

But in the last decade, as a consequence of Indochina and other frustrations of global engagement, some of our earlier impulses have reasserted themselves. Leadership opinion has, to an alarming degree, turned sharply against many of the internationalist premises of the postwar period. We now hear, and have for several years, that suffering is prolonged by American involvement, that injustice is perpetuated by American inaction, that defense spending is wasteful at best and produces conflict at worse, that American intelligence activities are immoral, that the necessary confidentiality of diplomacy is a plot to deceive the public, that flexibility is cynical and amoral—and that tranquillity is somehow to be brought about by an abstract purity of motive for which history offers no example.

This has a profound—and inevitable—impact on the national mood and on the national consensus regarding foreign policy. In the nation with the highest standard of living and one of the richest cultures in the world, in the nation that is certainly the most secure in the world, in the nation which has come closest of all to the ideals of civil liberty and pluralist democracy, we find a deep and chronic self-doubt, especially in the large urban centers and among presumptive leaders.

Will the American people support a responsible and active American foreign policy in these conditions? I deeply believe that they will—if their leaders, in and out of government, give them a sense that they have something to be proud of and something important to accomplish.

When one ventures away from Washington into the heart of America, one is struck by the confidence, the buoyancy, and the lack of any corrosive cynicism. We who sit at what my friend Stewart Alsop, a great journalist, once called "the center" tend to dwell too much on our problems; we dissect in overly exquisite detail our difficulties and our disputes.

I find it remarkable that two-thirds of the Americans interviewed in a nationwide poll in December, at a time of severe recession, still thought an active role in the world served their country's interests better than withdrawal. Even as other nations are closely watching the way we act in Washington, I suspect they marvel at the resiliency of our people and our institutions.

There is a great reservoir of confidence within America. We have the values, the means, and we bear the responsibility to strive for a safer and better world. And there is a great reservoir of confidence around the globe in this country's values and strength.

Where Do We Go From Here?

So, let us learn the right lessons from today's trials.

We shall have to pay the price for our setbacks in Indochina by increasing our exertions. We no longer have the margin of safety. In the era of American predominance, America's preferences held great sway. We could overwhelm our problems with our resources. We had little need to resort to the style of nations conducting foreign policy with limited means: patience, subtlety, flexibility. Today, disarray, abdication of responsibility, or shortsightedness exact a price that may prove beyond our means.

We are still the largest single factor in international affairs, but we are one nation among many. The weight of our influence now depends crucially on our purposefulness, our perseverance, our creativity, our power, and our perceived reliability. We shall have to work harder to establish the coherence and constancy of our policy—and we shall.

We must give up the illusion that foreign policy can choose between morality and pragmatism. America cannot be true to itself unless it upholds humane values and the dignity of the individual. But equally it cannot realize its values unless it is secure. No nation has a monopoly of justice or virtue, and none has the capacity to enforce its own conceptions globally. In the nuclear age especially, diplomacy—like democracy—often involves the compromise of clashing principles. I need not remind you that there are some 140 nations in the world, of which only a bare handful subscribe to our values.

Abstract moralism can easily turn into retreat from painful choices or endless interference in the domestic affairs of others; strict pragmatism, on the other hand, robs policy of vision and heart. Principles without security spell impotence; security without principles means irrelevance. The American people must never forget that our strength gives force to our principles and our principles give purpose to our strength.

Let us understand, too, the nature of our commitments. We have an obligation of steadfastness simply by virtue of our position as a great power upon which many others depend. Thus our actions and policies over time embody their own commitment whether or not they are enshrined in legal documents. Indeed, our actions and the perception of them by other countries may represent our most important commitments.

At the same time, diplomacy must be permitted a degree of confidentiality, or most serious exchange with other governments is destroyed. To focus the national debate on so-called secret agreements which no party has ever sought to implement and whose alleged subject matter has been prohibited by law for two years is to indulge what Mencken called the "national appetite for bogus revelation." It goes without saying that a commitment involving national action must be known to the Congress or it is meaningless.

One lesson we must surely learn from Viet-Nam is that new commitments of our nation's honor and prestige must be carefully weighed. As Walter Lippmann observed, "In foreign relations, as in all other relations, a policy has been formed only when commitments and power have been brought into balance." But after our recent experiences we have a special obligation to make certain that commitments we have made will be rigorously kept and that this is understood by all concerned. Let no ally doubt our steadfastness. Let no nation ever believe again that it can tear up with impunity a solemn agreement signed with the United States.

We must continue our policy of seeking to ease tensions. But we shall insist that the easing of tensions cannot occur selectively. We shall not forget who supplied the arms which North Viet-Nam used to make a mockery of its signature on the Paris accords.

Nor can we overlook the melancholy fact that not one of the other signatories of the Paris accords has responded to our repeated requests that they at least point out North Viet-Nam's flagrant violations of these agreements. Such silence can only undermine any meaningful standards of international responsibility.

At home, a great responsibility rests upon all of us in Washington.

Comity between the executive and legislative branches is the only possible basis for national action. The decade-long struggle in this country over executive dominance in foreign affairs is over. The recognition that the Congress is a coequal branch of government is the dominant fact of national politics today.

The executive accepts that the Congress must have both the sense and the reality of participation; foreign policy must be a shared enterprise. The question is whether the Congress will go beyond the setting of guidelines to the conduct of tactics; whether it will deprive the executive of discretion and authority in the conduct of diplomacy while at the same time remaining institutionally incapable of formulating or carrying out a clear national policy of its own.

The effective performance of our constitutional system has always rested on the restrained exercise of the powers and rights conferred by it. At this moment in our history there is a grave national imperative for a spirit of cooperation and humility between the two branches of our government.

Cooperation must be a two-way street. Just as the executive has an obligation to reexamine and then to explain its policies, so the Congress should reconsider the actions which have paralyzed our policies in the eastern Mediterranean, weakened our hand in relations with the U.S.S.R., and inhibited our dialogue in this hemisphere. Foreign policy must have continuity. If it becomes partisan, paralysis results. Problems are passed on to the future under progressively worse conditions.

When other countries look to the United States, they see one nation. When they look to Washington, they see one government. They judge us as a unit—not as a series of unrelated or uncoordinated institutions. If we cannot agree among ourselves, there is little hope that we can negotiate effectively with those abroad.

So one of the most important lessons to be drawn from recent events is the need to restore the civility of our domestic discourse. Over the years of the Viet-Nam debate rational dialogue has yielded to emotion, sweeping far beyond the issues involved. Not only judgments but motives have been called into question. Not only policy but character has been attacked. What began as consensus progressively deteriorated into poisonous contention.

Leaders in government must do their share. The Administration, following the President's example, will strive for moderation and mutual respect in the national dialogue. We know that if we ask for public confidence we must keep faith with the people.

Debate is the essence of democracy. But it can elevate the nation only if conducted with restraint.

The American people yearn for an end to the bitterness and divisiveness of the past decade. Our domestic stability requires it. Our international responsibilities impose it.

You, in this audience, are today in a unique position to contribute to the healing of the nation.

The Coming Agenda

Ralph Waldo Emerson once said "No great man ever complains [of] a want of opportunity." Neither does a great nation.

Our resources are vast; our leadership is essential; our opportunities are unprecedented and insistent.

The challenges of the coming decades will dwarf today's disputes. A new world order is taking shape around us. It will engulf us or isolate us if we do not act boldly. We cannot consume ourselves in self-destruction. We have great responsibilities:

—We must maintain the vigor of the great democratic alliances. They can provide the anchor of shared values and purposes as we grapple with a radically new agenda.

—We must overcome the current economic and energy crisis. A domestic energy program is thus an urgent national priority. Looking ahead, we envisage a fundamentally reformed international economic system, a Bretton Woods for the 1980's and beyond.

—We must stand up for what we believe in international forums, including the United Nations, and resist the politics of resentment, of confrontation, and stale ideology. International collaboration has a more vital role now than ever, but so has mutual respect among nations.

—We must meet our continuing responsibility for peace in many regions of the world, especially where we uniquely have the confidence of both sides and where failure could spell disaster beyond the confines of the region, as in the Middle East. We will not be pushed by threats of war or economic pressure into giving up vital interests. But equally, we will not, in the President's words, "accept stagnation or stalemate with all its attendant risks to peace and prosperity."

—We must stop the spiral, and the spread, of nuclear weapons. We can then move on to a more ambitious agenda: mutual reductions in strategic arms, control of other weaponry, military restraint in other environments.

—We must overcome two scourges of mankind: famine and the vagaries of nature. We reaffirm the food program announced at the World Food Conference last November.[5] Our fundamental challenge is to help others feed themselves so that no child goes to bed hungry in the year 2000.

—We must continue to reduce conflict and tensions with our adversaries. Over time, we hope that vigilance and conciliation will lead to more positive relationships and ultimately a true global community.

—We must insure that the oceans and space become areas of cooperation rather than conflict. We can then leave to future generations vast economic and technological resources to enrich life on this earth.

Our nation is uniquely endowed to play a creative and decisive role in the new order which is taking form around us. In an era of turbulence, uncertainty, and conflict, the world still looks to us for a protecting hand, a mediating influence, a path to follow. It sees in us, most of all, a tradition and vision of hope. Just as America has symbolized for generations man's conquest of nature, so too has America—with its banner of progress and freedom—symbolized man's mastery over his own future.

For the better part of two centuries our forefathers, citizens of a small and relatively weak country, met adversity with courage and imagination. In the course of their struggle they built the freest, richest, and most powerful nation the world has ever known. As we, their heirs, take America into its third century, as we take up the unprecedented agenda of the modern world, we are determined to rediscover the belief in ourselves that characterized the most creative periods in our country.

We have come of age, and we shall do our duty.

[5]Cf. Chapter 4 at note 10.

10. MEETING OF THE ANZUS COUNCIL

(Washington, April 24-25, 1975)

["We must maintain the vigor of the great democratic alliances," Secretary Kissinger had asserted in the course of his April 17 address to the American Society of Newspaper Editors.[1] One link in the globe-girdling network of free world security treaties negotiated during the first postwar decade was even then coming up for reaffirmation at a Washington session of the ANZUS Council, the periodic meeting of the Australian, New Zealand, and American Foreign Ministers held within the framework of the Tripartite Security Treaty concluded by the three Pacific powers in 1951.[2] Though Secretary Kissinger did not omit to make a personal appearance during the two-day meeting held on April 24-25, the United States was formally represented by Deputy Secretary of State Robert S. Ingersoll, Australia being represented by Foreign Minister Donald L. Willesee and New Zealand by Labor Minister Arthur J. Faulkner.

Few earlier meetings of this informal group had occurred amid political and military chaos of the sort that prevailed in parts of Asia and the Pacific during this final fortnight of 1975. Phnom Penh, Cambodia's capital, had finally fallen to its Communist besiegers just a week earlier, on April 17. Australia and New Zealand, in contrast to Washington's wait-and-see attitude, had shed few tears for the extinguished Khmer Republic but had promptly recognized the harsh successor regime, whose most visible leader was Deputy Premier and Defense Minister Khieu Samphan and whose first reported action was an order, rigorously enforced, for mass evacuation of the conquered capital. In Vietnam, meanwhile, the

[1] Chapter 9, Document 14.
[2] Tripartite Security Treaty between the Governments of Australia, New Zealand, and the United States, signed in San Francisco Sept. 1, 1951 and entered into force Apr. 29, 1952 (TIAS 2493; 3 UST 3420); text in *Documents, 1951*: 263-5.

Communists had continued to tighten the ring around a Saigon from which most Americans had already departed. President Thieu had formally resigned on April 21, and his successor, former Vice-President Tran Van Huong, was actively looking for someone who might be more successful than himself in opening negotiations with the increasingly imperious "Provisional Revolutionary Government," as the insurgent leadership called itself.

Unable to ignore the crumbling of a political structure that all three countries had shed blood to uphold, the representatives of the ANZUS powers nevertheless exhibited a public equanimity that would have been impressive even in quieter times. Aside from a few *pro forma* remarks on Indochina, the three ministers preferred to disregard the unsettling effects of the collapse and to emphasize in their communiqué (**Document 15**) such positive topics as the enduring nature of the ANZUS relationship, "the emergence of a new spirit of regional consciousness and self reliance in Southeast Asia," the continued value of such regional security arrangements as the South-East Asia Treaty Organization (SEATO) and the Five-Power Defense Arrangements centering on Malaysia and Singapore, and the prospective addition of Australian-administered Papua New Guinea to the "community of independent and self-governing states in the South Pacific." (Papua New Guinea was to become independent on September 16 as the 35th member of the Commonwealth of Nations). It would require the further dislocations attendant on the final collapse of the Republic of Vietnam to convince the ANZUS powers and their Asian allies that while ANZUS itself might continue indefinitely, regional security arrangements of the SEATO type had ceased to be viable under the conditions now prevailing in that part of the world.[3]]

(15) 24th Meeting of the ANZUS Council, Washington, April 24-25, 1975: Final communiqué.[4]

The ANZUS Council held its twenty-fourth meeting in Washington on April 24 and 25, 1975. Senator the Honorable Donald R. Willesee, Minister for Foreign Affairs, represented Australia; the Honorable Arthur J. Faulkner, Minister of Labor, represented New Zealand; and the Honorable Robert S. Ingersoll, Deputy Secretary of State, represented the U.S. Secretary of State Henry A. Kissinger also participated in the meeting.

The Ministers exchanged views on a wide range of strategic, political, and economic issues of concern to the ANZUS partners.

They reaffirmed the enduring nature of the relationship among the three countries, based as it is on a substantial community of interests and a shared heritage of representative democracy, individual freedom, and the rule of law. The ANZUS treaty and the regular consultations for which it provides are a natural expression of this close relationship.

The Ministers welcomed the continuing process of détente among the major powers, and efforts to work toward a more stable and cooperative relationship among states. They expressed hope that renewed efforts might bring about peace in areas of continuing conflict such as Indochina, and more peaceful and stable relationships in areas of recent or potential conflict such as the Near East.

The Ministers reviewed the situation in Indochina. The Ministers noted the plight of refugees in South Viet-Nam and regretted the continuing loss of life and the widespread human misery caused by the fighting. They recognized that an early end to the fighting, an adherence to the Paris Agreements, and a spirit of national reconciliation were prerequisites to an end to the suffering. The Council expressed the hope that the wounds of war in Cambodia would be speedily healed, and noted with satisfaction the continued peaceful evolution in Laos.

The Council welcomed the emergence of a new spirit of regional consciousness and self reliance in Southeast Asia and the practical measures being taken to develop the habit of regional cooperation. The Ministers applauded the progress made by the Association of Southeast Asian Nations and indicated the desire of their countries to assist this cooperation.

The Ministers agreed that the South East Asia Treaty Organization and the Five Power Defense Arrangements contributed to the climate of confidence in the area and provided a useful framework for practical cooperation.

The Council reviewed the world economic situation with special attention to its effects within the Asia/Pacific region. They discussed the difficulties caused by the present downturn in the world economic situation and also the collective international effort which has begun to evolve a more soundly-based world economic order. The Ministers agreed on the importance of close cooperation among themselves and with other nations on problems of international finance and trade. In particular, they agreed that in matters relating to trade in raw materials and primary products the interests of both producers and consumers should be taken into account. The Ministers expressed the hope that oil exporting and oil importing countries would seek to reconcile differences between them through dialogue. They affirmed the need for continued efforts aimed at liberalisation of international trade. The Ministers noted the special economic problems faced by the less developed countries of Asia and the Pacific and agreed on the need for efforts to see that the net flow of resources to those countries is not diminished.

The Council reviewed progress toward arms limitations and the limiting of the proliferation of nuclear weapons. The Ministers agreed that further measures of arms control are a necessary concomitant of the continuing trend toward détente and the establishment of a just and stable world order. Noting the need for progress toward reduction in nuclear weapons, the Council expressed the hope that the Strategic Arms Limitation Talks between the United States and the USSR will make further progress. The Council supported the continuing negotiations to achieve mutual and balanced force reductions in Europe as an important stage in the effort to bring about the limitation of conventional arms. The Ministers noted that a conference of the Parties will review the operation of the Non-Proliferation Treaty,[5] and expressed their hope for a strengthening of the non-proliferation regime. The Council noted the conclusion of a Threshold Test Ban Treaty[6] and reaffirmed its support for the early achievement of an effective Comprehensive Test Ban Treaty.

The Ministers welcomed the continued development of a community of independent and self-governing states in the South Pacific, including the forthcoming independence of Papua New Guinea. They noted with satisfaction the constructive role Australia has played in assisting the emergence of this new state.

In conclusion, the ANZUS partners reaffirmed the great value each placed on the Alliance. They agreed that the continuity symbolized by the ANZUS treaty was important in a period of significant change, and that the Alliance continued to play an important role in the evolution of stability and normal relationships among states in the Asia and Pacific area. The three partners agreed to continue to consult closely on all matters of common concern.

---

[5]Cf. Chapter 13 at note 1.
[6]Cf. note 13 to Chapter 13.

11. THE END IN VIETNAM

(April 29-30, 1975)

[Many pages would be needed to recount the tragic conclusion of the story whose final chapter had opened with President Ford's request of January 28 for a further $300 million in military assistance to the Saigon regime, followed on April 10 by an emergency request for an additional $722 million.[1] To Secretary Kissinger, the question ultimately posed by these requests had been "an elementary question of what kind of a people we are"—of whether the United States would "deliberately destroy an ally by withholding aid from it in its hour of extremity."[2] A more immediate concern for many members of Congress, however, had been the question whether Saigon could now survive even *with* additional American aid—and, in addition, whether renewed American support might not carry with it a danger of renewed military involvement. In the fortnight following the President's April 10 appeal, the Armed Services committees of both Senate and House decided by narrow margins *against* any recommendation of further military aid to the floundering Saigon regime.

So swiftly did events move during these April weeks that even an alternative bill to authorize funds for humanitarian and evacuation aid failed to clear the Congress in advance of the fall of Saigon and the final disappearance of the Republic of Vietnam.[3] With Communist forces already no more than eighteen to twenty miles away, President Huong had resigned on Sunday, April 27, to make room

[1]Cf. Chapter 3, Document 5, and Chapter 8, Document 13. For further developments cf. Chapter 10.

[2]News conference, Mar. 29, in *Bulletin*, 72: 462.

[3]The Vietnam Contingency Act of 1975, providing $250 million for humanitarian aid and $77 million for evacuation purposes, was approved by the Senate Apr. 25 but rejected by the House May 1. The later Indochina Migration and Refugee Assistance Act of 1975 (Public Law 94-23, May 23, 1975) did, however, authorize $455 million for assistance to refugees, of which $405 million was appropriated by a separate enactment of the same date (Public Law 94-24, May 23, 1975).

for the inauguration of General Duong Van ("Big") Minh, the best-known advocate of reconciliation among Vietnam's warring factions, on the following day. But hopes for a negotiated settlement, buoyed briefly by General Minh's advent, had been deflated once again by the increasing intransigence of the insurgents, whose political demands were again stepped up even as their military arm was bringing Tan Son Nhut airport, seat of the U.S. Defense Attaché's Office, under mortar and rocket fire.

By Tuesday, April 29 (local time), the rapidly deteriorating military situation had persuaded Washington that there was no longer any alternative to evacuating all remaining American personnel, together with as many "high risk" South Vietnamese as could still be removed. Evacuation by fixed-wing aircraft having become impossible amid the mass panic prevailing at Tan Son Nhut, a fleet of 81 helicopters was brought into action under the protection of nearly 1,000 Marines, with fighter-bomber cover provided by the Navy and Air Force. According to later tabulations, a total of 395 Americans and 4,475 South Vietnamese were successfully evacuated from Tan Son Nhut, and a further 978 Americans and 1,120 South Vietnamese were lifted from the U.S. Embassy in Saigon, where the prevalent confusion was aggravated by an insufficiency of landing and takeoff facilities.[4]

Some of the phantasmagoric quality of these events can still be glimpsed in the record of Secretary Kissinger's late afternoon news conference at Washington's Old Executive Office Building on April 29, Washington time (Wednesday, April 30, in Vietnam) **(Document 16)**. Still unreported as the Secretary spoke, but soon to be known to the entire world, was the formal surrender of President Minh and his colleagues to enemy military authorities following the failure of their attempt to arrange for a cease-fire and an orderly transfer of power. Although the victorious Provisional Revolutionary Government had continued to promise a policy of "national concord" and would in fact refrain from carrying out the "blood bath" so dreaded by former President Nixon, its reassuring words were powerless to stem a continuing flight of tens of thousands of refugees, some 145,000 of whom would eventually reach the United States.]

(16) Evacuation Efforts in South Vietnam: News Conference of Secretary of State Kissinger, April 29, 1975.[5]

Mr. Nessen: The briefing was delayed until the evacuation was completed, and the last helicopters are now in the air.

[4]*Keesing's*: 27203.
[5]Department of State Press Release 220, Apr. 29; text from *Bulletin*, 72: 625-33. The briefing was conducted by Ronald H. Nessen, Press Secretary to the President.

I would like to read a statement by the President.

During the past week, I had ordered the reduction of American personnel in the U.S. Mission in Saigon to levels that could be quickly evacuated during an emergency, while enabling that mission to continue to fulfill its duties.

During the day on Monday [April 28], Washington time, the airport at Saigon came under persistent rocket, as well as artillery, fire and was effectively closed. The military situation in the area deteriorated rapidly.

I therefore ordered the evacuation of all American personnel remaining in South Viet-Nam.

The evacuation has been completed. I commend the personnel of the Armed Forces who accomplished it as well as Ambassador Graham Martin and the staff of his mission, who served so well under difficult conditions.

This action closes a chapter in the American experience. I ask all Americans to close ranks, to avoid recrimination about the past, to look ahead to the many goals we share, and to work together on the great tasks that remain to be accomplished.

Copies of this statement will be available as you leave the briefing.

Now, to give you details of the events of the past few days and to answer your questions, Secretary of State Kissinger.

Secretary Kissinger: Ladies and Gentlemen, when the President spoke before the Congress [April 10],[6] he stated as our objective the stabilization of the situation in Viet-Nam.

We made clear at that time, as well as before many congressional hearings, that our purpose was to bring about the most controlled and the most humane solution that was possible and that these objectives required the course which the President had set.

Our priorities were as follows: We sought to save the American lives still in Viet-Nam. We tried to rescue as many South Vietnamese that had worked with the United States for 15 years in reliance on our commitments as we possibly could. And we sought to bring about as humane an outcome as was achievable under the conditions that existed.

Over the past two weeks, the American personnel in Viet-Nam have been progressively reduced. Our objective was to reduce at a rate that was significant enough so that we would finally be able to evacuate rapidly but which would not produce a panic which might prevent anybody from getting out.

[6]Chapter 8, Document 13.

Our objective was also to fulfill the human obligation which we felt to the tens of thousands of South Vietnamese who had worked with us for over a decade.

Finally, we sought, through various intermediaries, to bring about as humane a political evolution as we could.

By Sunday evening [April 27], the personnel in our mission had been reduced to 950 and there were 8,000 South Vietnamese to be considered in a particularly high-risk category—between 5,000 and 8,000. We do not know the exact number.

On Monday evening [April 28], Washington time, around 5 o'clock, which was Tuesday morning [April 29] in Saigon, the airport in Tan Son Nhut was rocketed and received artillery fire.

The President called an NSC [National Security Council] meeting. He decided that if the shelling stopped by dawn Saigon time, we would attempt to operate with fixed-wing aircraft from Tan Son Nhut Airport for one more day to remove the high-risk South Vietnamese, together with all the Defense Attache's Office [DAO], which was located near the Tan Son Nhut Airport.

He also ordered a substantial reduction of the remaining American personnel in South Viet-Nam.

I may point out that the American personnel in Saigon was divided into two groups; one with the Defense Attache's Office, which was located near the Tan Son Nhut Airport; the second one, which was related to the Embassy and was with the U.S. Mission in downtown Saigon.

The shelling did stop early in the morning on Tuesday, Saigon time, or about 9 p.m. last night, Washington time. We then attempted to land C-130's but found that the population at the airport had got out of control and had flooded the runways. It proved impossible to land any more fixed-wing aircraft.

The President thereupon ordered that the DAO personnel, together with those civilians that had been made ready to be evacuated, be moved to the DAO compound, which is near Tan Son Nhut Airport; and at about 11:00 last night, he ordered the evacuation of all Americans from Tan Son Nhut and from the Embassy as well.

This operation has been going on all day, which of course is night in Saigon, and under difficult circumstances, and the total number of those evacuated numbers about 6,500—we will have the exact figures for you tomorrow—of which about 1,000 are Americans.

Our Ambassador has left, and the evacuation can be said to be completed.

In the period since the President spoke to the Congress, we have therefore succeeded in evacuating all of the Americans who were in South Viet-Nam, losing the two marines last night to rocket fire and two pilots today on a helicopter.

We succeeded in evacuating something on the order of 55,000 South Vietnamese. And we hope we have contributed to a political evolution that may spare the South Vietnamese some of the more drastic consequences of a political change, but this remains to be seen. This last point remains to be seen.

As far as the Administration is concerned, I can only underline the point made by the President. We do not believe that this is a time for recrimination. It is a time to heal wounds, to look at our international obligations, and to remember that peace and progress in the world has depended importantly on American commitment and American conviction and that the peace and progress of our own people is closely tied to that of the rest of the world.

I will be glad to answer questions.

Q. Mr. Secretary, you made some reference a few weeks back to those who believe in the domino theory, and while I don't remember exactly your words, the point was it is easy to laugh at it but there is some justification for subscribing to that theory. Now that this chapter is over, can you give us your estimate of the security of Thailand and other countries in the area, or the near area?

Secretary Kissinger: I think it is too early to make a final assessment.

There is no question that the outcome in Indochina will have consequences not only in Asia but in many other parts of the world. To deny these consequences is to miss the possibility of dealing with them.

So, I believe there will be consequences. But I am confident that we can deal with them, and we are determined to manage and to progress along the road toward a permanent peace that we have sought; but there is no question that there will be consequences.

Q. Now that it is over, could you tell us, or elaborate in more detail, what we did through various intermediaries to bring about, I think you said, as humane a political solution as possible, and why those efforts seem to have failed?

Secretary Kissinger: I would not agree with the proposition that these efforts have failed because at least some of the efforts, especially those related to evacuation, were carried out through intermediaries. I think it is premature for me to go into all of the details, but we did deal with Hanoi and with the PRG [Provisional Revolutionary Government] through different intermediaries, and we were in a position to put our views and receive responses.

Q. May I follow on that by saying, why, then, was it necessary to stage a rescue operation in the final stages?

Secretary Kissinger: In the final stages, it was always foreseen that a helicopter lift for some contingents would be necessary. I believe that the dynamics of the situation in South Viet-Nam and the impatience of the North Vietnamese to seize power brought about an acceleration of events in the last day and a half.

But you will remember there was a period of about five days when both civilian and U.S. personnel were evacuated without any substantial opposition—in fact, more than five days, about a week.

Q. Mr. Secretary, on that point, do you now anticipate that the North Vietnamese intend to move in and forcefully seize Saigon? Do you anticipate there will be a bloody battle of Saigon, or is there still a chance for an orderly transition?

Secretary Kissinger: This is very difficult to judge at this moment. I think it is important to point out that the Communist demands have been escalating as the military situation has changed in their favor.

So, a week ago they were asking only for the removal of President Thieu. When he resigned, they immediately asked for the removal of his successor, specifying that General Minh would be acceptable. When President Huong resigned in favor of General Minh, he was now described as a member of a clique which includes all of the members of his administration.

A week ago, the Communist demand was for the removal of American military personnel. This quickly escalated into a removal of all American personnel.

Then a new demand was put forward for the dismantling of the South Vietnamese military apparatus. When that was agreed to, they added to it the demand for the dismantling of the South Vietnamese administrative apparatus. So, it is clear that what is being aimed at is a substantial political takeover.

Now, whether it is possible to avoid a battle for Saigon, it is too early to judge. I would hope—and we certainly have attempted to work in that direction—that such a battle can be avoided. And it is basically unnecessary because it seems to us that the South Vietnamese Government is prepared to draw the conclusions from the existing situation and, in fact, look forward to correspond to the demands of the Communist side.

Q. Mr. Secretary, do you consider the United States now owes any allegiance at all to the Paris pact? Are we now bound in any way by the Paris agreements?

Secretary Kissinger: Well, as far as the United States is concerned, there are not many provisions of the Paris agreement that are still relevant. As far as the North Vietnamese are concerned, they have stated that they wish to carry out the Paris accords, though by what definition is not fully clear to me. We would certainly support this if it has any meaning.

Q. May I ask one follow-up? Do you now favor American aid in rebuilding North Viet-Nam?

Secretary Kissinger: North Viet-Nam?

Q. North Viet-Nam.

Secretary Kissinger: No, I do not favor American aid for rebuilding North Viet-Nam.

Q. South Viet-Nam?

Secretary Kissinger: With respect to South Viet-Nam, we will have to see what kind of government emerges and indeed whether there is going to be a South Viet-Nam. We would certainly look at particular specific humanitarian requests that can be carried out by humanitarian agencies, but we do believe that the primary responsibility should fall on those who supply the weapons for this political change.

Q. Mr. Secretary, I would like to ask a question about the length of time that it took to complete this evacuation. First, the question of whether days went by after the end became obvious before ordering the evacuation; second, if after ordering it there was a one-hour delay in helicopter landings, apparently caused by military confusion; third, whether the evacuation was prolonged by picking up thousands of Vietnamese instead of concentrating on Americans; and fourth, whether this was delayed even further by Ambassador Martin's desire to be the last man to leave the sinking ship.

In other words, I tried to put the specifics in order to ask you, did it take too long to get out of there, to write this last chapter?

Secretary Kissinger: We got out, with all of the personnel that were there, without panic and without the substantial casualties that could have occurred if civil order had totally broken down. We also managed to save 56,000 people whose lives were in the most severe jeopardy.

We had to make a judgment every day how many people we

thought we could safely remove without triggering a panic and at the same time still be able to carry out our principal function and the remaining functions.

I think these objectives were achieved and they were carried out successfully. Therefore I do not believe that there was an undue delay, because an evacuation has been going on for two weeks.

The difference between the last stage and the previous period was that the last stage was done by helicopter and the previous stage had been done by fixed-wing.

I think the ability to conduct a final evacuation by helicopter without casualties during the operation, at least casualties caused by hostile action, is closely related to the policies that were pursued in the preceding two weeks.

As for Ambassador Martin, he was in a very difficult position. He felt a moral obligation to the people with whom he had been associated, and he attempted to save as many of those as possible. That is not the worst fault a man can have.

Q. Mr. Secretary, there have been numerous reports of American appeals to the Soviets, to the Chinese. Can you say today in the evacuation effort were either the Soviets or the Chinese helpful or unhelpful in this diplomatic effort?

Secretary Kissinger: I think that we received some help from the Soviet Union in the evacuation effort. The degree of it we will have to assess when we study the exchanges.

Q. Mr. Secretary, what caused the breakdown of the intent which was spoken of earlier on the Hill to try to achieve a measure of self-determination for the people of South Viet-Nam, and what is your total assessment now of the effectiveness or the noneffectiveness of the whole Paris accord operation, which you said at the outset was intended to achieve peace with honor for the United States?

Secretary Kissinger: Until Sunday night we thought there was some considerable hope that the North Vietnamese would not seek a solution by purely military means, and when the transfer of power to General Minh took place—a person who had been designated by the other side as a counterpart worth talking to, they would be prepared to talk with—we thought a negotiated solution in the next few days was highly probable.

Sometime Sunday night [April 27] the North Vietnamese obviously changed signals. Why that is, we do not yet know, nor do I exclude that now that the American presence is totally removed and very little military structure is left in South Viet-Nam, that there may not be a sort of a negotiation, but what produced this sudden shift to a military option or what would seem to us to be a sudden shift to a military option, I have not had sufficient opportunity to analyze.

As to the effectiveness of the Paris accords, I think it is important to remember the mood in this country at the time that the Paris accords were being negotiated. I think it is worth remembering that the principal criticism that was then made was that the terms we insisted on were too tough, not that the terms were too generous.

We wanted what was considered peace with honor, was that the United States would not end a war by overthrowing a government with which it had been associated. That still seems an objective that was correct.

There were several other assumptions that were made at that time that were later falsified by events that were beyond the control of— that indeed were unforeseeable by—anybody who negotiated these agreements, including the disintegration of or the weakening of ex-. ecutive authority in the United States for reasons unconnected with foreign policy considerations.

So, the premises of the Paris accords, in terms of aid, of the possibility of aid, and in terms of other factors, tended to disintegrate. I see no purpose now in reviewing that particular history. Within the context of the time, it seemed the right thing to do.

Q. Mr. Secretary, a follow-up question on that. What is the current relationship of the United States to the South Vietnamese political grouping, whatever you would call it?

Secretary Kissinger: We will have to see what grouping emerges out of whatever negotiations should now take place between the two South Vietnamese sides. After we have seen what grouping emerges and what degree of independence it has, then we can make a decision about what our political relationship to it is. We have not made a decision on that.

Q. Would you say diplomatic relations are in abeyance with the government in South Viet-Nam?

Secretary Kissinger: I think that is a fair statement.

Q. Mr. Secretary, looking back on the war now, would you say that the war was in vain, and what do you feel it accomplished?

Secretary Kissinger: I think it will be a long time before Americans will be able to talk or write about the war with some dispassion. It is clear that the war did not achieve the objectives of those who started the original involvement nor the objectives of those who sought to end that involvement, which they found on terms which seemed to them compatible with the sacrifices that had been made.

What lessons we should draw from it, I think we should reserve for another occasion. But I don't think that we can solve the problem of having entered the conflict too lightly by leaving it too lightly, either.

Q. Mr. Secretary, looking toward the future, has America been so stunned by the experience of Viet-Nam that it will never again come to the military or economic aid of an ally? I am talking specifically in the case of Israel.

Secretary Kissinger: As I pointed out in a speech a few weeks ago [April 17],[7] one lesson we must learn from this experience is that we must be very careful in the commitments we make but that we should scrupulously honor those commitments that we make.

I believe that the experience in the war can make us more mature in the commitments we undertake and more determined to maintain those we have. I would therefore think that with relation to other countries, including Israel, that no lessons should be drawn by the enemies of our friends from the experiences in Viet-Nam.

Q. Mr. Secretary, in view of the developments in the last week or so, would you agree that there was never any hope of stabilizing the South Vietnamese military situation after the withdrawal from the northern region?

Secretary Kissinger: When the President met with General Weyand in Palm Springs [April 5], the judgment was that there was a slim hope, but some hope. Somewhat less than 50—50, but still some hope.

The situation deteriorated with every passing day. Those of you whom I briefed at that time will remember that I said that whatever—and I said it in public testimony on innumerable occasions—that whatever objective we may set ourselves and whatever assessment we make about the outcome, the Administration had no choice except to pursue the course that we did, which was designed to save the Americans still in Viet-Nam and the maximum number of Vietnamese lives, should the worst come to pass.

Q. Mr. Secretary, could you tell us, are you now reassessing the amount of humanitarian aid which Congress should give to the

[7] Chapter 9, Document 14.

South Vietnamese, and also, can you tell us the President's reaction and mood during the past 24 hours?

Secretary Kissinger: With respect to humanitarian aid for South Viet-Nam, we spoke to the congressional leadership this morning, and we urged them to pass the humanitarian part of the aid request that we have submitted to the Congress.[8]

The President pointed out that he would make a later decision as to what part of that humanitarian aid could be used in South Viet-Nam after the political evolution in South Viet-Nam becomes clearer.

The President's mood was somber and determined, and we all went through a somewhat anxious 24 hours, because until the last helicopter had left, we could not really know whether an attack on any of these compounds might start and whether missiles might be used against our evacuation.

Q. Mr. Secretary, could I ask you to clarify something that seems rather important at this point? You said here and in the past that a weakening of the American executive authority was a factor in this whole outcome. Now, there have been reports that former President Nixon, with your advice, had decided in April of 1973 to resume the bombing of North Viet-Nam but that Watergate intruded and he could not carry through on that. Is that a historic fact or not?

Secretary Kissinger: To the best of my knowledge, President Nixon had never actually decided on any particular action. The Washington Special Action Group at that period was considering a number of reactions that could be taken to the beginning flagrant violations of the agreements.[9] This was done on an interdepartmental basis—including the Department of State, my office, the Department of Defense— and had reached certain options.

Then President Nixon, as it turned out, never made a final decision between these options. To what extent it was influenced by Watergate is a psychological assessment that one can only speculate about.

Q. Mr. Secretary, there is a new Asia developing after the Indochina situation. What will the priorities of the United States be in recognizing its existing commitments and in making new ones?

Secretary Kissinger: We will have to assess the impact of Indochina on our allies and on other countries in that area and on their

[8]Cf. note 3 above.
[9]Cf. *AFR, 1973:* 67-74.

perceptions of the United States, and we will have to assess also what role the United States can responsibly play over an indefinite period of time, because surely another lesson we should draw from the Indochina experience is that foreign policy must be sustained over decades if it is to be effective, and if it cannot be, then it has to be tailored to what is sustainable.

The President has already reaffirmed our alliance with Japan, our defense treaty with Korea, and we, of course, also have treaty obligations and important bases in the Philippines. We will soon be in consultation with many other countries in that area, including Indonesia and Singapore and Australia and New Zealand, and we hope to crystallize an Asian policy that is suited to present circumstances with close consultation with our friends.

Q. Mr. Secretary, are you confident that all the Americans that wanted to come out are out of Saigon, and do you have any idea of the number of Americans who remained behind?

Secretary Kissinger: I have no idea of the number of Americans that remained behind. I am confident that every American who wanted to come out is out, but how many chose to stay behind we won't know until tomorrow sometime. The last contingent that left was the Ambassador and some of his immediate staff, and we won't know really until we get the report from them.

Q. Mr. Secretary, is President Thieu welcome to seek asylum in this country, and is there any possibility that the United States would recognize an exile government of South Viet-Nam?

Secretary Kissinger: If President Thieu should seek asylum in the United States, he would be, of course, received.

The United States will not recognize an exile government of South Viet-Nam.

Q. Mr. Secretary, could you tell us what went wrong, what were the flaws in American foreign policy toward Indochina all these years? Why was it that so many Administrations repeatedly underestimated the power of the North Vietnamese and overestimated the capability on the part of the South Vietnamese?

Secretary Kissinger: As I said earlier, I think this is not the occasion, when the last American has barely left Saigon, to make an assessment of a decade and a half of American foreign policy, because it could equally well be argued that if five Administrations that were staffed, after all, by serious people dedicated to the welfare of their country came to certain conclusions, that maybe there was something in their assessment, even if for a variety of reasons the effort did not succeed.

As I have already pointed out, special factors have operated in recent years. But I would think that what we need now in this country, for some weeks at least, and hopefully for some months, is to heal the wounds and to put Viet-Nam behind us and to concentrate on the problems of the future. That certainly will be the Administration's attitude. There will be time enough for historic assessments.

Q. Mr. Secretary, you have repeatedly spoken of the potential consequences of what has happened in Southeast Asia. I would like to ask if you feel that your personal prestige and therefore your personal ability to negotiate between other countries has been damaged by what has happened?

Secretary Kissinger: If I should ever come to the conclusion that I could not fulfill what the President has asked of me, then I would draw the consequences from this. Obviously, this has been a very painful experience, and it would be idle to deny this has been a painful experience for many who have been concerned with this problem for a decade and a half.

I think the problems in Viet-Nam went deeper than any one negotiation and that an analysis of the accords at the time will require an assessment of the public pressures, of what was sustainable, but I don't think, again, that we should go into this at this particular moment, nor am I probably the best judge of my prestige at any particular point.

Q. Mr. Secretary, what was it in particular that led you to believe until Sunday night that Hanoi might be willing to go for a nonmilitary solution? Did you have some specific information from them to indicate that, because certainly the battlefield situation suggested otherwise?

Secretary Kissinger: Maybe to you, but the battlefield situation suggested that there was a standdown of significant military activity, and the public pronouncements were substantially in the direction that a negotiation would start with General Minh. There were also other reasons which led us to believe that the possibility of a negotiation remained open.

Q. Mr. Secretary, you have blamed the Soviets and the Red Chinese for breaking faith with the letter and the spirit of the Paris peace accords. The Soviet Union has apparently, through its broadcasts, encouraged a Communist takeover in Portugal. The Chinese have signed a joint communique with North Korea encouraging North Korea to unify South Korea by force.

My question is, why, in view of these violations in both the letter and in the spirit of détente, does the United States continue to believe in détente; secondly, are we ever going to take some obvious action showing American displeasure at the behavior of the two Communist superpowers?

Secretary Kissinger: First, I think it is important to keep in mind that our relationship with both the Soviet Union and the People's Republic of China is based on ideological hostility but practical reasons for cooperation in certain limited spheres.

With respect to the Soviet Union, they and we possess the capability to destroy mankind. The question of how to prevent a general nuclear war is a problem that some Administration must solve before consequences that would be irremedial. Therefore there is always a common interest, and indeed a common obligation, to attempt to deal with this particular problem.

With respect to the various points you made, it is important for us to recognize that we cannot, in this situation, ask of the Soviet Union that it does our job for us. On the one hand, as I pointed out previously, of course the Soviet Union and the People's Republic must be responsible for the consequences of those actions that lead to an upset of the situation in Indochina, or maybe in the Middle East; that is, the introduction of massive armaments that will in all probability be used offensively is an event that we cannot ignore.

On the other hand, I think it would be a grave mistake to blame the Soviet Union for what happened in Portugal.[10] It may have taken advantage of the situation in Portugal, but the fact that the Communist Party in Portugal has emerged despite the fact that it, in recent elections, had only 12 percent of the votes cannot be ascribed to Soviet machinations primarily, but due to causes that are much more complicated and also due to evolutions in Europe that have roots quite different from Soviet pressures.

So, we must not make the mistake of ascribing every reverse we have to our Communist opponents, because that makes them appear 10 feet tall. On the other hand, we must not make the mistake of lulling ourself, with a period of détente, into believing that all competition has disappeared.

Between these two extremes, we must navigate, seek to reduce tensions on the basis of reciprocity, and seek to promote a stabler world. When either of the Communist countries have attempted actively to bring foreign policy pressures, the United States has re-

[10]A new cabinet according strong representation to the Communist Party and related political groups took office in Portugal on Mar. 26.

sisted strenuously, and again we have called their attention to the fact that the fostering of international conflict will certainly lead to a breakdown of détente. But the individual examples which you gave cannot be ascribed to Communist actions primarily.

Q. In ordering the evacuation, to what extent were you responding exclusively to the military situation and to what extent were you responding either to a request by "Big" Minh for all Americans to get out or to your own feeling that a total evacuation might facilitate a political settlement?

Secretary Kissinger: When the President ordered total evacuation, it was done on the basis that Tan Son Nhut Airport had already been closed and that therefore the American personnel in Saigon—and there were 45 in the province—might soon become hostage to the approaching Communist forces.

The order to evacuate was made before any request had been received from General Minh, and the principal, indeed the only, reason was to guarantee the safety of the remaining Americans.

Q. Mr. Secretary, there was a report last night that the Communists were backing away from the airport, the rockets seemed to be moving back. Was that a direct result of negotiations and were they prepared to let us move refugees out or Americans out on fixed-wing aircraft?

Secretary Kissinger: I don't know that particular report, but the shelling stopped about 9 p.m., last night. We could not operate fixed-wing aircraft, because the control at the airport broke down. And it was at this point that the President decided that with Communist forces approaching on all sides and with the airport being closed that we had to go to helicopter evacuation.

Q. Mr. Secretary, there is a report in New York that last week you sent a further request for the good offices of the Council of Ministers of the Nine, the European Communities.

Secretary Kissinger: We did not approach the Nine last week.

Q. Mr. Secretary, do you see any possibility of a negotiated settlement, and also, with respect to that, what can and should the South Vietnamese Government do now?

Secretary Kissinger: I have already pointed out that the Communist demands have been escalating literally with every passing day, that as soon as one demand is met, an additional demand is put forward. So, we should have no illusions about what the Communist side is aiming for.

The South Vietnamese, as far as I can tell, have met every demand that has so far been put forward on the radio. There have not been any direct negotiations with which I am familiar.

What is attainable in the transfer of power that would preserve a vestige of other forces than the Communist forces, that remains to be seen.

12. CONFERENCE ON THE LAW OF THE SEA

(Geneva, March 17-May 9, 1975)

[Transcending even the fate of Indochina in its long-range implications was the future of the ocean spaces that cover some 70 percent of the earth's surface and provide essential conditions for the
existence of human and other forms of terrestrial life. A recognition of the crucial position of the sea in human affairs, and of the
multiple and growing threats to its integrity, had been the primary
reason for convening the Third United Nations Conference on the
Law of the Sea, which had begun its work in New York in December 1973, continued in Caracas in the summer of 1974, and held its
third (second substantive) session in Geneva from March 17 to May
9, 1975, with H.S. Amerasinghe of Sri Lanka presiding and some
1,700 delegates from 141 countries participating.[1]

The task assigned the conference by the U.N. General Assembly
amounted to nothing less than the elaboration of comprehensive
rules to govern the activities of nations in, on, and beneath those
portions of the sea that lay outside the limits of national jurisdiction—and, incidentally, to determine precisely where those limits
were located. The urgency of the endeavor had continued to increase as the conference proceeded. In the absence of early agreement to resolve a number of the more pressing issues on an international basis, it was evident that a number of countries would be
prepared to resort to unilateral measures aimed at furthering the
interests of their own nationals with minimal regard for wider considerations.

Two issues that had been of special concern to the United States
had to do with fisheries and with the exploitation of the mineral
wealth of the deep seabed. On fisheries, attempts had already been
made in Congress—thus far without success—to follow the example of some other maritime countries in asserting exclusive jurisdiction over a fishery zone extending seaward to a breadth of 200

[1]For background cf. *AFR, 1974*: 315-26.

miles. On the seabed minerals issue, American mining interests, supported by the Department of the Interior, were already making preparations to begin locating and bringing to the surface some of the manganese, nickel, copper, cobalt, and other mineral resources that they regarded as legitimate objects of commercial exploitation, but which were seen by the developing countries as part of a common heritage that should be exploited primarily for their benefit. While hopeful that the conflicting interests in such matters could still be harmoniously adjusted, official Washington clearly did not intend to sacrifice American interests in case the conference failed and a scramble for national advantage ensued.

Although the 1975 Geneva session did not achieve its assigned objective of wrapping up a comprehensive agreement on the law of the sea, American representatives went out of their way to insist that far from being a failure, the conference actually had made good progress and might possibly be able to complete its task in the course of the two further sessions that seemed likely to be held in 1976. The specific accomplishments of the Geneva session were set forth in some detail in a statement prepared for the Senate Foreign Relations Committee by Ambassador John R. Stevenson, the outgoing Special Representative of the President for the Law of the Sea Conference and Chief of the U.S. Delegation. The reading of Ambassador Stevenson's statement before a Foreign Relations subcommittee (**Document 17**) was followed by an assurance from Ambassador John Norton Moore, the Deputy Special Representative, that in view of the growing pressure of time, the U.S. administration had already undertaken a thorough reevaluation of its "interim policy" in order to ensure "that the necessary balance is found between our broad interest in a multilateral resolution of oceans' problems and our more immediate needs, particularly the protection of coastal fisheries stocks and access to the raw materials on the seabed."[2] Some important results of this reevaluation would later be made known by Secretary Kissinger in an August 19 address to the American Bar Association in Montreal.[3]]

(17) Third United Nations Conference on the Law of the Sea, Third (Second Substantive) Session, Geneva, March 17-May 9, 1975: Report to the Senate Foreign Relations Committee by Ambassador John R. Stevenson, Special Representative of the President for the Law of the Sea Conference and Chief of the United States Delegation, May 22, 1975.[4]

[2]U.S. Senate, 94th Cong., 1st sess., Committee on Foreign Relations, *Law of the Sea: Hearing* before the Subcommittee on Oceans and International Environment, May 22, 1975 (Washington: GPO, 1975): 7.

[3]Chapter 27, Document 45.

[4]Text from *Law of the Sea: Hearing*, cited: 2-5.

Once again, it is an honor and pleasure to report to the Senate Foreign Relations Committee to report on the progress in the Law of the Sea negotiations. The second substantive session of the Third United Nations Conference on the Law of the Sea was held in Geneva from March 17 to May 9, 1975. A third substantive session of eight weeks is planned for New York in 1976 commencing on March 29. The Conference also recommended that the United Nations General Assembly provide for an additional substantive session in the summer of 1976 if the third session of the Conference so decides and that the Conference be given priority by the General Assembly. Much to my regret our proposal that the Assembly expressly provide for completion of the treaty in 1976 was not approved.

I would summarize the results of the Geneva session as follows: the session concentrated on what it was supposed to—the translation of the general outlines of agreement reached at the first session in Caracas into specific treaty articles—and achieved a very considerable degree of progress; however, not as much progress as our Delegation had hoped or as the pressures for prompt agreement on a new law of the sea demand.

The decision of the Caracas session not to prolong general debate was respected—so much so that formal Plenary and Committee sessions were largely devoted to organizational and procedural matters. The substantive work of the session was carried on in informal Committee meetings (without records) and in working groups—both official and unofficial—with as many as fifteen different groups meeting in the course of a single day; and in private bilateral and multilateral consultations.

The official groups were handicapped by the insistence—a reflection of the acute sensitivity of many countries with respect to the sovereign equality of all states—that all such groups be open-ended. As a result they were generally ineffectual in dealing with controversial issues of general interest; such meetings were attended by a very large number of delegations who, by and large, restated their national positions rather than negotiating widely acceptable treaty language. The official working groups were much more effective in dealing with a number of articles which were relatively non-controversial or of interest to only a limited number of countries—such as the articles dealing with the baselines from which the territorial area is to be measured, innocent passage in the territorial sea, high seas law and, in the pollution area, articles on monitoring, environmental assessment and land-based sources of pollution.

The most effective negotiations and drafting of compromise treaty articles in major controversial areas took place in unofficial groups of limited but representative composition which were afforded interpretation and other logistical support by the Conference secretariat.

The Evensen group of some 30 to 40 participants, principally head of delegation, was organized by Minister [of Commerce and Shipping Jens] Evensen of Norway initially on the basis of cooperation by a group of international lawyers acting in their personal capacity, but functioning at Geneva more as representatives of their respective countries. The Evensen Group concentrated on the economic zone, the continental shelf, and vessel-source pollution. The dispute settlement group which met under the co-chairmanship of Mr. Adede of Kenya and Ambassadors Galindo Pohl of El Salvador and Harry of Australia, with Professor Louis Sohn of Harvard serving as Rapporteur, was open to all Conference participants and was attended at one time or another by representatives from more than 60 countries. Another informal group was organized by representatives of the United Kingdom and Fiji to work out a set of articles on unimpeded transit through straits as a middle ground between the free transit articles supported by many maritime countries and the innocent passage concept supported by a number of straits states.

In brief, the principal substantive accomplishments of the session were the large number of relatively noncontroversial treaty articles agreed to in the official working groups and the more controversial articles negotiated in the smaller unofficial groups which, while not as yet accepted by the Conference as a whole, do represent negotiated articles in large measure accommodating the main trends at the Conference.

The principal procedural achievement of the Geneva session was the preparation of an informal single negotiating text covering virtually all the issues before the Conference. This text was prepared by the Chairmen of the three Main Committees on their responsibility pursuant to the consensus decision of the Plenary, on the proposal of the Conference President, that they should prepare a negotiating (not negotiated) text as a procedural device to provide a basis for negotiations. Copies of the text[5] have been given to the Committee for your study, and possible inclusion in the record. The single Committee text does provide a means for focussing the Conference work in a way that should facilitate future negotiations with revisions and amendments reflecting the agreements and accommodations I hope will be reached at the next session.

There was clear evidence at the Geneva session of a widespread desire to conclude a comprehensive treaty on the Law of the Sea. Unfortunately, the nature of the negotiations was not geared to im-

[5]U.N. Document A/CONF.62/WP.8/Parts I-III, May 7, 1975; reproduced in *Law of the Sea: Hearing*: 37-116.

mediately visible results and the public impressions may have been that little progress was made. In fact, there were substantial achievements in some areas, although overall I was disappointed that the work schedule outlined by the General Assembly for conclusion of the treaty in 1975 will not be met. The informal single texts and the provision for a second meeting in 1976 if the Conference so decides, provides a procedural basis for concluding a treaty next year. It remains to be seen whether or not the will exists to reach pragmatic solutions where wide differences of view still exist. In this connection, I should also point out that a number of countries, particularly those with little to gain and in some cases much to lose from the establishment of a 200-mile economic zone, do not share our perception of the urgency of completing the treaty promptly. With the general expectation from the outset that at least one more full negotiating session would be scheduled in 1976, the United States was virtually isolated in urging major political compromise at the Geneva session on the very difficult Committee I deep seabed issues.

I believe that much common ground was found on navigation, fisheries, continental shelf resources and marine pollution issues. Significant differences remain with respect to the deep seabed regime and authority and, to a lesser degree, on scientific research and on the desires of landlocked and geographically disadvantaged states to participate in resources exploitation in the economic zone.

The juridical content of the 200-mile economic zone is probably the issue of the greatest interest to most countries.

The Evensen group made a considerable contribution to the Committee II single text by producing a chapter on the economic zone, including fisheries. These articles provide for comprehensive coastal-state management jurisdiction over coastal fisheries stocks out to 200 miles. There is also a coastal-state duty to conserve stocks and to fully utilize them by allowing access by foreign states to the catch in excess of the coastal state's harvesting capacity. The articles on anadromous species (e.g., salmon) were largely acceptable to the states most affected. These articles contain new, strong protections for the state in whose fresh waters anadromous fish originate. Attempts to negotiate acceptable articles on highly migratory species such as tuna were not successful at this session. Efforts to reach a negotiated solution in this area, however, will continue.

There was little opposition to a 12-mile territorial sea (Ecuador's proposal for a 200-mile territorial sea was supported only by a handful of countries and even some of the supporting statements were ambiguous). There was a strong trend in favor of a regime of unimpeded transit passage in straits used for international navigation. There was very widespread acceptance of freedom of navigation and overflight and other uses related to navigation and communication as well as freedom to lay submarine cables and pipelines in the 200-mile economic zone.

Coastal state exclusive rights to the non-living resources (principally petroleum and natural gas) in the economic zone were broadly supported. There was more controversy with respect to coastal state rights to mineral resources of the continental margin where it extends beyond 200 miles. As a possible compromise between opposing views, the United States suggested the establishment of a precise and reasonable outer limit for the margin coupled with an obligation to share a modest percentage of the well-head value of petroleum and natural gas production with the international community. I anticipate that there will be further negotiations in the Evensen group to determine a precise method for defining the outer limit of the continental margin beyond 200 miles and on a precise formula for revenue sharing.

Regarding protection of the marine environment, texts were completed in the official working groups on monitoring, environmental assessment and land-based pollution. Texts were almost completed on ocean dumping and continental shelf pollution. Negotiations were conducted in the Evensen group on vessel source pollution without reaching agreement; however, a trend did emerge against coastal state standard setting for vessel-source pollution throughout the economic zone.

The Group of 77, particularly those members who did not participate in the Evensen group, urged further strengthening of coastal state rights in the economic zone. The landlocked and geographically disadvantaged states were dissatisfied with the failure of the Evensen articles to afford them the legal right to participate in exploiting the natural resources of the economic zone on a basis of equality with coastal states.

There was a continuation of the debate between those states that demand consent for all scientific research conducted in the economic zone and those, such as the United States, that support the right to conduct such research subject to the fulfillment of internationally agreed obligations. A new approach sponsored by the Soviet Union attracted considerable attention. It requires consent for resource-related research and compliance with internationally agreed obligations for non-resource related research.

In the dispute settlement working group most states support binding dispute settlement procedures in areas of national jurisdiction although a minority opposed or wish to limit drastically their applicability (e.g., to navigation and pollution issues). Questions remain with respect to the relationship to coastal state resource jurisdiction and the scope and type of the dispute settlement mechanism. A compromise proposal permitting states to elect between three dispute settlement mechanisms—i.e., the International Court of Justice, arbitration, or a special Law of the Sea Tribunal—was acceptable to the vast majority of participants. However, some delegations considered that their preferred mechanism should be compulsory in all cases, while others favor a functional approach—different machinery for different types of disputes. General support exists for special dispute machinery for the deep seabed.

It is now clear that the negotiation on the nature of the deep seabed regime and authority is the principal stumbling block to a comprehensive Law of the Sea Treaty.

The basic problem is an ideological gap between those possessing the technological ability to develop deep seabed minerals and those developing countries which insist that the international Authority directly and effectively control all deep seabed mining and associated activities, and ultimately become the exclusive operator on the deep seabed. The developing countries' position in this area is reflective of their general concern expressed in other international forums for reordering the economic order with respect to access to and control over natural resources, particularly with respect to their price and rate of development.

The United States explored a number of approaches in an effort to be forthcoming with respect to developing country demands for participating in the exploitation system. We indicated our willingness to abandon the inclusion of detailed regulatory provisions in the treaty and to concentrate on basic conditions of exploitation. We agreed to consider a system of joint ventures and profit sharing with the Authority. In addition, we informally proposed the reservation of areas for exploration and exploitation by developing countries. Such areas would be equal in extent and potential to those which were not reserved. However, in the reserved area the Authority could negotiate for the most favorable financial terms it could obtain. The Soviet Union proposed a parallel system through the reservation of areas in which the Authority could exploit directly, while in other areas states could exploit under a separate system of regulation by the Authority. Both approaches were rejected by the Group of 77. Some developing country flexibility in the deep seabeds was demonstrated by their willingness to submit the entire exploration system to the control of the Seabed Authority Council and to include representatives of designated developed and developing country interest groups on that body in addition to those selected on the basis of equitable geographic representation

Mr. Chairman,[6] with over 140 states participating in a Confer-

[6]Senator John Sparkman (Democrat of Alabama) was Chairman of the Foreign Relations Committee. In Ambassador Stevenson's absence due to illness, his statement was inserted in the record by the Chairman of the Subcommittee on Oceans and International Environment, Senator Claiborne Pell (Democrat of Rhode Island).

ence affecting vital and complex economic, military, political, environmental and scientific interests, we could easily characterize the results of the Geneva session as a considerable success. However, it is no longer sufficient to make progress, even substantial progress, if the goal of the adoption of a widely acceptable, comprehensive treaty continues to elude us beyond the point at which many States will feel compelled to take matters into their own hands in protecting interests with which the existing law of the sea does not deal adequately or equitably.

Mr. Chairman, I have spent a considerable amount of time over the last six years working with those both within and outside our government who appreciate the imperative need of building a better legal order for the oceans. Throughout this period, the members of the Senate Foreign Relations Committee, and you in particular, have provided sound advice and unfailing support in this effort to resolve what appeared at first to be insolvable problems. Some still believe that failure is inevitable. I do not and cannot accept that view. Moreover, I do believe most strongly that we would be terribly remiss as a nation if we did not make every exertion necessary to achieve an acceptable treaty on what appears to be the final stretch of this long road we have travelled. I sincerely hope that this Committee and the Congress in general will give its support in our common endeavor to establish order in the oceans.

13. REVIEWING THE NUCLEAR NONPROLIFERATION TREATY

(Geneva, May 5-30, 1975)

[Among the more significant manifestations of the détente process initiated during the 1960s had been the Treaty on the Non-Proliferation of Nuclear Weapons, signed in London, Moscow, and Washington on July 1, 1968 and belatedly placed in force, after long delays occasioned primarily by the Soviet-organized invasion of Czechoslovakia, on March 5, 1970.[1] By its terms, all of the signatory parties— both those possessing and those lacking nuclear weapons— had undertaken to refrain from actions that would promote the acquisition of nuclear weapons or explosive devices by any member of the latter group. By the spring of 1975, when the operation of the treaty was due to be reviewed at a follow-up conference, its provisions had been accepted by some 94 countries, while 15 additional countries, including Japan, had signed but not yet ratified it. The three dozen or more holdout countries, however, included not only three nuclear powers—China, France, and India—but also a number of countries like Brazil, Israel, and Pakistan that were thought capable of themselves achieving nuclear-weapon status within a couple of years at most.

The already difficult problem of containing the spread of nuclear weapons had meanwhile been still further complicated by the growing diffusion of nuclear technology in connection with the peaceful applications of nuclear energy, a trend that had been stimulated by the world petroleum crisis and the heightened economic incentives to press ahead with the development of atomic power. India's success of May 18, 1974 in producing a "peaceful" nuclear explosion as a by-product of its atomic power program had alerted the United States and other advanced nuclear countries, including the Soviet Union, to the vital importance of reinforcing the existing nonproliferation machinery by developing new safeguards as well as securing the widest possible adherence to existing ones. One result had

[1]TIAS 6839 (21 UST 483); text in *Documents, 1968-9*: 62-8.

been the formation, on U.S. initiative, of what was to become known as the Nuclear Suppliers' Conference, an informal grouping that first met in London in April 1975 and included Canada, France, and the German Federal Republic as well as the U.S.S.R., the United Kingdom, and the United States. Another effect of the Indian explosion had been a strengthened determination on the part of the three latter powers, in their capacity as sponsors of the original nonproliferation treaty, to press for a strong reaffirmation of nonproliferation principles at the treaty review conference, which duly took place in Geneva on May 5-30, 1975, under the presidency of Inga Thorsson of Sweden and with 59 nations participating.

The main American contribution to the Geneva discussion was offered by Fred C. Iklé, Director of the U.S. Arms Control and Disarmament Agency and principal U.S. Representative, in a statement **(Document 18)** that placed the nonproliferation issue within the broader context of nuclear arms limitation. Not too dissimilar were the presentations put forward on behalf of the U.S.S.R. and the United Kingdom, the other participating nuclear-weapon states. As had often happened of late years, such differences as existed among the nuclear-weapon countries seemed less dramatic than those that separated the nuclear-weapon states as a group from the nuclear "have-not" countries. Running through the debate and the Final Declaration that concluded the conference[2]—in spite of reservations expressed by many of the participants—was an undertone of sharp criticism of the nuclear powers for failing to check their own arms race and hasten the advent of a disarmed and prosperous world. Most participants nevertheless appeared to agree that nuclear proliferation was indeed a serious problem; that the nonproliferation treaty had served a useful purpose during its first five years, but needed further strengthening through universal adherence to its terms; and that a second review conference could usefully be held in 1980. Subsequent developments, including the announcement the following month of a $5 billion, fifteen-year atomic cooperation agreement between West Germany and Brazil, could only heighten the feeling that critical decisions might have to be taken even before that date.]

(18) Review Conference of the Parties to the . Treaty on the Non-Proliferation of Nuclear Weapons, Geneva, May 5-30, 1975: Statement to the Conference by Fred C. Iklé, United States Representative and Director of the United States Arms Control and Disarmament Agency, May 6, 1975.[3]

[2]Final Declaration (Conference Document NPT/CONF/30/Rev.1) in *Bulletin*, 72: 924-9; U.S. interpretive statement in same, 73: 193-5.
[3]ACDA Press Release 75-16, May 6; text and subtitles from *Bulletin*, 72: 921-4.

It is my privilege to convey a message to this conference from the President of the United States:

This Review Conference offers an opportunity to focus new attention on our vital obligation to arrest the spread of nuclear weapons. It is a responsibility that confronts all nations equally and impartially. Nuclear energy can and should promote the fortunes of nations assembled at this conference. But its destructive potential can and must be contained.

Support for the Nonproliferation Treaty is a major tenet of American policy. Consequently, I hope this conference will:

—Convey the importance of nonproliferation to the security of all nations, hence to global stability;

—Promote international cooperation in peaceful uses of nuclear energy, while insuring that it not be misused as a means of mass destruction;

—Encourage the further development and wider application of effective safeguards and physical security measures for nuclear materials and facilities; and

—Review the considerable progress that has been made in arms control and disarmament since the treaty was signed, and promote efforts to build on what has been achieved.

We welcome the important recent additions to the roster of parties to the Nonproliferation Treaty,[4] as well as the indications that others are moving toward adherence. We recognize that the treaty's promise is not yet fully realized, but we take satisfaction from what has been achieved. We further recognize that no treaty by itself can prevent the proliferation of nuclear weapons. Yet we remain convinced that the Nonproliferation Treaty is an essential means of advancing this purpose.

Although we still have a long way to go, we see in reviewing the record that the cooperative undertaking to create a more stable world community is well underway.

I take this occasion therefore to rededicate the United States to the support of the Nonproliferation Treaty and to the high purpose of a stable peace which animates it.

Few international endeavors are more deserving of our attention and energy than containing the destructive potential of the atom. The stakes involved are enormous.

We cannot be complacent—and indeed we are not—about the nuclear arsenals that now exist. We must press ahead to make more

---

[4]See below, paragraph following note 5. Japan deposited its ratification June 8, 1976.

comprehensive the limitations which have been imposed and begin to reduce the potential for destruction, a potential that we can scarcely grasp.

But it would be a fatal error if we assumed that we could move forward in reducing the threat of nuclear destruction while nation after nation began to build its own nuclear arsenals. We cannot move forward and backward at the same time. The risk of nuclear destruction—by design, miscalculation, or accident—cannot be reduced if nuclear competition drives a dangerous wedge between neighboring nations throughout the world.

Let there be no mistake. The dangers resulting from nuclear proliferation are shared by all, nuclear powers and non-nuclear-weapon states alike.

We therefore have a common interest in the success of the Nonproliferation Treaty. It is my government's hope that this conference will focus attention on the treaty's essential role in promoting the security of all states and that it will provide a stimulus for cooperative international effort to make the treaty as effective and universally applicable as possible.

The basic provisions of the treaty, articles I and II, have been followed faithfully by the parties. The safeguards resulting from article III make an important additional contribution to the security of all states.[5]

But in our judgment, the effectiveness of all three articles can be strengthened best by securing the widest possible adherence to the treaty. Hence, it is most gratifying that several states have recently completed their ratification. The Republic of Korea ratified the treaty. Just last week major industrial countries of Western Europe also became parties to the treaty: Belgium, the Federal Republic of Germany, Italy, Luxembourg, and the Netherlands.

We welcome all the new parties. Several of them have attained world leadership in peaceful applications of nuclear technology. This offers telling evidence that the treaty is consistent with progress in the peaceful uses of the atom. In fact, the treaty not only supports peaceful uses but helps preserve the world order without which peaceful uses could not survive and expand.

The First Five Years of the Treaty

In its first five years, the treaty has clearly served to increase the volume of international nuclear commerce. The United States, for example, has entered into international arrangements for the enrichment of uranium to meet the needs of some 150 power reactors

---

[5]Articles I, II, and III of the treaty provide respectively for nontransfer and nonreceipt of nuclear weapons and for the acceptance of safeguards administered by the International Atomic Energy Agency.

in non-nuclear-weapon states, having a total capacity of about 120,000 megawatts. In addition, the United States has exported 35 nuclear reactors since 1970. Most of this cooperation has been with states now party to the Nonproliferation Treaty or with signatories whose ratification appears imminent.

The United States has shared its peaceful nuclear technology generously. It has provided information, offered training, supported research programs, supplied uranium enrichment services, and sold or donated research and power reactors embodying the most advanced technology.

Aid to the developing countries has also increased considerably since the treaty was opened for signature. We believe the developing countries party to the treaty should be given favored consideration in nuclear assistance. Last year, my government announced that parties will be given preference in the allocation of our in-kind contributions to the technical assistance program of the International Atomic Energy Agency. At the same time, we are increasing substantially the amount of our voluntary contribution for 1975.

Safeguards Over Peaceful Uses

A major purpose—indeed, a major accomplishment—of the Nonproliferation Treaty is to make possible the expansion of peaceful nuclear cooperation. But, as Secretary Kissinger stated to the United Nations last fall,[6] our policy of widely supplying nuclear fuels and other nuclear materials "cannot continue if it leads to the proliferation of nuclear explosives."

The rapid expansion of the peaceful uses of nuclear energy has raised massive new problems. One is meeting fuel-reprocessing needs in the safest and most economic way. Another is the disposal of the rapidly accumulating nuclear wastes. Fortunately, we still have some time to work out solutions. There is no economic need for reprocessing for several years to come, and spent fuel can still be kept in temporary storage. But nations must cooperate to solve these problems soon to protect the health and safety of all the people.

The promotion of peaceful uses of the atom is inseparably linked with safeguards to inspire international confidence that fissionable materials are not being diverted to destructive purposes. We can all take pride in what has been done about safeguards. Specifically, the International Atomic Energy Agency has accomplished a great deal. Its efforts deserve the wholehearted support of us all.

Virtually every party to this treaty with nuclear facilities requiring safeguards has negotiated an agreement with the Agency; and

[6]Statement to the General Assembly, Sept. 23, 1974, in *AFR, 1974*: 351.

almost every nuclear facility now operating in the non-nuclear-weapon states is subject to Agency safeguards or will be in the near future. This is a good record.

But much remains to be done. We need to insure:

—That all parties to the treaty conclude agreements with the Agency;

—That safeguards are effective and efficient; and

—That safeguards cover, as comprehensively as possible, the nuclear facilities of non-nuclear-weapon states not party to the treaty and preclude diversion of nuclear materials for any nuclear explosive device.

Also, we have to concern ourselves seriously with the threat of theft and other criminal seizure of nuclear material. We hope this conference will recognize the need for international measures to deal with this grim danger.

Peaceful Nuclear Explosions

Article V,[7] as we all know, was included in the treaty to insure that the non-nuclear-weapon states adhering to the treaty would not be deprived of any potential benefits of peaceful nuclear explosions that might be realized by the nuclear-weapon states.

In the United States, there has been much research and experimentation on the use of nuclear explosions for peaceful purposes. But we have not yet reduced any application to practice, nor have we obtained any commercial benefits from this technology. If and when we should succeed in doing so, we would of course make those benefits available as called for in the treaty.

Questions remain to be resolved regarding the feasibility and practicability of peaceful nuclear explosions. Moreoever, no request for such explosions has ever gone beyond the stage of preliminary feasibility studies. For these reasons, there has so far been no practical necessity to conclude the international agreement or agreements mentioned in article V. However, the United States stands ready to negotiate the requisite agreements when the practical need develops.

In the meantime, the United States is prepared to participate in consideration of the institutional arrangements that may be required to make the benefits of peaceful nuclear explosions available internationally. Toward this end, important steps have already been taken within the framework of the International Atomic Energy Agency. My government, as one of the potential suppliers

[7] Providing for sharing of the benefits of peaceful nuclear explosions with non-nuclear-weapon states.

of such services, has agreed to assist the Agency in a study of the related legal problems.

U.S.-Soviet Arms Control Agreements

When this treaty was opened for signature in 1968, the only other postwar arms control agreements were the Antarctic Treaty, the "Hotline" Agreement, the Limited Test Ban Treaty, and the Outer Space Treaty.[8] While these were solid accomplishments, they did not reduce the levels of existing nuclear armaments.

At the signing ceremony of the Nonproliferation Treaty, my government and the Soviet Government announced that we would open negotiations to limit offensive and defensive strategic arms.[9] The relationship between the treaty and this announcement was clear: the successful negotiation of this treaty had strengthened mutual confidence between the two largest nuclear-weapon powers and promised to keep nuclear arms control from becoming totally unmanageable.

Since then, serious and intensive negotiations on strategic arms limitations have continued steadily and received personal attention at the highest level of the two governments. The first fruits of these negotiations were the improved "Hotline" Agreement and the Agreement on Measures to Reduce the Risk of Outbreak of Nuclear War.[10]

The culmination of the Strategic Arms Limitation Talks in 1972 brought the Treaty on Anti-Ballistic Missile Systems[11] limiting each side to two marrowly circumscribed complexes. In my country it led in fact to dismantling an anti-ballistic-missile complex already well under construction. By renouncing major anti-ballistic-missile systems, the United States and the Soviet Union gave up a potential new weapons system that they were in a unique position to exploit. No other country could have built such systems.

Along with the Anti-Ballistic Missile Treaty, an interim agreement[12] was worked out to limit the number of strategic offensive launchers on both sides for five years, a period that would provide time to achieve more comprehensive limits.

At the summit meeting in the summer of 1974, the leaders of the

[8]*Documents, 1959*: 528-35; same, *1963*: 115-16 and 130-32; same, *1967*: 392-6.

[9]*Presidential Documents*, 4: 1044 (1968).

[10]*AFR, 1971*: 109-14.

[11]Treaty on the Limitation of Anti-Ballistic Missile Systems, signed in Moscow May 26, 1972 and entered into force Oct. 3, 1972 (TIAS 7503; 23 UST 3435); text in *AFR, 1972*: 90-95.

[12]Interim Agreement on Certain Measures with Respect to the Limitation of Strategic Offensive Arms, signed in Moscow May 26, 1972 and entered into force Oct. 3, 1972 (TIAS 7504; 23 UST 3462); text in *AFR, 1972*: 97-101.

United States and Soviet Union took a further important step by negotiating the Threshold Test Ban Treaty.[13] I should point out that this was not only an important arms control measure in its own right; it was also a positive step toward a comprehensive test ban, to which we remain firmly committed.

Last November, at Vladivostok, a major milestone was reached when President Ford and General Secretary Brezhnev established specific guidelines for a new agreement to limit strategic offensive arms.[14] Based on this accord, negotiations are now underway here in Geneva. The new agreement is to limit strategic offensive armaments, including strategic bombers and missiles equipped with multiple reentry vehicles (MIRV's), to equal totals on each side.

The implications of this breakthrough are far-reaching. By putting as overall ceiling on strategic armaments, we establish a promising basis for further reductions. We look forward to follow-on negotiations on further limitation and reduction as soon as the Vladivostok agreement is complete.

An encouraging precedent has already been set: only two years after the Anti-Ballistic Missile Treaty imposed comprehensive equal ceilings on these systems, both sides agreed to reduce the permitted deployment levels by one-half.[15]

Five years have now elapsed since the Nonproliferation Treaty went into effect. This period is only one-sixth of the nuclear era that began at the end of the Second World War. Yet, in this short time, far more has been accomplished in the control of nuclear arms than in the preceding 25 years. In historical perspective, the treaty has proven to be both a prerequisite and a catalyst for progress toward nuclear disarmament. That process is underway. And it is up to all of us to encourage and sustain it.

The Nonproliferation Treaty is indispensable to nuclear disarmament. It is indispensable to achieving the maximum peaceful benefits of nuclear energy. It is indispensable to the security of all. The task of this conference is to provide the support and forward movement that are needed to enable the treaty to fulfill its great promise.

[13]Treaty on the Limitation of Underground Nuclear Weapons Tests, signed in Moscow July 3, 1974 but not in force as of mid-1977; text in *AFR, 1974*: 229-33.

[14]Joint statement on the limitation of strategic offensive arms, released in Vladivostok Nov. 24, 1974; text in *AFR, 1974*: 508-9.

[15]Protocol to the Treaty on the Limitation of Anti-Ballistic Missile Systems, signed in Moscow July 3, 1974 and entered into force May 24, 1976 (TIAS 8276); text in *AFR, 1974*:226-8.

14. THE MAYAGÜEZ AFFAIR

(May 12-15, 1975)

[In their comments on the Vietnam debacle, the President and Secretary Kissinger did not fail to express their concern about the way in which America's allies and friends, in Southeast Asia and elsewhere, would view the destruction of a longstanding American protégé by hostile forces which the United States itself appeared unwilling to oppose either by force of arms or by timely material aid. Conceding that little if anything could now be done toward saving the Republic of Vietnam in light of the restrictions imposed by Congress, the two American spokesmen had nevertheless insisted that the Vietnam experience must not be thought to set a precedent for American inaction in other situations that might arise in the future.

An occasion that appeared to call for a vigorous demonstration of American resolve did in fact arise within a fortnight of the Vietnamese collapse with the receipt on Monday, May 12, of reports that a patrol boat of the newly installed Cambodian Government had intercepted and seized the U.S. containership *Mayagüez* at a point in the Gulf of Siam located some 60 miles from the Cambodian mainland and six and one-half miles from the small, Cambodian-claimed island of Poulo Wai. Protesting this "act of piracy" and demanding the immediate release of the vessel and its crew of 39, the United States over the next two days attempted without success to contact the Cambodian authorities through Chinese and other diplomatic channels. Concurrently, it initiated a number of measures looking toward eventual military action, among them the landing of a force of 1,100 Marines from Okinawa at the U Taphao air base in Thailand—in spite of a warning from Prime Minister Kukrit Pramoj that that country would not permit the use of its territory for any action against Cambodia.

By Tuesday, May 13 (Washington time), the *Mayagüez* had been conveyed by its captors to Koh Tang island, approximately half way to the mainland, and its crew had been placed on board a fishing boat en route to the port of Kompong Som, newly renamed Sihanoukville in honor of the nominal Cambodian Chief of State. In the continued absence of word from the Cambodians, the United States over the next two days initiated a series of military actions that began with air attacks on the fishing boat in an unsuccessful effort to make it change course. At 11:50 A.M. on Wednesday, May 14, the White House further reported that U.S. aircraft had begun efforts to block the movement of captive crewmen to the mainland, that three Cambodian patrol craft had been destroyed and about four others damaged and immobilized, but that one boat had succeeded in reaching Kompong Som.

Nine and one-half hours later, at 9:15 P.M. Washington time on May 14, it was announced that the President had ordered the Marines to board the *Mayagüez* and land on Koh Tang to rescue any crew members there, and that he had in addition ordered aircraft from the carrier Coral Sea "to undertake associated military operations in the area to protect and support the operations to regain the vessel and members of the crew." These latter operations, initiated after Cambodia had already given an indication of its readiness to release the vessel, not only led to a sharp local struggle at Koh Tang but also involved air attacks on the Ream airfield near Sihanoukville and on that port itself. Some fighting continued even after vessel and crew had been recovered late on Wednesday evening. American casualties were later reported as 15 killed, 3 missing, and 50 wounded; Cambodian losses, not surprisingly, were claimed to be substantially higher.[1]

Like earlier U.S. military ventures in Southeast Asia, these measures loosed a storm of domestic criticism directed both at the nature of the American action and at the quality of its execution. What President Ford, Secretary Kissinger, and others of those directly involved had apparently seen as a legitimate and necessary defense of American interests was depicted by unsympathetic critics as an act of *machismo*, an exercise in irresponsible muscle-flexing that recalled such Nixon-era performances as the 1970 invasion of the Cambodian mainland and the 1973 alert of U.S. military forces at the height of the Mideast crisis. Among its more readily measurable consequences was its distinctly negative impact on Thailand, an old-established U.S. ally which had already given evidence of an increasingly neutralist tendency, had recently called for an accelerated withdrawal of U.S. troops over the next twelve months, and would now begin agitating for a "phasing out" of the South-East Asia Treaty Organization (SEATO), the principal institutional bulwark of regional security in Southeast Asia.[2]

---

[1] Factual outline from *Keesing's*: 27239-40; White House announcements from *Presidential Documents*, 11: 511-12 and 514.
[2] *Keesing's*: 27071 and 27334-5; see further Chapter 34.

Some of the salient aspects of this controversial chapter in the history of American foreign policy are reflected in President Ford's terse official report on the *Mayagüez* incident **(Document 19)** and in the transcript of a news conference held by Secretary Kissinger a few hours after its conclusion **(Document 20).**]

(19) Report to Congress Under the War Powers Resolution: Letter from President Ford to the Speaker of the House and the President Pro Tempore of the Senate, May 15, 1975.[3]

Dear Mr. Speaker: (President Pro Tem)

On 12 May 1975, I was advised that the S.S. *Mayaguez,* a merchant vessel of United States registry en route from Hong Kong to Thailand with a U.S. citizen crew, was fired upon, stopped, boarded, and seized by Cambodia in international waters in the vicinity of Poulo Wai Island. The seized vessel was then forced to proceed to Koh Tang Island where it was required to anchor. This hostile act was in clear violation of international law.

In view of this illegal and dangerous act, I ordered, as you have been previously advised, United States military forces to conduct the necessary reconnaissance and to be ready to respond if diplomatic efforts to secure the return of the vessel and its personnel were not successful. Two United States reconnaissance aircraft in the course of locating the *Mayaguez* sustained minimal damage from small firearms. Appropriate demands for the return of the *Mayaguez* and its crew were made, both publicly and privately, without success.

In accordance with my desire that the Congress be informed on this matter and taking note of Section 4(a) (1) of the War Powers Resolution,[4] I wish to report to you that at about 6:20 a.m., 13 May, pursuant to my instructions to prevent the movement of the *Mayaguez* into a mainland port, U.S. aircraft fired warning shots across the bow of the ship and gave visual signals to small craft approaching the ship. Subsequently, in order to stabilize the situation and in an attempt to preclude removal of the American crew of the *Mayaguez* to the mainland, where their rescue would be more difficult, I directed the United States Armed Forces to isolate the island and interdict any movement between the ship or the island and the mainland, and to prevent movement of the ship itself, while still taking all possible care to prevent loss of life or injury to the U.S. captives. During the evening of 13 May, a Cambodian patrol boat attempting to leave the island disregarded aircraft warnings and was sunk. Thereafter, two other Cambodian patrol craft were de-

[3]Text from *Presidential Documents*, 11: 514-15.
[4]Public Law 93-148, Oct. 12, 1973; *AFR, 1973*: 486.

stroyed and four others were damaged and immobilized. One boat, suspected of having some U.S. captives aboard, succeeded in reaching Kompong Som after efforts to turn it around without injury to the passengers failed.

Our continued objective in this operation was the rescue of the captured American crew along with the retaking of the ship *Mayaguez*. For that purpose, I ordered late this afternoon [May 14] an assault by United States Marines on the island of Koh Tang to search out and rescue such Americans as might still be held there, and I ordered retaking of the *Mayaguez* by other marines boarding from the destroyer escort [*Harold E.*] *Holt*. In addition to continued fighter and gunship coverage of the Koh Tang area, these Marine activities were supported by tactical aircraft from the *Coral Sea*, striking the military airfield at Ream and other military targets in the area of Kompong Som in order to prevent reinforcement or support from the mainland of the Cambodian forces detaining the American vessel and crew.

At approximately 9:00 p.m. EDT on 14 May, the *Mayaguez* was retaken by United States forces. At approximately 11:30 p.m., the entire crew of the *Mayaguez* was taken aboard the [destroyer *Robert L.*] *Wilson*. U.S. forces have begun the process of disengagement and withdrawal.

This operation was ordered and conducted pursuant to the President's constitutional Executive power and his authority as Commander-in-Chief of the United States Armed Forces.

Sincerely,

GERALD R. FORD

(20) News Conference Statement by Secretary of State Kissinger, May 16, 1975.[5]

(Excerpts)

Q. Mr. Secretary, there have been public complaints from Thailand about our landing of marines. Was there a violation of Thai sovereignty in this caper? And secondly, can you tell us if there was any concern in the strafing of Cambodian gunboats that since we weren't too sure where our own men were, that we might—the crew was—that we might have hit the American crew?

Secretary Kissinger: Well, first of all of course, I have to reject the description of what happened this week as a "caper." It was a serious situation in which we were trying to save a group of Americans and recover a ship.

[5]Department of State Press Release 265, May 16; text from *Bulletin*, 72: 753-61.

With respect to Thailand, we have, of course, a treaty relationship with Thailand in SEATO. And we have had a series of base arrangements with them which over the period of years has led to a degree of cooperation in events in Indochina which were in the mutual interest and in which we have greatly appreciated the assistance that Thailand has given us.

In the course of this decade, it may be that a pattern of action has developed that made us assume that our latitude in using these bases was greater than the current situation in Southeast Asia would permit to the Thai Government. And therefore, insofar as we have caused any embarrassment to the Thai Government, we regret those actions.

At the same time, it is clear that any relationship between us and another country must be based on mutual interest. And we, I believe, have a reason, or have a right, to expect that those countries that have an alliance relationship with us look with some sympathy at matters that concern the United States profoundly.

If conditions in the area change, we are prepared to adjust our relationship to new conditions and to have discussions on that subject in a spirit of cooperation.

Q. Mr. Secretary, that was kind of a double-barreled question.

Secretary Kissinger: What was the second question?

Q. Since we were not so certain—

Secretary Kissinger: Oh, on the gunboats.

One of the most difficult and anguishing decisions we had to make was the risk to Americans in taking these gunboats under attack.

Now, we had to balance this, in our view, against the risk as we then saw it—of their being taken to the mainland—and we wanted to avoid a situation in which the United States might have to negotiate over a very extended period of time over a group of merchant seamen who had no connection whatever with any governmental activity.

There was one incident in which our pilots were told to determine, insofar as one can under those conditions, whether any Americans were likely to have been on the boat. There was one incident where a pilot beginning to take a boat under attack saw a group of individuals that looked to him as if they might have been Americans huddled on the boat, asked for instructions, and was told not to proceed with the attack. And that was one gunboat that reached Kompong Som. So we tried to take it into account, and fortunately it seems there was no injury to anybody.

Q. Mr. Secretary, in light of the Thai Prime Minister's recall of his Ambassador and his announcement of a complete review of all treaties and agreements between the two countries, could you give us your assessment of the diplomatic strains now developing? Also, have you had any communication as yet from the Thai Ambassador?

Secretary Kissinger: We have not had any formal communication from the Thai Ambassador. But I am assuming that the story is correct.

The Thai Government finds itself, in general, in a complicated position after the events of Indochina, quite independent of this recent operation.

We had, prior to this recent operation, made it clear that we are prepared to discuss with the Thai Government its conception of its requirements, or of the necessary adjustment in the present period. We are still prepared to do this, and we recognize that the Thai Government is under some strains and under some public necessities. And they have to understand, however, that we, too, have our necessities.

Q. Mr. Secretary, was there at any time in this crisis any chance to resolve it diplomatically?

Secretary Kissinger: There was no chance during this crisis to resolve it diplomatically. That is to say, we never received a communication, proposition, that would have enabled us to explore a diplomatic solution, and it was—when—by Wednesday evening [May 14] we had not yet received any reply that the President ordered the military operations to begin.

Mr. Lisagor [Peter Lisagor, Chicago Daily News].

Q. I would like to clear up one mystifying aspect of this: Why did the Chinese return the [U.S.] note [to Cambodia] 24 hours later? And did they indicate at the time that it had gotten through to the Cambodian authorities?

Secretary Kissinger: In this matter the Government of the People's Republic was not responsible for the content of the note. But I am assuming the Chinese Xerox machines can reproduce it within 24 hours.

Q. What was the significance of their returning it, Mr. Secretary?

Secretary Kissinger: Well, a degree of disassociation from the diplomatic process—

Q. Do you believe that they actually—

Secretary Kissinger: —a formal disassociation. I don't want to speculate on this, but I wouldn't be surprised.

Q. Mr. Secretary, in view of the attempts at détente with the People's Republic of China, are you dissatisfied with their apparent— or with the way they handled themselves in this situation?

Secretary Kissinger: The requirements of relationships with some of our potential adversaries have to be seen in a more complicated framework than is often stated.

Both the Chinese and we have certain common interests which have been laid down in the Shanghai communique,[6] which we have reaffirmed, and which we consider remain valid.

At the same time, we do have different perceptions in different areas, and there we will maintain our differences.

Thirdly, one has to keep in mind in asking other countries to play a role what their real possibilities are in any given situation.

And finally, one has to leave it to those countries to play the role, either publicly or privately—if they choose to—that they consider appropriate.

So on the whole, I don't believe that this is a useful area for me to comment on.

Q. Mr. Secretary, in view of the earlier incidents involving a Panamanian freighter being detained and a South Korean freighter being fired upon, why was there no effort by this government, earlier on, before the Mayaguez seizure, to warn U.S. vessels to stay out of that area?

Secretary Kissinger: Well, my understanding is that insurance companies had been notified and that it had been assumed that they would get in touch with these ships. So we were, frankly, not aware that there were any American ships in that area. And when the matter came to our attention—this was not a matter that had ever reached high levels of the government. It had been dealt with routinely by notification of the insurance companies, which are presumed to have the greatest interest in the preservation of these ships.

Bernie [Bernard Gwertzman, New York Times], you had a question before.

Q. I would like to go back to the Thailand question. Why was it,

[6]*AFR, 1972*: 307-11.

given the known sensitivities of the Thais to this situation in that area, that an effort was not made to at least consult with their government prior to the sending of the marines?

Secretary Kissinger: Well, the assumption was that we were in an emergency situation, in which, on occasion, we have acted without having had a full opportunity for consultation, and it was therefore thought that within the traditional relationship it would be a measure that would be understood.

In any event, it would have presented massive problems either way.

Q. Mr. Secretary, one of the effects of this incident appears to be a restoration of American credibility and, to some extent morale. My question is: To what extent was that a consideration in the American operation?

Secretary Kissinger: The thrust of our discussions concerned the recovery of the ship and the rescue of the men. If there were any by-products, that can be considered a bonus to the operation, but it was not the principal impetus behind the operation.

We believed that we had to draw a line against illegal actions and, secondly, against situations where the United States might be forced into a humiliating discussion about the ransom of innocent merchant seamen.

If it had these by-products—I think to some extent it did have this effect. But this was not the primary motivation behind the action.

Q. Mr. Secretary, the Cambodian Minister of Information and Propaganda has charged that our planes began systematically strafing and bombing the ship about 12 hours after it was seized—the area around the ship. Can you respond to that, please? This would be dawn on the morning of the 13th.

Secretary Kissinger: I would have to review the actual events. I don't have the log right here.

My recollection would be that it may have started somewhat later, but in any event, the decision was made. It was probably later than 12 hours afterward, but I don't want to tie myself to the time.

A decision was made to try to prevent ships from the mainland from reaching the ship—or ships from the island from reaching the mainland. That I think probably happened sometime during our night on Monday night. So the timing could be roughly correct—

Q. Mr. Secretary.

Secretary Kissinger: —but there must be some Defense Department statement of when the actual strafing started which would be correct.[7]

Q. I just wondered how long we waited for the diplomacy to work before force was used.

Secretary Kissinger: The methods that were used were not strafing at first. The methods that were used were to try to force ships back to the island.

Q. Mr. Secretary, the only basic criticism that has been directed at the Administration's actions this week is that perhaps the Administration moved much too quickly militarily and did not give diplomacy a chance to work.

Secretary Kissinger: Come on, Marvin [Marvin Kalb, CBS]— break down. Maybe we did something right. [Laughter.] Statistically we are bound to do it sometimes. [Laughter.]

Q. Well, in that spirit, could you tell us, or respond to that kind of criticism?

Secretary Kissinger: Well, when you say diplomacy was given no chance to work—if any communication had been received back, either from Cambodia or from any other source, then we would have had a subject matter for diplomacy on which to act. On the other hand, when this did not happen, and when we had received no communication whatsoever, we had to balance the risks that would occur if they tried to move the ship. Since we didn't know whether any of the crew was left on the ship or whether a Cambodian crew might have been put on the ship, we had to balance the risks if they tried to move the ship, the pressures we were under in neighboring countries, the difficulties that could arise. We therefore decided, after some 60 hours of diplomatic efforts, to try to seize the ship.

[7]Detailed chronologies prepared by the Congressional Research Service, the Department of State, and the Department of Defense were later published in an appendix to U.S. House of Representatives, 94th Cong., 1st sess., Committee on International Relations, *War Powers: A Test of Compliance: Hearings* before the Subcommittee on International Security and Scientific Affairs, May 7 and June 4, 1975 (Washington: GPO, 1975): 105-17.

It was a balance that had to be struck. We thought the risks of waiting another 24 to 48 hours in the absence of any communication whatsoever from any government were greater than the risks of going ahead.

Q. When the Cambodians did say that they would release the ship, why was it, as I understand it, that the bulk of the military action followed the Phnom Penh radio broadcast that they would release the ship?

Secretary Kissinger: The Phnom Penh radio broadcast was received in Washington—it was received in the White House at about 8:16 that evening [May 14]. At that time, we had 150 marines pinned down on the island, and we had the *Holt* approaching the ship. At that point, to stop all operations on the basis of a radio broadcast that had not been confirmed, whose precise text we did not at that moment have—all we had was a one-page summary of what it said—a broadcast, moreover, that did not say anything about the crew and referred only to the ship, it seemed to us it was too dangerous for the troops that had already been landed to stop the operation.

We therefore took rather drastic measures—drastic communications measures—of informing the Cambodian Government of the fact that we would stop all military operations as soon as the crew was released. And in order to make doubly sure, we released the statement that we had broadcast into Cambodia. We also released that statement to the press[8]—it was verbatim, the same statement—on the theory that perhaps they would read the news tickers faster than they could pick up the other means of communication that we were using.

About two and a half hours after that, the crew was released. And after that, we stopped all military operations except those which we judged necessary for the saving of Americans that were still on the island.

Q. Mr. Secretary, on that point, questions have been raised in Congress this morning as to whether there was a punitive intent by the United States. And secondly, in relation to that, wasn't there also a hazard that the bombing of the mainland could have hit the crewmen, because there were at least two circumstances where the crewmen could have been hit by American fire—while they were on the ship and while they were on the mainland?

Secretary Kissinger: Well, when you say "punitive intent," the

[8]*Presidential Documents,* 11: 512.

intent of the operation was as I described it—to rescue the men and to recover the ship. Obviously any damage that is done in the process has a punitive effect, whatever the intention is. We tried to gear the action as closely to the objective as was possible.

Now, as it turned out, there seems to have been some relationship between the release of the crew and the attacks on the mainland. That is to say, some members of the crew were told that they should tell the *Wilson*, or the officers on the *Wilson*, that they were being released on the assumption that this would end the bombing attacks. And when we received this word, around midnight—I mean this additional word, shortly after midnight—then all actions except those that were judged to be immediately necessary for the military operations were stopped. There was some risk. It was clear that either the attack on the island or the attack on the mainland could lead to American casualties if the Cambodians deliberately moved the prisoners into an area where they would be exposed to attack.

On the other hand, we tried to confine our attack to clearly military objectives, so that there would have had to be a very provocative intent on the part of the Cambodians.

But it was one of the balances that had to be struck.

Q. Mr. Secretary, when you referred to 60 hours of diplomacy, actually I am told there was fighting which ran through this whole sequence—that there was fighting the night of the 12th, there was some shooting at American vessels the night of the 12th. The Cambodians say that we began strafing at dawn on the 13th. So there was, by both sides' accounts, even though they don't match—there seemed to have been a considerable amount of shooting all during the period when the diplomacy was being attempted. Could we have a better breakdown on that, possibly?

Secretary Kissinger: For about 60 hours we made no attempt to seize the ship. We made it very clear from the very beginning—the President in his statement, the communications that were sent to whoever we thought might have a possibility of reaching the Cambodians, and in a number of statements that I made on Monday and Tuesday—we made it absolutely clear that we insisted on the release of the ship and the men.

Then we took collateral actions to make it more difficult for them to move the men and to speed up the pace of their deliberations.

Q. Are you satisfied, Mr. Secretary, that the American message reached the Cambodians? And if you are satisfied, what gives you that—

Secretary Kissinger: Well, I am positive that our message reached the Cambodians because we delivered it to the Cambodian Embassy in Peking, in addition to everything else.

Q. A technical question for a moment. In response to Bernie before, did you say there was no full consultation with Thailand or no consultation with Thailand?

Secretary Kissinger: Well, after the troops got into—

Q. Before.

Secretary Kissinger: Before, there was no consultation.

Q. At all.

Secretary Kissinger: No.

Q. Mr. Secretary, in Palm Springs[9] you said the United States would face a time of testing, what with events in Indochina. Now, granted that was a private conversation, but much of that conversation has since gone public anyway. I would like to ask you if you think this was indeed a time of international testing of the U.S. resolve; and also what useful purpose was served, that is, what has the world learned from the U.S. action regarding the Mayaguez?

Secretary Kissinger: I have said not only in private conversations, I have stated publicly, that events in Indochina would have international consequences and that they would affect other countries' perception of their position and of our own. I have also said that I believe those consequences were manageable if we were prepared to face them.

Now, this event could well have resulted from an isolated act of a local commander. I am not inclined to believe that this was a carefully planned operation on the part of the Cambodian authorities. Nevertheless, the impact on us was the same—and could have been the same as if it had been carefully planned if we had been drawn through irresolution into a negotiation over a period of months over the release of people that they had no right to seize to begin with.

What the impact of this may be internationally—I don't want to transform it into an apocalyptic event. The impact ought to be to make clear that there are limits beyond which the United States

[9]Secretary Kissinger met with President Ford and General Weyand in Palm Springs on Apr. 5.

cannot be pushed and that the United States is prepared to defend those interests and that it can get public support and congressional support for those actions. But we are not going around looking for opportunities to prove our manhood.

We will judge actions in the light of our interests and the extent of the provocation.

Q. Mr. Secretary, do you have any reason to anticipate a severance of relations with the United States by Thailand or that Thailand may move up the date by which we must remove our troops in that country, which I think is one year?

Secretary Kissinger: I do not personally anticipate a severance of relations with Thailand. I believe that relations with other countries must always be based on a mutuality of interest. We are doing other countries no favor when we have a well-considered alliance relationship, because it must be in the mutual interest. Other countries are doing us no favor by having diplomatic relations with us if it doesn't serve their interests. And therefore I am assuming that the Thai Government will look at its long-term interests as we will. We are prepared to discuss all issues with the Thai Government in a spirit of appreciation for what Thailand has done over several decades and with a cooperative attitude.

But, as I said the other day, we will not insist on arrangements that other countries no longer consider in their interests.

* * *

Q. Mr. Secretary, would you clarify for us the American communications with the Cambodians? Did we specify a deadline as to a specific time when we wanted the ship and the prisoners to be returned? And could you clarify why the marines landed on an island where obviously the prisoners were not being held? How does that whole sequence work there?

Secretary Kissinger: We did not give a time limit. We were considering at various times whether we should give a time limit. Every time we considered it we came to the conclusion that the risk of giving it to any military operation that might be contemplated and to the crewmembers were greater than the benefits to be achieved by giving a specific time limit—since most of those benefits were really domestic, so that we could say that we had given warning.

So by constantly increasing the severity of our requests we tried to convey an increasing sense of urgency, and therefore we approached the Secretary General. First of all, a number of public statements were made. Secondly, we approached on Wednesday the Secretary General of the United Nations with a letter, which was made public, indicating very clearly that we were going to invoke article 51 of the U.N. Charter, the right of self-defense of the U.N. Charter. And therefore we felt we had in effect given an ultimatum without giving a specific time.

We had, in fact, drafted something with a specific time as an alternative, but we felt the risks were too great.

Now, with respect to landing on an island on which the prisoners were not. Almost anything we did would in retrospect be subject to this sort of question. We did not know whether the prisoners were on the ship, whether the prisoners were on the island, or whether the prisoners were on the mainland. We tried to design an operation where we would, as close to simultaneously as possible, bring maximum pressure on the authorities in each place so that if they were on the mainland there was some reason for the mainland authorities to release them, if they were on the island we could seize them, and if they were on the ship, that would, of course, have been the happiest event of all.

We genuinely thought, or at least we suspected, that a number of them might have been brought to the mainland. We thought that a substantial number of them would probably be on the island. Had we not thought this, there was no reason to land on the island. As it turned out, the results achieved tend to justify what was attempted. There's no question that if it hadn't worked many of your questions would now be asked in a different atmosphere.

* * *

Q. Mr. Secretary, could one reasonably infer from several of your comments this morning that the United States would look with very great sympathy should the Thais decide to reconsider their involvement with SEATO and indeed conclude that it's in their best interests to withdraw from SEATO?

Secretary Kissinger: These are decisions which the Thai Government must make. We are in an existing relationship with the Thai Government. We have no reason on our side to change it. It is up to the Thai Government to decide what its interests require. And we will discuss the Thai concerns with the interest and sympathy that an old friend deserves. We are not suggesting to the Thai Government what position it should take.

Q. Mr. Secretary, let's get to something that might appear to be an inconsistency. I think you said that for 60 hours you waited before taking military action. Later on you said that we had to drive our point home with increasing severity. Did you mean that from the very beginning of this operation there was American military action taken to support existing diplomatic action?

Secretary Kissinger: No. What I meant by increasing severity—meant increasing severity of public statements. I did not mean increasing severity of military action. The military actions that were taken on Tuesday [May 13] our time were exclusively designed at that point to freeze the status quo as much as possible to keep them from moving the ship and keep them from moving the crewmen. They were not designed as such to bring diplomatic pressure, although they obviously had that result.

Q. Could I ask a question about the disengagement from the operation once the objective of releasing the men had been accomplished? Did some of the heaviest attacks actually occur after the men had been released?

Secretary Kissinger: I would have to check that. Some attacks occurred after the men had been released. At that point our biggest problem was that we had several hundred marines on the island who were under very heavy attack. There were also 2,400 Communist forces on the mainland, and we wanted to absorb their energies in other things than attempting to intervene with our disengagement efforts on the island. That was the general concept of the operation.

* * *

Q. Mr. Secretary, you spoke about the diplomatic results of the Cambodian operation as a bonus. Are you glad this happened?

Secretary Kissinger: Nobody can be glad to be put into a position where the lives of Americans are at stake. And the anguish of these operations for those who have the responsibility is very grave, because the consequences of failure are very serious and the loss of life is never one that is easy to contemplate. We would far have preferred if this had not happened.

Our problem was that we could not choose our involvement. We were forced into this. And then when the incident had occurred, we had to act on the basis of what we thought would most save lives and was most in the interests of the United States. But we were not looking for an opportunity.

Q. Mr. Secretary, the last raid on the airfield near Sihanoukville

[Kompong Som] was made a half an hour after the crew members were released, after the Cambodians had met the requirements for cessation of hostilities that the President laid down in his last public statement—that is, the ship was taken and the prisoners were released. Why was this raid not stopped?

Secretary Kissinger: Because we had some 200 marines on the island. And we were trying to extricate them, and we were trying to keep the military forces on the mainland from interfering with what could have been an extremely tricky and difficult operation.

The press: Thank you, Mr. Secretary.

15. REPORT ON PANAMA CANAL NEGOTIATIONS

(Seattle, May 22, 1975)

[Old-fashioned patriotism of the kind that surfaced in the *Mayagüez* affair was a familiar component of the American outlook, one that exerted its share of influence in every area of foreign policy and tended to become more assertive whenever it could be imagined that American preeminence was being insufficiently respected by the rest of the world. Competing with the emotional irritations of the Indochina involvement, such feelings had found a secondary outlet over the past dozen years in connection with the volatile relationship between the United States and the Republic of Panama—a relationship that centered, as always, upon the status of the Panama Canal and the U.S.-administered Canal Zone.

Intermittent negotiations, ostensibly concerned with fundamental modification of the binational arrangements originally established by the Panama Canal treaty of 1903, had been in progress through most of the eleven years since an outbreak of disorder within the Canal Zone in January 1964 had prompted the two governments to undertake a search for a new basis for their mutual coexistence.[1] The difficulties encountered along the way had been tiresome to the United States and definitely exasperating to Panama, which saw itself not merely as the victim of an historic injustice but also as the spearhead of an ideological crusade against manifestations of U.S. "imperialism" throughout the Americas. That other American governments were receptive to this view had been abundantly evident at the series of meetings held by the U.N. Security Council in Panama City early in 1973 for the purpose of listening to Panama's complaints.

Secretary Kissinger, assuming office later in 1973, had seemed

[1]For background cf. *AFR, 1971*: 486-93; same, *1973*: 119-20 and 126-39; also Document 21 below. The original Isthmian Canal Convention, signed at Washington Nov. 18, 1903 and entered into force Feb. 26, 1904, is printed in Department of State *Treaty Series*: 431.

well aware of the symbolic importance of the Panama Canal issue when he followed up his proposal for a new American "dialogue" by designating Ambassador Ellsworth Bunker to open talks with Panama on a new approach to a modernized canal treaty.[2] A few months later, in February 1974, the Secretary of State had personally gone to Panama to join with Foreign Minister Juan Antonio Tack in promulgating a statement of agreed negotiating principles that envisaged, among other things, the relinquishment by the United States of its past insistence on perpetual control of the canal and its appurtenances, and the acceptance of a fixed termination date for the new treaty.[3] But what was hailed by some of Dr. Kissinger's fellow citizens as a graceful accommodation to the spirit of the times had been seen by others as the threatened surrender of a vital national interest. As the U.S. Government appeared to move closer to agreement with Panama, resistance to this threatened "giveaway" had become more vocal. In Congress, opposition crystallized around a resolution opposing any surrender of U.S. rights which had been introduced by Republican Senator Strom Thurmond of South Carolina and eventually acquired 37 cosponsors, more than enough to block ratification of an eventual treaty.

Given the already exacerbated state of nationalist opinion in the smaller republic, the emergence of a corresponding movement within the United States did not bode well for settlement of the numerous issues still dividing the two governments. That "fundamental subjects" still remained to be negotiated was frankly acknowledged by the two parties in a joint report to the General Assembly of the Organization of American States, which held its Fifth Regular Session in Washington on May 8-19, 1975. Among other actions at this session, the Assembly also admitted the new West Indian state of Grenada as the 24th OAS member (not counting Cuba); elected Ambassador Alejandro Orfila of Argentina to succeed Galo Plaza Lasso of Ecuador for a five-year term as OAS Secretary-General; and decided to convoke a plenipotentiary conference later in the year to revise the basic Inter-American Treaty of Reciprocal Assistance.[4]

Ambassador Orfila was soon to emerge as an eloquent protagonist of the thesis that the evolving relationship between the United States and its southern partners might stand or fall with a prompt and amicable resolution of the Panama Canal issue. Ambassador Bunker, who appeared equally convinced of the urgency of a prompt settlement, went to Seattle a few days after adjourn-

---

[2] *AFR, 1973*: 412.
[3] Same, *1974*: 50-52.
[4] For documentation cf. *Bulletin*, 72: 879-83; for the San José conference see Chapter 23 below.

ment of the OAS meeting in order to deliver one of a series of public reports on the negotiations, prepared in the obvious hope of softening domestic opposition before it could crystallize in a manner harmful to the outcome.]

(21) "Panama and the United States—Toward a New Relationship": Address by Ambassador at Large Ellsworth Bunker, Chief United States Negotiator for the Panama Canal Treaty, before the Rainier Club, Seattle, May 22, 1975.[5]

I am happy to be with you this afternoon and to have this opportunity to speak on the efforts now underway to create a new relationship between Panama and the United States.

I know that the arrangements for the future operation of the Panama Canal are of great interest to a major maritime city such as Seattle.

But there are broader reasons why negotiations over the future of the canal should concern Americans. For the successful conclusion of a new agreement on the canal:

—Would demonstrate the possibility, in the conduct of our foreign relations, of resolving problems when they are susceptible to accommodation and compromise, rather than waiting until they raise the danger of confrontation and possible use of military force;

—Would provide concrete evidence of our country's willingness to move toward a more mature partnership with Latin America, where we have often in the past been accused of paternalism or neglect; and

—Would serve as an example of practical cooperation between a large and a small country, a developed and a less developed country. Such cooperation is indispensable if we are to achieve what the Secretary of State recently described as the aim of U.S. foreign policy: "to help shape a new structure of international relations which promotes cooperation rather than force; negotiation rather than confrontation; and the positive aspirations of peoples rather than the accumulation of arms by nations."[6]

In the past, when serving as a U.S. negotiator, I have made it a habit to keep my mouth shut publicly while negotiations were in progress. The fact that I have decided to discuss today some of the

[5]Department of State Press Release 284, May 22; text and titles from *Bulletin*, 72: 859-67.
[6]Houston address, Mar. 1, in same: 361

key issues in the current canal negotiations reflects another basic element of this Administration's conduct of foreign policy—the awareness that no foreign policy decision, and particularly no significant change in foreign policy, can take place without the advice and consent of Congress and the informed support of the American people, on the basis of candid and reasonable public discussion.

The story begins 72 years ago. In 1903 the newly independent Republic of Panama granted to the United States—in the Hay-Bunau-Varilla Treaty—a strip of its territory 10 miles wide and 50 miles long for the construction, maintenance, operation, and protection of a canal between the Atlantic and the Pacific. Panama also granted to the United States, in perpetuity, all of the rights, power, and authority to act within that strip of territory as "if it were the sovereign."

That the treaty favored the United States was acknowledged promptly. John Hay, then Secretary of State, told the Senate when it was considering the treaty for ratification, ". . . we shall have a treaty very satisfactory, vastly advantageous to the United States and, we must confess . . . not so advantageous to Panama." Hay added, in writing to Senator John C. Spooner, "You and I know very well how many points are in the Treaty to which many patriotic Panamanians would object." The Senate ratified the treaty promptly.

The exploits of Goethals, Gorgas, and Walter Reed led to a magnificent engineering achievement which has served us well and of which we are justly proud.

For 60 years world shipping has been served efficiently and at low tolls. Today the canal, despite its age, is still of value to the United States. Economically, we continue to benefit from the shortened shipping lines and lower transportation costs it permits. Recent studies have estimated, for example, that some 9 percent of the total value of our exports and imports transited the canal in 1972.

However, we must be careful in assessing the canal's long-term value. It appears now that trading patterns are evolving and that alternatives to the canal have begun to emerge. As canal users take advantage of these alternatives, it appears likely that the canal's value will generally decline relative to our economy.

Militarily, the canal has also been important to the United States. Although our largest warships cannot use the canal now, it clearly enables us to shorten our supply lines to some areas. Its large contributions during the Second World War, Korean war, and Viet-Nam war have been amply documented.

But again, we should bear in mind the canal's growing vulnerability to hostile attack, which points to the fact that we should not rely too heavily on it.

The point that I wish to make is that the canal's value, while of continuing importance, is probably not as great relatively speaking as in earlier years.

Moreover, our world today is a far different one than that of 1903.

No nation, including ours, would accept today a treaty which permits exercise of rights as if sovereign on a foreign land in perpetuity.

Panama has grown increasingly conscious of the fact that the treaty is heavily weighted in our favor. Consequently, the level of its consent to our presence there has, over the years, persistently declined. And by Panama, I mean the Panamanian people of all strata, not simply their governments.

Causes of Decline in Consent

Among the aspects of the 1903 treaty which have caused this decline in consent, Panama cites the following:

—The United States occupies a strip across the heartland of its territory, cutting the nation in two and curbing the natural growth of its urban areas.

—The United States rules as sovereign over this strip of Panama's territory, the Canal Zone.

—It maintains a police force, courts, and jails to enforce the laws of the United States, not only upon Americans but upon Panamanians as well.

—It operates, on Panama's territory, a full-fledged government—a government which has no reference to the Government of Panama, its host.

—It operates virtually all commercial enterprises within the Canal Zone and denies to Panama the jurisdictional rights which would permit private Panamanian enterprise to compete.

—It controls virtually all the deep-water port facilities which serve Panama.

—It holds idle large areas of land and water within the Canal Zone.

—The United States pays Panama $2.3 million annually for the immensely valuable rights it enjoys on Panamanian territory.

—Finally, and perhaps most importantly, the United States can do all these things, the treaty says, forever.

To these conditions Panama objects, saying that they deprive their country of dignity, of the ability to develop naturally, and indeed of full independence.

The United States attempted to respond to some of the Panamanian objections in the past. Treaty revisions were made in 1936 and 1955. But the most objectionable feature from Panama's viewpoint—U.S. exercise of rights as if sovereign in the Canal Zone in perpetuity—has remained unchanged.

Panamanian frustrations over this state of affairs, and over the apparent disinclination of the United States to alter it, have intensified over the years. These frustrations culminated in demonstrations and riots in January 1964 when 21 Panamanians and three Americans were killed. Diplomatic relations were broken.

Following a major reassessment of our policy toward Panama, President Johnson after consultations with President Truman and President Eisenhower committed us—publicly and with bipartisan support—to negotiate a wholly new treaty to replace the old one. President Nixon and President Ford subsequently renewed that commitment. Our purpose was, and continues to be this: to lay the foundations for a new, a more modern, relationship between the two countries.

Partnership and U.S. Interests

Without such a changed relationship I believe it safe to say that Panama's already low level of consent to our presence will become lower still. It will approach zero.

While it is true, of course, that we could attempt to maintain our present position with regard to the Panama Canal, we would have to do so in an increasingly hostile atmosphere. In these circumstances we would likely find ourselves engaged in hostilities with an otherwise friendly country—a conflict that, in my view, the American people would not long accept.

At the same time, we should bear in mind that the canal is vulnerable to sabotage and terrorist acts. We would find it difficult, if not impossible, to keep the canal running against all-out Panamanian opposition.

The problem, in my opinion, simply will not go away.

Attitudes, not only in Panama but in the hemisphere at large, have changed. The Latin American nations have made our handling of the Panama negotiation a test of our intentions in the hemisphere.

When the Latin American Foreign Ministers met in Bogotá, Colombia, in November 1973,[7] they voted to put the Panama question on the agenda of the new dialogue proposed by Secretary Kissinger.

---

[7] Cf. *AFR, 1973*: 412.

In March of this year the Presidents of Colombia, Costa Rica, and Venezuela publicly expressed their support for Panama's cause. More recently, the General Assembly of the Organization of American States, meeting in Washington in the last two weeks, approved unanimously a resolution reaffirming their interest in the negotiation.[8]

We no longer can be—nor would we want to be—the only country in the world exercising extraterritoriality on the soil of another country.

The evidence, it seems to me, strongly favors some form of partnership with Panama.

Partnership with Panama would help the United States preserve what it needs most respecting the canal. Partnership would provide an environment conducive to effective operation and defense of the canal by the United States. It would provide Panama with a meaningful stake in the operation and defense of the canal. It would help stimulate the cooperation and friendship both of the Panamanian people and of whatever government exists in Panama at any given time.

In short, partnership would mean that the United States would not have to divert any of its energies in Panama from the functions required for the efficient operation of the canal.

Putting it simply, I believe our interest in keeping the canal open and operating for our own strategic and economic purposes is best served by a partnership agreement for a reasonable additional period of time. The plain fact of the matter is that geography, history, and the economic and political imperatives of our time compel the United States and Panama to a joint venture in the Panama Canal.

We must learn to comport ourselves as partners and friends, preserving what is essential to each, protecting and making more efficient an important international line of communication, and, I suggest, creating an example for the world of a small nation and a large one working peacefully and profitably together.

Such a new relationship involves giving up something of what we now possess. We want to keep the power but discard what is nonessential to our purpose in Panama. Three examples should serve to explain my meaning:

—First, we will retain control over canal operations for the duration of the treaty, but Panama will participate progressively in these operations in preparation for its future role.

—Second, we will keep the lands and facilities we need to control and defend the canal but return what we can do without.

[8]OAS Document AG/RES. 174 (V-0/75), in *Bulletin*, 72: 882-3.

—Third, we will have defense rights but perform our defense tasks with Panamanian participation.

Simply stated, we will work together with Panama, but for the treaty's life we will operate the canal. We will secure the lands we need by releasing what we do not need. By having Panamanian participation in operation and defense we will have a more secure canal. In sum, we see a new treaty as the most practical means for protecting our interest.

Whereas continuance of the status quo will lead surely to prolonged problems—possible loss of what we are trying to preserve—partnership promises a greater assurance of success in achieving our essential interest: a canal that is open, efficient, and neutral.

The Negotiating Process

Turning to the negotiations, they have proceeded step by step during the past 21 months through three stages.

Stage 1 ended 15 months ago when Secretary of State Kissinger journeyed to Panama to initial with the Panamanian Foreign Minister a set of eight principles to serve as guidelines in working out the details of a new treaty.[9] Perhaps General [Omar] Torrijos [Herrera], the Chief of Government in Panama, best characterized these principles when he said they constitute "a philosophy of understanding." Their essence is that:

—Panama will grant the United States the rights, facilities, and lands necessary to continue operating and defending the canal; and
—The United States will return to Panama jurisdiction over its territory and arrange for the participation by Panama in the canal's operation and defense.

We have also agreed in the principles that the treaty will provide for any expansion of canal capacity in Panama that may eventually be needed, that Panama will get a more equitable share of the benefits resulting from the use of its geographical location, and—last but surely not least—that the new treaty shall not be in perpetuity but rather for a fixed period.

Stage 2 involved the identification of the major issues under each of the eight principles. This in turn provided the basis for substantive discussions.

Stage 3 began last June and continues. For almost one year now we have been discussing, with the helpful cooperation and support

[9]*AFR, 1974*: 50-52.

of the Department of Defense, the substantive issues associated with the statement of principles to which we agreed in February 1974.

Economic Benefits, Land Use, and Duration

We have made significant advances in important subjects, including agreements relating to jurisdiction, canal operation, and canal defense.

Besides these three issues several other major elements of a treaty package still require resolution. They concern:

—Increased economic benefits to Panama;
—Some capability to expand the canal should we wish to do so;
—The size and location of the land/water areas we will need for control of canal operation and defense; and
—Finally, and perhaps most importantly, the extent of duration of the treaty period.

I shall comment now on only three of these questions—economic benefits, land use, and duration—and then only in a general way.

On economic benefits, Panama for many years has complained that it receives a direct annuity of only $2.3 million. It has complained that the low tolls charged to canal users mean in effect that Panama has been subsidizing world shipping.

Moreover, Panama believes that it can obtain additional benefits from greater Panamanian exploitation of its geographic position and the presence of the canal by developing a wide range of commercial and service activities in the canal area and by deriving tax revenues from these activities—something Panama could do once it exercised jurisdiction over the area. For example, Panama says it could develop certain unused land areas; improve the Atlantic and Pacific ports by installing larger, more efficient cranes for handling cargo and developing greater port facilities; and expand the Colón Free Zone. Already Panama has plans which call for construction of an oil pipeline which would reduce the cost of transporting petroleum across the isthmus.

The United States agreed in the eight principles that Panama would receive greater economic benefits from the operation of the canal.

As for the issue of land use—that is, the land and water areas that the United States will need to continue to operate and defend the canal—it is not easily susceptible to rapid resolution.

Panama wishes to recover sizable land and water areas, especially those adjacent to its urban centers, that are now under U.S.

jurisdiction and would be the most logical areas for urban expansion. For our part we want use, through the life of the treaty, of those lands and waters that are necessary for the operation and defense of the canal. The problem will be to insure that we get sufficient areas to efficiently perform these functions while at the same time reducing the physical presence which is so objectionable to Panama.

Closely linked to the question of land use is the issue of treaty duration. Panama has publicly said that "there is no colonial situation which lasts for 100 years or a Panamanian who could endure it." For the United States it is difficult to predict with any accuracy the duration of the canal's utility to us. And yet we believe that the canal will have an importance for an extended period of time.

The agreements we reach on these issues will determine the final outcome of the negotiation. For better or worse, they could shape our relationship with Panama—and indeed with all Latin America—over the next decades. Although we have no fixed timetable, we are proceeding, as I have said, with all deliberate speed.

Misconceptions To Be Overcome

There is opposition in both countries.

In Panama some stand ready to challenge any "surrender" by their government of Panamanian aspirations to immediate control of the canal.

Here at home, I recognize that there are some who hold the view that we should not relinquish any rights acquired under the 1903 treaty. I understand this point of view. But for the reasons I have mentioned I believe it is time for a new relationship. I hope that it will be understood:

—That a new relationship means good foreign policy and good defense policy;
—That a new relationship based on partnership is consistent with good business management; and
—That a new relationship signals a new era of cooperation between the United States and the rest of the hemisphere.

We need to overcome several misconceptions. I will mention four:

First, we need to overcome the belief that sovereignty is essential to our needs.

In reality we have never claimed sovereignty over the Canal Zone. Under the 1903 treaty we have extensive rights. The new treaty would grant us continued rights to operate and defend the canal, but we would relinquish some rights which we don't need to accomplish these missions. Our essential requirement is not abstract sovereignty but the specific rights—accepted by Panama—that give the control we need.

Second, we need to overcome the idea that perpetuity is essential to defense and operation of the canal.

On the contrary, U.S. insistence on perpetual control is likely to create the kind of hostile environment which will jeopardize our ability to operate and defend the canal for an extended period of time. What is required is a relationship based on mutual respect and dignity.

Third, we must overcome the belief that the Canal Zone is part of the United States or a U.S. territory.

In the 1903 treaty Panama granted us "rights, power and authority within the zone . . . which the United States would possess . . . if it were the sovereign of the territory. . . ." We were not granted "sovereignty" as such. The United States for many years has considered the Canal Zone as Panamanian territory, albeit under U.S. jurisdiction.

Fourth, and last, we must overcome the notion that a new treaty will somehow lead inevitably to the canal's closure and loss.

This concern appears based upon an erroneous view of the Panamanians as well as a lack of knowledge about our negotiating objectives. There are still people who believe that Panamanians lack the technical aptitude and the inclination to manage the operation of the canal. These people ignore the fact that Panamanians already comprise over three-quarters of the employees of the canal enterprise. While it is true that many of these employees have not held supervisory positions, no one who has been to Panama and seen its thriving economy can persuasively argue that Panamanians, given the proper training, would not be able to keep the canal operating effectively and efficiently.

Whereas Panama's participation in the canal's operation and defense would increase its stake in the canal and provide it with a greater incentive to help us keep the canal open and operating efficiently, adherence to the status quo would more likely lead to the canal's closure and loss.

I firmly believe that our most critical problem at home is not fundamental antipathy to a new relationship with Panama. It is ignorance of why the new relationship is needed to protect our interests. We need a straightforward and productive dialogue. Considerable public education is needed if a new treaty is not to be regarded as bad politics domestically.

Debate on an issue of such national import is not only inevitable but desirable. After education, dialogue, and debate I believe that we will emerge with a reasonable and mutually satisfactory treaty which will be examined and which will stand on its merits.

16. MEETING OF THE CENTO COUNCIL
(Ankara, May 22-23, 1975)

[The *Mayagüez* affair had occurred at a significant moment in terms of its possible educational effect on other governments, allied and otherwise. Two allied leaders, the Prime Minister of the Netherlands (Johannes M. den Uyl) and the Shah of Iran, had actually been in Washington and were received at the White House in the course of that critical mid-May week, the Dutchman at the height of the crisis on May 14 and the Shah in its triumphant aftermath two days later. A day or two later still, Secretary Kissinger departed for Europe and the Near East for a scheduled round of conferences that included a meeting with Soviet Foreign Minister Andrei A. Gromyko in Vienna on May 20, a morale-sustaining visit to West Berlin on May 21, and a two-day stop in Ankara on May 22-23 for the annual Council meeting of the Central Treaty Organization (CENTO) and for discussions with Turkish Government and opposition representatives. Returning briefly to Washington at the Memorial Day weekend, the Secretary would soon be off to Paris again for meetings of the International Energy Agency and the Organization for Economic Cooperation and Development (OECD), followed at the end of May and the beginning of June by a summit meeting of the NATO Council in Brussels and participation in visits by President Ford with General Franco of Spain, President Sadat of Egypt, Pope Paul VI, and other dignitaries.[1]

Dr. Kissinger's personal attendance at what would be his first meeting of the CENTO Council was proof in itself of the importance the United States continued to attach to the security of its friends in the Middle East's "northern tier," long viewed as a kind of geopolitical barrier between the Soviet Union and the countries of the Middle East, the Mediterranean, and the Indian Ocean.

---

[1]For documentation on the Kissinger trips see especially *Bulletin,* 72: 799-824, 837-55, and 885-914, and Chapters 17-19 below. (The meeting with President Sadat took place in Salzburg, Austria.)

Among other indications of Washington's concern for maintenance of a "position of strength" in this part of the world had been the lifting on February 24, following a visit from Pakistan's Prime Minister Zulfikar Ali Bhutto, of a ten-year-old ban on sales of military equipment to Pakistan and India[2]—a step designed to gratify Pakistan even at the foreseeable cost of severe irritation in India, which was accustomed to obtain the bulk of its own armaments from the Soviet Union and was consequently not dependent on U.S. supplies.

Iran, with its rapidly growing oil wealth, had already emerged as one of the world's most assiduous purchasers of American arms, and the cordiality of U.S.-Iranian relations, so recently cemented by one of the Shah's periodic visits, was not to be shaken by such untoward incidents as the terrorist murder on May 21 of two colonels attached to the 3,000-man U.S. Military Assistance Advisory Group in that country. A source of particular satisfaction to both the Iranian and the American governments had been the recent settlement of Iran's longstanding differences with Iraq, the result of a personal encounter between the Shah and Iraq's Vice-President, Sadam Hussein Takriti, at an OPEC meeting in Algiers in March. The chief victims of this reconciliation had been the insurgent Kurds of Iraq, whose stubborn and long-continued resistance to the Baghdad government had collapsed with the abrupt cessation of the clandestine support that had hitherto been accorded them by Iran in tacit cooperation with the United States.[3]

More immediately worrisome to the Secretary of State, as he arrived in the Turkish capital on the eve of the CENTO meeting, was the still unsettled issue of American military aid to Turkey, a U.S. ally in NATO as well as CENTO but one whose recent conduct in Cyprus, in the eyes of a majority in Congress, had at least temporarily disqualified it for further American arms aid. With military aid shipments suspended since February 5—and with the fear of a Turkish counterstroke increasing from week to week—the Senate on May 19 had finally yielded to administration representations and passed, by a vote of 41 to 40, the pending Mansfield-Scott bill (S. 846) authorizing the President to lift the suspension of aid and requiring a monthly report on progress toward a Cyprus settlement.[4] Although unmatched as yet by any parallel move in the

[2]*Bulletin*, 72: 269-71 and 331-2.
[3]Details in Honore M. Catudal, Jr., "The War in Kurdistan: End of a Nationalist Struggle?" *International Relations* (London), May 1976, 1024-44. On the U.S. involvement cf. U.S. House of Representatives, 94th Cong., report of the Select Committee on Intelligence, Jan. 1976, as excerpted in *Village Voice* (New York), Feb. 16, 1976: 85, 87.
[4]For earlier discussion see Chapter 8 at note 13; for subsequent developments see Chapter 22.

House, this action afforded the Secretary of State at least condi-tional backing in his attempts to retain the loyalty of the Turkish Government, now headed by Prime Minister Süleyman Demirel, as well as the other governments composing the CENTO alliance.]

(22) 22nd Session of the Council of Ministers of the Central Treaty Organization, Ankara, May 22-23, 1975: Statement to the Council by Secretary of State Kissinger, May 22, 1975.[5]

Mr. Secretary General [Umit Bayülken], Mr. Prime Minister [Süleyman Demirel], Your Excellencies, distinguished guests, dele-gates, ladies and gentlemen: I am privileged to be here for the first time representing my country at the 22d meeting of Foreign Minis-ters of the nations of the Central Treaty Organization.

I would like to take this opportunity to thank the Prime Minister and the Foreign Minister of Turkey [Ihsan Caglayangil] for the characteristically warm reception we have received and for the ex-cellent arrangements they have made.

We meet at a timely moment when the United States is deter-mined to reaffirm its ties to its allies. We meet at a moment when this region—at the crossroads of Europe, the Mediterranean, the Persian Gulf, the Middle East, and South Asia—has taken on an ever greater strategic, economic, and global importance.

We live in an era of rapid economic change and political turbu-lence. There have been disturbing tensions in the eastern Mediterra-nean. The Middle East stands poised on the brink either of new up-heaval or of a hopeful process of movement toward peace. This re-gion reflects, therefore, all the problems and hopes of a new era of international affairs. If our nations can thrive and maintain our collaboration, we will achieve much for ourselves, and we will con-tribute even more for the resolution of issues far wider in their im-pact and implications. We will demonstrate to our peoples and set an example for all peoples that even in an era of change men remain the masters of their own future.

President Ford has repeated before the Congress that "We will stand by our friends, we will honor our commitments, and we will uphold our country's principles."[6] The American people have learned, through experience that is irreversible, that our fate is closely linked with the rest of the world.

The world faces a new agenda—of economic progress, of rela-tions between consumers and producers, of relations between de-veloped and developing countries, of issues such as the law of the sea—in which the United States is in a unique position to make a

[5]Department of State Press Release 289, May 22; text from *Bulletin*, 72: 816-18.
[6]Chapter 8, Document 13.

vital contribution and determined to do so. And at this moment, after some months of trial, the American people are perhaps more conscious than in the recent past of the need to reaffirm our steadfastness of our dedication toward international peace, progress, and security.

Central to our foreign policy is the close relationship with our allies in NATO, of which Turkey is such an important member, and in Japan, and with our friends in other treaty relationships. Our relationships are based on considerations beyond security. Next week the Foreign Ministers of the International Energy Agency and the OECD will meet in Paris to underline the importance of economic cooperation and economic progress. At the end of the week President Ford will meet with his colleagues at a summit in Brussels to emphasize America's ties to its friends.

In today's world our associations aim at peace and not confrontation. We seek to engage the Communist powers in constructive relations on the basis of our continued strength and security, individual and collective. But as we strive for peace we shall never give up our principles or abandon our friends.

In recent years the United States has attempted to build a more durable and constructive relationship with the Soviet Union, as my colleagues here have similarly done. We have taken historic steps of strategic arms limitation, of bilateral cooperation in various fields, and of resolution of differences in such areas as Berlin—which I visited yesterday. At the same time we are determined that in areas where our interests are not parallel to the Soviet Union's there must be a practice of reciprocal restraint and responsibility. We have always insisted, and we shall continue to insist, that the easing of tensions cannot occur selectively.

The United States, as you know, has also taken historic steps in recent years to end decades of estrangement with the People's Republic of China. This new relationship has served the cause of peace not only in Asia but globally. The development and improvement of this relationship is one of the priorities of American policy.

All the members of this organization have been similarly outward-looking in their policies. We all have important relationships which have strengthened each of us and thus served a common interest.

Within this region, we face a new era of challenges more complex than those when this organization was created:

—Pakistan's economic progress since its trials of three and a half years ago has been extraordinary. The United States takes pride in having been associated with this endeavor.

Prime Minister Bhutto had a highly productive visit to Washington. The territorial integrity of Pakistan remains a principal interest of the United States. At the same time the United States strongly supports the promising process of accommodation on the subcontinent which was begun at Simla.[7]

—The rapidity of Iran's modernization is one of the most impressive demonstrations of national dedication in the world today. The recent Washington visit of His Imperial Majesty was the occasion for deepening American-Iranian friendship and for increasing the already close economic cooperation. Iran's role for peace and stability in the region is vital. We welcome the improvement in its relations with its neighbors, including Iraq.

—The United States regards Turkey as a valued friend and ally. We will make very effort for further progress in restoring our normal defense relationship with Turkey. The United States strongly supports efforts aimed at ending the disputes between Turkey and Greece; for we consider their relationship important to the security of both countries, to the security of the Mediterranean, and to the security of Europe. We also will continue to do our utmost in the Cyprus dispute to encourage a just and durable solution that promotes the welfare of the people on the island and maintains the sovereignty, territorial integrity, and independence of Cyprus.

—The Arab-Israeli conflict remains a dangerous problem for the entire world. The two disengagement agreements established a momentum toward peace that the United States is committed to sustain. The challenge to diplomacy in the Middle East is to achieve agreement among the parties that will assure the territorial integrity, security, and right to national existence of all the states of the region and that will be seen to take into account the legitimate interests of all its peoples. Since the suspension of negotiations in March,[8] we have reviewed the various approaches of assisting the parties to continue their progress. Our reassessment is still underway. But we are convinced that the present stalemate must not be allowed to continue. The United States has every intention of remaining actively involved; we shall promote practical progress toward a just and durable peace pursuant to Security Council Resolutions 242 and 338. Our challenges—as previous speakers have pointed out—are not confined to the political field. Indeed, in an era of interdependence, peace must be built on many pillars.

—Energy is an area of increasing importance to all of us. This organization embraces countries which are consumers, others which are producers, and developing nations seriously affected by the recent crisis of shortage and increase in price. The well-

[7]Cf. *AFR, 1972*: 229.
[8]Cf. Chapter 6.

being of all our countries is affected in different ways. My government believes that a fair solution can be found serving all our interests—the consumers in a reliable supply at reasonable price, the producers in reliable long-term income for development, and the poorer nations' need for special consideration. This promise cannot be realized through tactics of confrontation or by taking advantage of temporarily favorable market conditions; such tactics will produce counter organization, and by undermining the world economic structure, will ultimately hurt producers as well as consumers. The United States will spare no effort to find a cooperative solution.

The accomplishments of CENTO in the political, security, and recently, economic fields are considerable. The cohesion of this organization, now in its third decade of existence, is a remarkable testimony to the common interests and values of the nations comprising it.

With the wise leadership of our distinguished new Secretary General, and with renewed determination that this alliance shall be a vehicle for close collaboration in all fields, CENTO can make a fresh contribution to this region's security and economic progress.

The President has asked me to underscore the continued commitment of my country to these fundamental aims. The United States is deeply conscious of our responsibility. We know that the future of the world depends very much on our contribution and perseverance. We will remain fully engaged because of our own self-interest, because of the responsibility our wealth and power confer upon us, and because only by standing by our friends can we be true to the values of freedom that have brought progress and hope to our people.

(23) Press Communiqué Issued at the Conclusion of the Meeting, May 23, 1975.[9]

ANKARA, *May 23, 1975*—The Council of Ministers of the Central Treaty Organization (CENTO) held its 22nd Session in Ankara on May 22-23, 1975.

The delegations were led by:

Iran	H.E. Dr. Abbas Ali Khalatbary, Minister of Foreign Affairs;
Pakistan	H.E. Mr. Aziz Ahmed, Minister of State for Defence and Foreign Affairs;

[9]Text from *Bulletin*, 72: 818-19.

Turkey   H.E. Mr. Ihsan Sabri Caglayangil, Minister of
                  Foreign Affairs;
United Kingdom The Rt. Hon. Roy Hattersley, M.P. Minister of
                  State, Foreign and Commonwealth Office;
United States   The Hon. Dr. Henry A. Kissinger, Secretary of
                  State.

The meeting was opened by H.E. Mr. Umit Halûk Bayülken, Secretary General of the Central Treaty Organization.

The Session was inaugurated by the message of H.E. Mr. Fahri Korutürk, President of the Republic of Turkey.

Following an address by H.E. Mr. Süleyman Demirel, Prime Minister of Turkey, opening statements were made by the leaders of delegations and the Secretary General of CENTO, expressing their thanks for the gracious message of the President of the Republic of Turkey and for the warm hospitality extended to them by the Turkish government.

H.E. Mr. Ihsan Sabri Caglayangil, Foreign Minister of Turkey, as representative of the Host Government presided at the Session.

In their discussions, held in a cordial and friendly atmosphere, the Council examined the international situation since their meeting last year in Washington and noted with satisfaction that peace, stability and economic and social progress were maintained in the CENTO Region. The Ministers noted with regret, however, that many problems posing a threat to world peace still remained unresolved. During these discussions, particular attention was given to matters of interest in the CENTO Region and the Ministers reviewed intensively the prospects for further promoting cooperation within the Alliance in all possible fields.

The Ministers, affirming that their efforts for peace and stability would also contribute to world peace, confirmed their support for all constructive steps that would help strengthen the cause of peace.

Members of the Council also made statements regarding problems of peace and security which are of special interest to their countries.

The Ministers reiterated their firm support for respect for the principles and the purposes of the United Nations and stressed the necessity of strengthening its role in the service of world peace and stability.

The Council took note of the recent developments in the relations between Iran and Iraq, conducive to the settlement of their disputes.

Having reviewed the situation in the Middle East, the Ministers agreed that the prolonged conflict in the area continued to constitute a grave threat to world peace and emphasized the urgent need for the establishment of a just, honourable and lasting peace in the Middle East in accordance with the principles and provisions of the United Nations Security Council Resolutions 242 of November 22, 1967 and 338 of October 22, 1973.

The Council of Ministers exchanged views on developments in Europe, especially with reference to the Conference on Security and Co-operation in Europe (CSCE) and the talks on Mutual and Balanced Force Reductions (MBFR). They expressed the hope that the CSCE would complete its work successfully in the near future and that there would soon be corresponding progress in MBFR. In this context, the Ministers stressed that security in the CENTO Region constituted an important element in European security.

The Ministers noted the progress made during the past year towards the normalization of the situation in the South Asia Region. They expressed their appreciation of the efforts made by Pakistan despite difficulties, and expressed the hope that these efforts would continue between Pakistan and India with a view to paving the way towards a durable peace and security in the Region.

The Ministers re-affirmed the vital importance they attached to the preservation of the independence and territorial integrity of each of the member states in this region.

The Council reviewed the Report of the Military Committee. They took note that combined forces of the Member Countries had gained valuable experience during the year from naval, ground and air exercises, successfully carried out under the auspices of CENTO. The Ministers emphasized that the sole purpose of these exercises was to enhance the ability of their countries to safeguard their security and legitimate national interests.

The Council reaffirmed its agreement that the economic programme constitutes an important element of the CENTO partnership.

The Council, bearing in mind the important contributions made by CENTO to the strengthening of the economic links between the Regional Countries, endorsed the recommendations of the Economic Committee to consider support for activities related to rural development, agriculture and agro-industries.

The Council approved the Report of the Twenty-third Session of the Economic Committee and noted that the programme of scientific cooperation and cultural exchanges continued to create still better understanding among the peoples of the region.

Reviewing the work of the Multilateral Technical Cooperation Programme and of the CENTO Scientific programme, the Council noted that their projects were increasing in number and diversity and were making significant inputs to the technical and scientific advancement of the region. The Council noted that contributions to the Multilateral Science Fund would be increased for the coming year.

The Ministers considered the continuing threats of subversion directed towards the region and expressed the determination of their Governments to meet any such subversion with all the means at their disposal.

Concluding their review, the Ministers noted with appreciation the Annual Report of the Secretary General and extended a warm welcome to him on his first attendance at the Ministerial Council as the Secretary General of CENTO.

The Ministers were received by the President of the Republic of Turkey.

The Council accepted the invitation of the Government of the United Kingdom to hold the next session in May 1976 in London.[10]

[10]The CENTO Council held its 23rd Session in London on May 26-27, 1976; cf. *Keesing's*: 27912 (1976).

17. MEETING OF THE INTERNATIONAL ENERGY AGENCY
(Paris, May 27, 1975)

[In his April 10 address on the "State of the World," President Ford had referred to the need for close collaboration among the Western nations and had announced his intention to join the other leaders of the Atlantic alliance at a "Western summit" in the very near future.[1] That such a meeting of allied leaders (later set for May 29-30 in Brussels) would range well beyond the traditional issues of military security and East-West relations was emphasized by Secretary Kissinger in a subsequent discussion of the problems posed for the Western world by the growing interrelationship between economic, political, and security elements. Far from attempting to confine the alliance to the military field as they might have done a couple of years earlier, the Secretary of State asserted, most allied countries now insisted on the proposition "that the economic policies of the industrialized countries must be brought into some relationship with each other if there is to be any effective future." It was no accident, Dr. Kissinger added, that the Western summit was to take place at the end of a week that would begin with a meeting of the newly established International Energy Agency (IEA) and would continue, in steadily expanding focus, with a meeting of the Organization for Economic Cooperation and Development (OECD) that would help the leaders of the Western alliance "look at the whole architecture of their relationship and develop a concept of security transcending the purely military aspect."[2]

The first in this series of diplomatic encounters, held May 27 in Paris, brought together high-level representatives of most of the major energy consuming nations (other than France) in the first meeting at ministerial level of the Governing Board of the International Energy Agency—an organization designed, in Secretary Kissinger's words, "to enable the consumers to take some control over their economic destiny by cooperative programs of conservation,

[1]Chapter 8 at note 12.
[2]News conference, May 24, in *Bulletin*, 72: 799-800.

alternative sources, and financial solidarity." The purpose of the Paris meeting, according to the Secretary of State, would be to "take stock of the past and look into the future";[3] the ultimate objective, he was to tell the assembled delegates, "must be to construct a world energy system capable of providing, on terms fair to all, the fuels needed to continue and extend the progress of our economies and our societies."[4]

Although the Secretary of State permitted himself on one occasion to refer to the new IEA as "one of the success stories of the recent period,"[5] it was already evident that such terminology could not be applied so confidently to the performance of some of the organization's individual member states—most notably to that of the United States itself, whose position as consumer of fully half the industrialized world's energy inevitably conferred preponderant importance on both its action and its inaction. Not only had no systematic effort been made, thus far, to cut back energy consumption from its current wasteful levels. Congress, engaged primarily in fighting the President's plan to reduce consumption by imposing special fees on each barrel of imported petroleum, had done almost nothing as yet to implement his broader proposals looking toward independence of foreign energy sources by 1985. "We are today worse off than we were in January," Mr. Ford complained in a nationwide broadcast on May 27. ". . .We cannot continue to depend on the price and supply whims of others. . . . The Congress cannot drift, dawdle, and debate forever with America's future."[6] Yet it was scarcely avoidable that inaction at home should breed some doubt about the long-term efficacy of U.S. petroleum diplomacy overseas.]

(24) Meeting at Ministerial Level of the Governing Board of the International Energy Agency, Paris, May 27, 1975: Statement to the meeting by Secretary of State Kissinger.[7]

Today we begin a week of deliberation on the central problems of the industrial democracies: energy, economic prosperity, the building of a constructive relationship with the developing nations, and insuring the security of our own countries.

Of these, no issue is more basic to the future than the challenge of energy. The fundamental achievements of our economies, and

[3]Same: 800.
[4]Document 24, below.
[5]*Bulletin*, 72: 800.
[6]*Presidential Documents*, 11: 565.
[7]Department of State Press Release 298, May 27; text and subtitles from *Bulletin*, 72: 838-44.

the modern civilization they sustain, have been built upon the ready availability of energy at reasonable prices.

The energy crisis of 1973 first brought home to us the full implications of the new reality of global interdependence. Energy stands as the first and most fundamental of these new problems; its magnitude compels us to cooperation. Without that cooperation we risk a return to nationalistic rivalry and economic decline comparable to the bitter experience of the thirties. Now all nations—rich and poor, industrialized and developing—must decide whether growing interdependence will foster common progress or common disaster.

Our objective must be to construct a world energy system capable of providing, on terms fair to all, the fuels needed to continue and extend the progress of our economies and our societies. The path that the members of this Agency have chosen begins with consumer solidarity. But a durable international system must ultimately encompass, and be built by, both the consumers and the producers of the world's energy.

This Agency has made remarkable progress since the Washington Energy Conference 15 months ago.[8] We recognized at Washington that the energy crisis was the most severe challenge to industrial civilization since the Second World War. For a generation North America, Europe, and Japan increasingly allowed oil imports to replace their own energy production. In 1950 the industrialized world imported 5 percent of its requirements. In 1960, this had grown to 17 percent; by 1972, it had reached 39 percent.

The embargo and price rises of 1973 taught us how vulnerable we had become. We saw that neither the supply nor the price of a central factor in our economies was any longer under our control. Our well-being and progress had become hostage to decisions in which we could not take part. At the Washington Energy Conference we recognized that only collective action could reduce our excessive dependence on imported oil and restore to our governments mastery over our own economies and foreign policies. Separately we could never create conditions for lower oil prices. Nor could any one of us, except at exorbitant cost, defend against a new embargo. Our security, our economic growth, our role in the world, were at risk.

Nothing so vividly demonstrates the cooperative vitality of the industrial democracies as the speed and imagination with which this Agency acted on these conclusions. It articulated a realistic strategy for attacking the problems of price and supply and launched a series of major steps which together make up the elements of a comprehensive program:

[8]*AFR, 1974*: 33-48.

—To safeguard against future energy emergencies, we committed ourselves to build stocks of oil and, in the event of an embargo, to cut our consumption by an equal percentage and to share available oil.

—For financial solidarity, the nations comprising the OECD agreed on a fund of $25 billion to protect against financial disruption from oil deficits or from arbitrary shifts of funds by the producers.[9]

—To prevent an increase in our vulnerability over the next few years, we set conservation goals and agreed on procedures to verify their implementation.

—To lessen our long-term vulnerability, we agreed on an ambitious policy to develop new energy sources through cooperation on individual development projects and safeguarded by a minimum price mechanism.

—To develop the technology to achieve independence by the end of the century, we established a far-reaching program of cooperation in energy research and development.

—Finally, we recognized the reality of the new economic and political conditions in which we are acting. Over the long term, a stable world energy economy must have the support and serve the interests of both consumers and producers. Therefore we in this Agency have committed ourselves to seek a long-term cooperative economic relationship with the energy-producing nations. This Agency has been the principal forum for our preparation for the dialogue with the producers.

In the short term, our objective in this Agency has been to restore the balance in the international energy market. Through rigorous conservation and the development of alternative sources, we have sought to create such a surplus of capacity that the flexibility of decision of the producers will be reduced. As our conservation policies gain momentum, our dependence on imported oil can at least be kept constant, while our economies recover from the recent recession. As the proportion of our energy needs from our own production increases, the producers' market will begin to shrink, first relatively and then in absolute terms. The producers will have to distribute ever-larger cutbacks among themselves to maintain the high prices, and even larger cutbacks to support an increase. Individual producers, especially those with ambitious development, de-

---

[9]Agreement Establishing a Financial Support Fund of the Organization for Economic Cooperation and Development, done at Paris Apr. 9, 1975; text in *Digest of United States Practice in International Law, 1975*: 651-65. Submitted to Congress June 6, 1975 (*Presidential Documents*, 11: 602-3), the agreement had not been ratified or accepted by the U.S. as of mid-1977.

fense, and other spending programs, will be under pressure to increase sales or at least to refuse further production cuts. Thus at some point, if this process succeeds, the cartel will have lost the exclusive and arbitrary control over prices.

We acknowledged from the start that our countries vary widely in energy needs and potential. Some of us have major and as yet untapped oil, gas, and coal reserves. Others must rely almost entirely on nuclear energy and new technology to reduce national dependence on imported oil.

This very diversity gives a strong impetus to our cooperation. Because of our interdependence, we all have an interest in each other's success. The action each country takes to reduce its vulnerability reduces the vulnerability of us all. And the decision to work cooperatively assures an equitable sharing of costs and benefits. The sacrifices of one country will not simply be offset by the failure of other nations.

All elements of our strategy are linked. Plans to deal with an emergency will prove empty if we permit our dependence on imported oil to mount year by year. Efforts to develop a new relationship with the producers will be thwarted if we fail to create the objective conditions for a new equilibrium through programs of conservation and the development of alternative supplies.

Many of the basic building blocks of our strategy are in place. But much remains to be done. This first ministerial meeting of the IEA faces the following urgent tasks:

—To impose determined conservation programs before our economies begin to expand again;
—To put into effect strong new incentives for developing alternative sources;
—To accelerate research on long-term development of nonconventional energy supplies; and
—To prepare thoroughly for a dialogue with the producers.

Let me deal with each of these in turn.

The cardinal objective of any energy program must be the limitation of growth of consumption. However much we augment our own energy production, in the medium term it cannot keep pace with the extravagant annual consumption increases of the 1960's.

Conservation will be particularly important over the next few years. Until North Sea and Alaskan oil and additional coal and nuclear power become available in quantity, it is the only means we have to limit our vulnerability.

In February, we agreed that the IEA countries should save 2 million barrels a day by the end of this year. The recession has put us ahead of that target. But the reduction in consumption caused by the recession has also led to complacency about the need for a strong conservation policy. This has delayed—in America and elsewhere—the imposition of conservation measures that will assure us of future savings.

We must recognize that most of our current savings result not from policy decisions but from the reduction in overall economic activity caused by the recession. During this spring's decline in demand for oil, the oil producers have absorbed the production cuts required to keep supply in line with demand, leaving the basic price structure intact. Price rises have been difficult. But as growth resumes in the industrial economies, and with a normal or cold winter, our demand for oil will inevitably increase.

Unless we convert our recession-induced conservation to policy-induced conservation, the producers will benefit from a stronger market. We will become increasingly vulnerable to price rises and the political manipulation of energy supply. Indeed, we have already been warned of new price increases. These would be economically unjustified, for there is much surplus production capacity, inflation is slowing, and oil prices are already at historic highs. Yet the market remains under the substantial control of the producers; it will become more so unless we impose upon ourselves a rigorous energy program and put immediate impetus behind our conservation efforts.

In January, President Ford set a goal for the United States of saving 2 million barrels a day by the end of 1977. Later today, the President will announce additional measures to discourage the consumption of imported oil.[10]

Together with actions already taken, this will bring the total estimated U.S. savings to 1.2 million barrels a day by the end of 1977. The President hopes that the Congress will join him in common action to bring about the remaining savings needed to meet our goal of 2 million barrels. But should this not prove possible, he is prepared to use the powers available to him to assure that the United States does its part in the common conservation effort.

We believe it essential that the IEA develop conservation goals which will prevent our vulnerability from increasing during 1976 and 1977. Because the United States is responsible for half the total oil consumption of IEA members, it pledges itself to half the savings. If, together, we can save 4 million barrels a day by the end of 1977, we can prevent our collective imports of oil from increasing above present levels even after a period of economic growth. OPEC's ability to raise prices arbitrarily will have been diminished.

---

[10] In his broadcast cited at note 6 above, the President announced a doubling of the existing import fee of $1 per barrel and the submission of a plan to decontrol the price of "old" (previously discovered) domestic oil.

And we will have reduced our oil payments deficit by many billions of dollars. But should we fail, the cost will be not only higher prices but also increasing economic and political vulnerability.

Alternative Sources

Over the longer term, our dependence on imported oil will become irreversible unless we rapidly develop new energy sources—oil, gas, coal, nuclear power. This is all the more urgent because the economic costs of the current level of high prices will multiply over time. At present, much of the producers' surplus revenues are recycled into investments in the industrialized countries. This is welcome as a short-term alleviation of the balance-of-payments drain. But, if current prices hold, sooner or later the imports of producers will rise dramatically. There will occur an increasing drain of goods and services from our economies.

If we are to lessen our vulnerability, energy production from alternative sources must, at a minimum, substantially reduce current IEA imports of 25 million barrels per day. Three actions are needed to accomplish this:

—We must remove or modify many of our governmental constraints on energy production. Energy development is encumbered everywhere by legal, environmental, and regulatory limitations. Many of these reflect valid social goals; others could usefully be reviewed or modified, or alternative safeguards could be devised. We should use this organization as a clearing-house for ideas to remove unnecessary obstacles to alternative energy sources.

—We must make sure that sufficient financing is available to assure energy development. Enormous amounts of capital will be required—perhaps a thousand billion dollars in the next 10 years. Each country should decide the arrangements best suited to meet this requirement, but we should proceed now to establish an IEA framework for project-by-project cooperation, including joint guarantees or other financial assistance to large cooperative projects.

—We must insure that our energy investments are protected against disruptive competition. For much of the Persian Gulf, production costs are only about 25 cents a barrel. Most of the major continental energy sources—new Alaskan North Slope oil, the U.S. outer continental shelf, North Sea oil, nuclear power everywhere—will be many times more costly to produce. If the cartel decides to undercut alternative sources by temporary, predatory price-cutting, investment in alternative sources may be inhibited or abandoned. The producers' pricing policies could thus keep us in a permanent state of dependence, and we would hardly have assurance that the price would not be raised again once our dependence was confirmed.

This is why we in the IEA have agreed in principle on the safeguard price mechanism. Only if consumers develop massive new energy sources will the oil producers lose their ability to set prices at high, artificial levels. But these sources will not be developed if producers retain the ability to thwart our energy programs by temporary, predatory price cuts. A minimum safeguard price—well below the current world price level—can help insure that these alternative sources will be developed.

We are obviously not proposing a guaranteed price for OPEC. On the contrary, if our policy succeeds, and as large quantities of new energy become available, OPEC's selling price could fall below the protected level. The minimum safeguard price can be implemented in a variety of ways—through tariffs, quotas, or variable levies. The difference between the world price and the higher domestic price would thus accrue to our governments in the form of import taxes and levies. These could be used for social programs or rebates or other national programs of our own choosing. In short, the minimum safeguard price is not a device for maintaining artificially high world oil prices. On the contrary, it is a device for making sure that they come down. And it can be designed to yield the benefits from such reduction to the industrial countries.

The agreed deadline for elaboration of the IEA overall alternative sources program is July 1. We must meet it. President Ford has asked me to emphasize the urgency of this task. Without clear incentives for major new energy investments rapidly put into place, IEA countries can never hope to reduce their current excessive vulnerability.

Nuclear Power for Energy Production

In the quest for greater energy self-reliance, nuclear power will be critical. By 1985, the European Community hopes that nuclear power will generate about one-quarter of its electricity; Japan, a third; the United States, perhaps a third. But there are major problems associated with the orderly, safe, and prudent introduction of this important new technology.

In all our countries, the growth of nuclear power produces both hope and anxiety. On the one hand, we recognize it as the only potential large-scale energy substitute for the inevitable exhaustion of supplies of oil and gas which would occur by the end of this century. On the other hand, there are increasing doubts that sufficient nuclear fuel will become available. Enormous amounts of capital will be needed to build reactors, severely straining existing capital markets. And we all know of the questions raised by the public and some legislators regarding the environmental impact of the widespread construction of nuclear facilities.

Thus we must move urgently and decisively within the IEA on the following program:

—We must insure that needed uranium enrichment facilities are constructed on schedule. In this regard, the United States recognizes its responsibility to continue providing nuclear fuel under long-term contract. Our policy is to bring into being— preferably by private industry but by the Federal Government if necessary—additional enrichment capacity which will insure adequate future supply. Negotiations are now underway with a potential private source. These discussions will proceed quickly, and by June 30, the President will decide which course of action, private or public, is in the best interests of our own country and those abroad who rely on us. We will then be in a position to accept long-term orders.

—We must intensify our joint efforts to map and analyze future demand and supply of fuel, including assessing the availability of uranium resources.

—We should jointly project the capital requirements of the nuclear sector for the next 10 years and consider how our governments, individually and cooperatively, can assist in meeting those requirements.

—We should evaluate the economic necessity, plant requirements, and safety implications of plutonium reprocessing, recycling, and storage.

—We must undertake intensive efforts to improve the safety and security of nuclear materials, equipment, and operation.

—And finally, we should develop balanced information programs to bring perceptions of the risks and benefits of nuclear energy in line with reality.

Several of the technical issues involved are already being dealt with by the OECD's Nuclear Energy Agency. That work should of course continue.

Research and Development

Beyond the next decade, a central issue will be how to create new nonconventional energy sources. It is in developing these new sources that IEA's program of cooperation may make its most important and lasting contribution.

For the long-range energy future depends not on the Persian

Gulf, or the North Sea, or Alaska. It does depend on what we do in our laboratories to make better use of conventional newer sources and to develop more exotic sources.

The advanced nations have vast scientific and technical capabilities. Over the past year and half, IEA member countries have expanded their national programs in energy research and development. In the United States our new Energy Research and Development Administration will spend more than $2 billion in the fiscal year beginning next month. American industry will invest far more than that.

The U.S. program emphasizes improving the efficiency of energy generation, transportation, and use; improving the recovery of oil and new uses of coal; and converting coal to synthetic oil and gas. These projects are designed to produce major advances in energy production and use in this century. For the period beyond the year 2000, only three known potential sources of energy have virtually infinite potential for expansion: the breeder reactor, nuclear fusion, and solar energy. These all have a high priority in the U.S. program.

The IEA program in these fields reflects the conviction that technical advance will be accelerated through cooperative efforts and facilitate the flow of information and knowledge. We have decided to link our national programs through coordinated planning, intensified information exchange, and through joint projects which pool our capital, industrial skills, and technology.

The early results are promising. We have moved forward rapidly on nine joint projects ranging from energy conservation to nuclear power. Important programs in coal processing, which involve substantial joint investments of money and manpower, are about to begin.

But a sustained program of cooperation requires much more. We have identified the existing and potential technologies that will have a critical impact on the future. We must now ascertain when these technologies can be implemented, what their production potential is, and which are best suited to large-scale joint projects.

As our cooperation expands, projects will increasingly operate at the frontier of technology. We will each have to recognize that we cannot retain the most promising projects solely for our own national purposes. We must establish guidelines which, while taking account of understandable concern over the sharing of information and the possible loss of commercial advantage, give impetus to multilateral cooperation.

Therefore, I propose that our leading research and development officials meet in early autumn at the special session of the Governing Board. Their goal would be to complete the design of a joint energy research and development program that will receive high priority in all of our national planning.

Relations with Producers

The final element of our energy strategy is the development of a cooperative relationship with producers. We must face the fact that the producers have the ability now and for some time to come to determine the supply and the price of our oil. But the decisions we make now on conservation and alternative sources will determine whether in the future prices will be set by political decision or economic competition.

Yet there exists no institution or agreed framework in which the exercise of the undoubted powers of both groups can be subject to discussion and mutual accommodation.

Since its start, IEA has been committed to the search for a new relationship with the producers which would take into account the needs and aspirations of both sides. The solidarity we have achieved in IEA is a necessary condition for building that broader structure.

Before the recent preparatory conference between producers and consumers,[11] the IEA agreed on several possible areas for joint action by producers and consumers. These remain fruitful topics for dialogue:

—First, we should discuss the management of financial recycling. Both producers and consumers have an interest in the effective reinvestment of surplus funds.

—Second, we should jointly examine the incoming-investment policies of the industrialized countries. The oil producers need attractive outlets for their revenues; the industrial countries, while they welcome new investment, will want to retain control of those sectors of their economies which they consider critical.

—Third, we can examine cooperative efforts to accelerate the development programs in producer countries. New industries can be established, combining the technology of the industrialized world with the energy and capital of the producers. Fertilizer is a promising example.

—Fourth, the oil-producing countries and the industrial consuming countries share responsibility for easing the plight of the poorest nations. International development efforts have been undermined by the current economic crisis; high prices for energy have shattered the hopes of developing nations for industrialization; high petrochemical costs have made needed fertil-

[11]Cf. Chapter 7.

izer prohibitively expensive and compounded the difficulties of producing enough food to feed the hungry. Special efforts must be made on behalf of those most seriously affected. The newly rich producing nations have an obligation to join us in this effort.

—And finally, there is an obvious need for a forum in which producers and consumers can discuss the difficult issues of oil prices and security of supply. This dialogue is not, of course, a substitute for our own efforts on conservation and the development of new supplies. But while we cannot protect these vital interests only by discussions with producers, both consumers and producers can benefit from a serious dialogue regarding their respective interests and objectives.

It has become clear—as a result of the April preparatory meeting—that the dialogue between the producers and consumers will not progress unless it is broadened to include the general issue of the relationship between developing and developed countries.

We in the IEA have no reason to recoil from a discussion of all the issues of concern to developing countries. I recently set forth my country's ideas on raw materials and commodities problems;[12] I proposed that these now be addressed in the multilateral trade negotiations, in individual commodity groups, and in the World Bank. I shall put forward further proposals at the OECD tomorrow.[13] I hope that these ideas as well as proposals put forward by others can help overcome the impasse in the producer-consumer dialogue.

The United States is prepared to have the preparatory meeting reconvene in Paris in the same format as before. In order to carry its work forward, commissions should be created to deal with critical areas such as energy, problems of the most seriously affected nations, and raw materials. Each commission would review the range of issues under its heading: finance, investment, trade, production. The commissions could meet consecutively or simultaneously, but without an arbitrary deadline for concluding their work. The commissions on raw materials and the problems of the most seriously affected nations would not supplant the already substantial work which is being done elsewhere. Rather, they would monitor, supplement, and orient that work and give it needed impetus.

Membership in these commissions should be limited if they are to be effective. We suggest that this be decided by objective criteria. In energy, for example, countries exporting or importing more than a certain volume of energy in the world market should be members.

---

[12]Kansas City address, May 13, in *Bulletin*, 72: 713-19; cf. Chapter 18 at note 2.
[13]Cf. Chapter 18, Document 26.

On the commission dealing with the most seriously affected countries, those with the lowest per capita income would participate along with traditional and new aid donors. The commission on commodities could include the principal exporters and importers of food and non-oil raw materials.

We suggest that the IEA discuss these concepts and coordinate our contacts with the countries that attended the April meeting, and especially with France as the convening country, to determine when and how the preparatory meeting could be reassembled.[14]

This Agency has already demonstrated what can be accomplished if nations have the vision to perceive their interest and the will to act upon it. We have set ourselves important goals including broadening the pattern of cooperation already established here. We are called upon to make concrete progress; this will require readiness to look beyond our own concerns as industrialized nations to the broader needs of all mankind.

The progress we have made in a short 15 months should give us great hope for the future. Goethe said that "The web of this world is woven of necessity and chance." We stand at a point where those strands intertwine. We must not regard necessity as capricious nor leave change to chance. Necessity impels us to where we are but summons us to choose where we go. Our interdependence will make us thrive together or decline together. We can drift, or we can decide. We have no excuse for failure. We have it in our power to build a better future.

(25) *Communiqué Issued at the Conclusion of the Meeting, May 27, 1975.*[15]

PARIS, *27th May, 1975.*

The Governing Board of the International Energy Agency met at Ministerial level in Paris on 27th May, 1975, under the Chairmanship of Mr. Renaat van Elslande, Minister for Foreign Affairs of the Kingdom of Belgium.

1. Ministers noted that the events of recent years have highlighted the importance for the world economy of a regular and stable energy supply. Solutions to current economic problems must rest upon the principles of inter-dependence of all countries, mutual support and shared responsibility, so that all countries, whatever their level of development, may be recognised as partners in the world economic system. Their continued economic and social de-

---

[14]A second session of the Preparatory Meeting was held in Paris Oct. 13-16; cf. Chapter 43 at note 3.

[15]Text from *Bulletin*, 72: 844-6.

velopment must be based upon world economic growth in conditions of stability and equity.

Ministers reiterated their determination that the Agency should contribute, as far as problems connected with energy were concerned, towards achievement of these objectives.

2. Ministers reviewed developments in the world energy situation since the establishment of the Agency on 15th November, 1974. They laid down guidelines and priorities for the Agency's future work and for the full implementation of the International Energy Program [IEP] and re-affirmed their commitment to work for the development of a co-operative multilateral relationship among oil producing and oil consuming countries.

3. They noted with approval that an emergency system has now been established to reduce oil consumption and to allocate oil supplies in conditions of shortage. This emergency system can be brought into operation at short notice if required, and will substantially reduce the economic effects of any future oil supply difficulties. They noted the importance of emergency reserves to insure the effectiveness of the emergency system, and noted that the Governing Board would reach a decision by 1st July, 1975, as to the date by which these emergency reserves should be raised to 90 days supply.

4. Ministers noted the importance of the collection and analysis of information on the oil market in order to ensure greater understanding and transparency in international oil trade. They agreed that the oil market information system should be promptly completed and evaluated.

5. Ministers confirmed their determination to begin the implementation of a programme on long-term co-operation on energy by 1st July, 1975, with a view to achieving the overall objectives of the Agency by making more efficient use of the world's limited available resources of energy in the interest of the world economy; by diversifying the sources of energy; and by reducing dependence on imported oil.

Ministers agreed that co-operation in the Long-Term Program, to be equitable and effective, should take into due consideration the specific economic and social conditions of Member countries. The program should ensure that the burdens and benefits deriving from joint efforts of participating countries are shared among them on an equitable basis, and that policies directed at achieving such a balance should be implemented within existing legislative and constitutional limitations. They further stressed that the overall efforts and undertakings of each participating country with respect to energy conservation, production of energy and research and development in the energy field should be regularly reviewed within the Agency.

6. Ministers noted with satisfaction the progress that has been made in the field of conservation, in particular through the adoption of a group conservation target for 1975.

Ministers decided that the work of the Agency should be actively continued, and agreed that governments of the participating countries would need to increase their efforts to ensure that the energy conservation objectives of the Agency are achieved.

Ministers laid down as priorities for future work:

—the consideration of conservation objectives for the group for 1976 and 1977;

—the establishment of medium-term goals for 1980 and 1985; and

—the intensification of individual country reviews to strengthen the effectiveness of conservation programmes.

7. The Ministers agreed on the need to elaborate a co-ordinated programme of co-operation for the accelerated development of alternative energy sources as provided in the decision already taken by the Governing Board, including in particular a commitment to increase, encourage and safeguard investment by general and specific measures.

The Ministers agreed that the Agency should initiate promptly an examination of the potential for expanded co-operation in the area of nuclear energy. This co-operation in all fields will be directed toward ensuring the development of this important alternative source of energy with due regard to safety and environmental conditions. Amongst other questions shall be discussed the availability of nuclear fuel and technology to meet the problems of safety and waste management.

On the basis of the above mentioned decision Ministers insisted on the importance of the establishment of co-operative projects in the research and development fields specified in the IEP Agreement, particularly coal and nuclear questions. In this connection, they agreed to build further upon the progress already achieved by the Agency in the area of energy research and development. They resolved that productive results in this area will require a sustained effort to develop concrete international co-operation. In support of this objective, they agreed that a special session of the Governing Board, with attendance by senior research and development officials, should be held in the Autumn of 1975 to complete the formulation of a research and development program.

8. Ministers reviewed the relations among oil producing and oil consuming countries, developing and developed alike. With this in view they were aware of the important and pressing problems of the developing countries which are not directly related to energy, and

they were determined that these should be tackled with political determination and within a reasonable time-frame. Ministers noted that the Council of the OECD meeting at Ministerial level on May 28th and 29th proposes to discuss the problems of development and of commodities, including foodstuffs, and expressed the hope that steps will be taken toward effective action for finding solutions to these problems. For its part, the Agency will do all within its competence to work for the solution of the problems of the developing countries, so far as they are concerned with energy.

Ministers noted that the Preparatory Meeting held in Paris from 7th-16th April, 1975, had provided an opportunity for full and serious discussion of the means of establishing closer relations among oil producing and oil consuming countries.

Ministers declared themselves ready to pursue discussions at any time and in any manner found mutually convenient, and reaffirmed their common willingness to continue the dialogue and to encourage initiatives directed towards further progress.

Ministers exchanged views on possible ways of pursuing the dialogue. They agreed to continue bilateral contacts with interested countries. They instructed their representatives in the Governing Board to address these questions as a matter of urgency, to co-ordinate their efforts to ensure that formal deliberations responsive to the interest of all countries concerned can be held as soon as possible, and to examine the manner in which the dialogue should be continued.

9. Ministers agreed that the work carried out in the Agency thus far has made an important contribution towards meeting the difficulties that have been encountered in the energy field. They stressed the importance of the solidarity among the Member countries, and emphasised the need for an intensification and, wherever possible, a broadening of co-operative efforts undertaken in this area. Acting in its operational capacity, the Agency will continue to develop further its co-operative energy programme in order to improve the overall energy supply and demand situation, which is of vital importance to the further development of the world economy as a whole.

18. MEETING OF THE OECD COUNCIL

(Paris, May 28-29, 1975)

[Having assured themselves that their countries' energy strategies were proceeding in parallel, participants in the IEA session joined colleagues from other industrialized countries at a two-day meeting of the Organization for Economic Cooperation and Development (OECD), the institutional parent of the IEA and the principal instrument of economic policy coordination for the advanced, free market economy nations. With 24 governments and the European Communities represented and with an agenda from which no aspect of international economic affairs could be entirely excluded, the ministerial meeting of the OECD Council was broader in both participation and focus than the preceding energy discussion. The presence of both Secretary Kissinger and Secretary of the Treasury Simon bore witness to the importance the U.S. Government attached to this encounter of free world economic authorities at a moment when some observers were beginning to glimpse the possibility of an economic upturn that might spell an end to the current recession.

Like most of the international economic gatherings of the mid-1970s, this OECD meeting was to be dominated to a large extent by different facets of the familiar "North-South" relationship between developed and developing countries—the relationship that lay at or near the heart of the current world crisis and had already provoked such lively debate at the recent North-South "Preparatory Conference."[1] That matters of concern to the developing world could not be allowed to remain in the stalemated condition in which they had been left at "Prepcon I" had been recognized by the United States no less than by other governments, and some adjustments in American thinking, notably on the central issue of raw material pricing, had already been outlined by Secretary Kissinger

[1]Chapter 7.

211

in advance of the OECD meeting.[2] A further elaboration of these new ideas provided the main interest of Dr. Kissinger's formal presentation to the OECD Council on May 28 **(Document 26)**.

Although it was evident from the two Kissinger statements that Washington continued to reject the concept of "indexation," or formal linkage of raw material prices to the prices of industrial commodities, it was also apparent that the United States was in the process of overcoming its reluctance to discuss new arrangements for individual commodities on a case-by-case basis. In addition, Dr. Kissinger announced, his government was now prepared to examine new financial expedients that might help protect developing countries against excessive fluctuations in their export income, thus aiding the poorest developing countries in meeting the double burden of higher import prices and recession-depressed export earnings. The really critical requirement, according to Dr. Kissinger, was to refrain from "self-indulgent rhetoric or self-righteous propaganda" and address the world's "practical concerns . . . with realism, maturity, mutual understanding, and common sense."

Something of this spirit of accommodation appeared to animate the other participants in the OECD meeting, whose final communiqué **(Document 27)** included a somewhat qualified acknowledgment of the Kissinger proposals together with an expression of hope for early resumption of the North-South dialogue. As evidence of their good will, the ministers appended to their communiqué a special "Declaration on Relations with Developing Countries" in which they reiterated their firm determination to pursue the dialogue "in all appropriate fora," including the forthcoming Special Session of the U.N. General Assembly[3] as well as the more restricted type of grouping, originally proposed by President Giscard d'Estaing, which had recently come together as "Prepcon I."[4]]

(26) Meeting at Ministerial Level of the Council of the Organization for Economic Cooperation and Development, Paris, May 28-29, 1975: Statement to the Council by Secretary of State Kissinger, May 28, 1975.[5]

When free nations join forces for the common good they can achieve great things.

This organization embodies the legacy and the hope of the Mar-

[2]Kansas City speech, May 13, in *Bulletin*, 72: 713-19.
[3]Cf. Chapter 30.
[4]Cf. Chapter 7.
[5]Department of State Press Release 302, May 28; text and subtitles from *Bulletin*, 72: 849-55.

shall plan, one of the most creative achievements of international collaboration. The nations represented here have every reason to be proud of the advances which they have achieved for their peoples during the past 30 years. Our progress has fostered global progress. Our success has demonstrated that hope, prosperity, and human dignity are not utopian dreams; they can become practical possibilities for all nations.

But the economic system which we labored so hard to construct is now under stress. The energy crisis of 1973 first dramatized the forces of change which threaten to outrun our capacity for cooperative action. A food crisis, a global recession, and a rate of inflation unprecedented in the postwar period have further strained the structure of international cooperation. At the same time, the poorer nations have increasingly pressed their demands for greater benefits and more participation in the international system.

Economic expansion in the industrial world and economic cooperation with the less developed countries go hand in hand. Only economic growth can satisfy competing demands for more income and more opportunity within and among countries. An expanding world economy is essential for development. It stimulates trade, investment, and technology; it supports necessary bilateral and multilateral aid programs; it assures growing markets for the raw materials, manufactures, and agricultural products of the developing countries; it provides the best framework for accommodation on the difficult, potentially divisive issues of food, energy, raw materials, trade, and investment.

These issues go far beyond economic considerations. Economic stagnation breeds political instability. For the nations of the industrialized world, the economic crisis has posed a threat to much more than our national income. It has threatened the stability of our institutions and the fabric of our cooperation on the range of political and security problems. Governments cannot act with assurance while their economies stagnate and they confront increasing domestic and international pressures over the distribution of economic benefit. In such conditions, the ability to act with purpose—to address either our national or international problems—will falter. If they are to contribute to world security and prosperity, the industrialized nations must be economically strong and politically cohesive.

The Organization for Economic Cooperation and Development reminds us of our strengths. It calls attention to the wisdom of our predecessors, who saw that we multiply our effectiveness by our cooperation. This organization was originally created to promote cooperation among those few nations which were already most advanced. This is still a worthwhile objective, but today's realities demand that we also increasingly base our policies on the recognition that growth in the industrial world is inextricably linked to our relationship with the rest of the world.

We thus face two important challenges:

—First, the challenge to the nations of the industrial world to restore sustained and stable economic growth, so essential to maintain confidence in their institutions.

—A challenge to all nations to improve the system of international economic cooperation, and thus provide greater opportunity for the less developed countries to share both the benefits and responsibilities of a growing world economy.

The industrialized nations are now experiencing the most serious economic crisis since the Great Depression of the thirties. We see it in widespread recession. We encounter it in the inflation that has become the bane of our societies. We note it in the increasing difficulty of governments to manage their economies and even to control their budgets. We observe it in the declining incentives to investment that many of the industrial democracies are willing to offer.

We see now how much all our social and economic objectives depend on the general trend of prosperity. A democratic society thrives on a political and social consensus. The distribution of economic benefit must be broadly accepted as just or as offering opportunity for those who seek it. Otherwise escalating wage and price demands, lagging work performance, and labor unrest will undermine productivity; and inflation, which destroys growth and shatters hope, will be the arbiter of social priorities. Stagnation magnifies all our difficulties; stable growth enhances our possibilities.

The Finance Ministers, meeting tomorrow, will discuss specific measures to achieve our goal. Secretary Simon will then describe in detail the trend of American economic recovery. Today, let me offer some general propositions about our long-term future.

Our first task is to rebuild confidence through decisive, coordinated, and mutually supportive action to promote sustained expansion. We must recognize, especially in the short- and medium-term management of our economies, that the economic policies of one nation can have a profound impact on others. And the United States, because of the size and impact of its economy, has a particular obligation to recognize the magnitude of its responsibility.

In the past we have kept each other informed on short-term policy measures. In a new departure, this past winter President Ford consulted with Chancellor Schmidt, Prime Minister Wilson, President Giscard d'Estaing, and former Prime Minister Tanaka on our efforts to combat the recession.[6] The major industrial countries need to do so. It will greatly improve the chances of avoiding the sequence of boom and bust experienced these last three years. The United States is prepared to cooperate fully in such efforts.

Second, we must collaborate to sustain the growth of international trade and investment. The great postwar effort to liberalize trade, to lessen barriers to investment, and to maintain free monetary exchanges has nourished our prosperity for over a generation. Trade has consistently expanded at a rate twice that of our domestic economy. We must carry this momentum forward in the OECD by renewing our pledge not to resort to restrictive trade measures to cover deficits resulting from current world economic difficulties.[7] And we must take advantage of the multilateral trade negotiations to lower tariffs and nontariff barriers and improve the world trading system.

Third, as I outlined yesterday in the IEA,[8] we must collectively adopt strong national and international policies on energy conservation and the development of alternative energy sources. This is indispensable if we are to lower prices and inhibit the political exploitation of a scarce resource. We must end, or at least reduce, the vulnerability of our economies to external economic or political manipulation.

Finally, we must develop longer term growth strategies by systematically addressing some fundamental questions:

—How can the industrial nations bring about the massive capital formation required over the next decade for an adequate rate of growth and for a new quality of life?
—What policies are needed to restore a noninflationary environment, without which long-term growth cannot occur?
—How can we encourage the research and development necessary to advance the technology vital to growth and to share it with others?

To begin the search for answers to such questions, I propose that we constitute a special group of distinguished economists both in and out of government. Their purpose should be to identify measures that OECD nations can adopt to assure long-term growth. This group should draw on the projections now being

[6]For the meetings with Messrs. Kakuei Tanaka, Giscard d'Estaing, and Helmut Schmidt, cf. *AFR, 1974*: 492-6, 550-55, and 559-61. Prime Minister Wilson met with President Ford in Washington on Jan. 30-31, 1975.
[7]*AFR, 1974*: 150-51.
[8]Chapter 17, Document 24.

developed within the Economic Policy Committee and turn them into policy recommendations for the next ministerial meeting.

The importance of our economic cooperation transcends immediate economic utility; it also fosters our sense of community and common interest. If we are to cooperate in times of political and military crisis, we cannot, in calmer periods, afford to be economically weak, or disunited, or preoccupied with clashing economic interests. The interrelationship of our political, economic, and security interests which the United States suggested two years ago[9] is a fact, not a theory.

Moreover, eased relations with the Communist world presuppose the political unity and economic vitality of the industrialized countries. The East's incentive to play a responsible role in the world economy and to improve political relationships with the industrialized nations will be enhanced as its stake in our economic success grows. This has been one of the more hopeful trends of recent years and it is up to us to assure its continuation.

Cooperation With the Developing Nations

Let me now turn to another crucial issue: the relationship between the industrialized nations and the developing world.

The world's prosperity will depend primarily on the industrialized nations since we account for 65 percent of the world's output and 70 percent of its trade. But our economic well-being depends on a structure of international cooperation in which the developing countries are, and perceive themselves to be, participants. The new problems of our era—insuring adequate supplies of food, energy, and raw materials—require a world economy that accommodates the interests of developing as well as developed countries.

We in this organization all face the same challenge, and we must face it together. The political evolution and economic growth of the last 30 years have brought about a new diffusion of power. No nation or bloc can dominate any longer. Economic issues are turning into central political issues. Thus it has become a central test of statesmanship to insure the orderly reconciliation of conflicting interests and to prevent a slide into political and economic warfare. Misused economic power—as the past two years have borne stark witness—can reverse the trend of worldwide growth and retard progress for everyone. An international system will be stable only so long as its economic benefits are widely shared and its arrangements are perceived as just. The United States, and I am sure all of us in this room, are ready to seek solutions to the problems of international cooperation with imagination and compassion.

⁹Kissinger address, Apr. 10, 1973, in *AFR, 1973*: 181-9.

But it is evident that others must be ready to follow a similar course. Confrontation and cooperation cannot be carried on simultaneously. International meetings that exhaust themselves in self-indulgent rhetoric or self-righteous propaganda help no one and no cause. We do not consider it constructive to participate in such exercises; we have a clear interest in resisting bloc pressure tactics or attempts to impose solutions through hostility. Such methods are futile and counterproductive. If the terribly complex issues before us are to be resolved through tests of strength, it is not the advanced industrial powers who will pay the highest price. Instead, it will be the poorest and most disadvantaged—those in whose name and for whose benefit these tactics are purportedly used.

It is time to end the theoretical debate over whether we are seeking a new order or improving the existing one. Let us deal in reality, not rhetoric. Let us address the practical common concerns of all the world's peoples with realism, maturity, mutual understanding, and common sense. The United States welcomes a dialogue in that spirit. We will do all we can to make it succeed.

Simple labels falsify the many real communities of interest which exist—some overlapping, some competitive, some complementary. One of the striking features of the modern world economy is the diversity of its participants. Among the countries formerly classed as "developing," there have emerged in the last decade new economic powers with a growing capacity to export manufactures and raw materials. The most successful have fostered investment and growth at home. To these emerging powers have now been added the oil-rich countries. Any nation with a moral claim to world leadership—we as well as the newly wealthy—must contribute to easing the plight of the poorest countries. For who can deny that every economic problem—stagnation, inflation, high energy prices, food shortages—hits them hardest?

The United States recognizes the responsibility that accompanies its economic power. We are prepared to do our part, in a spirit of equality, mutual respect, and cooperation. Yesterday I discussed our proposals for achieving a successful multilateral energy dialogue. Today let me turn to food, raw materials, and trade and finance. A breakdown of the system in these areas would foster economic chaos and instability. Successful collaboration could usher in a new era of economic advance and human progress.

Food—A Moral and Political Challenge

The global problems in food are a central moral and political challenge. A world order in which tens of millions starve and millions more are undernourished will never be accepted as just.

The good harvests expected this year should not make us complacent, for the world's total food requirements continue to grow dramatically. The gap between what developing countries can produce and what they need currently amounts to about 25 million tons. At current rates of production and population growth, that gap is expected to double or triple in 10 years. Unless we act now, the world may face a series of increasingly unmanageable food crises over the next quarter century.

For the short term, food aid will continue to be vital to feed the victims of poverty and natural disaster. It is an international responsibility—to be shared by all financially able countries. The United States has pledged that it will make every effort to provide at least 4 million tons of food aid annually.

But this will not be enough. A long-term solution to the food problem requires that world food production capacity be greatly increased, especially in the developing countries, and an international system of grain reserves be created.

Let me turn to the U.S. proposals in these areas.

Fortunately, the less developed nations which are in greatest need also have the greatest potential for increased production. They possess large quantities of unused water and cultivatable land and the greatest possibility for improvement in crop yields. Their success, however, requires vast amounts of capital, new methods of planning and funding, and more effective agricultural policies and practices.

To these ends, the United States supports two new international mechanisms:

First, the International Fund for Agricultural Development—this Fund, proposed by the oil-producing nations, is designed to bring together all nations who are prepared to contribute additional resources, over some agreed base year, to agricultural development. President Ford has asked me to announce that the United States will participate in the creation of such a fund. We believe its resources should total at least $1,000 million a year.

The link between funding and effective agricultural development strategies should be provided by a second organization, the Consultative Group on Food Production and Investment, which has already been organized as a result of the World Food Conference. This Group, sponsored by the World Bank, the U.N. Development Program, and the Food and Agriculture Organization, plans its first meeting in July. It should be the central mechanism for cooperation among traditional donors, new donors, and the developing countries.

A crucial element in a long-term food strategy is grain reserves. Short-term fluctuations in food production, due to weather or natural or other catastrophes, cause sharp swings in price and availability of precious grains and cause plagues of starvation. A system of grain reserves would make it possible to alleviate famine in bad years as well as reduce pressures on supply and markets.

At the Rome Food Conference we agreed to negotiate a new international system of nationally held grain reserves. I recently outlined the suggested principles for such a system which the United States is prepared to begin negotiating immediately:[10]

—First, total world reserves must be large enough to meet potential shortfalls in food-grains production.

—Second, grain exporters and importers should agree on a fair allocation of reserve holdings, taking into account wealth, productive capacity, and volume of trade.

—Third, there should be agreed international rules or guidelines to encourage members to build up reserves in times of good harvest.

—Fourth, each participating country should be free to determine how its reserves will be maintained and what incentives will be provided for their buildup and maintenance.

—Fifth, rules or guidelines should be agreed for the drawdown of reserves, triggered by shortfalls in world production. There must be a clear presumption that all members will make reserves available when needed and, conversely, that reserves will not be released prematurely or excessively, thereby depressing market prices.

—Sixth, in times of shortage the system must assure access to supplies for participating countries.

—Seventh, there must be special provisions to meet the needs of the poorer countries.

—Finally, the system must encourage expanded and liberalized trade in grains.

The United States is prepared to hold an important part of an agreed level of world reserves. If others join us, agreement on the outlines of a reserve system can be achieved before the end of the year.

Commodity Issues, Trade, and Finance

A second area of increasing concern is commodities. The time is ripe for a detailed look at problems of commodity trade—for solutions that will benefit producers and consumers alike. The current system is marked by volatile prices, disruption of supplies, investment disputes, and increasing hostility to the private capital invest-

---

[10]Cf. note 2 above. On the 1974 World Food Conference cf. Chapter 4 at note 10.

ment which remains indispensable for the transfer of resources and management skills.

Thus consumers as well as producers have an interest in effective arrangements. The consuming nations seek reliable supplies and prices. The producing countries seek reliable and growing export earnings to finance development and an adequate return on investments. All nations share an interest in ending the friction which characterizes the issue of raw materials. The debate is becoming more polarized and has already damaged other efforts for international cooperation. The failure of the preparatory energy conference last month is but a symptom of the larger problem we now confront. The longer we delay, the more difficult and painful it will be to find solutions.

The United States offers the following suggestions:

—First, we propose that new rules and procedures for access to markets and supplies be negotiated in the multilateral trade negotiations now taking place in Geneva.

—Second, we do not believe that exclusive producers organizations are the best way to solve the commodity problem. In our view consumers and producers should jointly discuss their problems and possible remedial actions. We are prepared to do so. Specifically we are ready to discuss new arrangements for individual commodities on a case-by-case basis. We have already made proposals for a new International Coffee Agreement. We are ready to discuss other commodities as circumstances warrant.

—Third, I have recently suggested that the World Bank increase its financing of resource investments and explore new ways of combining its financing with private management, skills, technology, and capital.

—Finally, for most less developed countries, the key issue is the need for reliable long-term stability and growth in export earnings. Proposals have been made to review mechanisms for the stabilization of earnings, notably that of the IMF [International Monetary Fund] to protect the developing countries against excessive fluctuations in their export income. We are prepared to join others in this effort.

Others here will have their own views on how to proceed and on new ways of addressing the concerns of the developing nations. Cooperative action among the industrialized nations will multiply the effectiveness of our individual efforts and will insure that we have a clear understanding of common needs. The United States therefore strongly supports the OECD recommendation of a high-level group to study proposals on commodities.

The traditional areas of international economic cooperation, trade and finance, remain central elements of the economic structure. We cannot adequately provide for new areas of cooperation unless we first assure that the trading and monetary system is functioning effectively. While the present system has come through the last few years quite well, two problems stand out:

—First, developing countries with large and growing industrial sectors, particularly in East Asia and Latin America, require expanding markets for their manufactured goods. The Tokyo Declaration's pledge to provide improved access to industrial world markets for developing countries[11] must be implemented urgently for these countries. And they should be given an opportunity to participate in the negotiations.

—Second, the poorest countries are badly in need of additional financial help. They now bear a double burden of higher prices for imported energy, food, fertilizer, and industrial goods and of reduced export earnings due to worldwide recession. We therefore support the creation by 1976 of a special trust fund of up to $2,000 million under the IMF. We have proposed that gold now held by the IMF be supplemented by other contributions, especially from oil producers, and be used to provide resources for half of this total. I hope that the countries of the OECD could put this proposal forward for action at the meetings of the IMF Interim Committee and IMF—IBRD Development Committee two weeks from now.[12]

In short, we propose to base the relationship between developed and developing nations on a spirit of cooperation and good will. We urge the developing countries to approach the issue with the same attitude. We must all realize that the actual diversity of parties and interests demands a variety of responses, that no single solution can be adequate, and that cooperation among the parties most concerned is the most effective means of addressing common problems.

The United States welcomes the Secretary General [Emile van Lennep]'s proposal for a comprehensive review of our economic relationships with developing countries. We also support the proposal of the Government of Japan for a major study within the OECD of the longer run development of the advanced industrial societies in harmony with the less developed countries.

It is not often in history that a fundamental challenge is so clearly visible and presents such an opportunity to shape our future. We

[11] *AFR, 1973*: 393.
[12] Cf. Chapter 31 at note 8.

are summoned to seize the possibilities inherent in the new era which the whole world is now entering. We should be confident and not timid; others are seeking to join in what we have built. Our challenge is to encourage progress and not abstract ideological confrontation. With this attitude we can look forward with optimism to the major international deliberations before us such as the seventh special session of the U.N. General Assembly this fall.[13]

Politically as well as economically, our era has been shaped by the Industrial Revolution and the progressive economic growth that it brought. Its impact has been rapid, its results prodigious, its effects remarkable. It has created a new age of well-being and helped rapid economic growth, which was confined to Western Europe and the United States a century ago, expand into many parts of the globe.

At home, this economic progress has been an essential underpinning of our democracies. It is the basis of a stable, progressive, and just political and social environment.

The new nations now striving to industrialize have, with our help, a similar opportunity. We have every reason to expect similar success in working together with them on the new challenges of food, raw materials, and energy. But progress will not happen automatically.

So a great deal depends on our determination and vision. There are no plateaus in the affairs of mankind. What is not a step forward is at best stagnation; more often, it is a pause before retreat. There is no need to be dismayed by the problems we face, for progress implies problems. Circumstances have already provided the nations of the world with a unique perception of their interdependence. The opportunity to write a new and enduring chapter in the story of international cooperation is up to us.

We are prepared to respond to the imperatives we face. We have the awareness, the tools, and the determination. Let us now resolve to build the new era that our times demand.

(27) Communiqué and Declaration Issued at the Conclusion of the Meeting, May 29, 1975.[14]

COMMUNIQUE

PARIS, *29th May, 1975.*

1. The Council of the OECD met at Ministerial level on 28th May, under the chairmanship of the Right Honourable James Callaghan, MP, United Kingdom Secretary of State for Foreign and Commonwealth Affairs, and on 29th May, with the Right

---

[13]Cf. Chapter 30.
[14]Text from *Bulletin*, 72: 856-8.

Honourable Denis Healey, MBE, MP, United Kingdom Chancellor of the Exchequer, in the chair.

The Economic Situation

2. Ministers expressed confidence that the policies of OECD governments will lead to a recovery of demand and employment and that this will be combined with further reductions in the average rate of inflation. They are determined to achieve these goals, and to ensure, by timely adjustments of policies, that the recovery is under-pinned should this prove necessary, and that, once under way, it does not degenerate into a new period of excessive demand pressures and inflationary tendencies. Ministers noted that the substantial international payments deficit on current account of OECD countries as a group, which has recently declined, is nevertheless likely to persist for some years. They also underlined the importance of ensuring that economic policies are such as to secure, among OECD countries, a less unbalanced distribution of current account positions, more compatible with a sustainable pattern of capital flows. Given such policies, Ministers were confident that, backed by official bilateral and multilateral arrangements, the financing of existing and prospective deficits could be continued on an orderly basis; in this connection they welcomed the steps being taken to obtain early ratification of the agreement establishing the OECD Financial Support Fund.[15]

3. Ministers stressed that policy decisions concerned with the immediate future had to be related to the unforeseeable medium and longer-term problems of structural change, and to broad strategies for resolving them. Ministers agreed that the OECD should carry forward and accelerate its re-assessment of the prospects for sustained economic growth and the constraints on such growth, particularly those arising from inflation, under the changing circumstances. They noted with interest the proposal made by the United States Government that a number of economists of international repute should be invited, drawing on this work, to examine the policy issues and make recommendations. In a broader and longer run context, Ministers also noted with interest a proposal initiated by the Japanese Government for a study of the future development of advanced industrial societies in harmony with that of developing countries.

Trade

4. Ministers[16] decided to renew, for a further period of one year,

[15]Cf. note 9 to Chapter 17.
[16]The Government of Portugal is not, at this stage, in a position to renew the Declaration. [Footnote in original.]

the Declaration adopted on 30th May, 1974,[17] stating the determination of all OECD governments to avoid recourse to new restrictions on trade and other current account transactions and the artificial stimulation of visible and current invisible exports. In renewing the Declaration, Ministers stressed that the present situation required a high degree of economic co-operation. Noting that there had been a marked difference in the balance-of-payments situations of OECD Member countries, they welcomed the economic measures taken by certain of them; and they reaffirmed that, in the present state of the world economy, it remained of the highest importance to follow an economic policy which combatted inflation but also aimed at maintaining a high level of employment and expansion of world trade. The way in which this policy should be implemented must take account of the respective situations of Member countries.

5. Ministers agreed that, given the importance of the terms of export credits in international competition, an arrangement of a general nature in this respect, between as many as possible of the industrialised countries of the OECD, should be achieved. This would constitute significant progress in international co-operation. They also agreed on the need to continue close consultations on exchange-rate developments in the appropriate bodies. They noted that the problems of the developing Member countries have become more serious in several respects during the past year, and deserve to be considered with special attention within the OECD.

6. Ministers reaffirmed that liberal and expanded trade was of the utmost importance for the further development of the world economy and that, to this end, they would work together for the success of the multilateral trade negotiations now under way.

Energy

7. Ministers stressed the importance they attached to continuing and developing co-operation in the field of energy. A report from the Belgian Foreign Minister, Mr. Renaat van Elslande, Chairman of the Governing Board of the International Energy Agency's meeting at Ministerial level on 27th May,[18] described the progress being made and the new impulse given to energy co-operation within that body.

8. Ministers agreed that increased co-operation between producer and consumer countries was needed in order to ensure equitable and stable conditions in the world energy market.

Commodities

9. Ministers stressed that adequate supplies of commodities at

---

[17] AFR, 1974: 150-51.
[18] Chapter 17, Document 25.

equitable and remunerative prices are essential to the world economy. They recognised the interdependence and common interest of producers and consumers, both developed and developing countries, particularly in relation to the avoidance of excessive fluctuations in commodity markets, as well as the importance attached by producers to assured access to markets and by consumers to secure supplies. These questions, together with other aspects of the commodity problem, are of special concern to the developing countries in making the best possible use of their natural resources to foster economic development.

10. In responding to the concerns of developing countries in the commodity field and while recognising that circumstances vary greatly between commodities or groups of commodities and that this must be taken into account when working out practical arrangements, Ministers agreed on the need for a more active and broadly based approach to commodity problems aiming in particular, at:

—reducing market instability and promoting a better balance between production and consumption, including, where appropriate, through commodity agreements;

—ensuring adequate levels of investment in production of commodities;

—improving and increasing market outlets and local processing of commodities.

In addition, Ministers indicated their readiness to consider improved international mechanisms to stabilize export earnings of developing producing countries.

11. Ministers stressed the need for progress in the various international discussions on grains. In this context they noted that the better agricultural crops expected this year offered the opportunity to begin rebuilding stocks of essential foodstuffs, notably grains, and to ensure greater world food security. Ministers also re-iterated their readiness to contribute to the efforts needed to increase food production in the developing countries.

12. Ministers agreed that these questions should be pursued actively in all appropriate bodies with a view to reaching concrete solutions based on co-operation between producing and consuming countries. They welcomed the establishment of a high level group in the OECD to further develop Member countries' attitudes both on general aspects of their commodity policies and on specific action concerning particular commodities.

Relations with Developing Countries

13. Ministers adopted an OECD Declaration on Relations with

Developing Countries (annexed to this Communiqué). They further agreed on a review within the OECD of economic relations between Member countries and developing countries, with a view to identifying what new and other constructive approaches could be adopted on selected substantive issues, and to giving support and new impetus to negotiations in other bodies working on specific problems. Ministers invited the ad hoc high-level Group which has been created for this purpose to begin its work as quickly as possible and to submit a preliminary progress report before the end of July 1975.

14. Ministers agreed on the need to continue the dialogue between developed and developing countries. They recognised that, concurrently with the problems of energy and oil, there are other problems such as commodities, including foodstuffs, development questions and the intensified difficulties of the most seriously affected countries, which will have to be tackled with increased vigour in co-operation with all countries concerned. The need for renewed efforts along these lines was a recurring theme throughout the meeting of the OECD Ministers. Ministers expressed the hope that their deliberations will have provided a basis for the resumption at an early date of the dialogue which was initiated in Paris last April.[19]

OECD DECLARATION ON RELATIONS WITH DEVELOPING COUNTRIES

PARIS, *28th May, 1975.*

1. Ministers of OECD Governments meeting in Paris on 28th May, 1975, discussed relations with developing countries and agreed that, in the present situation, the widest measure of international co-operation is required.

2. They considered that while many developing countries have made major progress in their economic and social development, a large number of them have not been in a position to advance sufficiently and many are still faced with extremely severe problems of poverty.

3. Recalling the contribution which their countries have made to further the economic development of the developing countries, Ministers resolved to intensify their efforts to co-operate with these countries in their endeavours to improve the conditions of life of their people and to participate increasingly in the benefits of an improved and expanding world economy.

4. Given the fact of world economic interdependence, they

[19]Chapter 7. For the second session of the Preparatory Meeting, held in Paris Oct. 13-16, cf. Chapter 43 at note 3.

believed that progress could best be made through practical measures which command wide support among all concerned— developed and developing nations alike.

5. They determined to consider policies aimed at strengthening the position of the developing countries in the world economy and expressed their willingness to discuss with the developing countries the relevant issues, with particular emphasis on food production, energy, commodities and development assistance for the most seriously affected countries.

6. They therefore expressed their firm determination to pursue the dialogue with the developing countries, in all appropriate fora, in particular the forthcoming Seventh Special Session of the United Nations General Assembly,[20] and in more restricted fora along the lines suggested by the President of the French Republic, in order to make real progress towards a more balanced and equitable structure of international economic relations.

[20]Chapter 30.

19. SUMMIT MEETING OF THE NATO COUNCIL

(Brussels, May 29-30, 1975)

[Crowning the week of Western diplomatic encounters was the summit meeting of the North Atlantic Council—the third such top-level session in NATO's 26-year history—that took place at NATO Headquarters in Brussels on May 29-30. Originally suggested by British Foreign Secretary James Callaghan as a means of concerting allied policies in advance of the European summit at Helsinki, the NATO meeting had subsequently broadened its focus in response to such unforeseen events as the Communist victories in Vietnam and Cambodia and a related flare-up of allied uncertainties about the reliability and long-range intentions of the United States. Leaders of all of the fifteen allied governments came to Brussels for the occasion, though President Giscard d'Estaing avoided the actual summit and contented himself with attending a state dinner given by the King of the Belgians and joining in a private conference with President Ford.

A further element of tension involved the still pending decision of the Belgian, Danish, Dutch, and Norwegian governments on the choice of a new fighter aircraft to replace the F-104G Starfighters they had acquired in the 1960s. Their determination, announced a few days later, to emulate the U.S. Air Force in preferring the General Dynamics Corporation's F-16 to the Northrop Corporation's F-17 or France's Mirage F1-E (which had been pressingly recommended to them as a "European" solution) not only threw some $2 billions' worth of business in General Dynamics' direction but further exacerbated French irritations, which were not assuaged by the subsequent disclosure that a former French Air Force general who had criticized the Mirage had served as a consultant on Northrop's payroll.

That the United States was not about to turn its back on Europe or retreat into isolation had meanwhile been evidenced once again by the action of the House of Representatices in rejecting, by a vote of 311 to 95, the latest in the long series of moves directed toward reducing U.S. military forces overseas. This issue had been distinctly overemphasized, President Ford suggested in reporting to a post-summit news conference the indications given by "many allies . . . that they did not feel the need of any special American reassurances concerning our commitment to the Alliance."[1] His own address at the opening session **(Document 28)** had been less an appeal for trust in the United States than an adjuration to America's allies to do *their* part toward ironing out disagreements, assuring a strong and credible defense, strengthening their democratic institutions, and encouraging the growth of democratic processes "everywhere."

Although the other allied leaders joined in issuing the customary statement on the need for allied strength and solidarity in a troubled time **(Document 29)**, they reacted with scant enthusiasm to President Ford's specific suggestion that Franco Spain, in view of its longstanding bilateral relationship with the United States, had earned the right to a recognized place in the Western defense system. Prime Minister den Uyl of the Netherlands articulated a widespread feeling when he suggested that any military gain that might accrue from a gesture toward the Spanish regime "would be offset by the loss of political credibility that the Alliance would incur." There was also some nervously inconclusive discussion, in and around the summit, of the implications for the alliance of the left-wing tendencies that were asserting themselves within the Portuguese administration currently led by Prime Minister Vasco dos Santos Gonçalves. In another sensitive area, Prime Ministers Constantine Caramanlis of Greece and Süleyman Demirel of Turkey voiced the expected criticism of allied actions in the Cyprus conflict and afterward.[2]

For President Ford, the talks in Brussels occurred at the outset of a week-long European tour whose other highlights would include a reception by General Franco and other Spanish dignitaries in Madrid; a stopover in Salzburg, Austria, for meetings with President Sadat of Egypt as well as Chancellor Bruno Kreisky of the host country; and conferences in Rome and Vatican City with Italian President Giovanni Leone, Prime Minister Aldo Moro, and Pope Paul VI.[3] Returning in time to take part in the graduation and commissioning ceremonies at the U.S. Military Academy, the President said he had found at the summit "a new sense of unity, a new sense of confidence in the United States." "I am convinced," he added, "that our major alliances are strong and firm. I am con-

[1] *Presidential Documents*, 11: 580.
[2] *Keesing's*: 27194; further details in Kissinger news conference, Brussels, May 29, in *Bulletin*, 72: 907-11.
[3] Documentation in *Presidential Documents*, 11: 583-93 (*Bulletin*, 72: 894-906).

vinced that our allies' confidence in us is not misplaced. I am confident that our cause is just and right."[4]j

(28) Meeting of the North Atlantic Council with the Participation of Heads of State and Government, Brussels, May 29-30, 1975: Address to the Council by President Ford, May 29, 1975.[5]

Mr. Secretary General,[6] members of the Council:

President Truman, in 1949, transmitted the text of the North
Atlantic Treaty to the Congress of the United States with his assessment of its importance. "Events of this century," he wrote, "have
taught us that we cannot achieve peace independently. The world
has grown too small. The security and welfare of each member of
this community depends on the security and welfare of all. None of
us alone can achieve economic prosperity or military security. None
of us alone can assure the continuance of freedom."[7] So spoke
President Truman. These words, describing the interdependence of
the North Atlantic Nations, are as accurate today as they were a
quarter century ago.

On the twenty-fifth anniversary of the signing of the North
Atlantic Treaty, leaders of the NATO nations met here in Brussels
to reaffirm the Declaration on Atlantic Relations,[8] the fundamental purposes of an Alliance that had fulfilled its promises by providing for the security, promoting the welfare, and maintaining the
freedom of its members.

We meet here today to renew our commitment to the Alliance.
We meet to remind our citizens in the 15 member nations, by our
presence, of the strength and stability of the transatlantic ties that
unite us and to restate our pledge to collective self-defense. We are
assembled to address the serious problems we face and to review
the steps we must take to deal with them.

Renewal of our commitment to the Alliance is the most important of these purposes. The United States of America unconditionally and unequivocally remains true to the commitments undertaken when we signed the North Atlantic Treaty, including the
obligation in Article 5 to come to the assistance of any NATO na-

---

[4]Remarks of June 4 in *Presidential Documents*, 11: 597.

[5]Text from *Presidential Documents*, 11: 574-8.

[6]Joseph M.A.H. Luns (The Netherlands).

[7]Message of Apr. 12, 1949; paraphrased from *Public Papers, 1949*: 206-7. The text
of the North Atlantic Treaty, signed at Washington Apr. 4, 1949 and entered into
force Aug. 24, 1949 (TIAS 1964), appears in *Documents, 1949*: 612-15.

[8]*AFR, 1974*: 198-201.

tion subjected to armed attack. As treaties are the supreme law of my land, these commitments are juridically binding in the United States. These commitments are strategically sound, politically essential, and morally justifiable and, therefore, command broad support in the United States. They remain the firm foundation, as they have for 26 years, on which our relationship rests. This foundation has well served the purposes for which it was created. It will go on serving these purposes, even in the face of new difficulties, as long as we continue our common resolve.

In the treaty we signed 26 years ago, and from which we drew confidence and courage, we pledged:

— To live in peace with all peoples and all governments;
— To safeguard the freedom, common heritage, and civilization of our peoples founded on the principles of democracy, individual liberty, and the rule of law;
— To promote stability and well-being in the North Atlantic area;
— To settle by peaceful means any international dispute in which any one of us may be involved;
— To eliminate conflict in international economic policies and encourage economic collaboration;
— To maintain and develop our individual and collective capacity to resist armed attack by means of continuous and effective self-help and mutual aid;
— To consult together when any one of us is threatened;
— To consider an armed attack against one as an armed attack against all.

There is no need today to improve on that statement of principles and purposes. It remains as clear, as resolute, and as valid today as when first adopted. But it is worth reminding ourselves of these pledges as we turn our attention and energies to the problems we now face both outside and within the Alliance—problems very different from those we confronted 26 years ago. As NATO heads of governments and friends, we have a duty to be frank and realistic with one another. Therefore, I must cite the following matters of concern to the United States and of importance to the Alliance:

— In Indochina, the events of recent months have resulted in enormous human suffering for the people of Cambodia and Vietnam, an ordeal that touches all human hearts. Because of the United States' long involvement in Indochina, these events have led some to question our strength and reliability. I believe that our strength speaks for itself: Our military power remains and will continue to remain second to none—of this let there be no doubt; our economy remains fundamentally sound and productive; and our political system has emerged from the shocks of the past year stronger for the way in which it met a severe internal test. Our actions will continue to confirm the durability of our commitments.

— There have been strains and difficulties within the Alliance during the past year. Serious disagreements have marred relations among some members. The unity of the Alliance and our common resolve have come into question.

— There are some problems that relate directly to our defense capabilities. I refer to increasing pressures to reduce the level of military commitments to NATO, despite the fact that the forces of our potential enemies have grown stronger. We also face basic problems of military effectiveness. A generation after its creation, the Alliance wastes vast sums each year, sacrificing military effectiveness. We have simply not done enough to standardize our weapons. We must correct this. We must also agree among ourselves on a sensible division of weapons development programs and production responsibilities. And we must do more to enhance our mutual capacity to support each other both in battle and logistically. The pressures on defense budgets throughout the Alliance should by now have convinced each of us that we simply must rationalize our collective defense.

— In the field of energy, we are still not immune from the political pressures that result from a heavy dependence on external sources of energy. Indeed, we are becoming more vulnerable each month. We have made joint progress in offsetting the effect of the action taken last year by the major oil producing countries, but we have far more to do.

— In the Middle East, there remains a possibility of a new war that not only could involve the countries in the area but also sow discord beyond the Middle East itself, perhaps within our Alliance.

This is a formidable array of problems. However, we have faced formidable problems before. Let us master these new challenges with all the courage, conviction, and cohesion of this great Alliance. Let us proceed. It is time for concerted action.

At this important stage in the history of the Alliance, we must pledge ourselves to six primary tasks:

— First, we must maintain a strong and credible defense. This must remain the foremost objective of the Alliance. If we fail in this task, the others will be irrelevant. A society that does not have the vigor and dedication to defend itself cannot survive—neither can an alliance. For our part, our commitment not to engage in any unilateral reduction of U.S. forces committed to NATO remains valid. But that is not enough. We must make more effective use of our defense resources. We need to achieve our longstanding goals of common procedures and equipment. Our research and development efforts must be more than the sum of individual parts. Let us become truly one in our allocation of defense tasks, support, and production.

— Second, we must preserve the quality and integrity of this Alliance on the basis of unqualified participation, not on the basis of partial membership or special arrangements. The commitment to collective defense must be complete if it is to be credible. It must be unqualified if it is to be reliable.

— Third, let us improve the process of political consultation. We have made considerable progress in recent months, but there is—as each of us knows—room for improvement by all parties if we are to maintain our solidarity. This is of particular importance if we are to move forward together in our efforts to reduce the tensions that have existed with the Warsaw Pact nations for more than a quarter of a century. We should further cultivate the habit of discussing our approaches to those matters which touch the interests of all, so that we can develop common policies to deal with common problems.

— Fourth, let us cooperate in developing a productive and realistic agenda for détente, an agenda that serves our interests and not the interests of others who do not share our values. I envision an agenda that anticipates and precludes the exploitation of our perceived weaknesses. One item on that agenda must be to assure that the promises made in the Conference on Security and Cooperation in Europe are translated into action to advance freedom and human dignity for all Europeans. Only by such realistic steps can we keep CSCE in perspective, whatever euphoric or inflated emphasis the Soviet Union or other participants may try to give it. Another agenda item should be the negotiations on mutual and balanced force reductions in Europe. We in NATO should be prepared to take appropriate initiatives in these negotiations if they will help us to meet our objectives. But the Soviet Union and its allies should also be prepared to respond in good faith on the common objectives both sides should be working toward—undiminished security for all, but at a lower level of forces.

— Fifth, let us look to the future of the West itself. We must strengthen our own democratic institutions and encourage the growth of truly democratic processes everywhere. Let us also look beyond our Alliance as it stands today. As an important topic on this agenda, we should begin now to consider how to relate Spain with Western defense. Spain has already made and continues to make an important contribution to Western military security as a result of its bilateral relationship with the United States.

— Sixth, we should rededicate ourselves to the Alliance as a great joint enterprise, as a commitment to follow common approaches to shared aspirations. We must build on the contribution our Alliance already makes through the Committee on the Challenges of Modern Society in coping with the environmental problems of industrialized societies. We must address the issues of population, food, and raw materials. We must find ways to strengthen the world trading and monetary system and to meet the imperatives of energy development and conservation. With the wealth and technological skills which are the products of our free systems, we can make progress toward a better standard of life in all of our countries if we work together.

These six primary tasks of the Alliance illustrate the breadth and depth of our responsibilities and opportunities. They reflect how very complex the world has become and how much more difficult it is to manage the Alliance today than a generation ago. Then, our problems were relatively simple to define; it was easier to agree on common solutions. Today, the problem of definition seems more complicated. In many of our countries there has been a fragmentation of public and parliamentary opinion, which has made it more difficult for governments to mobilize support for courses of action of importance to the Alliance.

But there are constants as well, and they are—in the final analysis—more important than the complexities. Together we continue to be the greatest reservoir of economic, military, and moral strength in the world. We must use that strength to safeguard our freedom and to address the grave problems that confront us.

I am proud of America's role in NATO, and I am confident of the future of our Alliance.

As President of the United States—but also as one who has been a participant and close observer of the American political scene for close to 30 years—I assure you that my country will continue to be a strong partner. On occasion, in the public debate of our free society, America may seem to stray somewhat off course. But the fact is that we have the willpower, the technical capability, the spiritual drive, and the steadiness of purpose that will be needed. Today, we in the United States face our NATO commitments with new vision, new vigor, new courage, and renewed dedication.

America's emphasis is on cooperation, cooperation within NATO and throughout the world. From diversity we can forge a new unity. Together, let us build to face the challenges of the future.

(29) Final Communiqué Issued at the Conclusion of the Meeting, May 30, 1975.[9]

The North Atlantic Council met in Brussels on 29th and 30th May, 1975 with the participation of Heads of State and Government.

2. As a result of their review of developments since the Ottawa Declaration on Atlantic Relations was signed in Brussels last year,[10] the Allied leaders are strengthened in their resolve to preserve the solidarity of the Alliance and restore it where impaired by removing the causes which disturb it among Allies. They reaffirm that the essential purpose of the Alliance is to safeguard the independence and security of its members and make possible the creation of a lasting structure of peace.

3. Serious problems confront the Allies in the pursuit of this purpose. The armed forces of the Warsaw Pact continue to grow in strength beyond any apparent defensive needs. At the same time, the maintenance of the Allied defence effort at a satisfactory level encounters new difficulties arising from the world-wide economic situation. The Allies are resolved to face such challenges together and with determination.

4. The collective security provided by the Alliance, on the basis of a credible capacity to deter and defend, is a stabilising factor, beneficial to international relations as a whole, and indeed an essential condition of détente and peace. In a troubled world subject to rapid transformation the Allies reaffirm that the security of each is of vital concern to all. They owe it, not only to themselves but to the international community, to stand by the principles and the spirit of solidarity and mutual assistance which brought them together as Allies. Accordingly the Allies stress their commitment to the provisions of the North Atlantic Treaty, and in particular Article 5 which provides for common defence.

5. The security afforded by the Treaty enables the Allies to pursue policies reflecting their desire that understanding and co-operation should prevail over confrontation. An advance along this road

[9]Text from *Presidential Documents*, 11: 578-9.
[10]Cf. above at note 8.

would be made if the Conference on Security and Co-operation in Europe were concluded on satisfactory terms and its words translated into deeds. The Allies hope that progress in the negotiations will permit such a conclusion in the near future.[11] They reaffirm that there is an essential connection between détente in Europe and the situation relating to Berlin. The Allies participating in the negotiations in Vienna emphasise that the development of understanding and co-operation also requires mutual and balanced force reductions in Central Europe in a manner which would contribute to a more stable relationship and enhanced security for all.

6. The peoples of the Alliance share in the universal aspiration for justice and social progress. They desire that through concerted efforts there should emerge an international order which reflects the political, economic and social realities of our time. The Allies are resolved to co-operate with the other members of the international community on global problems such as those of population, food, energy, raw materials and the environment. The well-being of mankind depends on success in these common tasks.

7. The Allied leaders meeting in Council recall that the future of democracy and freedom throughout the world is closely linked to the future of those countries whose common heritage embraces these ideals and where they enjoy the widest popular support. With this in mind, they unanimously affirm that they will enhance the effectiveness and vitality of their association within the framework of the North Atlantic Treaty, which is fundamental not only to the security of the Allied nations but also to the preservation of the values to which they are deeply attached.

[11] Cf. Chapter 25.

20. CONFERENCE OF THE INTERNATIONAL WOMEN'S YEAR

(Mexico City, June 19-July 2, 1975)

[Few of the international events of 1975 will be more vividly remembered than the World Conference of the International Women's Year, a mammoth United Nations-sponsored gathering that took place in Mexico City from June 19 to July 2 with the participation of delegates from 133 countries, 10 intergovernmental bodies, 23 U.N. organs and specialized agencies, 8 liberation movements, 113 nongovernmental organizations, and 3 dependent territories. Designed as the crowning event of the International Women's Year, 1975, a year-long observance on the theme of "equality, development and peace," the conference was to mark an epoch both in the worldwide struggle for equality of the sexes and in the progressive enlargement of the subject matter of international relations. Given the special political conditions of the mid-1970s, it was also destined to open a new phase in an ongoing ideological conflict in which the United States and a dwindling handful of like-minded countries were engaged in a series of last-ditch stands against an increasingly exigent majority of "third world," anticolonial, and Communist nations.

No serious criticism could be directed against the U.S. position in Mexico City with respect to the central issues of the conference, despite some faultfinding by American feminists outside the official delegation headed by Patricia Hutar, U.S. Representative on the U.N. Commission on the Status of Women. (Administrator Daniel Parker of the Agency for International Development served as co-head of the U.S. delegation during the first three days.) Mrs. Hutar's opening statement **(Document 30)** was emphatic in its reiteration of the American commitment to equality of the sexes; and the United States not only offered no objection to the principal document produced by the conference, a lengthy, nonbinding "World Plan of Action for the Implementation of the Objectives

239

of International Women's Year," but itself sponsored or cosponsored six resolutions dealing with various aspects of women's rights.[1]

What made the conference a painful occasion for the United States was the intrusion, as at some other recent U.N. meetings, of sensitive political issues that were not directly related to the business in hand but did reflect the vehement feelings professed by less developed, anticolonial, and "third world" countries with the support of the Communist bloc. The U.S. delegation, for instance, could see no great necessity for a conference on the woman question to pass resolutions on such matters as Palestine, Chile, the Panama Canal, or Vietnam. Still less could it approve the introduction by a group of 74 developing countries of a kind of socioeconomic manifesto, the so-called "Declaration of Mexico, 1975" **(Document 31)**, which not only reiterated standard feminist positions but entered the political arena with repeated denunciations of Zionism (among other political movements) and approving references to various economic tenets known to be unacceptable to the United States. Unable to interest the conference in an alternative, nonprovocative formulation submitted in concert with the United Kingdom and West Germany, the United States eventually joined with Israel in lonely opposition as the conference proceeded to adopt the Declaration by an overwhelming vote of 89 to 2 with 18 abstentions. (Denmark originally voted "No" but later said it had intended to abstain.)

In a concluding statement **(Document 32)** in which she voiced the U.S. delegation's regret that the conference must end with a declaration unacceptable to a number of countries, Mrs. Hutar made clear that the United States was in disagreement not only with the references to Zionism but also with the references to the Declaration on the Establishment of a New International Economic Order and the Charter of Economic Rights and Duties of States, both adopted by the General Assembly in 1974.[2] Notwithstanding such disagreements, however, the U.S. Representative reiterated "the intention of the U.S. delegation and women [*sic*] throughout the United States to work with determination and good will to implement the World Plan of Action, the only major document unanimously adopted."]

[1] Texts of all documents adopted by the conference appear in *Report of the World Conference of the International Women's Year, Mexico City, 19 June-2 July 1975* (U.N. Document E/CONF.66/34; U.N. sales no. E.76.IV.1): 2-113. The main texts of the World Plan of Action and of the resolutions sponsored or cosponsored by the U.S. are also printed in *Bulletin*, 73: 238-61.

[2] Cf. Chapter 7 at notes 1 and 2.

(30) World Conference of the International Women's Year, Mexico City, June 19-July 2, 1975: Statement in Plenary Session by Patricia Hutar, United States Representative, June 20, 1975.[3]

I wish to extend my congratulations to President Ojeda Paullada on his unanimous election to head the international conference.

Ladies and gentlemen: I would like to begin by bringing you the personal greetings from the First Lady of the United States, Betty Ford:

> As I am unable to be with you in Mexico City, I send my cordial greetings to President Echeverría and Mrs. Echeverría, to President of the Conference Ojeda Paullada, to Secretary General Waldheim, Secretary General of the Conference Mrs. Sipila, and to all who are attending this historic conference.
>
> I wish you to know that the people and Government of the United States are firmly committed to the goals of the conference and to the work that must follow it if these goals are to be reached.
>
> The high purpose of International Women's Year—to promote the equality of women—truly enhances the equality of us all. As my husband said on the occasion of announcing our own National Commission for the Observance of International Women's Year, the search to secure rights for women frees both sexes from restrictive stereotypes.[4] Liberation of the spirit opens new possibilities for the future of all individuals and of all nations. I am awed by the task you face. I am inspired by the opportunity you have for progress.
>
> I know that the leaders of the U.S. delegation will work unceasingly with you in a spirit of cooperation to make the Conference on International Women's Year a landmark in the history of women's affairs and of humanity's search for peace and understanding.

We are deeply grateful to President Echeverría for gracing our deliberation this afternoon and to the Government of Mexico for its generosity in volunteering to host this international conference.

---

[3]Text from *Bulletin*, 73: 233-7. Persons mentioned in the opening paragraphs include Pedro Ojeda Paullada, Attorney General of Mexico; Luis Echeverría Alvarez, President of Mexico; Kurt Waldheim, Secretary-General of the United Nations; and Helvi Sipila of Finland, Assistant Secretary-General of the United Nations and Secretary-General of the Conference.

[4]*Presidential Documents*, 11: 379.

We thank the Government of Mexico for all the work it has done in making arrangements for us. The vibrance and beauty of this capital city are a stimulus to achievement. The hospitality of the Mexican people enhances our enjoyment of our brief time among them. We also wish to praise the extraordinary competence of those members of the U.N. Secretariat at all levels who completed the enormous task of preparing for a world conference of this magnitude in an unprecedentedly short period of time.

The representatives of the United States of America come to this conference with a deep sense of empathy and solidarity with women in all parts of the world. We desire to work together on the many concerns that are common to us all.

Discrimination based on sex is the most widely known kind of discrimination. It is found in all developed and developing societies, either openly or covertly, and it is manifested in diverse forms. The time is long overdue for women to eliminate discrimination based on sex. No rhetoric, however attractive it may be, should postpone the achievement of equal rights and responsibilities for women.

We in the United States had long felt the need for all countries of the world to come together to discuss the most important problems that affect over half the world's population, the women of the world. Therefore, with the cosponsorship of nine developing nations, we introduced a U.N. resolution to establish a World Conference for International Women's Year.[5] We all are aware that declarations and statements of principle enunciated by the United Nations, though of great value, were not enough. There was a need to focus worldwide attention to dramatize the problems faced by women.

We will work with the other delegations to produce a plan of action that will impact on national governments for the implementation of the principles of International Women's Year—equality, development, and peace. But plans are not enough. Mechanisms need to be established to insure that real progress is made.

We in the United States expect to learn much from the accomplishments of our sisters around the world. In exchange, we offer to share with you the substantial progress made in the United States to further women's rights and responsibilities.

Much has been done, but there is much more that needs to be done to overcome the limitations and discriminatory practices of the past, reinforced by centuries of laws, traditions, and customs. We are proud in the United States of the legislation and government action that has been taken in the past several years to prohibit employment discrimination based on sex. Such legislation provides

[5]Economic and Social Council Resolution 1851 (LVI), May 16, 1974.

for equal pay for work of equal value, nondiscrimination in hiring, in discharging, and in compensation. Another piece of important legislation prohibits discrimination on the basis of sex in educational programs or activities.

These antidiscrimination laws and other social change have come about in our country through the joint efforts of voluntary organizations and the government. Traditionally the Government of the United States does not plan social change in the sense that some other governments do—it responds to the demands for reform made by citizens and/or voluntary associations and works with them in charting the mechanisms of social change.

We are also proud of the fact that we have established various national machinery to continue to monitor and implement nondiscrimination on the basis of sex. Some of these include a Special Assistant to the President of the United States for Women and an Office of Women's Programs in the White House; the Women's Bureau in our Department of Labor, established in 1920; a Women's Action Program in the Department of Health, Education, and Welfare; and a Federal Women's Program Coordinator to monitor employment practices in every governmental body. We also have citizens actively involved in this machinery, including a President's Advisory Council on the Status of Women, Advisory Councils to the Secretaries of Labor, Defense, and Health, Education, and Welfare.

Equality and Integration in Development

Though many general economic, political, and social changes are modifying the basic situation of women throughout the world—both in those countries now undergoing arduous processes of development and those which have already experienced the impact of industrialization—these changes will not automatically redress the balance. It requires positive efforts to identify and cope with the many factors which limit women and stand in the way of their full integration in development. I need mention only the lack of access to employment, education, and political integration to make the point that women are prevented from making their full and responsible contribution to the life of their societies and their full contribution to their families, their communities, and their nations.

International Women's Year has chosen as two of its basic goals equality for women and their integration in development. These goals are inextricably interrelated. Each is indispensable to the other.

Equality without development means shared misery and frustration. Development without equality may mean a worsened situation for many women, both those who are homemakers and those who are in the labor force. Similarly, achieving one of the goals helps achieve the other. Development creates new situations and changes which make it possible for women to win a new and more equal status. And the full, equal participation of women in the development process can make the difference between success and failure of development itself.

The U.S. Government is prepared to introduce at this conference a draft declaration on equality and development that embraces these two basic goals of the Year, which I have stated are intertwined.

But women cannot wait, with arms folded, for men to achieve a new order before women can achieve equality. On the contrary, women must continue their work, already begun, to achieve a truly equal partnership. Women must be in decisionmaking positions in the power structure along with men to build a more just world order.

Women have a strong sense of social responsibility and are searching for opportunities to share their vision of a new society free of hunger and poverty. We must have, though, the understanding and commitment of men to reach the goal of equality. We have heard pledges of such commitment already in this conference in our opening session. We welcome this pledge of partnership.

Increasing Participation in Decisionmaking

The third goal of International Women's Year is to strengthen the role of women in establishing world peace. To achieve it, women must mobilize their potential political power to assure that governments actively pursue the goal of disarmament.

The United States believes that disarmament negotiations should be directed toward general and complete disarmament under strict international control. It is our profound hope that women will not only use their influence to keep governments working toward this end but we believe also that women must equip themselves for and assert their right to serve in agencies of government and on international delegations that are responsible for arms control and disarmament.

Basically, the issue and challenge which we face is to develop and utilize the untapped potential of over half the world's population. There is a great scarcity of women in policymaking positions in the world. Women remain significantly absent from high-level posts in governments, in international affairs, in the professions, and in business.

Women want to share with men the responsibilities and the duties involved in decisions affecting peace and development as well as in decisions that affect their lives. But unless they are able to move into the top positions in their fields, their impact in national and world affairs will be negligible and the possibilities of helping other women to move ahead in their roles will be nil.

Women's presence must be felt if we want the policies of the public and the private sector to be altered so as to be more equitable for women and men. This is one of the major areas of concern and focus of our U.S. National Commission on the Observance of International Women's Year.

At this conference we must insist that the United Nations and its specialized agencies provide opportunities for women to rise to the highest levels.

During the last General Assembly the U.S. delegation introduced a resolution, inspired by Senator Charles Percy, designed to assure that priority is given to projects within the U.N. Development Program that integrate women into the development process.[6] This is a step in the right direction; our responsibility now, though, is to assure that this resolution is carried out.

At the initiative of the U.S. delegation, too, the U.N. Secretariat has set up a personnel committee to make sure that there shall be no discrimination against women in hiring or promotion within the U.N. Secretariat. The next step is to secure the establishment of other personnel committees throughout the entire U.N. system.

Developing Strategies for Change

Action by national governments will have a still broader effect upon the status of women than the international actions proposed above. A majority of governments have committed themselves to the principles of equality and of integrating women in development through their adherence to U.N. conventions and resolutions on these subjects.

This conference must build a plan of action that includes specific national measures for translating principles into action. Upon leaving this conference, participants must assume the responsibility for assuring that each of their governments puts into action the policy recommendations and provides the necessary resources to adopt the measures called for by the plan of action.

The U.S. delegation and the National Commission on the Observance of International Women's Year have held several meetings with our nongovernmental leaders to discuss the implementation of the World Plan of Action. We have a commitment to work together to insure the full implementation of the plan of action in our country upon our return from Mexico City.

I am pleased that so many nongovernmental leaders from around

[6]General Assembly Resolution 3342 (XXIX), Dec. 17, 1974.

the world have assembled here in Mexico City to attend this conference and also the International Women's Year Tribune.[7] I think that one of the strongest assets of the world conference is the interest of the nongovernmental organizations and the input they will provide the delegations to this U.N. conference.

In order to escalate the process of equality for women and for integration in development, we must devise strategies to change attitudes and behavior that have resulted from cultural conditioning. We cannot accomplish this by institutional change alone. Escalating strategies directed at attitudinal change involves not only the way men see women but also how women see themselves.

Women are learning that to compete is all right, for they are looking at themselves in a new light. They are learning that women must build support systems within existing structures—whether business, government, political, academic, or agriculture. Women must develop support systems to change the degrading sex-role stereotype and images of women in the mass media which perpetuate false depictions of women.

A myth prevails that women are not competitive—that they seem to lack motivation to progress and to participate in all phases of society.

However, we must keep in mind why this is perceived to be the case. We must remember the impact that conditioning has had on women. From the moment they are born, women's role in society has been dictated by culture and tradition. This affects the way their role is perceived by men, by the society, and by themselves.

We must examine and reassess old myths that society holds about the capacities, potential, and lifestyles of girls and women. Self-images for women are beginning to change, but the inaccurate and destructive sexist image projected must be rooted out.

We must make changes in the portrayal of women in program content and commercials in mass media—radio, television, newspapers. Educational materials in the schools—textbooks, visual aids, curricula—all need to be reexamined and changed to reflect the changing role of women and men in the society and to eliminate sex-role stereotyping.

To effect change in any area of life, women must seek and achieve leadership roles in management and public administration. Change will be accelerated when women serve in program planning, policymaking and decisionmaking roles in society.

Under the office of the Assistant Secretary for Education, the highest ranking official of education in the United States—currently a woman[8] and a member of our delegation, I am proud to

---

[7] An independent function organized by the Conference of Non-Governmental Organizations in Consultative Status with the U.N. Economic and Social Council.
[8] Virginia Trotter.

say— has developed programs based on special women's research being conducted at the National Institute of Education on changing sex roles in American culture, female role ideology, and educational aspiration, to mention a few.

Finally, this conference should serve as a stimulus to men as well as to women throughout the world. We hope that from this conference men will gain a vision of a more just society in which an equality for women and participation by them will mean a more varied and equitable sharing, to the benefit of men as well as women. It is the conviction of women globally that the goals of International Women's Year—of equality, development, and peace— are not goals for *women* but serious goals for a world society and that men no less than women stand to gain. It should be the objective of the conference to make this conviction take root and grow.

(31)   The Declaration of Mexico, adopted July 2, 1975. [9]

DECLARATION OF MEXICO ON THE EQUALITY OF WOMEN
AND THEIR CONTRIBUTION TO DEVELOPMENT AND PEACE, 1975

The World Conference of the International Women's Year,

Aware that the problems of women, who constitute half of the world's population, are the problems of society as a whole, and that changes in the present economic, political and social situation of women must become an integral part of efforts to transform the structures and attitudes that hinder the genuine satisfaction of their needs,

Recognizing that international co-operation based on the principles of the Charter of the United Nations should be developed and strengthened in order to find solutions to world problems and to build an international community based on equity and justice,

Recalling that in subscribing to the Charter, the peoples of the United Nations undertook specific commitments: "to save succeeding generations from the scourge of war . . ., to reaffirm faith in fundamental human rights, in the dignity and worth of the human person, in the equal rights of men and women and of nations large and small, and to promote social progress and better standards of life in larger freedom",

Taking note of the fact that since the creation of the United Nations very important instruments have been adopted, among which the following constitute landmarks: the Universal Declaration of

[9]Text from *Report of the World Conference of the International Women's Year* (cited in note 1): 2-7; adopted by a vote of 89-2 (U.S.)-18.

Human Rights,[10] the Declaration on the Granting of Independence to Colonial Countries and Peoples,[11] the International Development Strategy for the Second United Nations Development Decade,[12] and the Declaration and Programme of Action for the Establishment of a New International Economic Order[13] based on the Charter of Economic Rights and Duties of States,[14]

Taking into account that the United Nations Declaration on the Elimination of Discrimination against Women[15] considers that: "discrimination against women is incompatible with human dignity and with the welfare of the family and of society, prevents their participation, on equal terms with men, in the political, social, economic and cultural life of their countries and is an obstacle to the full development of the potentialities of women in the service of their countries and of humanity",

Recalling that the General Assembly, in its resolution 3010 (XXVII) of 18 December 1972, proclaimed 1975 as International Women's Year and that the Year was to be devoted to intensified action with a view to: promoting equality between men and women, ensuring the integration of women in the total development effort, and increasing the contribution of women to the strengthening of world peace,

Recalling further that the Economic and Social Council, in its resolution 1849 (LVI) of 16 May 1974, adopted the Programme for International Women's Year, and that the General Assembly, in its resolution 3275 (XXIX) of 10 December 1974, called for full implementation of the Programme,

Taking into account the role played by women in the history of humanity, especially in the struggle for national liberation, the strengthening of international peace, and the elimination of imperialism, colonialism, neo-colonialism, foreign occupation, zionism, alien domination, racism and *apartheid*,

Stressing that greater and equal participation of women at all levels of decision-making shall decisively contribute to accelerating the pace of development and the maintenance of peace,

Stressing also that women and men of all countries should have equal rights and duties and that it is the task of all States to create the necessary conditions for the attainment and the exercise thereof,

---

[10]General Assembly Resolution 217 A (III), Dec. 10, 1948, in *Documents, 1948*: 430-35.
[11]General Assembly Resolution 1514 (XV), Dec. 19, 1960, in same, *1960*: 575-7.
[12]General Assembly Resolution 2626 (XX), Oct. 24, 1970, in same, *1970*: 324-31.
[13]*AFR, 1974*: 103-7.
[14]Same: 528-41.
[15]General Assembly Resolution 2263 (XXII), Nov. 7, 1967.

Recognizing that women of the entire world, whatever differences exist between them, share the painful experience of receiving or having received unequal treatment, and that as their awareness of this phenomenon increases they will become natural allies in the struggle against any form of oppression, such as is practised under colonialism, neo-colonialism, zionism, racial discrimination and *apartheid*, thereby constituting an enormous revolutionary potential for economic and social change in the world today,

Recognizing that changes in the social and economic structure of societies, even though they are among the prerequisites, cannot of themselves ensure an immediate improvement in the status of a group which has long been disadvantaged, and that urgent consideration must therefore be given to the full, immediate and early integration of women into national and international life,

Emphasizing that under-development imposes upon women a double burden of exploitation, which must be rapidly eliminated, and that full implementation of national development policies designed to fulfil this objective is seriously hindered by the existing inequitable system of international economic relations,

Aware that the role of women in child-bearing should not be the cause of inequality and discrimination, and that child-rearing demands shared responsibilities among women, men and society as a whole,

Recognizing also the urgency of improving the status of women and finding more effective methods and strategies which will enable them to have the same opportunities as men to participate actively in the development of their countries and to contribute to the attainment of world peace,

Convinced that women must play an important role in the promotion, achievement and maintenance of international peace, and that it is necessary to encourage their efforts towards peace, through their full participation in the national and international organizations that exist for this purpose,

Considering that it is necessary to promote national, regional and international action, in which the implementation of the World Plan of Action adopted by the World Conference of the International Women's Year should make a significant contribution, for the attainment of equality, development and peace,

Decides to promulgate the following principles:

1. Equality between women and men means equality in their dignity and worth as human beings as well as equality in their rights, opportunities and responsibilities.

2. All obstacles that stand in the way of enjoyment by women of equal status with men must be eliminated in order to ensure their

full integration into national development and their participation in securing and in maintaining international peace.

3. It is the responsibility of the State to create the necessary facilities so that women may be integrated into society while their children receive adequate care.

4. National non-governmental organizations should contribute to the advancement of women by assisting women to take advantage of their opportunities, by promoting education and information about women's rights, and by co-operating with their respective Governments.

5. Women and men have equal rights and responsibilities in the family and in society. Equality between women and men should be guaranteed in the family, which is the basic unit of society and where human relations are nurtured. Men should participate more actively, creatively and responsibly in family life for its sound development in order to enable women to be more intensively involved in the activities of their communities and with a view to combining effectively home and work possibilities of both partners.

6. Women, like men, require opportunities for developing their intellectual potential to the maximum. National policies and programmes should therefore provide them with full and equal access to education and training at all levels, while ensuring that such programmes and policies consciously orient them towards new occupations and new roles consistent with their need for self-fulfilment and the needs of national development.

7. The right of women to work, to receive equal pay for work of equal value, to be provided with equal conditions and opportunities for advancement in work, and all other women's rights to full and satisfying economic activity are strongly reaffirmed. Review of these principles for their effective implementation is now urgently needed, considering the necessity of restructuring world economic relationships. This restructuring offers greater possibilities for women to be integrated into the stream of national economic, social, political and cultural life.

8. All means of communication and information as well as all cultural media should regard as a high priority their responsibility for helping to remove the attitudinal and cultural factors that still inhibit the development of women and for projecting in positive terms the value to society of the assumption by women of changing and expanding roles.

9. Necessary resources should be made available in order that women may be able to participate in the political life of their countries and of the international community since their active participation in national and world affairs at decision-making and other levels in the political field is a prerequisite of women's full ex-

ercise of equal rights as well as of their further development, and of the national well-being.

10. Equality of rights carries with it corresponding responsibilities; it is therefore a duty of women to make full use of opportunities available to them and to perform their duties to the family, the country and humanity.

11. It should be one of the principal aims of social education to teach respect for physical integrity and its rightful place in human life. The human body, whether that of woman or man, is inviolable and respect for it is a fundamental element of human dignity and freedom.

12. Every couple and every individual has the right to decide freely and responsibly whether or not to have children as well as to determine their number and spacing, and to have information, education and means to do so.

13. Respect for human dignity encompasses the right of every woman to decide freely for herself whether or not to contract matrimony.

14. The issue of inequality, as it affects the vast majority of the women of the world, is closely linked with the problem of underdevelopment, which exists as a result not only of unsuitable internal structures but also of a profoundly unjust world economic system.

15. The full and complete development of any country requires the maximum participation of women as well as of men in all fields; the under-utilization of the potential of approximately half of the world's population is a serious obstacle to social and economic development.

16. The ultimate end of development is to achieve a better quality of life for all, which means not only the development of economic and other material resources but also the physical, moral, intellectual and cultural growth of the human person.

17. In order to integrate women into development, States should undertake the necessary changes in their economic and social policies because women have the right to participate and contribute to the total development effort.

18. The present state of international economic relations poses serious obstacles to a more efficient utilization of all human and material potential for accelerated development and for the improvement of living standards in developing countries aimed at the elimination of hunger, child mortality, unemployment, illiteracy, ignorance and backwardness, which concern all of humanity and women in particular. It is therefore essential to establish and implement with urgency the New International Economic Order, of which the Charter of Economic Rights and Duties of States constitutes a basic element, founded on equity, sovereign equality, interdependence, common interest, co-operation among all States ir-

respective of their social and economic systems, on the principles of peaceful coexistence and on the promotion by the entire international community of economic and social progress of all countries, especially developing countries, and on the progress of States comprising the international community.

19. The principle of full and permanent sovereignty of every State over its natural resources, wealth and all economic activities and its inalienable right of nationalization as an expression of this sovereignty, constitute fundamental prerequisites in the process of economic and social development.

20. The attainment of economic and social goals, so basic to the realization of the rights of women, does not, however, of itself bring about the full integration of women in development on a basis of equality with men unless specific measures are undertaken for the elimination of all forms of discrimination against them. It is therefore important to formulate and implement models of development that will promote the participation and advancement of women in all fields of work and provide them with equal educational opportunities and such services as would facilitate housework.

21. Modernization of the agricultural sector of vast areas of the world is an indispensable element for progress, particularly as it creates opportunities for millions of rural women to participate in development. Governments, the United Nations, its specialized agencies and other competent regional and international organizations should support projects designed to utilize the maximum potential and develop the self-reliance of rural women.

22. It must be emphasized that, given the required economic, social and legal conditions as well as the appropriate attitudes conducive to the full and equal participation of women in society, efforts and measures aimed at a more intensified integration of women in development can be successfully implemented only if made an integral part of over-all social and economic growth. Full participation of women in the various economic, social, political and cultural sectors is an important indication of the dynamic progress of peoples and their development. Individual human rights can be realized only within the framework of total development.

23. The objectives considered in this Declaration can be achieved only in a world in which the relations between States are governed, inter alia, by the following principles: the sovereign equality of States, the free self-determination of peoples, the unacceptability of acquisition or attempted acquisition of territories by force and the prohibition of recognition of such acquisition, territorial integrity, and the right to defend it, and non-interference in the domestic affairs of States, in the same manner as relations between human beings should be governed by the supreme principle of the equality of rights of women and men.

24. International co-operation and peace require the achievement of national liberation and independence, the elimination of colonialism and neo-colonialism, foreign occupation, zionism, *apartheid*, and racial discrimination in all its forms as well as the recognition of the dignity of peoples and their right to self- determination.

25. Women have a vital role to play in the promotion of peace in all spheres of life: in the family, the community, the nation and the world. Women must participate equally with men in the decision-making processes which help to promote peace at all levels.

26. Women and men together should eliminate colonialism, neo-colonialism, imperialism, foreign domination and occupation, zionism, *apartheid*, racial discrimination, the acquisition of land by force and the recognition of such acquisition, since such practices inflict incalculable suffering on women, men and children.

27. The solidarity of women in all countries of the world should be supported in their protest against violations of human rights condemned by the United Nations. All forms of repression and inhuman treatment of women, men and children, including imprisonment, torture, massacres, collective punishment, destruction of homes, forced eviction and arbitrary restriction of movement shall be considered crimes against humanity and in violation of the Universal Declaration of Human Rights and other international instruments.

28. Women all over the world should unite to eliminate violations of human rights committed against women and girls such as: rape, prostitution, physical assault, mental cruelty, child marriage, forced marriage and marriage as a commercial transaction.

29. Peace requires that women as well as men should reject any type of intervention in the domestic affairs of States, whether it be openly or covertly carried on by other States or by transnational corporations. Peace also requires that women as well as men should also promote respect for the sovereign right of a State to establish its own economic, social and political system without undergoing political and economic pressures or coercion of any type.

30. Women as well as men should promote real, general and complete disarmament under effective international control, starting with nuclear disarmament. Until genuine disarmament is achieved, women and men throughout the world must maintain their vigilance and do their utmost to achieve and maintain international peace.

Wherefore,

The World Conference of the International Women's Year,

1. *Affirms* its faith in the objectives of the International Wom-

en's Year, which are equality, development and peace;

2. *Proclaims* its commitment to the achievement of such objectives;

3. *Strongly urges* Governments, the entire United Nations system, regional and international intergovernmental organizations and the international community as a whole to dedicate themselves to the creation of a just society where women, men and children can live in dignity, freedom, justice and prosperity.

(32)   Concluding Statement by Mrs. Hutar, July 2, 1975.[16]

The U.S. delegation regrets that this conference must conclude with a declaration which remains unacceptable to a number of countries.

There are, to be sure, many paragraphs and ideas in the declaration which we strongly support. Many of these paragraphs— dealing with the problems and concerns of women for which this conference was convened—are very similar to those in the draft declaration which we cosponsored.[17] We believe this illustrates the closeness of our views on the women's issues and the solidarity of our efforts here to gain full and equal participation of women as decision-makers in the economic, political, and social life of their countries and to eliminate sexism.

My delegation, along with the delegations of the United Kingdom and the Federal Republic of Germany, made repeated efforts to enter into serious negotiations about other political and economic points in the Group of 77's draft on which there was disagreement. However, there was no opportunity to pursue such negotiations. We deeply regret, therefore, there was no chance to work out language on those parts of the draft declaration which we could not accept.

We find this all the more disappointing because we share the deep concern expressed at this conference for the role of women in the developing countries. We have joined in supporting resolutions designed to improve their status and assure their participation in society on an equal basis with men.

The draft declaration of principles before the conference today also contains certain formulations and references to certain U.N.

---

[16]Text from *Bulletin*, 73: 237-8.

[17]A draft declaration cosponsored by the Federal Republic of Germany, the United Kingdom, and the United States (Document E/CONF.66/C.1/L.22) was not pressed to a vote. It differed from the Declaration of Mexico mainly in the omission of "highly political issues, such as references to the word Zionism and to the Charter of Economic Rights and Duties of States." (*Digest of United States Practice in International Law, 1975*: 209.)

documents which the United States has consistently opposed. For this reason, the United States voted against operative paragraphs 18 and 19 when the draft was considered in the First Committee. The United States remains willing to enter into serious negotiations to narrow the remaining differences where they exist on specific economic issues, but we obviously cannot do so at this conference.

An additional reason for our position today is the inclusion of four paragraphs which unnecessarily encumber the declaration with specific political viewpoints not shared by many delegations. References to "Zionism" appear to associate this conference with a campaign against the State of Israel, and carry the implication that the State of Israel should be eliminated. The United States strongly opposes any provisions of this nature directed against one member of the United Nations.

In conclusion, Mr. President, my delegation has been guided throughout this conference by the belief that this was a meeting of all nations of the world to promote the status and the role of women throughout the world. We believe we should fairly reflect, therefore, the concerns of all those represented here. We should try to reach conclusions with which we can all agree.

We have been able to do so to a considerable extent at this conference. However, differences do remain. What [*sic*] they do, and on matters of importance, my delegation must register its disagreement.

Accordingly, Mr. President, my delegation voted against the declaration. In doing so, I also wish to reiterate the intention of the U.S. delegation and women throughout the United States to work with determination and good will to implement the World Plan of Action, the only major document unanimously adopted.

21. A NEW PACIFIC COMMONWEALTH?

(July 1, 1975)

[The conclusion of the struggle in Indochina occurred, for the United States, in the midst of a series of complex maneuvers initiated some years earlier and aimed at fortifying the nation's strategic frontier in the Pacific. The shrinkage of American military power in Southeast and East Asia over the past few years had spurred a revival of official interest in the strategic potentialities of the Trust Territory of the Pacific Islands (Micronesia), the far-flung, sparsely populated collection of former Japanese-held islands which was administered by the United States, nominally on behalf of the United Nations, under a special strategic trust agreement concluded in 1947.[1]

Negotiations looking toward a revision in the status of these islands, along lines that hopefully might do justice both to Micronesian political aspirations and to U.S. strategic requirements, had been under way since the mid-1960s, without, as yet, producing an acceptable formula. Given the difficulty of reaching agreement with Micronesia as a whole, the United States since 1972 had also been seeking a separate, more limited understanding with representatives of the Mariana Islands, the northern section of the trust territory that included the strategically important islands of Tinian and Saipan. By early 1975, these latter negotiations had led to agreement on a constitutional document known as the "Covenant to Establish a Commonwealth of the Northern Mariana Islands in Political Union with the United States of America."[2] Under its terms, it was contemplated that the Northern Marianas should in due course acquire a status comparable to that of Puerto Rico, with the 14,000-odd inhabitants exercising self-government in internal affairs while the United States would

---

[1]Trusteeship Agreement for the Former Japanese Mandated Islands, approved by the U.S. and entered into force July 18, 1947 (TIAS 1665); text in *Documents, 1947*: 394-8.

[2]Text annexed to Public Law 94-241, Mar. 24, 1976.

retain responsibility for foreign affairs and defense, including the right to lease substantial military base areas on Tinian and elsewhere.

Actuated at least in part by calculations of economic self-interest, the legislature and people of the Northern Marianas did not appear unduly disturbed by the disapproval of other Micronesians, who laid more stress on the importance of maintaining the unity of the territory. In a plebiscite observed by a U.N. mission and supervised on behalf of President Ford by Erwin D. Canham, editor emeritus of the *Christian Science Monitor*, the covenant won popular approval on June 17 with a 95 percent turnout of the Northern Marianas' registered voters and an affirmative vote of 78.8 percent of those participating.

Just two weeks later, President Ford in a letter to congressional leaders (**Document 33**) urged prompt approval of the covenant as a first step toward the administrative separation of the Northern Marianas and their eventual establishment as a commonwealth in political union with the United States. As had also been explained to the U.N. Trusteeship Council, this final step was not thought likely to occur before 1980 or 1981, by which time it was hoped that arrangements for self-determination would have been completed by the other peoples of Micronesia so that the U.N. trusteeship agreement could be terminated simultaneously for all parts of the territory.[3]

Only three weeks were needed for the House of Representatives to approve the proposed legislation, though final action by the Senate, where three separate committees were involved, was held over until early in the following year. Approved by a Senate vote of 66 to 23 on February 24, 1976, the covenant was to become law for the United States with the President's signature on March 24, 1976.[4] Still to be faced, however, would be the possibly more formidable difficulties involved in getting the arrangement approved at the international level.]

(33) Commonwealth Status for the Northern Mariana Islands: Letter from President Ford to the Speaker of the House of Representatives and the President of the Senate, July 1, 1975.[5]

Dear Mr. Speaker: (Dear Mr. President:)

I am transmitting herewith a proposed Joint Resolution which

---

[3] *U.S. Participation, 1975*: 280-81.
[4] Public Law 94-241, Mar. 24, 1976.
[5] Text from *Presidential Documents*, 11: 695-6. The letter was addressed to Speaker of the House Carl Albert and President of the Senate Nelson A. Rockefeller.

would provide Congressional approval of the "Covenant to Establish A Commonwealth of the Northern Mariana Islands in Political Union with the United States of America."

On June 17, 1975, the people of the Northern Mariana Islands of the Trust Territory of the Pacific Islands overwhelmingly approved the Covenant in a United Nations-observed plebiscite. This historic act of self-determination was the capstone of more than twenty years of continuous effort on the part of the people of the Marianas District to enter into close union with the United States. This action has now cleared the way for the submission of the Covenant to the Congress of the United States for its formal consideration.

The passage by the Congress of the Joint Resolution approving the Northern Mariana Islands Commonwealth Covenant will set into motion a series of progressive steps which will result in: the administrative separation of the Northern Mariana Islands from the Government of the Trust Territory of the Pacific Islands; the adoption of a locally-drafted and popularly-approved Constitution for the Northern Mariana Islands; and finally, following the termination of the Trusteeship Agreement for all of the Trust Territory of the Pacific Islands, the conferral of Commonwealth status on the Northern Mariana Islands as a territory of the United States as provided for by the Covenant.

The Covenant Agreement I am presenting to the Congress today was signed on February 15, 1975, by the Marianas Political Status Commission for the Northern Mariana Islands and by Ambassador F. Haydn Williams for the United States. It is the result of more than two years of negotiations between the United States and a broadly representative delegation from the Northern Mariana Islands. Prior to and during the talks, the people of the Northern Mariana Islands actively participated in open discussions of the various aspects of the proposed relationship. Likewise, the Executive Branch consulted frequently with members of the U.S. Congress regarding the progress of the negotiations and actively sought the advice and guidance of the Congress, much of which is reflected in the final provisions of the Covenant.

Following the signing, the Covenant was submitted to the Marianas District Legislature for its review and approval. On February 20, 1975, the elected representatives of the people of the Northern Mariana Islands through the District Legislature unanimously approved the Covenant and requested the United States to arrange for an early Plebiscite. The Plebiscite was carried out in accordance with an Order issued by the Secretary of the Interior on April 10, 1975. It was conducted under the supervision of my personal representative, Mr. Erwin D. Canham, whom I appointed to serve as Plebiscite Commissioner. On June 22, 1975, Commissioner

Canham certified that 78.8 percent of the people in the Marianas who voted had approved the Covenant.

The next step in the approval process is action by the U.S. Congress. The enclosed Joint Resolution, when approved, will provide the authority to begin the gradual and progressive implementation of the terms of the Covenant. This process hopefully will have been completed by 1981 when we expect the Trusteeship over all of the Trust Territory of the Pacific Islands will have been terminated following a similar act of self-determination by the other districts of the TTPI.

All of the provisions of the Covenant are the product of detailed negotiations extending over a two year period. I want to call your attention particularly to the financial assistance provisions in light of the new procedures established by the Congressional Budget Act.[6]

Article VII of the resolution specifically constitutes a commitment and pledge of the full faith and credit of the United States for the payment, as well as for the appropriation, of guaranteed levels of direct grant assistance totalling $14,000,000 per year, in 1975 constant dollars, to the Government of the Northern Mariana Islands for each of the first seven full fiscal years after approval by the Federal Government of the locally adopted Constitution. The same amount would be paid in future years unless changed by the Congress. A pro rata share of the $14,000,000 is authorized to be appropriated for the first partial fiscal year after the Constitution has been approved. Article VIII of the resolution authorizes the appropriation of $19,520,600 to be paid to the Government of the Northern Mariana Islands for the 50 year lease, with the option of renewing the lease for another 50 years at no cost, of approximately 18,182 acres of lands and waters immediately adjacent thereto.

In addition to these specific authorizations for appropriations, Article VII authorizes the Government of the Northern Mariana Islands to receive the full range of Federal programs and services available to the territories of the United States, as well as the proceeds of numerous Federal taxes, duties and fees—the same treatment as is presently afforded to the Territory of Guam.

I urge the Senate and the House to take early, positive action to approve the Northern Mariana Islands Commonwealth Covenant which will thereupon become law in accordance with its provisions. Favorable consideration by the Congress will represent one more important step in the fulfillment of the obligations which the United States undertook when the Congress approved by joint resolution the Trusteeship Agreement on July 18, 1947. Congressional approval of the freely expressed wish of the people of the

[6]Cf. note 5 to Chapter 4.

Northern Mariana Islands will enable them to move toward their long sought goal of self-government in political union with the United States. The final realization of this desired goal will be an historic event for the people of the Northern Mariana Islands and for the United States—an event to which I look forward with great pleasure.

    Sincerely,

GERALD R. FORD

22. TROUBLE WITH TURKEY

(July 1975)

[Throughout the first six months of 1975, the Ford administration had been a prey to constant anxieties arising from the situation created by the Turkish intervention in Cyprus in the summer of 1974. Greece, incensed by the failure of its allies to prevent the *de facto* partition of Cyprus by Turkish armed force, had withdrawn its own armed forces from NATO command and, more recently, rescinded permission for the U.S. Sixth Fleet to use the harbor of Eleusis, near Athens. Turkey, on its side, had been enraged by the cutoff of U.S. military aid, much of it in the form of weapons already bought and paid for, which had taken effect on February 5, 1975 in spite of anguished pleas to Congress by President Ford and Secretary Kissinger. Progress toward a political settlement in Cyprus had meanwhile remained at a virtual standstill in spite of the resumption of intermittent, U.N.-sponsored contacts between Greek and Turkish Cypriot representatives.[1]

In May, as previously noted, the U.S. Senate had passed by a 41 to 40 vote the so-called Mansfield-Scott bill, which would authorize the President to lift the Turkish aid ban and would require a monthly report on progress toward a Cyprus settlement. No parallel action had, however, been taken in the House, where a "Greek" faction led by Democratic Representatives Paul S. Sarbanes of Maryland, John Brademas of Indiana, and Benjamin S. Rosenthal of New York was adamantly opposed to resuming military aid in the absence of accommodating moves by Turkey. Tired of waiting on developments in Washington, the Turkish Government announced in mid-June, not long after the CENTO Council's meeting in Ankara, that it had decided to place the twenty-odd U.S. bases and intelligence-gathering facilities in the country on provisional status and to commence a renegotiation of the relevant agreements on the following July 17.

Faced with the possible loss of installations it considered highly

[1]For background cf. Chapter 8 at note 13 and Chapter 16 at note 4.

important to the monitoring of Soviet military activities, the Ford administration redoubled its appeals to the House of Representatives to pass the Mansfield-Scott resolution or some similar alternative measure (**Document 34**). Its efforts failed when, after several days of lobbying and tense debate, the Mansfield-Scott bill fell short of House approval on July 24 by a vote of 206 in favor to 223 against. President Ford's immediate expression of alarm (**Document 35**) was soon justified by the action of the Ankara government, which announced next day that it was immediately suspending activities at all joint defense installations (except for NATO activities at the Incirlik air base) and placing them under full control and supervision of the Turkish armed forces.

President Ford, already preparing to leave for the windup of the European Security Conference in Helsinki, immediately voiced a further appeal to the House "to reconsider its refusal to restore the traditional U.S.-Turkish defense relationship" (**Document 36**). From Bonn, on July 28, he reiterated his appeal in a cabled message to Speaker Carl Albert (**Document 37**). At a meeting with Turkish Prime Minister Demirel in Helsinki at the end of the month, he reaffirmed past offers to furnish Turkey with $50 millions' worth of weapons on a grant basis, but was given the usual response that Turkey would not accept as a gift what it was not allowed to buy for cash.[2]

A bipartisan effort to retrieve the situation had meanwhile been initiated in the Senate, where the substance of the defeated Mansfield-Scott bill was incorporated in an amendment to a Board for International Broadcasting authorization that passed on July 31 by a vote of 47 to 46. Though not considered by the House until after the August recess, this provision (which was to become law on October 6)[3] would eventually provide the key to at least a partial restoration of U.S.-Turkish amity—and, just possibly, a push toward eventual diplomatic resolution of the Cyprus impasse.]

(34) United States Military Aid to Turkey: Letter from the President to the Speaker of the House of Representatives, July 9, 1975.[4]

Dear Mr. Speaker:

I wish to share with you my concern about a complex foreign policy problem that relates to the deteriorating situation in the Eastern Mediterranean, the threat to our North Atlantic Alliance

[2]Kissinger news conference, Helsinki, July 31, in *Bulletin*, 73: 319-21.
[3]Sec. 2, Public Law 94-104, Oct. 6, 1975.
[4]Text (reprinted from *Congressional Record*) from *Presidential Documents*, 11: 722-3.

relationships, the plight of the people of Cyprus and the role of the United States. Both the Congress and the Executive Branch share a responsibility to reexamine this critical situation with care. This is not a partisan matter or one where the rights and wrongs of a decades-old dispute can easily be judged—particularly by outsiders. Our overriding objective must be to help in the peaceful settlement of a problem that involves two valued Allies and a people whose history as an independent nation has been riven by strife.

The strategic situation must also be weighed. At a time of uncertainty in the Middle East, we should consider carefully any action which could add to the tensions that already exist. Our facilities in Turkey and our mutual defense arrangements have played and continue to play a vital role in the security of the area and, more directly, in the security of our own forces. Mutual defense links that have stood us well for thirty years should not be lightly cast aside.

I have spent much time studying these issues and have talked in Brussels with the leaders of Turkey and Greece.[5] I am convinced that U.S. and Western security interests require the urgent passage by the House of legislation enabling the resumption of our long-standing security relationship with Turkey. The Senate has already acted favorably on a bill to accomplish this purpose.

Existing legislation passed by Congress last December 18,[6] with an effective date of February 5, 1975, has been in force for nearly five months. This action has: (1) called into question the ability of an Ally to continue to fulfill its essential NATO responsibilities, thus undermining NATO's strength in the Eastern Mediterranean; (2) jeopardized vital common defense installations which Turkey and the U.S. jointly maintain; (3) contributed to tensions which are not helpful to Greece; and (4) reduced American influence to move the Cyprus negotiations toward a peaceful conclusion acceptable to all parties.

The legislation voted against Turkey last December is sweeping in its effect. It is more extensive than similar legislation enacted in October, 1974,[7] with which the Administration was in full compliance. The December legislation provides for not only a total embargo on grant military assistance, and cash and credit sales of defense items by the U.S. Government, but prohibits as well the issuance of licenses to permit the export of military equipment purchased from American firms. Practically all nations of the world can purchase in this country at least some items that are forbidden to Turkey. It is now impossible for Turkey to procure most items produced in third countries under U.S. license; nor can Turkey

---

[5]Cf. Chapter 19.

[6]Foreign Assistance Act of 1974 (Public Law 93-559, Dec. 30, 1974); extract in *AFR, 1974*: 574-5.

[7]Same: 377-8.

even take possession of merchandise in the U.S. which it paid for prior to February 5 and which is now ready for shipment. The result is that a relationship of trust and confidence with this important NATO Ally, built up over many years, has been seriously eroded. Continuation of the embargo risks further deterioration, jeopardizing our security interests throughout the Eastern Mediterranean area.

For all these reasons, it is my strong view that the Administration and the Congress must join in legislative action that will remedy the present situation. The form that legislation should take to achieve this end is for Congress itself to decide, but it is clear that only legislation can produce the actions which are necessary in this case.

I know that in the minds of many in the Congress there remains the issue of how American-supplied arms were used last summer. The Cyprus problem is one where neither moral nor legal judgments, on the arms issue or any other, can be easily or lightly made. Yet, the effect of the embargo is to ascribe blame totally to one of the parties in a dispute that has its roots in centuries of animosity and for which both sides must share some responsibility.

Where we can all agree, and where I believe we must all act together, is in our sense of anxiety and concern over the Cyprus problem and in a consensus that the only way to achieve what we all seek—a just and broadly acceptable settlement—is through negotiations in which we maintain maximum flexibility with all the parties. Unless some progress is made in the negotiations, the humanitarian plight facing the people of Cyprus, including particularly the refugee problem, cannot be solved.

The United States will continue to work, as it has done continuously since last July, as hard and as determinedly as possible to move the parties of the Cyprus conflict toward a negotiated settlement. Recent U.S. diplomatic activity in Ankara, Athens and Brussels has contributed to the start of a Greek-Turkish dialogue which has defused the tense situation and hopefully laid the groundwork for Greek-Turkish cooperation.

As we pursue our efforts, we want the continued friendship of both Greece and Turkey, and our sympathy and concern extend to all the people of Cyprus. We want an end to human suffering and misery, and the rebuilding of an island where all can live in freedom and security.

At present, our ability to urge this view persuasively is compromised by the erosion of our influence. I ask the Congress' cooperation and assistance, therefore, in enacting legislation which will assure that America's influence is not further weakened and U.S. interests further threatened at this time of critical concern in Cyprus and throughout the Eastern Mediterranean.

Sincerely,

GERALD R. FORD

(35) Defeat of the Mansfield-Scott Resolution in the House of Representatives: Statement by President Ford, July 24, 1975.[8]

I am deeply disappointed by the refusal of the House of Representatives to partially lift the embargo on the shipment of arms to Turkey. It is my strong conviction that this negative vote can only do the most serious and irreparable damage to the vital national security interests of the United States, including our normally excellent relations with the Government of Turkey, U.S. security interests in the Atlantic Alliance and the Eastern Mediterranean, and U.S. efforts to assist the governments of Greece, Turkey, and Cyprus to reach a just and equitable Cyprus settlement. It will also seriously affect important interests elsewhere.

I and members of my Administration worked hard to persuade Members of the House of Representatives that vital, national defense interests are at stake in this issue. I am very proud of those 206 Members of Congress of both parties as well as the Members of the Senate who supported a similar measure, for casting their votes in the national interest. I deeply appreciate the efforts of the bipartisan leadership of the Congress and the members of the House and Senate Committees on International Relations and Foreign Affairs who supported the legislation. I will continue to make every effort to assist in achieving an equitable settlement of the Cyprus dispute. I will work to reassure our allies, Turkey and Greece, of our continuing desire to maintain strong and effective relationships with them despite this setback. I hope the House of Representatives will reconsider its failure to act affirmatively.

(36) Turkish Takeover of Joint Defense Installations: Statement by President Ford, July 25, 1975.[9]

I deeply regret the announcement of the Government of Turkey to suspend all American activities at joint U.S.-Turkish defense installations and to take over control and supervision of these important installations.

I repeatedly warned the House of Representatives of extremely serious consequences, such as this, if the United States failed to restore military sales and credits to our Turkish allies. I again want to praise those House members of both parties who voted in the national interest. Now, as a result of yesterday's 223-206 vote in the House of Representatives, Turkey has today announced actions which I believe will work to the detriment of critically important U.S. security interests.

In view of these damaging developments, I urge the House of

[8]Text from *Presidential Documents*, 11: 777.
[9]Text from same, 11: 783.

Representatives to reconsider its refusal to restore the traditional U.S.-Turkish defense relationship. Prompt, affirmative action by the House of Representatives is essential to the vital national defense interests of the United States, our partners in the Eastern Mediterranean, and our allies in the Atlantic Alliance.

(37) Appeal for Legislative Reconsideration: Message from the President to the Speaker of the House of Representatives, Bonn, July 28, 1975.[10]

Dear Mr. Speaker:

The consequences of the House action in failing to lift the arms embargo on Turkey are now becoming apparent. As President of the United States my responsibility for the national security and conduct of foreign affairs have led me to urge in the strongest terms that the House lift the embargo. Despite the House action and subsequent events, I do not believe that the situation is irretrievable today.

It is difficult to overstate the importance of the major installations we will lose in Turkey if we cannot remedy the action. Their loss would seriously downgrade our capabilities in major areas of national security. These installations are not replaceable.

In reviewing the debates of the last several months, any fairminded person would agree that there is not a fundamental dispute on the objective of achieving a peaceful and equitable solution to the tragic Cyprus problem. The Congress has chosen means to accomplish that end which in my judgment would not only delay and impede a Cyprus settlement but, as now can be seen clearly, cause a disastrous deterioration in our security relations with Turkey and in the Eastern Mediterranean in general. In addition, these effects will certainly not make for an improvement in relations between Greece and Turkey, without which a Cyprus settlement is not possible.

My Administration has been and will continue to pursue the cause of a just and peaceful settlement in Cyprus. But I must emphasize in the strongest terms how seriously hobbled our efforts will be if the embargo against Turkey is maintained.

I, therefore, urge through you, Mr. Speaker, the immediate reconsideration of last week's House action. Only if we preserve our vital security relations with Turkey will I be able usefully to assist the parties in the area toward better relations.

    Sincerely,

GERALD R. FORD

[10]Text from same, 11: 801.

23. REVISING THE RIO TREATY

(San José, July 16-26, 1975)

[The summer of 1975 brought major developments affecting the political organization of two of the earth's regions, Europe and the Americas. In Helsinki, Finland, the concluding sessions of the Conference on Security and Cooperation in Europe (CSCE) on July 30-August 1 for the first time placed a seal of international acceptance on the political relationships that had grown up in Europe since World War II. In San José, Costa Rica, between July 16 and July 29, member countries of the Organization of American States (OAS) not only agreed to a substantial revision of the basic inter-American security treaty but also undertook to lift an eleven-year-old ban on diplomatic and commercial relations with the Castro regime in Cuba.

The impetus to revise the institutional structure of the existing inter-American system had been given by the OAS General Assembly in March 1973, when a special OAS committee, known from its Spanish initials as CEESI, had been established to propose remedies for what had been described at that time as the "general dissatisfaction" with its functioning and results.[1] Proceeding within the parameters of the new "dialogue" proposed by Secretary Kissinger, CEESI by early 1975 had held five major sessions and developed recommendations looking toward far-reaching revision of the basic Inter-American Treaty of Reciprocal Assistance (Rio Treaty),[2] the original collective security treaty concluded in 1947 in line with the regional security provisions of the U.N. Charter. After examining CEESI's report, the OAS General Assembly had decided in May 1975 that a formal Protocol of Amendment to the Rio Treaty should be completed and signed at a special plenipotentiary conference—which, after further prepara-

---

[1] *AFR, 1973*: 120 and 407-8.
[2] Opened for signature at Rio de Janeiro Sept. 2, 1947 and entered into force Dec. 3, 1948 (TIAS 1838); text in *Documents, 1947*: 534-40.

tory work, took place in San José on July 16-26 and was attended by 21 of the 22 states signatory to the Rio Pact, only Cuba being unrepresented.

The changes that would be brought about by the Protocol of Amendment that was signed at San José[3]—assuming its ratification by the necessary two-thirds of the signatory states—were conveniently listed in an official summary **(Document 38)** that accompanied the President's subsequent message asking the Senate's advice and consent to ratification **(Document 39).** Apart from technical changes, the protocol reformulated the basic mutual security concept of the Rio Treaty—". . . an armed attack by any State against an American State shall be considered as an attack against all the American States"—by narrowing its geographic zone of application and limiting it to an attack on an American state *party to the treaty*, thus excluding Canada and other American states that had not signed the Rio Pact. In a second significant change, which will be considered further in the next chapter, the protocol reduced the majority required for the lifting of OAS sanctions—such as those currently in effect against Cuba—from a two-thirds to a simple majority.

One other article in the Protocol of Amendment recalled the battles over economic policy that were currently taking up so much of the time of the United Nations and other international forums. In an action that was frowned upon by the United States on the ground that it was not germane to the purpose in hand, Latin American delegates insisted on the inclusion in the Protocol of an article asserting that "collective economic security for the development of the [OAS] Member States. . . must also be guaranteed through suitable mechanisms to be established in a special treaty." To this the United States replied, in a formal reservation reminiscent of its stand on similar issues in the United Nations, that in signing the protocol it accepted "no obligation or commitment to negotiate, sign or ratify a treaty or convention on the subject of collective economic security." This stand would be reiterated in President Ford's request for Senate approval of the Protocol.]

(38) Protocol of Amendment to the Inter-American. Treaty of Reciprocal Assistance (Rio. Treaty), done at San José, July 26, 1975: Summary of amendments effected by the protocol, prepared by the Department of State.[4]

---

[3]Text in S. Ex. J, 94th Cong., 1st sess., Dec. 1, 1975, and in *Digest of United States Practice in International Law, 1975*: 793-7.
[4]Attached to letter of submittal to the President, Nov. 13, 1975; text from S. Ex. J, 94th Cong., 1st sess., Dec. 1, 1975: 1-4.

SUMMARY OF AMENDMENTS EFFECTED BY THE PROTOCOL OF AMENDMENT TO THE INTER-AMERICAN TREAT OF RECIPROCAL ASSISTANCE

PREAMBLE

Although the Protocol of Amendment includes its own Preamble, the Preamble of the present Rio Treaty remains unchanged.

CONDEMNATION OF WAR AND PEACEFUL SETTLEMENT

In the existing Article 1 of the Rio Treaty the parties condemn war and undertake not to threaten or use force in any manner inconsistent with the U.N. Charter, OAS Charter, or this Treaty. The Protocol would simply add a reference to the OAS Charter.

The present Article 2 in the Treaty provides for submitting disputes among parties to inter-American procedures before referral to the General Assembly or the Security Council of the United Nations. The Protocol of Amendment adopts language modeled on Article 52 of the United Nations Charter, mentioning that the parties should seek peaceful settlement within the Inter-American System before resorting to the Security Council. It also makes a specific reference to the obligations of the states party under Articles 34 and 35 of the U.N. Charter.

ARMED ATTACK

In the Treaty Article 3 presently states that "an armed attack by any state against an American State shall be considered as an attack against all the American States, and consequently each one of the said Contracting Parties undertakes to assist in meeting the attack . . ." In negotiating the amendment of this Article, efforts to exclude attacks of extra-hemispheric origin from coverage of the Treaty were defeated; the compromise language set out in the Protocol would establish a distinction between extra-hemispheric attacks, and those within the hemisphere, by treating them in two separate subparagraphs, but there would be no substantive difference in the obligations of the member states in the two situations. Thus, the specific obligation entered into by the parties in paragraph 1 of the new Article 3 is reiterated in the two immediately following paragraphs (dealing with attacks from within and from outside the hemisphere).

Whereas the present Article 3 applies to all American states, under the Protocol of Amendment it would apply only to states which are party to the Rio Treaty.

ZONE OF COVERAGE

Under the new Article 4 the zone of coverage of the Rio Treaty would be somewhat narrowed. It still would include all of Canada, but would exclude Greenland and substantial high seas areas, especially in the Northern Pacific. (The South Atlantic coverage would be slightly expanded). It would include all of the other land areas in and around North, Central, and South America, and the Caribbean, and the margins extend in all cases for at least several hundred miles off the coasts of the continent. As in the present Article, the area is defined in the new Article in terms of map coordinates, and that definition has no effect on territorial or jurisdictional claims within the hemisphere.

OTHER THREATS TO THE PEACE

The present Article 6 of the Rio Treaty (Article 5 as renumbered in the Protocol), the provision which gives the Organ of Consultation jurisdiction over threats to the peace that do not involve armed attack, would be modified by the Protocol of Amendment although there are no major substantive changes. In place of the catch-all phrase "by an extra-continental or intracontinental conflict or by any other act or situation that might endanger the peace of America" the new Article includes "a conflict or serious event that might endanger the peace of America."

The new Article also makes a distinction between matters involving other states which are not parties. Pursuant to the new Article action may be taken under Article 5 with respect to armed attacks against American states not parties to the Treaty (which are excluded from coverage under Article 3), or when such states are "affected by a conflict or serious event that might endanger the peace of America."

MEASURES UNDER THE TREATY

While measures specified in the present Article 8 of the Rio Treaty remain essentially unchanged by the Protocol, a specific reference to "other means of communication" is incorporated.

Also included is a specific reference to conciliatory or peace-making steps which may be taken by the Organ of Consultation, recognizing explicitly a function which the Organ of Consultation has performed on a number of occasions in the past.

DEFINITION OF AGGRESSION

The definition of aggression incorporated in the new Article 9 presented in the Protocol of Amendment is an expanded version of that presently found in the Treaty and closely follows the one adopted by the U.N. General Assembly in 1974.[5] Despite some difference in the language, there is only one significant departure from the U.N. definition: the specific reference to "marine and air fleets" is deleted. It was established in the record of the San Jose Conference that this deletion does not mean that attacks on marine or air fleets would not be considered aggression: In subparagraph 3 of the new Article, the Organ of Consultation has authority to determine that other specific cases are aggression.

REPORT TO THE UNITED NATIONS

The present Article 5 of the Treaty (Article 10 as renumbered in the Protocol) is not substantively changed.

VOTING

The new Article 20, which would modify the present Article 17, incorporates the most important single change in the Rio Treaty. Under the new provision it is explicitly recognized that recommendations (of a non-binding nature) as well as binding decisions, may be adopted by the Organ of Consultation. Pursuant to the new Article measures taken pursuant to Article 8[6] could be *rescinded* by an absolute majority vote of the states party; all other decisions continue to require a vote of two-thirds of the states party.

[5] Annexed to General Assembly Resolution 3314 (XXIX), Dec. 14, 1974.
[6] Article 8 of the Rio Treaty provides as follows: "For the purposes of this Treaty, the measures on which the Organ of Consultation may agree will comprise one or more of the following: recall of chiefs of diplomatic missions; breaking of diplomatic relations; breaking of consular relations; partial or complete interruption of economic relations or of rail, sea, air, postal, telegraphic, telephonic, and radiotelephonic or radio telegraphic communications; and use of armed force." For further discussion see Chapter 24.

DECISIONS AND RECOMMENDATIONS

The new Article 23 (the present Article 20) also explicitly recognizes that the Organ of Consultation may adopt recommendations to the states party as well as decisions (the application of which would be binding on all states). In addition, the new provision includes an additional paragraph based on Article 50 of the U.N. Charter, which would afford any party to the Treaty confronted with special economic problems arising from acts of the Organ of Consultation the right to consult with the Organ with regard to the solution to those problems. The right would not be available to the state or states against which the sanctions are directed.

CONSENT FOR ASSISTANCE

The Protocol of Amendment specifies a new Article 6 providing that the Organ of Consultation may not assist a state without the consent of that state. The intent of this change is to guard against what some states party to the Treaty view as a danger of intervention in internal political situations.

COLLECTIVE ECONOMIC SECURITY

The Protocol of Amendment provides for a new Article 11[7] in which the parties recognize that "collective economic security for the development of the member states . . . must also be guaranteed through suitable mechanisms to be established in a special treaty." The United States strongly opposed this provision and entered a reservation to it upon signing the Protocol.[8] The Article on collective economic security is, in the United States view, not germane to the Rio Treaty.

---

[7]The text of the proposed article reads as follows: "The High Contracting Parties recognize that, for the maintenance of peace and security in the Hemisphere, collective economic security for the development of the Member States of the Organization of American States must also be guaranteed through suitable mechanisms to be established in a special treaty."

[8]The Reservation of the United States reads as follows: "The United States, in signing this Protocol of Amendment to the Inter-American Treaty of Reciprocal Assistance, accepts no obligation or commitment to negotiate, sign or ratify a treaty or convention on the subject of collective economic security."

NON-INTERVENTION

A new Article 12 states that no provision of the Treaty may be interpreted as limiting or impairing the principle of non-intervention and the right of all states to choose freely their political, economic, and social organization. This Article reflects the desire of several states to make the principle of non-intervention even more explicit and to emphasize each state's right to choose freely its political system.

AMENDMENT OF THE TREATY

The new Article 27 provided for in the Protocol combines the existing Article 24 (providing that the Treaty enters into force when two-thirds of the signatories have ratified it) with a specific provision stipulating that future amendments of the Treaty shall take place at a special conference convoked for that purpose. The intent of this new Article is to provide for possible future Protocols of Amendment to the Rio Treaty, should the need again arise.

MISCELLANEOUS PROVISIONS

The final provisions of the Protocol deal with renumbering of articles otherwise unchanged (Article III) with changes in terminology (Article V), and with signature, ratification, and deposit (Articles VI and VII). Articles VII, IX, and XI provide for entry into force of this particular Protocol and for the eventual situation in which the amended Rio Treaty is the only document open for signature by new states party.

Article X concerns registration with the United Nations, while Article XII relates to the continuation in force of the existing Treaty and a provision specifying the application of the Treaty as amended after the Protocol enters into force.

Article XIII seeks to deal with the problems which will arise when the Protocol has entered into force and the Treaty as amended is therefore in force as between the States that have ratified the Protocol, but there remain other American States that have not ratified it and are therefore still bound only by the original provisions of the Treaty.

Article XI provides that when the Protocol enters into force, the Secretary General of OAS shall prepare a consolidated text of the Rio Treaty which contains the amendments effected by the Protocol.

(39) Request for Advice and Consent to Ratification: Message from President Ford to the Senate, November 29, 1975.[9]

To the Senate of the United States:

I am transmitting for the Senate's advice and consent to ratification the Protocol of Amendment to the Inter-American Treaty of Reciprocal Assistance (Rio Treaty) signed at San Jose July 26, 1975. I also am transmitting, for the information of the Senate, the report of the Department of State with respect to the Protocol.[10]

The signing of the Protocol of San Jose was a major development for the Inter-American System and a reaffirmation of the importance of our own relationship with the countries of Latin America. The Amendments, taken as a whole, do not alter the Rio Treaty's fundamental thrust; rather, they are for the most part constructive changes which will make the Treaty more flexible and politically viable in the years ahead.

The San Jose Conference of Plenipotentiaries for the amendment of the Rio Treaty constituted the final step in a process which began in April 1973 when the General Assembly of the Organization of American States, with the support of the United States, began an effort aimed at modernizing the instruments of the Inter-American System so as to make them more responsive to today's needs. The Protocol thus represents the end product of a conceptual and drafting process which began more than two years ago.

The most significant changes embodied in the Protocol in the Rio Treaty are (1) a provision for lifting sanctions by majority vote rather than the two-thirds vote required for all other decisions under the Treaty; (2) specific provision for non-binding recommendations and for conciliatory and peace-making steps as well as for binding measures; (3) a narrowing of the geographic area in which the "attack against one, attack against all" applies, eliminating Greenland and some high seas areas, and limiting its applicability to attacks against other states parties (instead of all "American states"); (4) the incorporation of a more complete definition of aggression than appeared in the original treaty, following the lines of the definition approved in 1974 by the General Assembly of the United Nations; and (5) the addition of an article providing that "collective economic security" shall be guaranteed by a special treaty (a provision to which the United States submitted a reservation at the time of signature). While the inclusion of an article on collective economic security represents an unfortunate detraction

[9]Text from S. Ex. J, 94th Cong., 1st sess., Dec. 1, 1975: iii-iv.
[10]Same: v-vii.

from the Protocol's balance and good sense, on the whole, the amendments improve this basic instrument of inter-American security and peacekeeping.

It is significant from the point of view of the United States that many other proposed changes were *not* embodied in the Protocol. For example, a proposal supported by some that would have limited the "attack against one, attack against all" concept to attacks coming from within the hemisphere was soundly defeated. Similarly, efforts to limit the authority of the Organ of Consultation to deal with a broad range of acts which could endanger the peace of America were unsuccessful. The result, in our view, was a reaffirmation of the basic principles of the Rio Treaty rather than a weakening of them. Nevertheless, I believe the protection of interests of the United States with respect to its position on the concept of collective economic security requires a formal reservation to that Article when the United States deposits its instrument of ratification, along the lines of the reservation made at the time of signing.

The various amendments to the Treaty are dealt with in detail in the enclosed report by the Department of State and the summary of amendments.

I strongly believe that it is in the national interest of the United States to ratify the proposed amendments. I therefore urge that the Senate give its advice and consent to ratification by the United States of the Amendment to the Rio Treaty contained in this Protocol, and that it do so as promptly as possible consistent with its constitutional responsibilities.[11]

GERALD R. FORD.

[11] A resolution of ratification (with the reservation quoted in note 8 above) was approved by a 95-0 vote of the Senate on July 19, 1977.

24. ENDING CUBAN SANCTIONS
(San José, July 29, 1975)

[For most of the delegates assembled at San José, the technicalities of the Rio Treaty and its Protocol of Amendment had less immediate interest than a separate question that was not on their formal agenda yet occupied the thoughts of almost everyone present. This was the question of what to do about the diplomatic and economic sanctions against the Castro regime in Cuba that had been ordered in 1964 by the American Foreign Ministers, acting in exercise of their prerogatives under the Rio Treaty,[1] and still remained on the books in spite of far-reaching changes in Cuba and elsewhere and a growing refusal on the part of some OAS members to go on observing them. By mid-1975, no fewer than nine of the organization's 24 active members[2] were listed as maintaining diplomatic and/or trade relations with the Havana regime, a state of affairs that reduced the eleven-year-old OAS restrictions to little more than symbolic importance.

Proposals by various OAS members to rescind the 1964 decision had already led to the convocation of a special meeting of American Foreign Ministers which had been held at Quito, Ecuador, on November 8-12, 1974. That meeting, however, had ended inconclusively owing to the failure of the plan for revoking sanctions to enlist the two-thirds majority required under the terms of the Rio Treaty.[3] It was this experience, attributed largely to the refusal of the United States to take a firm position in favor of

---

[1] Resolution I of the Ninth Meeting of Consultation of Ministers of Foreign Affairs, Washington, July 26, 1964, in *Documents, 1964*: 294-5.
[2] Argentina, Barbados, Colombia, Jamaica, Mexico, Panama, Peru, Trinidad and Tobago, and Venezuela. (Barbados and Jamaica were not considered bound by the OAS restrictions, since they had not been members of the OAS at the time of the 1964 decisions.)
[3] *AFR, 1974*: 443-50.

revoking sanctions, that had motivated the decision of the plenipotentiary conference at San José to revise the Rio Treaty in such a way that the lifting of sanctions could in future be effected by a simple majority of Rio Treaty signatories.[4]

But since it might be two years or even longer before the Protocol of Amendment to the Rio Pact could be ratified and declared in force, the anti-sanctions elements at San José—led, as in the past, by Costa Rican Foreign Minister Gonzalo J. Facio—had been eager to make another attempt to assemble a two-thirds majority that would suffice to terminate the sanctions even under the existing rules. The basic question at San José, indeed, was not whether such an attempt should be made, but whether it should be made immediately or should be postponed to a separate meeting to be held in Trinidad in August. Meeting in San José on July 25 as the OAS Permanent Council, the eligible delegates decided in favor of immediate action and undertook to convoke another Meeting of Consultation of Ministers of Foreign Affairs, to be held in San José on Tuesday, July 29.

Some Latin American delegates had appeared rather disgruntled at the failure of Secretary Kissinger, immersed in preparations for the Helsinki conference, to come to San José to meet with them. They could not, however, complain of any lack of cooperation from the delegation headed by Ambassador William S. Mailliard, the new U.S. Representative to the OAS. What was not generally known until much later was the fact that the United States itself had been engaged in secret contacts with Cuban emissaries, initiated as far back as November 1974 and involving a series of clandestine meetings at airports and hotels in Washington and New York in which the U.S. participants had been Secretary Kissinger's executive assistant, Lawrence S. Eagleburger, and William D. Rogers, Assistant Secretary of State for Inter-American Affairs.

Spurred by conciliatory statements from Secretary Kissinger and Premier Castro, these conversations had focused primarily on such longstanding bilateral issues as those related to Cuba's expropriation of an estimated $1.8 billion in U.S. property, the U.S. trade embargo and freezing of some $30 million in Cuban assets, and the emotional problems that centered on the status of the Guantánamo naval base, the fate of political prisoners in Cuba, and the possibility of measures to reunite divided families. By the time of the San José conference, the chances for an overall settlement of such problems had begun to appear by no means unfavorable, although they were destined to recede again later in the year as the direct result of Cuba's military intervention in Angola.[5]

[4]Cf. Chapter 23 at note 6.
[5]David Binder in *New York Times*, March 29, 1977.

Consistent with the tone of these secret U.S.-Cuban exchanges was the attitude of the U.S. delegation at San José, not only in supporting the convocation of a special Foreign Ministers' meeting but also in agreeing to back the discontinuance of the mandatory sanctions decreed in 1964. This was accomplished by means of a brief resolution **(Document 40)**, adopted on July 29 by a decisive majority of 16 to 3 with 2 abstentions,[6] in which the Foreign Ministers, acting as Organ of Consultation under the Rio Treaty, reaffirmed the historic principle of nonintervention and simply left it up to the individual signatories of the Rio Treaty to manage their relations with Cuba in whatever way they thought best. Although the United States seemed not to envisage any immediate or major change in its own relationship with Havana, the abrogation of the sanctions program would at least remove one irritant from its relations with other nations of the hemisphere.]

(40) Relations with Cuba: Resolution I of the Sixteenth Meeting of Consultation of Ministers of Foreign Affairs, San José, July 29, 1975.[7]

I

FREEDOM OF ACTION OF THE STATES PARTIES TO THE
INTER-AMERICAN TREATY OF RECIPROCAL ASSISTANCE TO
NORMALIZE OR CONDUCT THEIR RELATIONS WITH THE REPUBLIC
OF CUBA AT THE LEVEL AND IN THE FORM THAT EACH STATE
DEEMS ADVISABLE

The Sixteenth Meeting of Consultation of Ministers of Foreign Affairs, acting as Organ of Consultation, in application of the Inter-American Treaty of Reciprocal Assistance (Rio Treaty),

CONSIDERING:

That the States Parties to the Rio Treaty have reiterated their adherence to the principles of inter-American solidarity and

[6] The complete vote was as follows:

In favor: Argentina, Bolivia, Colombia, Costa Rica, Dominican Republic, Ecuador, El Salvador, Guatemala, Haiti, Honduras, Mexico, Panama, Peru, Trinidad and Tobago, U.S., Venezuela.

Opposed: Chile, Paraguay, Uruguay.

Abstaining: Brazil, Nicaragua.

[7] Text from *Sixteenth Meeting of Consultation of Ministers of Foreign Affairs . . . Final Act* (OAS Document OEA/Ser.C/11.16): 4.

cooperation, nonintervention, and reciprocal assistance set forth in the Rio Treaty and the Charter of the OAS[8] and

DESIRING:

To further inter-American relations in the broadest possible sense,

RESOLVES:

1. To solemnly reaffirm the principle of nonintervention and to call upon the States Parties to ensure its observance in this hemisphere, in accordance with the Charter of the Organization, for which purpose they once again proclaim their solidarity and reiterate their will to constantly cooperate with a view to fully achieving the goals of a policy of peace.

2. To leave the States Parties to the Rio Treaty free to normalize or conduct in accordance with the national policy and interests of each their relations with the Republic of Cuba at the level and in the form that each State deems advisable.

3. To transmit the text of this resolution to the Security Council of the United Nations.

[8]Signed at Bogotá Apr. 30, 1948 and entered into force Dec. 31, 1951 (TIAS 2361; 2 UST 2394; text in *Documents, 1948*: 484-502); Protocol of Amendment signed at Buenos Aires Feb. 27, 1967 and entered into force Feb. 27, 1970 (TIAS 6847; 21 UST 607; summary in *Documents, 1968-69*: 399-401).

25. THE HELSINKI SUMMIT

(Helsinki, July 30-August 1, 1975)

[The concluding phase of the Conference on Security and Cooperation in Europe (CSCE), held in Finland's capital of Helsinki on July 30-August 1, 1975, is assured high rank among the diplomatic spectacles of the twentieth century, however its substantive accomplishment may ultimately be judged. Since its ceremonial opening phase in Helsinki on June 3-7, 1973,[1] this long-planned conference had been immersed in a laborious second or "working" stage that had continued at Geneva over the 22-month period from September 18, 1973 to July 21, 1975. The windup "at the summit," attended by heads of state or comparable dignitaries from 33 European countries (all European states except Albania) together with Canada and the United States, made up in glitter and prestige for anything it may have lacked in political substance.

From the Soviet point of view, the Helsinki summit also represented the culmination of years of effort to obtain some formal, international acknowledgment of the European territorial and political setup established, largely by force of Soviet arms, during and following World War II. Such an acknowledgement was included, by implication at least, among the general principles set forth in the Final Act of the conference, which stated among other things that the participating states "regard as inviolable all one another's frontiers as well as the frontiers of all States in Europe." For the United States and its Western allies, such an affirmation was tantamount to a final abandonment of any notion of pushing back the frontiers of Communism and reclaiming all or part of Soviet-dominated Central and Eastern Europe for the democratic world, let alone challenging the U.S.S.R.'s absorption of the formerly independent states of Estonia, Latvia, and Lithuania.

The verbal price exacted for this act of renunciation was also written into the 30,000-word text of the Helsinki Final Act, particularly the section devoted to "Cooperation in Humanitarian and

[1] *AFR, 1973:* 287-8 and 291-8.

Other Fields" and known informally as "Basket Three" to distinguish it from the sections on "Security in Europe" (Basket One), "Cooperation in the Field of Economics, of Science and Technology and of the Environment" (Basket Two), "Follow-Up Measures" (Basket Four), and a special section on "Security and Cooperation in the Mediterranean" incorporated at the request of Malta and other Mediterranean states. Included in the third basket were detailed provisions inspired by a Western hope that the Security Conference would open the door to intensified East-West exchanges in the areas of human contacts, information, culture, and education. In common with other parts of the document, Basket Three laid special emphasis upon the concern of the participating states for human rights and fundamental freedoms, as well as their determination to make détente a continuing process and thus contribute to the strengthening of universal peace, progress, and well-being.

Yet no one who was acquainted with the current status of human rights within the Soviet Union and the other Communist-governed countries could fail to be aware of a significant gap between the present-day reality and the ideals set forth in the Final Act. That the significance of this document would depend almost entirely upon the way it was implemented in the future was a point particularly stressed by President Ford in his address to the Helsinki conference (**Document 41**), delivered shortly before the actual signature of the Final Act (**Document 42**) on August 1.

Visibly unhappy about some aspects of the procedure—and obviously disturbed as well by the current crisis in U.S.-Turkish relations[2] and the mounting fear of a leftist takeover in Portugal[3]—the President and Secretary Kissinger had arranged to incorporate the Helsinki pilgrimage in a broader tour that had commenced with brief visits to West Germany and Poland and was to continue (after meetings in Helsinki with General Secretary Brezhnev, Prime Minister Demirel of Turkey, and others) with further stopovers in Romania and Yugoslavia.[4]

By dramatizing America's interest in those East European countries with which the United States traditionally had maintained the warmest relationship, the President undoubtedly hoped to combat any idea that his administration had "given up" on Eastern Europe or—as was being suggested in right-wing and émigré circles at home—was sacrificing the freedom of that region in return for

[2]Cf. Chapter 22.
[3]Cf. note 11 to Chapter 28.
[4]For full documentation see *Presidential Documents*, 11: 787-804 and 807-32 (*Bulletin*, 73: 289-351 and 363-76).

empty promises that Moscow had no intention of fulfilling. Despite his vigorous rejection of such imputations, this charge was to be frequently repeated—and as frequently denied—throughout the fifteen-month period leading up to the American presidential election in November 1976.]

(41) Conference on Security and Cooperation in Europe:. Third Stage, Helsinki, July 30-August 1, 1975: Address to the Conference by President Ford, August 1, 1975.[5]

Mr. Chairman,[6] *my distinguished colleagues:*

May I begin by expressing to the Governments of Finland and Switzerland, which have been superb hosts for the several phases of this Conference, my gratitude and that of my associates for their efficiency and hospitality.

Particularly to you, President [Urho K.] Kekkonen, I must convey to the people of the Republic of Finland, on behalf of the 214 million people of the United States of America, a reaffirmation of the long-standing affection and admiration which all my countrymen hold for your brave and beautiful land.

We are bound together by the most powerful of all ties, our fervent love for freedom and independence, which knows no homeland but the human heart. It is a sentiment as enduring as the granite rock on which this city stands and as moving as the music of Sibelius.

Our visit here, though short, has brought us a deeper appreciation of the pride, industry, and friendliness which Americans always associate with the Finnish nation.

The nations assembled here have kept the general peace in Europe for 30 years. Yet there have been too many narrow escapes from major conflict. There remains, to this day, the urgent issue of how to construct a just and lasting peace for all peoples.

I have not come across the Atlantic to say what all of us already know—that nations now have the capacity to destroy civilization, and, therefore, all our foreign policies must have as their one supreme objective the prevention of a thermonuclear war. Nor have I come to dwell upon the hard realities of continuing ideological differences, political rivalries, and military competition that persist among us.

I have come to Helsinki as a spokesman for a nation whose vision has always been forward, whose people have always demanded

---

[5]Text from *Presidential Documents*, 11: 809-14.
[6]Walter Kieber, Head of Government and Foreign Minister of Liechtenstein.

that the future be brighter than the past, and whose united will and purpose at this hour is to work diligently to promote peace and progress not only for ourselves but for all mankind.

I am simply here to say to my colleagues: We owe it to our children, to the children of all continents, not to miss any opportunity, not to malinger for one minute, not to spare ourselves or allow others to shirk in the monumental task of building a better and a safer world.

The American people, like the people of Europe, know well that mere assertions of good will, passing changes in the political mood of governments, laudable declarations of principles are not enough. But if we proceed with care, with commitment to real progress, there is now an opportunity to turn our people's hopes into realities.

In recent years, nations represented here have sought to ease potential conflicts. But much more remains to be done before we prematurely congratulate ourselves.

Military competition must be controlled. Political competition must be restrained. Crises must not be manipulated or exploited for unilateral advantages that could lead us again to the brink of war. The process of negotiation must be sustained, not at a snail's pace, but with demonstrated enthusiasm and visible progress.

Nowhere are the challenges and the opportunities greater and more evident than in Europe. That is why this Conference brings us all together. Conflict in Europe shakes the world. Twice in this century we have paid dearly for this lesson; at other times, we have come perilously close to calamity. We dare not forget the tragedy and the terror of those times.

Peace is not a piece of paper.

But lasting peace is at least possible today because we have learned from the experiences of the last 30 years that peace is a process requiring mutual restraint and practical arrangements.

This Conference is a part of that process—a challenge, not a conclusion. We face unresolved problems of military security in Europe; we face them with very real differences in values and in aims. But if we deal with them with careful preparation, if we focus on concrete issues, if we maintain forward movement, we have the right to expect real progress.

The era of confrontation that has divided Europe since the end of the Second World War may now be ending. There is a new perception and a shared perception of a change for the better, away from confrontation and toward new possibilities for secure and mutually beneficial cooperation. That is what we all have been saying here. I welcome and I share these hopes for the future.

The postwar policy of the United States has been consistently directed toward the rebuilding of Europe and the rebirth of

Europe's historic identity. The nations of the West have worked together for peace and progress throughout Europe. From the very start, we have taken the initiative by stating clear goals and areas for negotiation.

We have sought a structure of European relations, tempering rivalry with restraint, power with moderation, building upon the traditional bonds that link us with old friends and reaching out to forge new ties with former and potential adversaries.

In recent years, there have been some substantial achievements.

We see the Four-Power Agreement on Berlin of 1971[7] as the end of a perennial crisis that on at least three occasions brought the world to the brink of doom.

The agreements between the Federal Republic of Germany and the states of Eastern Europe and the related intra-German accords[8] enable Central Europe and the world to breathe easier.

The start of East-West talks on mutual and balanced force reductions[9] demonstrate a determination to deal with military security problems of the continent.

The 1972 treaty between the United States and the Soviet Union to limit anti-ballistic missiles and the interim agreement limiting strategic offensive arms[10] were the first solid breakthroughs in what must be a continuing, long-term process of limiting strategic nuclear arsenals.

I profoundly hope that this Conference will spur further practical and concrete results. It affords a welcome opportunity to widen the circle of those countries involved in easing tensions between East and West.

Participation in the work of détente and participation in the benefits of détente must be everybody's business—in Europe and elsewhere. But détente can succeed only if everybody understands what détente actually is.

First, détente is an evolutionary process, not a static condition. Many formidable challenges yet remain.

Second, the success of détente, of the process of détente, depends on new behavior patterns that give life to all our solemn declarations. The goals we are stating today are the yardstick by which our performance will be measured.

The people of all Europe, and, I assure you, the people of North America are thoroughly tired of having their hopes raised and then shattered by empty words and unfulfilled pledges. We had better say what we mean and mean what we say, or we will have the anger of our citizens to answer.

[7]*AFR, 1971*: 162-70; same, *1972*: 158-62.
[8]*AFR, 1971*: 163-4; same, *1972*: 148 and 173-4.
[9]*AFR, 1973*: 552-3 and 557-63.
[10]*AFR, 1972*: 89-101; cf. notes 11 and 12 to Chapter 13.

While we must not expect miracles, we can and we do expect steady progress that comes in steps—steps that are related to each other that link our actions with words in various areas of our relations.

Finally, there must be an acceptance of mutual obligation. Détente, as I have often said, must be a two-way street. Tensions cannot be eased by one side alone. Both sides must want détente and work to achieve it. Both sides must benefit from it.

Mr. Chairman, my colleagues, this extraordinary gathering in Helsinki proves that all our peoples share a concern for Europe's future and for a better and more peaceful world. But what else does it prove? How shall we assess the results?

Our delegations have worked long and hard to produce documents which restate noble and praiseworthy political principles. They spell out guidelines for national behavior and international cooperation.

But every signatory should know that if these are to be more than the latest chapter in a long and sorry volume of unfulfilled declarations, every party must be dedicated to making them come true.

These documents which we will sign represent another step—how long or short a step only time will tell—in the process of détente and reconciliation in Europe. Our peoples will be watching and measuring our progress. They will ask how these noble sentiments are being translated into actions that bring about a more secure and just order in the daily lives of each of our nations and its citizens.

The documents produced here represent compromises, like all international negotiations, but these principles we have agreed upon are more than the lowest common denominator of governmental positions:

— They affirm the most fundamental human rights: liberty of thought, conscience, and faith; the exercise of civil and political rights; the rights of minorities.

— They call for a freer flow of information, ideas, and people; greater scope for the press, cultural and educational exchange, family reunification, the right to travel and to marriage between nationals of different states; and for the protection of the priceless heritage of our diverse cultures.

— They offer wide areas for greater cooperation: trade, industrial production, science and technology, the environment, transportation, health, space, and the oceans.

— They reaffirm the basic principles of relations between states: nonintervention, sovereign equality, self-determination, territorial integrity, inviolability of frontiers, and the possibility of change by peaceful means.

The United States gladly subscribes to this document because we subscribe to every one of these principles.

Almost 200 years ago, the United States of America was born as a free and independent nation. The descendants of Europeans who proclaimed their independence in America expressed in that declaration "a decent respect for the opinions of mankind" and asserted not only that all men are created equal but they are endowed with inalienable rights to life, liberty, and the pursuit of happiness.

The founders of my country did not merely say that all Americans should have these rights, but all men everywhere should have these rights. And these principles have guided the United States of America throughout its two centuries of nationhood. They have given hopes to millions in Europe and on every continent.

I have been asked why I am here today.

I am here because I believe, and my countrymen believe, in the interdependence of Europe and North America—indeed in the interdependence of the entire family of man.

I am here because the leaders of 34 other governments are here— the states of Europe and of our good neighbor, Canada, with whom we share an open border of 5,526 miles, along which there stands not a single armed soldier and across which our two peoples have moved in friendship and mutual respect for 160 years.

I can say without fear of contradiction that there is not a single people represented here whose blood does not flow in the veins of Americans and whose culture and traditions have not enriched the heritage which we Americans prize so highly.

When two centuries ago the United States of America issued a declaration of high principles, the cynics and doubters of that day jeered and scoffed. Yet, 11 long years later our independence was won and the stability of our Republic was really achieved through the incorporation of the same principles in our Constitution.

But those principles, though they are still being perfected, remain the guiding lights of an American policy. And the American people are still dedicated, as they were then, to a decent respect for the opinions of mankind and to life, liberty, and the pursuit of happiness for all peoples everywhere.

To our fellow participants in this Conference: My presence here symbolizes my country's vital interest in Europe's future. Our future is bound with yours. Our economic well-being, as well as our security, is linked increasingly with yours. The distance of geography is bridged by our common heritage and our common destiny. The United States, therefore, intends to participate fully in the affairs of Europe and in turning the results of this Conference into a living reality.

To America's Allies: We in the West vigorously pursue the course upon which we have embarked together, reenforced by one another's strength and mutual confidence. Stability in Europe requires equilibrium in Europe. Therefore, I assure you that my country will continue to be a concerned and reliable partner. Our partnership is far more than a matter of formal agreements. It is a reflection of beliefs, traditions, and ties that are of deep significance to the American people. We are proud that these values are expressed in this document.

To the countries of the East: The United States considers that the principles on which this Conference has agreed are a part of the great heritage of European civilization, which we all hold in trust for all mankind. To my country, they are not cliches or empty phrases. We take this work and these words very seriously. We will spare no effort to ease tensions and to solve problems between us. But it is important that you recognize the deep devotion of the American people and their Government to human rights and fundamental freedoms and thus to the pledges that this Conference has made regarding the freer movement of people, ideas, information.

In building a political relationship between East and West, we face many challenges.

Berlin has a special significance. It has been a flashpoint of confrontation in the past; it can provide an example of peaceful settlement in the future. The United States regards it as a test of détente and of the principles of this Conference. We welcome the fact that, subject to Four-Power rights and responsibilities, the results of CSCE apply to Berlin as they do throughout Europe.

Military stability in Europe has kept the peace. While maintaining that stability, it is now time to reduce substantially the high levels of military forces on both sides. Negotiations now underway in Vienna on mutual and balanced force reductions so far have not produced the results for which I had hoped. The United States stands ready to demonstrate flexibility in moving these negotiations forward, if others will do the same. An agreement that enhances mutual security is feasible—and essential.

The United States also intends to pursue vigorously a further agreement on strategic arms limitations with the Soviet Union. This remains a priority of American policy. General Secretary Brezhnev and I agreed last November in Vladivostok on the essentials of a new accord limiting strategic offensive weapons for the next 10 years.[11] We are moving forward in our bilateral discussions here in Helsinki.

[11] *AFR, 1974*: 506-9; cf. note 14 to Chapter 13.

The world faces an unprecedented danger in the spread of nuclear weapons technology. The nations of Europe share a great responsibility for an international solution to this problem. The benefits of peaceful nuclear energy are becoming more and more important. We must find ways to spread these benefits while safeguarding the world against the menace of weapons proliferation.

To the other nations of Europe represented at this Conference: We value the work you have done here to help bring all of Europe together. Your right to live in peace and independence is one of the major goals of our effort. Your continuing contribution will be indispensable.

To those nations not participating and to all the peoples of the world: The solemn obligation undertaken in these documents to promote fundamental rights, economic and social progress, and well-being, applies ultimately to all peoples.

Can we truly speak of peace and security without addressing the spread of nuclear weapons in the world or the creation of more sophisticated forms of warfare?

Can peace be divisible between areas of tranquillity and regions of conflict?

Can Europe truly flourish if we do not all address ourselves to the evil of hunger in countries less fortunate than we?

— To the new dimensions of economic and energy issues that underline our own progress?

— To the dialog between producers and consumers, between exporters and importers, between industrial countries and less developed ones?

— And can there be stability and progress in the absence of justice and fundamental freedoms?

Our people want a better future. Their expectations have been raised by the very real steps that have already been taken—in arms control, political negotiations, and expansion of contacts and economic relations. Our presence here offers them further hope. We must not let them down.

If the Soviet Union and the United States can reach agreement so that our astronauts can fit together the most intricate scientific equipment, work together and shake hands 137 miles out in space, we as statesmen have an obligation to do as well on Earth.

History will judge this Conference not by what we say here today, but by what we do tomorrow—not by the promises we make, but by the promises we keep.

Thank you very much, Mr. Chairman.

(42)   Final Act of the Conference, Signed in Helsinki August 1, 1975.[12]

CONFERENCE ON SECURITY
AND CO-OPERATION IN EUROPE
FINAL ACT

The Conference on Security and Co-operation in Europe, which opened at Helsinki on 3 July 1973 and continued at Geneva from 18 September 1973 to 21 July 1975, was concluded at Helsinki on 1 August 1975 by the High Representatives of Austria, Belgium, Bulgaria, Canada, Cyprus, Czechoslovakia, Denmark, Finland, France, the German Democratic Republic, the Federal Republic of Germany, Greece, the Holy See, Hungary, Iceland, Ireland, Italy, Liechtenstein, Luxembourg, Malta, Monaco, the Netherlands, Norway, Poland, Portugal, Romania, San Marino, Spain, Sweden, Switzerland, Turkey, the Union of Soviet Socialist Republics, the United Kingdom, the United States of America and Yugoslavia.

During the opening and closing stages of the Conference the participants were addressed by the Secretary-General of the United Nations as their guest of honour. The Director-General of UNESCO [United Nations Educational, Scientific and Cultural Organization] and the Executive Secretary of the United Nations Economic Commission for Europe addressed the Conference during its second stage.

During the meetings of the second stage of the Conference, contributions were received, and statements heard, from the following non-participating Mediterranean States on various agenda items: the Democratic and Popular Republic of Algeria, the Arab Republic of Egypt, Israel, the Kingdom of Morocco, the Syrian Arab Republic, Tunisia.

Motivated by the political will, in the interest of peoples, to improve and intensify their relations and to contribute in Europe to peace, security, justice and co-operation as well as to rapprochement among themselves and with the other States of the world,

Determined, in consequence, to give full effect to the results of the Conference and to assure, among their States and throughout Europe, the benefits deriving from those results and thus to broaden, deepen and make continuing and lasting the process of détente,

---

[12]Official English-language text from U.S. Department of State, Bureau of Public Affairs, Office of Media Services, *Conference on Security and Co-operation in Europe: Final Act, Helsinki 1975* (Department of State Publication 8826; Washington: GPO, 1975).

The High Representatives of the participating States have solemnly adopted the following:

QUESTIONS RELATING TO SECURITY IN EUROPE

["Basket One"]

The States participating in the Conference on Security and Co-operation in Europe,

Reaffirming their objective of promoting better relations among themselves and ensuring conditions in which their people can live in true and lasting peace free from any threat to or attempt against their security;

Convinced of the need to exert efforts to make détente both a continuing and an increasingly viable and comprehensive process, universal in scope, and that the implementation of the results of the Conference on Security and Co-operation in Europe will be a major contribution to this process;

Considering that solidarity among peoples, as well as the common purpose of the participating States in achieving the aims as set forth by the Conference on Security and Co-operation in Europe, should lead to the development of better and closer relations among them in all fields and thus to overcoming the confrontation stemming from the character of their past relations, and to better mutual understanding;

Mindful of their common history and recognizing that the existence of elements common to their traditions and values can assist them in developing their relations, and desiring to search, fully taking into account the individuality and diversity of their positions and views, for possibilities of joining their efforts with a view to overcoming distrust and increasing confidence, solving the problems that separate them and co-operating in the interest of mankind;

Recognizing the indivisibility of security in Europe as well as their common interest in the development of co-operation throughout Europe and among themselves and expressing their intention to pursue efforts accordingly;

Recognizing the close link between peace and security in Europe and in the world as a whole and conscious of the need for each of them to make its contribution to the strengthening of world peace and security and to the promotion of fundamental rights, economic and social progress and well-being for all peoples;

Have adopted the following:

1.

(a)   Declaration on Principles Guiding Relations between Participating States

The participating States,

Reaffirming their commitment to peace, security and justice and the continuing development of friendly relations and co-operation;

Recognizing that this commitment, which reflects the interest and aspirations of peoples, constitutes for each participating State a present and future responsibility, heightened by experience of the past;

Reaffirming, in conformity with their membership in the United Nations and in accordance with the purposes and principles of the United Nations, their full and active support for the United Nations and for the enhancement of its role and effectiveness in strengthening international peace, security and justice, and in promoting the solution of international problems, as well as the development of friendly relations and co-operation among States;

Expressing their common adherence to the principles which are set forth below and are in conformity with the Charter of the United Nations, as well as their common will to act, in the application of these principles, in conformity with the purposes and principles of the Charter of the United Nations;

Declare their determination to respect and put into practice, each of them in its relations with all other participating States, irrespective of their political, economic or social systems as well as of their size, geographical location or level of economic development, the following principles, which all are of primary significance, guiding their mutual relations:

I. Sovereign equality, respect for the rights inherent in sovereignty

The participating States will respect each other's sovereign equality and individuality as well as all the rights inherent in and encompassed by its sovereignty, including in particular the right of every State to juridical equality, to territorial integrity and to freedom and political independence. They will also respect each other's right freely to choose and develop its political, social, economic and cultural systems as well as its right to determine its laws and regulations.

Within the framework of international law, all the participating States have equal rights and duties. They will respect each other's right to define and conduct as it wishes its relations with other States in accordance with international law and in the spirit of the present Declaration. They consider that their frontiers can be changed, in accordance with international law, by peaceful means and by agreement. They also have the right to belong or not to belong to international organizations, to be or not to be a party to bilateral or multilateral treaties including the right to be or not to be a party to treaties of alliance; they also have the right to neutrality.

II. Refraining from the threat or use of force

The participating States will refrain in their mutual relations, as well as in their international relations in general, from the threat or use of force against the territorial integrity or political independence of any State, or in any other manner inconsistent with the purposes of the United Nations and with the present Declaration. No consideration may be invoked to serve to warrant resort to the threat or use of force in contravention of this principle.

Accordingly, the participating States will refrain from any acts constituting a threat of force or direct or indirect use of force against another participating State. Likewise they will refrain from any manifestation of force for the purpose of inducing another participating State to renounce the full exercise of its sovereign rights. Likewise they will also refrain in their mutual relations from any act of reprisal by force.

No such threat or use of force will be employed as a means of settling disputes, or questions likely to give rise to disputes, between them.

III. Inviolability of frontiers

The participating States regard as inviolable all one another's frontiers as well as the frontiers of all States in Europe and therefore they will refrain now and in the future from assaulting these frontiers.

Accordingly, they will also refrain from any demand for, or act of, seizure and usurpation of part or all of the territory of any participating State.

IV. Territorial integrity of States

The participating States will respect the territorial integrity of each of the participating States.

Accordingly, they will refrain from any action inconsistent with the purposes and principles of the Charter of the United Nations against the territorial integrity, political independence or the unity of any participating State, and in particular from any such action constituting a threat or use of force.

The participating States will likewise refrain from making each other's territory the object of military occupation or other direct or indirect measures of force in contravention of international law, or the object of acquisition by means of such measures or the threat of them. No such occupation or acquisition will be recognized as legal.

V. Peaceful settlement of disputes

The participating States will settle disputes among them by peaceful means in such a manner as not to endanger international peace and security, and justice.

They will endeavour in good faith and a spirit of co-operation to reach a rapid and equitable solution on the basis of international law.

For this purpose they will use such means as negotiation, enquiry, mediation, conciliation, arbitration, judicial settlement or other peaceful means of their own choice including any settlement procedure agreed to in advance of disputes to which they are parties.

In the event of failure to reach a solution by any of the above peaceful means, the parties to a dispute will continue to seek a mutually agreed way to settle the dispute peacefully.

Participating States, parties to a dispute among them, as well as other participating States, will refrain from any action which might aggravate the situation to such a degree as to endanger the maintenance of international peace and security and thereby make a peaceful settlement of the dispute more difficult.

VI. Non-intervention in internal affairs

The participating States will refrain from any intervention, direct or indirect, individual or collective, in the internal or external affairs falling within the domestic jurisdiction of another participating State, regardless of their mutual relations.

They will accordingly refrain from any form of armed intervention or threat of such intervention against another participating State.

They will likewise in all circumstances refrain from any other act of military, or of political, economic or other coercion designed to subordinate to their own interest the exercise by another participating State of the rights inherent in its sovereignty and thus to secure advantages of any kind.

Accordingly, they will, inter alia, refrain from direct or indirect assistance to terrorist activities, or to subversive or other activities directed towards the violent overthrow of the regime of another participating State.

VII. Respect for human rights and fundamental freedoms, including the freedom of thought, conscience, religion or belief

The participating States will respect human rights and fundamental freedoms, including the freedom of thought, conscience, religion or belief, for all without distinction as to race, sex, language or religion.

They will promote and encourage the effective exercise of civil, political, economic, social, cultural and other rights and freedoms all of which derive from the inherent dignity of the human person and are essential for his free and full development.

Within this framework the participating States will recognize and respect the freedom of the individual to profess and practise, alone or in community with others, religion or belief acting in accordance with the dictates of his own conscience.

The participating States on whose territory national minorities exist will respect the right of persons belonging to such minorities to equality before the law, will afford them the full opportunity for the actual enjoyment of human rights and fundamental freedoms and will, in this manner, protect their legitimate interests in this sphere.

The participating States recognize the universal significance of human rights and fundamental freedoms, respect for which is an essential factor for the peace, justice and well-being necessary to ensure the development of friendly relations and co-operation among themselves as among all States.

They will constantly respect these rights and freedoms in their mutual relations and will endeavour jointly and separately, including in co-operation with the United Nations, to promote universal and effective respect for them.

They confirm the right of the individual to know and act upon his rights and duties in this field.

In the field of human rights and fundamental freedoms, the participating States will act in conformity with the purposes and principles of the Charter of the United Nations and with the Universal Declaration of Human Rights.[13] They will also fulfil their obliga-

[13]General Assembly Resolution 217 A (III), Dec. 10, 1948; text in *Documents, 1948*: 430-35.

tions as set forth in the international declarations and agreements in this field, including inter alia the International Covenants on Human Rights,[14] by which they may be bound.

VIII. Equal rights and self-determination of peoples

The participating States will respect the equal rights of peoples and their right to self-determination, acting at all times in conformity with the purposes and principles of the Charter of the United Nations and with the relevant norms of international law, including those relating to territorial integrity of States.

By virtue of the principle of equal rights and self-determination of peoples, all peoples always have the right, in full freedom, to determine, when and as they wish, their internal and external political status, without external interference, and to pursue as they wish their political, economic, social and cultural development.

The participating States reaffirm the universal significance of respect for and effective exercise of equal rights and self-determination of peoples for the development of friendly relations among themselves as among all States; they also recall the importance of the elimination of any form of violation of this principle.

IX. Co-operation among States

The participating States will develop their co-operation with one another and with all States in all fields in accordance with the purposes and principles of the Charter of the United Nations. In developing their co-operation the participating States will place special emphasis on the fields as set forth within the framework of the Conference on Security and Co-operation in Europe, with each of them making its contribution in conditions of full equality.

They will endeavour, in developing their co-operation as equals, to promote mutual understanding and confidence, friendly and good-neighbourly relations among themselves, international peace, security and justice. They will equally endeavour, in developing their co-operation, to improve the well-being of peoples and contribute to the fulfilment of their aspirations through, inter alia, the benefits resulting from increased mutual knowledge and from progress and achievement in the economic, scientific, technologi-

[14]International Covenant on Civil and Political Rights, adopted by U.N. General Assembly Dec. 16, 1966 and entered into force Mar. 23, 1976; International Covenant on Economic, Social and Cultural Rights, adopted by the U.N. General Assembly Dec. 16, 1966 and entered into force Jan. 3, 1976. (Neither covenant had been signed by the U.S. as of mid-1977.)

cal, social, cultural and humanitarian fields. They will take steps to promote conditions favourable to making these benefits available to all; they will take into account the interest of all in the narrowing of differences in the levels of economic development, and in particular the interest of developing countries throughout the world.

They confirm that governments, institutions, organizations and persons have a relevant and positive role to play in contributing toward the achievement of these aims of their co-operation.

They will strive, in increasing their co-operation as set forth above, to develop closer relations among themselves on an improved and more enduring basis for the benefit of peoples.

X. Fulfilment in good faith of obligations under international law

The participating States will fulfil in good faith their obligations under international law, both those obligations arising from the generally recognized principles and rules of international law and those obligations arising from treaties or other agreements, in conformity with international law, to which they are parties.

In exercising their sovereign rights, including the right to determine their laws and regulations, they will conform with their legal obligations under international law; they will furthermore pay due regard to and implement the provisions in the Final Act of the Conference on Security and Co-operation in Europe.

The participating States confirm that in the event of a conflict between the obligations of the members of the United Nations under the Charter of the United Nations and their obligations under any treaty or other international agreement, their obligations under the Charter will prevail, in accordance with Article 103 of the Charter of the United Nations.

All the principles set forth above are of primary significance and, accordingly, they will be equally and unreservedly applied, each of them being interpreted taking into account the others.

The participating States express their determination fully to respect and apply these principles, as set forth in the present Declaration, in all aspects, to their mutual relations and co-operation in order to ensure to each participating State the benefits resulting from the respect and application of these principles by all.

The participating States, paying due regard to the principles above and, in particular, to the first sentence of the tenth principle, "Fulfilment in good faith of obligations under international law", note that the present Declaration does not affect their rights and obligations, nor the corresponding treaties and other agreements and arrangements.

The participating States express the conviction that respect for these principles will encourage the development of normal and friendly relations and the progress of co-operation among them in all fields. They also express the conviction that respect for these principles will encourage the development of political contacts among them which in turn would contribute to better mutual understanding of their positions and views.

The participating States declare their intention to conduct their relations with all other States in the spirit of the principles contained in the present Declaration.

(b) Matters related to giving effect to certain of the above Principles

(i) The participating States,

Reaffirming that they will respect and give effect to refraining from the threat or use of force and convinced of the necessity to make it an effective norm of international life,

Declare that they are resolved to respect and carry out, in their relations with one another, inter alia, the following provisions which are in conformity with the Declaration on Principles Guiding Relations between Participating States:

— To give effect and expression, by all the ways and forms which they consider appropriate, to the duty to refrain from the threat or use of force in their relations with one another.
— To refrain from any use of armed forces inconsistent with the purposes and principles of the Charter of the United Nations and the provisions of the Declaration on Principles Guiding Relations between Participating States, against another participating State, in particular from invasion of or attack on its territory.
— To refrain from any manifestation of force for the purpose of inducing another participating State to renounce the full exercise of its sovereign rights.
— To refrain from any act of economic coercion designed to subordinate to their own interest the exercise by another participating State of the rights inherent in its sovereignty and thus to secure advantages of any kind.
— To take effective measures which by their scope and by their nature constitute steps towards the ultimate achievement of general and complete disarmament under strict and effective international control.
— To promote, by all means which each of them considers

appropriate, a climate of confidence and respect among peoples consonant with their duty to refrain from propaganda for wars of aggression or for any threat or use of force inconsistent with the purposes of the United Nations and with the Declaration on Principles Guiding Relations between Participating States, against another participating State.

— To make every effort to settle exclusively by peaceful means any dispute between them, the continuance of which is likely to endanger the maintenance of international peace and security in Europe, and to seek, first of all, a solution through the peaceful means set forth in Article 33 of the United Nations Charter.

— To refrain from any action which could hinder the peaceful settlement of disputes between the participating States.

(ii) The participating States,

Reaffirming their determination to settle their disputes as set forth in the Principle of Peaceful Settlement of Disputes;

Convinced that the peaceful settlement of disputes is a complement to refraining from the threat or use of force, both being essential though not exclusive factors for the maintenance and consolidation of peace and security;

Desiring to reinforce and to improve the methods at their disposal for the peaceful settlement of disputes;

1. Are resolved to pursue the examination and elaboration of a generally acceptable method for the peaceful settlement of disputes aimed at complementing existing methods, and to continue to this end to work upon the "Draft Convention on a European System for the Peaceful Settlement of Disputes" submitted by Switzerland during the second stage of the Conference on Security and Co-operation in Europe, as well as other proposals relating to it and directed towards the elaboration of such a method.

2. Decide that, on the invitation of Switzerland, a meeting of experts of all the participating States will be convoked in order to fulfil the mandate described in paragraph 1 above within the framework and under the procedures of the follow-up to the Conference laid down in the chapter "Follow-up to the Conference".

3. This meeting of experts will take place after the meeting of the representatives appointed by the Ministers of Foreign Affairs of the participating States, scheduled according to the chapter "Follow-up to the Conference" for 1977; the results of the work of this meeting of experts will be submitted to Governments.

2.

Document on confidence-building measures
and certain aspects of security and disarmament

The participating States,

Desirous of eliminating the causes of tension that may exist among them and thus of contributing to the strengthening of peace and security in the world;

Determined to strengthen confidence among them and thus to contribute to increasing stability and security in Europe;

Determined further to refrain in their mutual relations, as well as in their international relations in general, from the threat or use of force against the territorial integrity or political independence of any State, or in any other manner inconsistent with the purposes of the United Nations and with the Declaration on Principles Guiding Relations between Participating States as adopted in this Final Act;

Recognizing the need to contribute to reducing the dangers of armed conflict and of misunderstanding or miscalculation of military activities which could give rise to apprehension, particularly in a situation where the participating States lack clear and timely information about the nature of such activities;

Taking into account considerations relevant to efforts aimed at lessening tension and promoting disarmament;

Recognizing that the exchange of observers by invitation at military manoeuvres will help to promote contacts and mutual understanding;

Having studied the question of prior notification of major military movements in the context of confidence-building;

Recognizing that there are other ways in which individual States can contribute further to their common objectives;

Convinced of the political importance of prior notification of major military manoeuvres for the promotion of mutual understanding and the strengthening of confidence, stability and security;

Accepting the responsibility of each of them to promote these objectives and to implement this measure, in accordance with the accepted criteria and modalities, as essentials for the realization of these objectives;

Recognizing that this measure deriving from political decision rests upon a voluntary basis;

Have adopted the following:

I

Prior notification of major military manoeuvres

They will notify their major military manoeuvres to all other participating States through usual diplomatic channels in accordance with the following provisions:

Notification will be given of major military manoeuvres exceeding a total of 25,000 troops, independently or combined with any possible air or naval components (in this context the word "troops" includes amphibious and airborne troops). In the case of independent manoeuvres of amphibious or airborne troops, or of combined manoeuvres involving them, these troops will be included in this total. Furthermore, in the case of combined manoeuvres which do not reach the above total but which involve land forces together with significant numbers of either amphibious or airborne troops, or both, notification can also be given.

Notification will be given of major military manoeuvres which take place on the territory, in Europe, of any participating State as well as, if applicable, in the adjoining sea area and air space.

In the case of a participating State whose territory extends beyond Europe, prior notification need be given only of manoeuvres which take place in an area within 250 kilometres from its frontier facing or shared with any other European participating State, the participating State need not, however, give notification in cases in which that area is also contiguous to the participating State's frontier facing or shared with a non-European non-participating State.

Notification will be given 21 days or more in advance of the start of the manoeuvre or in the case of a manoeuvre arranged at shorter notice at the earliest possible opportunity prior to its starting date.

Notification will contain information of the designation, if any, the general purpose of and the States involved in the manoeuvre, the type or types and numerical strength of the forces engaged, the area and estimated time-frame of its conduct. The participating States will also, if possible, provide additional relevant information, particularly that related to the components of the forces engaged and the period of involvement of these forces.

Prior notification of other military manoeuvres

The participating States recognize that they can contribute further to strengthening confidence and increasing security and stability, and to this end may also notify smaller-scale military manoeuvres to other participating States, with special regard for those near the area of such manoeuvres.

To the same end, the participating States also recognize that they may notify other military manoeuvres conducted by them.

Exchange of observers

The participating States will invite other participating States, voluntarily and on a bilateral basis, in a spirit of reciprocity and goodwill towards all participating States, to send observers to attend military manoeuvres.

The inviting State will determine in each case the number of observers, the procedures and conditions of their participation, and give other information which it may consider useful. It will provide appropriate facilities and hospitality.

The invitation will be given as far ahead as is conveniently possible through usual diplomatic channels.

Prior notification of major military movements

In accordance with the Final Recommendations of the Helsinki Consultations[15] the participating States studied the question of prior notification of major military movements as a measure to strengthen confidence.

Accordingly, the participating States recognize that they may, at their own discretion and with a view to contributing to confidence-building, notify their major military movements.

In the same spirit, further consideration will be given by the States participating in the Conference on Security and Co-operation in Europe to the question of prior notification of major military movements, bearing in mind, in particular, the experience gained by the implementation of the measures which are set forth in this document.

Other confidence-building measures

The participating States recognize that there are other means by which their common objectives can be promoted.

In particular, they will, with due regard to reciprocity and with a view to better mutual understanding, promote exchanges by invitation among their military personnel, including visits by military delegations.

* * *

[15]*Bulletin*, 69: 181-8 (1973).

In order to make a fuller contribution to their common objective of confidence-building, the participating States, when conducting their military activities in the area covered by the provisions for the prior notification of major military manoeuvres, will duly take into account and respect this objective.

They also recognize that the experience gained by the implementation of the provisions set forth above, together with further efforts, could lead to developing and enlarging measures aimed at strengthening confidence.

II

Questions relating to disarmament

The participating States recognize the interest of all of them in efforts aimed at lessening military confrontation and promoting disarmament which are designed to complement political détente in Europe and to strengthen their security. They are convinced of the necessity to take effective measures in these fields which by their scope and by their nature constitute steps towards the ultimate achievement of general and complete disarmament under strict and effective international control, and which should result in strengthening peace and security throughout the world.

III

General considerations

Having considered the views expressed on various subjects related to the strengthening of security in Europe through joint efforts aimed at promoting détente and disarmament, the participating States, when engaged in such efforts, will, in this context, proceed, in particular, from the following essential considerations:

—The complementary nature of the political and military aspects of security;

—The interrelation between the security of each participating State and security in Europe as a whole and the relationship which exists, in the broader context of world security, between security in Europe and security in the Mediterranean area;

—Respect for the security interests of all States participating in the Conference on Security and Co-operation in Europe inherent in their sovereign equality;

—The importance that participants in negotiating fora see to it that information about relevant developments, progress and results is provided on an appropriate basis to other States participating in the Conference on Security and Co-operation in Europe and, in return, the justified interest of any of those States in having their views considered.

CO-OPERATION IN THE FIELD OF ECONOMICS, OF SCIENCE AND TECHNOLOGY AND OF THE ENVIRONMENT

["Basket Two"]

The participating States,

Convinced that their efforts to develop co-operation in the fields of trade, industry, science and technology, the environment and other areas of economic activity contribute to the reinforcement of peace and security in Europe and in the world as a whole,

Recognizing that co-operation in these fields would promote economic and social progress and the improvement of the conditions of life,

Aware of the diversity of their economic and social systems,

Reaffirming their will to intensify such co-operation between one another, irrespective of their systems,

Recognizing that such co-operation, with due regard for the different levels of economic development, can be developed, on the basis of equality and mutual satisfaction of the partners, and of reciprocity permitting, as a whole, an equitable distribution of advantages and obligations of comparable scale, with respect for bilateral and multilateral agreements,

Taking into account the interests of the developing countries throughout the world, including those among the participating countries as long as they are developing from the economic point of view; reaffirming their will to co-operate for the achievement of the aims and objectives established by the appropriate bodies of the United Nations in the pertinent documents concerning development, it being understood that each participating State maintains the positions it has taken on them; giving special attention to the least developed countries,

Convinced that the growing world-wide economic interdependence calls for increasing common and effective efforts towards the solution of major world economic problems such as food, energy, commodities, monetary and financial problems, and therefore emphasizes the need for promoting stable and equitable international economic relations, thus contributing to the continuous and diversified economic development of all countries,

Having taken into account the work already undertaken by relevant international organizations and wishing to take advantage of the possibilities offered by these organizations, in particular by the United Nations Economic Commission for Europe, for giving effect to the provisions of the final documents of the Conference,

Considering that the guidelines and concrete recommendations contained in the following texts are aimed at promoting further development of their mutual economic relations, and convinced that their co-operation in this field should take place in full respect for the principles guiding relations among participating States as set forth in the relevant document,

Have adopted the following:

1. Commercial Exchanges

General provisions

The participating States,

Conscious of the growing role of international trade as one of the most important factors in economic growth and social progress,

Recognizing that trade represents an essential sector of their co-operation, and bearing in mind that the provisions contained in the above preamble apply in particular to this sector,

Considering that the volume and structure of trade among the participating States do not in all cases correspond to the possibilities created by the current level of their economic, scientific and technological development,

are resolved to promote, on the basis of the modalities of their economic co-operation, the expansion of their mutual trade in goods and services, and to ensure conditions favourable to such development;

recognize the beneficial effects which can result for the development of trade from the application of most favoured nation treatment;

will encourage the expansion of trade on as broad a multilateral basis as possible, thereby endeavouring to utilize the various economic and commercial possibilities;

recognize the importance of bilateral and multilateral intergovernmental and other agreements for the long-term development of trade;

note the importance of monetary and financial questions for the development of international trade, and will endeavour to deal with them with a view to contributing to the continuous expansion of trade;

will endeavour to reduce or progressively eliminate all kinds of obstacles to the development of trade;

will foster a steady growth of trade while avoiding as far as possible abrupt fluctuations in their trade;

consider that their trade in various products should be conducted in such a way as not to cause or threaten to cause serious injury— and should the situation arise, market disruption—in domestic markets for these products and in particular to the detriment of domestic producers of like or directly competitive products; as regards the concept of market disruption, it is understood that it should not be invoked in a way inconsistent with the relevant provisions of their international agreements; if they resort to safeguard measures, they will do so in conformity with their commitments in this field arising from international agreements to which they are parties and will take account of the interests of the parties directly concerned;

will give due attention to measures for the promotion of trade and the diversification of its structure;

note that the growth and diversification of trade would contribute to widening the possibilities of choice of products;

consider it appropriate to create favourable conditions for the participation of firms, organizations and enterprises in the development of trade.

Business contacts and facilities

The participating States,

Conscious of the importance of the contribution which an improvement of business contacts, and the accompanying growth of confidence in business relationships, could make to the development of commercial and economic relations,

will take measures further to improve conditions for the expansion of contacts between representatives of official bodies, of the different organizations, enterprises, firms and banks concerned with foreign trade, in particular, where useful, between sellers and users of products and services, for the purpose of studying commercial possibilities, concluding contracts, ensuring their implementation and providing after-sales services;

will encourage organizations, enterprises and firms concerned with foreign trade to take measures to accelerate the conduct of business negotiations;

will further take measures aimed at improving working conditions of representatives of foreign organizations, enterprises, firms and banks concerned with external trade, particularly as follows:

—by providing the necessary information, including information on legislation and procedures relating to the establishment and operation of permanent representation by the above mentioned bodies;

—by examining as favourably as possible requests for the establishment of permanent representation and of offices for this purpose, including, where appropriate, the opening of joint offices by two or more firms;

—by encouraging the provision, on conditions as favourable as possible and equal for all representatives of the above-mentioned bodies, of hotel accommodation, means of communication, and of other facilities normally required by them, as well as of suitable business and residential premises for purposes of permanent representation;

recognize the importance of such measures to encourage greater participation by small and medium sized firms in trade between participating States.

Economic and commercial information

The participating States,

Conscious of the growing role of economic and commercial information in the development of international trade,

Considering that economic information should be of such a nature as to allow adequate market analysis and to permit the preparation of medium and long term forecasts, thus contributing to the establishment of a continuing flow of trade and a better utilization of commercial possibilities,

Expressing their readiness to improve the quality and increase the quantity and supply of economic and relevant administrative information,

Considering that the value of statistical information on the international level depends to a considerable extent on the possibility of its comparability,

will promote the publication and dissemination of economic and commercial information at regular intervals and as quickly as possible, in particular:

—statistics concerning production, national income, budget, consumption and productivity;

—foreign trade statistics drawn up on the basis of comparable classification including breakdown by product with indication of volume and value, as well as country of origin or destination;
—laws and regulations concerning foreign trade;
—information allowing forecasts of development of the economy to assist in trade promotion, for example, information on the general orientation of national economic plans and programmes;
—other information to help businessmen in commercial contacts, for example, periodic directories, lists, and where possible, organizational charts of firms and organizations concerned with foreign trade;

will in addition to the above encourage the development of the exchange of economic and commercial information through, where appropriate, joint commissions for economic, scientific and technical co-operation, national and joint chambers of commerce, and other suitable bodies;

will support a study, in the framework of the United Nations Economic Commission for Europe, of the possibilities of creating a multilateral system of notification of laws and regulations concerning foreign trade and changes therein;

will encourage international work on the harmonization of statistical nomenclatures, notably in the United Nations Economic Commission for Europe.

Marketing

The participating States,

Recognizing the importance of adapting production to the requirements of foreign markets in order to ensure the expansion of international trade,

Conscious of the need of exporters to be as fully familiar as possible with and take account of the requirements of potential users,

will encourage organizations, enterprises and firms concerned with foreign trade to develop further the knowledge and techniques required for effective marketing;

will encourage the improvement of conditions for the implementation of measures to promote trade and to satisfy the needs of users in respect of imported products, in particular through market research and advertising measures as well as, where useful, the establishment of supply facilities, the furnishing of spare parts, the functioning of after sales services, and the training of the necessary local technical personnel;

will encourage international co-operation in the field of trade promotion, including marketing, and the work undertaken on these subjects within the international bodies, in particular the United Nations Economic Commission for Europe.

2. Industrial co-operation and projects of common interest

Industrial co-operation

The participating States,

Considering that industrial co-operation, being motivated by economic considerations, can

—create lasting ties thus strengthening long-term overall economic co-operation,
—contribute to economic growth as well as to the expansion and diversification of international trade and to a wider utilization of modern technology,
—lead to the mutually advantageous utilization of economic complementarities through better use of all factors of production, and
—accelerate the industrial development of all those who take part in such co-operation,

propose to encourage the development of industrial co-operation between the competent organizations, enterprises and firms of their countries;

consider that industrial co-operation may be facilitated by means of intergovernmental and other bilateral and multilateral agreements between the interested parties;

note that in promoting industrial co-operation they should bear in mind the economic structures and the development levels of their countries;

note that industrial co-operation is implemented by means of contracts concluded between competent organizations, enterprises and firms on the basis of economic considerations;

express their willingness to promote measures designed to create favourable conditions for industrial co-operation;

recognize that industrial co-operation covers a number of forms of economic relations going beyond the framework of conventional trade, and that in concluding contracts on industrial co-operation the partners will determine jointly the appropriate forms and conditions of co-operation, taking into account their mutual interests and capabilities;

recognize further that, if it is in their mutual interest, concrete forms such as the following may be useful for the development of industrial co-operation: joint production and sale, specialization in production and sale, construction, adaptation and modernization of industrial plants, co-operation for the setting up of complete industrial installations with a view to thus obtaining part of the resultant products, mixed companies, exchanges of "know-how", of technical information, of patents and of licences, and joint industrial research within the framework of specific co-operation projects;

recognize that new forms of industrial co-operation can be applied with a view to meeting specific needs;

note the importance of economic, commercial, technical and administrative information such as to ensure the development of industrial co-operation;

Consider it desirable:

—to improve the quality and the quantity of information relevant to industrial co-operation, in particular the laws and regulations, including those relating to foreign exchange, general orientation of national economic plans and programmes as well as programme priorities and economic conditions of the market; and
—to disseminate as quickly as possible published documentation thereon;

will encourage all forms of exchange of information and communication of experience relevant to industrial co-operation, including through contacts between potential partners and, where appropriate, through joint commissions for economic, industrial, scientific and technical co-operation, national and joint chambers of commerce, and other suitable bodies;

consider it desirable, with a view to expanding industrial co-operation, to encourage the exploration of co-operation possibilities and the implementation of co-operation projects and will take measures to this end, *inter alia*, by facilitating and increasing all forms of business contacts between competent organizations, enterprises and firms and between their respective qualified personnel;

note that the provisions adopted by the Conference relating to business contacts in the economic and commercial fields also apply to foreign organizations, enterprises and firms engaged in industrial co-operation, taking into account the specific conditions of this co-operation, and will endeavour to ensure, in particular, the existence of appropriate working conditions for personnel engaged in the implementation of co-operation projects;

consider it desirable that proposals for industrial co-operation projects should be sufficiently specific and should contain the necessary economic and technical data, in particular preliminary estimates of the cost of the project, information on the form of co-operation envisaged, and market possibilities, to enable potential partners to proceed with initial studies and to arrive at decisions in the shortest possible time;

will encourage the parties concerned with industrial co-operation to take measures to accelerate the conduct of negotiations for the conclusion of co-operation contracts;

recommend further the continued examination—for example within the framework of the United Nations Economic Commission for Europe—of means of improving the provision of information to those concerned on general conditions of industrial co-operation and guidance on the preparation of contracts in this field;

consider it desirable to further improve conditions for the implementation of industrial co-operation projects, in particular with respect to:

—the protection of the interests of the partners in industrial co-operation projects, including the legal protection of the various kinds of property involved;
—the consideration, in ways that are compatible with their economic systems, of the needs and possibilities of industrial co-operation within the framework of economic policy and particularly in national economic plans and programmes;

consider it desirable that the partners, when concluding industrial co-operation contracts, should devote due attention to provisions concerning the extension of the necessary mutual assistance and the provision of the necessary information during the implementation of these contracts, in particular with a view to attaining the required technical level and quality of the products resulting from such co-operation;

recognize the usefulness of an increased participation of small and medium sized firms in industrial co-operation projects.

Projects of common interest

The participating States,

Considering that their economic potential and their natural resources permit, through common efforts, long-term co-operation in the implementation, including at the regional or sub-regional level, of major projects of common interest, and that these may contribute to the speeding-up of the economic development of the countries participating therein,

Considering it desirable that the competent organizations, enterprises and firms of all countries should be given the possibility of indicating their interest in participating in such projects, and, in case of agreement, of taking part in their implementation,

Noting that the provisions adopted by the Conference relating to industrial co-operation are also applicable to projects of common interest,

regard it as necessary to encourage, where appropriate, the investigation by competent and interested organizations, enterprises and firms of the possibilities for the carrying out of projects of common interest in the fields of energy resources and of the exploitation of raw materials, as well as of transport and communications;

regard it as desirable that organizations, enterprises and firms exploring the possibilities of taking part in projects of common interest exchange with their potential partners, through the appropriate channels, the requisite economic, legal, financial and technical information pertaining to these projects;

consider that the fields of energy resources, in particular, petroleum, natural gas and coal, and the extraction and processing of mineral raw materials, in particular, iron ore and bauxite, are suitable ones for strengthening long-term economic co-operation and for the development of trade which could result;

consider that possibilities for projects of common interest with a view to long-term economic co-operation also exist in the following fields:

—exchanges of electrical energy within Europe with a view to utilizing the capacity of the electrical power stations as rationally as possible;

—co-operation in research for new sources of energy and, in particular, in the field of nuclear energy;

—development of road networks and co-operation aimed at establishing a coherent navigable network in Europe;

—co-operation in research and the perfecting of equipment for multimodal transport operations and for the handling of containers;

recommend that the States interested in projects of common interest should consider under what conditions it would be possible to establish them, and if they so desire, create the necessary conditions for their actual implementation.

3. Provisions concerning trade and industrial co-operation

Harmonization of standards

The participating States,

Recognizing the development of international harmonization of standards and technical regulations and of international co-operation in the field of certification as an important means of eliminating technical obstacles to international trade and industrial co-operation, thereby facilitating their development and increasing productivity,

reaffirm their interest to achieve the widest possible international harmonization of standards and technical regulations;

express their readiness to promote international agreements and other appropriate arrangements on acceptance of certificates of conformity with standards and technical regulations;

consider it desirable to increase international co-operation on standardization, in particular by supporting the activities of intergovernmental and other appropriate organizations in this field.

Arbitration

The participating States,

Considering that the prompt and equitable settlement of disputes which may arise from commercial transactions relating to goods and services and contracts for industrial co-operation would contribute to expanding and facilitating trade and co-operation,

Considering that arbitration is an appropriate means of settling such disputes,

recommend, where appropriate, to organizations, enterprises and firms in their countries, to include arbitration clauses in commercial contracts and industrial co-operation contracts, or in special agreements;

recommend that the provisions on arbitration should provide for arbitration under a mutually acceptable set of arbitration rules, and permit arbitration in a third country, taking into account existing intergovernmental and other agreements in this field.

Specific bilateral arrangements

The participating States,

Conscious of the need to facilitate trade and to promote the application of new forms of industrial co-operation,

will consider favourably the conclusion, in appropriate cases, of specific bilateral agreements concerning various problems of mutual interest in the fields of commercial exchanges and industrial co-operation, in particular with a view to avoiding double taxation and to facilitating the transfer of profits and the return of the value of the assets invested.

4. Science and technology

The participating States,

Convinced that scientific and technological co-operation constitutes an important contribution to the strengthening of security and co-operation among them, in that it assists the effective solution of problems of common interest and the improvement of the conditions of human life,

Considering that in developing such co-operation, it is important to promote the sharing of information and experience, facilitating the study and transfer of scientific and technological achievements, as well as the access to such achievements on a mutually advantageous basis and in fields of co-operation agreed between interested parties,

Considering that it is for the potential partners, i.e. the competent organizations, institutions, enterprises, scientists and technologists of the participating States to determine the opportunities for mutually beneficial co-operation and to develop its details,

Affirming that such co-operation can be developed and implemented bilaterally and multilaterally at the governmental and non-governmental levels, for example, through intergovernmental and other agreements, international programmes, co-operative projects and commercial channels, while utilizing also various forms of contacts, including direct and individual contacts,

Aware of the need to take measures further to improve scientific and technological co-operation between them,

Possibilities for Improving Co-operation

Recognize that possibilities exist for further improving scientific and technological co-operation, and to this end, express their intention to remove obstacles to such co-operation, in particular through:

—the improvement of opportunities for the exchange and dissemination of scientific and technological information among the parties interested in scientific and technological research and co-operation including information related to the organization and implementation of such co-operation;
—the expeditious implementation and improvement in organization, including programmes, of international visits of scientists and specialists in connexion with exchanges, conferences and co-operation;
—the wider use of commercial channels and activities for applied scientific and technological research and for the transfer of achievements obtained in this field while providing information on and protection of intellectual and industrial property rights;

Fields of co-operation

Consider that possibilities to expand co-operation exist within the areas given below as examples, noting that it is for potential partners in the participating countries to identify and develop projects and arrangements of mutual interest and benefit:

Agriculture

Research into new methods and technologies for increasing the productivity of crop cultivation and animal husbandry; the application of chemistry to agriculture; the design, construction and utilization of agricultural machinery; technologies of irrigation and other agricultural land improvement works;

Energy

New technologies of production, transport and distribution of energy aimed at improving the use of existing fuels and sources of hydroenergy, as well as research in the field of new energy sources, including nuclear, solar and geothermal energy;

New technologies, rational use of resources

Research on new technologies and equipment designed in particular to reduce energy consumption and to minimize or eliminate waste;

Transport technology

Research on the means of transport and the technology applied to the development and operation of international, national and urban transport networks including container transport as well as transport safety;

Physics

Study of problems in high energy physics and plasma physics; research in the field of theoretical and experimental nuclear physics;

Chemistry

Research on problems in electrochemistry and the chemistry of polymers, of natural products, and of metals and alloys, as well as the development of improved chemical technology, especially materials processing; practical application of the latest achievements of chemistry to industry, construction and other sectors of the economy;

Meteorology and hydrology

Meteorological and hydrological research, including methods of collection, evaluation and transmission of data and their utilization for weather forecasting and hydrology forecasting;

Oceanography

Oceanographic research, including the study of air/sea interactions;

Seismological research

Study and forecasting of earthquakes and associated geological changes; development and research of technology of seism-resisting constructions;

Research on glaciology, permafrost and problems of life under conditions of cold

Research on glaciology and permafrost; transportation and construction technologies; human adaptation to climatic extremes and changes in the living conditions of indigenous populations;

Computer, communication and information technologies

Development of computers as well as of telecommunications and information systems; technology associated with computers and telecommunications, including their use for management systems, for production processes, for automation, for the study of economic problems, in scientific research and for the collection, processing and dissemination of information;

Space research

Space exploration and the study of the earth's natural resources and the natural environment by remote sensing in particular with the assistance of satellites and rocket-probes;

Medicine and public health

Research on cardiovascular, tumour and virus diseases, molecular biology, neurophysiology; development and testing of new drugs; study of contemporary problems of pediatrics, gerontology and the organization and techniques of medical services;

Environmental research

Research on specific scientific and technological problems related to human environment.

Forms and methods of co-operation

Express their view that scientific and technological co-operation should, in particular, employ the following forms and methods:

—exchange and circulation of books, periodicals and other scientific and technological publications and papers among interested organizations, scientific and technological institutions, enterprises and scientists and technologists, as well as participation in international programmes for the abstracting and indexing of publications;

—exchanges and visits as well as other direct contacts and communications among scientists and technologists, on the basis of mutual agreement and other arrangements, for such purposes as consultations, lecturing and conducting research, including the use of laboratories, scientific libraries, and other documentation centres in connexion therewith;

—holding of international and national conferences, symposia, seminars, courses and other meetings of a scientific and technological character, which would include the participation of foreign scientists and technologists;

—joint preparation and implementation of programmes and projects of mutual interest on the basis of consultation and agreement among all parties concerned, including, where possible and appropriate, exchanges of experience and research results, and correlation of research programmes, between scientific and technological research institutions and organizations;

—use of commercial channels and methods for identifying and transferring technological and scientific developments, including the conclusion of mutually beneficial co-operation arrangements between firms and enterprises in fields agreed upon between them and for carrying out, where appropriate, joint research and development programmes and projects;

consider it desirable that periodic exchanges of views and information take place on scientific policy, in particular on general problems of orientation and administration of research and the question of a better use of large-scale scientific and experimental equipment on a co-operative basis;

recommend that, in developing co-operation in the field of science and technology, full use be made of existing practices of bilateral and multilateral co-operation, including that of a regional or sub-regional character, together with the forms and methods of co-operation described in this document;

recommend further that more effective utilization be made of the possibilities and capabilities of existing international organizations, intergovernmental and non-governmental, concerned with science and technology, for improving exchanges of information and experience, as well as for developing other forms of co-operation in fields of common interest, for example:

—in the United Nations Economic Commission for Europe, study of possibilities for expanding multilateral co-operation, taking into account models for projects and research used in various international organizations; and for sponsoring conferences, symposia, and study and working groups such as those which would bring together younger scientists and technologists with eminent specialists in their field;

—through their participation in particular international scientific and technological co-operation programmes, including those of UNESCO and other international organizations, pursuit of continuing progress towards the objectives of such programmes, notably those of UNISIST [World Science Information System] with particular respect to information policy guidance, technical advice, information contributions and data processing.

5. Environment

The participating States,

Affirming that the protection and improvement of the environment, as well as the protection of nature and the rational utilization of its resources in the interests of present and future generations, is one of the tasks of major importance to the well-being of peoples and the economic development of all countries and that many environmental problems, particularly in Europe, can be solved effectively only through close international co-operation,

Acknowledging that each of the participating States, in accordance with the principles of international law, ought to ensure, in a spirit of co-operation, that activities carried out on its territory do not cause degradation of the environment in another State or in areas lying beyond the limits of national jurisdiction,

Considering that the success of any environmental policy presupposes that all population groups and social forces, aware of their responsibilities, help to protect and improve the environment, which necessitates continued and thorough educative action, particularly with regard to youth,

Affirming that experience has shown that economic development and technological progress must be compatible with the protection of the environment and the preservation of historical and cultural values; that damage to the environment is best avoided by preventive measures; and that the ecological balance must be preserved in the exploitation and management of natural resources,

Aims of co-operation

Agree to the following aims of co-operation, in particular:

—to study, with a view to their solution, those environmental problems which, by their nature, are of a multilateral, bilateral, regional or sub-regional dimension; as well as to encourage the development of an interdisciplinary approach to environmental problems;

—to increase the effectiveness of national and international measures for the protection of the environment, by the comparison and, if appropriate, the harmonization of methods of gathering and analyzing facts, by improving the knowledge of pollution phenomena and rational utilization of natural resources, by the exchange of information, by the harmonization of definitions and the adoption, as far as possible, of a common terminology in the field of the environment;

—to take the necessary measures to bring environmental policies closer together and, where appropriate and possible, to harmonize them;

—to encourage, where possible and appropriate, national and international efforts by their interested organizations, enterprises and firms in the development, production and improvement of equipment designed for monitoring, protecting and enhancing the environment.

Fields of co-operation

To attain these aims, the participating States will make use of every suitable opportunity to co-operate in the field of environment and, in particular, within the areas described below as examples:

Control of air pollution

Desulphurization of fossil fuels and exhaust gases; pollution control of heavy metals, particles, aerosols, nitrogen oxides, in particular those emitted by transport, power stations, and other industrial plants; systems and methods of observation and control of air pollution and its effects, including long-range transport of air pollutants;

Water pollution control and fresh water utilization

Prevention and control of water pollution, in particular of transboundary rivers and international lakes; techniques for the improvement of the quality of water and further development of ways and means for industrial and municipal sewage effluent purification; methods of assessment of fresh water resources and the improvement of their utilization, in particular by developing methods of production which are less polluting and lead to less consumption of fresh water;

Protection of the marine environment

Protection of the marine environment of participating States, and especially the Mediterranean Sea, from pollutants emanating from land-based sources and those from ships and other vessels, notably the harmful substances listed in Annexes I and II to the London Convention on the Prevention of Marine Pollution by the

Dumping of Wastes and Other Matters;[16] problems of maintaining marine ecological balances and food chains, in particular such problems as may arise from the exploration and exploitation of biological and mineral resources of the seas and the sea-bed;

Land utilization and soils

Problems associated with more effective use of lands, including land amelioration, reclamation and recultivation; control of soil pollution, water and air erosion, as well as other forms of soil degradation; maintaining and increasing the productivity of soils with due regard for the possible negative effects of the application of chemical fertilizers and pesticides;

Nature conservation and nature reserves

Protection of nature and nature reserves; conservation and maintenance of existing genetic resources, especially rare animal and plant species; conservation of natural ecological systems; establishment of nature reserves and other protected landscapes and areas, including their use for research, tourism, recreation and other purposes;

Improvement of environmental conditions in areas of human settlement

Environmental conditions associated with transport, housing, working areas, urban development and planning, water supply and sewage disposal systems; assessment of harmful effects of noise, and noise control methods; collection, treatment and utilization of wastes, including the recovery and recycling of materials; research on substitutes for non-biodegradable substances;

Fundamental research, monitoring, forecasting and assessment of environmental changes

Study of changes in climate, landscapes and ecological balances under the impact of both natural factors and human activities; forecasting of possible genetic changes in flora and fauna as a result of environmental pollution; harmonization of statistical data, development of scientific concepts and systems of monitoring networks, standardized methods of observation, measurement and assessment of changes in the biosphere; assessment of the effects of

[16]Opened for signature Dec. 29, 1972 and entered into force Sept. 27, 1975 (TIAS 8165; 26 UST 2403).

environmental pollution levels and degradation of the environment upon human health; study and development of criteria and standards for various environmental pollutants and regulation regarding production and use of various products;

Legal and administrative measures

Legal and administrative measures for the protection of the environment including procedures for establishing environmental impact assessments.

Forms and methods of co-operation

The participating States declare that problems relating to the protection and improvement of the environment will be solved on both a bilateral and a multilateral, including regional and subregional, basis, making full use of existing patterns and forms of co-operation. They will develop co-operation in the field of the environment in particular by taking into consideration the Stockholm Declaration on the Human Environment,[17] relevant resolutions of the United Nations General Assembly and the United Nations Economic Commission for Europe Prague symposium on environmental problems.

The participating States are resolved that co-operation in the field of the environment will be implemented in particular through:

—exchanges of scientific and technical information, documentation and research results, including information on the means of determining the possible effects on the environment of technical and economic activities;
—organization of conferences, symposia and meetings of experts;
—exchanges of scientists, specialists and trainees;
—joint preparation and implementation of programmes and projects for the study and solution of various problems of environmental protection;
—harmonization, where appropriate and necessary, of environmental protection standards and norms, in particular with the object of avoiding possible difficulties in trade which may arise from efforts to resolve ecological problems of production processes and which relate to the achievement of certain environmental qualities in manufactured products;
—consultations on various aspects of environmental protection, as agreed upon among countries concerned, especially in con-

[17]*AFR, 1972*: 470-75.

nexion with problems which could have international consequences.

The participating States will further develop such co-operation by:

—promoting the progressive development, codification and implementation of international law as one means of preserving and enhancing the human environment, including principles and practices, as accepted by them, relating to pollution and other environmental damage caused by activities within the jurisdiction or control of their States affecting other countries and regions;
—supporting and promoting the implementation of relevant international Conventions to which they are parties, in particular those designed to prevent and combat marine and fresh water pollution, recommending States to ratify Conventions which have already been signed, as well as considering possibilities of accepting other appropriate Conventions to which they are not parties at present;
—advocating the inclusion, where appropriate and possible, of the various areas of co-operation into the programmes of work of the United Nations Economic Commission for Europe, supporting such co-operation within the framework of the Commission and of the United Nations Environment Programme, and taking into account the work of other competent international organizations of which they are members;
—making wider use, in all types of co-operation, of information already available from national and international sources, including internationally agreed criteria, and utilizing the possibilities and capabilities of various competent international organizations.

The participating States agree on the following recommendations on specific measures:

—to develop through international co-operation an extensive programme for the monitoring and evaluation of the long-range transport of air pollutants, starting with sulphur dioxide and with possible extension to other pollutants, and to this end to take into account basic elements of a co-operation programme which were identified by the experts who met in Oslo in December 1974 at the invitation of the Norwegian Institute of Air Research;
—to advocate that within the framework of the United Nations

Economic Commission for Europe a study be carried out of procedures and relevant experience relating to the activities of Governments in developing the capabilities of their countries to predict adequately environmental consequences of economic activities and technological development.

6. Co-operation in other areas

Development of transport

The participating States,

Considering that the improvement of the conditions of transport constitutes one of the factors essential to the development of co-operation among them,

Considering that it is necessary to encourage the development of transport and the solution of existing problems by employing appropriate national and international means,

Taking into account the work being carried out on these subjects by existing international organizations, especially by the Inland Transport Committee of the United Nations Economic Commission for Europe,

note that the speed of technical progress in the various fields of transport makes desirable a development of co-operation and an increase in exchanges of information among them;

declare themselves in favour of a simplification and a harmonization of administrative formalities in the field of international transport, in particular at frontiers;

consider it desirable to promote, while allowing for their particular national circumstances in this sector, the harmonization of administrative and technical provisions concerning safety in road, rail, river, air and sea transport;

express their intention to encourage the development of international inland transport of passengers and goods as well as the possibilities of adequate participation in such transport on the basis of reciprocal advantage;

declare themselves in favour, with due respect for their rights and international commitments, of the elimination of disparities arising from the legal provisions applied to traffic on inland waterways which are subject to international conventions and, in particular, of the disparity in the application of those provisions; and to this end invite the member States of the Central Commission for the Navigation of the Rhine, of the Danube Commission and of other bodies to develop the work and studies now being carried out, in particular within the United Nations Economic Commission for Europe;

express their willingness, with a view to improving international rail transport and with due respect for their rights and international commitments, to work towards the elimination of difficulties arising from disparities in existing international legal provisions governing the reciprocal railway transport of passengers and goods between their territories;

express the desire for intensification of the work being carried out by existing international organizations in the field of transport, especially that of the Inland Transport Committee of the United Nations Economic Commission for Europe, and express their intention to contribute thereto by their efforts;

consider that examination by the participating States of the possibility of their accession to the different conventions or to membership of international organizations specializing in transport matters, as well as their efforts to implement conventions when ratified, could contribute to the strengthening of their co-operation in this field.

Promotion of tourism

The participating States,

Aware of the contribution made by international tourism to the development of mutual understanding among peoples, to increased knowledge of other countries' achievements in various fields, as well as to economic, social and cultural progress,

Recognizing the interrelationship between the development of tourism and measures taken in other areas of economic activity,

express their intention to encourage increased tourism on both an individual and group basis in particular by:

—encouraging the improvement of the tourist infrastructure and co-operation in this field;

—encouraging the carrying out of joint tourist projects including technical co-operation, particularly where this is suggested by territorial proximity and the convergence of tourist interests;

—encouraging the exchange of information, including relevant laws and regulations, studies, data and documentation relating to tourism, and by improving statistics with a view to facilitating their comparability;

—dealing in a positive spirit with questions connected with the allocation of financial means for tourist travel abroad, having

regard to their economic possibilities, as well as with those connected with the formalities required for such travel, taking into
account other provisions on tourism adopted by the Conference;
—facilitating the activities of foreign travel agencies and
passenger transport companies in the promotion of international
tourism;
—encouraging tourism outside the high season;
—examining the possibilities of exchanging specialists and
students in the field of tourism, with a view to improving their
qualifications;
—promoting conferences and symposia on the planning and
development of tourism;

consider it desirable to carry out in the appropriate international
framework, and with the co-operation of the relevant national
bodies, detailed studies on tourism, in particular:

—a comparative study on the status and activities of travel agencies as well as on ways and means of achieving better co-operation among them;
—a study of the problems raised by the seasonal concentration
of vacations, with the ultimate objective of encouraging tourism
outside peak periods;
—studies of the problems arising in areas where tourism has in-
jured the environment;

consider also that interested parties might wish to study the
following questions:

—uniformity of hotel classification; and
—tourist routes comprising two or more countries;

will endeavour, where possible, to ensure that the development
of tourism does not injure the environment and the artistic, historic
and cultural heritage in their respective countries;
will pursue their co-operation in the field of tourism bilaterally
and multilaterally with a view to attaining the above objectives.

Economic and social aspects of migrant labour

The participating States,

Considering that the movements of migrant workers in Europe have reached substantial proportions, and that they constitute an important economic, social and human factor for host countries as well as for countries of origin,

Recognizing that workers' migrations have also given rise to a number of economic, social, human and other problems in both the receiving countries and the countries of origin,

Taking due account of the activities of the competent international organizations, more particularly the International Labour Organisation, in this area,

are of the opinion that the problems arising bilaterally from the migration of workers in Europe as well as between the participating States should be dealt with by the parties directly concerned, in order to resolve these problems in their mutual interest, in the light of the concern of each State involved to take due account of the requirements resulting from its socio-economic situation, having regard to the obligation of each State to comply with the bilateral and multilateral agreements to which it is party, and with the following aims in view:

to encourage the efforts of the countries of origin directed towards increasing the possibilities of employment for their nationals in their own territories, in particular by developing economic co-operation appropriate for this purpose and suitable for the host countries and the countries of origin concerned;

to ensure, through collaboration between the host country and the country of origin, the conditions under which the orderly movement of workers might take place, while at the same time protecting their personal and social welfare and, if appropriate, to organize the recruitment of migrant workers and the provision of elementary language and vocational training;

to ensure equality of rights between migrant workers and nationals of the host countries with regard to conditions of employment and work and to social security, and to endeavour to ensure that migrant workers may enjoy satisfactory living conditions, especially housing conditions;

to endeavour to ensure, as far as possible, that migrant workers may enjoy the same opportunities as nationals of the host countries of finding other suitable employment in the event of unemployment;

to regard with favour the provision of vocational training to migrant workers and, as far as possible, free instruction in the language of the host country, in the framework of their employment;

to confirm the right of migrant workers to receive, as far as possible, regular information in their own language, covering both their country of origin and the host country;

to ensure that the children of migrant workers established in the host country have access to the education usually given there, under the same conditions as the children of that country and, furthermore, to permit them to receive supplementary education in their own language, national culture, history and geography;

to bear in mind that migrant workers, particularly those who have acquired qualifications, can by returning to their countries after a certain period of time help to remedy any deficiency of skilled labour in their country of origin;

to facilitate, as far as possible, the reuniting of migrant workers with their families;

to regard with favour the efforts of the countries of origin to attract the savings of migrant workers, with a view to increasing, within the framework of their economic development, appropriate opportunities for employment, thereby facilitating the reintegration of these workers on their return home.

Training of personnel

The participating States,

Conscious of the importance of the training and advanced training of professional staff and technicians for the economic development of every country,

declare themselves willing to encourage co-operation in this field notably by promoting exchange of information on the subject of institutions, programmes and methods of training and advanced training open to professional staff and technicians in the various sectors of economic activity and especially in those of management, public planning, agriculture and commercial and banking techniques;

consider that it is desirable to develop, under mutually acceptable conditions, exchanges of professional staff and technicians, particularly through training activities, of which it would be left to the competent and interested bodies in the participating States to discuss the modalities—duration, financing, education and qualification levels of potential participants;

declare themselves in favour of examining, through appropriate channels, the possibilities of co-operating on the organization and carrying out of vocational training on the job, more particularly in professions involving modern techniques.

QUESTIONS RELATING TO SECURITY AND
CO-OPERATION IN THE MEDITERRANEAN

The participating States,

Conscious of the geographical, historical, cultural, economic and political aspects of their relationship with the non-participating Mediterranean States,

Convinced that security in Europe is to be considered in the broader context of world security and is closely linked with security in the Mediterranean area as a whole, and that accordingly the process of improving security should not be confined to Europe but should extend to other parts of the world, and in particular to the Mediterranean area,

Believing that the strengthening of security and the intensification of co-operation in Europe would stimulate positive processes in the Mediterranean region, and expressing their intention to contribute towards peace, security and justice in the region, in which ends the participating States and the non-participating Mediterranean States have a common interest,

Recognizing the importance of their mutual economic relations with the non-participating Mediterranean States, and conscious of their common interest in the further development of co-operation,

Noting with appreciation the interest expressed by the non-participating Mediterranean States in the Conference since its inception, and having duly taken their contributions into account,

Declare their intention:

—to promote the development of good-neighbourly relations with the non-participating Mediterranean States in conformity with the purposes and principles of the Charter of the United Nations, on which their relations are based, and with the United Nations Declaration on Principles of International Law concerning Friendly Relations and Co-operation among States[18] and accordingly, in this context, to conduct their relations with the non-participating Mediterranean States in the spirit of the principles set forth in the Declaration on Principles Guiding Relations between Participating States;

—to seek, by further improving their relations with the non-participating Mediterranean States, to increase mutual confidence,

[18]General Assembly Resolution 2625 (XXV), Oct. 24, 1970.

so as to promote security and stability in the Mediterranean area as a whole;

—to encourage with the non-participating Mediterranean States the development of mutually beneficial co-operation in the various fields of economic activity, especially by expanding commercial exchanges, on the basis of a common awareness of the necessity for stability and progress in trade relations, of their mutual economic interests, and of differences in the levels of economic development, thereby promoting their economic advancement and well-being;

—to contribute to a diversified development of the economies of the non-participating Mediterranean countries, whilst taking due account of their national development objectives, and to co-operate with them, especially in the sectors of industry, science and technology, in their efforts to achieve a better utilization of their resources, thus promoting a more harmonious development of economic relations;

—to intensify their efforts and their co-operation on a bilateral and multilateral basis with the non-participating Mediterranean States directed towards the improvement of the environment of the Mediterranean, especially the safeguarding of the biological resources and ecological balance of the sea, by appropriate measures including the prevention and control of pollution; to this end, and in view of the present situation, to co-operate through competent international organizations and in particular within the United Nations Environment Programme (UNEP);

—to promote further contacts and co-operation with the non-participating Mediterranean States in other relevant fields.

In order to advance the objectives set forth above, the participating States also declare their intention of maintaining and amplifying the contacts and dialogue as initiated by the CSCE with the non-participating Mediterranean States to include all the States of the Mediterranean, with the purpose of contributing to peace, reducing armed forces in the region, strengthening security, lessening tensions in the region, and widening the scope of co-operation, ends in which all share a common interest, as well as with the purpose of defining further common objectives.

The participating States would seek, in the framework of their multilateral efforts, to encourage progress and appropriate initiatives and to proceed to an exchange of views on the attainment of the above purposes.

CO-OPERATION IN HUMANITARIAN
AND OTHER FIELDS

["Basket Three"]

The participating States,

Desiring to contribute to the strengthening of peace and understanding among peoples and to the spiritual enrichment of the human personality without distinction as to race, sex, language or religion,

Conscious that increased cultural and educational exchanges, broader dissemination of information, contacts between people, and the solution of humanitarian problems will contribute to the attainment of these aims,

Determined therefore to co-operate among themselves, irrespective of their political, economic and social systems, in order to create better conditions in the above fields, to develop and strengthen existing forms of co-operation and to work out new ways and means appropriate to these aims,

Convinced that this co-operation should take place in full respect for the principles guiding relations among participating States as set forth in the relevant document,

Have adopted the following:

1. Human Contacts

The participating States,

Considering the development of contacts to be an important element in the strengthening of friendly relations and trust among peoples,

Affirming, in relation to their present effort to improve conditions in this area, the importance they attach to humanitarian considerations,

Desiring in this spirit to develop, with the continuance of détente, further efforts to achieve continuing progress in this field,

And conscious that the questions relevant hereto must be settled by the States concerned under mutually acceptable conditions,

Make it their aim to facilitate freer movement and contacts, individually and collectively, whether privately or officially, among persons, institutions and organizations of the participating States, and to contribute to the solution of the humanitarian problems that arise in that connexion,

Declare their readiness to these ends to take measures which they consider appropriate and to conclude agreements or arrangements among themselves, as may be needed, and

Express their intention now to proceed to the implementation of the following:

(a) Contacts and Regular Meetings on the Basis of Family Ties

In order to promote further development of contacts on the basis of family ties the participating States will favourably consider applications for travel with the purpose of allowing persons to enter or leave their territory temporarily, and on a regular basis if desired, in order to visit members of their families.

Applications for temporary visits to meet members of their families will be dealt with without distinction as to the country of origin or destination: existing requirements for travel documents and visas will be applied in this spirit. The preparation and issue of such documents and visas will be effected within reasonable time limits; cases of urgent necessity—such as serious illness or death—will be given priority treatment. They will take such steps as may be necessary to ensure that the fees for official travel documents and visas are acceptable.

They confirm that the presentation of an application concerning contacts on the basis of family ties will not modify the rights and obligations of the applicant or of members of his family.

(b) Reunification of Families

The participating States will deal in a positive and humanitarian spirit with the applications of persons who wish to be reunited with members of their family, with special attention being given to requests of an urgent character—such as requests submitted by persons who are ill or old.

They will deal with applications in this field as expeditiously as possible.

They will lower where necessary the fees charged in connexion with these applications to ensure that they are at a moderate level.

Applications for the purpose of family reunification which are not granted may be renewed at the appropriate level and will be reconsidered at reasonably short intervals by the authorities of the country of residence or destination, whichever is concerned; under such circumstances fees will be charged only when applications are granted.

Persons whose applications for family reunification are granted may bring with them or ship their household and personal effects; to this end the participating States will use all possibilities provided by existing regulations.

Until members of the same family are reunited meetings and contacts between them may take place in accordance with the modalities for contacts on the basis of family ties.

The participating States will support the efforts of Red Cross and Red Crescent Societies concerned with the problems of family reunification.

They confirm that the presentation of an application concerning family reunification will not modify the rights and obligations of the applicant or of members of his family.

The receiving participating State will take appropriate care with regard to employment for persons from other participating States who take up permanent residence in that State in connexion with family reunification with its citizens and see that they are afforded opportunities equal to those enjoyed by its own citizens for education, medical assistance and social security.

(c) Marriage between Citizens of Different States

The participating States will examine favourably and on the basis of humanitarian considerations requests for exit or entry permits from persons who have decided to marry a citizen from another participating State.

The processing and issuing of the documents required for the above purposes and for the marriage will be in accordance with the provisions accepted for family reunification.

In dealing with requests from couples from different participating States, once married, to enable them and the minor children of their marriage to transfer their permanent residence to a State in which either one is normally a resident, the participating States will also apply the provisions accepted for family reunification.

(d) Travel for Personal or Professional Reasons

The participating States intend to facilitate wider travel by their citizens for personal or professional reasons and to this end they intend in particular:

—gradually to simplify and to administer flexibly the procedures for exit and entry;
—to ease regulations concerning movement of citizens from the other participating States in their territory, with due regard to security requirements.

They will endeavour gradually to lower, where necessary, the fees for visas and official travel documents.

They intend to consider, as necessary, means—including, in so far as appropriate, the conclusion of multilateral or bilateral consular conventions or other relevant agreements or understandings—for the improvement of arrangements to provide consular services, including legal and consular assistance.

*   *   *

They confirm that religious faiths, institutions and organizations, practising within the constitutional framework of the participating States, and their representatives can, in the field of their activities, have contacts and meetings among themselves and exchange information.

(e) Improvement of Conditions for Tourism on an Individual or Collective Basis

The participating States consider that tourism contributes to a fuller knowledge of the life, culture and history of other countries, to the growth of understanding among peoples, to the improvement of contacts and to the broader use of leisure. They intend to promote the development of tourism, on an individual or collective basis, and, in particular, they intend:

—to promote visits to their respective countries by encouraging the provision of appropriate facilities and the simplification and expediting of necessary formalities relating to such visits;
—to increase, on the basis of appropriate agreements or arrangements where necessary, co-operation in the development of tourism, in particular by considering bilaterally possible ways to increase information relating to travel to other countries and to the reception and service of tourists, and other related questions of mutual interest.

(f) Meetings among Young People

The participating States intend to further the development of contacts and exchanges among young people by encouraging:

—increased exchanges and contacts on a short or long term basis among young people working, training or undergoing education through bilateral or multilateral agreements or regular programmes in all cases where it is possible;

—study by their youth organizations of the question of possible agreements relating to frameworks of multilateral youth co-operation;

—agreements or regular programmes relating to the organization of exchanges of students, of international youth seminars, of courses of professional training and foreign language study;

—the further development of youth tourism and the provision to this end of appropriate facilities;

—the development, where possible, of exchanges, contacts and co-operation on a bilateral or multilateral basis between their organizations which represent wide circles of young people working, training or undergoing education;

—awareness among youth of the importance of developing mutual understanding and of strengthening friendly relations and confidence among peoples.

(g) Sport

In order to expand existing links and co-operation in the field of sport the participating States will encourage contacts and exchanges of this kind, including sports meetings and competitions of all sorts, on the basis of the established international rules, regulations and practice.

(h) Expansion of Contacts

By way of further developing contacts among governmental institutions and non-governmental organizations and associations, including women's organizations, the participating States will facilitate the convening of meetings as well as travel by delegations, groups and individuals.

2. Information

The participating States,

Conscious of the need for an ever wider knowledge and understanding of the various aspects of life in other participating States,

Acknowledging the contribution of this process to the growth of confidence between peoples,

Desiring, with the development of mutual understanding between the participating States and with the further improvement of their relations, to continue further efforts towards progress in this field,

Recognizing the importance of the dissemination of information from the other participating States and of a better acquaintance with such information,

Emphasizing therefore the essential and influential role of the press, radio, television, cinema and news agencies and of the journalists working in these fields,

Make it their aim to facilitate the freer and wider dissemination of information of all kinds, to encourage co-operation in the field of information and the exchange of information with other countries, and to improve the conditions under which journalists from one participating State exercise their profession in another participating State, and

Express their intention in particular:

(a) Improvement of the Circulation of, Access to, and Exchange of Information

(i) *Oral Information*

—To facilitate the dissemination of oral information through the encouragement of lectures and lecture tours by personalities and specialists from the other participating States, as well as exchanges of opinions at round table meetings, seminars, symposia, summer schools, congresses and other bilateral and multilateral meetings.

(ii) *Printed Information*

—To facilitate the improvement of the dissemination, on their territory, of newspapers and printed publications, periodical and nonperiodical, from the other participating States. For this purpose:

they will encourage their competent firms and organizations to conclude agreements and contracts designed gradually to increase the quantities and the number of titles of newspapers and publications imported from the other participating States. These agreements and contracts should in particular mention the speediest conditions of delivery and the use of the normal channels existing in each country for the distribution of its own publications and newspapers, as well as forms and means of payment agreed between the parties making it possible to achieve the objectives aimed at by these agreements and contracts;

where necessary, they will take appropriate measures to achieve the above objectives and to implement the provisions contained in the agreements and contracts.

—To contribute to the improvement of access by the public to periodical and non-periodical printed publications imported on the bases indicated above. In particular:

they will encourage an increase in the number of places where these publications are on sale;

they will facilitate the availability of these periodical publications during congresses, conferences, official visits and other international events and to tourists during the season;

they will develop the possibilities for taking out subscriptions according to the modalities particular to each country;

they will improve the opportunities for reading and borrowing these publications in large public libraries and their reading rooms as well as in university libraries.

They intend to improve the possibilities for acquaintance with bulletins of official information issued by diplomatic missions and distributed by those missions on the basis of arrangements acceptable to the interested parties.

(iii) *Filmed and Broadcast Information*

—To promote the improvement of the dissemination of filmed and broadcast information. To this end:

they will encourage the wider showing and broadcasting of a greater variety of recorded and filmed information from the other participating States, illustrating the various aspects of life in their countries and received on the basis of such agreements or arrangements as may be necessary between the organizations and firms directly concerned;

they will facilitate the import by competent organizations and firms of recorded audio-visual material from the other participating States.

The participating States note the expansion in the dissemination of information broadcast by radio, and express the hope for the continuation of this process, so as to meet the interest of mutual understanding among peoples and the aims set forth by this Conference.

(b) Co-operation in the Field of Information

—To encourage co-operation in the field of information on the basis of short or long term agreements or arrangements. In particular:

they will favour increased co-operation among mass media organizations, including press agencies, as well as among publishing houses and organizations;

they will favour co-operation among public or private, national or international radio and television organizations, in particular through the exchange of both live and recorded radio and television programmes, and through the joint production and the broadcasting and distribution of such programmes;

they will encourage meetings and contacts both between journalists' organizations and between journalists from the participating States;

they will view favourably the possibilities of arrangements between periodical publications as well as between newspapers from the participating States, for the purpose of exchanging and publishing articles;

they will encourage the exchange of technical information as well as the organization of joint research and meetings devoted to the exchange of experience and views between experts in the field of the press, radio and television.

(c) Improvement of Working Conditions for Journalists

The participating States, desiring to improve the conditions under which journalists from one participating State exercise their profession in another participating State, intend in particular to:

—examine in a favourable spirit and within a suitable and reasonable time scale requests from journalists for visas;

—grant to permanently accredited journalists of the participating States, on the basis of arrangements, multiple entry and exit visas for specified periods;

—facilitate the issue to accredited journalists of the participating States of permits for stay in their country of temporary residence and, if and when these are necessary, of other official papers which it is appropriate for them to have;

—ease, on a basis of reciprocity, procedures for arranging travel by journalists of the participating States in the country where they are exercising their profession, and to provide progressively greater opportunities for such travel, subject to the observance of regulations relating to the existence of areas closed for security reasons;

—ensure that requests by such journalists for such travel receive, in so far as possible, an expeditious response, taking into account the time scale of the request;

—increase the opportunities for journalists of the participating States to communicate personally with their sources, including organizations and official institutions;

—grant to journalists of the participating States the right to import, subject only to its being taken out again, the technical equipment (photographic, cinematographic, tape recorder, radio and television) necessary for the exercise of their profession;[19]

—enable journalists of the other participating States, whether permanently or temporarily accredited, to transmit completely, normally and rapidly by means recognized by the participating States to the information organs which they represent, the results of their professional activity, including tape recordings and undeveloped film, for the purpose of publication or of broadcasting on the radio or television.

The participating States reaffirm that the legitimate pursuit of their professional activity will neither render journalists liable to expulsion nor otherwise penalize them. If an accredited journalist is expelled, he will be informed of the reasons for this act and may submit an application for re-examination of his case.

3. Co-operation and Exchanges in the Field of Culture

The participating States,

Considering that cultural exchanges and co-operation contribute to a better comprehension among people and among peoples, and thus promote a lasting understanding among States,

Confirming the conclusions already formulated in this field at the multilateral level, particularly at the Intergovernmental Conference on Cultural Policies in Europe, organized by UNESCO in Helsinki in June 1972, where interest was manifested in the active

[19]While recognizing that appropriate local personnel are employed by foreign journalists in many instances, the participating States note that the above provisions would be applied, subject to the observance of the appropriate rules, to persons from the other participating States, who are regularly and professionally engaged as technicians, photographers or cameramen of the press, radio, television or cinema. [Footnote in original.]

participation of the broadest possible social groups in an increasingly diversified cultural life,

Desiring, with the development of mutual confidence and the further improvement of relations between the participating States, to continue further efforts toward progress in this field,

Disposed in this spirit to increase substantially their cultural exchanges, with regard both to persons and to cultural works, and to develop among them an active co-operation, both at the bilateral and the multilateral level, in all the fields of culture,

Convinced that such a development of their mutual relations will contribute to the enrichment of the respective cultures, while respecting the originality of each, as well as to the reinforcement among them of a consciousness of common values, while continuing to develop cultural co-operation with other countries of the world,

Declare that they jointly set themselves the following objectives:

(a) to develop the mutual exchange of information with a view to a better knowledge of respective cultural achievements,
(b) to improve the facilities for the exchange and for the dissemination of cultural property,
(c) to promote access by all to respective cultural achievements,
(d) to develop contacts and co-operation among persons active in the field of culture,
(e) to seek new fields and forms of cultural co-operation,

Thus *give expression to* their common will to take progressive, coherent and long-term action in order to achieve the objectives of the present declaration; and

Express their intention now to proceed to the implementation of the following:

Extension of Relations

To expand and improve at the various levels co-operation and links in the field of culture, in particular by:

—concluding, where appropriate, agreements on a bilateral or multilateral basis, providing for the extension of relations among competent State institutions and non-governmental organizations in the field of culture, as well as among people engaged in cultural activities, taking into account the need both for flexibility and the fullest possible use of existing agreements, and bearing in mind that agreements and also other arrangements constitute important means of developing cultural co-operation and exchanges;

—contributing to the development of direct communication and co-operation among relevant State institutions and non-governmental organizations, including, where necessary, such communication and co-operation carried out on the basis of special agreements and arrangements;

—encouraging direct contacts and communications among persons engaged in cultural activities, including, where necessary, such contacts and communications carried out on the basis of special agreements and arrangements.

Mutual Knowledge

Within their competence to adopt, on a bilateral and multilateral level, appropriate measures which would give their peoples a more comprehensive and complete mutual knowledge of their achievements in the various fields of culture, and among them:

—to examine jointly, if necessary with the assistance of appropriate international organizations, the possible creation in Europe and the structure of a bank of cultural data, which would collect information from the participating countries and make it available to its correspondents on their request, and to convene for this purpose a meeting of experts from interested States;

—to consider, if necessary in conjunction with appropriate international organizations, ways of compiling in Europe an inventory of documentary films of a cultural or scientific nature from the participating States;

—to encourage more frequent book exhibitions and to examine the possibility of organizing periodically in Europe a large-scale exhibition of books from the participating States;

—to promote the systematic exchange, between the institutions concerned and publishing houses, of catalogues of available books as well as of pre-publication material which will include, as far as possible, all forthcoming publications; and also to promote the exchange of material between firms publishing encyclopaedias, with a view to improving the presentation of each country;

—to examine jointly questions of expanding and improving exchanges of information in the various fields of culture, such as theatre, music, library work as well as the conservation and restoration of cultural property.

Exchanges and Dissemination

To contribute to the improvement of facilities for exchanges and the dissemination of cultural property, by appropriate means, in particular by:

—studying the possibilities for harmonizing and reducing the charges relating to international commercial exchanges of books and other cultural materials, and also for new means of insuring works of art in foreign exhibitions and for reducing the risks of damage or loss to which these works are exposed by their movement;

—facilitating the formalities of customs clearance, in good time for programmes of artistic events, of the works of art, materials and accessories appearing on lists agreed upon by the organizers of these events;

—encouraging meetings among representatives of competent organizations and relevant firms to examine measures within their field of activity—such as the simplification of orders, time limits for sending supplies and modalities of payment—which might facilitate international commercial exchanges of books;

—promoting the loan and exchange of films among their film institutes and film libraries;

—encouraging the exchange of information among interested parties concerning events of a cultural character foreseen in the participating States in fields where this is most appropriate, such as music, theatre and the plastic and graphic arts, with a view to contributing to the compilation and publication of a calendar of such events, with the assistance, where necessary, of the appropriate international organizations;

—encouraging a study of the impact which the foreseeable development, and a possible harmonization among interested parties, of the technical means used for the dissemination of culture might have on the development of cultural co-operation and exchanges, while keeping in view the preservation of the diversity and originality of their respective cultures;

—encouraging, in the way they deem appropriate, within their cultural policies, the further development of interest in the cultural heritage of the other participating States, conscious of the merits and the value of each culture;

—endeavouring to ensure the full and effective application of the international agreements and conventions on copyrights and on circulation of cultural property to which they are party or to which they may decide in the future to become party.

Access

To promote fuller mutual access by all to the achievements—works, experiences and performing arts—in the various fields of culture of their countries, and to that end to make the best possible efforts, in accordance with their competence, more particularly:

—to promote wider dissemination of books and artistic works, in particular by such means as:

facilitating, while taking full account of the international copyright conventions to which they are party, international contacts and communications between authors and publishing houses as well as other cultural institutions, with a view to a more complete mutual access to cultural achievements;

recommending that, in determining the size of editions, publishing houses take into account also the demand from the other participating States, and that rights of sale in other participating States be granted, where possible, to several sales organizations of the importing countries, by agreement between interested partners;

encouraging competent organizations and relevant firms to conclude agreements and contracts and contributing, by this means, to a gradual increase in the number and diversity of works by authors from the other participating States available in the original and in translation in their libraries and bookshops;

promoting, where deemed appropriate, an increase in the number of sales outlets where books by authors from the other participating States, imported in the original on the basis of agreements and contracts, and in translation, are for sale;

promoting, on a wider scale, the translation of works in the sphere of literature and other fields of cultural activity, produced in the languages of the other participating States, especially from the less widely-spoken languages, and the publication and dissemination of the translated works by such measures as:

encouraging more regular contacts between interested publishing houses;

developing their efforts in the basic and advanced training of translators;

encouraging, by appropriate means, the publishing houses of their countries to publish translations;

facilitating the exchange between publishers and interested institutions of lists of books which might be translated;

promoting between their countries the professional activity and co-operation of translators;

carrying out joint studies on ways of further promoting translations and their dissemination;

improving and expanding exchanges of books, bibliographies and catalogue cards between libraries;

—to envisage other appropriate measures which would permit, where necessary by mutual agreement among interested parties, the facilitation of access to their respective cultural achievements, in particular in the field of books;

—to contribute by appropriate means to the wider use of the mass media in order to improve mutual acquaintance with the cultural life of each;

—to seek to develop the necessary conditions for migrant workers and their families to preserve their links with their national culture, and also to adapt themselves to their new cultural environment;

—to encourage the competent bodies and enterprises to make a wider choice and effect wider distribution of full-length and documentary films from the other participating States, and to promote more frequent non-commercial showings, such as premières, film weeks and festivals, giving due consideration to films from countries whose cinematographic works are less well known;

—to promote, by appropriate means, the extension of opportunities for specialists from the other participating States to work with materials of a cultural character from film and audiovisual archives, within the framework of the existing rules for work on such archival materials;

—to encourage a joint study by interested bodies, where appropriate with the assistance of the competent international organizations, of the expediency and the conditions for the establishment of a repertory of their recorded television programmes of a cultural nature, as well as of the means of viewing them rapidly in order to facilitate their selection and possible acquisition.

Contacts and Co-operation

To contribute, by appropriate means, to the development of contacts and co-operation in the various fields of culture, especially among creative artists and people engaged in cultural activities, in particular by making efforts to:

—promote for persons active in the field of culture, travel and meetings including, where necessary, those carried out on the basis of agreements, contracts or other special arrangements and which are relevant to their cultural co-operation;
—encourage in this way contacts among creative and performing artists and artistic groups with a view to their working together, making known their works in other participating States or exchanging views on topics relevant to their common activity;
—encourage, where necessary through appropriate arrangements, exchanges of trainees and specialists and the granting of scholarships for basic and advanced training in various fields of culture such as the arts and architecture, museums and libraries, literary studies and translation, and contribute to the creation of favourable conditions of reception in their respective institutions;
—encourage the exchange of experience in the training of organizers of cultural activities as well as of teachers and specialists in fields such as theatre, opera, ballet, music and fine arts;
—continue to encourage the organization of international meetings among creative artists, especially young creative artists, on current questions of artistic and literary creation which are of interest for joint study;
—study other possibilities for developing exchanges and co-operation among persons active in the field of culture, with a view to a better mutual knowledge of the cultural life of the participating States.

Fields and Forms of Co-operation

To encourage the search for new fields and forms of cultural co-operation, to these ends contributing to the conclusion among interested parties, where necessary, of appropriate agreements and arrangements, and in this context to promote:

—joint studies regarding cultural policies, in particular in their social aspects, and as they relate to planning, town-planning, educational and environmental policies, and the cultural aspects of tourism;
—the exchange of knowledge in the realm of cultural diversity, with a view to contributing thus to a better understanding by interested parties of such diversity where it occurs;

—the exchange of information, and as may be appropriate, meetings of experts, the elaboration and the execution of research programmes and projects, as well as their joint evaluation, and the dissemination of the results, on the subjects indicated above;

—such forms of cultural co-operation and the development of such joint projects as:

international events in the fields of the plastic and graphic arts, cinema, theatre, ballet, music, folklore, etc.; book fairs and exhibitions, joint performances of operatic and dramatic works, as well as performances given by soloists, instrumental ensembles, orchestras, choirs and other artistic groups, including those composed of amateurs, paying due attention to the organization of international cultural youth events and the exchange of young artists;

the inclusion of works by writers and composers from the other participating States in the repertoires of soloists and artistic ensembles;

the preparation, translation and publication of articles, studies and monographs, as well as of low-cost books and of artistic and literary collections, suited to making better known respective cultural achievements, envisaging for this purpose meetings among experts and representatives of publishing houses;

the co-production and the exchange of films and of radio and television programmes, by promoting, in particular, meetings among producers, technicians and representatives of the public authorities with a view to working out favourable conditions for the execution of specific joint projects and by encouraging, in the field of co-production, the establishment of international filming teams;

the organization of competitions for architects and town-planners, bearing in mind the possible implementation of the best projects and the formation, where possible, of international teams;

the implementation of joint projects for conserving, restoring and showing to advantage works of art, historical and archaeological monuments and sites of cultural interest, with the help, in appropriate cases, of international organizations of a governmental or non-governmental character as well as of private institutions—competent and active in these fields—envisaging for this purpose:

periodic meetings of experts of the interested parties to elaborate the necessary proposals, while bearing in mind the need to consider these questions in a wider social and economic context;

the publication in appropriate periodicals of articles designed to make known and to compare, among the participating States, the most significant achievements and innovations;

a joint study with a view to the improvement and possible harmonization of the different systems used to inventory and catalogue the historical monuments and places of cultural interest in their countries;

the study of the possibilities for organizing international courses for the training of specialists in different disciplines relating to restoration.

* * *

National minorities or regional cultures. The participating States, recognizing the contribution that national minorities or regional cultures can make to co-operation among them in various fields of culture, intend, when such minorities or cultures exist within their territory, to facilitate this contribution, taking into account the legitimate interests of their members.

4. Co-operation and Exchanges in the Field of Education

The participating States,

Conscious that the development of relations of an international character in the fields of education and science contributes to a better mutual understanding and is to the advantage of all peoples as well as to the benefit of future generations,

Prepared to facilitate, between organizations, institutions and persons engaged in education and science, the further development of exchanges of knowledge and experience as well as of contacts, on the basis of special arrangements where these are necessary,

Desiring to strengthen the links among educational and scientific establishments and also to encourage their co-operation in sectors of common interest, particularly where the levels of knowledge and resources require efforts to be concerted internationally, and

Convinced that progress in these fields should be accompanied and supported by a wider knowledge of foreign languages,

Express to these ends their intention in particular:

(a) Extension of Relations

To expand and improve at the various levels co-operation and links in the fields of education and science, in particular by:

—concluding, where appropriate, bilateral or multilateral agreements providing for co-operation and exchanges among State institutions, non-governmental bodies and persons engaged in activities in education and science, bearing in mind the need both for flexibility and the fuller use of existing agreements and arrangements;

—promoting the conclusion of direct arrangements between universities and other institutions of higher education and research, in the framework of agreements between governments where appropriate;

—encouraging among persons engaged in education and science direct contacts and communications, including those based on special agreements or arrangements where these are appropriate.

(b) Access and Exchanges

To improve access, under mutually acceptable conditions, for students, teachers and scholars of the participating States to each other's educational, cultural and scientific institutions, and to intensify exchanges among these institutions in all areas of common interest, in particular by:

—increasing the exchange of information on facilities for study and courses open to foreign participants, as well as on the conditions under which they will be admitted and received;

—facilitating travel between the participating States by scholars, teachers and students for purposes of study, teaching and research as well as for improving knowledge of each other's educational, cultural and scientific achievements;

—encouraging the award of scholarships for study, teaching and research in their countries to scholars, teachers and students of other participating States;

—establishing, developing or encouraging programmes providing for the broader exchange of scholars, teachers and students, including the organization of symposia, seminars and collaborative projects, and the exchanges of educational and scholarly information such as university publications and materials from libraries;

—promoting the efficient implementation of such arrangements and programmes by providing scholars, teachers and students in good time with more detailed information about their placing in universities and institutes and the programmes envisaged for them; by granting them the opportunity to use relevant scholarly, scientific and open archival materials; and by facilitating their travel within the receiving State for the purpose of study or

research as well as in the form of vacation tours on the basis of
the usual procedures;
—promoting a more exact assessment of the problems of comparison and equivalence of academic degrees and diplomas by
fostering the exchange of information on the organization,
duration and content of studies, the comparison of methods of
assessing levels of knowledge and academic qualifications, and,
where feasible, arriving at the mutual recognition of academic
degrees and diplomas either through governmental agreements,
where necessary, or direct arrangements between universities
and other institutions of higher learning and research;
—recommending, moreover, to the appropriate international
organizations that they should intensify their efforts to reach a
generally acceptable solution to the problems of comparison and
equivalence between academic degrees and diplomas.

(c) Science

Within their competence to broaden and improve co-operation
and exchanges in the field of science, in particular:

To increase, on a bilateral or multilateral basis, the exchange and
dissemination of scientific information and documentation by such
means as:

—making this information more widely available to scientists
and research workers of the other participating States through,
for instance, participation in international information-sharing
programmes or through other appropriate arrangements;
—broadening and facilitating the exchange of samples and other
scientific materials used particularly for fundamental research in
the fields of natural sciences and medicine;
—inviting scientific institutions and universities to keep each
other more fully and regularly informed about their current and
contemplated research work in fields of common interest.

To facilitate the extension of communications and direct contacts between universities, scientific institutions and associations as
well as among scientists and research workers, including those
based where necessary on special agreements or arrangements, by
such means as:

—further developing exchanges of scientists and research
workers and encouraging the organization of preparatory
meetings or working groups on research topics of common interest;

—encouraging the creation of joint teams of scientists to pursue research projects under arrangements made by the scientific institutions of several countries;

—assisting the organization and successful functioning of international conferences and seminars and participation in them by their scientists and research workers;

—furthermore envisaging, in the near future, a "Scientific Forum" in the form of a meeting of leading personalities in science from the participating States to discuss interrelated problems of common interest concerning current and future developments in science, and to promote the expansion of contacts, communications and the exchange of information between scientific institutions and among scientists;

—foreseeing, at an early date, a meeting of experts representing the participating States and their national scientific institutions, in order to prepare such a "Scientific Forum" in consultation with appropriate international organizations, such as UNESCO and the ECE;

—considering in due course what further steps might be taken with respect to the "Scientific Forum".

To develop in the field of scientific research, on a bilateral or multilateral basis, the co-ordination of programmes carried out in the participating States and the organization of joint programmes, especially in the areas mentioned below, which may involve the combined efforts of scientists and in certain cases the use of costly or unique equipment. The list of subjects in these areas is illustrative; and specific projects would have to be determined subsequently by the potential partners in the participating States, taking account of the contribution which could be made by appropriate international organizations and scientific institutions:

—*exact and natural sciences*, in particular fundamental research in such fields as mathematics, physics, theoretical physics, geophysics, chemistry, biology, ecology and astronomy;

—*medicine*, in particular basic research into cancer and cardiovascular diseases, studies on the diseases endemic in the developing countries, as well as medico-social research with special emphasis on occupational diseases, the rehabilitation of the handicapped and the care of mothers, children and the elderly;

—*the humanities and social sciences*, such as history, geography, philosophy, psychology, pedagogical research, linguistics, sociology, the legal, political and economic sciences; comparative studies on social, socio-economic and cultural phenomena which are of common interest to the participating

States, especially the problems of human environment and urban development; and scientific studies on the methods of conserving and restoring monuments and works of art.

(d) Foreign Languages and Civilizations

To encourage the study of foreign languages and civilizations as an important means of expanding communication among peoples for their better acquaintance with the culture of each country, as well as for the strengthening of international co-operation; to this end to stimulate, within their competence, the further development and improvement of foreign language teaching and the diversification of choice of languages taught at various levels, paying due attention to less widely-spread or studied languages, and in particular:

—to intensify co-operation aimed at improving the teaching of foreign languages through exchanges of information and experience concerning the development and application of effective modern teaching methods and technical aids, adapted to the needs of different categories of students, including methods of accelerated teaching; and to consider the possibility of conducting, on a bilateral or multilateral basis, studies of new methods of foreign language teaching;

—to encourage co-operation between institutions concerned, on a bilateral or multilateral basis, aimed at exploiting more fully the resources of modern educational technology in language teaching, for example through comparative studies by their specialists and, where agreed, through exchanges or transfers of audio-visual materials, of materials used for preparing textbooks, as well as of information about new types of technical equipment used for teaching languages;

—to promote the exchange of information on the experience acquired in the training of language teachers and to intensify exchanges on a bilateral basis of language teachers and students as well as to facilitate their participation in summer courses in languages and civilizations, wherever these are organized;

—to encourage co-operation among experts in the field of lexicography with the aim of defining the necessary terminological equivalents, particularly in the scientific and technical disciplines, in order to facilitate relations among scientific institutions and specialists;

—to promote the wider spread of foreign language study among the different types of secondary education establishments and greater possibilities of choice between an increased number of European languages; and in this context to consider, wherever appropriate, the possibilities for developing the recruitment and training of teachers as well as the organization of the student groups required;

—to favour, in higher education, a wider choice in the languages offered to language students and greater opportunities for other students to study various foreign languages; also to facilitate, where desirable, the organization of courses in languages and civilizations, on the basis of special arrangements as necessary, to be given by foreign lecturers, particularly from European countries having less widely-spread or studied languages;

—to promote, within the framework of adult education, the further development of specialized programmes, adapted to various needs and interests, for teaching foreign languages to their own inhabitants and the languages of host countries to interested adults from other countries; in this context to encourage interested institutions to co-operate, for example, in the elaboration of programmes for teaching by radio and television and by accelerated methods, and also, where desirable, in the definition of study objectives for such programmes, with a view to arriving at comparable levels of language proficiency;

—to encourage the association, where appropriate, of the teaching of foreign languages with the study of the corresponding civilizations and also to make further efforts to stimulate interest in the study of foreign languages, including relevant out-of-class activities.

(e) Teaching Methods

To promote the exchange of experience, on a bilateral or multilateral basis, in teaching methods at all levels of education, including those used in permanent and adult education, as well as the exchange of teaching materials, in particular by:

—further developing various forms of contacts and co-operation in the different fields of pedagogical science, for example through comparative or joint studies carried out by interested institutions or through exchanges of information on the results of teaching experiments;

—intensifying exchanges of information on teaching methods used in various educational systems and on results of research into the process by which pupils and students acquire knowledge, taking account of relevant experience in different types of specialized education;

—facilitating exchanges of experience concerning the organization and functioning of education intended for adults and recurrent education, the relationships between these and other forms and levels of education, as well as concerning the means of adapting education, including vocational and technical training, to the needs of economic and social development in their countries;

—encouraging exchanges of experience in the education of youth and adults in international understanding, with particular reference to those major problems of mankind whose solution calls for a common approach and wider international co-operation;

—encouraging exchanges of teaching materials—including school textbooks, having in mind the possibility of promoting mutual knowledge and facilitating the presentation of each country in such books—as well as exchanges of information on technical innovations in the field of education.

* * *

National minorities or regional cultures. The participating States, recognizing the contribution that national minorities or regional cultures can make to co-operation among them in various fields of education, intend, when such minorities or cultures exist within their territory, to facilitate this contribution, taking into account the legitimate interests of their members.

FOLLOW-UP TO THE CONFERENCE

["Basket Four"]

The participating States,

Having considered and evaluated the progress made at the Conference on Security and Co-operation in Europe,

Considering further that, within the broader context of the world, the Conference is an important part of the process of improving security and developing co-operation in Europe and that its results will contribute significantly to this process,

Intending to implement the provisions of the Final Act of the Conference in order to give full effect to its results and thus to further the process of improving security and developing co-operation in Europe,

Convinced that, in order to achieve the aims sought by the Conference, they should make further unilateral, bilateral and multilateral efforts and continue, in the appropriate forms set forth below, the multilateral process initiated by the Conference,

1. *Declare their resolve*, in the period following the Conference, to pay due regard to and implement the provisions of the Final Act of the Conference:

(a) unilaterally, in all cases which lend themselves to such action;
(b) bilaterally, by negotiations with other participating States;
(c) multilaterally, by meetings of experts of the participating States, and also within the framework of existing international organizations, such as the United Nations Economic Commission for Europe and UNESCO, with regard to educational, scientific and cultural co-operation;

2. *Declare furthermore their resolve* to continue the multilateral process initiated by the Conference:

(a) by proceeding to a thorough exchange of views both on the implementation of the provisions of the Final Act and of the tasks defined by the Conference, as well as, in the context of the questions dealt with by the latter, on the deepening of their mutual relations, the improvement of security and the development of co-operation in Europe, and the development of the process of détente in the future;
(b) by organizing to these ends meetings among their representatives, beginning with a meeting at the level of representatives appointed by the Ministers of Foreign Affairs. This meeting will define the appropriate modalities for the holding of other meetings which could include further similar meetings and the possibility of a new Conference;

3. The first of the meetings indicated above will be held at Belgrade in 1977. A preparatory meeting to organize this meeting will be held at Belgrade on 15 June 1977. The preparatory meeting will decide on the date, duration, agenda and other modalities of the meeting of representatives appointed by the Ministers of Foreign Affairs;

4. The rules of procedure, the working methods and the scale of distribution for the expenses of the Conference will, *mutatis mutandis*, be applied to the meetings envisaged in paragraphs 1 (c), 2 and 3 above. All the above-mentioned meetings will be held in the participating States in rotation. The services of a technical secretariat will be provided by the host country.

The original of this Final Act, drawn up in English, French, German, Italian, Russian and Spanish, will be transmitted to the

Government of the Republic of Finland, which will retain it in its archives. Each of the participating States will receive from the Government of the Republic of Finland a true copy of this Final Act.

The text of this Final Act will be published in each participating State, which will disseminate it and make it known as widely as possible.

The Government of the Republic of Finland is requested to transmit to the Secretary-General of the United Nations the text of this Final Act, which is not eligible for registration under Article 102 of the Charter of the United Nations,[20] with a view to its circulation to all the members of the Organization as an official document of the United Nations.

The Government of the Republic of Finland is also requested to transmit the text of this Final Act to the Director-General of UNESCO and to the Executive Secretary of the United Nations Economic Commission for Europe.

Wherefore, the undersigned High Representatives of the participating States, mindful of the high political significance which they attach to the results of the Conference, and declaring their determination to act in accordance with the provisions contained in the above texts, have subscribed their signatures below:[21]

The Federal Republic of Germany:
HELMUT SCHMIDT, *Federal Chancellor*

The German Democratic Republic:
ERICH HONECKER, *First Secretary of the Central Committee of the Socialist Unity Party of Germany*

The United States of America:
GERALD R. FORD, *President of the United States of America*

The Republic of Austria:
BRUNO KREISKY, *Federal Chancellor*

The Kingdom of Belgium:
LEO TINDEMANS, *Prime Minister*

---

[20] Article 102 of the U.N. Charter provides in part as follows:

"1. Every treaty and every international agreement entered into by any Member of the United Nations after the present Charter comes into force shall as soon as possible be registered with the Secretariat and published by it. . . ."

[21] The document was signed in the alphabetical order of the country names in the French language. The signatures are here presented in simplified form as printed in *Bulletin*, 73: 349-50.

The People's Republic of Bulgaria:
TODOR JIVKOV [ZHIVKOV], *First Secretary, Central Committee of the Communist Party of Bulgaria and President of the Council of State of the People's Republic of Bulgaria*

Canada:
PIERRE ELLIOTT TRUDEAU, *Prime Minister*

The Republic of Cyprus:
His Beatitude Archbishop MAKARIOS III, *President of the Republic of Cyprus*

Denmark:
ANKER JORGENSEN, *Prime Minister*

Spain:
CARLOS ARIAS NAVARRO, *Head of the Government*

The Republic of Finland:
URHO KEKKONEN, *President of the Republic*

The French Republic:
VALERY GISCARD D'ESTAING

The United Kingdom of Great Britain and Northern Ireland:
The Rt. Hon. HAROLD WILSON, O.B.E., M.P., F.R.S., *First Lord of the Treasury and Prime Minister of the United Kingdom of Great Britain and Northern Ireland*

The Hellenic Republic:
CONSTANTIN CARAMANLIS, *Prime Minister*

The Hungarian People's Republic:
JANOS KADAR, *First Secretary of the Central Committee of the Hungarian Socialist Workers' Party, Member of the Presidential Council of the Hungarian People's Republic*

Ireland:
LIAM COSGRAVE, *Prime Minister*

Iceland:
GEIR HALLGRIMSSON, *Prime Minister*

The Italian Republic:
ALDO MORO, *Prime Minister of the Italian Republic and in his capacity as President in office of the Council of the European Communities*

The Principality of Liechtenstein:
WALTER KIEBER, *Head of Government*

The Grand Duchy of Luxembourg:
GASTON THORN, *Prime Minister, Minister for Foreign Affairs*

The Republic of Malta:
DOM MINTOFF, *Prime Minister, Minister for Commonwealth and Foreign Affairs*

The Principality of Monaco:
ANDRE SAINT-MLEUX, *Minister of State, President of the Government Council, Representing H.S.H. the Prince of Monaco*

Norway:
TRYGVE BRATTELI, *Prime Minister*

The Kingdom of the Netherlands:
J.M. DEN UYL, *Prime Minister*

Polish People's Republic:
EDWARD GIEREK, *First Secretary of the Central Committee of the Polish United Workers' Party*

Portugal:
FRANCISCO DA COSTA GOMES, *President of the Republic*

The Socialist Republic of Romania:
NICOLAE CEAUSESCU, *President of the Socialist Republic of Romania*

San Marino:
GIAN LUIGI BERTI, *Secretary of State for Foreign and Political Affairs*

The Holy See:
Son Excellence Monseigneur AGOSTINO CASAROLI, *Secretary of the Council for Church Public Affairs, Special Delegate of His Holiness Pope Paul VI*

Sweden:
OLOF PALME, *Prime Minister*

The Swiss Confederation:
PIERRE GRABER, *President of the Confederation, Head of the Federal Political Department*

The Czechoslovak Socialist Republic:
GUSTAV HUSAK, *Secretary-General of the Communist Party of Czechoslovakia and President of the Czechoslovak Socialist Republic*

The Republic of Turkey:
SULEYMAN DEMIREL, *Prime Minister*

The Union of Soviet Socialist Republics:
L. BREJNEV [BREZHNEV], *General Secretary of the CC of the CPSU*

The Socialist Federal Republic of Jugoslavia:
JOSIP BROZ TITO, *President of the Socialist Federal Republic of Jugoslavia*

26. A VISITOR FROM JAPAN

(August 5-6, 1975)

[Returning late on August 4 from his swing through Southeast-
ern Europe, President Ford had barely time to prepare for a meeting next day with Japanese Prime Minister Takeo Miki, the veteran
Liberal Democratic statesman who had succeeded Kakuei Tanaka
shortly after the President's visit to Tokyo in November 1974.[1]
There was symbolic fitness in this sequence of presidential meetings
with leaders from both sides of the globe; for Japan, with its
110,000,000 people and its phenomenal economic drive, represented an element in many ways no less essential than Europe in current
U.S. foreign policy conceptions. Ex-President Nixon's "pen-
tagonal world,"[2] Dr. Kissinger's "Year of Europe,"[3] and the doctrines of the unofficial but influential Trilateral Commission were
at one in ascribing to Japan a position at least formally coordinate
with the new, multinational political and economic complex that
had been evolving in Western Europe.

Recent developments in Southeast and East Asia had if anything
accentuated the importance of the Japanese-American tie as an influence for stability in a sometimes volatile region. The Communist
victories in Indochina, essentially unresisted by the United States,
had sent shock waves not only through Southeast Asia but
throughout the Pacific basin. Especially worrisome, from a
Japanese as well as an American point of view, had been a recent
revival of tension in nearby Korea, where the militant behavior of
the North Korean Communists led by President Kim Il Sung had
raised fears of a new northern crusade against the anti-Communist
Republic of Korea under President Park Chung Hee in the south.
In recent comments on the Korean situation, Defense Secretary

---

[1]Cf. *AFR, 1974*: 492.
[2]Cf. same, *1972*: 301.
[3]Same, *1973*: 177-89.

Schlesinger and President Ford had emphasized that the United States, as South Korea's ally, would make a vigorous response and might even consider a resort to tactical nuclear weapons in the event of renewed aggression from the north.[4]

So far as Japan's own safety was concerned, Secretary Kissinger had assured the Japan Society in a New York address on June 18[5] that "Our fidelity to our commitments will be as strong in one part of the globe as in the other." The United States' resolve "to maintain the peace and security of the Korean Peninsula," the Secretary added, reflected an awareness of its "crucial importance to Japan and all of Asia." Not only in this regard but in all the prerequisites to global peace, Dr. Kissinger emphasized, Japan and the United States shared vital responsibilities which could only be discharged in common.

A comparable emphasis pervaded the joint statements issued by President Ford and Prime Minister Miki at the conclusion of their two-day Washington meeting on August 5-6. Over and above the usual joint communiqué summarizing their discussions (**Document 43**), the two leaders also released a special statement enumerating some of the lofty principles professed by the two nations in their joint endeavors to build "a more open and free international community" (**Document 44**). Almost hieratic in its language, this latter document sounded a ceremonial note that would be heard again when Emperor Hirohito and Empress Nagako paid their long-awaited visit to the United States on September 30-October 13. "Never before in history," as the Emperor was to say on that much-photographed occasion, "have two such distant and different peoples forged such close bonds of friendship. I am confident that friendship, so well tested through a number of trials in the past, is an enduring one which will withstand whatever vicissitude there may be in future history."[6]]

(43) Visit of Prime Minister Takeo Miki to Washington, August 5-6, 1975: Joint announcement to the press following the meetings between President Ford and Prime Minister Miki, August 6, 1975.[7]

1. Prime Minister Miki and President Ford met in Washington August 5 and 6 for a comprehensive review of various subjects of

[4]Schlesinger in *New York Times*, June 21, 1975; Ford news conference, June 25, in *Presidential Documents*, 11: 678.

[5]*Bulletin*, 73: 1-8.

[6]Toast, Oct. 3, in *Presidential Documents*, 11: 1114. For full documentation see same: 1104-5, 1109-10, and 1113-14 (*Bulletin*, 73: 615-19).

[7]Text from *Presidential Documents*, 11: 833-5.

mutual interest. The discussions between the two leaders, in which Minister for Foreign Affairs [Kiichi] Miyazawa and Secretary of State Kissinger participated, were conducted in an informal and cordial atmosphere. Their meetings were productive and reflected the strength and breadth of the existing friendship between Japan and the United States.

2. The Prime Minister and the President reaffirmed the basic principles and common purposes underlying relations between Japan and the United States as set forth in the Joint Communique of November 20, 1974,[8] on the occasion of the President's visit to Japan. In so doing, the Prime Minister and the President noted that Japan and the United States, while sharing basic values and ideals, differ in their national characteristics and the circumstances in which they are placed; and yet the two nations, acting together, have drawn upon the strengths inherent in such diversity to build a mature, mutually beneficial and complementary relationship.

They emphasized the fundamental importance in that relationship of constructive and creative cooperation between the two countries toward the shared goals of world peace and prosperity. Expressing satisfaction with the open and frank dialogue which has developed between the two Governments, they pledged to maintain and strengthen this consultation. To this end, the Minister for Foreign Affairs and the Secretary of State will review twice a year bilateral and global matters of common concern.

3. The Prime Minister and the President discussed developments in Asia following the end of armed conflict in Indochina. The President, recognizing the importance of Asia for world peace and progress, reaffirmed that the United States would continue to play an active and positive role in that region and would continue to uphold its treaty commitments there. The Prime Minister and the President welcomed the efforts being made by many nations in Asia to strengthen their political, economic and social bases. They stated that Japan and the United States were prepared to continue to extend assistance and cooperation in support of these efforts. They agreed that the security of the Republic of Korea is essential to the maintenance of peace on the Korean peninsula, which in turn is necessary for peace and security in East Asia, including Japan. They noted the importance of the existing security arrangements for maintaining and preserving that peace. At the same time they strongly expressed the hope that the dialogue between the South and North would proceed in order to ease tensions and eventually to achieve peaceful unification. In connection with the Korean question in the United Nations,[9] the Prime Minister and the Presi-

[8] AFR, 1974: 492-5.
[9] Cf. Chapter 32 at notes 12-14.

dent expressed the hope that all concerned would recognize the importance of maintaining a structure which would preserve the armistice now in effect.

4. The Prime Minister and the President expressed their conviction that the Treaty of Mutual Cooperation and Security between Japan and the United States[10] has greatly contributed to the maintenance of peace and security in the Far East and is an indispensable element of the basic international political structure in Asia, and that the continued maintenance of the Treaty serves the long-term interests of both countries. Further, they recognized that the United States nuclear deterrent is an important contributor to the security of Japan. In this connection, the President reassured the Prime Minister that the United States would continue to abide by its defense commitment to Japan under the Treaty of Mutual Cooperation and Security in the event of armed attack against Japan, whether by nuclear or conventional forces. The Prime Minister stated that Japan would continue to carry out its obligations under the Treaty. The Prime Minister and the President recognized the desirability of still closer consultations for the smooth and effective implementation of the Treaty. They agreed that the authorities concerned of the two countries would conduct consultations within the framework of the Security Consultative Committee on measures to be taken in cooperation by the two countries.

5. The Prime Minister and the President discussed various international issues of common concern. The President noted that the United States would continue to seek an early conclusion to negotiations of the second agreement between the United States and the Soviet Union on the limitation of strategic arms. The Prime Minister and the President expressed their strong hope that prompt progress be made through current efforts toward a peaceful settlement in the Middle East.

6. The Prime Minister and the President expressed their concern over the recent trend toward nuclear proliferation in the world, and agreed that Japan and the United States should participate positively in international efforts for the prevention of nuclear proliferation and the development of adequate safeguards. They emphasized that all nuclear-weapon states should contribute constructively in the areas of nuclear arms limitation, the security of non-nuclear weapon states, and the use of nuclear energy for peaceful purposes. The Prime Minister expressed his intention to proceed with the necessary steps to bring about Japan's ratification of the

[10]Signed at Washington Jan. 19, 1960 and entered into force June 23, 1960 (TIAS 4509; 11 UST 1632); text and related documents in *Documents, 1960*: 425-31.

nuclear non-proliferation treaty at the earliest possible opportunity.[11]

7. In light of the increasing economic interdependence of the nations of the world, the Prime Minister and the President agreed that Japan and the United States share a special responsibility toward the development of a stable and balanced world economy. They agreed that the two countries would work in close consultation toward the resolution in a manner beneficial to all nations of problems relating to the general condition of the world economy, international finance, trade, energy, and cooperation between developed and developing nations. They noted with satisfaction that trade and investment relations between the two countries are expanding in a steady and mutually beneficial manner.

8. Observing the importance of free and expanding trade to the world economy, the Prime Minister and the President emphasized the need for an open international trading system, and affirmed that Japan and the United States would continue to play a positive and constructive role in the Tokyo Round of multilateral trade negotiations currently underway in Geneva within the framework of the General Agreement on Tariffs and Trade.

9. Recognizing that there remain elements of instability in the world energy situation, the Prime Minister and the President expressed their satisfaction with the progress thus far achieved in cooperation among consumer nations.

They agreed to maintain and strengthen cooperation between Japan and the United States in this field and in the development of their respective national energy efforts. Agreeing that mutual understanding and cooperation among all nations is fundamental to the solution of the international energy problem, they noted the urgent need for the development of harmonious relations between oil producing and consuming nations. In this connection, they welcomed steps now being taken to resume the dialogue between oil producer and consumer nations, and expressed their determination that the two countries should further strengthen and coordinate their cooperative efforts for that purpose.

10. Noting the desirability of establishing adequate supply and distribution to meet the world's growing demand for food, the Prime Minister and the President agreed upon the importance of cooperation in agricultural development assistance to promote the food production capabilities of developing countries. The President further noted the need for the early establishment of an internationally coordinated system of nationally-held grain reserves.

[11] Japan deposited its ratification of the Nuclear Nonproliferation Treaty (listed in Chapter 13 at note 1) on June 8, 1976.

The Prime Minister stressed the need for a steady expansion of trade in agricultural products through cooperation between exporting and importing countries to their mutual benefit. The Prime Minister and the President reaffirmed the interest of the two countries in maintaining and strengthening the mutually beneficial agricultural trade between them.

11. Noting the need to assist the efforts of the developing countries to promote their own economic development and to meet the human aspirations of their peoples, the Prime Minister and the President agreed upon the importance of increased cooperation, both between Japan and the United States and with the developing countries, in such areas as development assistance and trade, including that of primary commodities.

12. The Prime Minister and the President expressed appreciation for the achievements recorded during the past decade by existing bilateral cooperative programs in the fields of medicine, science, and technology, and for the work underway in the panel for the review of Japan/U.S. Scientific and Technological Cooperation. They declared their satisfaction at the signing on August 5 by the Minister for Foreign Affairs and the Secretary of State of a new agreement between the two countries for cooperation in environmental protection.[12] They recognized further that the promotion of mutual understanding through cultural and educational exchange is of basic importance to the strengthening of friendly relations between the Japanese and American peoples. In this regard, the Prime Minister expressed his intention of continuing to expand such exchange in addition to the promotion of Japanese studies in the United States and other projects thus far carried out by Japan, notably through the Japan Foundation. Welcoming the Prime Minister's statement, the President expressed his intention to continue his efforts to make expanded resources available for further promoting cultural and educational exchange with Japan.[13]

13. The Prime Minister conveyed on behalf of the people of Japan sincere congratulations to the people of the United States as they celebrate the 200th anniversary of their independence in the coming year. The President thanked the Prime Minister for these sentiments and expressed the deepest appreciation of the American people.

[12]Documentation in *Bulletin*, 73: 385-6.
[13]Use of certain funds for these purposes was authorized by the Japan-United States Friendship Act (Public Law 94-118, Oct. 20, 1975).

(44) Joint Statement by President Ford and Prime Minister Miki at the Conclusion of Their Meetings, August 6, 1975.[14]

The Prime Minister of Japan and the President of the United States, recognizing that the Japanese and American peoples share fundamental democratic values and are joined together by ties of mutual trust and cooperation, affirm that their two nations will continue to work together to build a more open and free international community, and state as follows:

— A more stable and peaceful world order requires the acceptance by all nations of certain principles of international conduct, and the establishment of a creative international dialogue—transcending differences of ideology, tradition or stages of development.
— Those principles must include respect for the sovereignty of all nations, recognition of the legitimate interests of others, attitudes of mutual respect in international dealings, determination to seek the peaceful resolution of differences among nations, and firm commitment to social justice and economic progress around the globe.
— Japan and the United States pledge to support these principles, and to nurture a dialogue among nations which reflects them. They will expand and strengthen their cooperation in many fields of joint endeavor. Recognizing that equitable and durable peace in Asia is essential to that of the entire world, Japan and the United States will extend every support to efforts of the countries of the region to consolidate such a peace.
— International economic and social relations should promote the prosperity of all peoples and the aspirations and creativity of individuals and nations. The interests of developed as well as developing countries, and of consumers as well as producers of raw materials, must be accommodated in a manner which advances the well being of all and brings closer the goal of social and economic justice.
— In a world made small by science and technology, as well as by trade and communications, interdependence among nations has become a reality affecting the lives and welfare of all peoples. International economic institutions and systems

[14]Text from *Presidential Documents*, 11: 835-6.

must function in a manner reflecting that interdependence and promoting a cooperative rather than a confrontational approach to economic issues.

— The suffering caused by disease and hunger is a most serious and poignant impediment to a humane international economic and social order. The financial, educational and technological resources of developed countries give them a special responsibility for the alleviation of these conditions. It is imperative that there be an increasingly effective sharing of knowledge, resources and organizational skill among all countries to hasten the day when these scourges will be eliminated from the earth. In these endeavors also, Japan and the United States will contribute fully.

27. THE CRISIS OF WORLD LAW

(Montreal, August 11, 1975)

[Such events as the Helsinki conference bore witness to the general desire for a harmonious form of international coexistence such as could, in the last analysis, be safeguarded only to the extent that the behavior of states was governed by moral principles and legal rules. A continuation of the centuries-old endeavor to elaborate a body of law that would effectively regulate the conduct of national governments in their relations with one another was an important part of the work of the United Nations, the Organization of American States, and other contemporary international bodies. The Third United Nations Conference on the Law of the Sea, which had held its second working session at Geneva during the spring of 1975,[1] provided a specially vivid illustration of the importance, as well as the complexity, of this effort.

Secretary of State Kissinger discussed the place of international law in American foreign policy in an important address to the annual convention of the American Bar Association at Montreal on August 11. Conventionally identified with a simplistic "balance-of-power" approach to international affairs, the Secretary on this occasion was at pains to emphasize that while an equilibrium of forces was indeed essential to international stability, it represented no more than the beginning of a just and viable international order. The current moment, Dr. Kissinger insisted, was one that not only permitted but imperatively demanded a reshaping of international institutions and practices in order to meet "a new standard of international restraint and cooperation."

Particularly urgent, in Dr. Kissinger's view, was a resolution of the major issues that had thus far prevented the conference on the Law of the Sea from completing its task. The United States, he warned, could not "indefinitely sacrifice its own interest" by waiting for international agreement in areas of maritime endeavor

[1]Cf. Chapter 12.

in which it not only was prepared to act, but was resolved to act independently if agreement was not forthcoming. Advancing a new proposal aimed at accommodating the various interests at stake in the exploitation of the deep seabed, the Secretary also warned that "unregulated and indiscriminate fishing" off the U.S. coasts would undoubtedly be barred by Congress if the international community failed to deal with the matter by agreement.

But neither in this area nor in such fields as the restraint of international terrorism did the Secretary of State succeed in galvanizing the international community into timely action—or, in the most acute case, in delaying unilateral action by the United States itself. The most noticeable sequel to the Montreal speech was the approval by the U.S. House of Representatives on October 9, by a vote of 208 to 101, of a bill asserting U.S. jurisdiction, on an interim basis, over all ocean fishing to a distance of 200 miles from the American coast. In spite of strong opposition by the administration, which had believed that U.S. interests could be adequately safeguarded through the conclusion of new bilateral agreements with the principal fishing nations, a similar bill was to clear the Senate by a vote of 77 to 19 on January 28, 1976. The formal establishment of a 200-mile interim fishery zone, to remain in effect from March 1, 1977 until such time as the issue might be satisfactorily resolved by international agreement, would be accomplished with the final passage and signature of the so-called Fishery Conservation and Management Act of 1976, approved by President Ford (albeit with manifest reluctance) on April 13, 1976.[2]]

(45) "International Law, World Order, and Human Progress": Address by Secretary of State Kissinger before the annual convention of the American Bar Association at Montreal, Canada, August 11, 1975.[3]

President Fellers [James D. Fellers, President of the American Bar Association], President-elect [Lawrence E.] Walsh, ladies and gentlemen: I wonder if any of you have commented on the tableau we present today: an American Secretary of State addressing an assemblage of distinguished American attorneys on American attitudes toward international law in a foreign country. That this meeting should take place in Montreal with no hint of the inappropriate testifies to the understanding, mutual respect, and cooperation which surround the vast network of interconnections be-

[2]Public Law 94-265, Apr. 13, 1976.
[3]Department of State Press Releases 408, Aug. 11, and 408A, Aug. 12; titles and text from *Bulletin*, 73: 353-62.

tween the United States and Canada to an extent virtually without parallel among sovereign nations.

Our meeting here today is also witness to the openness of Canadian society and to its respect for open debate and honest differences. On several issues I will discuss today, Canadian and American positions are not identical; but the differences between us in the realm of international law and cooperation run only to details. The Canadian commitment to international cooperation in all areas and on a global scale is second to none. The United States shares this commitment and has welcomed the cooperation of Canada as we work toward common goals. I wish to acknowledge this kindred spirit as we benefit from Canadian hospitality today.

My friends in the legal profession like to remind me of a comment by a British judge on the difference between lawyers and professors:

> It's very simple (said Lord Denning). The function of lawyers is to find a solution to every difficulty presented to them; whereas the function of professors is to find a difficulty with every solution.

Today the number of difficulties seems to be outpacing the number of solutions—either because my lawyer friends are not working hard enough or because there are too many professors in government.

Law and lawyers have played a seminal role in American public life since the founding of the Republic. In this century lawyers have been consistently at the center of our diplomacy, providing many of our ablest Secretaries of State and diplomats and often decisively influencing American thinking about foreign policy.

This is no accident. The aspiration to harness the conflict of nations by standards of order and justice runs deep in the American tradition. In pioneering techniques of arbitration, conciliation, and adjudication, in developing international institutions and international economic practices, and in creating a body of scholarship sketching visions of world order, American legal thinking has reflected both American idealism and American pragmatic genius.

The problems of the contemporary world structure summon these skills and go beyond them. The rigid international structure of the cold war has disintegrated; we have entered an era of diffused economic power, proliferating nuclear weaponry, and multiple ideologies and centers of initiative. The challenge of our predecessors was to fashion stability from chaos. The challenge of our generation is to go from the building of national and regional institutions and the management of crises to the building of a new international order which offers a hope of peace, progress, well-being, and justice for the generations to come.

Justice Holmes said of the common law that it "is not a brooding omnipresence in the sky but the articulate voice of some sovereign or quasi-sovereign that can be identified." But international politics recognizes no sovereign or even quasi-sovereign power beyond the nation-state.

Thus in international affairs the age-old struggle between order and anarchy has a political as well as a legal dimension. When competing national political aims are pressed to the point of unrestrained competition, the precepts of law prove fragile. The unrestrained quest for predominance brooks no legal restraints. In a democratic society law flourishes best amidst pluralistic institutions. Similarly in the international arena stability requires a certain equilibrium of power. Our basic foreign policy objective inevitably must be to shape a stable and cooperative global order out of diverse and contending interests.

But this is not enough. Preoccupation with interests and power is at best sterile and at worst an invitation to a constant test of strength. The true task of statesmanship is to draw from the balance of power a more positive capacity to better the human condition—to turn stability into creativity, to transform the relaxation of tensions into a strengthening of freedoms, to turn man's preoccupations from self-defense to human progress.

An international order can be neither stable nor just without accepted norms of conduct. International law both provides a means and embodies our ends. It is a repository of our experience and our idealism—a body of principles drawn from the practice of states and an instrument for fashioning new patterns of relations between states. Law is an expression of our own culture and yet a symbol of universal goals. It is the heritage of our past and a means of shaping our future.

The challenge of international order takes on unprecedented urgency in the contemporary world of interdependence. In an increasing number of areas of central political relevance, the legal process has become of major concern. Technology has driven us into vast new areas of human activity and opened up new prospects of either human progress or international contention. The use of the oceans and of outer space, the new excesses of hijacking, terrorism, and warfare, the expansion of multinational corporations, will surely become areas of growing dispute if they are not regulated by a legal order.

The United States will not seek to impose a parochial or self-serving view of the law on others. But neither will we carry the quest for accommodation to the point of prejudicing our own values and rights. The new corpus of the law of nations must benefit all peoples equally; it cannot be the preserve of any one nation or group of nations.

The United States is convinced in its own interest that the extension of legal order is a boon to humanity and a necessity. The traditional aspiration of Americans takes on a new relevance and urgency in contemporary conditions. On a planet marked by interdependence, unilateral action and unrestrained pursuit of the national advantage inevitably provoke counteraction and therefore spell futility and anarchy. In an age of awesome weapons of war, there must be accommodation or there will be disaster.

Therefore there must be an expansion of the legal consensus, in terms both of subject matter and participation. Many new and important areas of international activity, such as new departures in technology and communication, cry out for agreed international rules. In other areas, juridical concepts have advanced faster than the political will that is indispensable to assure their observance—such as the U.N. Charter provisions governing the use of force in international relations. The pace of legal evolution cannot be allowed to lag behind the headlong pace of change in the world at large. In a world of 150 nations and competing ideologies, we cannot afford to wait upon the growth of customary international law. Nor can we be content with the snail's pace of treatymaking as we have known it in recent years in international forums.

We are at a pivotal moment in history. If the world is in flux, we have the capacity and hence the obligation to help shape it. If our goal is a new standard of international restraint and cooperation, then let us fashion the institutions and practices that will bring it about.

This morning I would like to set forth the American view on some of those issues of law and diplomacy whose solution can move us toward a more orderly and lawful world. These issues emphasize the contemporary international challenge—in the oceans, where traditional law has been made obsolete by modern technology; in outer space, where endeavors undreamed of a generation ago impinge upon traditional concerns for security and sovereignty; in the laws of war, where new practices of barbarism challenge us to develop new social and international restraint; and in international economics, where transnational enterprises conduct their activities beyond the frontier of traditional political and legal regulation.

I shall deal in special detail with the law of the sea in an effort to promote significant and rapid progress in this vitally important negotiation.

The Law of the Sea

The United States is now engaged with some 140 nations in one of the most comprehensive and critical negotiations in history, an international effort to devise rules to govern the domain of the oceans. No current international negotiation is more vital for the long-term stability and prosperity of our globe.

One need not be a legal scholar to understand what is at stake. The oceans cover 70 percent of the earth's surface. They both unite and divide mankind. The importance of free navigation for the security of nations, including our country, is traditional; the economic significance of ocean resources is becoming enormous.

From the 17th century until now, the law of the seas has been founded on a relatively simple precept: freedom of the seas, limited only by a narrow belt of territorial waters generally extending three miles offshore. Today the explosion of technology requires new and more sophisticated solutions.

—In a world desperate for new sources of energy and minerals, vast and largely untapped reserves exist in the oceans.

—In a world that faces widespread famine and malnutrition, fish have become an increasingly vital source of protein.

—In a world clouded by pollution, the environmental integrity of the oceans turns into a critical international problem.

—In a world where 95 percent of international trade is carried on the seas, freedom of navigation is essential.

Unless competitive practices and claims are soon harmonized, the world faces the prospect of mounting conflict. Shipping tonnage is expected to increase fourfold in the next 30 years. Large self-contained factory vessels already circle the globe and dominate fishing areas that were once the province of small coastal boats. The worldwide fish harvest is increasing dramatically, but without due regard to sound management or the legitimate concerns of coastal states. Shifting population patterns will soon place new strains on the ecology of the world's coastlines

The current negotiation may thus be the world's last chance. Unilateral national claims to fishing zones and territorial seas extending from 50 to 200 miles have already resulted in seizures of fishing vessels and constant disputes over rights to ocean space. The breakdown of the current negotiation, a failure to reach a legal consensus, will lead to unrestrained military and commercial rivalry and mounting political turmoil.

The United States strongly believes that law must govern the oceans. In this spirit, we welcomed the U.N. mandate in 1970 for a multilateral conference to write a comprehensive treaty governing the use of the oceans and their resources.[4] We contributed substan-

---

[4]General Assembly Resolution 2750 C (XXV), Dec. 17, 1970, quoted in *AFR, 1974*: 316.

tially to the progress that was made at Caracas last summer[5] and at Geneva this past spring, which produced a "single negotiating text" of a draft treaty.[6] This will focus the work of the next session, scheduled for March 1976 in New York. The United States intends to intensify its efforts.

The issues in the law of the sea negotiation stretch from the shoreline to the farthest deep seabed. They include:

—The extent of the territorial sea and the related issues of guarantees of free transit through straits;
—The degree of control that a coastal state can exercise in an offshore economic zone beyond its territorial waters; and
—The international system for the exploitation of the resources of the deep seabeds.

If we move outward from the coastline, the first issue is the extent of the *territorial sea*, the belt of ocean over which the coastal state exercises sovereignty. Historically, it has been recognized as three miles; that has been the long-established U.S. position. Increasingly, other states have claimed 12 miles or even 200.

After years of dispute and contradictory international practice, the Law of the Sea Conference is approaching a consensus on a 12-mile territorial limit. We are prepared to accept this solution, provided that the unimpeded transit rights through and over straits used for international navigation are guaranteed. For without such guarantees, a 12-mile territorial sea would place over 100 straits— including the Straits of Gibraltar, Malacca, and Bab el Mandeb— now free for international sea and air travel under the jurisdictional control of coastal states. This the United States cannot accept. Freedom of international transit through these and other straits is for the benefit of all nations, for trade and for security. We will not join in an agreement which leaves any uncertainty about the right to use world communication routes without interference.

Within 200 miles of the shore are some of the world's most important fishing grounds as well as substantial deposits of petroleum, natural gas, and minerals. This has led some coastal states to seek full sovereignty over this zone. These claims, too, are unacceptable to the United States. To accept them would bring 30 percent of the oceans under national territorial control—in the very areas through which most of the world's shipping travels.

The United States joins many other countries in urging international agreement on a 200-mile offshore *economic zone*. Under this proposal, coastal states would be permitted to control fisheries and

[5]Same: 315-26.
[6]Cf. Chapter 12 at note 5.

mineral resources in the economic zone, but freedom of navigation and other rights of the international community would be preserved. Fishing within the zone would be managed by the coastal state, which would have an international duty to apply agreed standards of conservation. If the coastal state could not harvest all the allowed yearly fishing catch, other countries would be permitted to do so. Special arrangements for tuna and salmon, and other fish which migrate over large distances, would be required. We favor also provisions to protect the fishing interests of landlocked and other geographically disadvantaged countries.

In some areas the *continental margin* extends beyond 200 miles. To resolve disagreements over the use of this area, the United States proposes that the coastal states be given jurisdiction over continental margin resources beyond 200 miles, to a precisely defined limit, and that they share a percentage of financial benefit from mineral exploitation in that area with the international community.

Beyond the territorial sea, the offshore economic zone, and the continental margin lie *the deep seabeds*. They are our planet's last great unexplored frontier. For more than a century we have known that the deep seabeds hold vast deposits of manganese, nickel, cobalt, copper, and other minerals, but we did not know how to extract them. New modern technology is rapidly advancing the time when their exploration and commercial exploitation will become a reality.

The United Nations has declared the deep seabeds to be the "common heritage of mankind."[7] But this only states the problem. How will the world community manage the clash of national and regional interests or the inequality of technological capability? Will we reconcile unbridled competition with the imperative of political order?

The United States has nothing to fear from competition. Our technology is the most advanced, and our Navy is adequate to protect our interests. Ultimately, unless basic rules regulate exploitation, rivalry will lead to tests of power. A race to carve out exclusive domains of exploitation on the deep seabeds, even without claims of sovereignty, will menace freedom of navigation and invite a competition like that of the colonial powers in Africa and Asia in the last century.

This is not the kind of world we want to see. Law has an opportunity to civilize us in the early stages of a new competitive activity.

We believe that the Law of the Sea Treaty must preserve the right of access presently enjoyed by states and their citizens under inter-

[7]General Assembly Resolution 2749 (XXV), Dec. 17, 1970.

national law. Restrictions on free access will retard the development of seabed resources. Nor is it feasible, as some developing countries have proposed, to reserve to a new international seabed organization the sole right to exploit the seabeds.

Nevertheless the United States believes strongly that law must regulate international activity in this area. The world community has a historic opportunity to manage this new wealth cooperatively and to dedicate resources from the exploitation of the deep seabeds to the development of the poorer countries. A cooperative and equitable solution can lead to new patterns of accommodation between the developing and industrial countries. It could give a fresh and conciliatory cast to the dialogue between the industrialized and so-called Third World. The legal regime we establish for the deep seabeds can be a milestone in the legal and political development of the world community.

The United States has devoted much thought and consideration to this issue. We offer the following proposals:

—An international organization should be created to set rules for deep seabed mining.

—This international organization must preserve the rights of all countries, and their citizens, directly to exploit deep seabed resources.

—It should also insure fair adjudication of conflicting interests and security of investment.

—Countries and their enterprises mining deep seabed resources should pay an agreed portion of their revenues to the international organization, to be used for the benefit of developing countries.

—The management of the organization and its voting procedures must reflect and balance the interests of the participating states. The organization should not have the power to control prices or production rates.

—If these essential U.S. interests are guaranteed, we can agree that this organization will also have the right to conduct mining operations on behalf of the international community primarily for the benefit of developing countries.

—The new organization should serve as a vehicle for cooperation between the technologically advanced and the developing countries. The United States is prepared to explore ways of sharing deep seabed technology with other nations.

—A balanced commission of consumers, seabed producers, and land-based producers could monitor the possible adverse effects of deep seabed mining on the economies of those developing countries which are substantially dependent on the export of minerals also produced from the deep seabeds.

The United States believes that the world community has before it an extraordinary opportunity. The regime for the deep seabeds can turn interdependence from a slogan into reality. The sense of community which mankind has failed to achieve on land could be realized through a regime for the oceans.

The United States will continue to make determined efforts to bring about final progress when the Law of the Sea Conference reconvenes in New York next year. But we must be clear on one point: The United States cannot indefinitely sacrifice its own interest in developing an assured supply of critical resources to an indefinitely prolonged negotiation. We prefer a generally acceptable international agreement that provides a stable legal environment *before* deep seabed mining actually begins. The responsibility for achieving an agreement before actual exploitation begins is shared by all nations. We cannot defer our own deep seabed mining for too much longer. In this spirit, we and other potential seabed producers can consider appropriate steps to protect current investment and to insure that this investment is also protected in the treaty.

The conference is faced with other important issues:

—Ways must be found to encourage marine scientific research for the benefit of all mankind while safeguarding the legitimate interests of coastal states in their economic zones.

—Steps must be taken to protect the oceans from pollution. We must establish uniform international controls on pollution from ships and insist upon universal respect for environmental standards for continental shelf and deep seabed exploitation.

—Access to the sea for landlocked countries must be assured.

—There must be provisions for compulsory and impartial third-party settlement of disputes. The United States cannot accept unilateral interpretation of a treaty of such scope by individual states or by an international seabed organization.

The pace of technology, the extent of economic need, and the claims of ideology and national ambition threaten to submerge the difficult process of negotiation. The United States therefore believes that a just and beneficial regime for the oceans is essential to world peace.

For the self-interest of every nation is heavily engaged. Failure would seriously impair confidence in global treatymaking and in the very process of multilateral accommodation. The conclusion of a comprehensive Law of the Sea Treaty on the other hand would mark a major step toward a new world community.

The urgency of the problem is illustrated by disturbing developments which continue to crowd upon us. Most prominent is the problem of fisheries.

The United States cannot indefinitely accept unregulated and indiscriminate foreign fishing off its coasts. Many fish stocks have been brought close to extinction by foreign overfishing. We have recently concluded agreements with the Soviet Union, Japan, and Poland which will limit their catch; and we have a long and successful history of conservation agreements with Canada. But much more needs to be done.

Many within Congress are urging us to solve this problem unilaterally. A bill to establish a 200-mile fishing zone passed the Senate last year;[8] a new one is currently before the House.

The Administration shares the concern which has led to such proposals. But unilateral action is both extremely dangerous and incompatible with the thrust of the negotiations described here. The United States has consistently resisted the unilateral claims of other nations, and others will almost certainly resist ours. Unilateral legislation on our part would almost surely prompt others to assert extreme claims of their own. Our ability to negotiate an acceptable international consensus on the economic zone will be jeopardized. If every state proclaims its own rules of law and seeks to impose them on others, the very basis of international law will be shaken, ultimately to our own detriment.

We warmly welcome the recent statement by Prime Minister Trudeau reaffirming the need for a solution through the Law of the Sea Conference rather than through unilateral action. He said:

> Canadians at large should realize that we have very large stakes indeed in the Law of the Sea Conference and we would be fools to give up those stakes by an action that would be purely a temporary, paper success.

That attitude will guide our actions as well. To conserve the fish and protect our fishing industry while the treaty is being negotiated, the United States will negotiate interim arrangements with other nations to conserve the fish stocks, to insure effective enforcement, and to protect the livelihood of our coastal fishermen. These agreements will be a transition to the eventual 200-mile zone. We believe it is in the interests of states fishing off our coasts to cooperate with us in this effort. We will support the efforts of other states, including our neighbors, to deal with their problems by similar agreements. We will consult fully with Congress, our states, the public, and foreign governments on arrangements for implementing a 200-mile zone by virtue of agreement at the Law of the Sea Conference.

Unilateral legislation would be a last resort. The world simply

[8] Cf. *AFR, 1974*: 321 n. 11.

cannot afford to let the vital questions before the Law of the Sea Conference be answered by default. We are at one of those rare moments when mankind has come together to devise means of preventing future conflict and shaping its destiny rather than to solve a crisis that has occurred or to deal with the aftermath of war. It is a test of vision and will and of statesmanship. It must succeed. The United States is resolved to help conclude the conference in 1976, before the pressure of events and contention places international consensus irretrievably beyond our grasp.

Outer Space and the Law of Nations

The oceans are not the only area in which technology drives man in directions he has not foreseen and toward solutions unprecedented in history. No dimension of our modern experience is more a source of wonder than the exploration of space. Here, too, the extension of man's reach has come up against national sensitivities and concerns for sovereignty. Here, too, we confront the potential for conflict or the possibility for legal order. Here, too, we have an opportunity to substitute law for power in the formative stage of an international activity.

Space technologies are directly relevant to the well-being of all nations. Earth-sensing satellites, for example, can dramatically help nations to assess their resources and to develop their potential. In the Sahel region of Africa we have seen the tremendous potential of this technology in dealing with natural disasters. The United States has urged in the United Nations that the new knowledge be made freely and widely available.

The use of satellites for broadcasting has a great potential to spread educational opportunities and to foster the exchange of ideas.

In the nearly two decades since the first artificial satellite, remarkable progress has been made in extending the reach of law to outer space. The Outer Space Treaty of 1967[9] placed space beyond national sovereignty and banned weapons of mass destruction from earth orbit. The treaty also established the principle that the benefits of space exploration should be shared. Supplementary agreements have provided for the registry of objects placed in space,[10] for liability for damage caused by their return to earth,[11]

[9]Signed Jan. 27 and entered into force Oct. 10, 1967 (TIAS 6347; 18 UST 2410); text in *Documents, 1966*: 391-8.
[10]Opened for signature Jan. 14, 1975 and entered into force Sept. 15, 1976 (TIAS 8480).
[11]Signed Mar. 29, 1972 and entered into force for the U.S. Oct. 9, 1973 (TIAS 7762; 24 UST 2389).

and for international assistance to astronauts in emergencies.[12] Efforts are underway to develop further international law governing man's activities on the moon and other celestial bodies.

Earth-sensing and broadcasting satellites, and conditions of their use, are a fresh challenge to international agreement. The United Nations Committee on the Peaceful Uses of Outer Space is seized with the issue, and the United States will cooperate actively with it. We are committed to the wider exchange of communication and ideas. But we recognize that there must be full consultation among the countries directly concerned. While we believe that knowledge of the earth and its environment gained from outer space should be broadly shared, we recognize that this must be accompanied by efforts to insure that all countries will fully understand the significance of this new knowledge.

The United States stands ready to engage in a cooperative search for agreed international ground rules for these activities.

Hijacking, Terrorism, and War

The modern age has not only given us the benefits of technology; it has also spawned the plagues of aircraft hijacking, international terrorism, and new techniques of warfare. The international community cannot ignore these affronts to civilization; it must not allow them to spread their poison; it has a duty to act vigorously to combat them.

Nations already have the legal obligation, recognized by unanimous resolution of the U.N. General Assembly,[13] "to refrain from organizing, instigating, assisting or participating (or) acquiescing in" terrorist acts. Treaties have been concluded to combat hijacking, sabotage of aircraft,[14] and attacks on diplomats.[15] The majority of states observe these rules; a minority do not. But events even in the last few weeks dramatize that present restraints are inadequate.

The United States is convinced that stronger international steps must be taken—and urgently—to deny skyjackers and terrorists a safehaven and to establish sanctions against states which aid them, harbor them, or fail to prosecute or extradite them.

---

[12]Signed Apr. 22 and entered into force Dec. 3, 1968 (TIAS 6599; 19 UST 7570): text in *Documents, 1967*: 292-6.
[13]Resolution 2625 (XXV), Oct. 24, 1970.
[14]Details in *AFR, 1972*: 515-16.
[15]Convention on the Prevention and Punishment of Crimes Against Internationally Protected Persons, Including Diplomatic Agents, done at New York Dec. 14, 1973 and entered into force Feb. 20, 1977 (TIAS 8532); text in *AFR, 1973*: 586-94.

The United States in 1972 proposed to the United Nations a new international Convention for the Prevention and Punishment of Certain Acts of International Terrorism, covering kidnaping, murder, and other brutal acts.[16] This convention regrettably was not adopted, and innumerable innocent lives have been lost as a consequence. We urge the United Nations once again to take up and adopt this convention or other similar proposals as a matter of the highest priority.

Terrorism, like piracy, must be seen as outside the law. It discredits any political objective that it purports to serve and any nations which encourage it. If all nations deny terrorists a safehaven, terrorist practices will be substantially reduced—just as the incidence of skyjacking has declined sharply as a result of multilateral and bilateral agreements. All governments have a duty to defend civilized life by supporting such measures.

The struggle to restrain violence by law meets one of its severest tests in the law of war. Historically nations have found it possible to observe certain rules in their conduct of war. This restraint has been extended and codified especially in the past century. In our time, new, ever more awesome tools of warfare, the bitterness of ideologies and civil warfare, and weakened bonds of social cohesion have brought an even more brutal dimension to human conflict.

At the same time our century has also witnessed a broad effort to ameliorate some of these evils by international agreements. The most recent and comprehensive are the four Geneva Conventions of 1949 on the protection of war victims.[17]

But the law in action has been less impressive than the law on the books. Patent deficiencies in implementation and compliance can no longer be ignored. Two issues are of paramount concern: First, greater protection for civilians and those imprisoned, missing, and wounded in war; and second, the application of international standards of humane conduct in civil wars.

An international conference is now underway to supplement the 1949 Geneva Conventions on the laws of war.[18] We will continue to press for rules which will prohibit nations from barring a neutral country, or an international organization such as the International Committee of the Red Cross, from inspecting its treatment of prisoners. We strongly support provisions requiring full accounting

[16]*AFR, 1972*: 501-7.

[17]TIAS 3362-5; 6 UST 3114, 3217, 3316, 3516.

[18]The second session of the Diplomatic Conference on the Reaffirmation and Development of International Humanitarian Law Applicable in Armed Conflicts was held in Geneva on Feb. 3-Apr. 18, 1975; details in *Digest of United States Practice in International Law, 1975*: 803-11.

for the missing in action. We will advocate immunity for aircraft evacuating the wounded. And we will seek agreement on a protocol which demands humane conduct during civil war, which bans torture, summary execution, and the other excesses which too often characterize civil strife.

The United States is committed to the principle that fundamental human rights require legal protection under all circumstances, that some kinds of individual suffering are intolerable no matter what threat nations may face. The American people and government deeply believe in fundamental standards of humane conduct; we are committed to uphold and promote them; we will fight to vindicate them in international forums.

Multinational Enterprises

The need for new international regulation touches areas as modern as new technology and as old as war. It also reaches our economic institutions, where human ingenuity has created new means for progress while bringing new problems of social and legal adjustment.

Multinational enterprises have contributed greatly to economic growth in both their industrialized home countries, where they are most active, and in developing countries where they conduct some of their operations. If these organizations are to continue to foster world economic growth, it is in the common interest that international law, not political contests, govern their future.

Some nations feel that multinational enterprises influence their economies in ways unresponsive to their national priorities. Others are concerned that these enterprises may evade national taxation and regulation through facilities abroad. And recent disclosures of improper financial relationships between these companies and government officials in several countries raise fresh concerns.

But it remains equally true that multinational enterprises can be powerful engines for good. They can marshal and organize the resources of capital, initiative, research, technology, and markets in ways which vastly increase production and growth. If an international consensus on the proper role and responsibilities of these enterprises could be reached, their vital contribution to the world economy could be further expanded.

A multilateral treaty establishing binding rules for multinational enterprises does not seem possible in the near future. However, the United States believes an agreed statement of basic principles is achievable. We are prepared to make a major effort and invite the participation of all interested parties.

We are now actively discussing such guidelines and will support the relevant work of the U.N. Commission on Transnational Corporations.[19] We believe that such guidelines must:

—Accord with existing principles of international law governing the treatment of foreigners and their property rights.
—Call upon multinational corporations to take account of national priorities, act in accordance with local law, and employ fair labor practices.
—Cover all multinationals, state owned as well as private.
—Not discriminate in favor of host-country enterprises except under specifically defined and limited circumstances.
—Set forth not only the obligations of the multinationals but also the host country's responsibilities to the foreign enterprises within their borders.
—Acknowledge the responsibility of governments to apply recognized conflict-of-laws principles in reconciling regulations applied by various host nations.

If multinational institutions become an object of economic warfare, it will be an ill omen for the global economic system. We believe that the continued operation of transnational companies, under accepted guidelines, can be reconciled with the claims of national sovereignty. The capacity of nations to deal with this issue constructively will be a test of whether the search for common solutions or the clash of ideologies will dominate our economic future.

Since the early days of the Republic, Americans have seen that their nation's self-interest could not be separated from a just and progressive international legal order. Our Founding Fathers were men of law, of wisdom, and of political sophistication. The heritage they left is an inspiration as we face an expanding array of problems that are at once central to our national well-being and soluble only on a global scale.

The challenge of the statesman is to recognize that a just international order cannot be built on power, but only on restraint of power. As Felix Frankfurter said:

Fragile as reason is and limited as law is as the expression of the institutionalized medium of reason, that's all we have standing between us and the tyranny of mere will and the cruelty of unbridled, unprincipled, undisciplined feeling.

If the politics of ideological confrontation and strident nationalism become pervasive, broad and humane international agreement will grow ever more elusive and unilateral actions will

[19]Cf. *U.S. Participation, 1975*: 139-41.

dominate. In an environment of widening chaos the stronger will survive and may even prosper temporarily. But the weaker will despair, and the human spirit will suffer.

The American people have always had a higher vision: a community of nations that has discovered the capacity to act according to man's more noble aspirations. The principles and procedures of the Anglo-American legal system have proven their moral and practical worth. They have promoted our national progress and brought benefits to more citizens more equitably than in any society in the history of man. They are a heritage and a trust which we all hold in common. And their greatest contribution to human progress may well lie ahead of us.

The philosopher Kant saw law and freedom, moral principle and practical necessity, as parts of the same reality. He saw law as the inescapable guide to political action. He believed that sooner or later the realities of human interdependence would compel the fulfillment of the moral imperatives of human aspiration.

We have reached that moment in time where moral and practical imperatives, law, and pragmatism point toward the same goals.

The foreign policy of the United States must reflect the universal ideals of the American people. It is no accident that a dedication to international law has always been a central feature of our foreign policy. And so it is today—inescapably—as for the first time in history we have the opportunity and the duty to build a true world community.

28. POWER AND FOREIGN POLICY

(Minneapolis, August 19, 1975)

[As was natural in addressing a gathering of lawyers, Secretary Kissinger in his Montreal speech had stressed the role of law as an essential regulator of the interactions of the world's sovereign states. Not less natural was President Ford's determination, when he appeared at the Minneapolis Convention Center on August 19 to address the 57th National Convention of the American Legion, to emphasize the importance of national power as an essential guarantee of national security and international peace. The annual conventions of the American Legion and of the Veterans of Foreign Wars (whom President Ford had addressed exactly a year earlier)[1] were favorite occasions for the evocation of patriotic feeling and the deployment of presidential rhetoric about the need for a strong national defense. In this respect the Minneapolis address did not fall short of similar performances by Mr. Ford's predecessors.

Developments of the spring and summer of 1975 undoubtedly lent a special timeliness to a discussion of the role of military power in a world that had lately seemed to many observers to be dominated, for good or ill, by the phenomena of East-West détente. The gradual slackening of East-West tensions and the conclusion of the Vietnam adventure had not been favorable to the reestablishment of an American consensus on foreign policy matters. Such consensus as currently existed, indeed, had appeared to spring from nothing more positive than a somewhat uncritical impulse to relegate foreign affairs to a secondary position and give priority attention to domestic issues.

Responding to this trend, the two houses of Congress had already moved to trim the defense estimates submitted by the President in his January budget for the Fiscal Year 1976 and the three-month "transition quarter" ending September 30, 1976.[2] In a first

[1]Cf. *AFR, 1974*: 286.
[2]Cf. Chapter 4, Document 7.

trial of the new congressional budget process, House and Senate had agreed in May[3] to impose defense reductions totaling $7 billion in recommended budget authority and $3.3 billions in budget outlays, in part because of developments in Indochina and partly in implementation of a general shift of priorities in favor of the home front. Similar cuts were now being made in the annual military procurement authorization bill, the final version of which[4] would, among other things, prohibit any expenditure (in the absence of further authorizing legislation) for production of the B-1 bomber aircraft on which the administration was counting to help maintain "essential equivalence" in strategic armaments with the U.S.S.R.

In the meantime, however, the concept of East-West détente on which a majority in Congress still appeared to rely was being called in question by a visible slowdown in the progress of U.S.-Soviet relations. It was true that bilateral trade did not appear to have been adversely affected by the collapse of administration plans to grant the Soviet Union most-favored-nation treatment and large-scale credits (although the U.S.S.R.'s reentry into the American market as a substantial grain purchaser had once again occasioned anxiety from the standpoint of its possible impact on supplies and prices).[5] But the bitterness occasioned by the January trade fiasco still lingered; and the President's recent visit to Helsinki had elicited fresh criticism on the part of those Americans who disbelieved in the possibility—or the usefulness—of any genuine détente with a power so differently constituted as the Soviet Union. Less dramatic, though surely not less serious in the long run, was the apparent failure of the U.S. and Soviet SALT negotiators to advance toward the announced goal of a second-stage agreement on the limitation of strategic offensive arms that could be signed in 1975.

President Ford could offer no definite word on any of these matters in his August 19 speech to the American Legion. What he could, and did, do was to appeal for the support of his listeners in ensuring that the United States would not let down its guard but would continue, with or without a SALT agreement, to maintain the strength required by the defense of its own interests and those of the "free world" as a whole.]

---

[3]House Concurrent Resolution 218, 94th Cong., 1st sess., May 14, 1975.
[4]Department of Defense Appropriation Authorization Act, 1976 (Public Law 94-106, Oct. 7, 1975).
[5]Cf. Chapter 35.

(46) Détente and National Security: Remarks by President Ford before the 57th National Convention of the American Legion, Minneapolis, August 19, 1975.[6]

* * *

As a fellow Legionnaire of 30 years and as a member of the Furniture City Post Number 258, I am proud to be here with all of you as a fellow Legionnaire. I am proud of the organization, locally, nationally, and otherwise.

I strongly commend the American Legion for its constant patriotism in peace as well as in war. This great organization has given life and meaning to our motto, "For God and Country." As President, I salute you and say for all Americans: Hang in there!

I am very, very happy to have this opportunity to talk with my fellow Legionnaires about two things which the American Legion has always held dear: freedom and peace—for our country and for the world.

Freedom always comes first. Let there be no doubt about that. Patrick Henry answered that question for all of us some 200 years ago. The Marines, the seamen, and the airmen who rescued the *Mayaguez* gave the same clear answer which was heard 'round the world. All Americans are terribly proud of their success.

But in today's world of technological terror, with weapons of awesome sophistication and destructiveness, it is difficult to see how freedom as we know it could survive another all-out war. It is even questionable whether a free society such as ours could survive an all-out, unrestricted arms race.

We are, therefore, confronted with this dilemma that has faced the American people and their Government since the postwar Administrations of Presidents Truman and Eisenhower. The question is this: How do we preserve, protect, and defend our freedom and that of our allies? How do we advance the cause of freedom worldwide? And how do we, at the same time, preserve the general peace and create conditions that reduce the chances of war? How do we control the tremendous cost of maintaining the capabilities required for a potential major war?

These are exceedingly difficult questions to answer. At times, we have come perilously close to a major military confrontation. We have suffered some serious setbacks. And we are still unable to

[6]Text from *Presidential Documents*, 11: 869-74 (salutatory remarks omitted).

resolve some dangerous conflicts festering on nearly every continent in the world.

But we have prevented world war III. We have preserved civilization. Few who remember the immediate postwar period after World War II would say that the world is not calmer and better off today than it was.

The free world, as we define it, is essentially intact after 30 years of uneasy peace between the super powers, instability in former colonial areas, and sporadic outbreaks of local and regional violence. And three decades of imperfect peace have permitted unprecedented gains in productivity and economic progress for much of mankind, including the United States.

Some fundamental lessons were learned in this period. They must not be forgotten.

First, the military might, the material strength, and moral purpose of the United States were absolutely essential to achieve the present level of international stability. They remain absolutely essential. We are still the principal defender of freedom throughout the world.

Second, our enormous defense capability and its economic base have been reinforced by the growing resources of our allies in Europe and in the Pacific and by the increasing interdependence of industrial democracies in both military and economic areas. They must continue.

Third, the policies of five American Presidents before me for strong national defense, for reduction of East-West tension and the threat of thermonuclear war, and for the bolstering of our essential allies have had the unswerving and nonpartisan support of the Congress and the American people. I will continue to seek that support. But today I ask you, my fellow Legionnaires, to help me achieve that objective, and I know that I can count on your support.

We share a very deep concern over the cracks now appearing in the foundations of essential national unity on defense and foreign policy.

Without a clear consensus among 214 million Americans, the role of the United States as the champion of freedom and peace throughout the world would be crippled—crippled very seriously, if not fatally. The ability of a President to carry out his constitutional duties would be dangerously diminished. The temptation to potential adversaries to take advantage of any apparent weakness, disunity, and indecision could become irresistible. With your support and that of other Americans, my Administration will give them no such temptation.

George Washington, our first President, said the best way to preserve peace is to be prepared for war. In one way or another, each of President Washington's successors has repeated that truth. Unfortunately, we have historically ignored it. We have abruptly demobilized after every war, and the next generation—the next generation of Americans—paid very dearly for this folly. I see some danger signs of our doing it again, with the stakes infinitely higher than ever before.

That is why I say to you, I am determined to resist unilateral disarmament. I am equally committed to keeping America's defenses second to none.

Now that Americans are no longer fighting on any front, there are many sincere but, in my judgment, shortsighted Americans who believe that the billions for defense could be better spent for social programs to help the poor and disadvantaged.

But I am convinced that adequate spending for national defense is an insurance policy, an insurance policy for peace we cannot afford to be without. It is most valuable if we never need to use it. But without it, we could be wiped out.

Certainly the most important social obligation of government is to guarantee all citizens, including the disadvantaged, sufficient protection of their lives and freedoms against outside attack. Today, that protection is our principal hope of peace. What expense item in our Federal budget is more essential?

This is one place where second best is worth nothing. The proportion of Federal spending for national security and the proportion of our gross national product going for defense requirements have declined in recent years. The dollar figures in the Federal budget go up, but simply because of inflation. But the weapons we can purchase and the personnel we can afford have declined.

During the Vietnam war, defense spending concentrated—and properly so—on current combat requirements, shortchanging our long-range research and development efforts. If our technological lead is not rapidly recovered, this could be fatal to our qualitative superiority in the future. Scientific progress in the Pentagon must be an equal partner with the best in personnel and the best in weapons in maintaining peace and deterring war.

Our potential adversaries are certainly not reducing the levels of their military power. The United States, as a result, must be alert and strong, and it will be. The defense budget which I submitted for fiscal year 1976 represents, under these circumstances, the bare minimum required for our national security. I will vigorously resist all major cuts in every way I can, and I hope I have your help.

For the next fiscal year—1977—I honestly and sincerely hope to hold down our spending on nuclear forces. This tentative judgment is conditioned on real progress in SALT II. But the Congress and the American people must realize that, unless agreement is achieved, I will have no choice but to recommend to the Congress an additional $2 billion to $3 billion for strategic weapons programs in current and coming fiscal years.

In recent weeks, there has been a great deal said about the subject of détente. Today, let me tell you what I personally think about détente.

First of all, the word itself is confusing. Its meaning is not clear to everybody. French is a beautiful language, the classic language of diplomacy. But I wish there were one simple English word to substitute for détente. Unfortunately, there isn't.

Relations between the world's two strongest nuclear powers can't be summed up in a catch phrase. Détente literally means "easing" or "relaxing," but definitely not—and I emphasize not—the relaxing of diligence or easing of effort. Rather, it means movement away from the constant crisis and dangerous confrontations that have characterized relations with the Soviet Union.

The process of détente—and it is a process—looks toward a saner and safer relationship between us and the Soviet Union. It represents our best efforts to cool the cold war, which on occasion became much too hot for comfort.

To me, détente means a fervent desire for peace—but not peace at any price. It means the preservation of fundamental American principles—not their sacrifice. It means maintaining the strength to command respect from our adversaries and provide leadership to our friends—not letting down our guard or dismantling our defenses or neglecting our allies. It means peaceful rivalry between political and economic systems—not the curbing of our competitive efforts.

Since the American system depends on freedom, we are confident that our philosophy will prevail. Freedom is still the wave of the future. Détente means moderate and restrained behavior between two super powers—not a license to fish in troubled waters. It means mutual respect and reciprocity—not unilateral concessions or one-sided agreements.

With this attitude, I shall work with determination for a relaxation of tensions. The United States has nothing to fear from progress toward peace.

Although we have still a long way to go, we have made some progress: a defusing of the Berlin time bomb, the ABM treaty, the first SALT agreements and progress on SALT II, the start of mutual and balanced force reductions in Europe,[7] and other arms

[7] For references cf. Chapter 25 at notes 7-10.

control agreements regarding space,[8] the seabeds,[9] and germ warfare.[10]

We have established the basis for progress toward détente and cooperation in Europe as a result of the summit meeting of some 35 nations in Helsinki. But the principles we adopted there now must be put into practice—principles, I should say, will be put into practice. We cannot raise the hopes of our people and shatter them by unkept promises.

We are now carefully watching some serious situations for indications of the Soviet attitude toward détente and cooperation in European security. The situation in Portugal is one of them. We are deeply concerned about the future of freedom in Portugal, as we have always been concerned about the future of people throughout the world.

The reality of the Portuguese situation is apparent to all. The wishes of a moderate majority have been subverted by forces more determined than representative.[11] We are hopeful that the sheer weight of numbers—the 80 percent of the Portuguese people who support the democratic process—will prevail in this conflict of ideologies. But they must find the solution in an atmosphere that is free from the pressures of outside forces.

So far, my meetings with General Secretary Brezhnev in Vladivostok and Helsinki have been constructive and helpful. Future success will, of course, depend on concrete developments.

Peace is the primary objective of the foreign and defense policies of the United States. It is easy to be a cold warrior in peacetime. But it would be irresponsible for a President to engage in confrontation when consultation would advance the cause of peace.

So, I say to you—as I said to Mr. Brezhnev and the leaders of

[8]Cf. note 11 to Chapter 27.

[9]Treaty on the Prohibition of the Emplacement of Nuclear Weapons and Other Weapons of Mass Destruction on the Seabed and the Ocean Floor and in the Subsoil Thereof, opened for signature Feb. 11, 1971 and entered into force May 18, 1972 (TIAS 7337; 23 UST 701); text in *Documents, 1970*: 69-73.

[10]Convention on the Prohibition of the Development, Production and Stockpiling of Bacteriological (Biological) and Toxin Weapons and on Their Destruction, opened for signature Apr. 10, 1972 and entered into force Mar. 26, 1975 (TIAS 8062; 26 UST 583); text in *AFR, 1971*: 90-95.

[11]Increasing political tension in Portugal during the spring and early summer of 1975 had led to the establishment of a three-man collective leadership and the formation on July 31 of a transitional cabinet headed by the pro-Communist General Vasco dos Santos Gonçalves (who, however, was replaced on Aug. 29 by the more conservative Vice Admiral José Baptista Pinheiro de Azevedo).

other European nations and Canada in Helsinki[12]—peace is crucial, but freedom must come first.

Those who proclaimed American independence almost 200 years ago asserted not merely that all Americans should enjoy life, liberty, and the pursuit of happiness, but that all men everywhere are endowed by their Creator with such inalienable rights.

I told the leaders of Europe that these principles, though still being perfected, remain the guiding lights of American policy, that the American people are still dedicated to the universal advancement of individual rights and human freedom implicit in the Helsinki declaration.

It gave me great pride, as the spokesman of the United States at Helsinki, to say to both East and West: My country and its principles of freedom have given hope to millions in Europe and on every continent, and still does.

On the other hand, I emphasize that we are tired of having our hopes raised and then shattered by empty words and unkept promises.

I reminded all there in Helsinki that détente must be a two-way street because tensions cannot be eased with safety and security by one side alone.

Through détente, I hope that we are on a two-way street with the Soviet Union. But until I am certain of real progress, I must reserve final judgments about the defense budget and particularly our plans for strategic nuclear forces.

We will, therefore, continue to seek meaningful arms agreements. But this will be possible only with sufficient and credible strength of our own and in concert with our allies. Moreover, any agreements we reach must be verifiable for our security. To put it very practically, that is, we must possess the means of making sure that they are being honored. The time has not yet come when we can entrust our hopes for peace to a piece of paper.

Thus, another essential element of any real arms limitation, whether of strategic systems or conventional forces, is our own intelligence capability. Sweeping attacks, overgeneralization, against our intelligence activities jeopardize vital functions necessary to our national security. Today's sensations must not be the prelude to tomorrow's Pearl Harbor.

I certainly do not condone improper activities or violations of the constitutional rights of Americans by any personnel or any agency of the Federal Government. On the basis of the comprehensive studies of our intelligence agencies by the Rockefeller Commission[13] and by the [Robert] Murphy Commission on the conduct of

[12]Chapter 25, Document 41.
[13]Cf. Introduction at note 5.

foreign policy,[14] I will take administrative action and recommend legislation to the Congress for whatever must be done to prevent future abuses.

Intelligence in today's world is absolutely essential to our national security—even our survival. It may be even more important in peace than in war. Any reckless Congressional action to cripple the effectiveness of our intelligence services in legitimate operations would be catastrophic. Our potential adversaries and even some of our best friends operate in all intelligence fields with secrecy, with skill, and with substantial resources. I know and I know you know that what we need is an American intelligence capacity second to none.

Finally—and this relates both to our vital intelligence installations and to the imperative need to strengthen key alliances such as NATO—let us now consider our relations with our friend and ally of many years, Turkey.[15] How do you explain to a friend and an ally why arms previously ordered and paid for are not being delivered? How do you explain to your other allies the potential damage that this may cause to our NATO Alliance? How do you justify to the American people the loss of strategic intelligence data, with its attendant effect on our national security, that this action has caused?

I don't know, because I am at a loss to explain it myself. As a man of the Congress, and proudly so, for 25 years, the last thing I seek is confrontation with my friends, my former colleagues on Capitol Hill, both Democrats and Republicans.

Obviously, I am troubled that the House of Representatives has refused to permit the shipment of arms to Turkey. But I respect the sincerity and the motives of those who support this position. However, I know when the bottom line of any issue is the ultimate security of the United States, which it is in this case, the Congress and the President always found a way to close ranks and to act as one.

This does not mean that one side or the other capitulates blindly. Let us put this issue on the table and once again debate it, not in a climate of fire and fury, but in a reasoned approach based on what is right and what is best for America.

I am convinced from my personal talks last month with the leaders of Greece and Turkey and Cyprus that their differences can be settled peacefully.

We can help—the Congress, the President, and the American

---

[14]*Report of the Commission on the Organization of the Government for the Conduct of Foreign Policy, June 27, 1975* (Washington: GPO, 1975).
[15]Cf. Chapter 22.

people. We can help cool the passions that caused so much heartbreak in the Mediterranean.

The American political system is one of checks and balances. But it works best when the checks do not become roadblocks. As President, I need the cooperation and the full support of the Congress, which I know is as concerned as I am about our Nation's security.

Just as important, your representatives in the Congress need to know where you stand. They have to realize that you place America's security above personal and political considerations.

This morning I am deeply honored to have had this great opportunity to meet with you here in the heartland of America and to share some of my deep concerns and some of my personal thoughts on the future of our Nation.

But talk is only the starting point, and so I ask each of you, as well as this great organization, to join with me in the commitment that I have made for the reinforcement of lasting peace and the enlargement of human freedom. I ask this not only for ourselves but for our posterity and for all peoples who pray that the torch of liberty will continue to burn bright.

God helping us, freedom and peace will both prevail.

Thank you very much.

29. ANOTHER STEP IN THE MIDEAST

(September 1-October 13, 1975)

[Most intricate by far among the diplomatic achievements of 1975 was the agreement on a second-stage military disengagement in the Sinai Peninsula that was negotiated by Secretary Kissinger in a thirteen-day bout of shuttle diplomacy in late August, initialed by Israeli and Egyptian representatives in the presence of the Secretary of State in Jerusalem and Alexandria on September 1, and formally signed in Geneva on September 4. "The interim agreement being initialed . . . this evening," President Ford declared in announcing the success of the Kissinger mission, "reduces the risk of war in the Middle East and provides fresh opportunities for further progress toward peace for a troubled area whose turmoil has affected the lives and prosperity of peoples of all nations."[1]

A number of important developments had occurred in the Middle East since the breakdown of Dr. Kissinger's earlier disengagement effort in March.[2] King Faisal of Saudi Arabia had been slain by a demented nephew and succeeded by his half-brother, Khalid, while another half-brother, Prince Fahd, had become Crown Prince and virtual *de facto* head of government with the title of First Deputy Prime Minister. In Lebanon, an outbreak of fighting between Palestinian guerrillas and the militia of the right-wing Phalangist Party had precipitated a convulsive civil war that had already claimed hundreds of victims and was expected to exert profound if still obscure effects upon the Mideast balance of power.

Within the Arab-Israeli zone of conflict, the mandates of the two United Nations forces that were helping to maintain the disengagement arrangements in the Sinai and the Golan Heights had been extended by the Security Council,[3] and the Suez Canal, which had

[1]Statement of September 1, in *Bulletin*, 73: 460.
[2]Chapter 6.
[3]The U.N. Emergency Force in the Sinai was renewed for three months by Security Council Resolution 368 (1975) of Apr. 17, and for a further three months by Resolution 371 (1975) of July 24. The U.N. Disengagement Observer Force in the Golan Heights was extended for six months by Resolution 369 (1975) of May 28, 1975.

been closed since 1967, had been reopened (though not to Israel) in partial fulfillment of a commitment given by Egypt at the time of the original Sinai disengagement in 1974.[4] In the meantime, the "reassessment" of American policy that had been promised in the wake of the March fiasco had failed to shake the basic U.S. commitment to Israel, the depth of which had been specifically reaffirmed on May 21 in an open letter to the President signed by 76 Senators, more than three-fourths of the entire membership. In another manifestation of congressional support for Israel, plans to strengthen the self-defense capacity of neighboring Jordan had been temporarily blocked by resistance from within the House of Representatives to the proposed sale of a Hawk air defense system to that country.

Acknowledging that numerous obstacles still barred the way toward negotiations for a comprehensive Mideast settlement, President Ford and Secretary Kissinger had continued to urge the desirability of a second disengagement in the Sinai as the best available means of maintaining a peaceful momentum. Some new ideas concerning the possible characteristics of such an agreement had been discussed at the President's meetings with President Sadat in Salzburg on June 1-2, and with Prime Minister Rabin in Washington on June 10-13;[5] and by August 20, further discussion had supplied sufficient details to permit the Secretary of State, accompanied by a numerous retinue, to undertake one further mission to the Middle East in what was to be the last and most spectacular of his celebrated essays in "shuttle diplomacy."[6]

The salient features of the new Egyptian-Israeli agreement initialed on September 1 (**Document 47**) included (1) an eastward withdrawal of Israeli military forces to positions east of the Sinai passes and the oilfields, on a line running 20 to 40 miles east of the Suez Canal; (2) an eastward shift and enlargement of the existing U.N. buffer zone, to a width varying between 8 and 35 miles and with a southward extension encompassing the oil-producing areas along the Gulf of Suez; and (3) a corresponding eastward shift in the forward positions occupied by the Egyptian forces. What persuaded the two adversary countries to accept these changes was the acceptance by the United States of direct responsibility for the operation, under the supervision of American civilian personnel, of an electronic Early Warning System to be established in the area of

[4]*AFR, 1974*: 20.
[5]*Bulletin*, 72: 897-903; same, 73: 9-14.
[6]The negotiations are covered in some detail in Sheehan, *The Arabs, Israelis, and Kissinger*: 164-94, and in Golan, *The Secret Conversations of Henry Kissinger*: 243-54.

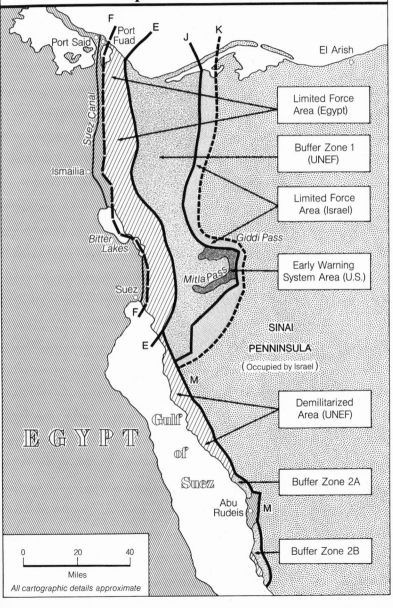

EGYPT - ISRAEL DISENGAGEMENT AGREEMENT
September 1, 1975

the Gidi and Mitla passes. A so-called U.S. "Proposal" detailing these arrangements, drawn up in the form of parallel agreements between the United States and Israel and between the United States and Egypt, was included as an integral part of the overall disengagement agreement.

Additional elements of this complex diplomatic package were contained in a series of written pledges by the United States to Israel and to Egypt (**Document 48**), originally made available only to the Congress but leaked in mid-September by the *Washington Post* and *New York Times*[7] and later formally declassified by the Senate Foreign Relations Committee. To Israel, the United States promised maximum responsiveness in the meeting of its defense, energy, and economic needs—including, apparently, such sophisticated military items as F-16 aircraft and, presumptively, Pershing ground-to-ground missiles with conventional warheads—as well as support on a variety of key political and diplomatic matters. Separate assurances to Egypt, whose acceptance of another partial agreement was being severely condemned by Syria and other Arab governments, featured Washington's intention to urge further negotiations between Syria and Israel and to be helpful with Egypt's economic development.

The existence of still other "assurances, undertakings, . . . commitments" and "declarations of intention" on the part of the United States was acknowledged by Secretary Kissinger in a later statement to the Senate Foreign Relations Committee, although he also insisted that everything the administration considered legally binding on the United States had been duly submitted to the Congress in connection with its request for prompt congressional approval of American participation in the Early Warning System.[8] Despite procedural qualms and strong reluctance to approve a new American engagement overseas, a resolution sanctioning the despatch of up to 200 American volunteer technicians to implement the agreement was approved by a 341 to 69 vote of the House on October 8, confirmed by a 70 to 18 vote of the Senate on October 9, and signed by the President on October 13 (**Document 49**).

However gratifying and significant the completion of this difficult step, President Ford observed in signing the Joint Resolution, "neither the United States nor Egypt nor Israel see it as an end in itself. . . . We must continue our diplomatic efforts with the parties in order to sustain the momentum toward peace generated by the Sinai agreement, and the United States must accept the responsibilities which flow from our stake in peace in the Middle East and

---

[7] *Washington Post*, Sept. 16, and *New York Times*, Sept. 17-18, 1975.
[8] Statement of Oct. 7, in *Bulletin*, 73: 609-13.

from our bilateral relationships which form the foundation for success in our diplomatic efforts. . . . I reaffirm today that we will not accept stagnation or stalemate in the Middle East. The participation of United States civilians in the Sinai early warning system demonstrates that determination."[9]]

(47) Interim Agreement on Disengagement of Egyptian and Israeli Military Forces, made public September 1, 1975.[10]

(a) Basic Agreement between Egypt and Israel, initialed at Jerusalem and Alexandria September 1 and signed at Geneva September 4, 1975.[11]

Agreement Between Egypt and Israel

The Government of the Arab Republic of Egypt and the Government of Israel have agreed that:

Article I

The conflict between them and in the Middle East shall not be resolved by military force but by peaceful means.

The Agreement concluded by the Parties January 18, 1974, within the framework of the Geneva Peace Conference,[12] constituted a first step towards a just and durable peace according to the provisions of Security Council Resolution 338 of October 22, 1973.[13]

They are determined to reach a final and just peace settlement by means of negotiations called for by Security Council Resolution 338, this Agreement being a significant step towards that end.

---

[9]*Presidential Documents*, 11: 1168; cf. further Chapter 36.

[10]Text from *Bulletin*, 73: 466-70.

[11]The agreement was initialed in Jerusalem by Avraham Kidron, Director-General of the Israeli Foreign Ministry, and Lieut. Gen. Mordecai Gur, Chief of Staff; thereafter it was initialed in Alexandria by the Egyptian Chief of Staff, Lieut. Gen. Mohammed Ali Fahmy, and the Egyptian Ambassador to the U.N. in Geneva, Ahmed Osman. The agreement was signed at Geneva on Sept. 4, 1975 by Maj. Gen. Taha al Magdoub (head of delegation) and Ahmed Osman of Egypt, and by Mordecai Gazit (head of delegation) and Maj. Gen. Herzl Shafir (Army Chief of Staff) of Israel. It was witnessed on behalf of the U.N. by Lieut. Gen. Ensio Siilasvuo of Finland, Chief Coordinator of the United Nations Peacekeeping Missions in the Middle East.

[12]*AFR, 1974*: 17-18.

[13]Same, *1973*: 459.

Article II

The Parties hereby undertake not to resort to the threat or use of force or military blockade against each other.

Article III

The Parties shall continue scrupulously to observe the ceasefire on land, sea and air and to refrain from all military or para-military actions against each other.

The Parties also confirm that the obligations contained in the Annex[14] and, when concluded, the Protocol shall be an integral part of this Agreement.

Article IV

A. The military forces of the Parties shall be deployed in accordance with the following principles:

(1) All Israeli forces shall be deployed east of the lines designated as Lines J and M on the attached map.

(2) All Egyptian forces shall be deployed west of the line designated as Line E on the attached map.

(3) The area between the lines designated on the attached map as Lines E and F and the area between the lines designated on the attached map as Lines J and K shall be limited in armament and forces.

(4) The limitations on armament and forces in the areas described by paragraph (3) above shall be agreed as described in the attached Annex.

(5) The zone between the lines designated on the attached map as Lines E and J, will be a buffer zone. In this zone the United Nations Emergency Force will continue to perform its functions as under the Egyptian-Israeli Agreement of January 18, 1974.

(6) In the area south from Line E and west from Line M, as defined on the attached map, there will be no military forces, as specified in the attached Annex.

B. The details concerning the new lines, the redeployment of the forces and its timing, the limitation on armaments and forces,

[14]Document 47b.

aerial reconnaissance, the operation of the early warning and surveillance installations and the use of the roads, the United Nations functions and other arrangements will all be in accordance with the provisions of the Annex and map which are an integral part of this Agreement and of the Protocol which is to result from negotiations pursuant to the Annex and which, when concluded, shall become an integral part of this Agreement.

Article V

The United Nations Emergency Force is essential and shall continue its functions and its mandate shall be extended annually.[15]

Article VI

The Parties hereby establish a Joint Commission for the duration of this Agreement. It will function under the aegis of the Chief Coordinator of the United Nations Peacekeeping Missions in the Middle East in order to consider any problem arising from this Agreement and to assist the United Nations Emergency Force in the execution of its mandate. The Joint Commission shall function in accordance with procedures established in the Protocol.

Article VII

Non-military cargoes destined for or coming from Israel shall be permitted through the Suez Canal.

Article VIII

This Agreement is regarded by the Parties as a significant step toward a just and lasting peace. It is not a final peace agreement.

The Parties shall continue their efforts to negotiate a final peace agreement within the framework of the Geneva Peace Conference in accordance with Security Council Resolution 338.

---

[15]The mandate of the U.N. Emergency Force was extended by Security Council Resolution 378 (1975) of Oct. 23 for a full year ending Oct. 24, 1976.

Article IX

This Agreement shall enter into force upon signature of the Protocol and remain in force until superseded by a new agreement.

Done at _____ on the _____ 1975, in four original copies.

For the Government of the
Arab Republic of Egypt

For the Government of
Israel

_____

_____

WITNESS

_____

(b) Annex to the Basic Agreement.

Annex to Egypt-Israel Agreement

Within 5 days after the signature of the Egypt-Israel Agreement, representatives of the two Parties shall meet in the Military Working Group of the Middle East Peace Conference at Geneva to begin preparation of a detailed Protocol for the implementation of the Agreement. The Working Group will complete the Protocol within 2 weeks.[16] In order to facilitate preparation of the Protocol and implementation of the Agreement, and to assist in maintaining the scrupulous observance of the ceasefire and other elements of the Agreement, the two Parties have agreed on the following principles, which are an integral part of the Agreement, as guidelines for the Working Group.

1. Definitions of Lines and Areas

The deployment lines, areas of limited forces and armaments, Buffer Zones, the area south from Line E and west from Line M, other designated areas, road sections for common use and other features referred to in Article IV of the Agreement shall be as indicated on the attached map (1:100,000—U.S. Edition).[17]

2. Buffer Zones

(a) Access to the Buffer Zones will be controlled by the United

[16]Officially completed Sept. 22, the Protocol (U.N. Document S/11818/Add. 5) provided among other things for completion of Israeli withdrawal from the Gulf of Suez oilfields by Dec. 1, 1975 and from other areas by Feb. 22, 1976. The protocol was signed by Egypt on Sept. 22 and by Israel on Oct. 10, 1975, after the U.S. role in the Early Warning System had been approved by Congress.
[17]The official map was issued as U.N. Document S/11818/Add. 3, Sept. 8, 1975. More detailed maps accompany the Protocol described in note 16.

Nations Emergency Force, according to procedures to be worked out by the Working Group and the United Nations Emergency Force.

(b) Aircraft of either Party will be permitted to fly freely up to the forward line of that Party. Reconnaissance aircraft of either Party may fly up to the middle line of the Buffer Zone between E and J on an agreed schedule.

(c) In the Buffer Zone, between line E and J there will be established under Article IV of the Agreement an Early Warning System entrusted to United States civilian personnel as detailed in a separate proposal, which is a part of this Agreement.[18]

(d) Authorized personnel shall have access to the Buffer Zone for transit to and from the Early Warning System; the manner in which this is carried out shall be worked out by the Working Group and the United Nations Emergency Force.

3. *Area South of Line E and West of Line M*

(a) In this area, the United Nations Emergency Force will assure that there are no military or para-military forces of any kind, military fortifications and military installations; it will establish checkpoints and have the freedom of movement necessary to perform this function.

(b) Egyptian civilians and third country civilian oil field personnel shall have the right to enter, exit from, work, and live in the above indicated area, except for Buffer Zones 2A, 2B and the United Nations Posts. Egyptian civilian police shall be allowed in the area to perform normal civil police functions among the civilian population in such numbers and with such weapons and equipment as shall be provided for in the Protocol.

(c) Entry to and exit from the area, by land, by air or by sea, shall be only through United Nations Emergency Force checkpoints. The United Nations Emergency Force shall also establish checkpoints along the road, the dividing line and at other points, with the precise locations and number to be included in the Protocol.

(d) Access to the airspace and the coastal area shall be limited to unarmed Egyptian civilian vessels and unarmed civilian helicopters and transport planes involved in the civilian activities of the area as agreed by the Working Group.

(e) Israel undertakes to leave intact all currently existing civilian installations and infrastructures.

(f) Procedures for use of the common sections of the coastal road along the Gulf of Suez shall be determined by the Working Group and detailed in the Protocol.

4. *Aerial Surveillance*

There shall be a continuation of aerial reconnaissance missions

[18]Document 47c.

by the United States over the areas covered by the Agreement (the area between lines F and K), following the same procedures already in practice. The missions will ordinarily be carried out at a frequency of one mission every 7-10 days, with either Party or the United Nations Emergency Force empowered to request an earlier mission. The United States Government will make the mission results available expeditiously to Israel, Egypt and the Chief Coordinator of the United Nations Peacekeeping Missions in the Middle East.

5. *Limitation of Forces and Armaments*

(a) Within the Areas of Limited Forces and Armaments (the areas between lines J and K and lines E and F) the major limitations shall be as follows:

(1) Eight (8) standard infantry battalions

(2) Seventy-five (75) tanks

(3) Seventy-two (72) artillery pieces, including heavy mortars (i.e. with caliber larger than 120 mm), whose range shall not exceed twelve (12) km.

(4) The total number of personnel shall not exceed eight thousand (8,000).

(5) Both Parties agree not to station or locate in the area weapons which can reach the line of the other side.

(6) Both Parties agree that in the areas between lines J and K, and between line A (of the Disengagement Agreement of January 18, 1974) and line E, they will construct no new fortifications or installations for forces of a size greater than that agreed herein.

(b) The major limitations beyond the Areas of Limited Forces and Armament will be:

(1) Neither side will station nor locate any weapon in areas from which they can reach the other line.

(2) The Parties will not place antiaircraft missiles within an area of ten (10) kilometres east of Line K and west of Line F, respectively.

(c) The United Nations Emergency Force will conduct inspections in order to ensure the maintenance of the agreed limitations within these areas.

6. *Process of Implementation*

The detailed implementation and timing of the redeployment of forces, turnover of oil fields, and other arrangements called for by the Agreement, Annex and Protocol shall be determined by the Working Group, which will agree on the stages of this process, including the phased movement of Egyptian troops to line E and

Israeli troops to line J. The first phase will be the transfer of the oil fields and installations to Egypt. This process will begin within two weeks from the signature of the Protocol with the introduction of the necessary technicians, and it will be completed no later than eight weeks after it begins. The details of the phasing will be worked out in the Military Working Group.

Implementation of the redeployment shall be completed within 5 months after signature of the Protocol.

For the Government of the   For the Government of
Arab Republic of Egypt   Israel

_____   _____

WITNESS

_____

(c) United States Proposal on the Early Warning System, signed at Jerusalem and Alexandria September 1, 1975.[19]

Proposal

In connection with the Early Warning System referred to in Article IV of the Agreement between Egypt and Israel concluded on this date[20] and as an integral part of that Agreement, (hereafter referred to as the Basic Agreement), the United States proposes the following:

1. The Early Warning System to be established in accordance with Article IV in the area shown on the map attached to the Basic Agreement will be entrusted to the United States. It shall have the following elements:

a. There shall be two surveillance stations to provide strategic early warning, one operated by Egyptian and one operated by Israeli personnel. Their locations are shown on the map attached to the Basic Agreement. Each station shall be manned by not

[19]Duplicate versions were signed in Jerusalem by Secretary Kissinger and Israeli Prime Minister Rabin, and in Alexandria by Secretary Kissinger and Egyptian Prime Minister Mamdouh Mohammed Sadem. The two agreements were subsequently published by the U.S. as TIAS 8155 and 8156 (26 UST 2271 and 2278).
[20]Document 47a.

more than 250 technical and administrative personnel. They shall perform the functions of visual and electronic surveillance only within their stations.

b. In support of these stations, to provide tactical early warning and to verify access to them, three watch stations shall be established by the United States in the Mitla and Giddi Passes as will be shown on the map attached to the Basic Agreement. These stations shall be operated by United States civilian personnel. In support of these stations, there shall be established three unmanned electronic sensor fields at both ends of each Pass and in the general vicinity of each station and the roads leading to and from those stations.

2. The United States civilian personnel shall perform the following duties in connection with the operation and maintenance of these stations.

a. At the two surveillance stations described in paragraph 1 a. above, United States civilian personnel will verify the nature of the operations of the stations and all movement into and out of each station and will immediately report any detected divergency from its authorized role of visual and electronic surveillance to the Parties to the Basic Agreement and to the United Nations Emergency Force.

b. At each watch station described in paragraph 1 b. above, the United States civilian personnel will immediately report to the Parties to the Basic Agreement and to the United Nations Emergency Force any movement of armed forces, other than the United Nations Emergency Force, into either Pass and any observed preparations for such movement.

c. The total number of United States civilian personnel assigned to functions under this Proposal shall not exceed 200. Only civilian personnel shall be assigned to functions under this Proposal.

3. No arms shall be maintained at the stations and other facilities covered by this Proposal, except for small arms required for their protection.

4. The United States personnel serving the Early Warning System shall be allowed to move freely within the area of the System.

5. The United States and its personnel shall be entitled to have such support facilities as are reasonably necessary to perform their functions.

6. The United States personnel shall be immune from local criminal, civil, tax and customs jurisdiction and may be accorded

any other specific privileges and immunities provided for in the United Nations Emergency Force Agreement of February 13, 1957.

7. The United States affirms that it will continue to perform the functions described above for the duration of the Basic Agreement.

8. Notwithstanding any other provision of this Proposal, the United States may withdraw its personnel only if it concludes that their safety is jeopardized or that continuation of their role is no longer necessary. In the latter case the Parties to the Basic Agreement will be informed in advance in order to give them the opportunity to make alternative arrangements. If both Parties to the Basic Agreement request the United States to conclude its role under this Proposal, the United States will consider such requests conclusive.

9. Technical problems including the location of the watch stations will be worked out through consultation with the United States.

HENRY A. KISSINGER
Secretary of State

Accepted by:

(48) United States Assurances to Israel and Egypt.[21]

(a) Memorandum of Agreement between Israel and the United States, September 1, 1975.

SEPTEMBER 1, 1975.

MEMORANDUM OF AGREEMENT BETWEEN THE GOVERNMENTS
OF ISRAEL AND THE UNITED STATES

The United States recognizes that the Egypt-Israel Agreement initialed on September 1, 1975,[22] (hereinafter referred to as the Agreement), entailing the withdrawal from vital areas in Sinai, constitutes an act of great significance on Israel's part in the pursuit of final peace. That Agreement has full United States support.

[21]Texts from U.S. Senate, 94th Cong., 1st sess., Committee on Foreign Relations, *Early Warning System in Sinai: Hearings . . . on Memoranda of Agreements between the Governments of Israel and the United States, Oct. 6 and 7, 1975* (Washington: GPO, 1975): 249-53.
[22]Document 47a.

UNITED STATES-ISRAEL ASSURANCES

1. The United States Government will make every effort to be fully responsive, within the limits of its resources and Congressional authorization and appropriation, on an on-going and long-term basis to Israel's military equipment and other defense requirements, to its energy requirements and to its economic needs. The needs specified in paragraphs 2, 3 and 4 below shall be deemed eligible for inclusion within the annual total to be requested in FY76 and later fiscal years.

2. Israel's long-term military supply needs from the United States shall be the subject of periodic consultations between representatives of the United States and Israeli defense establishments, with agreement reached on specific items to be included in a separate United States-Israeli memorandum. To this end, a joint study by military experts will be undertaken within 3 weeks. In conducting this study, which will include Israel's 1976 needs, the United States will view Israel's requests sympathetically, including its request for advanced and sophisticated weapons.

3. Israel will make its own independent arrangements for oil supply to meet its requirements through normal procedures. In the event Israel is unable to secure its needs in this way, the United States Government, upon notification of this fact by the Government of Israel, will act as follows for five years, at the end of which period either side can terminate this arrangement on one-year's notice.

(a) If the oil Israel needs to meet all its normal requirements for domestic consumption is unavailable for purchase in circumstances where no quantitative restrictions exist on the ability of the United States to procure oil to meet its normal requirements, the United States Government will promptly make oil available for purchase by Israel to meet all of the aforementioned normal requirements of Israel. If Israel is unable to secure the necessary means to transport such oil to Israel, the United States Government will make every effort to help Israel secure the necessary means of transport.

(b) If the oil Israel needs to meet all of its normal requirements for domestic consumption is unavailable for purchase in circumstances where quantitative restrictions through embargo or otherwise also prevent the United States from procuring oil to meet its normal requirements, the United States Government will promptly make oil available for purchase by Israel in accordance with the International Energy Agency conservation and allocation formula as applied by the United States Government, in order to meet Israel's essential requirements. If Israel is unable to secure the necessary means to transport such oil to Israel, the United States Government will make every effort to help Israel secure the necessary means of transport.

Israeli and United States experts will meet annually or more frequently at the request of either party, to review Israel's continuing oil requirement.

4. In order to help Israel meet its energy needs, and as part of the overall annual figure in paragraph 1 above, the United States agrees:

(a) In determining the overall annual figure which will be requested from Congress, the United States Government will give special attention to Israel's oil import requirements and, for a period as determined by Article 3 above, will take into account in calculating that figure Israel's additional expenditures for the import of oil to replace that which would have ordinarily come from Abu Rodeis and Ras Sudar (4.5 million tons in 1975).

(b) To ask Congress to make available funds, the amount to be determined by mutual agreement, to the Government of Israel necessary for a project for the construction and stocking of the oil reserves to be stored in Israel, bringing storage reserve capacity and reserve stocks now standing at approximately six months, up to one-year's need at the time of the completion of the project. The project will be implemented within four years. The construction, operation and financing and other relevant questions of the project will be the subject of early and detailed talks between the two Governments.

5. The United States Government will not expect Israel to begin to implement the Agreement before Egypt fulfils its undertaking under the January 1974 Disengagement Agreement to permit passage of all Israeli cargoes to and from Israeli ports through the Suez Canal.[23]

6. The United States Government agrees with Israel that the next agreement with Egypt should be a final peace agreement.

7. In case of an Egyptian violation of any of the provisions of the Agreement, the United States Government is prepared to consult with Israel as to the significance of the violation and possible remedial action by the United States Government.

8. The United States Government will vote against any Security

---

[23]A first Israeli cargo passed through the Canal aboard a Greek freighter on Nov. 2, 1975.

Council resolution which in its judgment affects or alters adversely the Agreement.

9. The United States Government will not join in, and will seek to prevent efforts by others to bring about consideration of proposals which it and Israel agree are detrimental to the interests of Israel.

10. In view of the long-standing United States commitment to the survival and security of Israel, the United States Government will view with particular gravity threats to Israel's security or sovereignty by a world power. In support of this objective, the United States Government will in the event of such threat consult promptly with the Government of Israel with respect to what support, diplomatic or otherwise, or assistance it can lend to Israel in accordance with its constitutional practices.

11. The United States Government and the Government of Israel will, at the earliest possible time, and if possible, within two months after the signature of this document, conclude the contingency plan for a military supply operation to Israel in an emergency situation.

12. It is the United States Government's position that Egyptian commitments under the Egypt-Israel Agreement, its implementation, validity and duration are not conditional upon any act or developments between the other Arab states and Israel. The United States Government regards the Agreement as standing on its own.

13. The United States Government shares the Israel position that under existing political circumstances negotiations with Jordan will be directed toward an overall peace settlement.

14. In accordance with the principle of freedom of navigation on the high seas and free and unimpeded passage through and over straits connecting international waters, the United States Government regards the Straits of Bab-el-Mandeb and the Strait of Gibraltar as international waterways. It will support Israel's right to free and unimpeded passage through such straits. Similarly, the United States Government recognizes Israel's right to freedom of flights over the Red Sea and such straits and will support diplomatically the exercise of that right.

15. In the event that the United Nations Emergency Force or any other United Nations organ is withdrawn without the prior agreement of both Parties to the Egypt-Israel Agreement and the United States before this Agreement is superseded by another agreement, it is the United States view that the Agreement shall remain binding in all its parts.

16. The United States and Israel agree that signature of the Protocol of the Egypt-Israel Agreement and its full entry into effect shall not take place before approval by the United States Congress

of the United States role in connection with the surveillance and observation functions described in the Agreement and its Annex.[24] The United States has informed the Government of Israel that it has obtained the Government of Egypt agreement to the above.

YIGAL ALLON,
Deputy Prime Minister and
Minister of Foreign Affairs
(For the Government of Israel).

HENRY A. KISSINGER,
Secretary of State
(For the Government of the United States).

(b) *Memorandum of Agreement between Israel and the United States Relating to the Geneva Peace Conference, September 1, 1975.*

MEMORANDUM OF AGREEMENT BETWEEN THE GOVERNMENTS OF ISRAEL
AND THE UNITED STATES

THE GENEVA PEACE CONFERENCE

1. The Geneva Peace Conference will be reconvened at a time coordinated between the United States and Israel.

2. The United States will continue to adhere to its present policy with respect to the Palestine Liberation Organization, whereby it will not recognize or negotiate with the Palestine Liberation Organization so long as the Palestine Liberation Organization does not recognize Israel's right to exist and does not accept Security Council Resolutions 242 and 338. The United States Government will consult fully and seek to concert its position and strategy at the Geneva Peace Conference on this issue with the Government of Israel. Similarly, the United States will consult fully and seek to concert its position and strategy with Israel with regard to the participation of any other additional states. It is understood that the participation at a subsequent phase of the Conference of any possible additional state, group or organization will require the agreement of all the initial participants.

3. The United States will make every effort to ensure at the Conference that all the substantive negotiations will be on a bilateral basis.

[24]Cf. note 16 above.

4. The United States will oppose and, if necessary, vote against any initiative in the Security Council to alter adversely the terms of reference of the Geneva Peace Conference or to change Resolutions 242 and 338 in ways which are incompatible with their original purpose.

5. The United States will seek to ensure that the role of the cosponsors will be consistent with what was agreed in the Memorandum of Understanding between the United States Government and the Government of Israel of December 20, 1973.[25]

6. The United States and Israel will concert action to assure that the Conference will be conducted in a manner consonant with the objectives of this document and with the declared purpose of the Conference, namely the advancement of a negotiated peace between Israel and each one of its neighbors.

YIGAL ALLON,
*Deputy Prime Minister and
Minister of Foreign Affairs*
(For the Government of Israel).

HENRY A. KISSINGER,
Secretary of State
(For the Government of
the United States).

(c) United States Assurances to Israel Relating to Military and Economic Assistance.

ASSURANCES FROM USG TO ISRAEL

On the question of military and economic assistance to Israel, the following conveyed by the U.S. to Israel augments what the Memorandum of Agreement[26] states.

The United States is resolved to continue to maintain Israel's defensive strength through the supply of advanced types of equipment, such as the F-16 aircraft. The United States Government agrees to an early meeting to undertake a joint study of high technology and sophisticated items, including the Pershing ground-to-ground missiles with conventional warheads, with the view to giving a positive response. The U.S. Administration will submit annually for approval by the U.S. Congress a request for military and economic assistance in order to help meet Israel's economic and military needs.[27]

---

[25]Cf. *AFR, 1973*: 606.
[26]Document 48a.
[27]Cf. Chapter 36.

(d) United States Assurances to Egypt.

ASSURANCES FROM USG TO EGYPT

1. The United States intends to make a serious effort to help bring about further negotiations between Syria and Israel, in the first instance through diplomatic channels.

2. In the event of an Israeli violation of the Agreement, the United States is prepared to consult with Egypt as to the significance of the violation and possible remedial action by the United States.

3. The United States will provide technical assistance to Egypt for the Egyptian Early Warning Station.

4. The U.S. reaffirms its policy of assisting Egypt in its economic development, the specific amount to be subject to Congressional authorization and appropriation.

(49) Joint Congressional Resolution on the Early Warning System: Public Law 94-110, October 13, 1975.

JOINT RESOLUTION

To implement the United States proposal for the early-warning system in Sinai.

Whereas an agreement[28] signed on September 4, 1975, by the Government of the Arab Republic of Egypt and the Government of Israel may, when it enters into force, constitute a significant step toward peace in the Middle East;

Whereas the President of the United States on September 1, 1975, transmitted to the Government of the Arab Republic of Egypt and to the Government of Israel identical proposals[29] for United States participation in an early-warning system, the text of which has been submitted to the Congress, providing for the assignment of no more than two hundred United States civilian personnel to carry out certain specified noncombat functions and setting forth the terms and conditions thereof;

Whereas that proposal would permit the Government of the United States to withdraw such personnel if it concludes that their safety is jeopardized or that continuation of their role is no longer necessary; and

Whereas the implementation of the United States proposal for the early-warning system in Sinai may enhance the prospect of compliance in good faith with the terms of the Egyptian-Israeli

[28]Document 47a.
[29]Document 47c.

agreements and thereby promote the cause of peace: Now, therefore, be it

Resolved by the Senate and House of Representatives of the United States of America in Congress assembled, That the President is authorized to implement the "United States Proposal for the Early Warning System in Sinai": *Provided, however*, That United States civilian personnel assigned to Sinai under such proposal shall be removed immediately in the event of an outbreak of hostilities between Egypt and Israel or if the Congress by concurrent resolution determines that the safety of such personnel is jeopardized or that continuation of their role is no longer necessary. Nothing contained in this resolution shall be construed as granting any authority to the President with respect to the introduction of United States Armed Forces into hostilities or into situations wherein involvement in hostilities is clearly indicated by the circumstances which authority he would not have had in the absence of this joint resolution.

SEC. 2. Any concurrent resolution of the type described in the first section of this resolution which is introduced in either House of Congress shall be privileged in the same manner and to the same extent as a concurrent resolution of the type described in section 5(c) of Public Law 93-148 is privileged under section 7 of such law.[30]

SEC. 3. The United States civilian personnel participating in the early warning system in Sinai shall include only individuals who have volunteered to participate in such system.

SEC. 4. Whenever United States civilian personnel, pursuant to this resolution, participate in an early warning system, the President shall, so long as the participation of such personnel continues, submit written reports to the Congress periodically, but no less frequently than once every six months, on (1) the status, scope, and anticipated duration of their participation, and (2) the feasibility of ending or reducing as soon as possible their participation by substituting nationals of other countries or by making technological changes. The appropriate committees of the Congress shall promptly hold hearings on each report of the President and report to the Congress any findings, conclusions, and recommendations.

SEC. 5. The authority contained in this joint resolution to implement the "United States Proposal for the Early Warning System in Sinai" does not signify approval of the Congress of any other agreement, understanding, or commitment made by the executive branch.

[30]*AFR, 1973*: 488-9.

30. TURNING POINT IN DEVELOPMENT?

(New York, September 1, 1975)

[The initialing on September 1 of the Egyptian-Israeli disengagement agreement coincided with a second important act of American foreign policy, this one addressed to the problems of economic development that so deeply preoccupied the majority of the world's nations. While Secretary Kissinger was taking part in the Sinai initialing ceremonies in Jerusalem and Alexandria, a special session of the United Nations General Assembly was convening in New York in order to consider the state of world development and international economic cooperation and to initiate any needed action to implement the International Development Strategy adopted for the ongoing Second U.N. Development Decade. The main event of the session's opening day, after the customary remarks by the President of the Session, Abdelaziz Bouteflika of Algeria, and U.N. Secretary-General Kurt Waldheim, was the reading of a voluminous statement that had been prepared for delivery by Secretary Kissinger himself but was read to the Assembly in his absence by Ambassador Daniel Patrick Moynihan, the new U.S. Representative to the United Nations.

The need for a special General Assembly session on development problems, originally planned in December 1973,[1] might have been thought questionable by the summer of 1975 in view of the intensifying dialogue between industrialized and developing countries that had meanwhile been undertaken in such forums as "Prepcon," the preparatory phase of the North-South conference that had been suggested by President Giscard d'Estaing and was to meet in plenary session in December.[2] But none of the discussions initiated to date had led to really substantial results, primarily because of the seemingly unbridgeable chasm, ideological and practical, that separated most developing countries from the United States and other industrialized nations.

[1]General Assembly Resolution 3172 (XXVIII), Dec. 17, 1973; cf. *AFR, 1973*: 583.
[2]Cf. Chapters 7 and 43.

Political relationships between the United States and the hundred or more "third world" governments that were now setting the tone in the United Nations and many of its specialized agencies had also failed to improve in recent months. Even before the dispute over Zionism at the International Women's Year conference in Mexico City,[3] there had been a partial U.S. walkout from the annual conference of the International Labour Organisation in protest against that body's grant of observer status to the Palestine Liberation Organization. (Later in 1975, the United States was to give notice of its intention to quit the ILO entirely in view of the Geneva-based agency's increasing "politicization" and deviation from basic principles.)[4] Ambassador Moynihan, whose forensic reputation was already well established, had meanwhile received his own baptism of fire as a U.N. delegate at two Security Council meetings in August. At the first, on August 6, the Council had disappointed the United States by failing to endorse an application for U.N. membership from the Republic of Korea. Responding on August 11, Ambassador Moynihan had disappointed the other members of the Council, as well as many other member states, by vetoing the endorsement of separate membership applications from North and South Vietnam.[5]

All the more exhilarating, in light of this discordant background, was the sense of rebirth engendered by the reading of Dr. Kissinger's 90-minute address **(Document 49)**. Embodying the results of a process of internal discussion that had been going forward within the U.S. Government since early in the year and had already received some public exposure at the time of the May meeting of the OECD Council, it offered what amounted to a comprehensive development strategy involving dozens of concrete proposals and what appeared to be a definite softening of the U.S. position on commodity problems and other controversial points. The extent to which the gulf with the developing countries was narrowed, in psychological terms at least, could be measured by the substantial overlap between the Kissinger proposals and the omnibus resolution on "Development and International Economic Cooperation" that was adopted by the Assembly—with only *pro forma* American dissent—before the adjournment of the session on September 16.[6]

[3]Chapter 20.
[4]Letter from Secretary Kissinger to ILO Director General Francis Blanchard, Nov. 5, in U.N. Document A/C.5/1704, Annex, Nov. 6, 1975 (*Digest of United States Practice in International Law, 1975*: 70-73).
[5]The vote of 7 (U.S.)-6-2 in favor of the Korean application fell short of the required two-thirds majority, while the vote of 13-1 (U.S.)-1 in favor of the two Vietnamese applications failed to carry because of the negative vote of a permanent member.
[6]Resolution 3362 (S-VII), Sept. 16, 1975; text in *Bulletin*, 73: 558-66. Specific points of disagreement with the resolution were outlined, following its adoption by consensus, by U.S. Representative Jacob M. Myerson (same: 557-8).

To the congressional advisory group that had helped prepare the new U.S. position, this outcome marked "a significant turning point in U.S. relations with the developing countries" and might even set the stage for "a new era of economic partnership between rich and poor nations." To Secretary Kissinger, returning to address the Assembly's regular session a few days later, the special session offered ground for hope "that—at least for the immediate future—a choice has been made to turn away from confrontation toward cooperation."[7]]

(49) Seventh Special Session of the United Nations General Assembly, New York, September 1-16, 1975: Statement by Secretary of State Kissinger, read to the General Assembly by Ambassador Daniel P. Moynihan, United States Representative, September 1, 1975.[8]

We assemble here this week with an opportunity to improve the condition of mankind. We can let this opportunity slip away, or we can respond to it with vision and common sense.

The United States has made its choice. There are no panaceas available—only challenges. The proposals that I shall announce today on behalf of President Ford are a program of practical steps responding to the expressed concerns of developing countries. We have made a major effort to develop an agenda for effective international action; we are prepared in turn to consider the proposals of others. But the United States is committed to a constructive effort.

For some time the technical capacity has existed to provide a tolerable standard of life for the world's 4 billion people. But we, the world community, must shape the political will to do so. For man stands not simply at a plateau of technical ability; he stands at a point of moral choice. When the ancient dream of mankind—a world without poverty—becomes a possibility, our profound moral convictions make it also our duty. And the convening of this special session bears witness that economic progress has become a central and urgent concern of international relations.

The global order of colonial power that lasted through centuries has now disappeared; the cold war division of the world into two rigid blocs has now also broken down, and major changes have taken place in the international economy. We now live in a world of some 150 nations. We live in an environment of continuing conflicts, proliferating weapons, new ideological divisions and economic rivalry. The developing nations have stated their claim for a

[7]*U.S. Participation, 1975*: 104-5; Chapter 32, Document 51.
[8]Department of State Press Release 450, Sept. 1; text and subtitles from *Bulletin*, 73: 425-41.

greater role, for more control over their economic destiny, and for a just share in global prosperity. The economically advanced nations have stated their claim for reliable supplies of energy, raw materials, and other products at a fair price; they seek stable economic relationships and expanding world trade, for these are important to the well-being of their own societies.

These economic issues have already become the subject of mounting confrontation—embargoes, cartels, seizures, countermeasures—and bitter rhetoric. Over the remainder of this century, should this trend continue, the division of the planet between North and South, between rich and poor, could become as grim as the darkest days of the cold war. We would enter an age of festering resentment, increased resort to economic warfare, a hardening of new blocs, the undermining of cooperation, the erosion of international institutions—and failed development.

Can we reconcile our competing goals? Can we build a better world, by conscious purpose, out of the equality and cooperation of states? Can we turn the energies of all nations to the tasks of human progress? These are the challenges of our time.

We profoundly believe that neither the poor nor the rich nations can achieve their purposes in isolation. Neither can extort them from the other—the developing countries least of all, for they would pay the greater cost of division of the planet, which would cut them off needlessly from sources of capital and markets essential to their own progress.

The reality is that ample incentives exist for cooperation on the basis of mutual respect. It is not necessarily the case that if some grow worse off, others will be worse off. But there is an opposite proposition, which we believe is true: that an economic system thrives if all who take part in it thrive. This is no theory; it is our own experience. And it is an experience that we, a people uniquely drawn from all the other peoples of the world, truly desire and hope to share with others.

Therefore it is time to go beyond the doctrines left over from a previous century that are made obsolete by modern reality.

History has left us the legacy of strident nationalism—discredited in this century by its brutal excesses a generation ago and by its patent inadequacy for the economic needs of our time. The economy is global. Recessions, inflation, trade relations, monetary stability, gluts and scarcities of products and materials, the growth of transnational enterprises—these are international phenomena and call for international responses.

History has also left us discredited doctrines of economic determinism and struggle. One of the ironies of our time is that systems based on the doctrine of materialism that promised economic justice have lagged in raising economic welfare.

And contrary to the ideologies of despair, many developing countries have been increasing their per capita incomes at far faster rates than obtained historically in Europe and North America in comparable stages of their growth.

It is also ironic that a philosophy of nonalignment, designed to allow new nations to make their national choices free from the pressure of competing blocs, now has produced a bloc of its own. Nations with radically different economic interests and with entirely different political concerns are combined in a kind of solidarity that often clearly sacrifices practical interests. And it is ironic also that the most devastating blow to economic development in this decade came not from "imperialist rapacity" but from an arbitrary, monopolistic price increase by the cartel of oil exporters.

The reality is that the world economy is a single global system of trade and monetary relations on which hinges the development of all our economies. The advanced nations have an interest in the growth of markets and production in the developing world; with equal conviction we state that the developing countries have a stake in the markets, technological innovation, and capital investment of the industrial countries.

Therefore the nations assembled here have a choice: We can offer our people slogans, or we can offer them solutions. We can deal in rhetoric, or we can deal in reality. My government has made its choice.

The United States firmly believes that the economic challenges of our time must unite us, and not divide us.

So let us get down to business. Let us put aside the sterile debate over whether a new economic order is required or whether the old economic order is adequate. Let us look forward and shape the world before us. Change is inherent in what we do and what we seek. But one fact does not change: that without a consensus on the realities and principles of the development effort, we will achieve nothing.

—There must be consensus, first and foremost, on the principle that our common development goals can be achieved only by cooperation, not by the politics of confrontation.

—There must be consensus that acknowledges our respective concerns and our mutual responsibilities. All of us have rights, and all of us have duties.

—The consensus must embrace the broadest possible participation in international decisions. The developing countries must have a role and voice in the international system, especially in decisions that affect them. But those nations who are asked to provide resources and effort to carry out the decisions must be accorded a commensurate voice.

We have learned from experience that the methods of development assistance of the 1950's and 60's are no longer adequate. Not only did the technical accomplishments of many programs fall short of expectations; the traditional approaches are less acceptable to the industrialized world because they have seemed to become an endless and one-sided financial burden. And they are less acceptable to the developing world because they have seemed to create a relationship of charity and dependency, inconsistent with equality and self-respect.

Therefore we must find new means. The United States offers today concrete proposals for international actions to promote economic development. We believe that an effective development strategy should concentrate on five fundamental areas:

—First, we must apply international cooperation to the problem of insuring basic economic security. The United States proposes steps to safeguard against the economic shocks to which developing countries are particularly vulnerable: sharp declines in their export earnings from the cycle of world supply and demand, food shortages, and natural disasters.

—Second, we must lay the foundations for accelerated growth. The United States proposes steps to improve developing countries' access to capital markets, to focus and adapt new technology to specific development needs, and to reach consensus on the conditions for foreign investment.

—Third, we must improve the basic opportunities of the developing countries in the world trading system so they can make their way by earnings instead of aid.

—Fourth, we must improve the conditions of trade and investment in key commodities on which the economies of many developing countries are dependent, and we must set an example in improving the production and availability of food.

—Fifth, let us address the special needs of the poorest countries, who are the most devastated by current economic conditions, sharing the responsibility among old and newly wealthy donors.

The determination of the developing nations to mobilize their own effort is indispensable. Without it, no outside effort will have effect. Government policies to call forth savings, to institute land reform, to use external aid and capital productively, to manage and allocate national resources wisely, to promote family planning— for these there are no substitutes.

But there must be international as well as national commitment. The United States is prepared to do its part. The senior economic officials of our government have joined with me in developing our approach. Treasury Secretary Simon, with whom I have worked closely on our program, will discuss it tomorrow in relation to the world economy.[9] The large congressional delegation that will attend the session, and the seriousness with which they and the executive branch have collaborated in preparing these proposals, are evidence of my country's commitment.

We ask in return for a serious international dialogue on the responsibilities which confront us all.

Insuring Economic Security

Our first task is to insure basic economic security.

The swings and shocks of economic adversity are a global concern tearing at the fabric of developed and developing nations alike. The cycle of good times and bad, abundance and famine, does vast damage to lives and economies. Unemployment, falling standards of living, and the ravages of inflation fuel social and political discontent. We have recently seen the corrosive effects in many countries.

Developing economies are by far the most vulnerable to natural and manmade disasters—the vagaries of weather and of the business cycle. Sharp increases in the prices of oil and food have a devastating effect on their livelihood. Recessions in the industrial countries depress their export earnings.

Thus economic security is the minimum requirement of an effective strategy for development. Without this foundation, sound development programs cannot proceed and the great efforts that development requires from poor and rich alike cannot be sustained.

And because economic security is a global problem, it is a global challenge:

—The industrial nations must work together more effectively to restore and maintain their noninflationary expansion;

—Nations which supply vital products must avoid actions which disrupt that expansion; and

—The international community must undertake a new approach to reduce drastic fluctuations in the export earnings of the developing countries.

Since the economic health of the industrial countries is central to the health of the global economy, their efforts to avoid the extremes of recession and inflation become an international, as well as a national, responsibility.

In a new departure this past year, the leaders of the United States and its major trading partners have begun closer coordination of

[9]Cf. Chapter 31, Document 50.

their national economic policies. A shared sense of urgency, and the exchange of information about trends and intentions, have already influenced important policy decisions. President Ford intends to continue and intensify consultations of this kind. The successful recovery of the industrial economies will be the engine of international stability and growth.

Global economic security depends, secondly, on the actions of suppliers of vital products.

Thus the United States has believed that the future of the world economy requires discussions on energy and other key issues among oil consuming and producing nations. The Government of France is inviting industrialized, oil-producing, and developing nations to relaunch a dialogue this fall on the problems of energy, development, raw materials, and related financial issues. The United States has supported this proposal and worked hard to establish the basis for successful meetings.

But this dialogue is based on an approach of negotiation and consensus, not the exercise of brute economic power to gain unilateral advantage. The enormous, arbitrary increases in the price of oil of 1973 and 1974 have already exacerbated both inflation and recession worldwide. They have shattered the economic planning and progress of many countries. Another increase[10] would slow down or reverse the recovery and the development of nearly every nation represented in this Assembly. It would erode both the will and the capacity in the industrial world for assistance to developing countries. It would, in short, strike a serious blow at the hopes of hundreds of millions around the world.

The forthcoming dialogue among consumers and producers is a test. For its part, the United States is prepared for cooperation. We will work to make it succeed, in our own self-interest and in the interest of all nations. We hope to be met in that same spirit.

The third basic factor in economic security is the stability of export earnings. The development programs—indeed, the basic survival—of many countries rest heavily on earnings from exports of primary products which are highly vulnerable to fluctuations in worldwide demand. Countries which depend on one product can find their revenues reduced drastically if its price drops or if exports fall precipitously. Most have insufficient reserves to cushion against sharp declines in earnings, and they cannot quickly increase the exports of other products. Facing such economic problems, most cannot borrow to offset the loss or can only do so at extremely high interest rates. In such situations countries are frequently forced to cut back on the imports on which their growth and survival depend. Thus the unpredictability of export earnings can make a mockery of development planning.

[10]Cf. note 27 to Introduction.

The question of stabilization of income from primary products has become central in the dialogue on international economic concerns. Price stabilization is not generally a promising approach. For many commodities it would be difficult to achieve without severe restrictions on production or exports, extremely expensive buffer stocks, or price levels which could stimulate substitutes and thereby work to the long-range disadvantage of producers. Even the most ambitious agenda for addressing individual commodities would not result in stabilization arrangements for all of them in the near term. And focusing exclusively on stabilizing commodity prices would not provide sufficient protection to the many developing countries whose earnings also depend on the exports of manufactured goods.

The U.S. Government has recently completed a review of these issues. We have concluded that, because of the wide diversity among countries, commodities, and markets, a new, much more comprehensive approach is required—one which will be helpful to exporters of all commodities and manufactured goods as well.

Let me set forth our proposal. The United States proposes creation in the International Monetary Fund (IMF) of a new development security facility to stabilize overall export earnings.

—The facility would give loans to sustain development programs in the face of export fluctuations; up to $2.5 billion, and possibly more, in a single year and a potential total of $10 billion in outstanding loans.

—Assistance would be available to all developing countries which need to finance shortfalls in export earnings, unless the shortfalls are caused by their own acts of policy.

—The poorest countries would be permitted to convert their loans into grants under prescribed conditions. These grants would be financed by the proceeds of sales of IMF gold channeled through the proposed $2 billion Trust Fund now under negotiation.[11]

—Eligible countries could draw most, or under certain conditions all, of their IMF quotas in addition to their normal drawing rights. Much of that could be drawn in a single year, if necessary; part automatically, part subject to balance-of-payments conditions, and part reserved for cases of particularly violent swings in commodity earnings.

—Shortfalls would be calculated according to a formula geared to future growth as well as current and past exports. In this way the facility helps countries protect their development plans.

[11]Cf. Chapter 18 at note 12, and note 8 to Chapter 31.

—This facility would replace the IMF's compensatory finance facility; it would not be available for industrial countries.

The United States will present its detailed proposals to the Executive Directors of the International Monetary Fund this month.

This development security facility would provide unprecedented protection against disruptions caused by reductions in earnings—both for countries whose exports consist of a few commodities and for those with diversified and manufactured exports, whose earnings also fluctuate with business cycles. In the great majority of countries, this new facility will cover nearly all the earnings shortfall.

This new source of funds also reinforces our more traditional types of assistance; without the stabilization of earnings, the benefits of concessional aid for developing countries are vitiated. For industrialized countries, it means a more steady export market. For developing countries, it helps assure that development can be pursued without disruption and makes them more desirable prospects in international capital markets. For consumers and producers, rich and poor alike, it buttresses economic security.

Thus the success of our efforts in this area will demonstrate that our interdependence can strengthen the foundations of prosperity for all while promoting progress in the developing countries.

Accelerating Economic Growth

It is not enough to insure the minimal economic security of the developing countries. Development is a process of growth, acceleration, greater productivity, higher living standards, and social change. This is a process requiring the infusion of capital, technology, and managerial skills on a massive scale.

Developing countries themselves will have to provide most of the effort, but international support is indispensable. Even a moderate acceleration of recent growth rates will require some $40 billion a year in outside capital by 1980. The requirement for technological innovation, though impossible to quantify, is similarly great.

How can these needs for capital, technology, and skills be met?

Bilateral concessional assistance from the industrialized countries has been one important source. Last year it amounted to some $7.2 billion. This must continue to grow. But realistically, we cannot expect the level to increase significantly over the coming years. To put it frankly, the political climate for bilateral aid has deteriorated. In the industrial countries, support for aid has been eroded by domestic economic slowdown, compounded by energy problems; in the developing countries, there is resentment at forms of assistance which imply dependence.

The oil exporters have only begun to meet their responsibility for assistance to the poorer countries. Last year their concessionary aid disbursements were roughly $2 billion; they could, and must, rise substantially this year.

But the industrial nations and the oil exporters cannot, even together, supply all the new resources needed to accelerate development. It follows inescapably that the remaining needs for capital and technology can only be met, directly or indirectly, from the vast pool of private sources. This investment will take place only if the conditions exist to attract or permit it. The United States therefore believes it is time for the world community to address the basic requirements for accelerating growth in developing countries:

—First, developing countries must have better access to capital markets.

—Secondly, we must promote the transfer of technology.

—Third, it is time to reach an international consensus on the principles to guide the beneficial operation of transnational enterprises.

Access to Capital Markets

First, access to capital markets: The private capital markets are already a major source of development funds, either directly or through intermediaries. The World Bank and the regional development banks borrow extensively to lend to developing nations. The United States urges the expansion of these programs. We are gratified that advanced countries outside of the Western Hemisphere are joining us shortly in a $6 billion expansion of the Inter-American Development Bank. We will participate in negotiations for replenishment of the Asian Development Bank, and we are seeking congressional authority to join the African Development Fund.[12]

But the developing countries that have been most successful and that no longer require concessional aid, especially in Asia and Latin America, have relied heavily on borrowing in the capital markets. Their future access must be assured.

We must now find new ways to enhance the opportunities of developing countries in the competition for capital. And we need to match in new ways potential sources of capital with the investment needs of developing countries.

Several courses of action offer promise.

[12]Increased participation in the Inter-American Development Bank and participation in the African Development Fund were authorized by Public Law 94-302, May 31, 1976.

First, the United States will support a major expansion of the resources of the World Bank's International Finance Corporation, the investment banker with the broadest experience in supporting private enterprise in developing countries. We propose a large increase in the IFC's capital, from the present $100 million to at least $400 million.

Second, the United States proposes creation of an International Investment Trust to mobilize portfolio capital for investment in local enterprises. The trust would attract new capital by offering investors a unique opportunity: participation in a managed broad selection of investments in developing country firms, public, private, and mixed. The International Finance Corporation would manage it and perhaps provide seed capital, but most of its funds would come from government and private investors. Investors would have their exposure to major losses limited by a $200 million loss reserve provided by governments of industrialized, oil-producing, and developing nations. This institution could be a powerful link between the capital markets and the developing world and could provide billions of dollars of essential resources.

Third, the United States will contribute actively to the work of the IMF-World Bank Development Committee to find ways to assist developing countries in their direct borrowing in the capital markets. It is encouraging that the Latin American countries are considering a regional financial safety net to underpin their access to capital markets by mutual commitments of financial backing.

Finally, we believe that all industrial countries should systematically review the conditions for developing-country access to their national markets to assure that they offer fair and open opportunity. The United States is prepared to provide technical assistance and expertise to developing countries ready to enter long-term capital markets, and we ask others to join us.

Transfer of Technology

Developing countries need not only new funds but also new technology. Yet the mechanisms for the transfer of technology and for its local development are limited and are seldom at the sole command of national governments, and the technologies of industrial countries must often be adapted to local economic and social conditions. New institutions and new approaches are therefore required.

For technology to spur development, it must spur growth in priority areas: energy, food, other resources strategic to the developing economies, and industrialization itself.

First, *energy* is critical for both agricultural and industrial development. The enormous rise in the cost of oil in the last two years has more than wiped out the total of the foreign aid that developing countries have received. It has undermined their balance of payments and has mortgaged their future by forcing them into larger borrowing at higher interest rates. There is no easy short-term solution; but if energy dependence is to be reduced, efforts to exploit new and diversified sources must be intensified now.

The United States invites other nations to join us in an increase of bilateral support for training and technical assistance to help developing countries find and exploit new sources of fossil fuel and other forms of energy.

Methods of discovering and using less accessible or low-grade resources must be fully utilized. So must technology to produce solar and geothermal power. And these techniques must be suited to the conditions of the developing countries.

The United States believes the topic of energy cooperation should be high on the agenda for the forthcoming dialogue between consumers and producers. We will propose, in this dialogue, creation of an International Energy Institute bringing together developed and developing, consumer and producer, on the particular problem of energy development. The International Energy Agency and the International Atomic Energy Agency should both find ways to give technical assistance and support to this institute.

A second critical area for technological innovation is *food production and improvement of nutrition*.

During the past decade, a number of international agricultural research centers have been established to adapt techniques to local needs and conditions. In 1971 the Consultative Group for International Agricultural Research was formed to coordinate these efforts. The United States is prepared to expand the capacity of these institutions. In collaboration with national research organizations with more skilled manpower and funds, they could grow into a worldwide research network for development of agricultural technology.

We are also supporting legislation in the Congress to enable our universities to expand their technical assistance and research in the agricultural field.

Nonfood agricultural and forestry products are a third strategic area for technological assistance. The export earnings of many of the poorest countries—and the livelihood of many millions of their people—depend on such products as timber, jute, cotton, and natural rubber, some of which have encountered serious problems in the face of synthetics. They urgently need assistance to improve the productivity and competitiveness of these products and to diversify their economies.

The United States therefore proposes creation of an organization to coordinate and finance such assistance. Its task will be to attract manpower and capital for research. The financing of this effort should be a priority task for the new International Fund for Agricultural Development.

But developing countries' need for technology is not only for development of strategic sectors but for the broad *promotion of industrialization* itself. This requires the broadest application of skills, resources, and information.

This is not an easy task. The storehouse of technology is already huge and is growing geometrically. Developing practical devices to transfer technology beyond those which already exist will require careful thought. We are prepared to join with other nations in examining new initiatives.

To this end the United States supports creation of an International Industrialization Institute to sponsor and conduct research on industrial technology together with the governments, industries, and research facilities of developing countries.

We support creation of an international center for the exchange of technological information, as a clearinghouse for the sharing of ongoing research and new findings relevant to development.

We will expand our bilateral support of industrial technology appropriate to developing country needs.

We will work with others in this organization in preparing guidelines for the transfer of technology and in the planning of a conference on science and technology for development.

Transnational Enterprises

Access to capital markets and special programs to transfer new technology are but two factors of accelerated growth. There is a third—which may well be one of the most effective engines of development—the transnational enterprise.

Transnational enterprises have been powerful instruments of modernization both in the industrial nations—where they conduct most of their operations—and in the developing countries, where there is often no substitute for their ability to marshal capital, management skills, technology, and initiative. Thus the controversy over their role and conduct is itself an obstacle to economic development.

It is time for the world community to deal with the problems, real and perceived, that have arisen. If the nations assembled here cannot reach consensus on the proper role of these enterprises, the developing countries could lose an invaluable asset. Let us make this issue a test of our capacity to accommodate mutual concerns in practical agreement.

For our part, the United States is prepared to meet the proper concerns of governments in whose territories transnational enterprises operate. We affirm that enterprises must act in full accordance with the sovereignty of host governments and take full account of their public policy. Countries are entitled to regulate the operations of transnational enterprises within their borders. But countries wishing the benefits of these enterprises should foster the conditions that attract and maintain their productive operation.

The United States therefore believes that the time has come for the international community to articulate standards of conduct for both enterprises and governments. The United Nations Commission on Transnational Corporations and other international bodies have begun such an effort. We must reach agreement on balanced principles. These should apply to transnational enterprises in their relations with governments, and to governments in their relations with enterprises and with other governments. They must be fair principles, for failure to reflect the interests of all parties concerned would exacerbate rather than moderate the frictions which have damaged the environment for international investment. Specifically, the United States believes that:

—Transnational enterprises are obliged to obey local law and refrain from unlawful intervention in the domestic affairs of host countries. Their activities should take account of public policy and national development priorities. They should respect local customs. They should employ qualified local personnel, or qualify local people through training.

—Host governments in turn must treat transnational enterprises equitably, without discrimination among them, and in accordance with international law. Host governments should make explicit their development priorities and the standards which transnational enterprises are expected to meet, and maintain them with reasonable consistency.

—Governments and enterprises must both respect the contractual obligations that they freely undertake. Contracts should be negotiated openly, fairly, and with full knowledge of their implications. Greater assurance that contracts will be honored will improve the international commercial environment, increase the flow of investment, and expand economic transactions. Destructive and politically explosive investment disputes, which spoil the climate for large commitments and investment, will occur less frequently.

—Principles established for transnational enterprises should apply equally to domestic enterprises, where relevant. Standards should be addressed not only to privately owned corporations, but also to state-owned and mixed transnational enterprises, which are increasingly important in the world economy.

A statement of principles is not the only or necessarily a sufficient way of resolving many of the problems affecting transnational enterprises. We must develop others:

—Governments must harmonize their tax treatment of these enterprises. Without coordination, host-country and home-country policies may inhibit productive investment.

—Factfinding and arbitral procedures must be promoted as means for settling investment disputes. The World Bank's International Center for the Settlement of Investment Disputes and other third-party facilities should be employed to settle the important disputes which inevitably arise.

—Laws against restrictive business practices must be developed, better coordinated among countries, and enforced. The United States has long been vigilant against such abuses in domestic trade, mergers, or licensing of technology. We stand by the same principles internationally. We condemn restrictive practices in setting prices or restraining supplies, whether by private or state-owned transnational enterprises or by the collusion of national governments.

—Insurance for foreign private investors should to the extent possible be multilateralized and should include financial participation by developing countries to reflect our mutual stake in encouraging foreign investment in the service of development.

—And there must be more effective bilateral consultation among governments to identify and resolve investment disputes before they become irritants in political relations.

The United States believes that just solutions are achievable—and necessary. If the world community is committed to economic development, it cannot afford to treat transnational enterprises as objects of economic warfare. The capacity of the international community to deal with this issue constructively will be an important test of whether the search for solutions or the clash of ideologies will dominate our economic future. The implications for economic development are profound.

Trade and Development

The third basic area for our attention is trade. Improving the world trading system will magnify our success in every other sphere of the development effort.

Trade has been a driving force in the unprecedented expansion of the world economy over the last 30 years. Comparative advantage and specialization, the exchange of technology and the movement of capital, the spur to productivity that competition provides—these are central elements of efficiency and progress. Open trade promotes growth and combats inflation in all countries.

For developing nations, trade is perhaps the most important engine of development. Increased earnings from exports help pay for both the imports that are essential to expand production and the food for growing populations. These earnings reduce dependence on aid, limit the accumulation of debt, and help finance essential borrowing. Growing export industries can provide jobs and increase the government revenues necessary for development programs. It is no accident, therefore, that the success stories in development of the past three decades have been those very countries that have taken full advantage of the opportunities in world trade.

But today the global trading system is threatened by the most serious recession since the Second World War. We face the danger of proliferating artificial barriers and unfair competition reminiscent of the 1930's, which contributed to economic and political disaster. Every day that economic recovery is delayed, the temptation grows to restrict imports, subsidize exports, and control scarce commodities. Concerted action is necessary now to safeguard and improve the open trading system on which the future well-being of all our countries depends.

The multilateral trade negotiations now taking place in Geneva are central to this effort. They will have a profound impact on the future of the world economy and the prospects for development. If these negotiations fail, all countries risk a slide into an increasingly fragmented, closed world of nationalism, blocs, and mounting frictions. If they succeed, all countries will benefit and there will be major progress toward a cooperative and prosperous world.

Many of the less developed nations are emerging as important commercial powers. But developing countries need assistance to take better advantage of trading opportunities, especially to help them open up new markets. In revising rules to govern trade we must take account of their particular needs. In this connection, regional trading associations can help many small countries by providing the economies of scale which result from larger markets.

Thus success in the negotiations depends critically on promoting the interests of the developing countries. For if they do not help to make the rules, assume part of the responsibility to maintain a stable trade system, and share in the benefits of trade, the rules will be subject to increasing challenge, the stability of the system undermined, and the benefits for all nations jeopardized.

The United States therefore believes that a major goal of the multilateral trade negotiations should be to make the trading system better serve development goals. Let me briefly outline our policy.

—First, there must be fundamental structural improvement in the relationship of the developing countries to the world trading system. In the earlier stages of their development, they should receive special treatment through a variety of means—such as preferences, favorable concessions, and exceptions which reflect their economic status. But as they progress to a higher level of development, they must gradually accept the same obligations of reciprocity and stable arrangements that other countries undertake. At some point they must be prepared to compete on more equal terms, even as they derive growing benefits.

—Second, we must improve opportunities for the manufacturing sectors of developing countries. These provide the most promising new areas for exports at the critical stage in development, but the tariffs of industrial countries are a substantial obstacle. To ease this problem the United States has agreed to join other industrial countries in instituting generalized tariff preferences to permit developing countries enhanced access to the markets of industrialized nations.

I am pleased to announce today that the U.S. program will be put into effect on January 1, 1976.[13] And before that date, we will begin consultations and practical assistance to enable exporting countries to benefit from the new trade opportunities in the American market, the largest single market for the manufactured goods of developing countries.

—Third, in keeping with the Tokyo Declaration,[14] we should adapt rules of nontariff barriers to the particular situation of developing countries. In setting international standards for government procurement practices, for example, the United States will negotiate special consideration for the developing countries. We will also negotiate on the basis that under prescribed conditions, certain subsidies may be permitted without triggering countervailing duties for a period geared to achieving particular development objectives.

—Fourth, we will work for early agreement on tariffs for tropical products, which are a major source of earnings for the developing world. Moreover, the United States will implement its tariff cuts on these products as soon as possible.

[13]Executive Order 11888, Nov. 24, 1975, in *Presidential Documents*, 11: 1312-15.
[14]*AFR, 1973*: 391-4.

—Finally, we are ready to join with other participants in Geneva to negotiate changes in the system of protection in the industrialized countries that favors the import of raw materials over other goods. Many countries impose low or no duties on raw materials and high duties on manufactured or processed goods; the tariff protection increases or "escalates" with the degree of processing. Nothing could be better calculated to discourage and limit the growth of processing industries in developing countries. The United States will give high priority in the Geneva negotiations to reducing these barriers.

The developing countries have obligations in return. The world needs a system in which no nation, developed or developing, arbitrarily withholds or interferes with normal exports of materials. This practice—by depriving other countries of needed goods—can trigger unemployment, cut production, and fuel inflation. It is therefore as disruptive as any of the other trade barriers I have discussed. We urge negotiations on rules to limit and govern the use of export restraints, a logical extension of existing rules on imports. The United States will join others in negotiating supply-access commitments as part of the reciprocal exchange of concessions.

But commodities can be addressed only in part in the context of the trade negotiations. For some serious commodity problems, special arrangements and different institutional structures are required. Let me now turn to that subject.

Commodity Trade and Productions

Exports of primary products—raw materials and other commodities—are crucial to the incomes of developing countries. These earnings can lift living standards above bare subsistence, generate profits to support the first steps of industrialization, and provide tax revenues for education, health, and other social programs for development. The history of the United States—and many other countries—confirms the importance of commodities.

But this path can be precarious in an uncertain global environment. Those developing countries which are not oil exporters rely on primary commodities for nearly two-thirds of their export earnings. Yet their sales of raw materials and agricultural products have not grown as fast as those of industrial countries. Agricultural commodities, particularly, are vulnerable to the whims of weather and swings of worldwide demand. The market in minerals is especially sensitive to the pendulum of boom-and-bust in the industrial countries. The result is a cycle of scarcity and glut, of underinvestment and overcapacity.

Developing countries are hit hard by commodity cycles also as consumers; higher prices for energy imports, swings in the price and supply of food, and greater costs for other essential raw materials have been devastating blows, soaking up aid funds and the earnings by which they hoped to finance imports. All this can make a mockery of development plans.

But the problems of commodities are not the problems only of developing countries. The industrialized countries are in fact the largest exporters of food and most minerals. Gyrating prices complicate economic decisions in industrial countries. And consumers in industrial countries have painfully learned that high commodity prices leave their inflationary impact long after the commodity market has turned around.

Therefore both industrial and developing countries would benefit from more stable conditions of trade and an expansion of productive capacity in commodities.

Many solutions have been put forward to benefit producers of particular products: cartelization, price indexing, commodity agreements, and other methods. But reality demonstrates the interdependence of all our economies and therefore the necessity for approaches that serve global rather than narrow interests.

Food Security

The most vital commodity in the world is food. The United States is its largest producer and exporter. We recognize our responsibility. We have also sought to make international collaboration in food a model for realistic and cooperative approaches to other international economic issues.

The U.S. policy is now one of maximum production. At home, we want a thriving farm economy and moderate prices for consumers. Internationally, we wish cooperative relations with nations that purchase from us, an open and growing market, and abundant supplies to meet the needs of the hungry through both good times and bad.

For hundreds of millions of people, food security is the single most critical need in their lives; for many it is a question of life itself. But food security means more than emergency relief to deal with crop failures, natural disasters, and pockets of famine. It means reasonable stability in the availability of food in commercial markets so that harvest failures in some parts of the world will not make food impossibly expensive elsewhere. We have seen with dramatic frequency in recent years how the international food market, strained to capacity, can shake the international economy. Its fluctuations have accelerated inflation, devastated development plans, and wreaked havoc with human lives. Yet in good times, the world community has not summoned the will to take obvious corrective steps to stabilize the market structure.

The United States believes that a global approach to food security, which contains elements that can apply to other commodities, should follow these basic principles:

—The problem must be approached globally, comprehensively, and cooperatively, by consultation and negotiation among all significant producers and consumers;

—Producers should recognize the global interest in stability of supply, and consumers should recognize the interest of producers in stability of markets and earnings;

—Special consideration should be given to the needs of developing countries; and

—Where volatile demand is combined with limited ability to make short-term increases in production, buffer stocks may be the best approach to achieving greater security for both consumers and producers.

At the World Food Conference last November,[15] which was convened at our initiative, the United States proposed a comprehensive international cooperative approach to providing food security. We proposed an international system of nationally held grain reserves, to meet emergencies and improve the market. The United States has since then offered specific proposals and begun negotiations.[16] But the international effort lagged when improved harvests seemed to diminish the immediate danger of worldwide shortage.

My government today declares that it is time to create this reserve system. If we do not, future crises are inevitable. Specifically, we propose:

—To meet virtually all potential shortfalls in food grains production, total world reserves must reach at least 30 million tons of wheat and rice. We should consider whether a similar reserve is needed in coarse grains.

—Responsibility for holding reserves should be allocated fairly, taking into account wealth, production, and trade. The United States is prepared to hold a major share.

—Acquisition and release of reserves should be governed by quantitative standards such as anticipated surpluses and shortfalls in production.

—Full participants in the system should receive assured access

[15]Cf. note 10 to Chapter 4.
[16]Cf. note 12 to Chapter 43.

to supplies. Among major producers, full participation should require complete exchange of information and forecasts.

—Special assistance should be extended to developing countries that participate, to enable them to meet their obligation to hold a portion of global reserves.

The United States is ready to negotiate the creation of such a system. Let us move ahead rapidly.

Other Primary Commodities

And let us apply the same approach of cooperation to other primary commodities that are similarly beset by swings of price and supply—and that are similarly essential to the global economy.

There is no simple formula that will apply equally to all commodities. The United States therefore proposes to discuss new arrangements in individual commodities on a case-by-case basis.

Buffer stocks can be an effective technique to moderate instability in supplies and earnings. On the other hand, price-fixing arrangements distort the market, restrict production, and waste resources for everyone. It is developing countries that can least afford this waste. Restricted production idles the costly equipment and economic infrastructure that takes years to build. Artificially high prices lead consumers to make costly investment in domestic substitutes, ultimately eroding the market power of the traditional producers.

Accordingly, the United States proposes the following approach to commodity arrangements:

—We recommend that a consumer-producer forum be established for every key commodity to discuss how to promote the efficiency, growth, and stability of its market. This is particularly important in the case of grains, as I have outlined. It is also important in copper, where priority should be given to creating a forum for consumer-producer consultation.

—The first new formal international agreement being concluded is on tin. We have participated actively in its negotiation. President Ford has authorized me to announce that the United States intends to sign the tin agreement, subject to congressional consultations and ratification.[17] We welcome its emphasis on buffer stocks, its avoidance of direct price fixing, and its balanced voting system. We will retain our right to sell from our strategic stockpiles, and we recognize the right of others to maintain a similar program.

[17]The Fifth International Tin Agreement, done at Geneva June 21, 1975, was signed by the U.S. Mar. 11, 1976 and entered into force provisionally July 1, 1976.

—We are participating actively in negotiations on coffee. We hope they will result in a satisfactory new agreement that reduces the large fluctuations in prices and supplies entering the market.[18]

—We will also join the forthcoming cocoa and sugar negotiations.[19] Their objective will be to reduce the risks of investment and moderate the swings in prices and supplies.

—We will support liberalization of the International Monetary Fund's financing of buffer stocks, to assure that this facility is available without reducing other drawing rights.

Comprehensive Program of Investment

I have already announced my government's broad proposal of a development security facility, a more fundamental approach to stabilizing the overall earnings of countries dependent on commodities trade. My government also believes that an effective approach to the commodities problem requires a comprehensive program of investment to expand worldwide capacity in minerals and other critical raw materials. This is basic to the health of both industrial and developing economies.

There are presently no shortages in most basic raw materials, nor are any likely in the next two or three years. But the adequacy of supplies in years to come will be determined by investment decisions taken now. Because the technology for processing lower grade ores is extremely complex and the financing requirements for major raw material investments are massive, new projects take several years to complete. In some countries the traditional source of funds—private foreign investment—is no longer as welcome, nor are investors as interested, as in the past.

The United States therefore proposes a major new international effort to expand raw material resources in developing countries.

The World Bank and its affiliates, in concert with private sources, should play a fundamental role. They can supply limited amounts of capital directly; more importantly, they can use their technical, managerial, and financial expertise to bring together funds from private and public sources. They can act as intermediary between private investors and host governments and link private and public effort by providing cross-guarantees on performance. World Bank loans could fund government projects, par-

[18]The International Coffee Agreement, 1976, done at London Dec. 3, 1975, was signed by the U.S. Feb. 27, 1976 and entered into force provisionally Oct. 1, 1976.
[19]The U.S. announced Jan. 16, 1976 that it would not sign the new International Cocoa Agreement unless certain provisions were renegotiated, but that it intended to participate actively in negotiations for a new International Sugar Agreement beginning in Sept. 1976 (*Bulletin*, 74: 242; further details in same, 74: 609-11).

ticularly for needed infrastructure, while the International Finance Corporation could join private enterprise in providing loans and equity capital. The World Bank Group should aim to mobilize $2 billion in private and public capital annually.

In addition, the United States will contribute to and actively support the new United Nations revolving fund for natural resources. This fund will encourage the worldwide exploration and exploitation of minerals and thus promote one of the most promising endeavors of economic development.

The Poorest Nations

Any strategy for development must devote special attention to the needs of the poorest countries. The fate of 1 billion people—half the developing world and a quarter of mankind—will be affected by what we do or fail to do.

For the last four years, per capita income in the poorest countries—already below minimal standards for development—has declined. Their exports are most concentrated in the least dynamic sectors of world demand. It is they who have been most cruelly affected by the rise in the costs of oil, food, and other essential imports.

Whatever adversity the rest of mankind endures, it is these peoples who endure the most. Whatever problems we have, theirs are monumental. Whatever economic consequences flow from the decisions that we all make, the consequences are greatest for them. If global progress in economic development falters, they will be submerged.

This challenge transcends ideology and bloc politics. No international order can be considered just unless one of its fundamental principles is cooperation to raise the poorest of the world to a decent standard of life.

This challenge has two dimensions. We must look to elemental economic security and the immediate relief of suffering. And we must give preference to these countries' needs for future economic growth.

Elemental Economic Security

First, security means balance-of-payments support for the poorest countries during periods of adversity. For them global recessions and wide swings in prices of key commodities have a particularly disastrous impact. Yet these countries have very little access to short- and medium-term capital to help them weather bad times. The little finance to which they have access often involves interest rates that are too high considering their chronic debt-repayment problems.

To provide greater balance-of-payments support at more acceptable rates of interest for the poor nations, the United States last November proposed a Trust Fund in the International Monetary Fund of up to $2 billion for emergency relief. Although this proposal met with wide support, it has been stalled by a dispute over an unrelated issue: the role of gold in the international monetary system. We cannot let this delay continue. The United States is making a determined effort to move forward the monetary negotiations at the IMF meetings now underway.[20] If others meet us in this same spirit, we could reach a consensus on the Trust Fund by the next meeting in January.

Second, security requires stable export earnings. The new approach that we are proposing today for earnings stabilization can provide major new economic insurance in the form of loans and grants for the poorest countries.

Third, security means having enough to eat. There must be determined international cooperation on food.

The World Food Conference set a target of 10 million tons of food aid annually. This fiscal year the U.S. food aid budget provides for almost 6 million tons of food grains—60 percent of the world target, and a 20 percent increase over last year. Other producers must also provide their share.

Another priority in the poorest countries must be to reduce the tragic waste of losses after harvest from inadequate storage, transport, and pest control. There are often simple and inexpensive techniques to resolve these problems. Investment in such areas as better storage and pesticides could have a rapid and substantial impact on the world's food supply; indeed, the saving could match the total of all the food aid being given around the world. Therefore we urge that the Food and Agriculture Organization, in conjunction with the U.N. Development Program and the World Bank, set a goal of cutting in half these postharvest losses by 1985, and develop a comprehensive program to this end.

Finally, security means good health and easing the strains of population growth. Disease ravages the poorest countries most of all and exacts a devastating economic as well as human cost. At the same time we face the stark reality that there will be twice as many people to feed by the end of this century as there are today. One of the most promising approaches to these problems is the integrated delivery of basic health services at the community level, combining medical treatment, family planning, and nutritional information and using locally trained paramedical personnel. The United States

[20]Cf. Chapter 31.

will support a major expansion of the efforts already underway, including those in cooperation with the World Health Organization, to develop and apply these methods. We strongly urge the help of all concerned nations.

Future Economic Growth

Programs to achieve minimum economic security, however essential, solve only part of the problem. We must help the poorest nations break out of their present stagnation and move toward economic growth.

This means, first of all, that they should have preferential access to official, concessionary financial aid. They have the least dynamic exports, but they lack the capital to develop new ones. They have the direst need for financing, but they have no access to capital markets and little ability to carry greater debt.

If these countries themselves can summon the effort required, outside assistance can be productive. All nations with the financial capacity must share the responsibility. We will do our part. More than 70 percent of our development assistance goes to low-income countries. More than 60 percent of this year's proposed programs is devoted to food and nutrition, which are of particular importance to the poorest.

The special financial needs of the poorest countries can be met particularly well by expanded low-interest loans of the international financial institutions. The International Development Association of the World Bank Group is a principal instrument whose great potential has not been fully realized. After congressional consultations, the United States will join others in a substantial fifth replenishment of the resources of the International Development Association, provided that the oil-exporting countries also make a significant contribution.[21]

An effective strategy for sustained growth in the poorest countries must expand their agricultural production, for external food aid cannot possibly fill their needs. The current gap between what the developing countries need and what they can produce themselves is 15 million tons; at present rates of growth, the gap is expected to double or triple within the next decade. Failure to meet this challenge will doom much of the world to hunger and malnutrition and all of the world to periodic shortages and higher prices.

Traditional bilateral aid programs to boost agricultural production remain indispensable. President Ford is asking Congress for

[21] A fifth replenishment of IDA resources, totaling $7.6 billion over a three-year period beginning in mid-1977, was recommended Mar. 15, 1977 at a meeting of interested governments in Vienna.

authorization to double our bilateral agricultural assistance this year to $582 million. We urge the other affluent nations to increase their contributions as well.

Clearly a massive program of international cooperation is also required. More research is needed to improve agricultural yields, make more efficient use of fertilizer, and find better farm management techniques. Technical assistance and information exchange are needed for training and for technological advance. Better systems of water control, transportation, and land management are needed to tap the developing countries' vast reserves of land, water, and manpower.

To mobilize massive new concessional resources for these purposes, the United States proposes the early establishment of the new International Fund for Agricultural Development. President Ford has asked me to announce that he will seek authorization of a direct contribution of $200 million to the fund, provided that others will add their support for a combined goal of at least $1 billion.[22]

The International Fund for Agricultural Development can be the major source of new capital to attack the most critical problems of the poorest developing countries. The United States urges the world community to give it prompt and major support.

The Political Dimension

In every area of endeavor that I have described—economic security, growth, trade, commodities, and the needs of the poorest—the developing countries themselves want greater influence over the decisions that will affect their future. They are pressing for a greater role in the institutions and negotiations by which the world economic system is evolving.

The United States believes that participation in international decisions must be widely shared, in the name of both justice and effectiveness. We believe the following principles should apply:

The process of decisions should be fair. No country or group of countries should have exclusive power in the areas basic to the welfare of others. This principle is valid for oil. It also applies to trade and finance.

The methods of participation must be realistic. We must encourage the emergence of real communities of interest between

---

[22]An agreement establishing the International Fund for Agricultural Development was concluded at Rome June 13, 1976 and signed by the U.S. Dec. 22, 1976 but had not yet entered into force as of mid-1977. An appropriation of $200 million for the Fund was authorized by the International Development and Food Assistance Act of 1975 (Public Law 94-161, Dec. 20, 1975).

nations, whether they are developed or developing, producer or consumer, rich or poor. The genuine diversity of interests that exists among states must not be submerged by bloc discipline or in artificial, unrepresentative majorities. For only genuine consensus can generate effective action.

The process of decision should be responsive to change. On many issues developing countries have not had a voice that reflects their role. This is now changing. It is already the guiding principle of two of the most successful international bodies, the IMF and the World Bank, where the quotas of oil-producing states will soon be at least doubled—on the basis of objective criteria. Basic economic realities, such as the size of economies, participation in world trade, and financial contributions, must carry great weight.

Finally, participation should be tailored to the issues at hand. We can usefully employ many different institutions and procedures. Sometimes we should seek broad consensus in universal bodies, as we are doing this week in this Assembly; sometimes negotiations can more usefully be focused in more limited forums, such as the forthcoming consumer-producer dialogue; sometimes decisions are best handled in large specialized bodies such as the IMF and World Bank, where voting power is related to responsibility; and sometimes most effective action can be taken in regional bodies.

Most relevant to our discussion here is the improvement of the U.N. system, so that it can fulfill its charter mandate "to employ international machinery for the promotion of the economic and social advancement of all peoples." We welcome the thoughtful report by the Secretary General's group of 25 experts on structural reform in the U.N. system.[23] We will seriously consider its recommendations. In our view, an improved U.N. organization must include:

—Rationalization of the U.N.'s fragmented assistance programs;
—Strengthened leadership within the central Secretariat and the entire U.N. system for development and economic cooperation;
—Streamlining of the Economic and Social Council;
—Better consultative procedures to insure effective agreement among members with a particular interest in a subject under consideration; and

[23]Cf. *U.N. Monthly Chronicle*, Oct. 1975: 13-14; same, Dec. 1975: 46.

—A mechanism for independent evaluation of the implementation of programs.

The United States proposes that 1976 be dedicated as a year of review and reform of the entire U.N. development system. An intergovernmental committee should be formed at this session, to begin work immediately on recommendations that can be implemented by the General Assembly in its 1976 session. We consider this a priority in any strategy for development.

Mr. President, Mr. Secretary General, colleagues, ladies and gentlemen: I began today with the statement that we have, this week, an opportunity to improve the condition of mankind. This fact alone represents an extraordinary change in the human condition. Throughout history, man's imagination has been limited by his circumstances—which have now fundamentally changed. We are no longer confined to what Marx called "the realm of necessity." And it has always been the case that the wisest realists were those who understood man's power to shape his own reality.

The steps we take now are not limited by our technical possibilities, but only by our political will. If the advanced nations fail to respond to the winds of change, and if the developing countries choose rhetoric over reality, the great goal of economic development will be submerged in our common failure. The speeches made here this week will be placed alongside many other lofty pronouncements made over decades past in this organization on this subject, buried in the archives of oblivion.

But we would not all be here if we did not believe that progress is possible and that it is imperative.

The United States has proposed a program of action. We are prepared to contribute, if we are met in a spirit of common endeavor.

—We have proposed steps to improve basic economic security—to safeguard the world economy, and particularly the developing countries, against the cruel cycles that undermine their export earnings.

—We have proposed measures to improve developing countries' access to capital, new technology, and management skills to lift themselves from stagnation onto the path of accelerating growth.

—We have proposed structural improvements in the world trading system, to be addressed in the ongoing multilateral trade negotiations, to enhance developing countries' opportunities to earn their own way through trade.

—We have proposed a new approach to improving market

conditions in food and other basic commodities, on which the economies and indeed the lives of hundreds of millions of people depend.

—We have proposed specific ways of giving special help to the development needs of the poorest countries.

My government does not offer these proposals as an act of charity, nor should they be received as if due. We know that the world economy nourishes us all; we know that we live on a shrinking planet. Materially as well as morally, our destinies are intertwined.

There remain enormous things for us to do. We can say once more to the new nations: We have heard your voices. We embrace your hopes. We will join your efforts. We commit ourselves to our common success.

31. MEETING OF THE BANK AND FUND

(September 1-5, 1975)

[As the General Assembly began its special New York session on the problems and prospects of economic development, other aspects of the world economic situation were coming under scrutiny in Washington at the 30th annual meeting of the Boards of Governors of the International Bank for Reconstruction and Development (IBRD) and the International Monetary Fund (IMF), key institutions in all questions of global economic management. This was a forum in which discussion of such long-range issues as those of economic growth and monetary reform was disciplined by an acute awareness of current economic trends; and President Ford seemed glad to strike a reassuring note in this regard in welcoming the delegates from 127 nations who were in Washington to attend the meeting. "In the United States, recovery is well underway," the President declared on September 2. "Each week brings additional evidence of renewed economic health, and I am determined to fight against an acceleration of inflation that could restrain this recovery." A durable recovery at home, Mr. Ford added, would be the best contribution the United States could make to the health of the world economy as a whole.[1]

Few nations at the moment could boast conditions as favorable as the United States; yet there were undoubtedly grounds for optimism in the way the world had managed to scrape through the crisis brought on by the oil price increase. No nation, it appeared, had totally succumbed to the recent economic and financial strains; and considerable ingenuity had been expended in devising emergency machinery to help temper their effect. The IMF itself had already extended and enlarged the special "oil facility" originally set up in 1974 to assist in recycling surplus oil revenues. The principal oil consuming nations had agreed through the OECD to establish a $25 billion financial support fund or "safety net" to assist in balance-of-payments emergencies. In June, agreement had

[1] *Bulletin*, 73: 443.

been reached on the establishment within the IBRD of a so-called "third window" to provide up to $1 billion in loans at moderate interest rates to those of the developing countries that were most seriously affected by the oil squeeze—though funds available for this purpose were not expected to exceed $500 million during the first year of operation.[2]

Preparations for a general overhaul of the international monetary system had also been going forward under the auspices of the IMF Interim Committee, established the year before to replace the earlier "Committee of Twenty." Meeting in Washington on the eve of the IBRD-IMF session, this twenty-member group had unveiled a comprehensive reform package that called, among other things, for a 32.5 percent increase in the quotas of IMF member states, with a doubling of the share held by major oil exporting countries; an increase in voting requirements for important decisions; and a reduction in the role of gold in the international monetary system through abolition of an official gold price, elimination of the obligation to use gold in transactions with the Fund, and a one-third reduction in the Fund's own gold holdings, half of this amount being sold for the benefit of developing countries and half returned to the Fund's members.[3] Other major problems, centering around the exchange rate system and a projected revision of the IMF Articles of Agreement, were to be taken up at a further meeting of the Interim Commiteee to be held in Jamaica in January 1976.[4]

These and other matters of current concern were reviewed by Secretary of the Treasury Simon on September 2 in a formal presentation of U.S. views **(Document 50)** that served as a kind of pendant to Secretary Kissinger's U.N. speech the day before. In tones a shade less optimistic than those employed by President Ford, the Secretary of the Treasury took note of the current recovery but voiced strong objection to the adoption of more stimulative economic policies such as were currently being urged upon the United States from various quarters. Equally noted were Mr. Simon's vigorous defense of the existing system of floating exchange rates and his opposition to returning to a system of fixed parities such as had prevailed before 1971. This was another issue on which France, in particular, held widely different views from the United States, and which would have to be resolved in some fashion before the work of monetary reform could go forward successfully.[5]]

[2]These and related matters are conveniently summarized in *Keesing's*: 27477-81; for further details cf. *IMF Survey, passim.*
[3]Communiqué, Aug. 31, in *Bulletin*, 73: 450-52.
[4]Cf. Chapter 38 at notes 2-3.
[5]For further developments cf. Chapter 38.

(50) Meeting of Boards of Governors of the International Bank for Reconstruction and Development and the International Monetary Fund: Statement by Secretary of the Treasury William E. Simon, United States Governor of the Bank and Fund, September 2, 1975.[6]

It is a privilege to address this distinguished audience once again and to share with you today the views of the United States on the major economic issues facing the world.

In general, the outlook for the international economy is now more hopeful than it was earlier this year. Most of the major industrial countries have adopted vigorous expansionary policies. Several nations, including the United States, have begun the process of recovery. Despite serious strains, the level of international cooperation remains undiminished. Few countries have resorted to policies which might yield domestic gains at the expense of their neighbors. And the more affluent nations are strengthening their efforts to assist those who are less fortunate.

Yet there can be no doubt that the pattern of progress is highly uneven. In a number of countries, the downward economic spiral continues still, becoming more prolonged and severe than once expected. The hardships created by an inflation of unparalleled strength, brutally sharp and unanticipated increases in the cost of energy, and a harsh recession—all of these remain a painful living reality in too many parts of the world. Thus, the urgent task still before us is to work together in restoring a broadly based forward momentum to the world economy which will provide the foundation for sustained, noninflationary growth in every nation.

As we press forward, it is essential that we maintain our bearings:

—We must carefully support and encourage the forces of recovery without yielding to the temptations of excessive stimulation.

—We must persevere in our efforts to control inflation without disrupting the process of recovery. A durable recovery will be possible only if we master the causes of inflation.

—We must reach a better accommodation on the problems of energy while continuing to support the oil-exporting nations in their quest for economic advancement.

—We must encourage economic development among poorer nations.

—And we must insure that we have a smoothly functioning monetary system.

[6]Department of the Treasury Press Release, Sept. 2; text and titles from *Bulletin*, 73: 443-50.

Let me turn now to a more detailed consideration of each of these issues.

Prospects for Economic Growth

The United States is acutely aware that its own economic policies bear heavily not only upon the livelihoods of our own citizens but upon those in other nations as well. While our economy is no longer as predominant in the world economy as it once was, our gross national product still amounts to over one-quarter of the world total and we represent the world's largest import market. Therefore the single most important contribution we can make to the health of the world economy is to achieve durable, noninflationary growth within our own borders.

Fortunately, there is now abundant evidence that an economic recovery is well underway in the United States. My government is determined to sustain this recovery while also bringing inflation under control and adopting those policy measures necessary for lasting growth.

We need not, and we should not, seek to choose among these objectives. We have learned from hard experience that all of our economic goals must be pursued simultaneously.

We will not provide excessive stimulation that would only intensify inflationary pressures, preempt the capital that is needed to sustain the recovery, and run the risk of setting off another vicious cycle of inflation and recession. Nor will we allow our concern with inflation to prevent us from actively supporting the natural forces of recovery or taking additional expansionary measures if they should be needed. We are not ready to acquiesce in either stagnation or inflation as a way of life.

Some have suggested that in order to help other nations out of recession, the United States should embark upon much more stimulative fiscal and monetary policies. We respectfully disagree. Too many of our current domestic troubles are rooted in such excesses in the past. Since 1965 the average U.S. Federal budget deficit and the average annual growth in our money supply have been about three times as large as in the preceding decade. It is no accident that during the earlier period our country enjoyed reasonable price stability while in recent years we have had increasing difficulty in containing inflation. And inflationary expectations are now so deeply embedded in our society that they will not disappear quickly.

The financial sins of a decade cannot be forgiven by a day of penance. Our policies in the United States must be designed to attack the causes of inflation, not their results. In the long run, that will bring the most lasting benefits to us all.

While the revival of the U.S. economy will help to bolster both the economic prospects and the confidence of other nations, it would be unrealistic to expect that any single country could lead the rest of the world out of recession. Expanded world trade should not be regarded as the source, but as the product, of recovery.

Indeed, let us recognize that the process of solving our economic troubles must begin at home, with each country acting on its own to make the tough decisions that are essential for sound, durable growth. As that process spreads from one nation to the next, it will become mutually reinforcing and all nations will realize greater benefits. In addition to the expansionary efforts undertaken by the United States earlier this year, several other major industrialized nations have now adopted more stimulative policies. Taken together, these actions should provide a forward thrust to the world economy.

As our policies of expansion gradually take effect, we ask ourselves: Have we done enough? Should we do more to speed up the effects? To the extent that some of our people believe we are not moving rapidly enough to create jobs and to restore our standard of living, there may be adverse social and political pressures. Yet it is equally clear that if we overheat our economies, we will reignite the fires of inflation and create another recession with more serious economic and social consequences.

Our highest responsibility as finance ministers, I would respectfully suggest, is to pursue sound, balanced policies which promote economic growth without encouraging renewed inflation. That often proves to be politically unpopular in the short run, but in the long run it will do far more to create jobs and serve the best interests of our people than the palliatives so often urged upon us. History is littered with the wreckage of governments that have refused to face up to the ravages of inflation; and none of us can afford, either through shortsightedness or lack of determination, to yield to these temptations.

Impact of Escalating Oil Prices

Beyond the problems of determining fiscal and monetary policies, nations must also deal with the difficulties created by high oil prices.

Almost two years after the first oil price shock, it is evident that we are only beginning to understand the full impact as well as the threat to our future which is posed by escalating oil prices. It is now obvious that the most serious consequences are not financial, but political and economic. While we must and will continue to devote special attention to the problems of the financial system in adjusting to new realities, we can be confident of our capacity to manage such problems. But the economic consequences of these oil policies—the higher costs that have come not just in energy but in many other vital commodities such as food, the structural adjustments that have been necessary, the loss of jobs, and the obstacles to economic growth—cannot be so easily managed.

In our view, current price levels for international oil can be justified on neither economic nor financial grounds. The present pricing policies of the OPEC countries mean that cheap energy remains in the ground and that the prosperity of all nations is diminished. Moreover, high oil prices lie at the root of much of the world's recent inflation and the recession that followed. Yet, now the possibility of another increase in oil prices looms on the horizon.[7] Let there be no misunderstanding about the result of another major price increase: it would seriously jeopardize the balance upon which global economic recovery now depends.

We urge the OPEC nations to recognize, as others have done in the past, that the prosperity of each nation is deeply intertwined with the prosperity of all nations.

Another price increase seems especially inappropriate in light of our efforts to address the legitimate problems facing the oil-exporting nations as well as other developing countries. We have taken significant steps to bring about a dialogue between producers and consumers. We have proposed the establishment of commissions to deal with critical problems in the areas of energy, raw materials, development, and related financial questions. Special bilateral programs have been set up with the oil-exporting countries, and considerable progress has been recorded.

All of these measures reflect our sincere desire to work cooperatively with the oil exporters as they strive for higher standards of living and more diversified economies. In turn, we urge that they work cooperatively with us and with other nations to enhance the prospects for a world economic recovery.

Let me add that the substantial financing requirements of industrial countries in this period of OPEC surpluses dictate that we continue to keep the adequacy of international financing arrangements under review. I am confident that in the future, as in the past two years, private financing mechanisms will continue to play the dominant role in channeling OPEC funds to various borrowers. At the same time, we welcome the prospective establishment of the Financial Support Fund agreed upon among the member countries of the Organization for Economic Cooperation and Development. That fund will supplement IMF resources and provide needed insurance in an uncertain period. Particularly important in present circumstances is the assurance thereby provided

[7] Cf. note 27 to Introduction.

that, if needed, financing will be available to facilitate the pursuit of sound expansionary policies by the industrial countries.

Problems of the Developing Countries

Those who have suffered the most from higher oil prices and the deterioration in world economic conditions have been those who least deserve to suffer and are least able to protect themselves—the poor and the needy of the developing countries. In the industrialized nations, the problems of inflation, exorbitant energy prices, and the resulting recession have often meant hardships, but they have not brought large numbers of people to the edge of desperation. Hopes for the future may have been dampened, but they have not been crushed. Sadly, the same cannot be said of the less fortunate nations of the world, where hunger and illness are the immediate result of reduced incomes.

In these circumstances, the United States and other industrial nations are determined to make special efforts to assist developing nations in their efforts to sustain the momentum of their economic and social progress. We do so from a sense of compassion and out of a realization that the prosperity of the developing world also serves to support our own continued prosperity.

The World Bank and the International Monetary Fund have already proven that they are highly effective instruments for working with developing countries in devising the most promising plans for economic growth. But we believe that more must now be done within the framework of those institutions to assist the developing countries.

Yesterday, in a speech read on his behalf at the United Nations, Secretary Kissinger set forth a range of proposals that he and I, under the leadership of President Ford, have developed together. Three of those proposals are of particular importance for the Fund and the Bank:

—First, the United States proposes as a matter of high priority that a development security facility be created in the IMF to meet the needs of those developing nations suffering from sharp fluctuations in export earnings. It would replace the existing compensatory finance facility. We fully recognize that excessive fluctuations in export earnings can disrupt development efforts and that many producing nations lack sufficient financial reserves to cushion themselves against sharp drops in their earnings. We believe that compensatory facilities to finance shortfalls in export earnings would be both more effective and more efficient in reducing such disruptions than commodity-pricing arrangements.

Shortly after the completion of these meetings, we will submit detailed proposals to the Executive Board of the IMF calling for the creation of the facility. They will also call for broadening the purposes of the proposed Trust Fund, enabling it to provide grants to the poorest countries experiencing export shortfalls and allowing some use of the Trust Fund resources to supplement the proposed facility.

—Secondly, we pledge our support to a major expansion of the International Finance Corporation (IFC), permitting that organization to serve as a more effective catalyst for growth of the private sector in developing countries. We agree with Mr. McNamara [Robert S. McNamara, President, IBRD] that the role of the IFC in mobilizing additional private investment is now more important than ever. There can be little doubt that much of the increase in living standards within developing countries must come from increased private sector production of goods and services.

Arrangements should be made in the next few months to give the International Finance Corporation better tools to assist the domestic private sector and to make the IFC a full partner in the Bank Group. Moreover, the IFC should play an active part in bringing together foreign and domestic investors. It should act aggressively to arrange financing for mineral production in developing countries, where, as an impartial international party, it can help to smooth relationships between international companies with technology and markets and national authorities who understandably wish to strike the best bargain for their countries. The IFC should also develop imaginative financial arrangements, including a new investment trust, so that equity shares in joint ventures can gradually be purchased by private individuals and firms in developing countries.

All of these activities will complement the ongoing work of the World Bank, which must continue to assist in financing related infrastructure such as ports and roads, and will, we expect, give higher priority to the most important aspect of identifying obstacles to private savings and domestic private investment in developing countries.

—Thirdly, the United States once again urges that agreement be promptly reached on the establishment of a Trust Fund managed by the IMF in order to provide highly concessional balance-of-payments financing for the poorest developing countries.[8] Nearly a year has passed since my government first proposed the Trust Fund and urged that a portion of the IMF gold

[8] Cf. Chaper 18 at note 12. Further efforts in this direction were recommended by the Interim Committee in the Aug. 31 communiqué cited in note 3 above.

be sold to help finance this worthy cause. We are pleased that there has been increasing recognition that the Trust Fund concept represents the most effective means of providing fast-disbursing financial support. This is one way we can move ahead immediately to respond to the severe financing needs faced by the developing countries; we can agree now to see a portion of IMF gold used without waiting for time-consuming amendments of the articles. Even as we have delayed in establishing this fund, the need for it has grown. Let us resolve to act promptly.

In addition to these major initiatives, other steps should be taken so that the Bank and the Fund can more adequately meet today's needs.

As the oil facility of the IMF phases out this year, we should take action to assure the immediate usability of all currencies held by the IMF. We also need to direct early attention to a review of the tranche policies of the Fund and to consider whether changes should be introduced in these policies in order to provide increased access to the Fund's regular drawing facilities. This would enable the Fund to play the expanded and more active role required of it in today's world.

The World Bank is by far the largest and most influential development lending institution and as such has a major role to play in assisting developing nations achieve their development goals. It is of the greatest importance that the quality of this work and the soundness of its financial position be sustained.

Since the lending program now being implemented by the Bank carries with it demanding assumptions about the Bank's long-term ability to borrow funds, it is important that the management and Executive Directors of the Bank work together to assess carefully the role the Bank should play in the development process in the next decade and to examine the implications of this for the capital of the Bank and the nature of its programs. With capital an increasingly scarce resource, critical for the growth of the developed as well as the developing countries, it is essential that we have a clear understanding of the priorities which should govern the lending of an institution whose borrowing now approaches $5 billion per year. The United States will continue to provide strong support to the Bank, and we will assist in helping it maintain a sound financial position.

As I said last year, we support a substantial increase in World Bank share ownership and voting power for countries newly able to make a major contribution to development through the Bank Group. Such an increase should be determined country by country, and increases in capital should be accompanied by commensurate contributions to the International Development Association (IDA) to help the poorest countries as well as the middle-level countries.

I stress the importance of IDA contributions because of the Association's central role in meeting the needs of the poorest and least developed countries. They have the least ability to deal with the impact of economic events on their development, and only a combined effort of present members and nations newly able to contribute will enable IDA to assist those countries adequately in the future. Mr. McNamara has announced that negotiations for the next replenishment of IDA will commence in November. A satisfactory agreement on extending IDA's resources[9] will be possible only with the full collaboration of all countries in a position to contribute.

Beyond these measures, developed nations must also support the longstanding development efforts such as the regional development banks and our bilateral assistance programs. These programs have shown their effectiveness over the years and deserve to be strongly supported. It is also important for all countries to open their capital markets to the borrowing of the Bank and of the developing countries themselves.

In setting forth these proposals today and reviewing the activities of the World Bank and the International Monetary Fund, I would be less than candid if I did not add that, in and of themselves, the measures I have outlined will not be sufficient to insure economic development. We must not mislead ourselves on this matter. Far more important to the developing nations than the financial assistance that industrialized countries may provide to them is the restoration of stable, noninflationary growth around the world. And in the long run, the policies and efforts of the developing countries themselves will be the most decisive. History has shown that no matter how generous others may be, those who have been helped the most are those who have helped themselves.

While the developed nations must provide financing and open up their markets, the effectiveness of such assistance depends heavily upon the ability of the developing countries themselves to assure the best use of all resources, domestic as well as foreign. Development assistance should be thought of not as an international welfare program to redistribute the world's wealth, but as an important element of an international investment program to increase the rate of economic growth in developing nations and to provide higher living standards for people of every nation. The effectiveness of international investment, private and public, depends fundamentally on the policies and efforts of each developing country.

[9]Cf. note 21 to Chapter 30.

I am particularly struck by the impressive economic and social progress made by countries which participate fully in the world market, which rely on market forces to provide incentives for efficient use of resources, and which maintain a favorable climate for foreign and domestic private investment.

In short, the process of economic development requires the cooperation and full efforts of each of us in pursuing economic policies to maximize production, income, and trade for all countries.

International Monetary Arrangements

Let me turn now to a discussion of international monetary issues.

We have achieved a significant breakthrough in our meetings this week in resolving many of the most difficult international monetary issues before us and in paving the way for a final comprehensive agreement in January. The technically complex—and politically sensitive—question of arranging a major quota increase and allocating national shares is substantially resolved. We have also succeeded in settling the thorny issues involved in phasing gold out of the international monetary system. Both of these agreements required concessions by many, but the result provides concrete evidence of the continuing spirit of cooperation and good will on which these institutions are founded. Once again we have demonstrated that through patient negotiation it is possible to arrive at an accommodation of conflicting views which is acceptable to each of us and beneficial to all of us.

Let us now proceed to the final component of our negotiations— an agreement on amendment of the exchange rate provisions of the articles—which will enable us to put into practice the accords reached here this week. Amended provisions are needed which give legal recognition to the realities of today's world and reflect the evolution of the system that has occurred in recent years.

Two and a half years ago the par value system gave way to a voluntary system of exchange rate practices under which some countries float independently, some float jointly, and some use pegged rates.[10] We are fortunate that this system was actually in place before the oil crisis hit, and its flexibility has served us well in difficult circumstances.

Let those who see stability in par values review again the chaos and disorder of the closing years of the Bretton Woods system. Think back to those days of market closures which disrupted trade and commerce. Recall that the only sure winners were the speculators, who could be assured that with time and persistence

[10]Cf. *AFR, 1973*: 89-91 and 94-9.

they would inevitably carry the day. Remember, too, the hurried international conferences to try to patch together some solution so that markets might open again. Think back to the duration and difficulty of the Smithsonian negotiations[11] and the tensions associated with those negotiations. Those were the days when our political cohesion was threatened by monetary difficulties.

The basic logic of the par value system implies a world which does not now exist—one in which prices are reasonably stable and in which current account balances adjust to capital flows that are relatively slow to change. But the world has changed, and we need a system that is adaptable and is appropriate for the world as it is today, not as it once was or as we might like it to be.

Today we have a system which is flexible and resilient. It has enabled exchange markets to remain open and viable in the face of pressures that would have previously been overwhelming. Even the massive accumulations by the OPEC countries and occasional significant fluctuations in particular exchange rates have not unsettled the system. It has been possible to relax or eliminate many of the extensive restrictions on capital movements and to find viable alternatives to restrictive current account measures. The large payments deficits of today have provoked fewer import restrictions by major countries than did the comparatively minor payments difficulties of earlier years. Although rates of inflation have varied enormously, from 6 percent in some countries to 25 percent in others, the flexibility of our system has allowed exchange rates to move so as to reflect these divergences in costs and prices. Attempts to maintain fixed exchange rates under these circumstances would have quickly and inevitably collapsed under the strain.

Some contend that the abandonment of par values is one of the causes of the tidal wave of inflation which has swept the world and that the voluntary system fails to provide the discipline needed to induce countries to restrain their inflation. I cannot agree. It was inflation which made floating necessary. Of course, floating does not prevent home-grown inflation or protect a country from drastic real changes from abroad such as the sudden jump in oil prices. It can, however, shield a country from imported inflation that results from overly expansive fiscal and monetary policies abroad. As for floating as an instrument of discipline, I believe that when a depreciating exchange rate in a free market directly increases the costs of imported goods, that has more meaning to the general public and political leaders than the level of central bank reserves or official borrowing.

[11]Cf. same, *1971:* 605-10.

U.S. policy is to have our own exchange rate determined essentially by market forces, and not by arbitrary official actions. We do not propose to object if foreign countries elect to establish fixed exchange rates among themselves—the essence of a voluntary system is to permit a free choice—so long as our own desire for essential freedom of the dollar exchange rate is respected. We are prepared to intervene whenever necessary to maintain orderly exchange market conditions. However, sizable movements in exchange rates over a period of several months are not necessarily indicators of disorderly markets—and the fact that such movements are sometimes reversed does not demonstrate that it would have been possible for governments to prevent the initial movement in rates, nor desirable to try.

When the pressures of inflation subside and economies recover, when periods of calm between unexpected shocks become longer, then the behavior of exchange rates will become more stable. The greater exchange stability we all would like to see can only be achieved through sound economic policies which result in greater domestic stability in all of our economies.

We believe strongly that countries must be free to choose their own exchange rate system and that all countries, whatever choice they make, must be subject to the same agreed-upon principles of international behavior. The right to float must be clear and unencumbered. In view of the great diversity in political systems, institutional arrangements, size of national economies, and degree of dependence on foreign trade and investment, our present world requires an open mind about the future.

I do not pretend to have the wisdom or the clairvoyance to predict the precise exchange arrangements the world may desire or require far in the future. Experience with the present articles provides clear evidence of the difficulty of specifying in rigid detail an exchange rate system that can be expected to last forever. We must deal with the world as it is today, and that now requires a system that can easily adapt to rapid change. I know this can be done. Our agreements this week on gold and quotas show that we can find answers to difficult problems—and that a mutually acceptable accommodation on exchange rates can be achieved. The United States will approach the search for a resolution of this problem with imagination and an appreciation of others' views. We know that others will do the same.

Ladies and gentlemen, it is apparent that the agenda for the future is formidable:

—To achieve lasting, noninflationary growth;
—To reach an accommodation on energy;

—To encourage economic development; and
—To maintain a monetary system adapted to today's needs.

Each of these demands our full attention. The agreements we have reached this week demonstrate that through cooperation and perseverance we can succeed. It is in that spirit that we must continue to move forward. I pledge to you that the United States will remain a reliable partner in this journey.

32. OPENING THE 30TH ASSEMBLY

(New York, September 16-22, 1975)

[Tuesday, September 16, 1975, marks an unusual date in the annals of the U.N. General Assembly, the world's supreme deliberative body and a barometer of attitudes and trends throughout the international community. On that day, the Assembly concluded both its Seventh Special Session, commenced September 1 and specifically focused on development and international economic cooperation,[1] and its 29th Regular Session, which had actually finished its work in December 1974 but had remained available for recall in light of the unsettled conditions in the Middle East. Finally, on that same September 16 the Assembly commenced still another Regular Session—its 30th—which was to continue until December 17 and would adopt a record 179 resolutions dealing with virtually every aspect of world affairs.

Included in the opening-day business of the 30th Session were the election of Prime Minister Gaston Thorn of Luxembourg as President of the Session, and the admission to U.N. membership of the former Portuguese territories of Cape Verde, Sao Tomé and Principe, and Mozambique as the world organization's 139th, 140th, and 141st member states. Three more new states were to be admitted later in the session, increasing the total membership of the organization to 144: Papua New Guinea on October 10, the Comoro Islands on November 12, and Surinam on December 4. No resolution was to be found, however, for the impasse that had developed over the admission of the two Vietnams and South Korea.[2] A renewed attempt to gain Security Council backing for the applications of North and South Vietnam was blocked on September 30 by two more U.S. vetoes, after the Council had again

[1]Cf. Chapter 30.
[2]Cf. Chapter 30 at note 5.

461

declined to take up the application submitted by the Republic of Korea as far back as 1949.[3]

A new approach to resolving the Korean stalemate—the convening of a conference to discuss ways of terminating the U.N. military command while preserving the 1953 armistice agreement—was proposed to the Assembly by Secretary Kissinger on September 22 in the course of a major address outlining the American Government's thinking on the entire range of current international questions (**Document 51**). "Building for peace," "building international security," "building economic well-being," and "building for justice" were the four imperatives of the international agenda as Dr. Kissinger defined it in this period when, as he said, "the bipolar confrontation of the last generation has given way to the beginning of dialogue and an easing of direct conflict"—and when, despite a lack of progress in the SALT talks, it still was possible to speak in terms of a "forthcoming" meeting of President Ford and General Secretary Brezhnev.

Another highlight of Dr. Kissinger's wide-ranging discourse was the suggested establishment of "multinational regional nuclear fuel cycle centers" to obviate a proliferation of nationally controlled reprocessing facilities that might prove a step toward broadened nuclear weapons capabilities. In no way minimizing the dangers inherent in this and other aspects of the current scene, the Secretary of State seemed none the less to have shaken off the sense of imminent catastrophe that had been so marked a feature of his U.N. address the year before.[4] "We have it in our power," Dr. Kissinger emphasized, "to prove to future generations that the last quarter of the 20th century was not an era of violence and conflict, but one of the creative epochs of world history. . . . Let us fashion together a new world order. . . . Let us all work together to enrich the spirit and to ennoble mankind."]

(51) "Building International Order": Address by Secretary of State Kissinger to the 30th Regular Session of the United Nations General Assembly, New York, September 22, 1975.[5]

At the outset, let me say how pleased we are that our deliberations this year take place under the Presidency of the distinguished Prime Minister of Luxembourg. His contribution to European co-

[3]The vote on including the Korean application on the agenda (Sept. 26) was 7 (U.S.)-7-1; the vote on the two draft resolutions recommending the Vietnamese applications (Sept. 30) was 14-1 (U.S.).
[4]*AFR, 1974*: 346-56.
[5]Department of State Press Release 496, Sept. 22; text and titles from *Bulletin*, 73: 545-53.

operation, his diplomatic skills, his dedication to democracy give us confidence that this 30th session will be marked by a constructive and creative spirit.

And I want also to pay tribute to the distinguished Secretary General, whose fairness, leadership, and tireless effort are dedicated to carrying this organization forward into a new era of cooperation for world peace.

This century has seen war and cataclysm on an unprecedented scale. It has witnessed the breakdown of established patterns of order and practices of international conduct. It has suffered global economic depression and cycles of famine. It has experienced the birth of thermonuclear weapons and the proliferation of armaments around the planet. Ours is a world of continuing turmoil and ideological division.

But this century has also seen the triumph of the principle of self-determination and national independence. A truly global community has begun to evolve, reflected in a multitude of institutions of international cooperation. We have shaped new methods of peaceful settlement, arms limitation, and new institutions to promote economic development and to combat hunger and disease worldwide. And our very presence here signifies the hope of all nations that disputes and conficts can be resolved by cooperative means.

As we deliberate the future, an event of potentially vast implication has just been achieved in this organization: the unanimous agreement produced by the seventh special session of the General Assembly on measures to improve the economic condition of mankind.[6] Despite differences of ideology and approaches to economic development, the nations assembled here began to move toward the recognition that our interdependence spells either common progress or common disaster, that in our age no nation or group of nations can achieve its aims by pressure or confrontation and that the attempt to do so would damage everyone. They agreed to transcend the stereotypes of the past in the search for a cooperative future. The special session forged a sense of common purpose based on the equality and cooperation of states. Now we must dedicate ourselves to implementing this consensus.

Let us carry forward the spirit of conciliation into the deliberations of this regular session. Let us address the issues of world peace—the foundation of all else we do on this planet—with this same consciousness of our common destiny.

It is our common duty to avoid empty slogans and endless recriminations. We must instead sustain, strengthen, and extend

[6]Cf. Chapter 30 at note 6.

the international environment we and our posterity will require for the maintenance of peace and the furtherance of progress.

Only in a structure of cooperation can disputes be settled and clashes contained. Only in an atmosphere of conciliation can the insecurity of nations, out of which so much conflict arises, be eased and habits of compromise and accommodation be nurtured. Social progress, justice, and human rights can thrive only in an atmosphere of reduced international tension.

The United States stands ready to dedicate itself to cooperative efforts to harmonize the different perspectives of the world community in creating a new sense of security and well-being. We do so not out of fear, for we are better able to sustain ourselves in situations of confrontation than most other nations. Nor do we do so out of a sense of guilt, for we believe that we have on the whole used our power for constructive ends.

We affirm our common destiny because of our recognition of global interdependence and because global peace requires it. Indeed, there is no realistic alternative to shared responsibility in dealing with the international agenda of peace, security, economic well-being, and justice.

Let me set forth the views of the United States on the work we face in each of these areas.

Building for Peace

Our first and transcendent concern is for peace in the world.

Peace is never automatic. It is more than the absence of war. And it is inseparable from security.

A world in which the survival of nations is at the mercy of a few would spell oppression and injustice and fear. There can be no security without equilibrium and no safety without restraint. Only when the rights of nations are respected, when accommodation supplants force, can man's energies be devoted to the realization of his deepest aspirations.

The United States will pursue the cause of peace with patience and an attitude of conciliation in many spheres:

—We shall nurture and deepen the ties of cooperation with our friends and allies.

—We shall strive to improve relations with countries of different ideology or political conviction.

—We shall always stand ready to assist in the settlement of regional disputes.

—We shall intensify our efforts to halt the spiral of nuclear armament.

—We shall strive to improve man's economic and social condition and to strengthen the collaboration between developed and developing nations.

—We shall struggle for the realization of fundamental human rights.

Relations With Allies and Friends

America's close ties with the industrial democracies of North America, Western Europe, and Japan have been the cornerstone of world stability and peace for three decades. Today, looking beyond immediate security and defense, we are working together on a range of new issues. Through our consultations, we have begun joint efforts to ease international tensions, to coordinate our national policies for economic recovery, to work together on common challenges such as energy and the environment, and to address the great issues that concern the developing countries.

These endeavors are in pursuit of universal goals; they are not directed at any nation or group of nations. They are designed as building blocks for a broader international community.

In the same spirit, the United States has opened a new dialogue with its neighbors in Central and Latin America. We have taken important steps toward resolving major political problems; we have begun close consultations for cooperation in promoting economic and social development. Alliance relations in the Western Hemisphere have a long history and great promise for the future. With imagination and dedication, we can make inter-American cooperation on the tasks of development an example and a pillar of the global community.

East-West Relations

Peace, to be secure, must place on a more durable and reliable basis the relations between the nations possessing the means to destroy our planet.

In recent years, the bipolar confrontation of the last generation has given way to the beginning of dialogue and an easing of direct conflict. In this body, of all organizations, there is surely an appreciation of the global importance of lessened tension between the nuclear superpowers. All nations have a stake in its success. When weapons of mass destruction can span continents in minutes, nuclear conflict threatens the survival of all mankind.

We recognize that the suspicion and rivalry of a generation will not be swept away with a document or a conference. Real ideological and political differences exist. We shall firmly defend our vital interests and those of our friends. But we shall never lose sight of the fact that in our age peace is a practical necessity as well as a moral imperative. We shall pursue the relaxation of tensions on the basis of strict reciprocity. We know the difference between posturing and policy; we will not encourage the belief that anyone can benefit from artificial tensions. We are deeply conscious that we owe it to future generations not to be swayed by momentary passions.

The state of U.S.-Soviet relations today and just a decade ago present a dramatic contrast. The world is no longer continually shaken by chronic and bitter confrontations. Periodic consultations—including at the highest level—encourage restraint and amplify areas of mutual interest. The forthcoming meeting between President Ford and General Secretary Brezhnev should strengthen this process.

Principles of mutual restraint have been enunciated at various summit meetings; they were reaffirmed by the Conference on Security and Cooperation in Europe two months ago.[7] These principles provide a standard of behavior by which our actions will be tested. If they are observed—as we insist—and if neither side seeks unilateral advantage, the specter of general war will be lifted not only from our own people but from all nations. There is no more important task before us.

We have likewise pursued more constructive and beneficial relationships with the countries of Eastern Europe. The United States has many traditional and deep-rooted bonds of friendship with the proud peoples of that region. We see widening possibilities for practical cooperation as the barriers between East and West in Europe diminish.

There is no relationship to which the United States assigns greater significance than its new ties with the People's Republic of China. We believe that the well-being and progress of a quarter of humanity is an important element in global stability.

The hostility of decades between our two nations has been replaced by a relationship of mutual respect which is now a durable feature of the world scene. It serves not only the interest of our two countries but also the broader interests of peace and stability in Asia and around the world. President Ford plans to visit the People's Republic of China later this year to confirm the vitality of our relationship and to advance the ties between us on the basis of the strict implementation of the Shanghai communique.[8] We take seriously the process of normalizing our relationship. We are dedicated to pursuing it.

[7] Chapter 25, Document 42.
[8] Cf. Chapter 40.

Containing Regional Conflicts

The world community must find a way to contain or resolve regional conflicts before they spread into global confrontations.

Nowhere has the danger been greater than in the *Middle East*. Nowhere has the need for persistent and imaginative negotiation between suspicious rivals been more evident. Nowhere is there greater promise of moving from perennial crisis toward peace. Nowhere has the U.N. Security Council established a clearer framework of principles than in its Resolutions 242 and 338.[9]

The road toward a lasting peace stretches long and hard before us. The Middle East has seen more than its share of dashed hopes and disappointment. But the conclusion of the recent Sinai agreement[10] marks a major step forward. It is the first agreement in the long and tragic history of the Arab-Israeli conflict which is not the immediate consequence of hostilities. It could mark a turning point.

The agreement deserves the support of all the countries assembled here, because every nation here has an interest in progress toward peace in the Middle East. It is another step in the process launched by Security Council Resolution 338. The alternative was a continuing stalemate which would have led over time to another war, creating a serious threat to world peace and the prospect of broad global economic dislocation.

Neither fear of the future nor pride should obscure the fact that an unusual opportunity for further progress on all issues now exists. But opportunities must be seized or they will disappear. I want to emphasize that the United States did not help negotiate this agreement in order to put an end to the process of peace, but to give it new impetus.

President Ford has stated that we will not accept stalemate and stagnation in the Middle East.[11] That was true before the Sinai agreement was signed; it remains true today. The objective of our policy is not merely to create another temporary truce, but to sustain the momentum of negotiations. The United States is determined to take every feasible step to help promote further practical progress toward final peace.

As a first step, it is essential that the Sinai agreement be carried out impeccably, within the terms and the time frame that are stipulated.

In the improved atmosphere thus created, the United States

---

[9]*Documents, 1967*: 169-70; *AFR, 1973*: 459.
[10]Chapter 29.
[11]Cf. Chapter 29 at note 9.

stands ready to participate in any promising initiative toward peace at the request of the parties concerned.

We have made clear that we are prepared to make a serious effort to encourage negotiations between Syria and Israel.

We also intend to consult over the coming weeks with all concerned regarding the reopening of the Geneva Conference, which met at an early crucial phase. As cochairmen of the Geneva Conference together with the Soviet Union, our two countries have special responsibilities in this regard.

We are prepared also to explore possibilities for perhaps a more informal multilateral meeting to assess conditions and to discuss the future.

The United States seeks no special benefit; we do not attempt to exclude any country. We will cooperate with any nation that is willing to make a contribution. We have no preference for any particular procedure. We will support whatever process seems most promising. Our approach will continue to be both flexible and determined.

The search for final peace must be conducted on a wide basis. We are in frequent touch with governments in the Middle East. We have already begun discussions with the Soviet Union with a view to assessing the current situation in the Middle East and weighing possible diplomatic approaches to bring about a just and durable peace in accordance with Security Council Resolutions 242 and 338. While we have had important differences with the Soviet Union, our two countries have held parallel views that the situation in the Middle East poses grave dangers and that partial steps must be part of and contribute to progress toward a comprehensive settlement.

The role of the world organization remains essential. If this organization had no other accomplishment than its effective peacekeeping role in this troubled area, it would have well justified itself. These soldiers of peace, wearing the blue beret of the United Nations as members of UNTSO, UNEF, UNDOF [U.N. Truce Supervision Organization, U.N. Emergency Force, U.N. Disengagement Observer Force], have become indispensable to the maintenance of the two 1974 disengagement accords as well as the Sinai agreement. I want to take this occasion to salute Secretary General Waldheim and his staff and General Siilasvuo, the Chief Coordinator of the U.N. peacekeeping missions in the Middle East, and all the men and women from many countries who have served in the forces without an enemy.

The deliberations of this Assembly regarding the Middle East also play a central role. They can encourage progress or exacerbate tensions.

Procedural decisions can be based on the recognition that dialogue requires universality of membership, or they can fuel a futile self-defeating effort to discriminate—in violation of the charter—against a member state whose participation is vital for a solution.

The Middle East will continue to be an area of anguish, turmoil, and peril until a just and durable peace is achieved. Such a peace must meet the principal concerns and interests of all in the area; among these are territorial integrity, the right to live in peace and security, and the legitimate interests of the Palestinians.

In the Middle East today there is a yearning for peace surpassing any known for three decades. Let us not doom the region to another generation of futile struggle. Instead, let the world community seize the historic opportunity before it. The suffering and bravery of all the peoples of the Middle East cry out for it; the hopes and interests of all the world's peoples demand it. The United States promises its full dedication to further progress toward peace.

The contribution of the United Nations to the process of peace is essential in *Cyprus* as well. The Secretary General has the responsibilities of organizing the peacekeeping forces on the island and of facilitating the talks between the leaders of the Greek and Turkish communities.

Strict maintenance of the cease-fire is imperative. For this we look to the restraint of the parties and the efficacy of the U.N. peacekeeping forces.

We know that the world community shares our sense of urgency that the negotiating process be resumed and that the parties demonstrate flexibility and statesmanship. The status quo on the island must not become permanent; a rapid and equitable solution is essential. The Secretary General has worked tirelessly and imaginatively under the most difficult circumstances to narrow the differences. He deserves the full support of the parties and of every nation here.

The details of a Cyprus settlement are for the two communities themselves to decide. However, in keeping with U.N. resolutions which the United States has fully supported, the following principles are essential:

—A settlement must preserve the independence, sovereignty, and territorial integrity of Cyprus.

—It must insure that both the Greek Cypriot and the Turkish Cypriot communities can live in freedom and have a large voice in their own affairs.

—The present dividing lines cannot be permanent. There must

be agreed territorial arrangements which reflect the economic requirements of the Greek Cypriot community and take account of its self-respect.

—There must be provision for the withdrawal of foreign military forces other than those present under the authority of international agreements.

—And there must be security for all Cypriots; the needs and wishes of the refugees who have been the principal victims and whose tragic plight touches us all must be dealt with speedily and with compassion.

These goals match the aspirations of the overwhelming majority of the Cypriot people as well as the interests of all neighboring states.

Another area where this organization will be called upon to take responsible action is *the Korean Peninsula*.

This requires, above all, maintenance of the armistice, pending agreement by all of the parties most directly concerned to replace it with a new arrangement. The existing armistice[12] is the only legal instrument committing the parties to maintain the peace. It is a carefully designed structure for monitoring and policing the military demarcation line.

The U.N. commander in chief is a signatory to that agreement. The armistice machinery functions daily. None of the signatories has repudiated it. Nor could they do so without serious risks to the peace of the world.

Since 1972, South and North Korea have pledged themselves to enter into a dialogue and to seek unification without resort to arms. This Assembly in 1973 and 1974 encouraged this process—first in a consensus resolution supporting talks between the two sides; then in a resolution which looked toward termination of the U.N. Command.[13] The United States agrees that 20 years after the end of the Korean war, it is timely to terminate the U.N. Command. We have, in fact, cosponsored a resolution to that effect which is now before you.[14]

It would be foolhardy, however, to terminate the U.N. Command without new arrangements to preserve the integrity of the armistice agreement. In the interest of peace, the United States cannot accept any solution which fails to provide for the continuing validity of the armistice agreement.

[12]Signed at Panmunjom July 27, 1953 (TIAS 2782; 4 UST 234); summary and excerpts in *Documents, 1953*: 289-93.

[13]For background cf. *AFR, 1971*: 375-8; same, *1972*: 340n.; same, *1973*: 300-301 and 578; same, *1974*: 496-500 and 519.

[14]Cf. Chapter 44 at note 5.

The Republic of Korea and the United States have stated their general readiness to meet with representatives of the other side and with other members of the Security Council to discuss termination of the U.N. Command while preserving the armistice agreement.[15]

Today I can be more specific. The United States and the Republic of Korea, looking forward to the time when a lasting solution of the Korean problem can be achieved, are herewith proposing to the parties of the armistice the convening of a conference to discuss ways to preserve the armistice agreement. At such a meeting, we would also be prepared to explore other measures to reduce tension on the Korean Peninsula, including the possibility of a larger conference to negotiate a more fundamental arrangement.

It would be in keeping with this spirit of dialogue for this body to open its doors to full membership for the two Korean Governments. The United States supports the dual entry of both South and North Korea into the United Nations without prejudice to their eventual reunification. For our part, if North Korea and its allies would move to improve their relations with the Republic of Korea, we would be prepared to take similar reciprocal actions.

It goes without saying that no proposal for security arrangements on the Korean Peninsula which attempts to exclude the Republic of Korea from the discussions can be accepted by the United States. The United Nations can contribute significantly to the process of peace on the Korean Peninsula by supporting a responsible approach.

Over the past year the United States has followed carefully and with great sympathy the efforts to reach peaceful settlements in *southern Africa*.[16]

We welcome the statesmanlike efforts of both black and white African leaders who are seeking to prevent violence and bloodshed and to promote a negotiated settlement in Rhodesia. The differences between the two communities in that country, while substantial, have been narrowed significantly in the last decade. Both sides in Rhodesia and Rhodesia's neighbors—black and white—have an interest in averting civil war. We will support all efforts to bring about a peaceful settlement.

In underlining our goal of peaceful change for southern Africa, I want to emphasize the importance of an early settlement in Namibia. My government's opposition to South Africa's continuing occupation of Namibia and our rejection of South Africa's apartheid system are well known. The United States has consistent-

---

[15]U.S. letter to the Security Council, June 27, in U.N. Document S/11737, June 27, 1975 (*Digest of United States Practice in International Law, 1975*: 820-22).
[16]For fuller discussion cf. Chapter 33.

ly conveyed our position on this subject to South Africa. We will continue to do so.

We believe that the people of Namibia should be given the opportunity within a short time to express their views on the political future and constitutional structure of their country freely and under U.N. supervision.

Building International Security

Peace in the world will be fragile and tenuous without a curb and eventually *an end of the arms race.* This is why the United States has embarked with the Soviet Union upon the difficult and complex negotiation to limit strategic arms. Our objectives are to prevent unchecked destabilizing competition in strategic armaments, to achieve reduction of these arms, to lessen further the likelihood of hasty decisions in time of crisis, and to ease the economic burden of the nuclear arms race.

The Vladivostok accord of last fall[17] marked a major step toward achieving these goals. When the agreement in principle is translated into a treaty, agreed ceilings will be placed on strategic force levels for a 10-year period. This unprecedented step will slow the pace of new arms programs, especially those driven by fear of major deployments by the other side. And it will enhance prospects for international stability and for political accommodation in other areas.

The United States is actively engaged in other arms control negotiations. Together with the Soviet Union, we have made progress toward establishing a regime for peaceful nuclear explosions. And we have agreed to set a threshold on the underground testing of nuclear weapons.[18] These are significant steps toward a verifiable comprehensive test ban.

In addition, the United States and the U.S.S.R. have presented to the Conference of the Committee on Disarmament texts of a Convention on the Prohibition of Military or Any Other Hostile Use of Environmental Modification Techniques.[19] These techniques are still at a primitive stage of development, but man's mastery of environmental forces continues to advance. Misuse of this knowledge might open new avenues of military competition and wreak untold and irreversible harm upon all humanity. We urge the conference to complete its consideration rapidly.

Another urgent task is a substantial reduction in the high levels of military forces now confronting each other in various parts of

[17]Cf. Chapter 13 at note 14.
[18]Cf. Chapter 13 at note 13.
[19]Details and text in *Bulletin,* 73: 417-20; for background cf. *AFR, 1974:* 234 and 543-4.

the world. The United States believes that the time has come to give new impetus to the negotiations on mutual and balanced force reductions in Central Europe. The significance of the Conference on Security and Cooperation in Europe depends importantly on whether we can achieve progress in this area. An agreement that enhances mutual security in Central Europe is feasible and essential. We will work toward this goal.[20]

The world faces a paradox with respect to *the proliferation of nuclear energy*. Men have fashioned from the atom weapons which can in minutes end the civilization of centuries. Simultaneously, the atom is fast becoming a more and more essential source of energy. It is clear that the cost and eventual scarcity of oil and other fossil fuel will increasingly spread nuclear power around the world in the decades ahead.

But the spreading of nuclear power poses starkly the danger of proliferating nuclear weapons capabilities—and the related risks of the theft of nuclear materials, blackmail by terrorists, accidents, or the injection of the nuclear threat into regional political conflicts. Now is the time to act. If we fail to restrain nuclear proliferation, future generations will live on a planet shadowed by nuclear catastrophe.

Over the past year, the United States has repeatedly urged new efforts among the supplier states to strengthen and standardize safeguards and controls on export of nuclear materials. We must not allow these safeguards to be eroded by commercial competition. We must insure the broad availability of peaceful nuclear energy under safe, economical, and reliable conditions.

The United States has intensified its efforts within the International Atomic Energy Agency (IAEA) and with other nations to broaden and strengthen international standards and safeguards and has proposed an international convention setting standards to protect the physical security of nuclear materials in use, storage, or transfer.

The United States continues to urge the widest possible adherence to the Nonproliferation Treaty[21] and the associated safeguard measures of the IAEA.

The greatest single danger of unrestrained nuclear proliferation resides in the spread under national control of reprocessing facilities for the atomic materials in nuclear power plants. The United States therefore proposes—as a major step to reinforce all other measures—the establishment of multinational regional nuclear fuel cycle centers. These centers would serve energy needs on a commercially sound basis and encourage regional energy

---

[20]Cf. Chapter 41.
[21]Cf. Chapter 13 at note 1.

cooperation. Their existence would reduce the incentive for small and inefficient reprocessing facilities, limit the possibility of diverting peaceful nuclear materials to national military use, and create a better framework for applying effective international safeguards.

We urge that groups of nations begin now to explore this concept and that all states support the IAEA's work in this field.

Building Economic Well-Being

In the last two years, the world community has been reminded dramatically to what extent economic relations are an essential foundation of the international order. Economic conditions not only underpin every society's ability to achieve its national goals, but all national economies are sustained by the global economic system. The conduct of our economic affairs will therefore determine to an extraordinary degree whether our political relations will be based on cooperation or conflict.

It would be one of history's most tragic ironies if, at a time when we are putting behind us the tensions of the cold war, we were to enter a new period of conflict between North and South, rich and poor. At the recently concluded special session, the United States called for an end to the sterile confrontation of the past.[22] We stated that when the ancient dream of mankind—a world without poverty—becomes a possibility, our moral convictions also make it a duty. And we emphasized that only cooperation—not extortion—can achieve this goal.

The special session gives us ground for hope that—at least for the immediate future—a choice has been made to turn away from confrontation toward cooperation. The United States is proud to support the final document which is the product of the arduous effort and dedication of so many in this chamber.

The United States considers the achievements of the special session a beginning, not an end. As recommended by the final report, we must now move forward in available forums to give reality and content to the objectives on which we have agreed. In the difficult negotiations ahead, my government will participate energetically in a cooperative and conciliatory spirit.

Building for Justice

Beyond peace, security, and prosperity lies a deeper universal aspiration for dignity and equal opportunity. Mankind will never be spared all the tragedies inherent in the cycle of life and death. But we do have it in our power to eliminate or ease the burden of social tragedy and of organized injustice.

[22]Chapter 30, Document 49.

The United States has therefore traditionally been an advocate of extending the reach of international law in international affairs. We have offered our help to the victims of disease and natural disaster. We have been a champion of liberty and a beacon to the oppressed. There is no longer any dispute that international human rights are on the agenda of international diplomacy.

The reach of international law must extend to the last frontiers of our planet, the oceans. They are the common heritage of mankind, but they can turn into arenas of conflict unless governed by law. They hold untapped sources of energy, minerals, and protein; their environmental integrity is crucial to our survival.

The United States welcomed the U.N. mandate for a comprehensive treaty governing the use of the oceans and their resources. Last month in Montreal, I set forth our approach to this negotiation and urged that next year's session of the Law of the Sea Conference move matters to a rapid and successful conclusion.[23] No international negotiation is more vital for long-term political and economic stability and the prosperity of our globe.

International law must also come to grips with international terrorism. Innumerable innocent lives have been lost as a consequence of the lack of internationally accepted standards specifically designed to avert unlawful and dangerous interference with civil aviation. The hijacking of aircraft, the kidnaping and murder of innocent civilian victims for presumed political gain remain a plague on civilized man. This remains one of the underdeveloped areas of international law which merits the most urgent attention of this organization.

Compassion for our fellow men requires that we mobilize international resources to combat the age-old scourges of mankind—disease, famine, and natural disaster. We are pleased that a concerted effort has been undertaken by the World Health Organization and interested governments, in response to our initiative at the last General Assembly, to control schistosomiasis, a disease which afflicts and debilitates over 200 million people in 70 countries and imposes a great human and economic cost.

The great human rights must be recognized, respected, and given reality in the affairs of nations. The earliest U.N. declarations and the recent Helsinki Conference leave no doubt that these are matters of international concern. The United States will support these principles. Throughout the world, in all continents, violations of human rights must be opposed whether they are inflicted by one race upon another—or upon members of the same race. Human rights must be cherished regardless of race, sex, or religion. There can be no double standard.

[23]Chapter 27, Document 45.

The U.N. Human Rights Commission has taken its first steps against gross violations of human rights where serious and reliable allegations are submitted by individuals. We support these steps. The organized concern of the world community can be a potent weapon in the war against degradation of human values.

One of the most persistent and serious problems is torture, a practice which all nations should abhor. It is an absolute debasement of the function of government when its overwhelming power is used not for people's welfare but as an instrument of their suffering.

The United States urges this Assembly to adopt the declaration of the recent world congress on this issue in Geneva.[24] In addition, we propose that this General Assembly establish a group of experts, to be appointed by the Secretary General, to study the nature and extent of torture in the world today and to report back to the next Assembly.

Mr. President, this organization was created in the belief that the universality of the human race can be reflected in the conduct of international affairs. This chamber symbolizes the hope that mankind places in the force of nations working together in the common interest with reason, responsibility, and mutual respect. The problems we face are complex and perilous. The sterile slogans of yesterday, the solutions of the past, the dwelling upon old resentments, can only widen the gaps between us and allow the dangers to peace and the well-being of our peoples to fester and grow.

We have it in our power to prove to future generations that the last quarter of the 20th century was not an era of violence and conflict, but one of the creative epochs of world history.

My country's history, Mr. President, tells us that it is possible to fashion unity while cherishing diversity, that common action is possible despite the variety of races, interests, and beliefs we see here in this chamber. Progress and peace and justice are attainable.

So we say to all peoples and governments: Let us fashion together a new world order. Let its arrangements be just. Let the new nations help shape it and feel it is theirs. Let the old nations use their strengths and skills for the benefit of all mankind. Let us all work together to enrich the spirit and to ennoble mankind.

---

[24]Declaration on the Protection of All Persons from being subjected to Torture and Other Cruel, Inhuman or Degrading Treatment or Punishment, recommended by the Fifth U.N. Congress on the Prevention of Crime and the Treatment of Offenders (Geneva, Sept. 1-12, 1975) and adopted as an annex to General Assembly Resolution 3452 (XXX), Dec. 9, 1975. (Secretary Kissinger's proposal regarding implementing measures was not acted upon because of lack of time.)

33. POLICY TOWARD AFRICA

(New York, September 23, 1975)

[Since his first appearance at the U.N. General Assembly in 1973, Secretary Kissinger had been in the habit of spending a few days in New York at the beginning of each annual session for conferences with Foreign Ministers and other diplomatic representatives from the U.S.S.R., allied nations, and countries associated with the major regional groupings of American, Arab, and African states. A dinner held September 23, 1975 in honor of the Foreign Ministers and Permanent Representatives of member states of the Organization of African Unity (OAU) thus afforded a natural occasion for one of the rather infrequent recapitulations of U.S. policy toward Africa.

It must be added that American policy as expounded by the Secretary of State on this occasion **(Document 52)** appeared to have evolved less rapidly than the *de facto* situation in Africa, where the collapse of Portugal's former colonial empire had created a revolutionary ferment of steadily mounting intensity. As in earlier pronouncements by President Nixon and others,[1] the United States seemed more than ready at this period to affirm a broad commitment to African economic betterment, racial justice, and political nonalignment. Up to this moment, however, it had scarcely begun to feel the pressures that would soon convert its abstract interest into a burning concern directly involving the administration's concepts of East-West relations and global security.

The reason for this impending change of attitude, still only dimly visible at the time of Dr. Kissinger's speech, was the increasing intervention of outside governments in what had been an internal power struggle in the territory of Angola, whose Portuguese rulers had promised to relinquish their authority on November 11, 1975.

In other parts of Portuguese Africa, the United States had ex-

---

[1] Cf. especially *AFR, 1971:* 380-85; same, *1972:* 353 and 381-2.

perienced no special difficulty in accepting the advent to power of the former nationalist resistance movements, notwithstanding the outspokenly left-wing character of such organizations as the African Independence Party (PAIGC) in Guinea-Bissau and, even more conspicuously, the Marxist-influenced Mozambique Liberation Front (FRELIMO), led by President Samora Machel, in Mozambique. In Angola, however, the independence movement had been split between at least three separate liberation fronts, each representing a distinct political tendency. In spite of OAU-sponsored mediation efforts, these movements had for many months been fighting one another, creating widespread hardship and terror within the country and provoking a mass exodus of persons of white and mixed ancestry. The discovery that the most leftist of the three movements, the Popular Movement for the Liberation of Angola (MPLA) led by Agostinho Neto, was receiving large-scale material assistance from the U.S.S.R. and Cuba[2] was directly responsible for Dr. Kissinger's dawning alarm at what he called "the interference of extracontinental powers who do not wish Africa well and whose involvement is inconsistent with the promise of true independence."

In other respects, the Kissinger speech broke little new ground. Expressing support for the British-backed effort to negotiate a peaceful solution in Southern Rhodesia, he made no direct reference to the abortive constitutional discussions that had taken place at Victoria Falls, on the Rhodesian-Zambian frontier, on August 25-26.[3] He did, however, voice the expectation— unwarranted, as matters turned out—that Congress would soon repeal the 1971 Byrd amendment barring the observance of Security Council sanctions against the importation of strategic materials from Southern Rhodesia.[4]

Concerning Namibia (South West Africa), Dr. Kissinger reaffirmed the American commitment to self-determination under U.N. principles, but avoided comment on the work of the so-called Windhoek conference, a South African-sponsored gathering that had recently hinted at the possibility of the territory's becoming independent—presumably under South African patronage—within three years.[5] Nor did he refer to the triple veto cast by France, Great Britain, and the United States on June 6 to kill a draft Securi-

[2] For background cf. Chapter 45, Document 67.
[3] Cf. *Keesing's*: 27397-401.
[4] For the Byrd amendment (Sec. 503, Public Law 92-156, Nov. 17, 1971), see *AFR, 1971*: 414-15 and 424-7. A bill to repeal the amendment (H.R. 1287, 94th Cong., 1st sess.) was rejected by the House of Representatives on Sept. 25, 1975 by a vote of 187 in favor to 209 opposed. The amendment was, however, eventually repealed by Public Law 95-12, Mar. 18, 1977.
[5] Cf. *Keesing's*: 27582-3 (1976).

ty Council resolution that had termed the situation in Namibia a threat to international peace and security and called for an arms embargo against South Africa.[6] Within South Africa itself, the Secretary of State implied, the signs of change in long-established racial patterns must be "encouraged and accelerated"; but he also warned that the United States would firmly oppose any repetition of the unsuccessful attempt of the year before to effect South Africa's expulsion from the United Nations.[7]]

(52) *United States Policy in Africa:. Toast by Secretary of State Kissinger at a dinner honoring Foreign Ministers and Permanent Representatives of States Members of the Organization of African Unity, New York, September 23, 1975.*[8]

Some 15 years ago Prime Minister Harold Macmillan added a new and durable phrase to the English language when, in speaking of Africa, he said, "The wind of change is blowing through the continent."[9] When the 20th century opened, Western colonialism stood at its zenith. Today, only the barest vestiges of Western colonialism remain in Africa. Never before in history has so revolutionary a reversal occurred with such rapidity. Morally and politically, the spread of national independence has already transformed world institutions and the nature of international affairs. Today we feel the winds of change blowing *from* Africa, and they will affect the course we set for generations to come.

The first official function at which I presided as Secretary of State two years ago was a luncheon here for the representatives of the Organization of African Unity. Since then the world has undergone continuing change—as much in Africa as anywhere else.

In Africa, the Portuguese African colonial empire has come to an end. The effects of that on southern Africa are being felt in Rhodesia, Namibia, and South Africa; and their full course has yet to be run.

Also of great importance, major changes have taken place in the international economy, as reflected in the recent special session.[10]

[6]U.N. Document S/11713, failed of adoption by a vote of 10-3 (U.S.)-2; details in *Bulletin*, 73: 42-6.
[7]Cf. *AFR, 1974*: 391-401. Suspended from participation in the Assembly's 29th Regular Session in 1974 (same: 401-6), South Africa refrained from participating in the 30th Regular Session in 1975.
[8]Department of State Press Release 500, Sept. 23; text and subtitles from *Bulletin*, 73: 571-5.
[9]Address to the South African Parliament, Feb. 3, 1960; cf. *The United States in World Affairs, 1960*: 162-3.
[10]Cf. Chapter 30.

The developing nations of Africa, Asia, and Latin America are claiming more control over their economic destiny and a greater share in global prosperity.

Africa continues to face enormous problems. The trials of economic development, exacerbated by the problems of the world economy and the exorbitant rises in the price of oil, continue to pose challenges for African nations despite the progress they have made. The arbitrary boundaries established by the colonial powers left many African countries vulnerable to ethnic strife. Social change and development, as they succeed, challenge national unity and cultural identity far more profoundly than other nations have experienced. The job of nation-building in Africa is formidable indeed.

The people of this country wish you well and offer you our help.

There is growing interest in America in African issues and African problems. Traditionally America has been dedicated to independence and self-determination and to the rights of man. We have been strong advocates of decolonization since the beginning of the postwar period. The special identification of black Americans with their African heritage intensifies our belief, and our will to demonstrate, that men of all races can live and prosper together.

Because of these ties, and with the economic interdependence of Africa and America becoming increasingly obvious, Americans owe it to ourselves and to Africa to define clearly and to state candidly our policy toward the continent of Africa. Therefore, today I would like to go beyond the usual toast for occasions such as this and talk with you informally about some of the important issues in relations between the United States and Africa.

America has three major concerns:

—That Africa attain prosperity for its people and become a strong participant in the economic order, an economic partner with a growing stake in the international system;

—That self-determination, racial justice, and human rights spread to all of Africa; and

—That the continent be free of great-power rivalry or conflict.

The United States seeks neither military allies nor ideological confrontation in Africa. As Adlai Stevenson once said here at the United Nations, "Africa for the Africans *means* Africa for the Africans and not Africa as a hunting ground for alien ambitions."[11]

---

[11]Statement to the U.N. Security Council, Feb. 15, 1961, in *Bulletin*, 39: 361 (1961).

Economic Development

The people of Africa entered the era of independence with high aspirations. Economic development has become both their highest national goal and a symbol of their drive for a more significant role in world affairs.

Much progress has been made. National incomes in Africa have risen rapidly in the last two decades. Africa's overall trade has increased about fourfold in the last 15 years.

But development hopes in Africa have too often been crushed by the cycles of natural disasters and the shocks of worldwide economic instability. No continent suffers so cruelly when crops fail for lack of rain. No continent endures a heavier burden when prices of primary commodities fluctuate violently in response to shifts in the world economy.

The United States has set as one of the fundamental goals of its foreign policy to help lay the foundations for a new era of international cooperation embracing developed and developing countries in an open and durable international system. Africa has an important role in this international system. Our mutual success will determine the nature of political and economic relations in the world over the remainder of this century.

The United States offered a comprehensive practical approach to economic development at the seventh special session.[12] My government was pleased that our suggestions formed the basis for a highly significant consensus among the developed and developing countries, which we hope will mark the end of a period of fruitless confrontation and misunderstanding.

Our major aims are:

—To make developing countries more secure against drastic economic difficulties arising from cyclical declines in export earnings and in food production;

—To accelerate economic growth by improving their access to capital, technology, and management skills;

—To provide special treatment to improve their opportunities in trading relations;

—To make commodity markets function more smoothly and beneficially for both producers and consumers; and

—To devote special attention to the urgent needs of the poorest countries.

Our proposals apply to all developing countries. But many of them are particularly appropriate to Africa:

[12]Chapter 30, Document 49.

—Sixteen of the world's twenty-five least developed countries are in Africa. Our bilateral assistance program is increasingly concentrated on the least developed. Above and beyond our emergency assistance to the Sahelian drought area,[13] our regular aid appropriation for Africa this fiscal year reflects an increase of about 60 percent over last year.

—We expect African countries to benefit particularly from the development security facility which we propose to create in the International Monetary Fund to counter drastic shortfalls in export earnings for economies which are particularly dependent on a few highly volatile primary commodities.

—But stabilizing earnings is not enough. The United States supports measures to improve markets for individual commodities, including coffee, cocoa, and copper, which are so important to Africa.

—We also propose to double our bilateral assistance to expand agricultural production.

—We will raise our proposed contribution to the African Development Fund to $25 million.[14]

—In addition to the proposals we made to the United Nations, the United States has attempted to mobilize international support for a coordinated long-term development program to provide basic economic security for the Sahelian countries. We have supported this effort already with massive assistance of more than $100 million.

The key to sustaining development over the long run is expanded trade and investment. Growing exports of manufactured, as well as primary, products generate the foreign exchange needed to buy the imports to fuel further development. The United States provides a large and growing market for the products of African countries. Our trade with Africa had grown to about $8 billion in 1974, almost eight times its volume in 1960. The rapid implementation of the U.S. generalized system of preferences should spell even greater expansion in the years to come.

American private investment has been a valuable source of the capital, management, and technology that are essential to African development. Direct U.S. investment in Africa has increased more than four times since 1960.

We are encouraged by these striking increases in the magnitude and relative importance of trade and investment relationships between the United States and independent black Africa. We expect

[13]Cf. *AFR, 1973*: 214-17 and 497.
[14]Cf. note 12 to Chapter 30.

this trend to continue, and we will do what we can to assure that it does so.

Southern Africa

Economic progress is of utmost importance to Africa; but at the same time, the political challenges of the continent, particularly the issue of southern Africa, summon the urgent attention of the world community.

We believe that these problems can and must be solved. They should be solved peacefully. We are mindful of the Lusaka Manifesto,[15] which combines a commitment to human dignity and equality with a clear understanding of what is a realistic and hopeful approach to this profound challenge.

No problem is more complex than the racial issues in South Africa itself. My country's convictions on apartheid are well known. It is contrary to all we believe in and stand for. The U.S. position has been longstanding and consistent. We note that the wind of change continues to blow, inexorably. The signs of change that are visible in South Africa must be encouraged and accelerated. We are pleased to see the constructive measures taken by African governments to promote better relations and peaceful change. We believe change is inevitable, and efforts to promote a progressive and peaceful evolution will have our support.

The United States also continues to support the International Court of Justice's advisory opinion of 1971 affirming the General Assembly's 1966 decision which terminated the South African mandate over Namibia.[16] The United States will take no steps that would legitimize South Africa's administration of the territory. We repeatedly have protested violations of the rights of black Namibians by the authorities there.

As I indicated in my address yesterday,[17] we believe that all Namibians should be given the opportunity to express their views freely, and under U.N. supervision, on the political and constitutional structure of their country. We have expressed this view consistently to South Africa. We will continue to do so. We welcome public statements of South African leaders that they accept the principle of independence and self-determination for Namibia.

For the past decade, Rhodesia has been a major international issue. The maintenance by force of an illegal regime based on white supremacy is of deep concern to African governments and to my

[15]Cf. *Documents, 1970*: 297 n. 14.
[16]*Documents, 1966*: 309-11; *AFR, 1971*: 403-5.
[17]Chapter 32, Document 51.

government. Over the past year, the United States has watched with sympathy the attempt to negotiate a peaceful solution in Rhodesia. We have noted, in particular, the statesmanlike efforts of the leaders of African countries—especially President Kaunda, Prime Minister Vorster, President Khama, President Nyerere, and President Machel[18]—to avert violence and bloodshed. We would encourage them to continue in their difficult task of bringing the parties together.

The United States intends to adhere scrupulously to the U.N.'s economic sanctions against Rhodesia. President Ford and his entire Administration continue to urge repeal of the Byrd amendment and expect this will be accomplished during the current session of the Congress.

The United Nations has tried in various ways to exert a positive influence on change in southern Africa. I should add, however, that we have opposed, and will continue to oppose, actions that are incompatible with the U.N. Charter. In particular, we will not retreat from our opposition to the expulsion of any member of the United Nations. We believe this would be contrary to the best interests and effectiveness of this organization. Universality is a fundamental principle that we stand for in this body. The charter's provisions for members' full exercise of their prerogatives are another. We do not believe that these principles can be ignored in one case and applied in another. This is why, despite our disapproval of South Africa's policies, we do not believe this organization can afford to start down the path of excluding members because of criticism of their domestic policies.

Former Portuguese Territories

Since we last sat down together, three more African nations— Mozambique, Sao Tome and Principe, and Cape Verde—have become independent. We welcome them to the U.N. family, and we look forward to establishing regular relations with them. We stand ready to assist in their economic development.

But I want to say a cautionary word about Angola. Events in Angola have taken a distressing turn, with widespread violence. We are most alarmed at the interference of extracontinental powers who do not wish Africa well and whose involvement is inconsistent with the promise of true independence. We believe a fair and peaceful solution must be negotiated, giving all groups representing the Angolan people a fair role in its future.

---

[18]Kenneth Kaunda (Zambia), Balthazar Johannes Vorster (South Africa), Sir Seretse Khama (Botswana), Julius K. Nyerere (Tanzania), Samora Machel (Mozambique).

The Spirit of Cooperation

Ladies and gentlemen, colleagues: Twenty years ago there were only three independent African states. Today you comprise more than one-third of the membership of the United Nations. Africa's numbers and resources and the energies of its peoples have given Africa a strong and important role in world affairs.

We do not expect you to be in concert with us on all international issues. We ask only that as we respect your interests, are mindful of your rights, and sympathize with your concerns, you give us the same consideration. Let us base our relations on mutual respect. Let us address our differences openly and as friends, in the recognition that only by cooperation can we achieve the aspirations of our peoples.

Let us be guided by the flexibility and the spirit of conciliation which were so evident during the special session. Let us replace the sterility of confrontation with the promise inherent in our collaboration. Let us search diligently for areas of agreement and strive to overcome any misunderstandings.

Strengthening the relationship between the United States and Africa is a major objective of American policy. We support your self-determination, sovereignty, and territorial integrity. We want to help you in your efforts to develop your economies and improve the well-being of your people. Like yours, our belief in racial justice is unalterable.

America has many ties to Africa and a deep commitment to its future.

It is my profound hope that this session of the General Assembly will be remembered as a time when we began to come together as truly united nations, a time when we earnestly searched for reasons to agree, a time when the interdependence of mankind began to be fully understood. The nations of Africa will have a major part in determining whether this will come to pass.

Ladies and gentlemen, please raise your glasses with me in a toast to the future of Africa, the Organization of African Unity, and the United Nations in a world of peace.

34. A FAREWELL TO SEATO

(New York, September 24, 1975)

[Another recurring feature of the New York diplomatic season was the annual ministerial-level meeting of the SEATO Council, the policy organ of the South-East Asia Treaty Organization established on American initiative in the wake of the Communist victories in Indochina in 1954. Set up originally to discourage armed attack and subversion against its member countries, SEATO had not been remiss in claiming credit for the relatively peaceful conditions that had prevailed in Southeast Asia for much of the ensuing period. But the resumption of large-scale warfare in Vietnam in the 1960s had severely damaged the organization's unity and prestige, and the incipient détente between the United States and China in the early 1970s had raised additional doubts about its contemporary relevance. In 1973, SEATO's remaining members—Australia, New Zealand, the Philippines, Thailand, the United Kingdom, and the United States—had decided that the organization's traditional military activities should be reduced in favor of increased attention to stability and development in the Philippines and Thailand, the two regional members.[1] By 1975, another round of Communist victories in Indochina had created a situation in which the organization's existence even in this modified form was being questioned by some of the very countries it had been set up to protect.

Not only had the world been shaken by the Communist conquest of South Vietnam and Cambodia, but even Laos was sliding into the Communist orbit by the time fixed for the SEATO Council meeting on September 24, 1975. The tripartite political arrangements established in that country in 1973[2] had failed to contain the deep-seated antagonism between its rightist forces, including the warlike Meo tribesmen trained and formerly subsidized by the

---

[1] *AFR, 1973*: 373-4 and 376-7.
[2] Same: 371-2 and 375-6.

United States, and the Communist-dominated Pathet Lao with its long-established ties to North Vietnam. Outbreaks of localized fighting had taken place in the spring of 1975 and had been followed by the flight of the right-wing ministers, an advance of Pathet Lao forces into areas hitherto barred to them, and a wave of anti-U.S. demonstrations that had led in June to the closing down of the U.S. Agency for International Development (AID) mission. By late August, the Pathet Lao had completed its takeover of the key Vientiane Province and begun a process that was to culminate in December in the abolition of the monarchy and the proclamation of a People's Democratic Republic under the nominal presidency of the leftist Prince Souphanouvong.[3]

The extension of Communist rule to all parts of Indochina had accelerated an ongoing process of diplomatic readjustment on the part of the remaining states of the region, five of which—Indonesia, Malaysia, the Philippines, Singapore, and Thailand—shared membership in the nonaligned Association of Southeast Asian Nations (ASEAN), while only two—the Philippines and Thailand—were members of SEATO as well. In common with the other ASEAN members, the two latter countries had been quick to recognize the new Cambodian regime; in addition, the leaders of both nations had visited Peking in June in order to establish diplomatic relations with the People's Republic of China. At the same time, Philippine President Ferdinand E. Marcos had announced a thorough review of his country's security relationship with the United States, while Prime Minister Kukrit Pramoj of Thailand, who had been particularly upset by developments in connection with the *Mayagüez* affair,[4] had insisted upon an accelerated withdrawal of the U.S. troops and aircraft that had remained in his country since the Vietnam war.[5]

Apparently undismayed by a recrudescence of pro-Chinese guerrilla activity in Thailand's volatile Northeast, Prime Minister Kukrit continued to stress the obsolescence of past arrangements in a tour of ASEAN countries during June and July. Concluding a visit to the Philippines on July 24, he joined with President Marcos in a public suggestion that while SEATO "had served its purpose commendably, . . . the organization should be phased out to make it accord with the new realities in the region."[6] Promptly endorsed by Australia, this view was ratified by the entire SEATO Council at its final ministerial meeting on September 24. Ordered with minimal publicity and with no audible expressions of regret, the

---

[3]Details in *Keesing's*: 27277-81 (1975) and 27541-3 (1976).
[4]Cf. Chapter 14 at note 2.
[5]Details in *Keesing's*: 27333-6 (1975).
[6]Same: 27335.

phasing-out process would presumably leave intact the underlying South-East Asia Collective Defense Treaty (Manila Pact) of 1954,[7] which had been concluded for an indefinite period and still called upon the parties to develop their individual and collective defense capability and accord each other mutual support in case of armed attack. Additional evidence of the continuing U.S. interest in the security of Southeast Asia would be given by President Ford in the course of a journey to the region later in 1975.[8]]

(53) *Twentieth Annual Meeting of the Council of the South-East Asia Treaty Organization, New York, September 24, 1975: Press statement issued at the conclusion of the meeting.*[9]

1. The Council of the South-East Asia Treaty Organization (SEATO), comprising Ministerial Representatives of Australia, New Zealand, the Philippines, Thailand, the United Kingdom and the United States, held their Twentieth Annual Meeting in New York on 24 September.

2. The Council reviewed events in the Treaty Area in the year since they had last met.[10] They considered the role of SEATO in light of the new situation in the South-East Asian region. While noting that the Organization had over the years made a useful contribution to stability and development in the region, they decided that in view of the changing circumstances it should now be phased out.

3. The Council accordingly instructed the Secretary-General[11] to prepare a detailed plan for the phasing out process to be conducted in an orderly and systematic manner. Recognizing that many of the projects and activities in which the Organization had been engaged were of substantial value and might be continued under other auspices, possibly with bilateral or multilateral technical and economic support, the Council requested the Secretary-General and the Negotiating Bodies to explore this subject further.

4. The Council expressed its appreciation to the Government of Thailand for having been the host to SEATO during its existence and for all the facilities accorded by the Government of Thailand to the Organization.

---

[7]Signed in Manila Sept. 8, 1954 and entered into force Feb. 19, 1955 (TIAS 3170; 6 UST 81); text in *Documents, 1954*: 319-23.
[8]Cf. Chapter 40.
[9]Text from *Bulletin*, 73: 575.
[10]For the Council's 1974 meeting see *AFR, 1974*: 370-73.
[11]Sunthorn Hongladarom (Thailand).

35. THE SOVIET GRAIN DEAL

(Moscow, October 20, 1975)

[The United States has long been a net exporter of agricultual products and a net importer of fuels, especially petroleum. Proposals to barter American food for foreign fuel did not, however, as a rule impress the U.S. Government as especially helpful, if only because the countries on which the United States depended for its oil supplies were not, in most cases, those most in need of American food. In one significant instance during 1975, however, the American Government did take the lead in trying to link an agreement on future grain exports with the assurance of a modest contribution to American petroleum needs.

That the Soviet Union had become heavily dependent on grain imports from American and other Western sources had been common knowledge ever since the disastrous harvest of 1972 had forced Moscow to look abroad for the satisfaction of some of its most urgent needs.[1] Recovering somewhat in 1973, Soviet grain output had again declined in 1974 and declined further in 1975, when the smallest crop since 1965 was harvested. Faced with a new wave of Soviet purchase orders at a time when the United States' own crop prospects were still uncertain, the American Government at the beginning of August had taken the by now familiar step of imposing temporary restrictions on grain exports to the Soviet Union (later extended to Poland) until the situation was clarified. To supplement the voluntary cooperation of U.S. traders, American longshoremen for several weeks had maintained a ban on the loading of grain for Soviet ports.

Noting the unsettling effects of the instability that had characterised the Soviet grain trade in recent years, President Ford had also announced on September 9 that an American mission was about to leave for Moscow to explore the possibilities of a long-term agreement that would alleviate these conditions and enable him to lift the

[1] Cf. *AFR, 1972*: 114-19.

current restrictions.[2] Six weeks later, on October 20, the President could announce that the U.S. delegation, which had been headed by Under Secretary of State Robinson, had not only concluded a five-year agreement on future grain sales to the U.S.S.R. but had persuaded Moscow to begin negotiations for a similar agreement covering U.S. purchases of Soviet oil.[3]

Details fo the Agreement on the Supply of Grain, which had been signed in Moscow on October 20,[4] were explained by Under Secretary Robinson in a later appearance before the House International Relations Committee **(Document 54)**. Barring extraordinary circumstances, he noted, the U.S.S.R. would be committed by its terms to purchase between 6 and 8 million metric tons of U.S. wheat and corn at market rates in each of the five years beginning October 1, 1976 and ending September 30, 1981. The expected benefits to the United States would include perhaps $1 billion in annual foreign sales, reduced uncertainty for American farmers, lessened fluctuations in world markets, and protection for livestock producers and others from the wide price swings occasioned by the Soviet Union's previous unregulated purchases.

President Ford, who had described the Moscow negotiations at one point as "just a matter of good, old Yankee trader actions," had recognized that the relative situation of the two parties was more favorable to a grain deal than to the oil agreement the United States hoped to negotiate at the same time. "We have the grain, we want a 5-year or longer term, and we want good arrangements. . . .I think we are probably going to have some results [on grain]," he said. But so far as oil was concerned, the President added, "that is a little more difficult. In that case, they have the commodity and we want it. So, they have somewhat better bargaining position in that case than we."[5]

Despite this built-in handicap, the letter of intent addressed by Under Secretary Robinson to the Soviet Foreign Trade Minister, N.S. Patolichev, at the conclusion of the Moscow negotiations[6] suggested that the two parties were near agreement on an annual sale to the United States of 10 million metric tons of Soviet crude oil and petroleum products— equivalent to about 3 percent of current U.S. imports—some part of which would be available for resale in Europe or elsewhere. Although the amount in question was small, Mr. Robinson explained, it would not only signify a

---

[2]*Presidential Documents*, 11: 977-8 (*Bulletin*, 73: 540-41).
[3]*Bulletin*, 73: 662-3.
[4]TIAS 8206; 26 UST 2971; text in *Bulletin*, 73: 663-4.
[5]News conference, Detroit, Oct. 10, in *Presidential Documents*, 11: 1158.
[6]*Bulletin*, 73: 664.

diversification of U.S. supply sources but would give the U.S.S.R. an incentive to expand its production more rapidly.

But despite these favorable auguries, little if any further progress had been registered by the end of the year, and the oil talks were to be recessed indefinitely in March 1976 amid continuing differences between the two governments on shipping rates and other matters.]

(54) *Grain and Oil Arrangements with the Soviet Union, October 20, 1975: Statement by Under Secretary of State Robinson before the House Committee on International Relations, October 28, 1975.* [7]

I welcome the opportunity to appear here today to describe new arrangements with the Soviet Union on trade in grains which I believe will significantly benefit the United States.

U.S.S.R. production and trade in grain currently are the two most unstable elements in the world grain economy, accounting for about 80 percent of the annual fluctuation in world trade in wheat—the principal food grain. Variations in Soviet imports of grain have been particularly marked in this decade. In the 1971 crop year, the Soviet Union imported about 8 million metric tons of grain, of which 2.9 million tons were from the United States. In the following crop year, imports totaled about 21 million tons, of which 13.7 were from the United States.

It is this extreme variation which makes planning production for the Soviet market by U.S. farmers difficult and which affects the availability of supplies not only for our other foreign customers but also American consumers—not just homemakers but our meat producers as well. In view of this situation, the President announced on September 9 that he had directed me to explore a long-term agreement with the Soviet Union, which was subsequently signed and announced on October 20.

The U.S.-U.S.S.R. agreement on grain sales primarily aims at reducing this heretofore unpredictable massive intervention in our market. The agreement:

—Unconditionally commits the Soviet Union to purchase a minimum of 6 million metric tons of wheat and corn annually.

—Permits the U.S.S.R. to purchase an additional 2 million tons annually without government-to-government consultation.

—Obliges the U.S. Government to facilitate Soviet purchases and not to exercise its authority to control shipments of these amounts unless the total U.S. grain supply (beginning stocks of

[7]Text from *Bulletin*, 73: 712-13.

all grains except rice plus the U.S. Department of Agriculture's estimate of production) falls below 225 million metric tons. In this event, the U.S. Government may reduce the amount which the Soviet side may purchase to less than 6 million tons.

The agreement also provides for consultation by the two governments in advance of purchases in excess of 8 million tons of wheat and corn in any one crop year. Shipment of grain under the agreement is to be in accord with the U.S.-U.S.S.R. maritime agreement.[8]

The Soviets have assured us that their additional purchases of grain in the current crop year will not be in a volume which could disrupt the U.S. market. As Secretary [of Agriculture Earl L.] Butz noted at the time this agreement was announced, we view this volume as 7 million metric tons.

In announcing the grain agreement, the President outlined its benefits to our economy. The agreement:

—Provides for a relatively stable long-term major market for U.S. grain, valued at about $1 billion annually.

—Increases the incentive for American farmers to maintain full production.

—Reduces fluctuations in U.S. and world markets by smoothing out Soviet purchases of U.S. grain.

—Stimulates not only agriculture but such related enterprise as farm machinery and ocean transport.

I will now turn briefly to the letter of intent to negotiate an agreement on sales of Soviet oil to the United States, which was also signed on October 20.

The Soviet Union is the world's largest producer of crude oil, at about 9.5 million barrels per day, having recently surpassed U.S. production. The United States is the world's largest consumer of petroleum with domestic production of about 8.9 million barrels per day and imports about 6 million barrels per day. The U.S.S.R. exports about 2.3 million barrels per day, mainly to Eastern and Western Europe.

The U.S. and Soviet Governments have agreed to commence negotiation promptly of an agreement under which:

—The U.S.S.R. would offer for sale to the United States 10

[8]Signed in Washington Oct. 14, 1972 (*AFR, 1972*: 119), the U.S.-Soviet maritime agreement was replaced by a new six-year agreement signed in Washington and Moscow Dec. 29, 1975 and effective Jan. 1, 1976.

million metric tons of crude oil and petroleum products annually (about 200,000 barrels per day) for five years.

—The U.S. Government would be free to purchase the oil for its own use; or by agreement, oil could be purchased by U.S. firms for resale, including in agreed areas outside the United States.

Prices are to be agreed at a mutually beneficial level, and efforts are to be made toward expanding technical cooperation in energy in ways to be agreed upon.

The volume of potential U.S. purchases under such an agreement is small, but their significance lies in the diversification of sources of supply it opens for the United States.

Such an agreement could also be an incentive to the Soviet Union to expand its production capacity more rapidly than would otherwise be the case.

This brief description highlights the main features and effects of the arrangements we have concluded with the Soviet Union. I welcome your questions, not only on these arrangements but on our foreign economic policy and current initiative in general.

36. MIDDLE EAST PRICE TAG

(October 30, 1975)

[Few of the diplomatic achievements of the Ford administration had given it more obvious satisfaction than the Egyptian-Israeli disengagement arrangements announced September 1 and formally accepted by Congress in the joint resolution approved October 13.[1] Apart from its potential importance in a Middle Eastern context, the agreement had appreciable domestic value at a time when the administration was embroiled with Congress on a variety of issues and, in addition, was coming under increasing attack in nationalist and right-wing circles that favored the presidential aspirations of former California Governor Ronald Reagan.

To obtain Egyptian and Israeli consent to a second disengagement, the United States had of course made lavish promises to both parties[2]—particularly to Israel, whose stubbornness earlier in the year had provoked the much-publicized "reassessment" of American policy but had failed to shake the basic American identification with Israeli interests. Now that the second-stage disengagement was acually on the verge of implementation, the time had come for the United States to begin redeeming its pledges. The scope of this operation was suggested by the message President Ford addressed to Congress on October 30, in which he sketched the details of a $4.6 billion security assistance program of which no less than $3.4 billion would be allocated to Israel and other countries of the Middle East.

As was explained in the message **(Document 55)**, this request in effect embodied the "security assistance" portion of the annual foreign aid program for the fiscal year 1976 and the three-month transitional period ending September 30, 1976. (A separate request for foreign economic assistance, submitted May 15, 1975,[3] was

[1]Public Law 94-110, Oct. 13 (Chapter 29, Document 49).
[2]Chapter 29, Document 48.
[3]Presidential letter, May 15, in *Presidential Documents*, 11: 517-18 (*Bulletin*, 72: 970); details in House Document 94-158, May 15, 1975.

already being dealt with in the pending International Development and Food Assistance Act of 1975, which had passed the House by a 244 to 155 vote on September 10 and would become law in December.)[4] Of the requested total of $4,533,000,000 for security assistance, the Military Assistance Program (MAP) of grant aid accounted for only $409 million; Security Supporting Assistance, a kind of defense-related economic aid, came to $1,800,000,000; and Foreign Military Sales (FMS) credits amounted to $2,324,000,000. By far the largest share of the total was allotted to Israel, with $740,000,000 in supporting assistance and $1,500,000,000 in credit sales. Egypt was offered $750,000,000 in supporting assistance, while other large recipients would include Jordan, Syria, South Korea, Greece, and Turkey (whose eligibility for limited military aid had been restored by Congress a few weeks earlier).[5]

Immediate action on a request of these proportions was not to be expected of a Congress that had grown used to asserting its independence and, moreover, had become increasingly dubious about the whole idea of foreign military and security assistance. No bill to implement the President's program had been reported in either house by the time the Congress adjourned in December. Indeed, it was not until June 30, 1976 that President Ford was able to sign the modified authorization and appropriation measures designed to implement his request.[6]]

(55) Security Assistance Programs for Fiscal Year 1976: Message from President Ford to the Congress, October 30, 1975.[7]

To the Congress of the United States:

I sent to the Congress on May 15 draft legislation to authorize foreign assistance programs for fiscal years 1976 and 1977, and for the transition period July 1, 1976, through September 30, 1976.[8] At that time, because of uncertainties caused by changing events, particularly in the Middle East and Indochina, I was unable to propose specific amounts for security assistance programs. I said I would return to the Congress with specific programs as soon as possible.

[4]Public Law 94-161, Dec. 20, 1975.
[5]Public Law 94-104, Oct. 6; cf. Chapter 22 at note 3.
[6]International Security Assistance and Arms Export Control Act of 1976 (Public Law 94-329) and Foreign Assistance and Related Programs Appropriations Act, 1976 (Public Law 94-330), both approved June 30, 1976.
[7]Text from *Presidential Documents*, 11: 1214-17.
[8]Same as note 3.

The review of security assistance programs now has been completed and my revisions to the draft legislation are being transmitted today. My initial legislative proposal was printed in the House of Representatives as House Document No. 94-158 and was introduced in the Senate as S. 1816. The revisions transmitted with this message will supersede sections 10, 11, 12, 15, 16, 17 and 18 of that proposal.

The world is different and far more complex than the world we knew in the 1950's. So are the problems confronting it. However, the United States Government still has a primary responsibility to take the lead in creating conditions which will insure justice, international cooperation and enduring peace. The program of security assistance I am transmitting today will contribute significantly toward meeting this responsibility.

PEACE IN THE MIDDLE EAST

Nothing so underscores how essential the American peacekeeping role is than our current efforts in the Middle East. Since the October 1973 War, our Middle East policy has been based on the following three principles.

— First, a firm resolution to work for a just and lasting settlement of the Arab-Israeli conflict taking into account the legitimate interests of all states and peoples in the area, including the Palestinians.
— Second, a commitment to the improvement of our relations with all the states of the Middle East on a bilateral basis, maintaining our support for Israel's security while strengthening our relations with the Arab countries.
— Third, continued dedication to avoiding great power confrontation in the Middle East.

The October 1973 War was the fourth, and most devastating, round of hostilities between Arab and Israeli forces. Moreover, the impact of this last collision between opposing forces was not confined to the Middle East. The spectre of armed confrontation between the United States and the Soviet Union hung over the crisis. Disruption of the economies of Western Europe, Japan and other nations was an important by-product of the conflict. In addition, the likelihood existed that the period immediately after October 1973 would merely represent a pause between the fourth and fifth rounds of conflict.

The quest for peace in the area was of the highest priority. Our most immediate objective was to encourage the disengagement of the contending military forces. Disengagement was accomplished in 1974. This year, we dedicated ourselves to the goal of withdrawal in the Sinai—and an agreement was negotiated as a result of the efforts of Secretary of State Kissinger. We believe that the step-by-step approach to negotiations offers the best prospects for establishing an enduring peace in the region. We expect to proceed on an incremental basis to the next stage of negotiation within the near future.

I believe the hope for a lasting solution to the Arab-Israeli dispute is stronger today than at any time in the previous quarter century. A new era also is opening in our relations with Arabs and Israelis. This security assistance program will give substance to these new relationships and help preserve the momentum toward peace.

My proposals have three basic purposes:

— First, to provide Israel with the assistance needed to maintain security and to persevere in the negotiating process.
— Second, to give tangible expression to our new and fruitful relations with the Arab nations most directly involved and to encourage those which are seriously prepared to work for peace.
— Third, to encourage the peaceful development of the area, thereby reducing the incentives to violence and conflict.

The Security Assistance Program I am transmitting to Congress is heavily weighted with requirements to sustain the peace in the Middle East. Fully 70 percent of the program for fiscal year 1976 is to be concentrated in this region.

It proposes:

— For Israel, $740 million in security supporting assistance and $1,500 million in military credits. Israel's ability to defend herself and to relieve some of the burdens of her defense reduces the prospect of new conflict in the Middle East.
— For Egypt, $750 million in supporting assistance. Egypt has made the bold decision to move from confrontation to negotiation as a means of resolving the Arab-Israeli dispute. Its leaders also must cope with serious economic problems whose resolution the United States is in a position to assist.
— For Jordan, $100 million in military assistance grants, $78 million in security supporting assistance, and $75 million in military credit sales. This assistance will strengthen Jordan's ability to hold to the course of moderation it has consistently followed.

— For Syria, $90 million in security supporting assistance. This assistance will enable our development cooperation with Syria to go forward, furthering our efforts to re-establish more normal bilateral relations.

— In addition, I am recommending a Special Requirements Fund this fiscal year of $50 million. The fund is to be used to reinforce the peace process in the area and, in particular, to defray the costs of stationing American civilian technicians in the Sinai area.

All of this aid will contribute to the confidence that Middle Eastern nations must have in the United States if we are to maintain our momentum toward peace.

EAST ASIA

The collapse of friendly governments in Indochina has necessitated a thorough review of the situation and of our policies and objectives throughout East Asia. The program I am proposing therefore recognizes the new realities as well as our enduring responsibilities as a leading participant in the affairs of the Asia Pacific region. For the first time, military sales credits exceed grants in our proposals for security assistance to Asian countries. These proposals include Foreign Military Sales credits in the amount of $80 million for the Republic of China, $126 million for Korea, and $37 million for Thailand, with smaller but no less significant amounts for Indonesia, Malaysia, and the Philippines. Grant assistance programs include $19 million for Indonesia, $74 million for Korea, $20 million for the Philippines, and $28 million for Thailand. This funding pattern reflects the improved economic circumstances of several of our allies, their decreasing dependence on grant aid, and a greater ability to pay for defense purchases on a deferred basis.

EUROPE

The program that I am proposing for Europe is focussed primarily on two countries with whom the United States shares extraordinary mutual defense interests: Greece and Turkey. For Greece, I am proposing more than $50 million in MAP and $110 million in FMS credits. Over the same period, Turkey would receive $75 million in MAP and $130 million in FMS credits. These amounts take into consideration urgent needs for defense articles and services on the part of these two important NATO allies. Implementation of the respective programs would allow the United States to resume its traditional cooperative role following the unfortunate disruptions occasioned by the Cyprus crisis. In this traditional role, the United States can work more effectively to alleviate regional tensions and rectify recent misunderstandings which have had an adverse impact on the interests of all our European allies.

AFRICA AND LATIN AMERICA

In these two geographic areas where there were widespread special development problems, I am proposing security assistance programs with emphasis on training as a common denominator. While the training programs are not individually costly, the fact that they are distributed among many countries should contribute to the strengthening of our regional relations well beyond the military sector. The only significant MAP proposal in either area involves a $12 million program for Ethiopia, where we have been committed to an armed forces modernization program of reasonable dimensions. No other grant aid funds are envisioned elsewhere in Africa. MAP proposals throughout Latin America are confined to small sums, mainly for vehicles, communications equipment and spare parts. FMS credits for Latin America are proposed in amounts commensurate with the relative sizes of the recipients' armed forces, their repayment ability and overall development needs. In Africa, the only significant FMS credit proposals are $10 million for Ethiopia and $19 million for Zaire.

SECURITY SUPPORTING ASSISTANCE

Aside from the special programs for the Middle East states which I have described previously, my proposals for security supporting assistance include $35 million for Cyprus, including $10 million for the United Nations Forces there, $55 million for Portugal, $65 million for Greece, and $23 million for Zaire. Other small programs and administrative expenses will total $33 million. In all instances, these programs reflect enlightened self-interest for the United States and a carefully documented need.

CONCLUSION

While the extraordinary recent developments in Indochina and the Middle East have necessitated a re-examination of our policies and changes in the focus of our security assistance programs, there can be no doubt that bilateral and multilateral cooperation in the defense sector remains a vital and necessary component of American foreign policy. The proposals that I am now able to make after this reappraisal are addressed specifically to a new global situation and to the extraordinary challenges and opportunities confronting us in the international sphere. Just as it would be a grievous mistake to base our current and future security assistance programs on the precepts of the past, it would be an even greater error to ignore our enduring responsibilities as a major world power by failing to exploit these opportunities. After twenty-five years of seemingly irreconcilable differences, two parties to the Middle East dispute at last have taken a decisive stride toward settling their differences, in joint reliance on our good offices and continuing support. In the strategic Eastern Mediterranean, two of our long-standing NATO allies look to us for a tangible sign of renewed support and traditional friendship. In East Asia, friends and allies are anxiously awaiting evidence that the United States intends to maintain its stabilizing role in Pacific affairs.

DEVELOPMENT ASSISTANCE

I am also pleased to note the progress made by the Congress on H.R. 9005, the International Development and Food Assistance Act of 1975, which authorizes funds for our development and disaster assistance programs. Although we have minor differences with the Congress on the formulation of this legislation, I expect these to be resolved in the legislative process. The 244-155 vote in the House clearly indicates that the Congress and the Executive Branch jointly endorse the current reorientation of our bilateral development assistance program focusing on basic human problems in the poor countries.

We must reaffirm our humanitarian commitment to some 800 million people in the Third and Fourth World, who live in poverty, facing the daily reality of hunger and malnutrition without access to adequate health and education services and with limited productive employment. Improving the quality of life for one-third of mankind living in conditions of despair has become a universal political demand, a technical possibility, and a moral imperative.

Our foreign assistance programs, both development and security, are essential for achieving world peace and for supporting an expanding international economy which benefits all nations. Our national security and economic well-being in a world more interdependent than ever before in the history of mankind warrant the fullest support of the American people and the Congress for our foreign assistance programs.

In regard to the impact of these proposals on overall federal budget levels, I fully recognize the proposed amounts are substantial. I should emphasize, however, that total fiscal year 1976 expenditures for all types of foreign aid including economic and military will still be roughly ten percent below the amounts originally contained in my January budget[9] because of the withdrawal of the request for Indochina funding.

I am confident the Congress shares my desire to see the United States continue to manifest to all nations its determination to play a role in the search for a more secure international environment which is worthy of its greatness as a nation.

GERALD R. FORD

The White House,
October 30, 1975.

---

[9]Cf. Chapter 4. The budget for Fiscal Year 1976, transmitted Feb. 3, 1975, projected total foreign aid expenditures of $6,880 million.

37. "THIS INFAMOUS ACT"

(New York, November 10, 1975)

[President Ford's October 30 message on security assistance was one of several interacting elements in the Middle Eastern situation during these climatic weeks. President Sadat of Egypt was making a state visit to the United States, in the course of which he conferred with President Ford in Washington and Jacksonville, lent his blessing to bilateral agreements on nuclear cooperation, agricultural sales, and the like,[1] and delivered an address to the U.N. General Assembly in which he insisted, among other things, that the Palestine Liberation Organization (PLO) should be represented at the Geneva peace conference on an equal footing with the other participants.[2] Although this recommendation conflicted with the strongly expressed views of Israel and the United States,[3] it was presently endorsed by the Assembly in one of a pair of resolutions in which that body not only voiced broad support for the PLO but established a tendentiously named, twenty-member "Committee on the Exercise of the Inalienable Rights of the Palestinian People."[4] Adopted by crushing majorities in spite of opposition by the United States and others, these resolutions reflected not so much the wisdom of the General Assembly as the numerical strength of the Afro-Asian-Third World-Communist majority that could now be counted upon to back the Arab side on virtually any aspect of the Mideast quarrel.

A more sensational, if not more edifying, expression of this majority attitude had been developing in connection with the program for the U.N.'s 1973-83 "Decade for Action to Combat Racism and Racial Discrimination." In an action that struck American

---

[1] Details in *Bulletin*, 73: 721-37 and 754-6.
[2] Summary of address (Oct. 29) in *UN Monthly Chronicle*, Nov. 1975: 53-4.
[3] Cf. Chapter 29, Document 48b.
[4] Resolutions 3375 and 3376 (XXX), adopted Nov. 10 by votes respectively of 101-8 (U.S.)-25 and 93-18 (U.S.)-27.

505

observers as running directly counter to the announced purpose of this occasion, a group of countries which included Cuba and various Afro-Asian states had put forward an amendment—later replaced by a full-fledged draft resolution—in which they declared that Zionism, the movement in support of a Jewish homeland, was "a form of racism and racial discrimination" and hence, by implication, an object of legitimate reprobation. Vigorously denounced by U.S. Representative Leonard Garment,[5] the resolution was nevertheless adopted by the Assembly's Third (Social, Humanitarian and Cultural) Committee on October 17 by the substantial majority of 70 to 29, with 27 abstentions.

Although this action was condemned "in the strongest terms" by President Ford, Secretary Kissinger, and others,[6] a three-week lobbying effort by the American delegation proved powerless to shake the resolution's supporters. On November 10, the full Assembly approved the committee's text **(Document 56)** by a vote of 72 in favor to 35 opposed—including, of course, the United States—with 32 abstentions. Even within the NATO group there were defections from the U.S. position, with Portugal and Turkey voting "yes" while the other thirteen voted "no."

"The United States of America," Ambassador Moynihan promptly warned the Assembly **(Document 57)**, "declares that it does not acknowledge, it will not abide by, it will never acquiesce in, this infamous act." In Washington and in the country, the reaction was equally strong. Next day, November 11, the Senate unanimously adopted a resolution condemning the U.N. action and calling for immediate hearings "to reassess the United States' further participation in the United Nations General Assembly."[7] A similar resolution, lacking only the reference to possible withdrawal from the Assembly, was adopted by the House of Representatives. But though U.S.-U.N. relations had clearly plummeted to their lowest depth since President Ford's assumption of office, the General Assembly's majority seemed undisturbed. Its voting record for the balance of the session would continue to reflect an equal measure of animosity toward Israel (and "Zionism") and indifference to the American delegation's pleas for objectivity and fairness.[8]]

---

[5]Cf. Introduction at note 11.
[6]Ford (Oct. 24) in *Bulletin*, 73: 790; Kissinger (Oct. 25) in same: 698.
[7]S. Con. Res. 73, 94th Cong., Nov. 11, 1975; text in *New York Times*, Nov. 13, 1975.
[8]For further developments cf. Chapter 44.

(56) *"Elimination of All Forms of Racial Discrimination":* *General Assembly Resolution 3379 (XXX), November 10, 1975.* [9]

The General Assembly,

Recalling its resolution 1904 (XVIII) of 20 November 1963, proclaiming the United Nations Declaration on the Elimination of All Forms of Racial Discrimination, and in particular its affirmation that "any doctrine of racial differentiation or superiority is scientifically false, morally condemnable, socially unjust and dangerous" and its expression of alarm at "the manifestations of racial discrimination still in evidence in some areas of the world, some of which are imposed by certain Governments by means of legislative, administrative or other measures",

Recalling also that, in its resolution 3151 G (XXVIII) of 14 December 1973, the General Assembly condemned, *inter alia*, the unholy alliance between South African racism and zionism,

Taking note of the Declaration of Mexico on the Equality of Women and Their Contribution to Development and Peace, 1975, [10] proclaimed by the World Conference of the International Women's Year, held at Mexico City from 19 June to 2 July 1975, which promulgated the principle that "international co-operation and peace require the achievement of national liberation and independence, the elimination of colonialism and neo-colonialism, foreign occupation, zionism, *apartheid* and racial discrimination in all its forms, as well as the recognition of the dignity of peoples and their right to self-determination",

Taking note also of resolution 77 (XII) adopted by the Assembly of Heads of State and Government of the Organization of African Unity at its twelfth ordinary session, [11] held at Kampala from 28 July to 1 August 1975, which considered "that the racist régimes in occupied Palestine and the racist régimes in Zimbabwe and South Africa have a common imperialist origin, forming a whole and having the same racist structure and being organically linked in their policy aimed at repression of the dignity and integrity of the human being",

Taking note also of the Political Declaration and Strategy to Strengthen International Peace and Security and to Intensify

[9]Text from U.N. General Assembly, *Official Records: 30th Session, Supplement No. 34* (A/10034): 83-4.
[10]Chapter 20, Document 31.
[11]See [U.N. Document] A/10297, annex II. [Footnote in original.]

Solidarity and Mutual Assistance among Non-Aligned Countries,[12] adopted at the Conference of Ministers for Foreign Affairs of Non-Aligned Countries held at Lima from 25 to 30 August 1975, which most severely condemned zionism as a threat to world peace and security and called upon all countries to oppose this racist and imperialist ideology,

Determines that zionism is a form of racism and racial discrimination.

(57) Views on the anti-Zionist Resolution: Statement to the Assembly by Ambassador Moynihan, November 10, 1975.[13]

The United States rises to declare before the General Assembly of the United Nations, and before the world, that it does not acknowledge, it will not abide by, it will never acquiesce in, this infamous act.

Not three weeks ago, the U.S. Representative in the Social, Humanitarian and Cultural Committee pleaded in measured and fully considered terms for the United Nations not to do this thing. It was, he said, "obscene." It is somethiing more today, for the furtiveness with which this obscenity first appeared among us has been replaced by a shameless openness.

There will be time enough to contemplate the harm this act will have done the United Nations. Historians will do that for us, and it is sufficient for the moment only to note one foreboding fact. A great evil has been loosed upon the world. The abomination of anti-Semitism—as this year's Nobel peace laureate, Andrei Sakharov, observed in Moscow just a few days ago—the abomination of anti-Semitism has been given the appearance of international sanction. The General Assembly today grants symbolic amnesty—and more—to the murderers of the 6 million European Jews. Evil enough in itself, but more ominous by far is the realization that now presses upon us—the realization that if there were no General Assembly, this could never have happened.

As this day will live in infamy, it behooves those who sought to avert it to declare their thoughts so that historians will know that we fought here, that we were not small in number—not this time—and that while we lost, we fought with full knowledge of what indeed would *be* lost.

Nor should any historian of the event, nor yet any who have participated in it, suppose that we have fought only as governments, as chancelleries, and on an issue well removed from the concerns of our respective peoples. Others will speak for their nations; I will speak for mine.

[12]A/10217 and Corr.1, annex, p. 3. [Footnote in original.]
[13]USUN Press Release 141, Nov. 10; text and subtitles from *Bulletin*, 73: 790-94.

In all our postwar history there has not been another issue which has brought forth such unanimity of American opinion.

The President of the United States has from the first been explicit: This must not happen. The Congress of the United States, in a measure unanimously adopted in the Senate and sponsored by 436 of 437 Representatives in the House, declared its utter opposition.[14]

Following only American Jews themselves, the American trade union movement was first to the fore in denouncing this infamous undertaking. Next, one after another, the great private institutions of American life pronounced anathema on this evil thing—and most particularly, the Christian churches have done so. Reminded that the United Nations was born in the struggle against just such abominations as we are committing today—the wartime alliance of the United Nations dates from 1942—the United Nations Association of the United States has for the first time in its history appealed directly to each of the 141 other delegations in New York not to do this unspeakable thing.

The proposition to be sanctioned by a resolution of the General Assembly of the United Nations is that "zionism is a form of racism and racial discrimination." Now, this is a lie. But as it is a lie which the United Nations has now declared to be a truth, the actual truth must be restated.

Term "Racism" Not Defined by United Nations

The very first point to be made is that the United Nations has declared Zionism to be racism—without ever having defined racism. "Sentence first—verdict afterwards," as the Queen of Hearts said. But this is not Wonderland, but a real world, where there are real consequences to folly and to venality.

Just on Friday, the President of the General Assembly, speaking on behalf of Luxembourg, warned not only of the trouble which would follow from the adoption of this resolution but of its essential irresponsibility—for, he noted, members have wholly different ideas as to what they are condemning. "It seems to me," he said, and to his lasting honor he said it when there was still time, "It seems to me that before a body like this takes a decision they should agree very clearly on what they are approving or condemning, and it takes more time."

Lest I be unclear, the United Nations has in fact on several occasions defined "racial discrimination." The definitions have been loose, but recognizable. It is "racism," incomparably the more serious charge—racial discrimination is a practice; racism is a

---

[14]S. Res. 288, 94th Cong., Oct. 28, 1975. The similar House resolution was not acted upon.

doctrine—which has never been defined. Indeed, the term has only recently appeared in U.N. General Assembly documents.

The one occasion on which we know its meaning to have been discussed was the 1644th meeting of the Third Committee on December 16, 1968, in connection with the report of the Secretary General on the status of the International Convention on the Elimination of All Forms of Racial Discrimination.[15]

On that occasion—to give some feeling for the intellectual precision with which the matter was being treated—the question arose as to what should be the relative positioning of the terms "racism" and "nazism" in a number of the preambular paragraphs. The distinguished delegate from Tunisia argued that "racism" should go first because nazism was merely a form of racism. Not so, said the no less distinguished delegate from the Union of Soviet Socialist Republics. For, he explained, nazism contained the main elements of racism within its ambit and should be mentioned first. This is to say that racism was merely a form of nazism.

The discussion wound to its weary and inconclusive end, and we are left with nothing to guide us, for even this one discussion of "racism" confined itself to word orders in preambular paragraphs and did not at all touch on the meaning of the words as such.

Still, one cannot but ponder the situation we have made for ourselves in the context of the Soviet statement on that not so distant occasion. If, as the distinguished delegate declared, racism is a form of nazism, and if, as this resolution declares, Zionism is a form of racism, then we have step by step taken ourselves to the point of proclaiming—the United Nations is solemnly proclaiming—that Zionism is a form of nazism.

What we have here is a lie—a political lie of a variety well known to the 20th century and scarcely exceeded in all that annal of untruth and outrage. The lie is that Zionism is a form of racism. The overwhelmingly clear truth is that it is not.

Racism Alien to Zionist Movement

The word "racism" is a creation of the English language, and relatively new to it. It is not, for instance, to be found in the Oxford English Dictionary. The term derives from relatively new doctrines—all of them discredited—concerning the human population of the world, to the effect that there are significant biological differences among clearly identifiable groups and that these differences establish, in effect, different levels of humanity. Racism, as defined by Webster's Third New International Dictionary, is "the assumption that . . . traits and capacities are determined by

[15] Adopted by General Assembly Resolution 2106 (XX), Dec. 21, 1965; not signed by the U.S.

biological race and that races differ decisively from one another."
It further involves "a belief in the inherent superiority of a particular race and its right to domination over others."

This meaning is clear. It is equally clear that this assumption, this belief, has always been altogether alien to the political and religious movement known as Zionism. As a strictly political movement, Zionism was established only in 1897, although there is a clearly legitimate sense in which its origins are indeed ancient. For example, many branches of Christianity have always held that, from the standpoint of the biblical prophets, Israel would be reborn one day. But the modern Zionist movement arose in Europe in the context of a general upsurge of national consciousness and aspiration that overtook most other people of Central and Eastern Europe after 1848 and that in time spread to all of Africa and Asia.

It was, to those persons of the Jewish religion, a Jewish form of what today is called a national liberation movement. Probably a majority of those persons who became active Zionists and sought to emigrate to Palestine were born within the confines of Czarist Russia, and it was only natural for Soviet Foreign Minister Andrei Gromyko to deplore, as he did in 1948, in the 299th meeting of the Security Council, the act by Israel's neighbors of "sending their troops into Palestine and carrying out military operations aimed"—in Mr. Gromyko's words—"at the suppression of the national liberation movement in Palestine."

Now, it was the singular nature—if I am not mistaken, it was the unique nature—of this national liberation movement that, in contrast with the movements that preceded it, those of that time, and those that have come since, it defined its members in terms not of birth, but of belief.

That is to say, it was not a movement of the Irish to free Ireland or of the Polish to free Poland, not a movement of Algerians to free Algeria nor of Indians to free India. It was not a movement of persons connected by historic membership in a genetic pool of the kind that enables us to speak loosely but not meaninglessly, say, of the Chinese people, nor yet of diverse groups occupying the same territory which enables us to speak of the American people with no greater indignity to truth.

To the contrary, Zionists defined themselves merely as Jews and declared to be Jewish anyone born of a Jewish mother or—and this is the absolutely crucial fact—anyone who converted to Judaism. Which is to say, in the terms of the International Convention on the Elimination of All Forms of Racial Discrimination, adopted by the 20th General Assembly, *anyone*—regardless of "race, colour, descent, or national or ethnic origin."

The State of Israel, which in time was the creation of the Zionist movement, has been extraordinary in nothing so much as the range of "racial stocks" from which it has drawn its citizenry. There are black Jews, brown Jews, white Jews, Jews from the Orient, and Jews from the West. Most such persons could be said to have been "born" Jews, just as most Presbyterians and most Hindus are "born" to their faith; but there are many Jews who are converts. With a consistency in the matter which surely attests to the importance of this issue to that religious and political culture, Israeli courts have held that a Jew who converts to another religion is no longer a Jew.

In the meantime the population of Israel also includes large numbers of non-Jews, among them Arabs of both the Moslem and Christian religions and Christians of other national origins. Many of these persons are citizens of Israel, and those who are not can become citizens by legal procedures very much like those which obtain in a typical nation of Western Europe.

Now, I should wish to be understood that I am here making one point, and one point only, which is that whatever else Zionism may be, it is not and cannot be "a form of racism." In logic, the State of Israel could be, or could become, many things—theoretically including many things undesirable—but it could not be and could not become racist unless it ceased to be Zionist.

Dangers to Cause of Human Rights

Indeed, the idea that Jews *are* a "race" was invented not by Jews, but by those who hated Jews. The idea of Jews as a race was invented by 19th-century anti-Semites such as Houston Stewart Chamberlain and Edouard Drumont, who saw that in an increasingly secular age, which is to say an age which made for fewer distinctions between people, the old religious grounds for anti-Semitism were losing force. New justifications were needed for excluding and persecuting Jews, and so the new idea of Jews as a race, rather than as a religion, was born. It was a contemptible idea at the beginning, and no civilized person would be associated with it. To think that it is an idea now endorsed by the United Nations is to reflect on what civilization has come to.

It is precisely a concern for civilization, for civilized values that are or should be precious to all mankind, that arouses us at this moment to such special passion. What we have at stake here is not merely the honor and the legitimacy of the State of Israel— although a challenge to the legitimacy of any member nation ought always to arouse the vigilance of all members of the United Nations. For a yet more important matter is at issue, which is the integrity of that whole body of moral and legal precepts which we know as human rights.

The terrible lie that has been told here today will have terrible consequences. Not only will people begin to say—indeed they have already begun to say—that the United Nations is a place where lies are told; but far more serious, grave, and perhaps irreparable harm will be done to the cause of human rights itself.

The harm will arise first because it will strip from racism the precise and abhorrent meaning that it still precariously holds today. How will the peoples of the world feel about racism, and about the need to struggle against it, when they are told that it is an idea so broad as to include the Jewish national liberation movement?

As this lie spreads, it will do harm in a second way. Many of the members of the United Nations owe their independence in no small part to the notion of human rights, as it has spread from the domestic sphere to the international sphere and exercised its influence over the old colonial powers. We are now coming into a time when that independence is likely to be threatened again. There will be new forces, some of them arising now, new prophets and new despots, who will justify their actions with the help of just such distortions of words as we have sanctioned here today.

Today we have drained the word "racism" of its meaning. Tomorrow, terms like "national self-determination" and "national honor" will be perverted in the same way to serve the purposes of conquest and exploitation. And when these claims begin to be made—as they already have begun to be made—it is the small nations of the world whose integrity will suffer. And how will the small nations of the world defend themselves, on what grounds will others be moved to defend and protect them, when the language of human rights, the only language by which the small can be defended, is no longer believed and no longer has a power of its own?

There is this danger, and then a final danger that is the most serious of all—which is that the damage we now do to the idea of human rights and the language of human rights could well be irreversible.

The idea of human rights as we know it today is not an idea which has always existed in human affairs. It is an idea which appeared at a specific time in the world and under very special circumstances. It appeared when European philosophers of the 17th century began to argue that man was a being whose existence was independent from that of the state, that he need join a political community only if he did not lose by that association more than he gained. From this very specific political philosophy stemmed the idea of political rights, of claims that the individual could justly make against the state; it was because the individual was seen as so separate from the state that he could make legitimate demands upon it.

That was the philosophy from which the idea of domestic and international rights sprang. But most of the world does not hold with that philosophy now. Most of the world believes in newer modes of political thought, in philosophies that do not accept the individual as distinct from and prior to the state, in philosophies that therefore do not provide any justification for the idea of human rights, and philosophies that have no words by which to explain their value. If we destroy the words that were given to us by past centuries, we will not have words to replace them, for philosophy today has no such words. But there are those of us who have not forsaken these older words, still so new to much of the world. Not forsaken them now, not here, not anywhere, not ever.

The United States of America declares that it does not acknowledge, it will not abide by, it will never acquiesce in, this infamous act.

38. THE RAMBOUILLET SUMMIT
(November 15-17, 1975)

[The usefulness of personal contact among the leaders of the Western democracies had often been demonstrated in recent years, not least in the resolution of economic issues that had sometimes festered for months and years at lower levels. Outstanding examples were the meetings between Presidents Nixon and Pompidou in the Azores in 1971, and between Presidents Ford and Giscard d'Estaing in Martinique in 1974.[1] But since most of the economic problems that faced the major industrialized nations were too complex to be successfully dealt with on a mere bilateral basis, it had also been natural to consider the possibility of holding a broader meeting or meetings, encompassing all or most of the interested heads of state or government.

The idea of a summit meeting dealing primarily with monetary issues had in fact been broached by President Giscard d'Estaing as early as May 1975—in part at least in hopes of winning broadened support for French ideas on international monetary reform, which conflicted significantly with those of the United States. Put forward officially at the time of the Helsinki conference in July, the idea was in due course accepted by the United States and other invited governments—on the understanding, however, that the agenda would be broadened in such a way as to embrace not only monetary affairs but all of the principal economic and financial issues of current concern. A lengthy preparatory process came to fruition in mid-November when the heads of state or government of France, West Germany, Italy, Japan, the United Kingdom, and the United States, accompanied by their Foreign and Finance Ministers, convened at the Château of Rambouillet near Paris for what they were to describe in a formal Declaration (**Document 58**) as ''a searching and productive exchange of views on the world

---

[1]*AFR, 1971*: 181, 604-7; same, *1974*: 558-61.

economic situation, on economic problems common to our countries, on their human, social and political implications, and on plans for resolving them.''

Immediate as well as longer-range problems of their interdependent economies had been on the participants' minds in the weeks that preceded this precedent-making encounter. Of most immediate concern had been the still lagging pace of recovery from the recent recession. Because recovery had progressed much faster in the United States than in most of the other industrialized countries, Washington had for months been under pressure to adopt a more expansionist policy designed to aid the recovery of its associates. American authorities, however, had remained exceedingly averse to taking such action lest they unchain a new round of inflation that would be damaging to all concerned. Discussion at Rambouillet, according to Secretary Kissinger's later account (**Document 59**), resulted in a better understanding of the American position and an abatement of the pressure on the United States to act against its better judgment.

In the longer range, the governments represented at Rambouillet continued to confront a host of issues in the field of trade and monetary reform, energy, and North-South relations, most of them already being worked on in more specialized groupings. Aside from a general resolve to invigorate the search for cooperative solutions, the main achievement at Rambouillet was the acceptance of a French-American compromise on the exchange rate regime in a reformed international monetary system—or, more crudely stated, the acceptance by France of the inevitability of floating exchange rates, and the abandonment of its longstanding campaign for a return to the system of fixed parities. An unpublished memorandum of understanding, initialed by the French and American financial representatives, established conditions for intervention to reduce erratic fluctuations in exchange rates, provided for more consultation and action by monetary authorities, and incorporated a draft of the pertinent article to be incorporated in the pending revision of the International Monetary Fund agreement.

At a technical level, this French-American accord—later approved by the other industrialized nations making up the Group of Ten[2]—would clear the way for an agreement on most features of the pending monetary reform at the meeting of the IMF Interim Committee that was to take place in Jamaica on January 7-8, 1976.[3] Another accomplishment of the Rambouillet meeting was a formal acknowledgment that the ''Tokyo Round'' of multilateral

[2]Group of Ten communiqué, Dec. 19, 1975, in *IMF Survey*, 1976:15-16.
[3]Interim Committee communiqué, Kingston, Jan. 8, 1976, in same: 18-19 and *Bulletin*, 74: 197-9.

trade negotiations, originally scheduled for conclusion in 1975, would fail to meet that deadline but might hopefully be completed in 1977. Possibly of even greater long-run significance, however, was a point made by President Ford in a subsequent report to Congress: "This meeting, and the accompanying bilateral talks I had with leaders of the major industrialized democracies, established a new spirit of cooperation and confidence stemming from a deeper understanding of our common destiny. They set the stage for our efforts to deal with a variety of specific international economic challenges facing us in 1976."[4]

(58) Meeting of Heads of State and Government at Rambouillet, France, November 15-17, 1975:. The Declaration of Rambouillet, issued at the conclusion of the meeting, November 17, 1975.[5]

The Heads of States and Governments of France, Federal Republic of Germany, Italy, Japan, the United Kingdom of Great Britain and Northern Ireland and the United States of America,[6] met in the Chateau de Rambouillet from 15th to 17th of November 1975, and agreed to declare as follows:

1. In these three days we held a searching and productive exchange of views on the world economic situation, on economic problems common to our countries, on their human, social and political implications, and on plans for resolving them.

2. We came together because of shared beliefs and shared responsibilities. We are each responsible for the government of an open, democratic society, dedicated to individual liberty and social advancement. Our success will strengthen, indeed is essential to democratic societies everywhere. We are each responsible for assuring the prosperity of a major industrial economy. The growth and stability of our economies will help the entire industrial world and developing countries to prosper.

3. To assure in a world of growing interdependence the success of the objectives set out in this declaration, we intend to play our own full part and strengthen our efforts for closer international cooperation and constructive dialogue among all countries,

[4]Message on the International Economic Report, Mar. 17, 1976, in *Presidential Documents*, 12: 440-41.

[5]Text from same, 11: 1292-4.

[6]Respectively President Valéry Giscard d'Estaing, Chancellor Helmut Schmidt, Prime Minister Aldo Moro, Prime Minister Takeo Miki, Prime Minister Harold Wilson, and President Gerald R. Ford.

transcending differences in stages of economic development, degrees of resource endowment and political and social systems.

4. The industrial democracies are determined to overcome high unemployment, continuing inflation and serious energy problems. The purpose of our meeting was to review our progress, identify more clearly the problems that we must overcome in the future, and to set a course that we will follow in the period ahead.

5. The most urgent task is to assure the recovery of our economies and to reduce the waste of human resources involved in unemployment. In consolidating the recovery it is essential to avoid unleashing additional inflationary forces which would threaten its success. The objective must be growth that is steady and lasting. In this way, consumer and business confidence will be restored.

6. We are confident that our present policies are compatible and complementary and that recovery is under way. Nevertheless, we recognize the need for vigilance and adaptability in our policies. We will not allow the recovery to falter. We will not accept another ouburst of inflation.

7. We are also concentrated on the need for new efforts in the areas of world trade, monetary matters and raw materials, including energy.

8. As domestic recovery and economic expansion proceed, we must seek to restore growth in the volume of world trade. Growth and price stability will be fostered by maintenance of an open trading system. In a period where pressures are developing for a return to protectionism, it is essential for the main trading nations to confirm their commitment to the principles of the OECD pledge[7] and to avoid resorting to measures by which they could try to solve their problems at the expense of others, with damaging consequences in the economic, social and political fields. There is a responsibility on all countries, especially those with strong balance of payments positions and on those with current deficits to pursue policies which will permit the expansion of world trade to their mutual advantage.

9. We believe that the multilateral trade negotiations should be accelerated. In accordance with the principles agreed in the Tokyo Declaration,[8] they should aim at achieving substantial tariff cuts, even eliminating tariffs in some areas, at significantly expanding agricultural trade and at reducing non-tariff measures. They should seek to achieve the maximum possible level of trade liberalization therefrom. We propose as our goal completion of the negotiations in 1977.

[7]Cf. Chapter 18 at note 16.
[8]*AFR, 1973*: 391-4.

10. We look to an orderly and fruitful increase in our economic relations with socialist countries as an important element in progress in détente, and in world economic growth.

11. We will also intensify our efforts to achieve a prompt conclusion of the negotiations concerning export credits.

12. With regard to monetary problems, we affirm our intention to work for greater stability. This involves efforts to restore greater stability in underlying economic and financial conditions in the world economy. At the same time, our monetary authorities will act to counter disorderly market conditions, or erratic fluctuations, in exchange rates. We welcome the rapprochement, reached at the request of many other countries, between the views of the U.S. and France on the need for stability that the reform of the international monetary system must promote. This rapprochement will facilitate agreement through the IMF at the next session of the Interim Committee in Jamaica on the outstanding issues of international monetary reform.

13. A co-operative relationship and improved understanding between the developing nations and the industrial world is fundamental to the prosperity of each. Sustained growth in our economies is necessary to growth in developing countries: and their growth contributes significantly to health in our own economies.

14. The present large deficits in the current accounts of the developing countries represent a critical problem for them and also for the rest of the world. This must be dealt with in a number of complementary ways. Recent proposals in several international meetings have already improved the atmosphere of the discussion between developed and developing countries.[9] But early practical action is needed to assist the developing countries. Accordingly, we will play our part, through the IMF and other appropriate international fora, in making urgent improvements in international arrangements for the stabilization of the export earnings of developing countries and in measures to assist them in financing their deficits. In this context, priority should be given to the poorest developing countries.

15. World economic growth is clearly linked to the increasing availability of energy sources. We are determined to secure for our economies the energy sources needed for their growth. Our common interests require that we continue to cooperate in order to reduce our dependence on imported energy through conservation and the development of alternative sources. Through these measures as well as international cooperation between producer and consumer countries, responding to the long term interests of

[9]Cf. Chapter 30.

both, we shall spare no effort in order to ensure more balanced conditions and a harmonious and steady development in the world energy market.

16. We welcome the convening of the Conference on International Economic Co-operation scheduled for December 16.[10] We will conduct this dialogue in a positive spirit to assure that the interests of all concerned are protected and advanced. We believe that industrialized and developing countries alike have a critical stake in the future success of the world economy and in the cooperative political relationships on which it must be based.

17. We intend to intensify our cooperation on all these problems in the framework of existing institutions as well as in all the relevant international organizations.

(59) Significance of the Rambouillet Summit: Comments by Secretary of State Kissinger and Secretary of the Treasury Simon, November 17, 1975.[11]

(Excerpts)

SECRETARY KISSINGER. The overall purpose of the meeting was to bring together the leaders of the industrial democracies at a time when their economies were in various states of recession.

When it was proposed, it was suggested that these leaders ought to meet to give confidence to their peoples and to convey to their peoples the sense that they were in control of their future and were not simply waiting for blind forces to play themselves out.

So, we thought it was a matter of great importance, one, because for 2 years we have been maintaining that the political and economic cohesion of the industrial democracies was central to the structure of the non-Communist world, secondly, because we believed that the interdependence of these economies makes isolated solutions impossible, and, thirdly, because we believed that there were a number of concrete issues on which work had to begin and in which common action was important.

We spent a great amount of effort within our Government to prepare for this meeting, and there are always many stories when there are disagreements in the Government, but this has been an unusual occasion, an unusual way in which all the departments working together worked out common positions, common philosophies, and achieved the basic proposals that were put before the other leaders.

[10]Cf. Chapter 43.
[11]Text from *Presidential Documents*, 11: 1295-1300. The comments were made in a question-and-answer session with a pool of four reporters on board Air Force One, the presidential aircraft.

When this conference was called, I think it is safe to say that some of our friends wanted to use it as an occasion to blame us or at least to imply that their economic difficulties could be solved primarily by American efforts, and others may have had the idea that especially in the monetary field it could be used to bring about rapid solutions in which the heads of government overruled the long negotiations that had gone on.

But as the preparation developed, I think a more sober spirit grew also, and one of our big themes was that economic recovery was meaningless if it started another spurt of inflation and that what we had to aim for was stable growth.

The second theme we had to get across is that the American economy was doing well and that, therefore, the concerns of other countries that our recovery was too slow for their own was unjustified.

Thirdly, we had in a number of areas specific ideas on how the interdependence of these countries could be carried out in the field of trade, in the field of economic relations with the socialist countries, in the field of monetary affairs, in the field of energy, and in the field of development.[12]

The discussions took place in a really unusually harmonious spirit. The fears which some of us had that the others would bring pressure on us to accelerate what we think is a well-conceived economic program proved unfounded, and after the President made his extensive intervention of the first day, explaining our economic program, the other countries substantially accepted this and indeed seemed to be appreciative of it.

I think this was a very important event because it meant that they had more confidence that in looking ahead to their own future they could count on steady growth in the United States, and since everybody agreed that a substantial percentage of the recession was psychological, I had the sense that a consensus emerged that this confidence that developed in our ability to handle the economic problems was a very major factor.

In fact, the confidence of the leaders in this process was shown by the fact that they would talk about general principles and then turned over the drafting to either ministers or experts and that the leaders only spent about an hour on the declaration. At first, we didn't want any declaration because we were afraid we would spend our whole time drafting it. And it didn't turn out that way, and that was important.

In the field of trade, there was an agreement, first, that the negotiations on the multilateral trade negotiations should be completed next year, secondly, a commitment by all of the countries

---

[12]Cf. Kissinger address, Pittsburgh, Nov. 11, in *Bulletin*, 73: 757-64.

there to bring about a substantial reduction of trade barriers, including in the agricultural field, and no attempt to hide behind community mandates or other obstacles.

There was also an agreement to accelerate or to foster the negotiations concerning export credits. Bill [Simon] will talk about the agreements in the monetary field which put an end to a debate of years about the nature of the floating system and the relation between floating and stability which should end in January in an agreement that should at least put the field of international finance on a more stable basis than it has been in a long time.

In the field of energy, there has been an agreement to cooperate closely or actively on the alternative sources and on conservation, and I believe this will show up in the program of the International Energy Agency which is in the process of being negotiated and which we hope to conclude by December 15.[13]

In the field of development, we identified the balance-of-payments deficits of the developing countries or their current account deficits as one of the major problems on which we would work jointly, but we also pointed out that there is a close relationship between that and the action that is taken with respect to oil prices. So, we believe that the consuming countries are in an excellent position for the beginning of the talks on international economic cooperation that are beginning in the middle of December. And we agreed to work together in all existing institutions.

To sum up, this unusual meeting of the heads of government of the countries that between them produce 70 percent of the world trade represented a commitment to the conception that our economic problems were long-term, that there were no quick fixes to them, that they required a steady cooperative effort, that their political relationship affected their economic relationship, and that their economic relationship in turn assisted their political cooperation.

And so, the free countries vindicated the concept of their interdependence and laid out a program and a method for cooperation which we hope will accelerate the recovery of all the peoples as well as their cooperation with the less-developed countries for the benefit of everybody.

But I think Bill ought to explain the monetary agreement because that is perhaps the single-most significant thing that happened there.

---

[13] The Governing Board of the International Energy Agency decided on Jan. 30, 1976 to adopt a program of long-term cooperation in the field of energy (*Bulletin*, 74: 261-2).

SECRETARY SIMON. There is no doubt that it was a significant agreement reached between the French and the United States which, I believe and most everyone believes, is going to pave the way for agreement at the Interim Committee on Overall Monetary Reform in January. I think that the agreements that we have reached are a fair and balanced compromise. Neither side won nor neither side lost.

Each has protected its very critical national interests in a spirit of cooperation. We have sought to bring a convergence of views, and this is important. What we are trying to do is build and expand on these areas of convergence. And as we succeed in doing this, the whole world community at large is going to benefit from this.

Now I think that the disparity of views of the past few years between the French and the United States in particular on various amendments to the articles of agreement have obscured the deep mutuality of interest to return to stable economic and financial conditions in the world and more orderly and stable exchange rates, and that is very significant because this instability that we have had contributed as well as resulted from tremendous institutional financial strains. Also, the instability created great problems for many of the countries in the world in taking care of the erratic price movements and setting economic policies and restoring stable growth in their own economies.

Now having said this, because one must look at the fundamental cause of the problem before we can begin to look for any of the solutions, which is important, it has been clear that the French and the United States share some fundamental agreements on the monetary system, there is no doubt about that. We both agree that the diversity of financial arrangements, the floating system, if you will, has served us well. Under the present circumstances, it is actually necessary to take care of the stresses and the strains that have been brought about by the severe inflation, recession, and, of course, the extraordinary oil increase.

So, having identified the causes, we then must set about in curing the fundamental problems of this economic instability, and, therefore, the communique, as it said, dealt with two aspects of the monetary issue: one, the operational and, two, the reform of the system.

On the operational side we have reached an understanding that to achieve durable and meaningful stability in the underlying economic and financial conditions, we have to provide for mutually cooperative and conciliatory policies among ourselves, but that national domestic economic policies must indeed be compatible. The world economy has suffered from all of the ills that I have spoken about and the underlying problem remains with the severe inflation and, of course, the recession which was caused by this inflation.

On exchange markets, we are going to deal with erratic movements in exchange rates which, of course, create again an instability. Erratic movements can be defined as movements that have no underlying economic reason. Ours is not an attempt to peg any of the currency rates at artificial levels, but there are erratic movements in financial markets on occasion that are not directly attributable to fundamental economic events, and at this point intervention policies will become mutually cooperative and compatible to smooth out these unstable periods.

Q. How is this stability going to be brought about, that is, how is this operation going to work?

SECRETARY SIMON. Well, in two ways. One, I think a session that was heavily devoted, as Secretary Kissinger said, to the economic aspects of the world's problems today, the needed policies—cooperative as well as individual—that are required for a return to stable economic and financial conditions are at the foundation of the answer to your question.

As far as the consultations and the mechanisms that are going to be established for smoothing out, there is going to be greatly expanded consultative mechanisms throughout the world done on a more orderly basis, on a more daily basis, if you will, by both the central banks, of course, who do this today, as well as the deputies to the Finance Ministers and the Finance Ministers themselves. There will be more constructive meetings of the Finance Ministers to deal specifically with this issue.

Q. Will there be a standing committee of some kind to advise intervention at a given point?

SECRETARY SIMON. No, the makeup of this committee has not been set yet, but we have many standing committees. We have the Interim Committee, which is the old Group of Twenty and the Group of Ten which will meet and direct itself right to this issue in December in Paris.

Q. The mechanism has not been set up yet—I mean the mechanism has not been designed as to how this consultative process will go forward?

SECRETARY SIMON. The mechanism has been designed in the Memorandum of Understanding that the French and the United

States initialed today and that the other Ministers who attended this session and were briefed fully on this are in general agreement, but until we bring all of the interested and affected parties together, we cannot say that this is going to be totally acceptable, although I believe it will be.

SECRETARY KISSINGER. It is safe to say that there will be a much expanded discussion or consultation among the Finance Ministers and their deputies as a result of this.

Q. Mr. Secretary, as long as we have still got some videotape left, let me ask you in realistic terms what you think this conference means to the average American. Does it mean more jobs or lower prices, and if so, how?

SECRETARY KISSINGER. Well, if this conference contributes to an acceleration of economic recovery worldwide, which it is intended to do, if it contributes to a lowering of trade barriers, as it is intended to do, and to greater financial stability, then it will mean more jobs, perhaps lower prices, better control over inflation, and a degree of cooperation among the industrialized nations that will benefit every American.

Q. When is this millennium going to come about? How fast will this process take effect?

SECRETARY KISSINGER. We have made clear that it is a long-term process, and we are not ever going to be able to say that on the next day a dramatic change occurred, but I think that the hopeful processes that are already going on can be accelerated by the results that occurred here. The major theme of this meeting was that we have got a long-term problem, that we are not trying to make quick fixes, but that we can get a stable, steady growth on the long-term basis.

* * *

Q. Mr. Secretary, on the basis of your Pittsburgh speech and some other indications, I think some of us had the idea that the American delegation went to Rambouillet hoping that out of this would evolve some continuing machinery for consultation, and the communique speaks only of using the existing machinery. Did we abandon some idea here?

SECRETARY KISSINGER. You have the machinery that was set up under the monetary arrangements in which the Finance Ministers will be in almost daily contact, and there are many other organizations. There was an agreement that the governments concerned would work cooperatively on all of these problems, and so there was no formal machinery set up except the one that grows out of the monetary group. And since the monetary arrangement is exactly the group we envisage to begin with, there wasn't any sense of setting up another one with a different hat.

Q. Was there any talk about another meeting of this sort a year from now?

SECRETARY KISSINGER. Yes, there was talk of another meeting, and the leaders will stay in touch with each other depending on conditions. If the conditions get critical, they will meet earlier. If conditions take the form that are now predicted, then they will meet some time during the course of the next year—within a year, roughly.[14]

* * *

[14]Heads of state and government of the Rambouillet participants and Canada met at Dorado Beach, Puerto Rico, on June 27-28, 1976. Their Joint Declaration appears in *Presidential Documents*, 12: 1091-4 (*Bulletin*, 75: 121-3).

39. "TO WHOM IT MAY CONCERN"
(Detroit, November 24, 1975)

[The success of the Rambouillet summit occurred at a moment when the United States was making few if any gains on other foreign policy fronts. Its discomfiture over the anti-Zionist resolution was maintained by other actions of the "third world"-Communist majority as the General Assembly session entered its closing weeks.[1] Continuing unrest in Portugal and Italy was causing grave uneasiness about the future of those two NATO countries.[2] At home, support for détente with the Soviet Union continued to erode as it became evident that there would be no SALT agreement, and no Brezhnev visit, before the year's end.

In the meantime, the Washington atmosphere had been transformed by the President's surprise announcement on November 3, 1975—approximately fifteen months after his assumption of office, and twelve months before the coming presidential election—of a major shakeup in his official family. Its most conspicuous victim was Defense Secretary Schlesinger, whose pessimistic assessment of East-West military trends was widely thought to have embarrassed the President and encouraged critics of the administration's détente policy. Dr. Schlesinger, it was now disclosed, was surrendering the leadership of the Defense Department to presidential assistant Donald Rumsfeld, a former Ambassador to NATO. Balancing this action to some degree was an apparent reduction in the responsibilities of Secretary of State Kissinger, regarded by many as the very incarnation of détente, whose concurrent functions as Assistant to the President for National Security Affairs were now taken over by his deputy, Brent Scowcroft. Other changes announced at the same time included the designation of George Bush, head of the U.S. Liaison Office in Peking, to succeed William E. Colby as

[1]Cf. Chapter 44.
[2]Cf. Chapter 42.

Director of Central Intelligence, and of Elliot L. Richardson, currently Ambassador to the United Kingdom, to succeed Rogers C.B. Morton as Secretary of Commerce.

The precise intent of these changes—designed, in President Ford's words, to "strengthen the Administration in the important area of national security affairs"—was difficult to pin down, particularly as they affected the hitherto impregnable status of Secretary Kissinger. Among their obvious effects, however, would be a heightened awareness that every administration move from this time forward would be carefully assessed in terms of its potential influence on the 1976 election.

On Capitol Hill, meanwhile, the administration not only found itself involved in a running controversy with the House and Senate intelligence committees[3] but continued to suffer one minor defeat after another as Congress worked its way through the annual defense and foreign affairs legislation. In its annual appropriation of funds for military construction, for instance, Congress just at this time decided to yield to administration pressure by providing $13.8 million to develop military support facilities on the British Indian Ocean island of Diego Garcia, but to prevent prompt use of the funds by stipulating that most of the money would remain unavailable until April 15, 1976.[4] The object of this restriction, which obviously reflected deep uncertainty about the meaning of contemporary events in the Indian Ocean area, was to reduce the danger of a U.S.-Soviet arms race in that part of the world and facilitate the negotiation of a regional arms restraint agreement. Whether it would in fact have such an effect was a matter of varying opinions.

Americans who leaned to a pessimistic view of Soviet intentions had been impressed by the evidence that far from seeking a hands-off arrangement in the Indian Ocean, the U.S.S.R. had already gained a foothold there with the development of a substantial military installation at Berbera, Somalia. By the autumn of 1975, moreover, most observers were even more dismayed by the increasingly open intervention of the U.S.S.R.—and Cuba—in the continuing civil conflict in Angola. That country's formal accession to independence on November 11 had little immediate effect upon the progress of the ongoing, three-way internal struggle among rival liberation movements, although the Luanda-based Popular Movement (MPLA), which benefited from substantial Soviet and Cuban support, seemed gradually to be gaining an edge over its rivals in

[3]Cf. Introduction at notes 7-9.
[4]Sec. 112, Military Construction Appropriation Act, 1976 (Public Law 94-138, Nov. 28, 1975).

the northern and southern sectors despite the limited assistance being accorded the latter by the United States, South Africa, and others. (Here again, congressional misgivings had hampered U.S. attempts to funnel assistance to the National Front for the Liberation of Angola [FNLA], the principal resistance movement in the north, by way of Zaïre.)[5]

A warning to Moscow and Havana to refrain from actions that could undermine the foundations of détente was the most prominent feature of an address on "what is right with America's foreign policy" that Secretary Kissinger delivered at a dinner sponsored by the Economic Club of Detroit and other local organizations on November 24 (**Document 60**). The U.S.S.R. and Cuba were not, however, the only parties addressed in the course of Dr. Kissinger's exposition, which included, among other things, a renewed complaint about "the rapid and exorbitant rise in energy prices" as well as a strong reaffirmation of America's interest in the Asian regions he would soon be visiting with President Ford.[6] Still another prominent feature of this omnibus presentation was an admonition to Americans, in Congress and out, to lay aside the various forms of neurotic behavior born of the recent past and join in meeting their responsibility "to help shape a national policy in a positive and cooperative spirit . . . to exercise creative leadership in a moment of uncertainty, in a world that cries out for inspiration."]

(60) "Building an Enduring Foreign Policy": Address by Secretary of State Kissinger before a dinner meeting cosponsored by the Economic Club of Detroit, November 24, 1975.[7]

* * *

I come before you tonight to talk about what is right with America's foreign policy.

This nation, no matter how much some may cast doubt on it, is still seen as the land of hope by all the millions around the world who cherish freedom, the dignity of man, and peace. Without us there can be no security. Without us there can be no hope for progress.

America has been true to its responsibility. And I am here to say that it will remain so.

Out of the ashes of World War II, we and our allies built a new world. We had learned from bitter experience that America's safety

[5]For details cf. Chapter 45.
[6]Cf. Chapter 40.
[7]Department of State Press Release 578, Nov. 24; text and titles from *Bulletin*, 73: 841-50 (introductory pleasantries omitted).

and world peace, America's prosperity and the world economy, were inextricably linked.

In this spirit the United States promoted the economic and political recovery of Western Europe and Japan. We strengthened our defense and forged our first peacetime alliances; they have preserved the global balance of power for a generation. We pioneered in arms control so that the specter of global cataclysm might never become a reality. We and our partners built a cooperative global economic system so that growth, prosperity, and development could be the common heritage of mankind. We have mediated conflicts and helped settle problems from the Middle East to Berlin. The technological and managerial genius of this country has been the driving force of global change; our science and communications have circled the planet and stretched to the moon and beyond. The American people have reached out with generosity to their fellow men afflicted by disease, hunger, deprivation, natural disaster, war, and oppression. More than any other nation, we have taken in immigrants and refugees, fed the starving, and educated the youth of other lands. We owe the world no apology for what we have done. We have much to be proud of.

And a generation after World War II, with conditions radically altered and the postwar period of international relations at an end—partially as a result of the success of previous policies—the United States successfully adapted its foreign policy to a new era. At the beginning of this decade we faced a number of urgent tasks:

The military balance was being altered by the growth of the Soviet nuclear arsenal and the acceleration of weapons technology.

We were bogged down in a war that we would not win and seemingly could not end.

For 20 years we had isolated ourselves from China; in other words, from one-quarter of the human race.

Our relations with the Soviet Union were characterized by constant tension and confrontation: on the access routes to Berlin, in the Middle East, and in the Caribbean.

Diplomatic relations with most Arab states were broken, and progress toward peace in the Middle East was stalemated.

The new strength and vitality of Europe and Japan required major adjustments in the practices and responsibilities of the previous two decades.

We have come a long way in the first half of this decade.

American foreign policy has been transformed:

We brought peace to our nation for the first time in over a decade and a half.

We have ended our isolation from China and opened a growing relationship with the world's most populous nation.

U.S.-Soviet relations have entered a new period. In place of continual crises there are continuing negotiations—on arms control, economic relations, and international issues—which give both sides a stake in peace and have lessened the chances that great-power confrontation will lead to nuclear Armageddon.

In the Middle East we have restored diplomatic relations with all of the key countries of the Arab world. We have helped to move the area from stagnation to hope. Three major agreements between Israel and its Arab neighbors have opened the path to peace, a path on which we are determined to persevere.

Our relations with Europe and Japan have been given new balance and impetus; as the recent economic summit demonstrated, they have never been better.

Above all, not only our country but the world is at peace. For the first time since the end of World War II, no nation anywhere is engaged in military conflict with another.

This is the true record of our foreign policy—not the debates, the innuendoes, and political wrangling that so often form the headlines of the day. It is the end result of the trips, the meetings, the summits, the agreements, the setbacks, and the achievements of the everyday conduct of foreign affairs. These are the building blocks of a dream all Americans share: the vision of a peaceful, just, humane, and progressive world.

We have had our disappointments, and we have made our mistakes. After the bitter experience of Viet-Nam, America has learned that it does not possess the power to right every wrong or to solve every problem. We know that our influence is finite, though the demands upon it and the injustices of the world often seem infinite. And we understand that America, like all human institutions, is fallible.

But the vast majority of Americans remain convinced—as your government is—that if we do not resist aggression, if we do not work for a better world economy, if we do not promote liberty and justice, no nation will do it for us, at least no nation that shares our values.

I want to speak tonight about the broader vision of a lasting peace and how America is needed to turn that vision into a reality.

America and Global Peace

The allied statesmen who built the postwar international order would not recognize the international landscape we see today. The evolution that has taken place over 30 years has transformed the environment in which America lives. The world of the last quarter of the 20th century will be vastly different from that to which we have grown accustomed—but it is a world that we must help to shape.

These are the broad tasks of our foreign policy:

In an age of continuing peril and exploding technology, we must maintain and improve our national defense. In the aftermath of Viet-Nam, we have strengthened and modernized our military forces. This process will continue. We know that peace requires an equilibrium of power, and this government will maintain it. No nation can remain great if it leaves its safety to the mercy or the good will of others. Any realistic hope of better relations with the Communist powers—and there is such hope—depends on a strong America which leaves other countries no realistic course except restraint and cooperation. So long as potential adversaries continue to expand and improve their forces, we will maintain a modern defense that cannot be challenged.

We will place our priority on our alliances with the great industrial democracies of the Atlantic community and Japan. In the new era, the industrial democracies have found that security involves more than common defense. We joined together out of fear; but we can stay united only if we find deeper and more positive common purposes. The moral unity of the democracies, in an era when their values are a minority in the world and buffeted by difficulties at home, is one of our greatest resources. A sense of solidarity in a turbulent world can help all of our peoples recover the confidence that their societies are vital, that they are the masters of their destinies, that they are not subject to blind forces beyond their control.

This is why the United States attaches so much importance to the economic summit just concluded in France. The agreement to cooperate in economic policy, energy, and development, the major progress made on monetary questions, could usher in a new era of unity and confidence among the industrial democracies. We will never forget that our most important relationships are with those nations which share our principles, our way of life, and our future.

We strongly support the words of the Declaration of Rambouillet[8] agreed to by President Ford and the leaders of Britain, France, Italy, Japan, and Germany:

We came together because of shared beliefs and shared responsibilities. We are each responsible for the government of an open, democratic society, dedicated to individual liberty and social advancement. Our success will strengthen, indeed is essential to democratic societies everywhere.

We will strive to transform the relationship with the major Communist powers. Foreign policy must be based on reality, not rhetoric. And today's reality is that we live in a world of nuclear equality. This has been imposed by technology; it could not have been prevented; it cannot be ignored or reversed by unilateral decision. It means that we must manage a fundamental conflict of values in the shadow of nuclear holocaust; we are striving to preserve peace while defending our essential principles and interest.

At the same time, the Communist monolith of a generation ago has fragmented into bitter rivalries, and many Communist countries have turned to the West for more constructive bilateral relationships. This provides the opportunity for a careful policy of relaxation of tensions. Future generations would not understand it if partisan controversy caused us to forget that in the nuclear age the relaxation of tensions is a moral imperative as well as a practical necessity. We will spare no effort in building habits of restraint and moderation among the superpowers.

But the easing of tensions cannot endure if we relax our vigilance. We must understand the need for both defense *and* relaxation of tension, both firm action in crises *and* willingness to resolve problems on a realistic and fair basis. We must be prepared for either course; the choice rests with our adversaries.

We cannot ignore, for example, the substantial Soviet buildup of weapons in Angola, which has introduced great-power rivalry into Africa for the first time in 15 years. This Soviet involvement is resented by African nations most of all. But the United States cannot be indifferent while an outside power embarks upon an interventionist policy—so distant from its homeland and so removed from traditional Russian interests. The Soviet Union still has an opportunity for a policy of restraint which permits Angolans to resolve their own differences without outside intervention. We would be glad to cooperate in such a course. But time is running out; continuation of an interventionist policy must inevitably threaten other relationships.

[8]Chapter 38, Document 58.

Nor can we ignore the thousands of Cubans sent into an African conflict. In recent months the United States has demonstrated, by deed as well as word, its readiness to improve relations with Cuba. We have cooperated with steps to ease the inter-American boycott against Cuba and to restore a more normal relationship between the nations of the Americas and Cuba.[9] But let there be no illusions: a policy of conciliation will not survive Cuban meddling in Puerto Rico or Cuban armed intervention in the affairs of other nations struggling to decide their own fate.

To Cuba, as to other nations with whom our relations have been strained, I say this: the United States has no higher goal than to ease the conflicts that have torn the globe for nearly a generation. We will be flexible and cooperative in settling conflicts. But we will never permit détente to turn into a subterfuge for unilateral advantage. The policy of relaxation of tensions is designed to promote peace, not surrender; we will be flexible, but we shall insist on reciprocity and restraint.

We shall work to shape a prosperous and equitable economy. The productivity and economic strength of this country is one of our greatest assets. We have used it to help consolidate the vitality of the industrial democracies, to stabilize political relations with potential adversaries, and to fashion new ties with the developing countries.

The division of the planet between North and South, industrial and developing, is now becoming as pressing an issue as the division between East and West. Yet our economies are interdependent, and neither North nor South can long accept growing division without paying a costly and unnecessary price. International order and a thriving world economy can only be built on the basis of cooperation; economic warfare will mean decline for everyone, but most of all for the developing world. Therefore, at the U.N. General Assembly special session in September[10] the United States put forward a practical program of collaborative endeavor on energy, food, trade, raw materials, and the needs of the poorest.

We will continue our efforts on all these fronts.

Cooperative solutions are our objective; but we will not accept the proposition that any group of nations, no matter what its temporary economic power, can exercise its strength arbitrarily to the detriment of the world economic system. The economies of the industrialized nations have been severely shaken by the rapid and exorbitant rise in energy prices; the balance of payments and development programs of the poorer countries have been undermined to a

---

[9] Cf. Chapter 24.
[10] Chapter 30.

point that no conceivable aid program could compensate.

International peace and stability now clearly require an international economic system that embraces the aspirations and needs of *all* nations. The United States will come to next month's Conference on International Economic Cooperation,[11] the consumer-producer conference, with every intention to help find cooperative arrangements just to all. But we cannot accept indefinitely placing our economy at the mercy of decisions made far away or being asked to redress hardships and meet deficits caused by the actions of others.

The Asian Dimension

Let me now discuss in some detail one part of the world of particular interest to all Americans: the continent of Asia.

Next week President Ford will travel to Asia to reaffirm our stake in that vast region's future and to strengthen important bilateral ties.

The United States is a Pacific power. Our history has been inextricably linked to Asia. No region is of greater importance to us. None is more dynamic. None merits more America's enduring interest and purpose.

The security interests of all the great world powers intersect in Asia. Japan, China, the Soviet Union, Western Europe, and the United States have important stakes in the region; all would be affected by any major conflict there. It is an area vast in population, rich in culture, and abundant in resources. The United States has been involved in three long and costly Asian wars in the past generation. We have learned, at painful cost, that equilibrium in Asia is essential to our own peace and safety and that no stable order in that region can be maintained without our active participation.

Through much of the postwar period, America engaged itself deeply in Asia to build up friendly nations and to contain Communist expansion. American policy achieved major and lasting successes: the emergence of a prosperous and democratic Japan in close alliance with us, the defeat of aggression in Korea, the continued independence and growing dynamism of the many small friendly nations in the region.

But by the late 1960's our policies needed to adjust to new realities. We were too directly committed militarily. At times America acted as if its stake in its allies' security was greater than their own.

Thus, throughout the first half of this decade we have sought to fashion a new Asian policy, a policy that gradually reduced our

[11]Chapter 43.

military presence and aimed instead at augmenting the strength and vitality of our allies. We sought to stabilize the region by fashioning a balance among the major powers, bringing our commitments into line with our interests.

American policy has had several basic objectives:

—To preserve the sovereignty and independence of our friends in Asia;

—To consolidate our alliance with Japan by giving our most important Asian ally a greater role and equal partnership;

—To open the door to constructive ties with the People's Republic of China;

—To reduce tensions and promote political solutions to Asian regional conflicts; and

—To encourage self-help and regional cooperation among smaller allies.

On all these fronts much progress has been made in the last few years. Our relations with both adversaries and friends have markedly improved. We have extended the range of our diplomacy without reneging on our commitments to our allies. We have adjusted our military posture to maintain a balance in Asia in the face of changing strategic requirements and political trends. We have expanded our economic relations in many countries.

Most importantly, the structure of Asian peace policy has proven strong enough to withstand the tragedy in Indochina. There was widespread initial apprehension that it might signal—or precipitate—a general American retreat from Asia and even from global responsibilities. Our policy since then has greatly eased those fears.

It is as clear as ever that no serious effort to resolve major problems in Asia can succeed without America's participation. The future of Japan and our other allies, the easing of tensions with potential adversaries, the problem of peace in Korea, the continuing independence of the nations of Southeast Asia—all depend significantly on a strong and responsible American policy.

This is why President Ford visited Japan and Korea a year ago on his first overseas trip.[12] This is why he will leave for Asia again at the end of this week to visit the People's Republic of China, the Philippines, and Indonesia.[13]

For the future we have set ourselves the following tasks:

We will maintain a continuing strong role in Asia. We know that military power alone will not guarantee security. National cohesion

[12] *AFR, 1974*: 491-500.
[13] Chapter 40.

and social justice are essential for effective resistance against subversion or external attack. We know, too, that nationalism and self-reliance are the dominant trends in the region. But foreign policy begins with security, and a military balance remains fundamental to peace and the easing of tension. Given Asia's importance to our security and well-being, we owe it to ourselves and to those whose future depends on us to preserve a firm and balanced military posture in the Pacific.

We will continue to strengthen our partnership with Japan. Japan is our principal Asian ally and largest overseas trading partner; Japan's participation is essential to international efforts to promote economic recovery. Our hopes for a peaceful and prosperous Asia depend in large part on Japan's creative collaboration on many international issues. Japan's experiment in political leadership without the attributes of military power is anchored in turn upon our security treaty, which threatens no one and is widely recognized as a pillar of regional stability.

In short, we regard Japan not as an occasional or temporary ally, but as a permanent friend.

In the early 1970's, in response to Japan's growing economic strength and some bilateral strains, we went through a period of adjustment in our relations. There were frictions, some avoidable by more thoughtful U.S. actions. But these tensions have been overcome by devoted effort on both sides. Today our relations are the best they have been in 30 years. We face no serious bilateral problems. We are collaborating on a vast agenda: to advance the prosperity of the industrial democracies, to ease tensions with the Communist countries, and to extend the new era of cooperation to the members of the less developed world.

Our bilateral relationship, which depends so much upon intangibles of conduct and understanding, has acquired a deeper quality. There have been important cultural exchanges, which have enhanced our sensitivity to each other's national style and values. The first visit by an American President to Japan last fall and the historic visit of the Emperor and the Empress to the United States[14]—and the warm reception that each people extended to the other's leader—demonstrated the extraordinary depth and strength of this friendship.

We do not propose to rest on the accomplishments of the past.

—We will preserve the Treaty of Mutual Cooperation and Security[15] while continuing to adapt its practical arrangements

[14]Cf. note 6 to Chapter 26.
[15]Cf. note 10 to Chapter 26.

to the changing military and political environment.

—We will strengthen our political consultation, in the full realization that we will not always pursue identical policies but that we have it in our power to assure compatible approaches and full understanding of occasional disagreements.

—We will harmonize even more closely our national policies to combat recession and promote economic expansion.

—We will continue to deepen the cultural dimension of our ties, which strengthens the bonds between our peoples.

In all our dealings we intend to honor a higher standard of concern and consultation than normally obtains even between allies—one that reflects the profound quality of our partnership.

We shall continue to advance our relationship with the People's Republic of China. For a generation our two great countries were separated by a gulf of suspicion and hostility. The reestablishment of ties in recent years has had a significance far beyond its impact on our two countries; it has transformed the international landscape.

There have long existed attachments of sentiment and high regard between the Chinese and American peoples, which we have never ceased to value. But the United States and the People's Republic of China came together again after two decades because of necessity. It was mutual interests that impelled us both—without illusions—to launch a new beginning. These mutual interests continue. They can be the foundation of a durable, growing relationship.

We and the People's Republic of China have parallel concerns that the world be free from domination by military force or intimidation—what our many joint communiques have termed "hegemony." We have affirmed that neither of our two countries should seek hegemony and that each would oppose the attempts of others to do so. Our commitment to this policy will not change. The United States will continue to resist expansionism as we have throughout the entire postwar period. But we will also avoid needless confrontations. We will not be swayed from our effort to improve relations with potential adversaries and to build a more stable international environment.

The United States and China have also agreed to pursue the normalization of our relations. The United States remains dedicated to the principles of the Shanghai communique.[16] We do not challenge the principle of one China—a principle that is maintained by Chinese on both sides of the Taiwan Strait. While time may yet be

[16]*AFR, 1972*: 307-11.

required to resolve our remaining differences on this issue, the direction of our policy is clear.

Since we lack the full range of diplomatic links with the People's Republic of China, and since so much depends on our mutual perceptions of the world scene, exchanges of views on the international scene between the President and the leaders of China are essential and assume special significance.

President Ford's visit to China next week will be the first contact between a U.S. President and Chinese leaders in nearly four years. We can expect the talks to be marked by the scope and the directness which have marked our previous encounters and which best serve leaders whose societies are different but whose policies are rooted in realism.

Disagreements in ideology and national interests exist; there will be no attempt to hide them. It is inevitable, therefore, that each side will determine its own policies according to its own situation and perception of its national interest; these are not subject to the instruction of the other. Both of us are self-reliant; both of us understand the difference between rhetoric and action, between tactics and basic strategy.

This spirit of candor and mutual respect has infused our new relationship with the People's Republic of China from its beginnings over four years ago. On this basis we are prepared to make our relationship an enduring and constructive feature of the world scene.

We shall continue to strive to reduce tensions and promote more durable arrangements for peace on the Korean Peninsula. An atmosphere of confrontation, regrettably, persists on the Korean Peninsula. The United States has a major stake in maintaining the peace and security of the Republic of Korea. American forces are still stationed there in keeping with our Mutual Defense Treaty with the Republic of Korea.[17] Our commitment to South Korea rests not only on our historic relationship with the Korean people, a bond forged by common sacrifice in war; it derives as well from the recognition that the security of Japan, our closest ally in the Pacific, is directly linked to the security of Korea. We will continue to work with our friends to preserve the balance. We will resist with determination any unilateral attempt to change or upset the equilibrium on the peninsula.

At the same time, we and the Republic of Korea are prepared to move to a more permanent solution. We have proposed a conference among North and South Korea, the United States, and the

[17]Signed at Washington Oct. 1, 1953 and entered into force Nov. 17, 1954 (TIAS 3097; 5 UST 2368); text in *Documents, 1953*: 312-13.

People's Republic of China to discuss the dissolution of the U.N. Command while preserving the Korean armistice agreement.[18] And in that context we are willing to consider other measures to reduce tensions, including a wider conference to negotiate more fundamental arrangements for peace in Korea.

We will not acquiesce in any proposals which would exclude the Republic of Korea from discussions about its future. And we will not allow our military presence, which derives from bilateral agreements, to be dictated by third parties. But we are prepared—now—to transform the armistice arrangements to a permanent peace. And we are ready to talk to any interested country, including North Korea, about the future of Korea, provided only that South Korea is present.

We shall seek a new structure of stability in Southeast Asia. This Administration inherited the conflict in Indochina and brought our involvement to an end. That chapter in our history, which occasioned so much anguish, is now closed. As for our relations with the new governments in that region, these will not be determined by the past; we are prepared to look to a more hopeful future. The United States will respond to gestures of good will. If those governments show understanding of our concerns and those of their neighbors, they will find us ready to reciprocate. This will be especially the case if they deal constructively with the anguish of thousands of Americans who ask only an accounting for their loved ones missing in action and the return of the bodies of Americans who died in Indochina. We have no interest to continue the Indochina war on the diplomatic front; we envisage the eventual normalization of relations. In the interim we are prepared to consider practical arrangements of mutual benefit in such fields as travel and trade.

One of the basic purposes of our original commitment in Indochina was to provide a buffer of security and time for the *many* nations of Southeast Asia to enable them to develop their own strength and cohesion. In this regard our efforts proved successful. These nations have preserved their independence; they are assuming increasing importance. We have a substantial stake in the well-being of the Philippines and Indonesia, which President Ford will visit next week. We have important links with Thailand and strong ties of friendship with Singapore and Malaysia. And we have a longstanding association with our ANZUS partners, Australia and New Zealand.

These nations are preserving their independence through economic development, a serious effort to relax tensions, and institu-

[18]Cf. Chapter 32 at note 15.

tions of regional cooperation. All of them are examples of self-reliance and national resilience. All of them also seek to maintain and broaden their association with us—and all of them wish the United States to remain actively engaged in Asia.

In short, the new Asia is an important pillar of the structure of global peace. It is a central element in the design of our foreign policy.

America's Responsibility

Thirty years ago, when we were first summoned to leadership, we were the only country to have survived World War II with its institutions and economy intact. In that era we were overwhelmingly predominant in nuclear weapons and in every measure of military and economic strength. The American people, with pride in their victory and fresh memory of the folly of isolationism, confidently assumed the responsibilities of world leadership.

Inevitably, with time, other nations—allies and adversaries—recovered and developed their strength. It was natural that decolonization and an expanding economy would produce new centers of economic power and political influence. And it was understandable that the American people would tire of the burdens of leadership and ask for another balancing of America's interests and commitments.

But history gives us no respite. To build peace, other nations must do more—but we must do our share. Today's foreign policy and today's international environment pose for us a novel psychological challenge. We can no longer overwhelm our problems with resources; we must learn foresight, tactical skill, and constancy. We can no longer expect our moral preferences to hold sway simply because of our power; we must possess patience and understanding. We cannot shape a new world by ourselves; we must elicit from others—friend and foe alike—a contribution to the arduous process of building a stable international order. America's challenge today is to demonstrate a new kind of leadership—guiding by our vision, our example, and our energy, not by our predominance.

Only rarely in history does a people have the chance to shape the international environment in which it lives. That opportunity is America's today. But we can meet the opportunity only as a united and confident nation.

In a world of thermonuclear weapons, shrunken distances, and widely dispersed power, we cannot afford disunity, disarray, or disruption in the conduct of our foreign affairs. Foreign policy requires authority. Our ability to maintain peace fundamentally involves the belief of other nations that our word counts, that we have a coherent policy, that we possess steadiness and resolve.

It is time, therefore, to end the self-flagellation that has done so much harm to this nation's capacity to conduct foreign policy. It is time that we outgrew some of the illusions that characterized the long-past period of our isolationism: the idea that we are always being taken in by foreigners; the fear that military assistance to allies leads to involvement rather than substitutes for it; the pretense that defense spending is wasteful and generates conflict; the delusion that American intelligence activities are immoral; the suspicion that the confidentiality of diplomacy is a plot to deceive the public; or the illusion that tranquillity can be achieved by an abstract purity of motive for which history offers no example.

In the nation with the highest standard of living and one of the richest cultures in the world, in the nation which has come closest of all to the ideals of civil liberty and democracy, it is long past time to put a stop to self-doubt about our example and role in the world.

We have already gone through a traumatic period—with assassinations, resignations from our two highest offices, and a political climate still poisoned by the residue of the war and domestic turbulence of the previous decade. And we are now one year before our Presidential election.

But this country cannot have a moratorium on a responsible foreign policy. Let us never forget that there are many in the world who do not wish us well, that there are crises and challenges which will not wait for our elections.

We must keep in mind that in a world where totalitarian government can manipulate friendly political parties, there is a gray area between foreign policy and overt intervention which we deny ourselves only at grave risk to our national security.

The bitterness that has marked so much of our national discourse for a decade no longer has reason or place. A great responsibility rests upon both the Congress and the executive. Our foreign policy has been most effective when it reflected broad bipartisan support. This spirit of cooperation has never been more essential than today. Our free debate once again must find its ultimate restraint in the recognition that we are engaged in a common enterprise.

The decade-long debate over executive predominance in foreign policy is now a thing of the past; Congress' reassertion of its role and prerogative is now a dominant and important fact in our political life. In recent years congressional investigations have served the country well in correcting many abuses. We must discover the excesses of the past, overcome the abuses that are uncovered, and insure that they will never be repeated—this is the deepest strength of a free society. But it should be possible to cleanse our institutions without disrupting the conduct of our nation's business abroad and buffeting all the instruments of our policy. When the most confidential documents are spread on the public record as a matter of routine, there is a danger that rather than cleanse our government we will produce timidity and obfuscation in our bureaucracy and loss of confidence abroad.

We must resist the myth that government is a gigantic conspiracy. The truth is that the vast majority of public servants are serious, dedicated, and compassionate men and women who seek no other reward than the consciousness of having served their country well.

We need nothing so much as a restoration of confidence in ourselves. President Ford, a man of Congress, has conducted his Administration with an unprecedented commitment to cooperation and conciliation with his colleagues of the House and Senate. But he has some fundamental obligations to the national interest:

—We cannot allow the intelligence services of this country to be dismantled.

—We must preserve our ability to maintain the confidentiality of other governments' dealings with us and our dealings with them.

—We must maintain our defenses and a prudent program of economic and military assistance to other countries with whom we have productive political relations.

—We must achieve a rational division of labor between Congress' defining of broad national commitments and the executive's constitutional responsibility for tactics, the execution of policy, and the conduct of negotiations.

Ladies and gentlemen: It is the responsibility of Americans—of all political persuasions, in both branches of government, in the public and the press—to help shape a national policy in a positive and cooperative spirit. It is the responsibility of this nation to exercise creative leadership in a moment of uncertainty, in a world that cries out for inspiration.

America is the only country whose destiny always seemed open, whose future always appeared more compelling than its past. We have been the hope of mankind, not only because we stood for freedom and offered a haven to the oppressed but because we have demonstrated time and again the resiliency and indestructible spirit of free men. We have not lost our understanding of our true interests or our humane concern for the fate of our fellow men.

This country's foreign policy is not a burden; it is a success and a promise. We have done great things. There are great things yet to do. If the American people stand together, we will leave as our legacy a more secure, prosperous, and just world than the one that we inherited.

40. NEW DOCTRINE FOR THE PACIFIC

(Honolulu, December 7, 1975)

[It was during a visit to the Pacific in the summer of 1969 that President Nixon, enunciating the principles that would become known as the "Nixon Doctrine,"[1] had stressed the need for some redefinition and reduction of American responsibilities in that area to correct what he regarded as a serious overcommitment of American power and resources. Six years later, the liquidation of the war in Vietnam, the reduction of U.S. troop strength elsewhere in the Pacific, the changing relationship between the United States and China, and the prospective "phasing out" of SEATO[2] had created a fundamentally altered situation in which it could be asked whether the process of withdrawal initiated under the Nixon administration was not in danger of being carried too far. The necessity of preserving "a flexible and balanced position of strength throughout the Pacific" thus became the cardinal element of the new "Pacific Doctrine" that was proclaimed by President Ford at Honolulu on Pearl Harbor Day, December 7, 1975, at the conclusion of a week-long Pacific tour with Secretary Kissinger that began in Alaska and included four days in mainland China as well as briefer stops in Indonesia and the Philippines.

President Ford's address at Honolulu's East-West Center (**Document 61**) offered the best concise account of his journey to a region where political changes had been occurring with startling suddenness of late.[3] Australia, perhaps America's stanchest Pacific ally, was currently going through a period of great uncertainty following the recent dismissal of Labor Prime Minister Gough Whitlam and the designation of Liberal-Country party leader Malcolm Fraser to organize a caretaker government and prepare

---

[1]Text in *Public Papers (Nixon), 1969*: 545-9; excerpts in *Documents, 1968-69*: 329-34.

[2]Chapter 34.

[3]Itinerary and documentation in *Presidential Documents*, 11: 1331-4, 1339-59, and 1369-70 (*Bulletin*, 73: 913-33).

for new elections (in which the conservatives were to win a resounding victory). New Zealand, too, was about to shift to the conservative column with the National Party's upset electoral victory on November 29 and the subsequent appointment of Robert D. Muldoon to succeed Laborite Wallace E. Rowling as Prime Minister.

Events in Southeast Asia were also crowding thick and fast. Even as President Ford began his visit to mainland China on December 1, the final steps in the establishment of Communist rule in Laos were being effected with the formal abolition of the monarchy and the installation of Prince Souphanouvong as President, and the Communist Kaysone Phomvihan as Prime Minister, of a "Democratic and Popular Republic." Hours after Mr. Ford's departure from Indonesia on December 6, that country sent its military forces to occupy and prepare for annexation of the adjacent Portuguese territory of East Timor, where a civil war between pro-independence and pro-Indonesian elements had been in progress since the preceding summer. (Demands for their withdrawal by the U.N. General Assembly and Security Council failed to shake the Indonesians' evident determination to retain possession.)

Potentially even more unstable was the situation in the People's Republic of China itself, where the ailing Premier Chou En-lai had less than six weeks to live and Deputy Premier Teng Hsiao-ping was currently exercising day-to-day responsibility. The American visitors' lengthy meeting with Mao Tse-tung, the aging Communist Party Chairman, could only emphasize the transitory nature of present-day political arrangements and the certainty that both powers would need to maintain a high degree of flexibility in the months to come. Other factors, including the United States' continuing friendship with and diplomatic recognition of the Republic of China on Taiwan, continued to delay the full "normalization of relations" envisaged in the Shanghai communiqué drawn up at the time of President Nixon's visit to the PRC in February 1972.[4] With these important qualifications, President Ford could nevertheless insist at Honolulu that the relationship between the two powers was becoming "a permanent feature of the international political landscape" and one that was of benefit not only to the two peoples but to "all peoples of the region and the entire world."]

[4]*AFR, 1972*: 307-11.

(61) "The Pacific Doctrine": Address by President Ford at the East-West Center, Honolulu, at the conclusion of his Pacific journey, December 7, 1975.[5]

* * *

. . . It is good to be home again in the United States. I have just completed, as many of you know, a 7-day trip to the State of Alaska, to the People's Republic of China, to our good friends, Indonesia and the Philippines, and now I am obviously happy to be home in our 50th State, Hawaii.

This morning I reflected on the past at the shrine of Americans who died on Sunday morning 34 years ago. I came away with a new spirit of dedication to the ideals that emerged from Pearl Harbor in World War II—dedication to America's bipartisan policy of pursuing peace through strength and dedication to a new future of interdependence and cooperation with all peoples of the Pacific.

I subscribe to a Pacific doctrine of peace with all and hostility toward none. The way I would like to remember or recollect Pearl Harbor is by preserving the power of the past to build the future. Let us join with new and old countries of that great Pacific area in creating the greatest civilization on the shores of the greatest of our oceans.

My visit here to the East-West Center holds another kind of meaning. Your center is a catalyst of America's positive concern for Asia, its people and its rich diversity of cultures. You advance our hope that Asia will gain a better understanding of the United States.

Last year we were pleased to receive and to welcome nearly 54,000 Asian students to the United States while thousands upon thousands of American students went to Asian countries. I applaud your contribution to partnership in education. Your efforts represent America's vision of an open world of understanding, freedom, and peace.

In Hawaii, the crossroads of the Pacific, our past and our future join.

I was deeply moved when I visited Japan last year and when I recently had the honor of welcoming the Emperor and the Empress

[5]Text from *Presidential Documents*, 11: 1354-8 (introductory pleasantries omitted),

of Japan to America.[6] The gracious welcome that I received and the warmth of the welcome the American people bestowed upon the Emperor and the Empress testify to a growing friendship and partnership between our two great countries. This is a tribute to what is best in man—his capacity to grow from fear to trust and from a tragedy of the past to a hopeful future. It is a superb example of what can be achieved in human progress. It inspires our new efforts in Asia to improve relations.

America, a nation of the Pacific Basin, has a very vital stake in Asia and a responsibility to take a leading part in lessening tensions, preventing hostilities, and preserving peace. World stability and our own security depend upon our Asian commitments.

In 1941, 34 years ago today, we were militarily unprepared. Our trade in the Pacific was very limited. We exercised jurisdiction over the Philippines. We were preoccupied with Western Europe. Our instincts were isolationist.

We have transcended that age. We are now the world's strongest nation. Our great commercial involvement in Asia is expanding. We led the way in conferring independence upon the Philippines. Now we are working out new associations and arrangements with the trust territories of the Pacific.[7]

The center of political power in the United States has shifted westward. Our Pacific interests and concerns have increased. We have exchanged the freedom of action of an isolationist state for the responsibilities of a great global power. As I return from this trip to three major Asian countries, I am even more aware of our interests in this part of the world.

The security concerns of great world powers intersect in Asia. The United States, the Soviet Union, China, and Japan are all Pacific powers. Western Europe has historic and economic ties with Asia. Equilibrium in the Pacific is absolutely essential to the United States and to the other countries in the Pacific.

The first premise of a new Pacific Doctrine is that American strength is basic to any stable balance of power in the Pacific. We must reach beyond our concern for security. But without security, there can be neither peace nor progress. The preservation of the sovereignty and the independence of our Asian friends and allies remain a paramount objective of American policy.

We recognize that force alone is insufficient to assure security. Popular legitimacy and social justice are vital prerequisites of resistance against subversion or aggression. Nevertheless, we owe it

[6] *AFR, 1974*: 492-5, and note 6 to Chapter 26, above.
[7] Cf. Chapter 21. The advent of Papua New Guinea to independence on Sept. 16, 1975 left the U.S.-administered Trust Territory of the Pacific Islands (Micronesia) as the only remaining U.N. trust territory.

to ourselves and to those whose independence depends upon our continued support to preserve a flexible and balanced position of strength throughout the Pacific.

The second basic premise of a new Pacific Doctrine is that partnership with Japan is a pillar of our strategy. There is no relationship to which I have devoted more attention, nor is there any greater success story in the history of American efforts to relate to distant cultures and to people. The Japanese-American relationship can be a source of great, great pride to every American and to every Japanese. Our bilateral relations have never been better. The recent exchange of visits symbolized a basic political partnership. We have begun to develop with the Japanese and other advanced industrial democracies better means of harmonizing our economic policy. We are joining with Japan, our European friends, and representatives of the developing nations this month to begin shaping a more efficient and more equitable pattern of North-South economic relations.[8]

The third premise of a new Pacific Doctrine is the normalization of relations with the People's Republic of China, the strengthening of our new ties with this great nation representing nearly one-quarter of mankind. This is another recent achievement of American foreign policy. It transcends 25 years of hostility.

I visited China to build on the dialog started nearly 4 years ago. My wide-ranging exchanges with the leaders of the People's Republic of China—with Chairman Mao Tse-tung and Vice Premier Teng Hsiao-ping—enhanced our understanding of each other's views and each other's policies.

There were, as expected, differences of perspective. Our societies, our philosophies, our varying positions in the world give us differing perceptions of our respective national interests.

But we did find a common ground. We reaffirmed that we share very important areas of concern and agreement. They say and we say that the countries of Asia should be free to develop in a world where there is mutual respect for the sovereignty and territorial integrity of all states; where people are free from the threat of foreign aggression; where there is noninterference in the internal affairs of others; and where the principles of equality, mutual benefit, and coexistence shape the development of peaceful international order. We share opposition to any form of hegemony in Asia or in any other part of the world.

I reaffirmed the determination of the United States to complete the normalization of relations with the People's Republic of China on the basis of the Shanghai communique. Both sides regarded our

[8] Cf. Chapter 43.

discussions as significant, useful, and constructive. Our relationship is becoming a permanent feature of the international political landscape. It benefits not only our two peoples but all peoples of the region and the entire world.

A fourth principle of our Pacific policy is our continuing stake in stability and security in Southeast Asia.

After leaving China, I visited Indonesia and the Philippines. Indonesia is a nation of 140 million people, the fifth largest population in the world today. It is one of our important new friends and a major country in that area of the world. The Republic of the Philippines is one of our oldest and dearest allies. Our friendship demonstrates America's longstanding interest in Asia.

I spent 3 days in Djakarta and Manila. I would have liked to have had time to visit our friends in Thailand, Singapore, and Malaysia. We share important political and economic concerns with these five nations who make up the Association of Southeast Asian Nations.

I can assure you that Americans will be hearing much more about the ASEAN organization. All of its members are friends of the United States. Their total population equals our own. While they are developing countries, they possess many, many assets— vital peoples, abundant natural resources, and well-managed agricultures. They have skilled leaders and the determination to develop themselves and to solve their own problems.

Each of these countries protects its independence by relying on its own national resilience and diplomacy. We must continue to assist them. I learned during my visit that our friends want us to remain actively engaged in the affairs of the region. We intend to do so.

We retain close and valuable ties with our old friends and allies in the Southwest Pacific—Australia on the one hand and New Zealand on the other.

A fifth tenet of our new Pacific policy is our belief that peace in Asia depends upon a resolution of outstanding political conflicts. In Korea, tension persists. We have close ties with the Republic of Korea. And we remain committed to peace and security on the Korean Peninsula, as the presence of our forces there attests.

Responding to the heightened tension last spring, we reaffirmed our support of the Republic of Korea.[9] Today, the United States is ready to consider constructive ways of easing tensions on the peninsula. But we will continue to resist any moves which attempt to exclude the Republic of Korea from discussion of its own future.

In Indochina, the healing effects of time are required. Our policies toward the new regimes of the peninsula will be determined by their conduct toward us. We are prepared to reciprocate gestures

[9]Cf. Chapter 26 at note 4.

of good will—particularly the return of remains of Americans killed or missing in action or information about them. If they exhibit restraint toward their neighbors and constructive approaches to international problems, we will look to the future rather than to the past.

The sixth point of our new policy in the Pacific is that peace in Asia requires a structure of economic cooperation reflecting the aspiration of all the peoples in the region.

The Asian-Pacific economy has recently achieved more rapid growth than any other region in the world. Our trade with East Asia now exceeds our transactions with the European community. America's jobs, currency, and raw materials depend upon economic ties with the Pacific Basin. Our trade with the region is now increasing by more than 30 percent annually, reaching some $46 billion last year. Our economies are increasingly interdependent as cooperation grows between developed and developing nations.

Our relations with the five ASEAN countries are marked by growing maturity and by more modest and more realistic expectations on both sides. We no longer approach them as donor to dependent. These proud people look to us less for outright aid than for new trading opportunities and more equitable arrangements for the transfer of science and technology.

There is one common theme which was expressed to me by the leaders of every Asian country that I visited. They all advocate the continuity of steady and responsible American leadership. They seek self-reliance in their own future and in their own relations with us.

Our military assistance to allies and friends is a modest responsibility, but its political significance far surpasses the small cost involved. We serve our highest national interests by strengthening their self-reliance, their relations with us, their solidarity with each other, and their regional security.

I emphasized to every leader I met that the United States is a Pacific nation. I pledged, as President, I will continue America's active concern for Asia and our presence in the Asian-Pacific region.

Asia is entering a new era. We can contribute to a new structure of stability founded on a balance among the major powers, strong ties to our allies in the region, an easing of tension between adversaries, the self-reliance and regional solidarity of smaller nations, and expanding economic ties and cultural exchanges. These components of peace are already evident. Our foreign policy in recent years and in recent days encourages their growth.

If we can remain steadfast, historians will look back and view the 1970's as the beginning of a period of peaceful cooperation and progress, a time of growing community for all the nations touched by this great ocean.

Here in the Pacific crossroads of Hawaii, we envision hope for a wider community of man. We see the promise of a unique republic which includes all the world's races. No other country has been so truly a free, multiracial society. Hawaii is a splendid example, a splendid showcase of America and exemplifies our destiny as a Pacific nation.

America's Pacific heritage emerged from this remarkable State. I am proud to visit Hawaii—the island star in the American firmament which radiates the universal magic of Aloha.

Let there flow from Hawaii—and from all of the States in our Union—to all peoples, East and West, a new spirit of interchange to build human brotherhood.

Thank you very much.

41. NATO LOOKS AT MBFR

(Brussels and Vienna, December 11-16, 1975)

[From affirmations of solidarity in the Pacific, America's leaders turned their attention once again to the perennial task of helping to assure the peace and security of Western Europe and the North Atlantic area. The recent Conference on Security and Cooperation in Europe, culminating in the Final Act of Helsinki,[1] had established a set of principles that theoretically would guarantee the future tranquility of that politically divided area. But formidable problems still remained in view of the doubtful political intentions of some of the Helsinki signatories, the formidable military strength maintained in Europe by the opposed alliance groups, and, possibly most important, the growing superiority of the forces of the Soviet-dominated Warsaw Pact to the NATO forces currently commanded by General Alexander M. Haig, Jr. According to NATO estimates, Warsaw Pact forces in the crucial Central European sector now outnumbered those of NATO (including France) by 925,000 to 777,000 in ground force personnel, by 16,000 to 6,000 in main battle tanks, and by 3,000 to 1,300 in tactical aircraft.

This situation had not gone unnoticed in NATO military quarters. Meeting in Brussels on December 9-10, 1975, the ministers composing NATO's Defense Planning Committee again "expressed their grave concern at current trends which are altering the relative military strengths of NATO and the Warsaw Pact. They noted the increasing fire power, mobility and armoured strength of the Warsaw Pact forces and their formidable capability in such areas as tactical nuclear, chemical and electronic warfare; the growth and world-wide deployment of the Soviet navy, including the introduction into service of large numbers of nuclear-propelled attack and missile carrying submarines; and most

---

[1]Chapter 25, Document 42.

recently, the change in emphasis from air defence to offensive operations in Warsaw Pact air forces, represented by the acquisition of new high performance bombers and tactical aircraft with deep penetration capabilities."[2]

Ironically, this military imbalance had developed at a time when the countries concerned had ostensibly been striving to check the European armaments race via the conference on mutual force reduction (MBFR) initiated in Vienna in the fall of 1973. Throughout the intervening months, the principal Western powers (other than France, which was not taking part) had persistently advocated a two-phased program of reductions in ground force manpower and tanks that would begin with a reduction of U.S. and Soviet ground forces, continue with reductions in the forces of other participating countries, and eventually equalize the ground forces of both sides by bringing them under a common, collective ceiling. But representatives of the Warsaw Pact group, who felt that this approach offered few if any advantages to their side, had continued to urge an alternative proposal which was much more favorable to them in that it called for proportional, across-the-board reductions of *all* forces—ground, air, and nuclear—of the participating countries over a three-year period ending in 1977.[3]

A new attempt to break this deadlock was the principal action approved by the North Atlantic Council at its December ministerial meeting, held at NATO headquarters in Brussels on December 11-12. Only vaguely referred to in the NATO communiqué (**Document 62**), the new Western proposal approved for tabling at the Vienna talks apparently sought to enhance the attractiveness of the basic Western plan by offering what amounted to a limited reduction of American nuclear and air forces to supplement the ground force reductions already proposed. Specifically, the Vienna conferees were advised when the new proposal was submitted on December 16 that the United States would be prepared, on a "one-time" basis, to withdraw from Europe 1,000 tactical nuclear warheads (out of an estimated 7,000) together with their related means of delivery, including 54 Phantom F-4 strike aircraft and 36 Pershing missiles. In return for this concession, the Warsaw Pact countries were asked to accept a two-phased reduction program culminating in the establishment of a common ceiling of 700,000 for ground forces (and 900,000 for ground plus air personnel) on either side. Also as a part of this overall process, the U.S.S.R. was invited to withdraw a complete tank army of 68,000 men and 1,700 main battle tanks in exchange for the withdrawal of 29,000 U.S. Army soldiers.[4]

[2]*NATO Review*, Feb. 1976: 25.
[3]Details from Lothar Ruehl, "The Negotiations on Force Reductions in Central Europe," *NATO Review*, Oct. 1976: 18-25.
[4]Same: 23; additional details from *Keesing's*: 27815 (1976).

No immediate response to this complex proposal was possible or expected, and it was not until February 19, 1976 that the Warsaw Pact came forward with a counterproposal amounting to a modified version of the original Soviet plan.[5] In the meantime, the Foreign Ministers of the Warsaw Pact countries, holding a routine meeting in Moscow on December 15-16, confined themselves to exchanging views on the status of the Vienna talks, reaffirming the determination "to exert tireless efforts in order to achieve real progress," and expressing confidence that the talks "must lead to effective and substantial reductions of armed forces and armaments on the basis of respect for the principle of not harming the security of any state."[6]]

(62) Meeting at Ministerial Level of the North Atlantic Council, Brussels, December 11-12, 1975: Communiqué issued at the conclusion of the meeting, December 12, 1975.[7]

1. The North Atlantic Council met in Ministerial session in Brussels on 11 and 12 December, 1975.

2. Ministers noted that there had been encouraging features in the development of East-West relations during recent months. They reaffirmed their determination to persevere in their efforts to place relations with the USSR and other Warsaw Pact countries on a more stable basis.

At the same time they noted that the beneficial effects of détente can develop only in so far as all the countries concerned do their best to reduce the risk of confrontation in both the political and military fields.

In the political sphere, détente requires tolerance and mutual understanding, and accordingly demands that the natural contest of political and social ideas should not be conducted in a manner incompatible with the letter and spirit of the Final Act of Helsinki. Furthermore, Ministers considered that attempts to take advantage of tension in any part of the world could have a negative impact on détente.

In the military sphere, Ministers viewed with concern, as on previous occasions, the continued rapid growth of the power of the land, air and naval forces of the Warsaw Pact, which exceeds its apparent defensive needs. They emphasized that détente and security are closely linked. In these circumstances they stressed the need to preserve the defensive strength of the Alliance which is important as a deterrent not only against military aggression but also against political pressure.

[5]*NATO Review*, Oct. 1976: 23-4.
[6]*Soviet News*, 1975: 437.
[7]Department of State Press Release 608, Dec. 15; text from *Bulletin*, 74: 57-8.

Ministers reaffirmed that the solidarity of the Alliance and the security which it provides are essential conditions for the improvement of East-West relations, and they restated the determination of their Governments, expressed in the Ottawa Declaration,[8] to maintain and improve the efficiency of their forces.

3. Ministers welcomed the adoption of the Final Act of the Conference on Security and Cooperation in Europe [CSCE] which provides guidelines for an evolution of relations between the participating states and between their peoples towards greater understanding and cooperation. They noted the fact that the results of the Conference apply throughout Europe, including, subject to Quadripartite rights and responsibilities, Berlin. The Allies attach high priority to the full implementation of the Final Act by all signatories in improving relations between states, in applying confidence building measures, in encouraging closer economic cooperation, and in lowering barriers between people. Noting that only a short time had elapsed since Helsinki, Ministers hoped that substantial progress would be seen during the coming months.

In accordance with the provisions of the Final Act, the Allies concerned have already notified all CSCE participants of a number of military maneuvers and have invited observers. The Allies look for the implementation of such measures also by the members of the Warsaw Pact.

4. Ministers heard a report from the United States Secretary of State on the continuing U.S. efforts towards the further limitation of strategic offensive arms. The Ministers expressed satisfaction with the substantial progress made since the Vladivostok Summit towards a SALT II Agreement. They expressed the hope that further efforts would lead to the conclusion of a satisfactory agreement. The Ministers also expressed appreciation for continuing consultations within the Alliance with respect to strategic arms limitation.

5. Ministers of the participating countries reviewed the state of the negotiations in Vienna on Mutual and Balanced Force Reductions. They recalled that it is the aim of these negotiations to contribute to a more stable relationship and to strengthening of peace and security in Europe.

These Ministers stressed again that the existing disparities in ground force manpower and tanks are the most destabilizing factor in Central Europe and that any agreement must deal adequately with these disparities. They reconfirmed, therefore, the Allied proposal to establish in the area of reductions approximate parity in ground forces in the form of a common collective ceiling for

[8]*AFR, 1974*: 198-201.

ground force manpower on each side. A first phase reductions agreement concerning United States and Soviet ground forces as proposed by the participating Allies would be an important and practical step towards this goal.

With a view to achieving these objectives, they approved important additional proposals and authorized their presentation at the appropriate moment in Vienna.

These Ministers reiterated their resolve to pursue vigorously all the Allied objectives in order to assure undiminished security for all parties. They proceed on the premise that the additional proposals will lead to the achievement of these objectives.

These Ministers noted with satisfaction that Allied solidarity has continued to prove itself in these negotiations. They reaffirmed the principle that NATO forces should not be reduced except in the context of a Mutual and Balanced Force Reductions agreement with the East.

6. The Ministers took note of the Declaration made by the Governments of France, the United Kingdom and the United States on 14 October, 1975,[9] that the rights and responsibilities of the Four Powers for Berlin and Germany as a whole remain unaffected by the Treaty of Friendship, Cooperation and Mutual Assistance concluded by the USSR and the GDR [German Democratic Republic] on the 7 October, 1975. They shared the view of the Government of the Federal Republic of Germany that its policy to work for a state of peace in Europe in which the German nation will regain its unity through free self-determination, is fully consistent with the Final Act of Helsinki.

Ministers underlined the essential connection between the situation relating to Berlin and détente, security and cooperation throughout Europe.

They emphasized in particular, that traffic and ties between Western sectors of Berlin and the Federal Republic of Germany and the representation abroad of the interests of those sectors by the Federal Republic of Germany continue to be important elements of the viability of the city.

7. Ministers reviewed developments in the Mediterranean area since their last meeting. They expressed concern at the possible dangers of new tensions that could affect the balance of forces in this region. They reaffirmed the importance they attach to the continuation of efforts designed to achieve an overall settlement resulting in a just and durable peace in the Middle East.

Ministers took note of the report on the situation in the Mediterranean prepared on their instructions. They requested the Council

[9]U.N. Document A/10328, Nov. 3, 1975.

to keep this question under review and to report back to them again at the next meeting.

8. The issue of the present fisheries dispute between Iceland and the United Kingdom was raised and discussed.

9. Ministers discussed various aspects of problems related to armaments and standardization with the aim of improving the military capability of the Alliance and of making more effective use of available resources, especially in view of the increasing pressures in national budgets. They agreed that the examination of these questions would be pursued by the Council and the other competent bodies of the Alliance in accordance with established procedures. They agreed to form for a limited time an *ad hoc* committee under the Council to prepare a specific program of action covering the interoperability of military equipment.

10. Ministers took note of the progress achieved by the Committee on the Challenges of Modern Society (CCMS). They endorsed resolutions on coastal water pollution and oil spills, noting the determination of the member countries to continue to combat pollution of the seas and to enhance the quality of the marine environment. Ministers noted and endorsed the initiation of a pilot study open to interested nations on the relationship between food and health, and the continuation of other studies relating to the environment and to energy. They noted the important contribution of the CCMS to effective international cooperation in areas of major concern to our societies.

11. Ministers reaffirmed the attachment of their nations to the democratic principles on which their free institutions are founded. They expressed their confidence in the ability of their countries to surmount the problems of our time. They considered the cohesion and vitality of the Alliance to be a sure source of mutual support and solidarity.

12. The next Ministerial session of the North Atlantic Council will be held in Oslo on 20 and 21 May, 1976.[10]

---

[10]Text of communiqué, May 21, 1976, in *Bulletin*, 74: 774-5.

42. EUROPE AFTER HELSINKI

(London, December 13-14, 1975)

[As always, the Brussels session of the NATO Council afforded Secretary Kissinger and his ministerial colleagues the opportunity for a wide-ranging review of current political concerns. Appearing for a brief news conference following adjournment of the meeting on December 12, Dr. Kissinger seemed particularly disturbed about the current situation in Angola. The Soviet Union, he asserted, by its "massive" support of "a military operation thousands of miles from Soviet territory in an area where there are no historic Russian interests," was engaged in what was at least "a new projection of Soviet power and Soviet interests" if not an attempt "to establish a new pattern of dominance." Such action, Secretary Kissinger declared in diplomatic language, was bound to affect the relations between the United States and the Soviet Union; and if it proved impossible for Angola to be handled as an African issue within an African framework, the United States itself would "try to prevent one party by means of massive introduction of outside equipment from achieving dominance."[1]

The Secretary of State seemed momentarily more relaxed about conditions in Portugal, where the defeat of an attempted left-wing coup on November 25-26 had strengthened the moderate regime of President Francisco da Costa Gomes and Prime Minister José Pinheiro de Azevedo. "I believe that, on the whole, the situation in Portugal has improved," Dr. Kissinger stated. "The danger of Portugal going Communist is less. The possibility of a pluralistic evolution seems better. . . . I think that the Soviet Union's role in Portugal is not as acute as its role in Angola."[2] Asked about the frequently mentioned possibility that Italy's large Communist party might before long be granted representation in the national government, the Secretary intimated that while he personally would

[1] *Bulletin*, 74: 54-5. For details on Angola see Chapter 45.
[2] *Bulletin*, 74: 55.

not favor such a development, "we consider the Italian domestic situation a matter for Italians to decide—all the more so as our advice is likely to have the opposite effect from the one we wish to bring about."[3]

A less permissive view of political trends in Italy and elsewhere in Western Europe was offered by the Secretary of State in an off-the-record briefing of U.S. ambassadors to European countries that took place in London over the December 13-14 weekend. To this presumably discreet professional audience, Dr. Kissinger voiced resolute opposition not only to "the dominance of Communist parties in the West"—which, he said plainly, was "unacceptable"—but even to "major Communist participation in Western governments," which would, he said, make the retention of U.S. ground forces in Europe "inconceivable" and would in effect destroy the Western alliance as it then existed. The stenographic notes of the Kissinger talk **(Document 63a)** could hardly fail to create a political and diplomatic sensation when made public, without official authorization, in the *New York Times* of April 7, 1976. Dr. Kissinger's subsequent insistence that these were merely "extemporaneous remarks . . . designed to generate comment"[4] did little to lesson the impact of a pronouncement that seemed to place allied governments in Europe on much the same footing as the late Allende government in Chile.

A parallel briefing on U.S. policy toward Eastern Europe, presented by Helmut Sonnenfeldt, the Counselor of the Department of State and a long-time Kissinger aide, was destined to evoke a different kind of criticism on its publication in similar, summarized form **(Document 63b)**. What struck most readers of the Sonnenfeldt document was a rather cryptic statement to the effect that the United States must "strive for an evolution that makes the relationship between the Eastern Europeans and the Soviet Union an organic one," avoiding "any excess of zeal" but "responding to the clearly visible aspirations in Eastern Europe for a more autonomous existence within the context of a strong Soviet geopolitical influence." Whatever the intent of this language, its publication early in the 1976 election year was destined to give it a notoriety perhaps exceeding its intrinsic significance. Where Dr. Kissinger was charged with ideological rigidity, his aide was promptly taxed with overhasty acquiescence in the Soviet domination of Eastern Europe and with insensitivity to congressional views on human rights matters. The resultant semantic controversy obscured what may have been the document's more permanent interest as one of the comparatively rare delineations of American official thinking about Eastern Europe in the period following the Helsinki conference.]

[3]Same: 57.
[4]*Bulletin,* 74: 568.

(63)   Europe East and West: Briefing of United States Ambassadors in London, December 13-14, 1975.

(a)   Communist Prospects in Western Europe: Summary of remarks by Secretary of State Kissinger.[5]

The problem of our age is how to manage the emergence of the Soviet Union as a superpower. In today's circumstances, neither side can gain a strategic advantage that can be translated into political utility. A perceived strategic gap would have only marginal political benefit. However, the prediction that many made in the mid-fifties, and that was wrong then, is true now—that the strategic balance provides increased opportunities for regional pressure. In these circumstances our task is to find ways to restrain Soviet power over an historical period. We need a foreign policy that we can sustain over time, not one geared to oscillations and cycles of crises.

If strategic forces are today less important, regional balances gain more significance. Without a U.S. consensus, it will be hard to contain Soviet power. We need a permanent conception of our national interests—a conception that is not based upon personal relations between leaders, nor on expectations drawn from previous periods, nor on the idea that the Soviets should have permanent changes in their domestic policies.

We must balance off Soviet power around the world through a combination of political, military and economic means. In the Far East, the P.R.C. [People's Republic of China] must be a part of our political calculations.

In the Middle East we must not separate ourselves from the dominant political currents. We must pursue there a policy relevant to regional balance.

The United States public must see its Government as being interested in the settlement of disputes. Truculence toward the Soviets, with everyone beating his chest, would create a situation in which opinion leaders and youth would say that we are needlessly jeopardizing peace. This would start the kind of debate that paralyzed us in the Vietnam War. We need a United States policy which would make it impossible even for those Western European parties which are anti-NATO to describe the United States connection as a threat to peace. Accordingly, we have made efforts at conciliation, as during the U.N. special session with regard to developing countries.[6]

[5] "Official State Department nonverbatim summary" as published with subtitles in *New York Times*, Apr. 7, 1976.

[6] Cf. Chapter 30.

We must contain the Soviets and prevent their expansion either through Western weakness or through the application of military force. To do this we must achieve domestic support for a long-term conception of our national interest. We must draw the Soviet Union into relationships which are both concrete and practical and we must create the maximum incentives for a moderate Soviet course. The Soviet system has not changed fundamentally. It is an amalgam of an ideology that cannot resist movement in Angola and a bureaucracy that mixes caution with persistence. But the Soviets are also subject to imperative, for example a bad economic situation, a failure to win ideological adherents, and pressure from the east. In such circumstances, for the West to engage in fratricidal conflict would be folly.

A great deal of what has gone wrong is not the result of détente or of Soviet policy. Examples are Portugal and Italy. The problems of Greece, Turkey and Cyprus are in part a result of domestic paralysis in the U.S. Even Angola represents as much a judgment by the Soviets of the domestic situation in the U.S.—as much a reaction to our intelligence investigations—as it does a long-term policy.

Our discomfort is at having to conduct foreign policy by relative means rather than by unilateral declarations. The fact is that, with the Soviet Union as an emerging superpower, we are doomed to coexistence. Thus to sum up, détente is not an amelioration of tone. Détente is the improvement of long-term relations with an emerging superpower. And that is a problem which will confront any American President no matter who he is.

Europe Is Backbone

Western Europe continues to be the backbone of our foreign policy. We are doing extremely well. Both the frequency and content of our mutual consultations are improving. There is presently a greater degree of real exchange of views than there has been during the past decade and a half. The period in which Europe was attempting to define itself is at least temporarily over. We are now closer to the Atlantic partnership that we envisaged with the Year of Europe in 1973.[7] But at the same time, the world has become even more interdependent and there are now new problems which must be addressed within the Atlantic context. This interdependence is the dominant fact of our international relationships. We have not yet achieved the degree of coherence in our relations with our European allies that is required in crisis situations, but we are making progress.

What is most worrisome is not the foreign policy of nations in Western Europe, but their domestic evolution. The growth of left-wing policies threatens to undermine the security relationship and

[7]Cf. *AFR, 1973*: 177-89.

defense policies on which the alliance has been constructed. And this growth is bound to affect the relations between Western Europe and the United States. In Italy, Spain and Portugal and maybe even France, we are witnessing the rising influence of Communist parties and we are facing the question of what we should do. The intellectual community in the United States is trying to resolve a paradox. We are accused of being soft on communism and hard on Communist parties. We are asked to be tough with Moscow but to have a dialogue with Communist parties in the West.

Dominance Unacceptable

One thing is clear, however, the dominance of Communist parties in the West is unacceptable. This has nothing to do with the reasonableness of these parties or with the degree of their independence with Russia. It is hard to imagine that, if one or the other of these parties takes control of a Western government, it will permit the democratic process to operate and thereby face the possibility that it may itself be removed from office. A Communist Party taking control of a government would find itself on a specific point in its line of development, regardless of what it may claim. It is unlikely to turn back the clock. More likely, once it is in power, it will seek to change the objective conditions of society so that the democratic process can no longer operate. We must do our utmost to assure the survival of democratic processes and to preserve the Western political orientation of Western European countries.

Secondly, we can have fruitful relations with Titoist Yugoslavia; we are prepared to improve our relations with that sort of government. But it is another thing to say that we could have a Titoist ally in NATO without fundamental changes in the alliance or in the U.S. perception of NATO. Irrespective of other factors, the primary appeal of Communists to the electorate has to do with their position on social and economic problems that bother the people of the country. Security issues would undoubtedly be low on their priority list if they came to power. This would have effects on the balance of European power and would, in turn, cause a reaction in the United States. We cannot encourage dialogue with Communist parties within NATO nations. We understand them and their aims, and we doubt they can be moderated by their dealings with the United States. If Communists get into power they will deal with us on the basis of their necessities at the time.

It is not our job to manipulate domestic policies. Our capacity is finite. But it is inconceivable that the United States could maintain ground forces in Europe if there is major Communist participation in Western governments. The foundation of our Atlantic security would therefore be eroded.

Cunhal Called Stalinist

There are those who think we are too intransigent in our attitude toward these Western European Communist parties. But we cannot encourage the progress of these parties nor permit the setting of a precedent in which by our inaction we have facilitated the success of a Communist Party. The extent to which such a party follows the Moscow line is unimportant. Even if Portugal had followed the Italian model, we would still have been opposed. It is not just because Cunhal [Alvaro Cunhal, Portuguese Communist leader] is a Stalinist that we are in opposition. Even the impact of an Italian Communist Party that seemed to be governing effectively would be devastating—on France, and on NATO, too.

It is difficult to see how we could continue to have NATO discussions if these various Communist parties did achieve control of Western European governments. We could, as with China, perhaps have parallel policies. But the alliance, as it is now, could not survive. The Western alliance has always had an importance beyond military security. The United States would be alone and isolated in a world in which we had no relations by values to other countries.

As for Socialists, we will continue to support them. We do so in Portugal. We must do so in Italy, although the Italian Socialist Party will be unreliable until the Christian Democrats can organize themselves. We have good relations with the S.P.D. [Social Democratic Party] in Germany. In Spain there must be an evolution toward democracy and better institutions without eroding the strength of the country and producing another Portugal. Political demonstrations in Spain will mean bloodshed and the Spanish, at least historically, are not used to resolving their differences peaceably.

Headache for Soviet

The Soviets are not the key element that is producing the present instabilities that we now face in Western Europe. A Communist Western Europe would be a headache for us. It would be a headache for the Soviets as well. They probably prefer not to see Communist powers taking over in Western Europe. But in the final analysis their ideology requires them to assist in these efforts. The U.S.S.R. has probably not been a decisive element in Portugal, but we cannot reasonably expect it to do nothing.

If Communist parties take power in several Western European democracies, there would be a shocking change in the established patterns of American policy. It could result in a situation where the United States would be an island in its own values, and thereby be forced to manipulate various Communist centers of power against each other. The United States could probably survive this situation, but only through the use of ruthless balance-of-power policy. If we were to have to do this, we would have lost the moral foundation we have operated on for our entire history.

There is an inconsistency perceived in the United States between our opposing Communist governments in Western Europe and our talking to them in Eastern Europe. We must overcome this problem in the public's mind.

(b) The Outlook for Eastern Europe: Summary of Remarks by Helmut Sonnenfeldt, Counselor of the Department of State.[8]

We are witnessing the emergence of the Soviet Union as a super-power on a global scale. This will be a long-term process. It is a process that is just beginning in global terms as the Soviets are just now breaking out of their continental mold. They are just now developing modalities for carrying out such a global policy.

The reason why it is possible for the United States and its Western European allies to develop the policies that will allow us to cope with this situation is that Soviet power is developing irregularly. It is subject to flaws and to requirements which in some cases only the outside world can meet.

Their thrust as an imperial power comes at a time well after the period when the last imperial power, Germany, made the plunge, and it hence comes at a time when different rules and perceptions apply. The Soviets have been inept. They have not been able to bring the attractions that past imperial powers brought to their conquests. They have not brought the ideological, legal, cultural, architectural, organizational and other values and skills that characterized the British, French and German adventures.

Tensions in the System

In addition, there are serious underlying pressures and tensions in the Soviet system itself.

The base from which imperialism asserts itself has serious problems in the economic and social sectors. There are also internal nationalist groups which are growing. Non-Russian nationalist groups in Russia are growing at a disproportionally faster rate, which will add to these tensions in the base whence springs Soviet imperialism.

The Soviets have been particularly unskilled in building viable international structures. They have nothing approaching the European Community or the many other successful Western institutions. In Eastern Europe particularly, the single most important unifying force is the presence of sheer Soviet military power. There has been no development of a more viable, organized structure.

[8] "Official State Department Summary" as published with subtitles in *New York Times*, Apr. 6, 1976.

If anything, the last 30 years have intensified the urges in Eastern European countries for autonomy, for identity. There has been an intensification of the desire to break out of the Soviet straitjacket. This has happened in every Eastern European country to one degree or another. There are almost no genuine friends of the Soviets left in Eastern Europe, except possibly Bulgaria.

Power at the Core

The Soviets' inability to acquire loyalty in Eastern Europe is an unfortunate historical failure, because Eastern Europe is within their scope and area of natural interest. It is doubly tragic that in this area of vital interest and crucial importance it has not been possible for the Soviet Union to establish roots of interest that go beyond sheer power.

It is, therefore, important to remember that the main, if not the only, instrument of Soviet imperialism has been power.

The reason we can today talk and think in terms of dealing with Soviet imperialism, outside of and in addition to simple confrontation, is precisely because Soviet power is emerging in such a flawed way. This gives us the time to develop and to react. There is no way to prevent the emergence of the Soviet Union as a superpower. What we can do is affect the way in which that power is developed and used. Not only can we balance it in the traditional sense, but we can affect its usage—and that is what détente is all about.

It is often asked how détente is doing. The question itself evades the central issue we are trying to pose, that is, what do you do in the face of increasing Soviet power? We will be facing this increased power if our relationship with the Russians is sweet or our relationship is sour. The day when the U.S. could choose its preferences from two alternatives is over: That is, turning our back on the world—usually behind the protection of another power like the British navy—or changing the world. That choice no longer exists for us. There is too much power in the world for us to ignore, not just the Soviets, but other industrial powers, raw-material producers, and even the combined political power of the dwarf states. Nor do we today have enough power to simply overwhelm these problems.

The Persistent Challenge

So the Soviets will be seen and heard on the world stage no matter what we do. Therefore, the question of whether or not détente is up or down at a particular moment is largely irrelevant. We Americans like to keep score cards, but the historic challenge of the Soviet Union will not go away and the problems of coping with the effects of that growing Soviet power also won't go away.

We don't have any alternative except to come to grips with the various forms of power which surround us in the world. We have to get away from seeing détente as a process which appeases or propitiates Soviet power. We have to see our task as managing or domesticating this power.

That is our central problem in the years ahead, not finding agreements to sign or atmospheres to improve, although those have some effect. Our challenge is how to live in a world with another superpower, and anticipate the arrival of a third superpower, China, in 20 years or so.

The debate in the United States on détente is illustrated by comments that Soviet trade is a one-way street. It seems that today you can't just get payment for the goods you sell—you must get Jewish emigration, or arms restraint, or any number of other things.

Our European friends have extended considerable credit to the Soviets and Eastern European countries, while the U.S. does not extend lines of credit but, rather, approves financing on the basis of each project. That feature gives us some control over the direction of Soviet economic development. The Europeans have surrendered on this point. While not falling into the trade trap, we have seen trade as a set of instrumentalities to address the set of problems we face with the Soviets. We have to find a way to develop a coherent trade strategy that goes beyond the commercial views of individual firms.

Concessions on Trade

The grain agreement[9] is a good but narrow example of what I am talking about. The Soviets were forced to accept that they need substantial imports from the United States. That gives us leverage, but only if it is done within a coherent framework of policies to achieve certain objectives. M.F.N. [most-favored-nation treatment] has been considered a concession to the U.S.S.R., and in a sense it is. The Soviets don't like paying interest—they prefer to earn their way as they go.

If this is an accurate assessment, then with M.F.N. and credit policies we can get the U.S.S.R. to be competitively engaged in our U.S. markets. If done skillfully, this forces them to meet the requirements of the sophisticated U.S. market. M.F.N. entry into U.S. markets can have an impact on Soviet behavior. This is not a trivial matter.

It is in our long-term interests to use these strengths to break down the autarchic nature of the U.S.S.R. There are consumer choices being made in the U.S.S.R. that, although more below the surface than those in the United States, can be exploited.

[9]Chapter 35.

This is just one illustration. There are many assets in the West in this area, and instead of looking at them as just commercial sales, we need to be using them to draw the Soviet Union into a series of dependencies and ties with the West. It is a long-term project.

When we lost the M.F.N. battle with Congress,[10] we lost [words omitted?] as we were able to do in the case of the grain deal. This is the real tragedy of losing that trade issue. In the long term, we have suffered a setback.

Influence on East Europe

With regard to Eastern Europe, it must be in our long term interest to influence events in this area—because of the present unnatural relationship with the Soviet Union—so that they will not sooner or later explode, causing World War III. This inorganic, unnatural relationship is a far greater danger to world peace than the conflict between East and West. There is one qualification to this statement. If Western Europe becomes so concerned with its economic and social problems that an imbalance develops, then perhaps the dangers to the United States' interests will be endangered by the simple change in the balance of power.

So it must be our policy to strive for an evolution that makes the relationship between the Eastern Europeans and the Soviet Union an organic one. Any excess of zeal on our part is bound to produce results that could reverse the desired process for a period of time, even though the process would remain inevitable within the next 100 years. But, of course, for us that is too long a time to wait.

So our policy must be a policy of responding to the clearly visible aspirations in Eastern Europe for a more autonomous existence within the context of a strong Soviet geopolitical influence. This has worked in Poland. The Poles have been able to overcome their romantic political inclinations which led to their disasters in the past. They have been skillful in developing a policy that is satisfying their needs for a national identity without arousing Soviet reactions. It is a long process.

A similar process is now going on in Hungary. [Party First Secretary] Janos Kadar's performance has been remarkable in finding ways which are acceptable to the Soviet Union, which develop Hungarian roots and the natural aspirations of the people. He has conducted a number of experiments in the social and economic areas. To a large degree he has been able to do this because the Soviets have four divisions in Hungary and, therefore, have not

[10]Cf. Chapter 1 at note 4.

been overly concerned. He has skillfully used their presence as a security blanket for the Soviets, in a way that has been advantageous to the development of his own country.

The Rumanian picture is different, as one would expect from their different history. The Rumanians have striven for autonomy, but they have been less daring and innovative in their domestic systems. They remain among the most rigid countries in the internal organization of their system.

The Yugoslav Position

We seek to influence the emergence of the Soviet imperial power by making the base more natural and organic so that it will not remain founded in sheer power alone. But there is no alternative open to us other than that of influencing the way Soviet power is used.

Finally, on Yugoslavia, we and the Western Europeans, indeed, the Eastern Europeans as well, have an interest which borders on the vital for us in continuing the independence of Yugoslavia from Soviet domination. Of course we accept that Yugoslav behavior will continue to be, as it has been in the past, influenced and constrained by Soviet power. But any shift back by Yugoslavia into the Soviet orbit would represent a major strategic setback for the West. So we are concerned about what will happen when Tito disappears, and it is worrying us a good deal.

So our basic policy continues to be that which we have pursued since 1948-49, keeping Yugoslavia in a position of substantial independence from the Soviet Union. Now at the same time we would like them to be less obnoxious, and we should allow them to get away with very little. We should especially disabuse them of any notion that our interest in their relative independence is greater than their own and, therefore, they have a free ride.

43. THE NORTH-SOUTH CONFERENCE BEGINS

(Paris, December 16-19, 1975)

[Roughly two years had now elapsed since the commencement of the worldwide politico-economic crisis precipitated by the OPEC nations' sudden escalations of petroleum prices. Despite persistence of the mutual irritations that had accompanied this process, there had of late been definite improvement in the tone of international debate about the energy crisis and other global economic questions. From shrill polemics about the "New International Economic Order" and the "Economic Rights and Duties of States,"[1] emphasis had shifted in some degree toward the search for areas of practical cooperation between developed and developing countries.

This atmospheric change could be attributed in considerable measure to the development of a more flexible attitude on the part of the United States itself, whose distaste for some third world economic concepts had been noticeably muted in the months since the failure of "Prepcon I," the preparatory meeting for the proposed North-South conference, in April 1975. Signs of an increasing elasticity in the American attitude, already discernable in Dr. Kissinger's speeches at the time of the OECD Council meeting in May, had seemed to be spectacularly confirmed by the Secretary's statement prepared for the special U.N. Assembly session at the beginning of September.[2]

The conciliatory spirit that had helped avoid a threatened clash on that occasion had still been evident a month later when the same group of developing and industrialized nations that had failed to agree in April had reassembled in Paris for a second—and this time successful—attempt to establish ground rules for the long-awaited North-South "Conference on International Economic Coopera-

---

[1]Cf. *AFR, 1974*: 103-12 and 525-41.
[2]Cf. respectively Chapters 7, 18, and 30.

tion" (CIEC). Working from proposals put forward by France, as originator of the project, this second Preparatory Meeting (Prepcon II) determined that the CIEC should consist of 26 countries, together with the European Economic Community (EEC); that it should meet at ministerial level in Paris in mid-December, and should hold a second ministerial meeting approximately a year later; and that its substantive responsibilities should be split up among four commissions dealing respectively with energy, raw materials, development, and financial affairs.[3]

The resolution of these critical issues reduced the area of possible disagreement at CIEC's formal opening, which took place in Paris on December 16-19 to the accompaniment of only minor polemics within and between groups. "Our dialogue here must be candid, but with a positive spirit and cooperative attitude," said Secretary Kissinger in the course of yet another survey of global economic problems as seen from an American perspective (**Document 64**). In activating the machinery of what might possibly turn out to be a quasi-permanent forum of North-South interchange, the assembled delegates acknowledged in their final communiqué (**Document 65**) that CIEC afforded "a unique opportunity" to address the problems of the international economic situation and "further international economic cooperation for the benefit of all countries and peoples."]

(64) Meeting at Ministerial Level of the Conference on International Economic Cooperation, Paris, December 16-19, 1975: Statement to the conference by Secretary of State Kissinger, December 16, 1975.[4]

The challenge of our time is to build a stable and just international structure. This task has two principal dimensions. There is the imperative of peace—the more traditional problems of building security, resolving conflicts, easing tensions. These issues dominate the agenda of relations between East and West. No less urgent is the imperative of justice—the compelling requirements of global economic progress and social advance. These are now the major issues in the relationship between North and South. They, too, carry the potential for either conflict or order. Neither the goal of peace nor that of social justice can be achieved in isolation. We must succeed in both quests or we will succeed in neither.

Social justice and economic progress are our concerns at this

[3]Final Declaration of the Preparatory Meeting, Oct. 16, in *Bulletin*, 73: 668-9.
[4]Department of State Press Release 612, Dec. 16; prepared text and subtitles from *Bulletin*, 74: 37-48.

conference. We meet here to launch the dialogue that has been so often urged and so long awaited. The convening of this meeting should itself be a reason for hope. For we believe it represents a commitment to the path of conciliation. It demonstrates a recognition that consumer and producer, industrial and agricultural, developed and developing, rich and poor, must together address the challenges of the global economy.

The United States will work with dedication and energy for a positive outcome. We will do so in our own self-interest and in the interest of a more just and prosperous community of nations. We will do our utmost to help mobilize the world's resources and the talents of men and women everywhere in the service of economic progress and common well-being.

In the past two years we have all learned that no nation or group of nations can solve its economic problems in isolation. In a world which is becoming increasingly interdependent, we have witnessed that inflation and recession affect us all. We have seen that no country can achieve redress by exporting its economic difficulties or by exacting an exorbitant economic price from others.

But our deepest challenge is political. Economic distress magnifies the problems of government in all our countries, clouding the prospects of social peace and democratic institutions. We have seen that national economic problems thus become international; they spawn clashes of interest and protectionist pressures that strain the fabric of collaboration even among traditional friends. We have all come to understand that, if unresolved, the competing claims of developed and developing, consumer and producer, will thwart any effort to build a stable and progressive international structure.

Our future depends now not on blind economic forces, but on choices that statesmen make. The world's nations can struggle in national or ideological contention—or they can acknowledge their interdependence and act out of a sense of community. The United States has chosen the path of cooperation.

The United States, as the world's strongest economy, has demonstrated its resilience; we are on the road to recovery. We might best survive any new round of economic warfare. But it is my country's conviction that tests of strength benefit no nation. The approach that we took at the seventh special session of the U.N. General Assembly in September reflects our vision of a more positive future.

The special session reached consensus on an impressive range of economic problems. This commitment to cooperation can become a benchmark in human affairs—if its spirit is carried forward. We owe our people solutions, not slogans. So let us set to work. Let us implement the consensus of the special session and take up its unfinished tasks. Let us make this conference a decisive step toward their achievement.

The Road to This Conference

We are here because two years ago the international structure was gravely tested by a crisis in energy. No problem on the international agenda is more crucial to the world economy. As this conference demonstrates, it has led us to a much broader consideration of the range of related issues.

The unprecedented expansion of the global economy in the decades since World War II relied upon the plentiful supply of energy at reasonable prices. It produced economic growth, fostered industrialization, and encouraged development in every quarter of the globe.

Thus the energy crisis—caused by a combination of the 1973 embargo and the fivefold increase in the price of oil—has dealt a serious blow to global stability and prosperity.

Inflation, recession, and payments balances significantly worsened in all the industrialized world and in those developing nations which had realized substantial progress toward industrialization. The poorest of the developing countries, struggling to make modest steps toward progress, were dealt the cruelest blow of all. Their hopes for growth were, and continue to be, thwarted. Their development planning has been disrupted. Even their agricultural production has been undermined by the increased cost of petrochemical fertilizers. For the vast majority of the developing world, economic justice was poorly served.

In response to the energy crisis, the United States sought first to reach a consensus among the industrialized nations. We worked together to assure basic security against future arbitrary disruptions in oil supply and against potential oil-induced financial difficulties. We pledged ourselves to long-term cooperation in energy conservation and the development of alternative energy supplies.[5] We agreed not to resort to protectionist measures;[6] and we began unprecedented cooperation in our economic policies, as dramatized by the recent economic summit in Rambouillet.[7]

These actions were not taken in a spirit of confrontation. Most are prudent steps of self-protection which have effect only if confrontation is provoked by others. Others involve an urgent program for the development of alternative sources to the benefit of all.

But the collaboration of the industrial countries has always been

[5]Cf. Chapters 5 and 17.
[6]Cf. Chapter 18 at notes 16-17.
[7]Cf. Chapter 38.

conceived as only part of a larger program for economic progress. From the beginning, we have foreseen an effort to develop a constructive dialogue leading to close and mutually beneficial long-term economic ties with oil-producing nations—so that our investment and technical support would contribute to their development and their prosperity would contribute to the worldwide expansion of trade and development. We recognize that the only durable basis for constructive relations is an economic system which fosters the prosperity of all. Each of us has a stake in the progress of others.

Last April, at the invitation of the President of France, we agreed to begin this discussion.[8] The industrial nations wanted to focus on energy. The oil-producing and other developing nations wanted to give equal priority to a wider range of development issues, including prices and markets for other raw materials, and to international financial questions. The industrial nations regarded these issues as too varied and complex to be addressed effectively in a single forum. The April preparatory conference failed to reconcile these positions.

To demonstrate its desire for a constructive and cooperative solution the United States worked closely with other participants in developing a mutually satisfactory arrangement: energy, the concerns of the less developed countries about raw materials, development, and related financial matters would be addressed as part of a discussion of global economic problems, while maintaining enough distinction between them for a useful dialogue.

The United States is committed to a serious and wide-ranging program of cooperation with the developing world. My country understands full well, and has shown in its many proposals, that this dialogue must encompass issues of concern to all sides—including the needs of the many nations not in attendance here. For us, this clearly requires a discussion of the effects of energy prices on the world economy. For cooperation depends on mutual respect, mutual understanding, and mutual benefit.

To this end, at the seventh special session of the U.N. General Assembly three months ago, the United States made a series of proposals in several areas:[9]

—To insure the economic security of developing countries against shortfalls in export earnings, food shortages, and natural disasters;
—To accelerate their economic growth by improving their access to capital markets, technology, and foreign investment;
—To better the conditions of trade and investment in key

[8]Cf. Chapter 7.
[9]Cf. Chapter 30, Document 49.

commodities on which many of their economies are dependent and to set an example in the vital area of food;

　—To improve the world trading system and make it better serve development goals, and realize through the multilateral trade negotiations a strengthening of developing-country participation; and

　—To address the especially urgent needs of the poorest countries devastated by current economic conditions.

The seventh special session ended on a note of conciliation and cooperation. The spirit of the session was carried forward to the October preparatory conference in Paris,[10] where the declaration laid the basis for our meeting today.

This will be the attitude of the United States here. Progress has been made in many areas, and this conference must move us forward.

The Work of the Commissions

The four commissions that this conference is establishing have much work before them:

　—The Commission on Energy should promote an effective world balance between energy demand and supply. It should work for practical cooperation among industrialized and developing countries to develop new energy supplies. And it should lay the foundations of a mutually beneficial long-term relationship between energy producers and consumers.

　—The Commission on Raw Materials should work to establish the conditions for stable longrun supplies of raw materials vital to global progress at prices that are remunerative to producers and fair to consumers.

　—The Commission on Development should strive to accelerate economic development in all nations, especially the poorest. In particular, it should bring together industrial nations and oil-wealthy nations to provide financial support for the development initiatives of the U.N. special session.

　—The Commission on Finance should address financial issues as they relate to the work of the other three commissions. It should seek to strengthen the sense of shared financial responsibility for the health and growth of the international economy.

With a cooperative approach, the commissions can give direction and impetus to related activity in other forums and organizations, under whose jurisdiction a number of these issues fall. They can

[10] Bulletin, 73: 665-72.

serve as clearinghouses for information and motivate other organizations doing similar work. They can identify areas where necessary work is not being done and devise new initiatives where needed.

The United States will support progress on a broad range of topics in the context of the four commissions. But we have a special interest in the following areas:

—First, the price of oil and the security of oil supply as they affect the international economy;
—Second, the serious balance-of-payments problems of developing countries;
—Third, the conditions of international investment;
—Fourth, the issues of key commodities, especially food;
—Fifth, the problems of trade; and
—Sixth, the urgent needs of the poorest countries.

Let me discuss each of these in turn.

Energy

First, energy. The application of science and technology to tap the vast energy potential imprisoned beneath the earth, radiated by the sun, generated by the movement of wind and water across the earth's surface, or locked in the core of matter is fundamental to the hopes of millions to pull themselves above a bare struggle for existence. For the expansion of the global economy for both developed and developing countries depends heavily on our harnessing and efficiently employing the world's energy resources.

Some nations are particularly well endowed with these resources; some have the scientific and technological expertise to explore and utilize that potential. The international flow of energy, investment capital required to produce it, and goods produced from fuels have become in effect a global energy system which sustains all our economies. Only through international cooperation can all nations benefit from these processes and can the world economy harness its energy resources most effectively.

The United States is committed to a cooperative approach. We have much to offer. We have produced more energy than any other nation in the history of mankind, our energy science and technology are the most advanced, and we have tremendous potential for future energy development in our country and abroad. The United States also has much to gain from cooperation. Our energy needs are the world's largest; our ability to raise living standards for all our citizens depends on greater energy production and the more efficient use of energy resources.

This dialogue and this conference have these tasks:

—First, it is time to reach a common evaluation of the relationship between changes in energy prices and the stability and performance of the world economy.

The abrupt and arbitrary increase in the price of oil has been a major factor in rates of inflation and unemployment unprecedented since the 1930's. It has led to serious balance-of-payments deficits, indirectly through global recession and directly through higher priced imports.

By extraordinary effort, the industrial countries, on the whole, put their payments back in balance over the last year, although at a high cost to the well-being of their peoples. Thus the immediate burden of the massive petrodollar deficit is now borne largely by the developing countries which have little or no oil resources.

Developing countries, by definition, tend to have less of a margin to reduce consumption, to restructure energy use, or to shift to alternative sources when the oil price rises. They are the most vulnerable—and the most wounded.

A lower oil price would make possible more rapid economic recovery around the globe. It would assist the developing countries by easing their enormous balance-of-payments burden and their debt burden and increasing foreign demand for their exports. A lower price, along with stability of supply, would also benefit producer nations over the long term by easing the urgency for consuming countries to develop alternative supply sources.

Conversely, any further increase in prices would seriously hamper economic recovery, retard international trade, compound the internal difficulties of many countries, weaken the ability of the advanced nations to assist the developing, and strain the fabric of international cooperation.

It is time for a serious discussion of this issue. We are prepared to make a sustained effort to achieve understanding.

—Second, we must collaborate to find new sources of energy and intensify our conservation efforts. All consuming countries, developed and developing, must use energy more efficiently and develop more abundant supplies. Producers need to prepare their economies for the day when they will have exhausted their easily accessible oil reserves.

Individually, the industrialized countries are accelerating the development of their own energy sources. The United States is developing its conventional fuels and also new sources, including nuclear power, to replace fossil fuels. We have committed massive resources to research and devoted our best talents to this effort; we expect it to result in a substantial increase in U.S. energy production. In Europe, major efforts have been launched along the same lines, with the North Sea as the most dramatic example of the potential. The development of alternative energy sources is vital.

In the near future, the industrial countries will take the first steps toward welding these national programs into a coherent cooperative program. These programs are designed to promote conservation and to accelerate the development of alternative energy supplies through large-scale joint projects and cooperation in research and development. We will demonstrate our commitment to the maximum development of new energy by agreeing not to permit imported oil to be sold in our internal markets below a common minimum safeguard price.

This effort will bring a better balance to the world energy market. But as it gathers support, it will bring important benefits to developing as well as industrial countries. The programs that the industrial countries are undertaking, and those that many developing countries have within their potential to undertake, can lead to additional and more secure supplies of energy, which can be a spur to their prosperity and development. All nations will have access to a larger pool of energy resources, and there will be less competition for oil. The efforts of developing countries to increase their own production of energy, if supported, can be the single most important step they take to secure their development for future generations.

At the seventh special session of the General Assembly, the United States proposed an International Energy Institute. Through such an organization, the developed countries and OPEC countries can assist poorer developing nations to utilize energy more efficiently, increase their own production, and improve allocation and distribution of existing resources. It could identify current or new energy technologies most relevant to their special needs. The institute can help oil-producing countries to improve the use of their own energy.

Using the most advanced techniques of analysis, the institute could help assess all countries' energy resources and requirements. Staffed by experts drawn from government, industry, and academic life in both industrialized and developing countries, it could provide training for local and regional technicians or specialists in energy problems. It could become a central point of contact where policymakers and experts could exchange ideas on plans and programs.

We see the institute as a first bridge between the massive effort the industrialized countries have now launched to develop alternative sources of energy and the effort which the developing countries must now undertake.

In addition, the United States has suggested a number of other means by which the talents and experience of the developed nations, collectively and individually, can assist developing states to find and exploit new energy sources and conserve their national patrimony. We will advance these proposals in the Energy Commission. We anticipate a full exchange of views on their scope and substance.

Oil producers and nations with the technology to help develop oil resources share an interest in cooperation on conservation and exploration. But this cooperation will be easier to forge in a stable energy market with a more appropriate structure of energy prices.

—Third, the United States seeks a greater participation and contribution of the oil-producing countries in the international economy. With the extraordinary transfer of wealth that has taken place, it is in the common interest that the oil-producing nations be constructive members, not challengers, of the world economic system, that investment and the latest technology be made available to them on a reimbursable basis for their development programs, and that the flow of goods and services be enhanced between producing and consuming countries.

We believe that these three issues—a better understanding of the effects of oil price increases on the world economy; cooperation on conservation and new production; and the orderly integration of OPEC economies into the global economy—are priority tasks for the energy forum.

Balance of Payments

The balance-of-payments problems of developing countries are an immediate and urgent task for this conference to address, closely related to the energy issue. Current projections indicate that the developing world in 1976 will be collectively in deficit by about $35 billion. Bilateral and multilateral aid, along with direct investment, will finance roughly $25 billion of this. The question is whether borrowing from international capital markets can again this year make up the remainder. If not, some countries will be forced to reduce imports, cut back development programs, and further mortgage their future. The deficits of the developing countries thus could endanger not only their own well-being but also the stability of the international trade and financial system.

A multitude of ideas and proposals are already before us. Let us address steps that can be taken now.

—First, the members of the IMF should promptly agree on the details of the Trust Fund which the United States has proposed to furnish concessional financing for the poorest countries. It would provide these countries additional resources of

$1-$2 billion a year, using the profits from IMF gold sales as well as national contributions. We are well on the way to resolving outstanding issues on IMF gold; let us take final action on the Trust Fund in January.

—Second, the members of the IMF should complete negotiations next month on the new development security facility. The United States made this major proposal to provide more substantial financing to countries facing temporary shortfalls in export earnings due to the world business cycle or commodity fluctuations. We proposed this on September 1; its realization in January would be an impressive demonstration of international resolve and responsiveness.

—Third, the IMF should approve a one-third increase in member quotas, thus expanding its potential financing for all members.

Final approval can and must be taken on each of these proposals at the meeting of the IMF Interim Committee in Jamaica in early January.[11] Together with substantial unused regular drawings still available to developing countries, these measures will add significantly to the capacity of developing countries to sustain their needed imports and their development programs.

But however substantial these facilities, they may not be enough. Once the Trust Fund and these other proposals have been implemented in January, we must determine how best to respond to the remaining balance-of-payments problems of the developing countries. The United States is committed to finding a constructive solution.

Our specific response will depend in part on whether there is a general across-the-board financing problem or one concentrating on a few countries. One promising approach would be to expand the credit that developing countries can draw from the IMF by liberalizing the rules governing access to regular IMF resources. The IMF Board could, for example, increase the size of each credit drawing, base them on expanded new quotas, or add a new drawing beyond those now available. Decisions on such proposals will need to be based on close analysis of their effect on the financial integrity of the IMF. Secretary Simon will present our analysis and proposals for increased use of the IMF at the Interim Committee meeting.

We cannot emphasize enough the need for immediate action in this area to supplement the long-term proposals which have already been made. The responsibility does not lie with the industrialized countries alone. We cannot be expected to bear the major burdens for remedying balance-of-payments problems in which the actions

[11]Cf. Chapter 38 at note 3.

of others play such a significant role. There is a collective obligation to act; there must be a joint program involving the industrialized as well as the oil-producing countries.

Investment and Technology for Development

The balance-of-payments deficits of the developing countries will perhaps moderate as the global economy recovers from recession. But sustained economic growth requires the continuous application of capital, technology, and management skills to development needs.

Private investment has always been a major factor in the growth of the global economy. My own country has benefited from foreign investment throughout its history. Today more than ever, the developing countries need this capital in addition to the limited supply of official development assistance.

To make this possible, governments of developing countries need better access to world capital markets. The United States has urged that technical assistance and expertise be provided to developing countries that are ready to enter long-term private capital markets for the first time. We have proposed a major expansion of the resources of the World Bank's International Finance Corporation (IFC) to strengthen the private sector in developing countries and to enhance their international competitiveness for private capital. We have recommended creation of an international investment trust to mobilize private portfolio capital for investment in local enterprises. And we are contributing to the work of the IMF-World Bank Development Committee to assist in removing impediments to developing countries' access to capital markets.

But we also believe that one of the most important vehicles for transferring capital, technology, and management skills to where they are most needed is private enterprise. There simply is not enough governmental capital available. Because of ideological considerations, these private enterprises operate in an investment climate increasingly clouded by unpredictable national legislation and uncertain rules of the game.

In this environment everybody suffers. Host countries are deprived of the capital resources, technology, and management which these enterprises uniquely provide, as well as a source of tax revenue. Home countries are deprived of the overseas markets, investment income, and the new ideas and techniques which come with foreign contact. And the enterprises themselves are squeezed at both ends, making overseas investment less worthwhile for them and reducing their contribution to home and host country alike and to the global product.

The United States has taken an active part in international efforts to facilitate international investment on a basis that serves the interests of all parties. We are willing to explore voluntary guidelines for the behavior of both transnational enterprises and governments. At the United Nations I stated four basic principles that should be included:

—Transnational enterprises must obey local law and refrain from unlawful intervention in the domestic affairs of host countries.

—Host governments must treat these enterprises equitably, without discrimination among them, and in accordance with international law.

—Both governments and businesses must respect the contractual obligations they freely undertake.

—Principles for transnational enterprises should apply to domestic enterprises where relevant.

But efforts should not be limited to general guidelines for investment. Other remedial measures are possible.

Taxation is one such area. Because they operate in multiple jurisdictions, transnational enterprises may sometimes be subject to either double taxation or inappropriate tax incentives. The result in either case is that investment patterns are distorted. We must find ways to enable both host and home countries to coordinate their tax policies and make them more equitable to each other and to productive enterprises.

A second area for improvement is intergovernmental consultation on investment disputes. This is especially important to developing countries whose progress is dependent on a climate conducive to an adequate flow of investment. It is time to develop generally accepted international rules for the settlement of investment disputes and the arbitration of differences and other guidelines for dealing with problems arising between governments and enterprises. The United States recommends that the World Bank's International Center for Settlement of Investment Disputes be given a greater role in solving important investment controversies.

International assistance for development must also focus on the advancement, selection, and application of modern technology. Many countries in the developing world are already on the path of industrialization. They have proved their capacity to take advantage of the vast storehouse of modern technology. The United States encourages this endeavor. We have long been in the forefront of the effort to train more managers, technicians, and researchers in the developing countries to carry this forward.

Most technology transfer takes place through international investment and the operations of transnational enterprises on a licensing, equity, or contract basis. The United States understands the concern of many developing countries not to become the repository of obsolescent technology. Technology must be suited to local needs, the terms and conditions must be mutually acceptable, and it must be effectively managed and utilized. Developing countries must be enabled to make their own informed choices of foreign or domestic technology, to adapt it to their own needs and conditions, and to manage its application skillfully. This technology transfer requires the development of human capabilities—the management and skills that constitute the infrastructure of technological development.

People—their training and their placement in a country's management systems—are the key to making technology a producing resource. International cooperation can make no greater contribution to development than to foster the training of a corps of specialists in each country competent to select, bargain for, and manage technologies. We see this requirement as an important topic for consideration by the Commission on Development, and we will make concrete proposals to this end.

Commodities

A healthy global economy requires that both producers and consumers find protection against the cycle of raw materials surplus and shortage which chokes growth and disrupts planning. We must insure more reliable supplies of vital commodities on terms fair to all.

The problem is most urgent in food, mankind's most critical need. The cycles of feast and famine, widely fluctuating prices of basic foodstuffs, and breakdowns in the system of storage and transportation continue to afflict mankind. These show few signs of abating. And in the long run, growth in demand for food threatens to outrun the expansion of supply.

As the world's largest producer and exporter of food, the United States recognizes its special responsibility. At home, we have been committed to policies of maximum food production and have removed all production restraints; internationally, we have proposed a system of grain reserves to help moderate fluctuations in world prices and supplies.[12]

---

[12]Detailed proposals for a system of nationally held grain reserves, based on the principles outlined in Secretary Kissinger's U.N. speech, had been presented by the U.S. to a working group of the International Wheat Council and were currently under preliminary discussion in connection with that body's preparations to formulate a new International Wheat Agreement. Action on the U.S. proposals, which involved a 30 million ton world security reserve stock of wheat and rice to be held by

We believe that our grain reserves proposal can be a model for cooperation on other commodity problems. It takes into account interests of producers and consumers. It makes special provision for the concerns of developing countries. Its reliance on buffer stocks minimizes the distortion of trade and improves the efficiency of the market. We now await the cooperation and commitment of others to help implement this proposal.

Most importantly, we are increasing our assistance to developing countries—not merely for short-term relief but to help them boost their own agricultural production. Our bilateral aid programs in this area have been expanded greatly. We also strongly support the proposal first made by oil-exporting countries for an International Fund for Agricultural Development.[13] We have announced our willingness to make a contribution of $200 million, or one-fifth of the worldwide goal of $1 billion.

Other commodities are of critical importance to many countries, either as producers or consumers. Many developing countries depend crucially on earnings from commodity exports to lift their people above subsistence levels, to support basic social programs, and to finance the beginnings of industrialization. The solution to commodity issues will affect not only the developing countries but also the industrial countries—who are in fact the largest producers, consumers, and exporters of commodities. The economies of all countries are affected by the instabilities of the market—the vulnerability of agricultural commodities to the vagaries of weather and shifts in world demand, the sensitivity of agricultural and mineral markets to fluctuations in the business cycle in industrial countries, and the higher prices of critical energy imports.

At the seventh special session a consensus was achieved that commodity issues should be approached cooperatively. The U.S. position is that a realistic and constructive approach will require that we:

—Establish producer-consumer forums for discussions of key commodities;
—Reduce obstacles to producers' access to markets and to consumers' access to supplies;

importers and exporters, was, however, delayed by the contention of the European Community that issues relating to grain stocks should be dealt with in the framework of the multilateral trade negotiations under the GATT. For details cf. the statement of Assistant Secretary of State Thomas O. Enders, Dec. 3, in *Bulletin*, 74: 33-4. A partial text of the proposals appears in *Digest of United States Practice in International Law, 1975*: 686-8.

[13] Cf. Chapter 30 at note 22.

—Rely more on buffer stocks, where feasible and necessary, in preference to restrictions on trade and production;

—Improve the productivity and marketability of agricultural raw materials; and

—Expand worldwide production capacity in other key commodities.

We now stand ready to cooperate in establishing producer-consumer forums to discuss copper, bauxite, and other commodities. We plan to address the question of supply and market access in the multilateral trade negotiations in the next several months. We have proposed that the IFC and the IBRD make available increased financing for mineral development and look forward to progress in the near future. We plan to support the U.N. Revolving Fund for Natural Resources Exploration. Finally, we have proposed establishment of an organization to finance and coordinate research on nonfood tropical products to improve their productivity and competitiveness.

We look forward to additional discussion of these measures in the Raw Materials Commission of this conference.

Trade

An expanding and more open international trading system is a principal factor in the growth and development of both developed and developing nations. We are committed to the strengthening of this system so it can better serve the needs of the international community and include importantly the developing nations.

Trade enables nations to earn their own way. It is most consistent with national dignity and with the efficiency of the economic system.

Over the last five years, in a major step of international cooperation, all the major industrial nations have committed themselves to establish a generalized system of tariff preferences, giving developing countries better access to the markets of all industrial nations.

The United States will implement its generalized system of preferences in two weeks' time.[14] Under this system we will eliminate duties on 2,724 tariff items, representing some 19 percent of dutiable non-oil imports from eligible countries in 1974. This will open up significant potential new markets for the products of developing countries in the United States.

Tropical products are a promising area of export expansion for many developing countries. The international trading system should encourage this expansion. In the multilateral trade negotia-

[14]Cf. Chapter 30 at note 13.

tions in Geneva, work is beginning on a package of tariff concessions on tropical products for early implementation. We attach much importance to this effort.

Tariff escalation—the process by which tariffs are progressively increased on goods as they move higher on the ladder of processing—is an obstacle to the exports and industrialization of many developing countries. At the U.N. special session, we proposed that reduction, or in some cases elimination, of tariff escalation be an important goal for the multilateral trade negotiations. The effort to identify and negotiate specific changes will begin next year.

This effort, however, is related in our view to the issue of access to supply of raw materials. Consumers cannot be expected to improve access to their markets for finished products if they face restrictions on supplies of related raw materials. Thus the Geneva negotiations must also improve access to supply as well as access to markets.

Reducing or eliminating nontariff barriers to trade is another major task facing the international trading community. We will make a particular effort to negotiate special and differential treatment for developing countries in this area.

An improved and strengthened world trading system would not be complete, however, if it did not insure greater sharing by developing countries of both benefits and responsibilities. Developing countries should gradually take on the normal obligations of reciprocity and trade rules as they progress.

The multilateral trade negotiations are the most effective forum for pursuing all these objectives.

The United States put forward proposals in many of these areas at the recent meeting of the Trade Negotiations Committee in Geneva as goals for 1976. The developing countries will also benefit from progress in all other areas of the negotiations, which we now hope will be completed in 1977.[15]

The United States is committed to a role of leadership in the multilateral trade negotiations. We will seek rapid progress for the benefit of both developing and developed countries. I believe that this conference and its relevant commissions should endorse the work of the multilateral trade negotiations. It should provide continued support for the negotiations by monitoring and contributing ideas to the work in Geneva.

Global Poverty

Our deliberations here must address the plight of the one-quarter of mankind whose lives are overwhelmed by poverty and hunger

[15]Cf. Chapter 38 at note 8.

and numbed by insecurity and despair. This group has suffered im-
measurably from high prices of food and fuel. Their export
revenues have been seriously undermined by global recession.

In these regions less than one person in five is literate; one baby
in ten dies in childhood, and in some areas closer to one out of two;
life expectancy is less than 50 years; and birth rates continue to be
intolerably high. Public expenditures for education and health care
are low—and their per capita income has been declining for the last
four years.

And so today, alongside the Third World with its increasing
power and assertiveness, there has come into being a fourth world,
where human beings still struggle for bare existence.

In one international conference after another, we have all
pointed to the fourth world with sincere intentions of giving immediate help, providing long-term assistance, and devising special
arrangements. We have agreed that this is a major test of a just international structure. It is time for all of us here to act on our
words. Three areas need immediate action:

—First, many of the poorest cannot finance balance-of-
payments deficits because they cannot gain access to capital
markets or because of high interest rates on what little finance
they can obtain. The Trust Fund which the United States proposed in the IMF to provide up to $2 billion for emergency relief
is of special benefit to them. Let us reach a consensus to create
this Trust Fund at next month's IMF meeting in Jamaica.

—The second area for immediate action is food aid. No
obligation is more basic than our insuring that the poorest are
fed. This fiscal year the United States expects to provide more
than 6 million tons of food aid—or more than 60 percent of the
10-million-ton global target set by the World Food Conference[16]
and a 20 percent increase over last year's contribution. Others
must donate their fair share.

—Third, the poorest countries need preferential and expanded
access to official concessionary financial aid. The United States
will do its part. More than 70 percent of our bilateral development assistance now goes to low-income countries. The concessional financing of the international financial institutions should
also be expanded.[17] At the seventh special session, my government pledged to support the fifth IDA [International Development Association] replenishment and the regional development
banks. We are making every effort to secure congressional appropriations for funds already committed. We hope that the
traditional and new donors will help the poorest through finan-

[16] *AFR, 1974*: 442.
[17] Cf. Chapter 30 at notes 12 and 21.

cial contributions to both bilateral and multilateral programs.

Let us urgently rededicate ourselves to action on behalf of the poorest among us. Such action is the responsibility of the entire world community—not just the industrial countries but also the more affluent in the developing world. While no one commission will be dealing with the totality of problems of the fourth world, each commission has a responsiblity to be conscious of the need for special consideration for the poorest.

Conclusion

Ladies and gentlemen: The nations and economies of the world are many; our differences are great. But our reasons for pulling together are far greater. Therefore our dialogue here must be candid, but with a positive spirit and cooperative attitude. The prosperity, the progress, and indeed the security of the world may depend upon whether we succeed in finding realistic answers to the kinds of problems before us at this conference. For lasting peace around the globe will depend not only on containing conflict but mounting progress. It requires not merely the preservation of stability but the fulfillment of human aspirations.

The issues we face are often technical, but their implications could not be more profound. They go to the heart of our future. Only rarely in history does mankind consciously swing out from familiar, well-marked paths to move in new directions. Only rarely does humanity comprehend as clearly as we do today that change is imminent and that the direction to be taken is subject to human decision. The nations of the world face such an opportunity now.

We have the possibility of forging international relationships that will govern world affairs for the next several decades. We can bring together developed and developing, producer and consumer, in common endeavors—or we can go our separate ways, with every one of us paying the price for a lack of vision in lower standards of living and increased international tensions. Mutual interest should bring us together; only blindness can keep us apart.

The American people have always believed in a world of conciliation rather than a world ruled by intimidation, pressure, or force. My country, in spite of its own strengths and advantages, has chosen the path of cooperation. We will remain committed to that path. But we cannot travel it alone; others will have to join us. All of us here must base our policies on the reality that we have a practical and moral stake in each other's well-being.

I am confident of our cooperation and of our success. The result will be a fair and prosperous world economy of benefit to all nations, and with it new hope, opportunity, and justice for all peoples.

(65)   Communiqué Issued at the Conclusion of the Meeting, Paris, December 19, 1975.[18]

1. The Conference on International Economic Cooperation met in Paris at ministerial level, from December 16 to December 19. Representatives of the following 27 members of the Conference took part: Algeria, Argentina, Australia, Brazil, Cameroon, Canada, EEC, Egypt, India, Indonesia, Iran, Iraq, Jamaica, Japan, Mexico, Nigeria, Pakistan, Peru, Saudi Arabia, Spain, Sweden, Switzerland, United States, Venezuela, Yugoslavia, Zaïre, Zambia. The ministerial representatives who attended the conference welcomed the presence of the Secretary-General of the United Nations.

2. The work of the Conference was opened by H.E. the President of the French Republic, Mr. Valéry Giscard d'Estaing.

3. The Hon. Allan J. MacEachen, Secretary of State for External Affairs of Canada, and Dr. Manuel Perez-Guerrero, Minister of State for International Economic Affairs of Venezuela, co-chairmen of the Conference on International Economic Cooperation, presided at the ministerial meeting.

4. The ministerial representatives at the Conference expressed their views with regard to the international economic situation. They made suggestions as to how the problems which they had identified might be resolved. Attention was drawn to the plight of the most seriously affected countries. They recognized that the Conference on International Economic Cooperation provides a unique opportunity to address these problems and to further international economic cooperation for the benefit of all countries and peoples.

5. The Conference decided to initiate an intensified international dialogue. To this end, it established four Commissions (on energy, raw materials, development and financial affairs) which will meet periodically through the coming year. It was agreed that each of the four Commissions would consist of fifteen members, ten of them representing developing countries, five of them representing industrialized countries.

6. The Commissions shall start their work on February 11, 1976. Preparation for the work of the four commissions shall be reviewed at a meeting of the co-chairmen of the Conference and of the four Commissions after consultation with the other participants in the Conference. This meeting will take place on January 26, 1976 within the framework of the general guidelines contained in paragraphs 10-14 of the final declaration of the Second Preparatory Meeting[19] which are approved by the Conference.

[18]Unofficial text from *Bulletin*, 74: 48-9.
[19]Cf. note 3 above.

7. The Conference agreed that the following participants should serve on the Commissions:

—Energy: Algeria, Brazil, Canada, Egypt, EEC, India, Iran, Iraq, Jamaica, Japan, Saudi Arabia, Switzerland, United States, Venezuela, Zaïre.
—Raw materials: Argentina, Australia, Cameroon, EEC, Indonesia, Japan, Mexico, Nigeria, Peru, Spain, United States, Venezuela, Yugoslavia, Zaïre, Zambia.
—Development: Algeria, Argentina, Cameroon, Canada, EEC, India, Jamaica, Japan, Nigeria, Pakistan, Peru, Sweden, United States, Yugoslavia, Zaïre.
—Finance: Brazil, EEC, Egypt, India, Indonesia, Iran, Iraq, Japan, Mexico, Pakistan, Saudi Arabia, Sweden, Switzerland, United States, Zambia.

The co-chairmen of the Commissions will be:

—Energy: Saudi Arabia and United States.
—Raw materials: Japan and Peru.
—Development: Algeria and EEC.
—Finance: EEC and Iran.

Joint meetings of the co-chairmen of the Conference and of the Commissions may be held if the need arises.

8. It was agreed that members of the Conference who wish to follow the work of a Commission to which they do not belong should be entitled to appoint a representative in the capacity of auditor without the right to speak.

9. The Conference decided that a number of intergovernmental functional organizations which are directly concerned with the problems to be considered would be able to make a useful contribution to their consideration. It therefore invited these organizations (United Nations Secretariat, OPEC, IEA, UNCTAD, OECD, FAO, GATT, UNDP, UNIDO, IMF, IBRD, SELA)[20] to be represented on a permanent basis in the relevant commissions. Their observers will have the right to speak but not the right to vote and hence will not participate in the formation of a consensus. Each commission may, in addition, invite appropriate intergovern-

[20]Organization of Petroleum Exporting Countries; International Energy Agency; United Nations Conference on Trade and Development; Organization for Economic Cooperation and Development; Food and Agriculture Organization; General Agreement on Tariffs and Trade; United Nations Development Program; United Nations Industrial Development Organization; International Monetary Fund; International Bank for Reconstruction and Development; Latin American Economic System.

mental functional organizations to participate as observers ad hoc in the examination of specific questions.

10. The Conference decided to establish an international secretariat with an exclusively administrative and technical function on the basis of proposals put forward by the two co-chairmen. It named Mr. Bernard Guitton [of France] as head of the secretariat and approved plans for its organization and operational procedures. The financial costs arising from the establishment of the secretariat and from future meetings of the Conference will be borne by members of the Conference on the basis of a formula agreed by the Conference.

11. It was agreed that the four Commissions should meet in Paris. Subsequent meetings of the Commissions will be convened by their co-chairmen.

12. One or several meetings of the Conference at the level of government officials may be held at least six months after this ministerial meeting. The Ministerial Conference agreed to meet again at ministerial level in about twelve months time.

13. The Conference adopted the rules of procedure recommended by the Preparatory Meeting which are based on the principle of consensus, according to which decisions and recommendations are adopted when the chair has established that no member delegation has made any objection. English, Arabic, Spanish and French are the official and working languages of the Conference. The rules of procedure apply to all the bodies of the Conference.

14. The Conference took note of the resolution of the General Assembly entitled "Conference on International Economic Cooperation" (Resolution 3515 (XXX))[21] and agreed to make reports available to the 31st session of the U.N. General Assembly.

15. The members of the Conference paid special tribute to President Giscard d'Estaing for the action he had taken to bring about the dialogue which is now engaged and expressed their warm appreciation to the Government of France for its hospitality and for the efforts and obligations it had undertaken in order to make the Ministerial Conference a success.

---

[21] Adopted without vote Dec. 15, 1975.

44. THE GENERAL ASSEMBLY CONCLUDES

(New York, December 17, 1975)

[The more equable spirit that had seemed to animate the Paris economic conference had failed to communicate itself to the U.N. Assembly, where the relations between the United States and the Communist-"third world" majority remained at the abysmal level to which they had been reduced by the resolution branding Zionism as "a form of racism and racial discrimination."[1] Time and again in the ensuing weeks, this signal rejection of U.S. purposes and beliefs had been reduplicated as the Assembly continued to trample on American sensibilities and to endorse positions the United States could not conceivably accept in view of its history and ethical outlook.

In most such cases, the United States was simply left behind by the galloping impetuosity of a majority whose course was subject to neither inward nor outward restraint. There had, however, been one original, if thoroughly ill-starred, American initiative in the form of a proposal calling for a worldwide amnesty for political prisoners. Put forward by Ambassador Moynihan on November 12, the proposal was withdrawn a mere nine days later after it had been rendered all but unrecognizable by the addition of "destructive" and politically motivated amendments.[2] Such a rebuff was only partially solaced by the Assembly's later adoption, without a formal vote, of a strongly worded, essentially hortatory "Declaration on the Protection of All Persons from being subjected to Torture and other Cruel, Inhuman or Degrading Treatment or Punishment."[3]

---

[1] Chapter 37, Document 57.
[2] *Bulletin*, 73: 867-74; *U.S. Participation, 1975*: 209-10.
[3] Annex to Resolution 3452 (XXX), Dec. 9, 1975 (*Bulletin*, 74: 87-8); cf. note 24 to Chapter 32.

In other political and ideological fields, the U.S. delegation as usual found itself devoting much of its time to fruitlessly opposing Assembly actions aimed, among other things, at denouncing the evils of colonialism, demanding more rapid progress in the SALT talks, endorsing the anti-Zionist expressions of the Conference on the International Women's Year, reaffirming the Charter of Economic Rights and Duties of States, and castigating Israel's policy in the occupied territories. (In addition, Ambassador Moynihan cast the United States' twelfth veto at a Security Council meeting on December 8 to block the adoption of an "unbalanced" resolution condemning recent Israeli air attacks on Palestinian targets in Lebanon but failing to mention Arab violence against Israel.)[4] Nor did American delegates hide their dismay at the Assembly's action in adopting two mutually contradictory recommendations on the Korean problem, one backing the U.S.-South Korean proposal for talks on dissolving the U.N. Command while maintaining the Armistice Agreement,[5] the other calling for dissolution of the U.N. Command and replacement of the Armistice Agreement by a peace agreement of unspecified character.[6]

Adding to the sense of hostile encirclement that affected the U.S. delegation at this period was a fairly widespread reaction against the personal style of Ambassador Moynihan, whose professorial manner and pungent rhetoric had given offense extending even beyond the numerous "third world" group. Ambassador Ivor Richard of the United Kingdom, for example, was quoted as publicly deprecating "confrontational" tactics and making caustic references to the "O.K. Corral" and "Wyatt Earp." Described at one point as being on the verge of resignation, Ambassador Moynihan was publicly backed by the President and Secretary Kissinger and was apparently persuaded to remain at least until after the end of the Assembly session.[7] Yet there were clearly valedictory overtones in the concluding statement (**Document 66**) in which, not long before its adjournment on December 17, the U.S. Representative again reproved the Assembly for committing "acts which we regard as abominations," lectured it upon its inherent limitations,

[4]U.N. Document S/11898 (*Bulletin*, 74: 26); failed of adoption by a vote of 13-1 (U.S.)-1 (Costa Rica).

[5]Resolution 3390 A (XXX), Nov. 18, 1975 (*Bulletin*, 73: 822-3); adopted by a vote of 59 (U.S.)-51-29.

[6]Resolution 3390 B (XXX), Nov. 18, 1975 (*Bulletin*, 73: 823-4); adopted by a vote of 54-43 (U.S.)-42.

[7]*New York Times*, Nov. 22, 1975; White House statement, Nov. 24, in *Presidential Documents*, 11: 1312. Ambassador Moynihan resigned Jan. 31, 1976.

and assured it that the United States remained unflaggingly dedicated to establishing "some minimal international standards by which governments treat their citizens."]

(66) Remarks by Ambassador Moynihan at the Closing Session of the 30th United Nations General Assembly, December 17, 1975.[8]

None will learn with surprise that for the United States, at very least, the 30th General Assembly has been a profound, even alarming disappointment. This splendid hall has, since the opening of the Assembly, been repeatedly the scene of acts which we regard as abominations. We have not sought to conceal this view. Nor is it our view alone. Throughout the world individuals and governments have observed this General Assembly with dismay.

Unquestionably, our distress was deepened by the contrast between this regular Assembly session and the special session which preceded it.[9] In the recent history, perhaps in the whole history, of the United Nations there has not been a more striking, even exhilarating example of what the General Assembly can accomplish than the example of the seventh special session. In two weeks of intensive, determined, and hardheaded negotiations, we worked out a set of principles and programs for the economic advance of the poorer nations of the world that will take us a decade to put into practice.

The United States took a lead in this enterprise, from the opening statement of the Secretary of State to the concluding dense and detailed agreement, which incorporated no fewer than 28 proposals we had initially set forth.

In the general debate of the 30th session that followed, one speaker after another rose to extol the achievement of the special session. Praise was unanimous—from every bloc, from nations of every size and condition. The Assembly was honored this year by the visit of His Majesty King Olav [V] of Norway, who appropriately made the last such general statement:

The successful conclusion of the seventh special session of the General Assembly has initiated a universal and cooperative process to effect changes in international economic relations which may have a far-reaching impact on the daily life of millions around our globe.

[8]USUN Press Release 190, Dec. 17; text and subtitles from Bulletin, 74: 139-43.
[9]Cf. Chapter 30.

Both Assemblies are now concluded, and the time is at hand to ask whether anything can be learned from them. For we do not want them forgotten. To the contrary, there are events that occurred in the 30th Assembly which the United States will never forget. Even so, we turn our attention just now to the question of whether it will be possible to avoid such events in the future. In that spirit, we would like to offer two general comments. We offer them in a spirit of reconciliation and of shared concern. We are trying to learn, and we ask if others will not seek to learn with us.

Limitations of the General Assembly

The first lesson is the most important, which is that the General Assembly has been trying to pretend that it is a parliament, which it is not. It is a conference made up of representatives sent by sovereign governments which have agreed to *listen* to its recommendations—recommendations which are, however, in no way binding.

It is usual to use the term "recommendatory" to describe the Assembly's powers, but for present purposes it seems more useful simply to say that there has been an agreement to take into consideration—to listen to—such proposals as the Assembly may make. For this directs our attention to the reality that unless such recommendations have the effect of persuading, they have no effect at all. Resolutions that condemn, that accuse, that anathematize, do not bring us any nearer to agreement. They have the opposite effect.

Hence the lesson of the seventh special session. What took place among us on that occasion was a negotiation. It was self-evident—money is said to clear the mind!—that no party to the negotiation was going to pay the least subsequent attention to any proposal to which he had not agreed. On the other hand, the authority of the unanimous agreement reached at the end of the session was very considerable. The United Nations on that occasion had served as a setting for reaching consensus—a very different thing from recording division, which is what so often happens.

Why is this lesson not self-evident, as it clearly was to those who drafted the charter? Here we come to the second of the general comments the United States would wish to offer in this closing statement. It is not an agreeable matter of which we now speak, nor yet one easily explained. Yet we must make the effort to state our views fully if we are to ask others to seek to understand them.

The Nature of the Crisis of the U.N.

The crisis of the United Nations is not to be found in the views of the majority of its members. Rather, it resides in the essential incompatibility of the system of government which the charter assumes will rule the majority of its members and the system of government to which the majority in fact adheres.

The charter assumes that most of the members of the General Assembly will be reasonably representative governments, committed at home no less than abroad to the maintenance of representative institutions.

It may be asked: How do we know? The answer has no greater—or lesser—authority than that of history and experience. The charter was conceived by an embattled American President and his British comrade-in-arms. American statesmen helped to draft the charter. American scholars may just possibly claim preeminence in their study and interpretation of the charter. Certainly the bulk of such scholarship has been American.

This is not, perhaps, surprising. Among the nations of the world we are the one most to be identified with constitutional government, in the sense of a written charter setting forth the powers and duties of government, a charter that is repeatedly amended and continuously interpreted. We would like to think that our long and really quite dedicated concern with constitutional representative government has given us at least some sense of such matters.

There are others whose experience of representative government is just as long or just as intense, and we feel that such nations may also be expected to speak with knowledge and insight. They have, in a sense, earned the right to do so.

Such nations or, more accurately, the governments of such nations, being of necessity sensitive to the nature of their own national institutions, will be similarly sensitive to the claims made by larger, multinational bodies.

Observe, for example, the great care and lengthy debate which has attended the development of multinational bodies among the nations of Western Europe. Genuine power, true authority, has been transferred from national to international bodies, but only with great and deserved caution. The parliaments of European nations slowly satisfied themselves that political and social conditions in that region had indeed evolved to the point where individuals were prepared, for certain purposes, to submit to the authority of supranational bodies. But they came to this judgment slowly and on the basis of fact.

Those who have submitted to this discipline—and obviously, at the level of individuals, this is not a variety of understanding confined to citizens of parliamentary states—will readily enough understand that the General Assembly has not attained to anything like the degree of acceptance and authority among its constituent members that warrants any transfer of genuine power of a parliamentary nature.

Now, and for the foreseeable future, it can only be a recommendatory body, a conference which adopts positions to which governments have agreed to listen. There is a certain evolution in these matters, and clearly the General Assembly has made some tiny movement in a parliamentary direction. But to pretend we are further than we are will serve only to set back what progress has in truth been made.

This goes to the question of legitimacy. What powers does an assembly have? How have they been conferred? How is it periodically reconfirmed that the population—be it of individuals or governments or whatever—over which such powers are exercised does indeed consent to that exercise?

This process—of definition, of conferral, of confirmation—is the essence of a representative institution. Those who understand it will readily enough understand what can and cannot be accomplished through the instrumentality of the General Assembly.

The Heart of the Matter

And now to the heart of the matter. Many governments—most governments—now represented in the General Assembly seem disposed to use this body as if it had powers which the General Assembly does not have, to enforce policies of a nature which the General Assembly ought not, at this stage, even to consider.

It took our 18th-century Congress well into the 19th century before it felt that political society in America had advanced to the point where an income tax could be imposed, and even then the act was declared unconstitutional; so that Congress was forced to await the 20th century to successfully impose such a tax in peacetime. Now, some see that as progress; others do not. But all see that the evolution of true consent is the first process of effective government. By contrast, before its third decade was out the General Assembly of the United Nations was proclaiming a New International Economic Order.[10]

There is a reason for this, of which we speak at the risk of offense but having no desire to offend; the reason is that most of the governments represented in the General Assembly do not themselves govern by consent. Assemblies for them, and for their peoples, are places in which decrees are announced. Where it is felt that "majorities" are needed to attest to the decree, well, such majorities are readily enough summoned.

We put the simple test. In how many of the 144 members of the

[10] *AFR, 1974*: 92-103.

United Nations is there a representative body which both has the power and periodically exercises the power of rejecting a decision of the government? Only a handful. By one competent count, there are now 28, possibly 29, functioning, representative democracies in the world, and one is not a member of the United Nations. Such governments will by instinct pay the greatest heed to winning consent, including winning consent in the General Assembly. Consent is the very essence of their being. Other governments will not pay such heed. At home they rule by decree, and it seems wholly natural to seek to emulate the same practice in the General Assembly.

We dare to believe that this reality is better known and understood in this Assembly than it might at first appear. If only a handful of the nations represented here have representative governments today, most of them—truly!—have had such in the life of the United Nations. This is a mournful fact for those of us committed to democratic institutions.

At their height, perhaps 15 years ago, there were two or three times as many democratic governments in the world as there are today. But this very fact suggests that there are still memories in most of the nations of the world as to just what representative institutions were like and that correspondingly there exists a much more widespread understanding of their nature than might at first appear.

Let it be clear that we do not entertain any delusions about a grand revival of democracy. We do not expect a reversal of its decline in the near term. (What we do hope to see, and hope to encourage, is more societies which will do something to protect some civil rights, even if they deny most political rights.) But we do think it is possible for there to be a greater understanding among members at large of the nature of a representative institution and the corresponding limits of the General Assembly. We would seek this understanding not to restrict what the United Nations can accomplish but, rather, to accentuate the positive and concentrate on real possibilities rather than to squander the opportunity that does exist by the mindless pretense of legislative omnipotence.

It may be that this objective would be well served if a "parliamentary caucus" were established within the General Assembly. This would be a group of nations constituted, let us say, along the lines of the membership criteria of the Council of Europe, which would attend not so much to policy issues as to institutional ones. Its concern would be to seek to encourage those practices and approaches which enhance the effectiveness of the General Assembly and to discourage, both by example and by pronouncement, those which do not.

Progress on Human Rights Issues

Surely we might especially hope to do this in the area of human rights. Let us accept the fact that the ideal of liberal democracy has sustained huge losses in the last decade. It is not likely that more than a few nations which are not democracies today will become democracies in the course of the last quarter of the century, so that we must expect continued difficulties in the General Assembly of the sort I have described.

Very well then, let us concentrate on things we can do. Of these, the most important is that of establishing some minimal international standards by which governments treat their citizens.

Let us, for example, try to agree that governments should not torture their subjects. Many do. Perhaps most do. And yet, as Gaston Thorn, our wholly admirable and universally admired President, said yesterday, we did make progress on human rights at this Assembly.

Specifically we adopted, unanimously, a resolution against "torture and other cruel, inhuman or degrading treatment or punishment in relation to detention and imprisonment." Citizens throughout the world may in years to come point to their governments' concurrence with that resolution as they demand rights or beg for mercy and humanity in their own societies.

The United States hoped for more progress than we actually made. This year, for example, we introduced a new practice with respect to the venerable issue of apartheid. It has seemed to us that our standard practice of mere denunciation has suffered from diminishing effectiveness.

Instead, this year the United States brought into the General Assembly what was in effect a bill of particulars.[11] With respect to violations of the standards of civil liberties which we would hope to see attained in South Africa—and throughout the world—we named prisoners, specified dates, cited statutes, quoted judges, described sentences, identified jails. There are indeed political prisoners in South Africa. But we feel they are no longer unknown political prisoners. We hope other nations may follow our precedent of lawyerlike, documented presentation of such issues.

For there are political prisoners the world over. Here again, the United States this year took an unprecedented initiative in submitting a resolution calling for amnesty for all political prisoners. We were not successful. But we said we would be back next year, and we will be. We will be there, and we may be equally sure that the political prisoners will be there also.

[11]Statement by U.S. Representative Clarence M. Mitchell, Nov. 28, in *Bulletin*, 73: 935-44.

Confession is good for the soul, and we confess to not having handled this issue well enough. There are more members in this Assembly that would support an amnesty proposal than the half-dozen who told us they would support ours. And if it should prove the case that it was American sponsorship that held off many, then clearly we will make no claims to sponsorship next time. But our determination in this matter is, if anything, strengthened by the feeling that we achieved so little this time.

We are not perfect, and we make no pretense to perfection. What we hope for, what some of us pray for, is simply that we should be concerned and engaged.

And on the issue of political prisoners we are just that. We are strengthened by the extraordinary statement of Andrei D. Sakharov, this year's winner of the Nobel Peace Prize and the recipient two years ago of the award of the International League for the Rights of Man.[12] Speaking of his hope for the final victory of the principles of peace and human rights, he said:

The best sign that such hopes can come true would be a general political amnesty in all the world, liberation of all prisoners of conscience everywhere. The struggle for a general political amnesty is the struggle for the future of mankind.

And so we will be back.

Farewell. We wish you peace in the New Year.

---

[12] Nobel Peace Prize acceptance statement, Oslo, Dec. 10, read in Sakharov's absence by his wife, Yelena Bonner Sakharov; text in *New York Times*, Dec. 11, 1975.

45. THE COLD WAR COMES TO AFRICA

(January 29, 1976)

[Throughout the 1970s, American world policy had been imped-
ed by a lack of effective teamwork between the administration and
the Congress, two branches of government with radically different
perceptions about the nature of the contemporary world and the requirements of the national interest. Unwaveringly insistent on its
dedication to peace, the Nixon-Kissinger-Ford administration had
sought to uphold American interests within a framework of traditional power relationships consistent, in its view, with the teachings
of history, the limitations of human nature, and the insufficiency
of mere good will in a world where force was often the decisive factor. Recoiling from so bleak a view of human affairs, many
members of the Congress had tended of late years to favor a more
idealistic position that assigned less weight to military power and
somewhat more to various types of humanitarian aspirations. Acting in response to its own priorities, Congress had done tenacious
battle with the administration on such issues as Vietnam, presidential war powers, Soviet trade, arms for Turkey, and Diego Garcia.
Now, in December 1975, it was about to "blow the whistle" on an
incipient U.S. involvement in African affairs that could, it feared,
contain the seeds of another Vietnam adventure despite the administration's categorical assurances to the contrary.

The administration itself had long professed a hope that Africa
could be preserved against the intrusion of great power rivalries,
and that the people of that continent could be left to settle their
problems without outside interference. So much the ruder had been
the awakening at the State Department and the White House when
it became evident in the course of 1975 that the Soviet Union, apparently forgetful of its three-year-old commitment to refrain from
seeking unilateral advantage at the expense of the United States,[1]

---

[1]"Basic Principles of Relations Between the United States and the U.S.S.R.,"
Moscow, May 29, 1972, in *AFR, 1972*: 76.

had intervened in the internal struggle in Angola on a scale that by December amounted, in Secretary Kissinger's words, to nothing less than "a new projection of Soviet power and Soviet interests."[2] What made matters still worse, in American eyes, was the fact that Cuba's Fidel Castro had actually sent some thousands of troops to the assistance of Angola's leftist Popular Movement (MPLA), apparently at the very time when the Organization of American States had undertaken to lift its boycott of the Havana regime and when even the United States had entered into secret discussions looking toward settlement of Cuban-U.S. issues.[3] To complicate matters still further, South Africa had also become obscurely involved in the military struggle in southern Angola, to the considerable embarrassment of those African factions and governments which, like Zaïre and Zambia, were themselves opposed to the MPLA and favorable to one or another of its rivals.

What proved to be the ultimate complication was the disclosure early in December that Washington, too, had covertly engaged itself in the Angolan quarrel by providing clandestine assistance to some of the neighboring states—principally to Zaïre, which was closely identified with the National Front (FNLA) movement led by Holden Roberto, a brother-in-law of President Mobutu Sese Seko. According to one account, as much as $25 million in arms and support funds had been channeled through the Central Intelligence Agency, mostly to Zaïre, over the past three months, with another $25 million already programed and a request to Congress for additional funds in the offing.[4] To a Congress still imperfectly recovered from the Vietnam experience, such reports were all too reminiscent of the news from Southeast Asia in the early 1960s. With a decisiveness surprising to all concerned, the Senate acted on December 19 to nip such ventures in the bud by adopting, by a vote of 54 to 22, an amendment to the pending Defense Department appropriation bill stipulating that none of the appropriated funds be used "for any activities involving Angola other than intelligence gathering."

Described by President Ford as "a deep tragedy" that would have "the gravest consequences for the long-term position of the United States and for international order in general,"[5] the Senate's action nevertheless would be emulated by a 323 to 99 vote of the House of Representatives on January 27, 1976, achieving legal status as part of the $112.3 billion Defense Department appropriation for the fifteen-month period ending September 30, 1976.[6] In

[2]Cf. Chapter 42 at note 1.
[3]Cf. Chapter 24 at note 5.
[4]David Binder in *New York Times*, Dec. 12, 1975.
[5]Remarks of Dec. 19, in *Presidential Documents*, 11: 1383.

the meantime, Soviet actions had clearly dealt détente a major blow, and hopes for a *rapprochement* with Cuba had flown out the window. "As I said earlier," Mr. Ford observed on December 20, "there are between 4,000 and 6,000 Cuban combat military personnel in Angola. The action of the Cuban Government in sending combat forces to Angola destroys any opportunity for improvement in relations with the United States. They have made a choice. It, in effect, and I mean very literally, has precluded any improvement in relations with Cuba."[7]

Civil war was still in progress in Angola, but the victory of the MPLA looked more and more certain, as Secretary Kissinger appeared on January 29, 1976 to offer his assessment of these developments to the Subcommittee on African Affairs of the Senate Foreign Relations Committee. Although his statement **(Document 67)** belongs properly to the records of the year 1976, it is included here because it presents perhaps the most coherent analysis, from an administration point of view, of a series of events that was to exert far-reaching influence not only on the situation in Africa but on the overall foreign policy of the United States.]

(67) "Implications of Angola for Future U.S. Foreign Policy": *Statement by Secretary of State Kissinger before the Subcommittee on African Affairs of the Senate Committee on Foreign Relations, January 29, 1976.*[8]

I appear before you not to score debating points in an abstract contest over executive-legislative prerogative. What faces us is a congressional decision of potentially grave magnitude taken after the executive branch had complied with all legal requirements for the kind of operation involved in Angola and after eight congressional committees had been briefed over 20 times without foreshadowing any opposition in principle. The issue is not "victory" of one branch over another. The issue is what constitutes a victory for the national interest.

I welcome this opportunity to explain the global significance of what is now happening in Angola, the events that have brought us to this point, the U.S. objectives, and the major consequences which can result if we fail to pursue those objectives.

The Soviet Union's massive and unprecedented intervention in the internal affairs of Africa—with nearly 200 million dollars'

[6]Title IV, Public Law 94-212, Feb. 9, 1976.
[7]News conference, Dec. 20, in *Presidential Documents*, 11: 1389.
[8]Department of State Press Release 40, Jan. 29, 1976; titles and text from *Bulletin*, 74: 174-82.

worth of arms and its military technicians and advisers, with 11,000 Cuban combat troops, and with substantial sea and airlift and naval cover in adjacent waters—is a matter of urgent concern. Not only are the interests of the countries directly affected at stake but also the interests of all nations in preserving global stability—which is the precondition for all else mankind aspires to accomplish.

In recent years the United States has sought to help build a new international order less tied to the traditional patterns of power balances. It was the United States which took the initiative in seeking to resolve the most dangerous problems of our time by negotiation and cooperation rather than by force of arms. It was we who saw that the historical necessity of this period required a more stable relationship between the two nations that possess the capacity to destroy civilization.

We have sought—and with some successes—to build more constructive relations with the U.S.S.R. across a broad range: to contain strategic arms; to institutionalize cooperation in economic, scientific, and cultural fields; to reduce tensions in areas where our vital interests impinge on one another; and to avoid destabilizing confrontations in peripheral areas of the globe—such as Angola. The classical pattern of accumulating marginal advantages must be overcome and mankind must build more constructive patterns if catastrophe is to be avoided. No one has been more dedicated than the President and I to working for these principles.

But our efforts have been founded upon one fundamental reality: peace requires a sense of security, and security depends upon some form of equilibrium between the great powers. And that equilibrium is impossible unless the United States remains both strong and determined to use its strength when required. This is our historic responsibility, for no other nation has the capacity to act in this way. While constantly seeking opportunities for conciliation, we need to demonstrate to potential adversaries that cooperation is the only rational alternative. Any other course will encourage the trends it seeks to accommodate; a challenge not met today will tempt far more dangerous crises tomorrow.

If a continent such as Africa, only recently freed from external oppression, can be made the arena for great-power ambitions, if immense quantities of arms can affect far-off events, if large expeditionary forces can be transported at will to dominate virtually helpless peoples—then all we have hoped for in building a more stable and rational international order is in jeopardy.

The effort of the Soviet Union and Cuba to take unilateral advantage of a turbulent local situation where they have never had any historical interests is a willful, direct assault upon the recent constructive trends in U.S.- Soviet relations and our efforts to improve relations with Cuba. It is an attempt to take advantage of our continuing domestic division and self-torment. Those who have acted so recklessly must be made to see that their conduct is unacceptable.

The history of the postwar period should give us pause. Military aggression, direct or indirect, has frequently been successfully dealt with, but never in the absence of a local balance of forces. U.S. policy in Angola has sought to help friends achieve this balance. Angola represents the first time since the aftermath of World War II that the Soviets have moved militarily at long distances to impose a regime of their choice. It is the first time that the United States has failed to respond to Soviet military moves outside their immediate orbit. And it is the first time that Congress has halted the executive's action while it was in the process of meeting this kind of threat.

Thus to claim that Angola is not an important country or that the United States has no important interests there begs the principal question. The objectives which the United States has sought in Angola have not been aimed at defending, or acquiring, intrinsic interests in that country. We are not opposing any particular faction. We could develop constructive relations with any Angolan government that derives from the will of the people. We have never been involved militarily in Angola. We are not so involved now. We do not seek to be so involved in the future.

Our objective is clear and simple: to help those African countries and those groups within Angola that would resist external aggression by providing them with needed *financial* support. Those whom we seek to assist are our friends; they share our hopes for negotiated solutions and for African self-determination. They played a larger role than the MPLA [Popular Movement for the Liberation of Angola] in striving toward Angolan independence.

But our deeper concern is for global stability. If the United States is seen to emasculate itself in the face of massive, unprecedented Soviet and Cuban intervention, what will be the perception of leaders around the world as they make decisions concerning their future security?

Will they feel they can proceed to develop their nations in an international climate which fosters cooperation and self-determination? How will they adjust their conduct in the context of such events? And what conclusion will an unopposed superpower draw when the next opportunity for intervention beckons?

America's modest direct strategic and economic interests in Angola are not the central issue. The question is whether America still maintains the resolve to act responsibly as a great power— prepared to face a challenge when it arises, knowing that preventive action now may make unnecessary a more costly response later.

Let there be no mistake about it—the culprits in the tragedy that is now unfolding in Angola are the Soviet Union and its client state Cuba. But I must note with some sadness that by its actions the Congress has deprived the President of indispensable flexibility in formulating a foreign policy which we believe to be in our national interest. And Congress has ignored the crucial truth that a stable relationship with the Soviet Union based on mutual restraint will be achieved only if Soviet lack of restraint carries the risk of counteraction.

The consequences may well be far-reaching and substantially more painful than the course we have recommended. When one great power attempts to obtain special positions of influence based on military interventions, the other power is sooner or later bound to act to offset this advantage in some other place or manner. This will inevitably lead to a chain of action and reaction typical of other historic eras in which great powers maneuvered for advantage, only to find themselves sooner or later embroiled in a major crisis and often in open conflict.

It is precisely this pattern that must be broken—and that we wanted to break until stopped—if a lasting easing of tensions is to be achieved. And if it is not broken now, we will face harder choices and higher costs in the future.

It is in this context that we have framed our goals in Angola. Simply put, we wish to see:

—A cease-fire, ending the tragic bloodshed in that country;
—Withdrawal of outside forces—Soviet, Cuban, and South African;
—Cessation of foreign military involvement; and
—Negotiations among the Angolan factions.

We are prepared to accept any solution that emerges from African efforts. And we are ready to offer economic assistance to the people of Angola when a legitimate government is established there.

We have consistently advocated such a government representing all three factions in Angola. We have never opposed participation by the Soviet-backed Popular Movement for the Liberation of Angola, the MPLA. What we do oppose is the massive Soviet and Cuban intervention and their expressed aim of denying the other two groups any part in governing the country. Our overriding goal has been to assure that Africans shape their own destiny and that traditional colonialism not be replaced by a more modern version.

For the United States to be found wanting as a credible friend, precisely at a time when moderate African states have clearly and repeatedly expressed their hope that America provide the necessary balance to the Soviet Union and Cuba, will have a major impact on those countries on the continent of Africa which resisted all pressures and stuck by their position even after the Senate cut off aid; on our allies in other parts of the world who look to us for security; on other countries that seek ties with us primarily because they see us as the guardian of international equilibrium.

The Record of Events in Angola

Let me briefly recount the course of events that has led us to this point.

In 1961, the United States declared its support for self-determination in Portugal's African territories.[9] At the time, the National Front for the Liberation of Angola, FNLA, was a leading force in the struggle for Angolan independence. Looking to the future, we sought to develop a relationship with the FNLA through providing it some financial, nonmilitary assistance. The U.S.S.R. had already established links with the Popular Movement for the Liberation of Angola, MPLA, through the Portuguese Communist Party.

The MPLA began military action against the Portuguese in the midsixties. The National Union for the Total Independence of Angola, UNITA, an offshoot of the FNLA, also began to fight on a small scale in the late 1960's. Although these various uncoordinated insurgency efforts caused considerable difficulties for Portugal, they posed no serious military threat to the dominance of Portuguese military forces in Angola.

However, the overthrow of the Portuguese Government in April 1974 and the growing strength of the Portuguese Communist Party apparently convinced Moscow that a "revolutionary situation" was developing in Angola. The Soviet Union began to exploit this situation in the fall of 1974 through shipments of some arms and equipment to the MPLA. The United States received requests for support from other Angolan elements at that same time, but turned them down.

The prospect of an independent Angola was clouded by the intense rivalry of the FNLA, MPLA, and UNITA which had developed over the years. Concerned about the three factions' failure to end their bitter quarrel, leaders of other African countries prevailed upon them to come together with Portugal and seek agreement. This effort led to the Alvor [Portugal] Accord of January [15] 1975. Under its terms a transitional coalition government was to be established and charged with preparing for a peaceful turnover of power by integrating the military forces of the three movements,

[9]*Documents, 1961*: 365-6.

writing a constitution, and organizing an election to take place before independence, scheduled for November 11, 1975.

This was the moment, when Portugal was trying to organize a peaceful transition to independence, for the exercise of restraint by all outside parties. But the U.S.S.R. and Portuguese Communists decided to put the MPLA in power in Angola through stepped-up shipments of arms. With this kind of encouragement, the MPLA had little incentive to fulfill the terms of the Alvor Accord, which would have prevented it from dominating any future coalition government.

It is no coincidence that major violence broke out in March 1975 when large shipments of Soviet arms began to arrive—thousands of infantry weapons, machineguns, bazookas, and rockets. On March 23 the first of repeated military clashes between the MPLA and FNLA occurred. They increased in frequency in April, May, and June, when deliveries of Communist arms and equipment, including mortars and armored vehicles, escalated by air and sea. In May the MPLA forced the FNLA out of the areas north and east of Luanda and in June took effective control of Cabinda. On July 9 all-out civil war began when the MPLA attacked the FNLA and UNITA, driving both organizations out of Luanda, thereby ending the short-lived coalition government. By mid-July the military situation radically favored the MPLA.

As the military position of the FNLA and UNITA deteriorated, the Governments of Zaïre and Zambia grew more and more concerned about the implications for their own security. Those two countries turned to the United States for assistance in preventing the Soviet Union and Cuba from imposing a solution in Angola, becoming a dominant influence in south-central Africa, and threatening the stability of the area.

It was at this point that President Ford decided to respond to requests for help and to provide military assistance to the FNLA and UNITA forces through neighboring black African countries.

In August intelligence reports indicated the presence of Soviet and Cuban military advisers, trainers, and troops, including the first Cuban combat troops. If statements by Cuban leaders are to be believed, a large Cuban military training program began in Angola in June, and Cuban advisers were probably there before then. By September the MPLA offensive had forced UNITA out of several major central and southern Angolan cities. It controlled most of the coastline except for a strip in the far north, much of the south, and a wide belt running from Luanda to the Zaïre border in the east.

In early September the poorly equipped UNITA forces turned in desperation to South Africa for assistance against the MPLA, which was overrunning UNITA's ethnic areas in the south. South Africa responded by sending in military equipment, and some military personnel, without consultation with the United States.

The UNITA forces launched a successful counteroffensive which swept the MPLA out of the southern and most of the central part of Angola. In the north the FNLA also made significant advances. By Independence Day—November 11—the MPLA controlled only the former colonial capital of Luanda and a narrow belt across north-central Angola.

In October massive increases in Soviet and Cuban military assistance began to arrive. More Cuban troops were ferried to Angola. Cuba inaugurated its own airlift of troops in late October. And the MPLA declared itself the Government of Angola, in violation of the Alvor Accord.

In the hope of halting a dangerously escalating situation, the United States—using the leverage provided by our financial support—undertook a wide range of diplomatic activity pointing toward a summit of the Organization of African Unity (OAU) scheduled for January 1976. Starting in October we made several overtures to the Soviet Union, expressing our concern over the scale and purpose of their intervention. We offered to use our influence to bring about the cessation of foreign military assistance and to encourage an African solution if they would do the same. Their responses were evasive but not totally negative.

We began to voice our concerns and our limited objectives publicly. Beginning with a speech in Detroit on November 24[10] we pointed out that Soviet continuation of an interventionist policy must inevitably threaten our other relationships and that our sole objective was an African resolution of an African problem.

The Administration undertook a new series of congressional consultations on the extent of our help to the Angolan factions resisting Soviet and Cuban aggression. I briefed the NATO Foreign Ministers and obtained significant understanding and support. Our diplomatic efforts with foreign governments, especially African governments, culminated with a mission by Assistant Secretary [for African Affairs William E.] Schaufele to five African countries and the dispatch of letters from President Ford to 32 African heads of state, as well as the Secretary General of the OAU,[11] stating America's policy.

[10]Chapter 39, Document 60.
[11]William Eteki Mboumoua (Cameroon).

Throughout this period the U.S. principles for a solution to the Angolan tragedy were unambiguous and straightforward:

—Angola is an African problem and should be left to Africans to solve.
—Foreign military involvement only escalates and prolongs the warfare there and should be ended.
—OAU efforts to promote a cease-fire should be supported.
—The United States pursues no unilateral interests in Angola and is exclusively concerned with seeing the people of that country live in peace, independence, and well-being.
—Angola should be insulated from great-power conflict.

Our diplomacy was effective so long as we maintained the leverage of a possible military balance. African determination to oppose Soviet and Cuban intervention was becoming more and more evident. On December 9 President Ford made a formal proposal to the Soviet Government through their Ambassador. Indeed, it appeared as if the Soviet Union had begun to take stock. They halted their airlift from December 9 until December 24.

By mid-December we were hopeful that the OAU would provide a framework for eliminating the interference of outside powers by calling for an end to their intervention. At that point, the impact of our domestic debate overwhelmed the possibilities of diplomacy. After the Senate vote to block any further aid to Angola, the Cubans more than doubled their forces and Soviet military aid was resumed on an even larger scale. The scope of Soviet-Cuban intervention increased drastically; the cooperativeness of Soviet diplomacy declined.

The weight of Soviet aid and advisers and the massive Cuban expeditionary force began to tip the scales of battle in December. By this point, most of the effective fighting for the MPLA was being done by Cubans. It was clear that the U.S.S.R., Cuba, and the MPLA hoped to achieve a decisive military victory on the eve of the Organization of African Unity's extraordinary summit conference in Addis Ababa a few weeks ago. [January 10-13, 1976.] Yet notwithstanding their reverses, the FNLA-UNITA forces still controlled about 70 percent of the territory and 70 percent of the population of Angola at the time of the conference. An OAU Reconciliation Commission, which had met earlier in 1975, took the position that none of the movements should be recognized as the government of Angola. The Commission called for a cease-fire and the formation of a government of national unity. Thus, those governments who recognized the MPLA were in violation of a decision of the OAU.

At the January OAU summit, 22 members of the OAU advocated recognition of the MPLA and condemnation of South Africa. But they were opposed, in an unusual demonstration of solidarity, by 22 other members who held out for a more balanced resolution, one that would include the following points:

1. An immediate cease-fire;
2. Condemnation of South Africa and immediate withdrawal of all South African forces;
3. Withdrawal of all foreign forces;
4. An end to the supply of arms to all factions; and
5. Reconciliation of all factions, with the aim of establishing a government of national unity.

The United States regarded this program as reasonable and responsive to the facts of the situation. But the Soviet Union and Cuba urged MPLA supporters to refuse to accept this solution. The summit ended in impasse.

The United States Position

This, then, is the significance of Angola and the record to date. In elaborating further the U.S. position, I want to respond directly to some of the issues raised in the current debate.

Our principal objective has been to respond to an unprecedented application of Soviet power achieved in part through the expeditionary force of a client state.

During 1975 the Soviet Union is estimated to have contributed nearly 200 million dollars' worth of military assistance to Angola. This equals the entire amount of all military aid from all sources to sub-Saharan Africa in 1974.

Soviet arms have included infantry weapons—machineguns, bazookas, mortars, and recoilless rifles—armored personnel carriers, heavy artillery, light and medium tanks, truck-mounted multitube rocket launchers, helicopters, and light aircraft. There are unconfirmed reports that the Soviet Union will provide the MPLA with MIG-21 aircraft to be piloted by Cubans.

A total of at least 46 flights of Soviet heavy and medium military transports have ferried Soviet military equipment from the U.S.S.R. to Luanda and Congo (Brazzaville), while a steady stream of Soviet and Cuban aircraft has continued to bring Cuban troops across the Atlantic. Soviet naval involvements clearly related to the Angolan event have continued in west African waters for several weeks.

The implications of Cuba's unprecedented and massive intervention cannot be ignored. It is a geopolitical event of considerable significance. For the first time, Cuba has sent an expeditionary force to another nation on another continent. About 11,000 Cuban military personnel have been sent to Angola.

If allowed to proceed unchecked, this blatant power play cannot but carry with it far-reaching implications—including the impact it will have on the attitudes and future conduct of the nations of this hemisphere. Indeed, friend and foe alike cannot fail to contrast the sending of a large Cuban expeditionary force with our apparent inability to provide even indirect financial assistance. The failure of the United States to respond effectively will be regarded in many parts of the world as an indication of our future determination to counter similar Communist interventions.

We have been asked why we do not respond with other pressures on the Soviet Union.

The first answer is that many of the links the Administration has tried to forge—such as trade and credit, which would have provided incentives for restraint and levers for penalties—have been precluded by earlier congressional actions. But two other instruments have been suggested: wheat sales and the Strategic Arms Limitation Talks.

A moratorium was placed on wheat sales for four months in 1975. To use this device every three months is to blunt it permanently. Above all, economic measures take too much time to affect a fast-moving situation like Angola; any longer term impact would be of little use to those immediately threatened. We should also ponder whether we want to return to the situation, now prevented by the grain agreement,[12] in which the U.S.S.R. can capriciously enter and leave the U.S. grain trade.

As for the Strategic Arms Limitation Talks, we have never considered these to be a favor which we grant to the Soviet Union to be turned on and off according to the ebb and flow of our relations. The fact is that limiting the growth of nuclear arsenals is an overriding global problem that must be dealt with urgently for our own sake and for the sake of world peace.

Still, we have made clear that a continuation of actions like those in Angola must threaten the entire web of Soviet-U.S. relations. In this sense, both negotiations and the overall relationship are in long-term jeopardy unless restraint is exercised. But there is no substitute for a local balance; indirect pressures can succeed only if rapid local victories are foreclosed.

[12]Cf. Chapter 35.

Have we really thought through the implications of our decisions? Do we really want the world to conclude that if the Soviet Union chooses to intervene in a massive way, and if Cuban or other troops are used as an expeditionary force, the United States will not be able to muster the unity or resolve to provide even financial assistance to those who are threatened? Can those faced with such a threat without hope of assistance from us be expected to resist? Do we want our potential adversaries to conclude that, in the event of future challenges, America's internal divisions are likely to deprive us of even minimal leverage over developments of global significance?

Our second objective is to help our friends in black Africa who oppose Soviet and Cuban intervention.

Only in recent years has Africa become free of great-power rivalry; it must not once again become an arena in which the ambitions of outside forces are pursued. We have sought with our African friends to maintain a local balance of power so there can be no imposed solution that would deprive the Angolan people of the right to determine their own destiny.

We are told that we need not concern ourselves, because in the final analysis and at some indefinite date in the future, African nationalism will reassert itself and drive out foreign influence. Even were this to prove true, it still ignores the fact that governments under pressure will be forced to yield whenever a threat develops. Those who are threatened cannot afford to wait; they must decide whether to resist or to adjust. Advice which counsels patience and confidence in the verdict of history is a mockery to those who are concerned for the fate of their country today. History rarely helps those who do not help themselves.

Some charge that we have acted in collusion with South Africa. This is untrue. We had no foreknowledge of South Africa's intentions and in no way cooperated with it militarily. Nor do we view South African intervention more benevolently than we do the intervention of other outside powers. Indeed, we have formally proposed that the removal of outside forces begin with those of South Africa and have asked—in vain—for an indication of how soon thereafter Soviet and Cuban forces would be withdrawn.

It is also claimed that because of our support for the side which later felt itself compelled to seek the aid of South Africa, we have lost influence in black Africa. One cannot generalize so easily about the perceptions of the African people, as the firm stand at Addis Ababa of 22 OAU members against OAU recognition of the MPLA should demonstrate. Behind this stand, which coincided with the U.S. position, was awareness that the MPLA represented only a minority of Angolans, and also a genuine apprehension over Soviet and Cuban, as well as South African, intervention. Indeed, it is our inability to support our African friends that will cost us influence in Africa.

We are firmly convinced that, had there been no outside interference initiated by the Soviet Union, the Africans would have found their own solution. No single movement would have been strong enough to take over. The resulting solution would have been more representative of the people of Angola than a government imposed by an outside power and representing only a minority faction.

The outcome in Angola will have repercussions throughout Africa. The confidence of countries neighboring Angola—Zambia and Zaïre—as well as other African countries, in the will and power of the United States will be severely shaken if they see that the Soviet Union and Cuba are unopposed in their attempt to impose a regime of their choice on Angola. They and others elsewhere may well adjust their policies to what they consider to be the forces of the future.

The means we have chosen have been limited, and explained to Congress.

Our immediate objective was to provide leverage for diplomatic efforts to bring about a just and peaceful solution. They were not conceived unilaterally by the United States; they represented support to friends who requested our financial assistance.

We chose covert means because we wanted to keep our visibility to a minimum; we wanted the greatest possible opportunity for an African solution. We felt that overt assistance would elaborate a formal doctrine justifying great-power intervention—aside from the technical issues such as in what budgetary category this aid should be given and how it could be reconciled with legislative restrictions against the transfer of U.S. arms by recipients.

The Angola situation is of a type in which diplomacy without leverage is impotent, yet direct military confrontation would involve unnecessary risks. Thus it is precisely one of those gray areas where covert methods are crucial if we are to have any prospect of influencing certain events of potentially global importance.

We chose a covert form of response with the greatest reluctance. But in doing so, we were determined to adhere to the highest standard of executive-legislative consultation. Eight congressional committees were briefed on 24 separate occasions. We sought in these briefings to determine the wishes of Congress. While we do not claim that every member approved our actions, we had no indication of basic opposition.

Between July and December 1975 we discussed the Angolan situation on numerous occasions with members of the foreign relations committees and the appropriations committees of both Houses and the committees of both Houses that have CIA oversight responsibilities. The two committees investigating CIA activities—the Church Committee and the Pike Committee—were also briefed. Altogether more than two dozen Senators, about 150 Congressmen, and over 100 staff members of both Houses were informed. I am attaching to my statement a list of all the briefings carried out.[13]

Mr. Chairman,[14] where are we now?

We are told that by providing money and arms in Angola we are duplicating the mistakes we made in Viet-Nam. Such an argument confuses the expenditure of tens of millions of dollars with the commitment of U.S. troops. If we accept such a gross distortion of history—if we accept the claim that we can no longer do anything to aid our friends abroad because we will inevitably do too much—then the tragedy of Viet-Nam will indeed be monumental.

We will have lost all ability to respond to anything less than direct and substantial challenge. And having lost that ability, we will eventually discover that by failing to respond at an early stage, our ultimate response will have to be greater and the stakes will be higher. If we do not exercise our responsibilities to maintain the international balance, if Congress and the executive are unable to act in concert when vital national interests are affected, then world security may well be seriously undermined.

Many of the members of this committee have expressed their general support for our policy of easing tensions with the Soviet Union. We in the executive branch are grateful for that support. But this process cannot be divided into those segments which the Soviets will honor and those which we will allow them to ignore. What the United States does when confronted with a challenge like Angola can be of great significance in shaping our future relationship with the Soviet Union. A demonstration of a lack of resolve could lead the Soviets to a great miscalculation thereby plunging us into a major confrontation which neither of us wants. Credibility determines, to a great degree, what a nation can accomplish without a resort to force. And as credibility is reduced, the eventual need to resort to force increases. And in the end, we are all the losers.

The United States must make it clear that Angola sets no prece-

---

[13]Reproduced in Department of State Press Release 40, Jan. 29, 1976, and in U.S. Senate, 94th Cong., 2nd sess., Committee on Foreign Relations, *Angola: Hearings* before the Subcommittee on African Affairs, Jan. 29-Feb. 6, 1976 (Washington: GPO, 1976): 21-3.

[14]Senator Dick Clark (Democrat of Iowa).

dent; this type of action will not be tolerated elsewhere. This must be demonstrated by both the executive and the Congress—in our national interest and in the interest of world peace.

To the Soviet Union and to Cuba, the Administration says: We will continue to make our case to the American public. We will not tolerate wanton disregard for the interests of others and for the cause of world peace.

To the American people, the Administration says: The time has come to put aside self-accusation, division, and guilt. our own country's safety and the progress of mankind depend crucially upon a united and determined America. Today, as throughout our 200 years, the world looks to us to stand up for what is right. By virtue of our strength and values we are leaders in the defense of freedom; without us there can be neither security nor progress.

To the Congress, the Administration says: Whatever our past disagreements, let the Congress and the executive now resolve to shape a cooperative relationship that will enable the United States to play a responsible international role. Both branches will have to do their share in restoring the kind of nonpartisan support that has served our foreign policy so well in the past.

On the issue of Angola, the Administration is now seriously considering overt financial aid, and we will soon be consulting with the Congress on this possibility. But whatever that decision, let us work together with an appreciation of the larger interests involved and with a sense of national responsiblity. A united America cannot be ignored by our adversaries. Together we will preserve the independence of those who face the prospect of oppression. Together we will hearten the friends of liberty and peace everywhere.

APPENDIX:
PRINCIPAL SOURCES

(The abbreviation GPO refers to the U.S. Government Printing Office.)

"AFR": *American Foreign Relations: A Documentary Record* (New York: New York University Press, for the Council on Foreign Relations; annual vols., 1971-).

"Bulletin": *The Department of State Bulletin* (Washington: GPO, weekly). The official source for material of State Department origin appearing in this volume; contains also numerous documents originated by the White House and other governmental and international bodies. Most references are to vols. 72 (Jan.-June 1975), 73 (July-Dec. 1975), and 74 (Jan.-June 1976).

Digest of United States Practice in International Law, 1975, by Eleanor C. McDowell (Department of State Publication 8865; Washington: GPO, 1976). Documents U.S. foreign relations from a legal standpoint.

"Documents": *Documents on American Foreign Relations* (annual vols., 1939-70). Volumes prior to 1952 published by Princeton University Press (Princeton, N.J.) for the World Peace Foundation; subsequent volumes published for the Council on Foreign Relations by Harper & Brothers/Harper & Row (New York and Evanston) for 1952-66 and by Simon and Schuster (New York) for 1967-70. For continuation volumes see *"AFR"* above.

Documents on Disarmament (Washington: GPO; annual vols. for 1960-74). The most comprehensive collection of documents on disarmament and related topics, published annually by the U.S. Arms Control and Disarmament Agency.

Golan, Matti, *The Secret Conversations of Henry Kissinger: Step-by-Step Diplomacy in the Middle East* (New York: Quadrangle/The New York Times Book Co., 1976). Based largely on unpublished Israeli records.

IMF Survey (Washington: International Monetary Fund, semi-monthly). The official bulletin of the International Monetary Fund. Most references are to vol. 4 (1975).

International Economic Report of the President, transmitted to the Congress March 1976 (Washington: GPO, 1976). Includes the annual report of the Council on International Economic Policy, covering developments of the year 1975.

International Legal Materials: Current Documents (Washington: American Society of International Law, bimonthly). Includes numerous documents of non-U.S. origin.

"Keesing's": Keesing's Contemporary Archives (Bristol: Keesing's Publications, Ltd., weekly). A detailed review of current developments throughout the world. Most references are to pp. 26877-27500 (1975).

NATO Review (Brussels: NATO Information Service, bimonthly). Contains documents and articles on NATO activities. Most references are to vols. 23 (1975) and 24 (1976).

The New York Times (New York: The New York Times Co., daily). Contains unofficial texts of numerous documents of international interest.

OECD Observer (Paris: OECD Information Service, bimonthly). The official review of the Organization for Economic Cooperation and Development.

"Presidential Documents": Weekly Compilation of Presidential Documents (Washington: GPO, weekly). The official source for White House materials reproduced in this volume. Much of the contents is later republished in *Public Papers*, and many texts relating to foreign affairs appear also in the Department of State *Bulletin* and/or *Documents on Disarmament*. Most references are to vol. 11 (1975).

Public Laws of the United States, cited in this volume by serial number and date of approval (e.g., Public Law 92-156, Nov. 17, 1971), are issued by the GPO in leaflet form (slip laws) and subsequently collected in the *United States Statutes at Large (Stat.)*.

"Public Papers": Public Papers of the Presidents of the United States (Washington: GPO, annual). Contains definitive texts of most presidential statements and some other material of White House origin, most of it previously published in *Presidential Documents*.

Sheehan, Edward R.F., *The Arabs, Israelis, and Kissinger: A Secret History of American Diplomacy in the Middle East* (New York: Reader's Digest Press/Thomas Y. Crowell Co., 1976). An expanded version of the author's article, "How Kissinger Did It: Step by Step in the Middle East," *Foreign Policy*, No. 22: 3-70 (Spring 1976).

Soviet News (London: Press Department of the Soviet Embassy, weekly). Includes unofficial texts or condensations of numerous

Soviet documents.

"TIAS": U.S. Department of State, *Treaties and Other International Acts Series* (Washington: GPO, published irregularly). This series presents the definitive texts of treaties and agreements to which the United States is a party, as authenticated by the Department of State. Issued in leaflet form under their individual serial numbers, items in this series are later republished with consecutive pagination in the official *United States Treaties and Other International Agreements* (UST) series, likewise published by the GPO on behalf of the Department of State.

United Nations General Assembly, *Official Records* (New York: United Nations). Includes official texts of all resolutions as well as much related material.

United Nations Security Council, *Official Records* (New York: United Nations). Includes official texts of all resolutions, with much related material.

The United States in World Affairs (annual vols., 1931-40, 1945-67, and 1970). The annual survey of U.S. foreign policy developments, published for the Council on Foreign Relations by Harper & Brothers/Harper and Row (New York and Evanston) from 1931 through 1966 and by Simon and Schuster (New York) for 1967 and 1970. Continued by the present series..

UN Monthly Chronicle (New York: United Nations Office of Public Information, monthly). The official account of current U.N. activities, with texts of major resolutions and other documents. Most references are to vols. 12 (1975) and 13 (1976).

U.S. Arms Control and Disarmament Agency, *15th Annual Report to the Congress* (ACDA Publication 88; Washington: GPO, 1976). Surveys arms control developments during 1975.

U.S. Department of State, Bureau of Public Affairs, Office of Media Services, *Selected Documents:*

    2. Results of the Seventh Special Session of the U.N. General Assembly, September 1-16, 1975 (Department of State Publication 8831, Nov. 1975).

    3. U.S. International Energy Policy, October 1973-November 1975 (Department of State Publication 8842, Dec. 1975).

    4. U.S. Policy in the Middle East: November 1974-February 1976 (Department of State Publication 8878, Oct. 1976).

    Selected reprints from the Department of State *Bulletin.*

U.S. House of Representatives, 94th Cong., 2nd sess., Committee on International Relations, *Congress and Foreign Policy—1975*, prepared by the Foreign Affairs and National Defense Division, Congressional Research Service, Library of Congress (Committee print; Washington: GPO, 1976).

U.S. Participation in the UN: Report by the President to the Con-

gress for the Year 1975 (Department of State Publication 8880; Washington: GPO, 1976). Published also as House Document 94-652, 94th Congress.

U.S. Senate, 95th Cong., 1st sess., Committee on Foreign Relations, *Legislative Activities Report of the Committee on Foreign Relations, United States Senate: Ninety-fourth Congress, January 14, 1975-October 1, 1976* (S. Rept. 95-21; Washington: GPO, 1977).

"USUN Press Releases": Press releases of the U.S. Mission to the United Nations, as reprinted in the Department of State *Bulletin*.

Yearbook of the United Nations (New York: United Nations Office of Public Information). A comprehensive review of U.N. activities, issued annually.

INDEX

A

ABM Treaty (Treaty Between the United States of America and the Union of Soviet Socialist Republics signed Moscow May 26, 1972), Iklé statement (Geneva, May 6, excerpt), 155; Ford remarks (Minneapolis, Aug. 19, excerpt), 392

Africa, 3, 8, 16-17, 61, 528-9, 559; *see also* country and organizational entries

African Development Fund, Kissinger address (New York, Sept. 1, excerpt), 427

Agency for International Development (AID), 239, 490

Albania, 283

Albert, Carl, letter from Ford on aid to Turkey (July 9), 264-6

Algeria, 186, 417

Allende Gossens, Salvador, 4, 5, 6, 560

Amerasinghe, H.S., 141

American Bar Association, Kissinger address (Montreal, Aug. 11), 370-85

American Legion, Ford remarks (Minneapolis, Aug. 19), 389-96

American Society of Newspaper Editors, Kissinger address (Apr. 17), 110-20

Amin Dada, Idi, 3, 16

Angola, 9, 17, 20, 477-8, 528-9, 603-18; Kissinger address (Detroit, Nov. 24), 533-4; Kissinger remarks (Dec. 12), 559; Kissinger statement (Jan. 29, 1976), 605-18

ANZUS Pact, 121-4; Council meeting (Washington, Apr. 24-5): communiqué, 122-4; Kissinger address (Detroit, Nov. 24, excerpt), 540

Arab-Israeli conflict, 7-8 75-82, 240, 397-416, 497-8, 505-14; Rabin-Kissinger remarks (Jerusalem, Mar. 23), 77-8; Nessen briefing (Mar. 24), 78-9; Kissinger statement on reassessment of U.S. policy (Mar. 26, excerpts), 79-84; Ford address (Apr.

623

B

D

E

F

G

H

I

J

K

N

O

P

U

Uganda, 3

Union of Soviet Socialist Republics (U.S.S.R.), 13, 14, 24, 388, 491-5; Kissinger statement on shelving of trade agreement (Jan. 14), 26-9; Ford address (Apr. 10), 103-4; Robinson statement on grain deal (Oct. 28), 493-5; Sonnenfeldt remarks (London, Dec. 13), 567-8; *see also* Angola, Disarmament, and other topical entries

United Kingdom, 11, 150, 240, 487; and Rhodesia, 487; and Diego Garcia, 528

U.N. Commission on the Status of Women, 239

U.N. Conference on the Law of the Sea, *see* Law of the Sea, U.N. Conference on

U.N. Development Decade, 417

U.N. General Assembly (7th Special Session, New York, Sept. 1-16), 10, 212, 417-46, 461; Kissinger statement (read by Moynihan Sept. 1), 419-46; same (Paris, Dec. 16, excerpt), 575-6

U.N. General Assembly (30th Regular Session, Sept. 16-Dec. 17, 1975), 8, 9-10, 461-76, 505-14, 593-601; Kissinger address (Sept. 22), 462-76; Moynihan remarks (Dec. 17), 595-601; and development, 418; and Korea, 418, 461-2, 594; and Declaration on Torture, 476, 593; and South Africa, 478-9; and anti-Zionist resolution, 8, 505-14, 594; and East Timor, 546; and political prisoners, 593; and International Women's Year, 239-55; and SALT, 594. *Resolution by number:* 3379 (XXX), Nov. 10, Elimination of all forms of racial discrimination (the anti-Zionist resolution), 507

U.N. Security Council, and Panama, 173; and Korea, 418, 461-2; and Middle East, 397, 594; and Vietnam, 418, 461; and Rhodesia, 478; and Namibia, 478-9; and East Timor, 546

U.N. Trusteeship Council, 258

United States, *see* appropriate topical, organizational and personal entries

V

Venezuela, 7, 24

Vietnam conflict, 1-2, 6, 14-15, 17-18, 32, 39-45, 91-2, 109, 121-2, 125-40; Ford message (Jan. 28), 41-3; Ford address (Apr. 10),